A FIRST COURSE IN FACTOR ANALYSIS

Second Edition

A FIRST COURSE
IN FACTOR ANALYSIS

Second Edition

Andrew L. Comrey
University of California, Los Angeles
Howard B. Lee
California State University, Northridge

LEA LAWRENCE ERLBAUM ASSOCIATES, PUBLISHERS
1992   Hillsdale, New Jersey   Hove and London

Lawrence Erlbaum Associates, Inc., Publishers
365 Broadway
Hlilsdale, New Jersey 07642

Library of Congress Cataloging-in-Publication Data

Comrey, Andrew Laurence.
A first course in factor analysis / by Andrew L. Comrey and Howard
B. Lee. — 2nd ed.
    p.   cm.
Includes bibliographical references and index.
ISBN 0-8058-1062-5
1. Factor analysis. I. Lee, Howard B. (Howard Bing), 1949–
II. Title.
QA278.5.C66 1992
519.5′354 — dc20   92-2896
                                      CIP

Printed in the United States of America
10 9 8 7 6 5 4 3 2 1

CONTENTS

PREFACE TO THE
FIRST EDITION

It is perhaps presumptuous for a nonmathematician to undertake the writing of a textbook on a topic such as factor analysis. After teaching the course in factor analysis for many years, however, I feel that I have been able to develop a clear picture of what students need in the way of an introduction to the topic. Furthermore, although good books on factor analysis have been published in recent years, they tend to be either too difficult for the typical student or else not sufficiently oriented toward providing an understanding of the underlying rationale for the technique.

I have tried to develop a book that will serve the needs of talented but mathematically unsophisticated advanced undergraduates, graduate students, and research workers who wish to acquire a basic understanding of the principles upon which factor analysis rests so that they can correctly apply these methods in their own work and intelligently evaluate what others are doing with them. I have tried to pitch the book at a level that will be a challenge for such readers but not so difficult as to discourage them. On the assumption that the emphasis in such a beginning text should be on more fundamental topics, I have minimized the amount of attention given to certain complex controversial issues, and I have omitted many recent developments. I feel, therefore, that this book represents not a substitute for such excellent advanced works as those of Harman and Horst but rather an introduction to them. After mastering the contents of this book, the typical student will find it much easier to read these more advanced books as well as new material in such technical journals as *Psychometrika*.

Another reason for my writing this book was to present in one volume some of the things I have learned about factor analysis that are not treated by other authors. For example, I have developed the minimum residual method of factor extraction and also an analytic method of factor rotation. These methods have been applied in my own research as integral parts of an overall research strategy that has given me good empirical results. I want to share these and other techniques I have developed with fellow research workers in the hope that they too will find them useful. Finally, I have taken this opportunity to present some of my own philosophical views on the use of factor analytic methods in scientific research.

I have been influenced by many people in developing my own conceptions about factor analysis: by my teacher, J. P. Guilford; my friends and colleagues, H. H. Harman, R. B. Cattell, and H. F. Kaiser; and many others. I would like to acknowledge this debt. Students from two separate classes have used the manuscript as a text and have offered many helpful suggestions. Some of the people who have been most instrumental in bringing about changes in the manuscript itself are Peter Bentler, Lee Cooper, Ken Ford, Richard Harshman, Diana Solar, and Mike Vandeman. Last but not least, I am indebted to my wife, Barbara Sherman Comrey, for encouraging me to write the book and for her continued support.

Andrew L. Comrey

PREFACE TO THE
SECOND EDITION

The first edition of this book (Comrey, 1973) was written prior to the rise in popularity of confirmatory factor analysis and structural equation modeling and the general availability of sophisticated computer programs to perform the intricate computations involved, e.g., LISREL and EQS. These newer methods have revolutionized factor analysis in the last few years so that any factor analysis textbook which ignores them is necessarily dated. The decision was made, therefore, to revise the original edition of this book to include at least an introduction to these newer methods. The mathematical basis of these newer methods is so complex and the topic is so extensive, however, that this book can only hope to provide the reader with a brief introduction to the topic and how it relates to more traditional factor analytic methods. Other parts of the original edition have been updated, newer material relating to the validation of the Comrey Personality Scales has been added, and the computer programs have been modifed and expanded in addition to making them available on convenient diskettes for ready transfer to readers' computer facilities. Both authors of the current edition have worked on all parts of the book, but more responsibility for writing the material on confirmatory factor analysis and structural equation models lay with the second author. The other chapters were written primarily by the first author.

The authors want to thank many students in the first author's classes on factor analysis, anonymous reviewers, and Professor Stanley A. Mulaik, all of whom have offered helpful suggestions for improving the book. Programmer Paul Hoffman of the UCLA Office of Academic Computing helped update some of the computer programs for the latest version of the

FORTRAN compiler. Programmer Eric Wu of Professor Peter Bentler's lab at UCLA helped adapt the programs for the IBM PC. In addition, the authors are especially endebted to Professor Peter M. Bentler for his critical reading of the chapters on confirmatory factor analysis and structural equation modeling. Dr. Bentler located several errors in the initial draft of the manuscript and made a number of very helpful editorial suggestions. Any errors and deficiencies that remain, however, are the sole responsibility of the authors.

Andrew L. Comrey
Howard B. Lee

1

Introduction

Discovering the nature of relationships between variables is a very important part of any scientific field. In the well-established sciences, the variables to be related are precisely defined and widely accepted by the scientific community as *the* important variables to study. The relationships of these variables with each other are frequently specified mathematically, and these mathematical relationships between variables in some cases are further organized into elaborate mathematical theories involving several interrelated variables. In the newer scientific fields the variables are less precisely defined, there is not so much agreement among scientists concerning what variables should be related to each other, and the nature of the relationships between variables is less clearly specified. Factor analysis represents a rapidly growing body of statistical methods that can be of great value in these less developed sciences. Factor analytic methods can help scientists to define their variables more precisely and decide what variables they should study and relate to each other in the attempt to develop their science to a higher level. Factor analytic methods can also help these scientists to gain a better understanding of the complex and poorly defined interrelationships among large numbers of imprecisely measured variables. The purpose of this book is to help the reader achieve some familiarity with these powerful methods of analysis.

This book has been written for advanced undergraduate students, graduate students, and research workers who need to develop a knowledge of factor analysis, either for the purpose of understanding the published research of others or to aid them in their own research. It is presumed that most readers will have a reasonable understanding of high school geometry, algebra, trigonometry, and a course in elementary statistics, even though the concepts in these areas may not have been reviewed recently. Some sections of the book make use of more advanced mathematical techniques than the typical high school graduate is exposed to, but this should not prove to be an obstacle of any significant proportions for the average reader. The authors have tried hard to present the material in a way that can be understood by interested students with only a modest mathematical background. Although the book has been designed to serve as a textbook for classes in factor analysis, it was also written with the expectation that many of the readers will be using it without the guidance of a teacher.

Factor analysis represents a class of procedures for treating data that are being applied with increasing frequency in the behavioral and health sciences and even in the physical sciences. Despite this popularity, however, factor analysis is not well understood by many of the scientists who use it. There are many reasons for this phenomenon. First of all, factor analysis is based on mathematical foundations that go beyond the level of quantitative sophistication and training possessed by the bulk of behavioral scientists who use it the most. Although there are several excellent books (e.g., Harman, 1967; Horst, 1965; Mulaik, 1972) that present the mathematical background of factor analysis, the average behavioral scientist is unable or unwilling to wade through these books, largely because of his or her limited mathematical skills.

Another problem with understanding factor analysis, however, is that it rests on empirical science as much as it does on mathematics. The person who is well trained in mathematics will have little difficulty with the mathematical aspects of the topic, but without training in empirical science applications of factor analysis, can be expected to have difficulty making effective use of these methods in practice. It is also true that the textbooks that are comprehensive with respect to the mathematical aspects of factor analysis do not deal with the nonmathematical parts of the subject with the same degree of adequacy.

Thus, neither mathematical skill nor scientific sophistication alone is sufficient to understand and use factor analysis effectively. Knowledge in both these areas is needed. An attempt is made in this book to present in both these realms the ideas that are necessary for a basic understanding of factor analysis and how to use it. No attempt has been made to provide an exhaustive coverage of all the methods used in factor analysis. Rather, the focus in this book is on the correct use and understanding of some practical, proven procedures. Step-by-step instructions are given that will permit the reader to apply these techniques correctly. In addition, an attempt has been made to explain the underlying rationale for these methods. Without a fundamental understanding of why certain procedures are supposed to work, application of factor analysis becomes a cookbook operation in which the user is not in a position to evaluate whether or not what is being done makes any sense. The first goal of this volume, therefore, is to promote understanding as a basis for proper application. Understanding is also the basis for intelligent evaluation of published applications of factor analysis by others. Most scientists need this capacity today whether or not they ever do a factor analysis.

This book provides more emphasis on the nonmathematical aspects of factor analysis than the books mentioned above. Although this book presents the essential aspects of the mathematical basis of factor analysis, it does so on a simpler level than that found in these more mathematical texts. It is hoped that the mastery of the content of this book will provide a ready avenue for progression to more advanced mathematical treatments of the subject. The nonmathematical aspects of the present treatment will also provide a useful background for placing more advanced mathematical material in proper perspective as well as making it easier to absorb. Some textbooks on factor analysis that may offer valuable assistance to the reader who wishes to explore the topic further include the following:

Cattell (1952), *Factor Analysis*. This is a book of intermediate difficulty in which simple structure is emphasized as a means of carrying out factor rotations. Ways of combining factor analysis with experimental design are described.

Cattell (1978), *The Scientific Use of Factor Analysis*. Cattell summarizes his major developments in the area of factor analysis since his 1952 book. Other important developments in factor analysis by other researchers besides Cattell and his students are also presented. The mathematics required to read this book are not extensive. Cattell addresses many issues that are still current in using factor analysis.

Fruchter (1954), *Introduction to Factor Analysis*. An elementary book that provides an easy introduction.

Gorsuch (1983), *Factor Analysis*. An intermediate level of difficulty and a balance between theory and applications.

Guertin and Bailey (1970), *Introduction to Modern Factor Analysis*. This book avoids mathematics and concentrates on how to use the computer to do factor analysis. It is easy to read but does not emphasize an understanding of the underlying theory.

Harman (1967, 1976), *Modern Factor Analysis*. A comprehensive treatment with a mathematical emphasis. Difficult to read.

Horst (1965), *Factor Analysis of Data Matrices*. Entirely algebraic treatment. Difficult for the non-mathematical reader.

Lawley and Maxwell (1963), *Factor Analysis as a Statistical Method*. This is a little book that presents, among others, Lawley's own maximum likelihood method. Some mathematical sophistication is required to read this book.

Mulaik (1972), *The Foundations of Factor Analysis*. A comprehensive treatment of the mathematical basis for factor analytic methods. Difficult for the nonmathematical reader.

Rummel, R. J. (1970), *Applied Factor Analysis*. A book of intermediate difficulty. Contains good chapters on matrix algebra and its use in factor analysis. Presents many of the traditional approaches but does not discuss extensively the issues involved in the use of different exploratory factor models. The author presents several examples using political science variables instead of psychological variables. The different factor models are well explained.

Thomson (1951), *The Factorial Analysis of Human Ability*. Presents the point of view of an important British historical figure in factor analysis. Easy to read.

Thurstone (1947), *Multiple Factor Analysis*. This is the classic historical work by the father of modern factor analysis. It still contains much of value to the advanced student.

The authors recommend that after mastering the material in the present text, the reader should go on to read other texts from the list above. Journal articles on factor analytic methods are to be found in such periodicals as *Psychometrika, Multivariate Behavioral Research, Educational and Psychological Measurement*, and *Applied Psychological Measurement*. Many other journals report research in which factor analysis has been used to treat data.

1.1.   FACTOR ANALYTIC GOALS AND PROCEDURES

There are many reasons why an investigator may undertake a factor analysis. Some of these are the following: (a) He or she may have measurements on a collection of variables and would like to have some idea about what constructs might be used to explain the intercorrelations among these variables; (b) there may be a need to test some theory about the number and nature of the factor constructs needed to account for the intercorrelations among the variables being studied; (c) there may be a desire to determine the effect on the factor constructs brought about by changes in the variables measured and in the conditions under which the measurements were taken; (d) there may be a desire to verify previous findings, either those of the investigator or those of others, using a new sample from the same population or a sample from a different population;

(e) there may be a need to test the effect upon obtained results produced by a variation in the factor analytic procedures used.

Whatever the goals of an analysis, in most cases it will involve all of the following major steps: (a) selecting the variables; (b) computing the matrix of correlations among the variables; (c) extracting the unrotated factors; (d) rotating the factors; and (e) interpreting the rotated factor matrix. The variables studied in a factor analysis may represent merely a selection based on what happens to be available to the investigator in the way of existing data. On the other hand, the variables chosen may represent the results of a great deal of very careful planning.

The factor analysis proper typically begins with a matrix of correlation coefficients between data variables that are being studied. In psychology, for example, these variables might consist of test scores on several short tests of personality, such as 1. Lack of Reserve, 2. Lack of Seclusiveness, 3. No Loss for Words, 4. Lack of Shyness, 5. Lack of Stage Fright, 6. Gregariousness, and 7. Sociability. These tests might be administered to several hundred students. A correlation coefficient would be computed between each pair of tests over the scores for all students tested. These correlation coefficients would then be arranged in a matrix as shown in Table 1.1. Numerical values would appear in an actual table rather than the symbols shown in Table 1.1. Thus, the correlation between variables 1 and 2 appears in the first row, second column of the correlation matrix, shown in Table 1.1 as r_{12}. The subscripts indicate the variable numbers involved in the correlation. It should be noted that the entry r_{21} (in row 2, column 1) involves the correlation between variables 2 and 1. This is the same as r_{12} since the same two variables are involved. The correlation matrix, therefore, is said to be "symmetric" since $r_{ij} = r_{ji}$, that is, the entries in the upper right-hand part of the matrix are identical to the corresponding entries in the lower left-hand part of the matrix.

The symbols shown in Table 1.1 are replaced by hypothetical numerical values to give the correlation matrix shown in Table 1.2. The matrix shown in Table 1.2 is a very small one, of course, being only a 7×7 matrix involving just seven variables. Matrices treated in actual research work frequently run to 60×60 or more, that is, involving 60 variables or more. The symmetric character of the matrix in Table 1.2 is seen by observing that the numbers above the main diagonal (the imaginary line through the blank cells in Table 1.2) are the same as those below the main diagonal. Also, the entries in row 1 are the same as those in column 1. The same thing holds for all other rows and columns that have the same number if the matrix is symmetric.

When the correlation matrix has large correlation coefficients in it, this indicates that the variables involved are related to each other, or overlap in what they measure, just as weight, for example, is related to height. On the

TABLE 1.1

A Symbolic Correlation Matrix

Variables	1	2	3	4	5	6	7
1. Lack of Reserve		r_{12}	r_{13}	r_{14}	r_{15}	r_{16}	r_{17}
2. Lack of Seclusiveness	r_{21}		r_{23}	r_{24}	r_{25}	r_{26}	r_{27}
3. No Loss for Words	r_{31}	r_{32}		r_{34}	r_{35}	r_{36}	r_{37}
4. Lack of Shyness	r_{41}	r_{42}	r_{43}		r_{45}	r_{46}	r_{47}
5. No Stage Fright	r_{51}	r_{52}	r_{53}	r_{54}		r_{56}	r_{57}
6. Gregariousness	r_{61}	r_{62}	r_{63}	r_{64}	r_{65}		r_{67}
7. Sociability	r_{71}	r_{72}	r_{73}	r_{74}	r_{75}	r_{76}	

TABLE 1.2

A Numerical Correlation Matrix

Variables	1	2	3	4	5	6	7
1. Lack of Reserve		.46	.66	.53	.36	.50	.59
2. Lack of Seclusiveness	.46		.55	.57	.27	.45	.50
3. No Loss for Words	.66	.55		.82	.46	.37	.45
4. Lack of Shyness	.53	.57	.82		.43	.45	.45
5. No Stage Fright	.36	.27	.46	.43		.38	.40
6. Gregariousness	.50	.45	.37	.45	.38		.55
7. Sociability	.59	.50	.45	.45	.40	.55	

average, tall people are heavier and short people are lighter, giving a correlation between height and weight in the neighborhood of .60. With a large number of variables and many substantial correlations among the variables, it becomes very difficult to keep in mind or even contemplate all the intricacies of the various interrelationships. Factor analysis provides a way of thinking about these interrelationships by positing the existence of underlying "factors" or "factor constructs" that account for the values appearing in the matrix of intercorrelations among these variables. For example, a "factor" of "Bigness" could be used to account for the correlation between height and weight. People could be located somewhere along a continuum of Bigness between very large and very small. Both height and weight would be substantially correlated with the factor of Bigness. The correlation between height and weight would be accounted for by the fact that they both share a relationship to the hypothetical factor of Bigness.

Whether or not it is more useful to use a single concept like Bigness or to use two concepts like height and weight is a question that cannot be answered by factor analysis itself. One common objective of factor analysis, however, is to provide a relatively small number of factor constructs that will serve as satisfactory substitutes for a much larger number of variables. These factor constructs themselves are variables that may prove to be more useful than the original variables from which they were derived.

A factor construct that has proved to be very useful in psychology is Extraversion-Introversion. It is possible to account for a substantial part of the intercorrelations among the variables in Table 1.2 by this single factor construct. This is because all of these variables are correlated positively with each other. With most large real data matrices, however, the interrelationships between variables are much more complicated, with many near-zero entries, so that it usually requires more than one factor construct to account for the intercorrelations that are found in the correlation, or **R**, matrix.

After the correlation matrix **R** has been computed, the next step in the factor analysis is to determine how many factor constructs are needed to account for the pattern of values found in **R**. This is done through a process called "factor extraction," which constitutes the third major step in a factor analysis. This process involves a numerical procedure that uses the coefficients in the entire **R** matrix to produce a column of coefficients relating the variables included in the factor analysis to a hypothetical factor construct variable. The usual procedure followed is to "extract" factors from the correlation matrix **R** until there is no appreciable variance left, that is, until the "residual" correlations are all so close to zero that they are presumed to be of negligible importance.

There are many methods of extracting a factor but they all end up with a column of numbers, one for each variable, that represent the "loadings" of the variables on that factor. Some factor analysts, mostly British, prefer the term "saturation" to the term "loading." These loadings represent the extent to which the variables are related to the hypothetical factor. For most factor extraction methods, these loadings may be thought of as correlations between the variables and the factor. If a variable has an extracted factor loading of .7 on the factor, then its correlation is to the extent of .7 with that hypothetical factor construct. Another variable might have a substantial negative loading on the factor, indicating that it is negatively correlated with the factor construct.

After the first factor is extracted (factor extraction methods will be explained in Chapters 3 and 4), the effect of this factor is removed from the correlation matrix **R** to produce the matrix of first factor "residual" correlations. How this is done is explained in greater detail later but suppose that the first factor extracted from the matrix in Table 1.2 had loadings of .7 for 1. Lack of Reserve and .8 for 3. No Loss for Words. Multiplying .7 × .8 gives .56 as the correlation between these two variables due to the first factor alone. Substracting .56 from .66 leaves only .10 for the first factor residual correlation between these two variables. If all the other first factor residuals were also as small as this or smaller, it would probably be unnecessary to extract a second factor. If substantial values remain in the first factor residual correlations, however, it is necessary to extract a second factor. If substantial values remain in the second factor residual correlations, a third factor must be extracted, and so on, until the residuals are too small to continue.

Once the factors that are needed to account for the correlations in the **R** matrix have been extracted, the values are arranged in a table that is referred to as the "matrix of unrotated loadings." Such a matrix might look something like the example given in Table 1.3. The first factor in Table 1.3 is the largest factor in the sense that the sum of squares of the factor loadings is largest for the first column (2.37). The subsequent factors become progressively smaller, with the last one in this example being only about one-fifth as large as the first (.53). The last column of the matrix in Table 1.3, headed by h^2, contains the "communalities" for the variables. In this table, the communalities equal the sums of squares of the loadings for the variables over the four factors. That is, the communality h_1^2 for variable 1, for example, is given by $.68 = (.48)^2 + (-.67)^2 + (-.01)^2 + (-.05)^2$, ignoring rounding errors. The communalities represent the extent of overlap between the variables and these four factors. If the communality for a variable were as high as 1.0, it would indicate that the variable overlaps totally with these four factors in what it measures. In this case, its scores could be predicted perfectly by a weighted combination of scores representing only these four factors. Another way of expressing this idea is to say that all the variance in this variable can be accounted for by scores for individuals representing their positions on the four factors. If one of these variables had a communality of zero, on the other hand, all four factor loadings for that variable would be zero and the variable would not share anything in common with any of the four factors. Communality values in between 1.0 and 0 indicate partial overlapping between the variables and the factors in what they measure.

In Table 1.3, the names of the variables have not been listed, contrary to what was done in Tables 1.1 and 1.2. Sometimes an author puts these names in the table of factor loadings and sometimes not. The sums of squares and the communalities also may or may not be shown. The decimal points on the correlations and factor loadings are included in most tables in this book, but these are often omitted for convenience in table preparation. Roman numerals are usually used to designate factors and arabic numerals to designate variables, although sometimes the factors also will be labeled with arabic numerals. The factors are almost always listed across the top of the table and the variables down the left side for tables of factor loadings.

The factor analysis does not stop, however, with the extraction of the

TABLE 1.3

An Unrotated Factor Matrix

Variable	Factors				
	I	II	III	IV	h^2
1	.48	−.67	−.01	−.05	.68
2	.38	−.63	.12	.08	.56
3	.40	−.65	−.14	−.10	.61
4	.51	.27	.36	−.17	.50
5	.61	.26	.37	−.02	.57
6	.46	.22	.46	.09	.48
7	.41	.26	−.11	−.40	.41
8	.55	.28	−.26	−.25	.52
9	.41	.31	−.42	.32	.54
10	.47	.37	−.38	.38	.65
SSQ[a]	2.37	1.82	.91	.53	—

[a] The sum of squares.

factors and the preparation of a table of unrotated factor loadings. Although this table gives a factor solution based on mathematically acceptable factor constructs, the factor constructs represented in an unrotated factor matrix are rarely useful in scientific work. The reason for this is that most methods of factor extraction are designed to extract approximately as much variance as possible with each successive factor, resulting in a sharp drop off in factor size from the first to the last factor, as shown by the sum of squares of the columns of factor loadings. This phenomenon is very apparent in the unrotated factor matrix shown in Table 1.3. These unrotated factors obtained by extracting as much variance as possible from the matrix of correlations at each factor extraction step tend to be highly complex factor constructs that relate to or overlap with many of the variables rather than with just a few. Factor I, for example (in Table 1.3), has appreciable loadings for all the variables. Factor II has high negative loadings for three variables and all the other variables have positive loadings of some importance. Five of the ten variables are related to factor III to about the same level. Such complex, overlapping factors are usually difficult to interpret and use for scientific description because they contain within them many unrelated parts. They are not homogeneous in character.

Using an unrotated factor for scientific description is not unlike describing human beings with a physical variable developed by adding equally weighted scores based on Intelligence, Weight, Bank Balance, and Number of Siblings. Such a composite variable would be complex indeed. Knowledge of a person's score on such a variable would be virtually useless because it would be impossible to tell from knowledge of the total score where the individual falls with respect to the component parts.

Fortunately, however, it is possible to "rotate" the factor matrix into another form that is mathematically equivalent to the original unrotated matrix but which represents factor constructs that are often much more useful for scientific purposes than the unrotated factor constructs. The unrotated factor matrix in Table 1.3, for example, can be rotated into the form shown in Table 1.4. The values shown in Table 1.4 are decimal proportions of 1.0 with either a positive or a negative sign attached. Thus, factor loadings are limited to values between -1.0 and $+1.0$. This does not apply to the case where covariances are analyzed instead of correlation coefficients. This practice is relatively rare, however, so the present text will be concerned primarily with the factor analysis of correlation matrices. Certain types of factor solutions, called "oblique" solutions, also permit the factor loadings to be larger than 1.0 but only when the factors are highly correlated with one another. Many factor analytic solutions are "orthogonal," which means that the factors are uncorrelated with each other.

The factor constructs represented by the rotated factor matrix in Table 1.4 are very different from those represented by the unrotated matrix in Table 1.3 even though the two matrices are mathematically equivalent in the sense that they both account equally well for the original correlation coefficients from which they were derived. Notice that factor I in Table 1.4 has high loadings for the first three variables and low loadings for all the rest. Factor II has high loadings for variables 4, 5, and 6 and much lower loadings for all the other variables. Factor III has high loadings for variables 7 and 8 with much lower loadings for all the other variables. Finally, factor IV has high loadings only for variables 9 and 10. Each

TABLE 1.4

A Rotated Factor Matrix

Variable	Factors				
	I	II	III	IV	h^2
1	.82	.04	.08	.01	.68
2	.73	.10	−.10	−.02	.56
3	.76	−.10	.14	.03	.61
4	.03	.64	.28	−.05	.50
5	.09	.72	.20	.08	.57
6	.05	.69	.00	.02	.48
7	−.02	.22	.60	.06	.41
8	.04	.24	.60	.31	.52
9	−.06	.12	.16	.70	.54
10	−.08	.21	.14	.76	.65

factor, then, in Table 1.4 is related highly to only a few variables and the variables related to each factor are different.

By inspecting the content of variables 1, 2, and 3, it would be possible to gain some inkling about the nature of the underlying factor construct. Similarly, factors II, III, and IV could be tentatively identified and described on the basis of the variables that are related to them. These factors will all be well differentiated from each other since each is represented by a different set of variables. The factor constructs derived from the rotated matrix in Table 1.4, therefore, are much more likely to have some scientific utility than those derived from the unrotated matrix in Table 1.3.

The communalities in the last column are the same in both Tables 1.3 and 1.4. This is one indication of the mathematical equivalence of the two matrices for describing the original correlation matrix. The procedures for rotating a matrix of unrotated factors into a mathematically equivalent rotated matrix that yields more interpretable factors are described and explained in later chapters.

Following the computation of the correlations, extraction of the unrotated factors, and the rotation of the unrotated factors, the factor analyst attempts to interpret what the factors are like, using any available knowledge about the variables as well as any other pertinent information. The variables that have high loadings on the rotated factor are studied carefully to determine what they share in common. Each such rotated factor is named on the basis of the common content that has been identified.

1.1.1.   FOLLOWING UP FACTOR ANALYTIC RESULTS

In many cases carrying out a factor analysis and naming the factors may represent only an exercise if we do not go beyond these procedures. The rotated factor matrix and its implied factor constructs provide one interpretation of the data, but there is no guarantee that this interpretation is the "correct" one. Factor analysis could be considered to be a way of generating hypotheses about nature. The factor constructs that emerge from a factor analysis may be very useful as variables for understanding and describing the relationships within a given scientific domain, but the correctness of interpretations based on factor analytic results must be confirmed by evidence outside the factor analysis itself.

There are many different methods of carrying out a factor analysis. Several different factor analysts can take the same data and come up with as many different solutions. This fact has led to a great deal of misunderstanding about factor analysis and not a little distrust of the method. It must be recognized, however, that all of these different solutions for the same data by different analysts represent interpretations of the original correlation matrix that may be equally correct from the mathematical point of view. The mathematical analyses merely show that the same data may be interpreted in a variety of ways. Some of these interpretations undoubtedly are more useful than others from the standpoint of scientific objectives, but there is nothing in the factor analytic methods themselves that can demonstrate that one factor solution is more scientifically useful than another. The factor analyst, therefore, must use other means than the factor analysis itself to demonstrate that the factor analytic results have scientific value. A failure to do so on the part of the factor analyst does not represent a fault that can be laid at the doorstep of factor analytic methods themselves.

1.2.   SOURCES OF DISAGREEMENT IN FACTOR ANALYTIC RESEARCH

There are many reasons why the solutions reached by different factor analysts do not always agree with each other. Some of the major reasons are outlined briefly in the following sections.

1.2.1.   COMMUNALITIES

The communality for a variable in a factor analysis has already been defined as the sum of squares of the factor loadings over all the factors, as shown in Tables 1.3 and 1.4. These are the communalities that emerge from the factor analysis. These values give an indication of the extent to which the variables overlap with the factors, or more technically, they give the proportion of variance in the variables that can be accounted for by scores in the factors. In many methods of factor extraction, however, estimates of the communality values must be inserted in the diagonal cells of the original correlation matrix before the factor analysis is carried out. Consequently, the factor loadings and the communalities that emerge from the factor analysis depend to some extent on the estimated communality values used at the beginning in the correlation matrix. Since these values are at best approximations to the "true" communalities, the resulting factor loadings are only approximately correct. Since there is no fully accepted mathematical solution to the "communality problem" at the present time, even using the same data, variations would be introduced into the results by different investigators by their choice of communality estimates.

1.2.2. METHODS OF FACTOR EXTRACTION

There are many different ways to extract factors. Even with the same communality estimates, these different methods do not always give the same results. In most cases, however, the results from different methods of factor extraction can be transformed by the rotation process so that they are reasonably comparable from method to method. The fact that this is possible, however, does not mean that it will be done in practice. The initially extracted factors may appear to be very different from one method to another and the rotations may never bring them into congruence.

1.2.3. NUMBER OF FACTORS EXTRACTED

No precise solution to the problem of how many factors to extract from the correlation matrix has been achieved in the ordinary empirical factor analysis. Many guidelines have been proposed and some have gained a measure of acceptance. Investigators differ in practice, however, in how they deal with this problem, which leads to variations in the results obtained. Differences between investigators in this area can lead to substantial variations in their final interpretive solutions.

1.2.4. HOW TO ROTATE THE FACTORS

Most factor analysts agree that the unrotated factors do not generally represent useful scientific factor constructs and that it is usually necessary to rotate, when there are two or more extracted factors, if useful and meaningful factor constructs are to be identified. All factor analysts agree that all rotated solutions, when the same number of factors are rotated, are mathematically equivalent to each other and to the unrotated solution in that all of them account for the original correlation matrix equally well. This is so because in the final analysis, different factor solutions, rotated or otherwise, merely represent different basis systems (or sets of coordinate axes) for the same vector space. Beyond this, however, there is little agreement on what method of rotation gives the "best" solution in some scientific sense. Every analyst has preferred procedures which he or she considers to be superior to the procedures used by other investigators. The fact that these disagreements occur, however, is not a reflection on the technique. It does point out that a matrix of intercorrelations between variables can be interpreted in many ways. Factor analytic procedures reveal the various possibilities that are mathematically valid. Subsequent experience, not factor analysis per se, will reveal which, if any, of these possibilities has scientific utility. Certain factor analytic procedures may produce useful scientific solutions much more consistently than other methods, but it is impossible to establish that one method is always preferable to other available methods.

1.3.   PLAN OF THE BOOK

The remaining chapters are now described briefly so that the reader will have an idea of what to expect and what can be temporarily omitted if the entire text is not to be read immediately.

1.3.1.   THE FACTOR ANALYTIC MODEL: CHAPTER 2

In this chapter, the basic equations and assumptions of factor analysis are presented in algebraic and matrix form. The bare minimum of matrix algebra needed to understand the theory is presented. Instead of first devoting a section or chapter to matrix theory, however, these ideas have been introduced as they are needed. This may not be very neat and orderly, but it does permit the reader to try immediately to grasp the ideas of factor analysis without first having to wade through a treatise on matrix theory that may offer little of intrinsic interest. The authors hope that this manner of presentation will raise reader interest sufficiently to offset any loss of organizational precision.

A good part of Chapter 2 is devoted to showing that the correlation matrix can be decomposed into the matrix product of two other matrices, the unrotated factor matrix **A** and its transpose matrix **A'**, where the rows of **A'** equal the columns of **A**, and vice versa. In schematic matrix form, this matrix equation looks like the diagram in Fig. (1.1). The factor extraction process that yields matrix **A**, the matrix of unrotated factors, is explained further, and an example is presented. The process of factor rotation, where matrix **A** is transformed into a matrix of rotated factors, is also explained further using a miniature example. Both factor extraction and rotation are treated in much greater depth in later chapters, but the intent in this chapter is to paint the broad outlines of the picture before filling in the details. This should help to maintain reader interest and facilitate understanding.

1.3.2.   FACTOR EXTRACTION BY THE CENTROID METHOD: CHAPTER 3

This chapter is devoted to explaining the basis for the centroid method of extracting factors and to presenting detailed how-to-do-it instructions. Although this method would not ordinarily be used today if the investigator has access to an electronic computer, it is a good method to use if only a

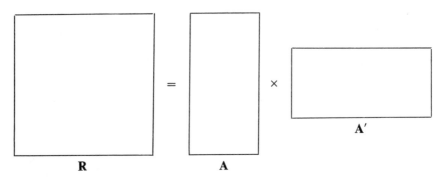

FIG. 1.1   Schematic Representation of Matrix Equation $\mathbf{R} = \mathbf{AA'}$

small calculator is available. It is also a good method to use for instructional purposes, particularly for individual class projects. Carrying out a factor analysis from beginning to end enables the student to obtain a much better grasp of what it is all about. The centroid method is ideal for this purpose because the computing involved is not too extensive. First, the chapter presents a small four-variable problem to illustrate the ideas and then a completely worked out 12-variable example to outline practical computing procedures.

1.3.3.   THE PRINCIPAL FACTOR AND MINIMUM RESIDUAL METHODS OF FACTOR EXTRACTION: CHAPTER 4

Prior to the advent of the computer, the centroid method was the most popular way of extracting factors. Today, however, the principal factor method is probably the most widely used. Some underlying theory and the Jacobi method of computing a principal factor solution are presented in this chapter. In addition, theory and computation procedures for extracting factors by the minimum residual method are given. This method does not require the use of communality estimates, and it also provides an automatic rule for terminating factor extraction. The close connection between the principal factor method and the minimum residual method is shown along with the procedure for obtaining a principal factor solution using the minimum residual algorithm.

1.3.4.   ORTHOGONAL HAND ROTATIONS: CHAPTER 5

When the unrotated factors are rotated to obtain the rotated factor matrix, the investigator may elect to leave the factor axes at right angles to each other, in which case the factors are uncorrelated and the solution is called an "orthogonal" solution; or the angles between the factor axes may be allowed to depart from 90°. If the angles between the factor axes depart from 90°, the factors are no longer uncorrelated with each other, and the solution is referred to as an "oblique" solution. Chapter 5 presents the traditional method of rotating the factor axes orthogonally, leaving the factor axes at right angles to each other. The mechanics of making plots of factor axes, determining what rotations to perform, and then carrying them out are explained by means of an actual example. Although the mechanics of making the rotations are the same no matter what principle is used in deciding what rotations to carry out, Thurstone's principles of "simple structure" are used as the criteria for deciding what rotations to perform in this particular example. The logic underlying simple structure principles is explained.

Although the hand rotational procedures described in Chapter 5 are not used as much today as they were before the advent of computers, these techniques are as good today as they ever were and probably should be used much more than they are. Too many investigators today wish to take short cuts by using computerized solutions that do not require them to make judgments about the rotations that should be performed. Unfortunately, such computerized solutions do not always represent a satisfactory substitute for the more traditional methods.

1.3.5.   OBLIQUE HAND ROTATIONS: CHAPTER 6

One of the reasons why many investigators prefer orthogonal rotations is that they are much easier to understand and simpler to compute than oblique solutions. This chapter takes up the geometric principles underlying the representation of data variables with respect to oblique factor axes and explains the procedures used in actually computing an oblique solution. An example is worked out to illustrate the principles presented. The oblique hand-rotated solution provides the most flexibility in choosing a model to represent the data. This is one of the more difficult chapters and can be omitted on the first reading of the book if desired. As long as the investigator sticks to orthogonal solutions, the material in this chapter can be ignored. On the other hand, this material should be mastered eventually if the reader expects to achieve a good understanding of factor analytic methodology.

1.3.6.   SIMPLE STRUCTURE AND OTHER
ROTATIONAL CRITERIA: CHAPTER 7

How to carry out rotations to achieve the most scientifically meaningful rotated factor solution has always been an area of heated controversy in factor analytic circles. For many years, simple structure was the dominant method. With the arrival of electronic computers, however, many new methods have been proposed. In this chapter, the underlying rationale for rotation is considered in some detail to give the reader sufficient under-standing of the principles involved so that reasonable decisions can be made about what rotational methods should be employed in a given situation. Simple structure and several other approaches to the rotation process, including the so-called "analytic" methods, are discussed. The underlying theory for two of these analytic methods will be presented in greater detail, the Kaiser Varimax method and the Tandem Criteria method, developed by the first author. The Kaiser Varimax method has become perhaps the most popular rotation method in use today. The Tandem Criteria method uses the correlation coefficients between the variables as an additional aid in positioning the factor axes. The method also provides a technique for determining how many factors should be used in the final rotated solution.

1.3.7. PLANNING THE STANDARD DESIGN FACTOR ANALYSIS: CHAPTER 8

It is often said of factor analysis that you only get out of it what you put into it. This is an oversimplification, but it is certainly true that a poorly planned factor analysis is much less likely to yield useful results than one that is well planned. The purpose of this chapter is to explain the principles of good factor analytic design. Different methods of obtaining the corre-lation coefficients are compared, and finally a number of common errors in the design and execution of a factor analysis are discussed. Attention is given to the concept of the factor hierarchy and its implications for factor analytic design and interpretation.

1.3.8. ALTERNATE DESIGNS IN FACTOR ANALYSIS: CHAPTER 9

The most common type of factor analytic design is that involving analysis of a matrix of correlations between data variables. Each correlation between two data variables is computed over a substantial sample of data objects or individuals. This design is referred to as "R-technique," following Cattell's terminology. Occasionally, however, other designs, such as "Q-technique," are used. In Q-technique, the correlation matrix is obtained by correlating pairs of data objects or individuals over a substantial sample of data variables. This method can be used in locating "types" or clusters of similar data objects. There are also other designs that are even less used than Q-technique but which are useful for special purposes. This chapter treats a specialized topic, however, and may be readily omitted in the first reading.

1.3.9.   INTERPRETATION AND APPLICATION OF FACTOR ANALYTIC RESULTS: CHAPTER 10

Even if it were possible to know that a particular factor analysis had been designed and executed perfectly, interpretation of the results would still leave room for disagreement between investigators. Typical procedures involved in factor interpretation are presented in this chapter and the meaning of factor constructs is discussed. Also, factor analysis is compared with multiple regression analysis to clarify their respective functions. In addition, this chapter presents several methods of computing factor scores and tells the reader how to write up reports of factor analytic research. Finally, there is a brief discussion of the purposes for which factor analysis can be used.

1.3.10.   DEVELOPMENT OF THE COMREY PERSONALITY SCALES; AN EXAMPLE OF THE USE OF FACTOR ANALYSIS: CHAPTER 11

This chapter presents first the author's approach to psychological test development and summarizes the factor analytic research based on that approach which has led to the development of a factored personality inventory, the Comrey Personality Scales. It gives the history and end results of the use of factor analysis in a programmatic research project leading to a tangible end product. This chapter should give the reader a good appreciation for the way factor analysis can be employed in test and scale development, one of its most common applications.

1.3.11.   CONFIRMATORY FACTOR ANALYSIS: CHAPTER 12

The first 11 chapters of this book are concerned with what are sometimes referred to as "exploratory" factor analytic methods to distinguish them from "confirmatory" methods. The first edition of this book was concerned exclusively with exploratory methods, which are those methods that traditionally have been called "factor analytic" methods. The first 11 chapters of the current edition are still devoted to exploratory methods. In recent years, however, powerful new statistical methods of treating correlational data have been developed which are also considered by many to be factor analytic methods. They are called "confirmatory" methods to distinguish them from the traditional factor analytic methods which in turn have been labeled "exploratory" to distinguish them from the later, more mathematically sophisticated procedures. These confirmatory factor analytic methods represent special cases within a larger class of methods variously known as causal modeling, structural equation modeling, path analysis, and so on. The popularity of these new methods has grown dramatically in the past decade, in large measure due to the widespread availability of elaborate professionally developed computer programs (e.g., LISREL and EQS) to carry out the analyses. A thorough treatment of this mathematically difficult subject is beyond the scope of this introduction to factor analysis. This chapter is designed, however, to provide at least an introduction to the use of these methods that will permit the reader to understand in a general way what they do, what their strengths and limitations are, and how they relate to more traditional exploratory factor analytic techniques. This chapter also should help the reader to decide when exploratory methods should be used and when confirmatory methods should be preferred. This chapter and the following chapter on structural equation modeling can be omitted in a first reading of the book.

1.3.12.   STRUCTURAL EQUATION MODELS: CHAPTER 13

In confirmatory factor analysis, programs like LISREL and EQS solve simultaneous linear equations to provide factor analytic solutions that come as close as possible to an hypothesized factor model. Much more elaborate models relating observed and latent variable constructs can be dealt with using the same general methods. It is even possible to test hypotheses concerning putative causal effects between certain variables, hence the term "causal" modeling that is often associated with these methods. This chapter presents a brief introduction to these methods for the purpose of giving the reader some idea of what purpose these more elaborate models can serve and how they do it without attempting to be a substitute for more complete sources such as the LISREL and EQS manuals.

1.3.13.   COMPUTER PROGRAMS: CHAPTER 14

Over the years the first author has developed several computer programs to carry out the numerical operations necessary to implement his own test development projects. FORTRAN listings of these programs are made available with this book since they are not readily available elsewhere. This chapter provides the documentation necessary to run these programs once they have been compiled and prepared for use at your own computer center. Programs are included to score tests, scale scores, prepare frequency distributions, compute correlations, extract and rotate factors by various methods. These programs are not available in the well-known profession-ally developed computer packages such as BMDP, SAS, SYSTAT, and SPSS.

1.3.14. SUMMARY

The mathematical basis of the exploratory factor analytic procedures treated in this book is presented in Chapters 2–6, and for analytic rotation in Chapter 7. Instructions on the steps necessary for carrying out a factor analysis if the simplest procedures are to be used are given in Chapters 3–5. These instructions can be followed without mastering the mathematical basis of the methods. Non-mathematical discussions of important aspects of correct factor analytic practice are presented in Chapters 7, 8, 10, and 11. Confirmatory factor analytic methods and structural equation models are described in Chapters 12 and 13. Some useful computer programs are described in Chapter 14. If the reader does not have a great deal of mathematical training and, therefore, many parts of the book do not appear clear on the first reading, rereadings are recommended. Against the background of an earlier reading, many more pieces of the puzzle will fall into place on the second reading. Many students will find it necessary to reread the entire text several times before achieving an adequate depth of understanding. Persistence in rereading the text will be sufficient to compensate for inadequate mathematical background for most students. Others are urged to start with the simpler books recommended earlier.

2

The Factor Analytic Model

In this chapter, some of the fundamental ideas underlying factor analysis are developed in order to provide the reader with a theoretical introduction to the subject. Many of the ideas treated are highly abstract. As a consequence the student may have difficulty relating them to previous experience. It is also assumed that the student has a working knowledge of elementary trigonometry, algebra, and statistics. For these reasons, the reader may need to review some mathematical concepts and read the chapter several times before everything falls into place. The other chapters should be less difficult to follow once the material in this chapter is mastered. Some of the later chapters consider in greater detail the topics that are introduced here.

2.1. THE SPECIFICATION EQUATION

In factor analysis, it is customary to start with a matrix of correlations among data variables and wind up with a matrix of factor loadings that can be interpreted in the orthogonal factor model as correlations between the data variables and certain hypothetical constructs, called "factors." At the basis of this whole procedure, however, lies a fundamental assumption which can be stated as follows: A standard score on a data variable can be expressed as a weighted sum of the common factor scores, the specific factors scores, and the error factor scores. That is,

$$z_{ik} = a_{i1}F_{1k} + a_{i2}F_{2k} + \ldots + a_{im}F_{mk} + a_{is}S_{ik} + a_{ie}E_{ik} \qquad (2.1)$$

where

z_{ik} is a standard score for person k on data variable i,

a_{i1} is a factor loading for data variable i on common factor 1,

a_{i2} is a factor loading for data variable i on common factor 2,

a_{im} is a factor loading for data variable i on the last common factor,

a_{is} is a factor loading for data variable i on specific factor i,

a_{ie} is a factor loading for data variable i on error factor i,

F_{1k} is a standard score for person k on common factor 1,

F_{2k} is a standard score for person k on common factor 2,

F_{mk} is a standard score for person k on common factor m, the last common factor,

S_{ik} is a standard score for person k on specific factor i,

E_{ik} is a standard score for person k on error factor i.

The z, F, S, and E scores in Eq. (2.1) are all standard scores that have a mean (M) of zero and a standard deviation (σ) of 1.0. Each a value in Eq. (2.1) is a numerical constant, or weight, called a factor loading, which will usually fall between -1.0 and $+1.0$. The z score on the left-hand side of Eq. (2.1) is empirically obtained as a data-variable score, whereas the F, S, and E scores are hypothetical factor scores not obtained by data collection. The F scores are sometimes computed or estimated as part of a factor analysis, but the S and E scores are rarely computed in practice. The a values, the factor loadings, are found by the process of factor analysis itself. Standard scores rather than raw scores are used in Eq. (2.1) and in other equations to follow because the equations are simpler when standard scores are used.

Raw scores obtained in data collection may be converted to standard scores (z scores) by the formula $z = (X - M)/\sigma$, where X is a raw score, M is the mean of the X scores, and, as before, σ is the standard deviation of the X scores. Conversion from raw scores to standard scores may also be accomplished through the use of normal curve tables that give the standard scores corresponding to percentile scores associated with the raw scores. Conversion of raw scores to standard scores by means of normal curve tables not only standardizes the scores, that is, makes $M = 0$ and $\sigma = 1.0$, but also normalizes the distribution of scores as well. Equation (2.1) is called a "linear" equation because the variables in the equation, the standard scores variables, are all to the first power. The weights, the a

values in Eq. (2.1) are different for each variable and for each factor but remain constant from person to person.

Equation (2.1) can be made more concrete by relating it to a specific example. Let z_{ik} represent the standard score of person k on an intelligence test, to be treated as a single data variable in this example. Further, suppose for the sake of argument that there are just five common factors concerned with human intelligence, Verbal Ability (V), Numerical Ability (N), Memory (M), Reasoning Ability (R), and Perceptual Ability (P). Assume that the standard scores in these ability factors are known for every person in a given population. Then, in Eq. (2.1), F_{1k} represents person k's standard score on the Verbal (V) factor, F_{2k} represents person k's standard score on the Numerical (N) factor, and F_{5k} ($m = 5$ in this case) represents person k's standard score on the Perceptual (P) factor. The term S_{ik} represents person k's standard score on a specific factor associated only with this intelligence test; E_{ik} represents person k's standard score on the error factor associated only with this intelligence test. The values $a_{i1}, a_{i2}, \ldots, a_{i5}, a_{is}$, and a_{ie} are the factor loadings for the intelligence test on the five common ability factors plus the specific and error factors. In the orthogonal factor model described here, these a values may be thought of as correlations between variable i and the factors $V, N, M, R, P, S_i,$ and E_i. The a values are also weights that indicate the relative importance of the various factors in performance on the intelligence test. Equation (2.1) states, therefore, that the intelligence test score of person k equals the weighted sum of his standard scores in common factors $V, N, M, R,$ and P plus a specific factor component plus an error factor component.

Selecting a particular individual to represent person k might result in the following standard score substitutions in Eq. (2.1):

$$1.96 = a_{i1}(1.5) + a_{i2}(1.0) + a_{i3}(2.5) + a_{i4}(-1.0)$$
$$+ a_{i5}(-.2) + a_{is}(-.3) + a_{ie}(1.0)$$

The standard scores substituted in Eq. (2.1) with rare exceptions will be values between -3.0 and $+3.0$. If hypothetical factor loadings are now substituted for the a values, the equation becomes:

$$1.96 = .50(1.5) + .40(1.0) + .40(2.5) + .37(-1.0)$$
$$+ .30(-.2) + .30(-.3) + .33(1.0)$$

Person k's standard score on the intelligence test, 1.96, is a relatively high one, with about 97.5% of the population below this score. When a mean of 100 and a standard deviation of 16 is used, this would correspond to an IQ of about 132. The student's best ability is Memory, with Verbal and Numerical also well above average. Reasoning and Perceptual abilities are below average. The below-average specific factor score is countered by an above-average error score, which boosted the intelligence score higher than it should be. It is clear that the data-variable score cannot be reproduced exactly by the common factors alone. The specific and error factors must be taken into account. The more reliable the test, however, the smaller will be the error factor loading.

Equation (2.1) may be represented in schematic matrix form for all values of i and k simultaneously, that is, for all data variables and all persons or other data-producing objects, as shown in Fig. (2.1).

The schematic matrix equation given in Fig. (2.1) may be represented by the following matrix equation:

$$\mathbf{Z} = \mathbf{A}_u \mathbf{F}_u \qquad (2.2)$$

Equation (2.2) states that the matrix of data-variable scores $\mathbf{Z}$ may be obtained by multiplying the matrix of factor loadings $\mathbf{A}_u$ by the matrix of factor scores $\mathbf{F}_u$. Matrix multiplication is explained below.

Each row of the data score matrix $\mathbf{Z}$ gives the standard scores for all the data-yielding subjects, persons, or objects, for one variable. A column of the $\mathbf{Z}$ matrix gives all the standard scores on all the data variables for a given person or other data-yielding object. The matrix of factor loadings $\mathbf{A}_u$ is partitioned into three sections for didactic purposes. The left-hand section contains the factor loadings for the n data variables on the m common factors. The middle section of $\mathbf{A}_u$ contains the factor loadings for the n data variables on the specific factors. The right-hand section of $\mathbf{A}_u$ contains the factor loadings for the n data variables on the error factors. The middle and right-hand sections of $\mathbf{A}_u$ contain nonzero entries only in the diagonal cells due to the assumption of the factor analytic model that each data variable has a loading in its own specific and error factors but not in the specific and error factors for any other data variables. Any factor with nonzero loadings for two or more variables would, by definition, be a "common factor" and therefore would belong in the first part of the $\mathbf{A}_u$ matrix. Specific and error factors, on the other hand, each have loadings for one and only one variable, and hence cannot be common factors. Each row of the matrix of factor scores $\mathbf{F}_u$ contains the factor scores for all data-yielding persons or objects for a given factor. The common factor scores appear in the first m rows of $\mathbf{F}_u$, the specific factor scores in the middle n rows, and the error factor scores in the last n rows.

By multiplying the matrix $\mathbf{A}_u$ by the matrix $\mathbf{F}_u$, then, Eq. (2.1) is represented for all persons, or all values of k, and for all observed data variables, or all values of i. The common factor portion of $\mathbf{A}_u$, the left-hand

FIG. 2.1. Schematic Matrix Representation of Equation (2.1)

section, will be called matrix **A** (without the subscript u), and the common factor portion of $\mathbf{F}_u$, the top section, will be called matrix **F**.

2.1.1.   MATRIX MULTIPLICATION

Matrix multiplication will be illustrated by an example. The first row of the matrix on the left is multiplied with the first column of the matrix on the right to give the entry in the first row and first column of the product matrix. In general, the ith row of the matrix on the left is multiplied with the jth column of the matrix on the right to give the ijth element of the product matrix. This row by column multiplication, called "inner multiplication," proceeds by multiplying the first element of the row on the left by the first element of the column on the right and adding this result to the products for the second elements, the third elements, and so on, as illustrated in Fig. (2.2).

The number of columns in the matrix on the left in Fig. (2.2) must equal the number of rows in the matrix on the right; otherwise a row of the matrix on the left will not have the right number of elements to permit inner multiplication with a column of the matrix on the right. The product matrix will have the same number of rows as the matrix on the left and the same number of columns as the matrix on the right. Referring back to Eq. (2.2), the product $\mathbf{A}_u\mathbf{F}_u$ will have n rows and N columns, as shown in the product matrix **Z**. It should be noted that matrix multiplication is not commutative as a rule; that is, the product of matrix **A** times **B** is not in general equal to the product of matrix **B** times **A**. In fact, such reversals of the order of multiplication are often not even possible because the number of columns of the matrix on the left must equal the number of rows of the matrix on the right.

$$\begin{bmatrix} 2 & 4 & 3 & 1 \\ 5 & 3 & 4 & 0 \end{bmatrix} \times \begin{bmatrix} 3 & 4 \\ 1 & 2 \\ 5 & 1 \\ 4 & 5 \end{bmatrix} = \begin{bmatrix} p_{11} & p_{12} \\ p_{21} & p_{22} \end{bmatrix} = \begin{bmatrix} 29 & 24 \\ 38 & 30 \end{bmatrix}$$

$p_{11} = (2 \times 3) + (4 \times 1) + (3 \times 5) + (1 \times 4) = 6 + 4 + 15 + 4 = 29$

$p_{12} = (2 \times 4) + (4 \times 2) + (3 \times 1) + (1 \times 5) = 8 + 8 + 3 + 5 = 24$

$p_{21} = (5 \times 3) + (3 \times 1) + (4 \times 5) + (0 \times 4) = 15 + 3 + 20 + 0 = 38$

$p_{22} = (5 \times 4) + (3 \times 2) + (4 \times 1) + (0 \times 5) = 20 + 6 + 4 + 0 = 30$

FIG. 2.2.   Matrix Multiplication

2.2.   THE FUNDAMENTAL EQUATION OF FACTOR ANALYSIS

Returning to matrix equation (2.2), if we wish to reproduce the score on variable 5 for person number 9, the fifth row of matrix $\mathbf{A}_u$ is inner multiplied with the ninth column of matrix $\mathbf{F}_u$. This would give

$$z_{59} = a_{51}F_{19} + a_{52}F_{29} + \ldots + a_{5m}F_{m9} + \ldots + 0 \cdot S_{19} +$$
$$0 \cdot S_{49} + a_{5s}S_{59} + 0 \cdot S_{69} + \ldots + 0 \cdot S_{n9} + \ldots 0 \cdot E_{19}$$
$$+ 0 \cdot E_{49} + a_{5e}E_{59} + 0 \cdot E_{69} + \ldots + 0 \cdot E_{n9} \qquad (2.3)$$

Equation (2.3) is a form of Eq. (2.1), substituting 9 for k and 5 for i. Any value from 1 to N may be substituted for k in Eq. (2.1) and any value from 1 to n may be substituted for i. The upper case letter N will be used throughout the book to represent the number of persons or other data-yielding objects. The lower case letter n will always be used to represent the number of data variables for which scores are obtained from the data-yielding objects.

Substituting the subscript j for the subscript i in Eq. (2.1) yields an expression representing a standard score for person k in variable j:

$$z_{jk} = a_{j1}F_{1k} + a_{j2}F_{2k} + \ldots + a_{jm}F_{mk} + a_{js}S_{jk} + a_{je}E_{jk} \qquad (2.4)$$

If we now multiply Eq. (2.1) by Eq. (2.4), sum both sides over k from 1 to N, and divide both sides by N, the result after some simplification may be expressed as follows:

$$\frac{1}{N} \cdot \sum_{k=1}^{k=N} z_{ik}z_{jk} = \frac{a_{i1}a_{j1}}{N} \cdot \sum_{k=1}^{k=N} F_{1k}^2$$

$$+ \frac{a_{i2}a_{j2}}{N} \cdot \sum_{k=1}^{k=N} F_{2k}^2 + \ldots + \frac{a_{im}a_{jm}}{N} \cdot \sum_{k=1}^{k=N} F_{mk}^2$$

$$+ \frac{2a_{i1}a_{j2}}{N} \cdot \sum_{k=1}^{k=N} F_{1k}F_{2k} + \ldots + \frac{2a_{i(m-1)}a_{jm}}{N} \cdot \sum_{k=1}^{k=N} F_{(m-1)k}F_{mk}$$

$$+ \frac{a_{i1}a_{js}}{N} \cdot \sum_{k=1}^{k=N} F_{1k}S_{jk} + \ldots + \frac{a_{im}a_{js}}{N} \cdot \sum_{k=1}^{k=N} F_{mk}S_{jk}$$

$$+ \frac{a_{i1}a_{je}}{N} \cdot \sum_{k=1}^{k=N} F_{1k}E_{jk} + \ldots + \frac{a_{im}a_{je}}{N} \cdot \sum_{k=1}^{k=N} F_{mk}E_{jk}$$

$$+ \frac{a_{j1}a_{is}}{N} \cdot \sum_{k=1}^{k=N} F_{1k}S_{ik} + \ldots + \frac{a_{jm}a_{is}}{N} \cdot \sum_{k=1}^{k=N} F_{mk}S_{ik}$$

$$+ \frac{a_{j1}a_{ie}}{N} \cdot \sum_{k=1}^{k=N} F_{1k}E_{ik} + \ldots + \frac{a_{jm}a_{ie}}{N} \cdot \sum_{k=1}^{k=N} F_{mk}E_{ik}$$

$$+ \frac{a_{is}a_{js}}{N} \cdot \sum_{k=1}^{k=N} S_{ik}S_{jk} + \frac{a_{is}a_{je}}{N} \cdot \sum_{k=1}^{k=N} S_{ik}E_{jk}$$

$$+ \frac{a_{ie}a_{js}}{N} \cdot \sum_{k=1}^{k=N} E_{ik}S_{jk} + \frac{a_{ie}a_{je}}{N} \cdot \sum_{k=1}^{k=N} E_{ik}E_{jk} \tag{2.5}$$

The formula for the correlation coefficient in standard score form is:

$$r_{ij} = \frac{1}{N} \cdot \sum_{k=1}^{k=N} z_{ik}z_{jk} \tag{2.6}$$

The formula for the variance, that is, the standard deviation squared, of the set of standard scores is

$$\sigma_i^2 = \frac{1}{N} \sum_{k=1}^{k=N} z_{ik}^2 = 1.0 \tag{2.7}$$

The reader is reminded that the sign Σ means to add up the terms with the subscripts which are placed immediately after this summation sign. Thus

$$\sum_{k=1}^{k=N} z_{ik}z_{jk} = z_{i1}z_{j1} + z_{i2}z_{j2} + \ldots + z_{iN}z_{jN} \tag{2.8}$$

That is, the two standard scores in data variables i and j for the first person are multiplied together; then, the two standard scores in data variables i and j for the second person are multiplied together, and so on, until the two scores for the last person are multiplied together; then, all these products are added up to get the summation total which is the single number symbolized by the expression in Eq. (2.8). Any numerical constant appearing in such a summation of terms may be moved from the right- to the left-hand side of the summation sign as in the following, where a_{i1} is an example of such a constant:

$$\sum_{k=1}^{k=N} a_{i1}F_{1k}^2 = a_{i1}F_{11}^2 + a_{i1}F_{12}^2 + \ldots + a_{i1}F_{1N}^2$$

$$= a_{i1} (F_{11}^2 + F_{12}^2 + \ldots + F_{1N}^2)$$

$$= a_{i1} \sum_{k=1}^{k=N} F_{1k}^2 \tag{2.9}$$

Note that the summation is over the subscript k rather than the subscript i. For this reason, a_{i1} is a constant term as far as this summation is concerned since it contains no k subscript.

All the summation terms on the right-hand side of Eq. (2.5) after the first few involving sums of F^2 values equal zero since when divided by N they equal correlations between different sets of factor scores. These sums of cross products divided by N are like the formula in Eq. (2.6). Such values are assumed to be zero in the orthogonal factor analytic model. This causes all but the first few terms to vanish in Eq. (2.5). In a later chapter, a nonorthogonal, or oblique, factor analytic model is considered in which the factors are correlated with each other.

The term on the left-hand side of Eq. (2.5) is also a correlation, namely between variables i and j, but it is not assumed to be zero. All the summation terms on the right-hand side of Eq. (2.5) involving sums of F^2 values, when divided by N, equal the variance of a set of standard scores, like Eq. (2.7). These values are all equal to 1.0. Substituting zeros for the correlations between factors and 1.0 for the variances of factors in Eq. (2.5) results in simplifying the formula to

$$r_{ij} = a_{i1}a_{j1} + a_{i2}a_{j2} + \ldots + a_{im}a_{jm} \qquad (2.10)$$

In other words, Eq. (2.10) states that the correlation between data variables i and j is the sum of the products of their factor loadings in the common factors only. All the specific and error factor cross-product terms drop out of Eq. (2.5) as long as the factors are orthogonal, that is, uncorrelated, with each other. The term on the left of Eq. (2.5) and (2.10) is not equal to zero because it is a correlation between data variables rather than between factor scores. Where i equals j, the correlation is that of a variable with itself due to common factor variance only, with the specific factor variance omitted.

For all values of i and j simultaneously, Eq. (2.10) may be represented by the schematic matrix diagram shown on page 30.

The schematic matrix notation on page 30 represents Eq. (2.10) for all values of i and j simultaneously. The matrix equation corresponding to this schematic representation is

$$\mathbf{R} = \mathbf{AA'} \qquad (2.11)$$

Equation (2.11) states that the correlation matrix $\mathbf{R}$ with communalities in the diagonal cells may be represented as a product of the matrix of common factor loadings multiplied by the transpose of the matrix of common factor loadings. The transpose of a matrix is obtained by interchanging rows and columns; that is, row 1 of $\mathbf{A}$ is column 1 of $\mathbf{A'}$. A numerical example is shown below.

$$
\mathbf{R} = \begin{array}{c|ccccc} & 1 & 2 & 3 & \cdots & n \\ \hline 1 & r_{11} & r_{12} & r_{13} & \cdots & r_{1n} \\ 2 & r_{21} & r_{22} & r_{23} & \cdots & r_{2n} \\ 3 & r_{31} & r_{32} & r_{33} & \cdots & r_{3n} \\ \vdots & \vdots & \vdots & \vdots & \vdots & \vdots \\ n & r_{n1} & r_{n2} & r_{n3} & \cdots & r_{nn} \end{array}
$$

$$
= \mathbf{A} \times \mathbf{A'}
$$

$$
\mathbf{A} = \begin{array}{c|ccccc} & 1 & 2 & 3 & \cdots & m \\ \hline 1 & a_{11} & a_{12} & a_{13} & \cdots & a_{1m} \\ 2 & a_{21} & a_{22} & a_{23} & \cdots & a_{2m} \\ 3 & a_{31} & a_{32} & a_{33} & \cdots & a_{3m} \\ \vdots & \vdots & \vdots & \vdots & \vdots & \vdots \\ n & a_{n1} & a_{n2} & a_{n3} & \cdots & a_{nm} \end{array}
\qquad
\mathbf{A'} = \begin{array}{c|ccccc} & 1 & 2 & 3 & \cdots & n \\ \hline 1 & a_{11} & a_{21} & a_{31} & \cdots & a_{n1} \\ 2 & a_{12} & a_{22} & a_{32} & \cdots & a_{n2} \\ 3 & a_{13} & a_{23} & a_{33} & \cdots & a_{n3} \\ \vdots & \vdots & \vdots & \vdots & \vdots & \vdots \\ m & a_{1m} & a_{2m} & a_{3m} & \cdots & a_{nm} \end{array}
$$

If $\mathbf{P} = \begin{bmatrix} 1 & 2 \\ 4 & 5 \\ 7 & 3 \end{bmatrix}$ then $\mathbf{P'} = \begin{bmatrix} 1 & 4 & 7 \\ 2 & 5 & 3 \end{bmatrix}$

Just as the algebraic equation (2.10) could be derived by algebraic means from algebraic equation (2.1), so it is also possible to derive matrix equation (2.11), the matrix equivalent of algebraic equation (2.10), by matrix operations. First, consider the following matrix equation:

$$
\mathbf{R}_u = \frac{1}{N}(\mathbf{ZZ'}) \tag{2.12}
$$

Matrix equation (2.12) is represented schematically as shown on page 31 in Eq. (2.12a). A row i of matrix $\mathbf{Z}$ inner multiplied with a column j of matrix $\mathbf{Z'}$ gives a sum of cross products of standard scores. When this sum is divided by N, as required in Eq. (2.12), the resulting expression is a correlation coefficient between variables i and j as shown by the formula in Eq. (2.6). For the diagonal terms, the row by column multiplication gives variance terms, like those in Eq. (2.7), which are all equal to 1.0. When unities, rather than communalities, are placed in the diagonal cells, the correlation matrix will be designated by the symbol $\mathbf{R}_u$. With communalities

$$\mathbf{R}_u = \frac{1}{N}(ZZ') = \frac{1}{N} \times 3$$

	1	2	3	⋯	n
1	1.0	r_{12}	r_{13}	⋯	r_{1n}
2	r_{21}	1.0	r_{23}	⋯	r_{2n}
3	r_{31}	r_{32}	1.0	⋯	r_{3n}
⋯	⋯	⋯	⋯	⋯	⋯
n	r_{n1}	r_{n2}	r_{n3}	⋯	1.0

$n \times 3$

	1	2	3	⋯	N
1	z_{11}	z_{12}	z_{13}	⋯	z_{1N}
2	z_{21}	z_{22}	z_{23}	⋯	z_{2N}
3	z_{31}	z_{32}	z_{33}	⋯	z_{3N}
⋯	⋯	⋯	⋯	⋯	⋯
n	z_{n1}	z_{n2}	z_{n3}	⋯	z_{nN}

Z

$N \times 3$

	1	2	3	⋯	n
1	z_{11}	z_{21}	z_{31}	⋯	z_{n1}
2	z_{12}	z_{22}	z_{32}	⋯	z_{n2}
3	z_{13}	z_{23}	z_{33}	⋯	z_{n3}
⋯	⋯	⋯	⋯	⋯	⋯
N	z_{1N}	z_{2N}	z_{3N}	⋯	z_{nN}

Z'

Matrix equation (2.12a).

in the diagonal cells, the correlation matrix will be designated by the symbol **R** without the subscript.

Equation (2.2) states that $\mathbf{Z} = \mathbf{A}_u\mathbf{F}_u$; that is, the standard score matrix for the data variables is equal to the complete matrix of factor loadings multiplied by the complete matrix of factors scores. Substituting Eq. (2.2) into Eq. (2.12) gives

$$\mathbf{R}_u = \frac{1}{N}\, (\mathbf{A}_u\mathbf{F}_u)\, (\mathbf{A}_u\mathbf{F}_u)\,' \tag{2.13}$$

Using the fact that the transpose of a product of two matrices equals the product of their transposes in reverse order and relocating the position of the constant divisor N, Eq. (2.13) can be rewritten as follows:

$$\mathbf{R}_u = \mathbf{A}_u \left[\frac{\mathbf{F}_u\mathbf{F}_u{}'}{N} \right] \mathbf{A}_u' \tag{2.14}$$

The matrix product in parentheses on the right-hand side of Eq. (2.14), $\mathbf{F}_u\mathbf{F}_u'/N$, represents a matrix of correlations between factor scores, since each element of this product matrix is of the same form as Eq. (2.6). The matrix of correlations between these factor scores contains only elements of 1 and 0, depending on whether the correlation is that of a factor score with itself or with some other factor. The correlation of a factor with itself becomes a variance term, like that in Eq. (2.7), and hence equals 1.0. Such a matrix is termed an identity matrix **I**. It has ones in the diagonal cells and zeros in all other cells. Multiplying a matrix by an identity matrix leaves it unchanged; it is like multiplying by 1 in ordinary scalar algebra. Since the factor scores in this model are all uncorrelated, or orthogonal, the matrix $\mathbf{F}_u\mathbf{F}_u'/N$ looks like that shown in Fig. (2.3). Equation (2.14) may be rewritten, therefore, to give

$$\mathbf{R}_u = \mathbf{A}_u\mathbf{I}\mathbf{A}_u' \tag{2.15}$$

Dropping the identity matrix leaves

$$\mathbf{R}_u = \mathbf{A}_u\mathbf{A}_u' \tag{2.16}$$

where $\mathbf{R}_u$ is the correlation matrix among data variables with l's in the diagonal cells and $\mathbf{A}_u$ is the complete matrix of factor loadings, including common, specific, and error factors. The matrix $\mathbf{R}_u$ is symmetric; that is, an element r_{ij} equals the element r_{ji}. Putting it another way, the elements above the diagonal are the same as those below the diagonal so that $\mathbf{R}_u = \mathbf{R}_u'$. Matrix $\mathbf{A}_u$ values also represent correlations between the data variables and the factors. These correlations are called factor loadings in the orthogonal

	1	2	3	...	m	1	2	3	...	n	1	2	3	...	n
1	1														
2		1													
3			1					0					0		
...				...											
m					1										
1						1									
2							1								
3			0					1					0		
...									...						
n										1					
1											1				
2												1			
3			0					0					1		
...														...	
n															1

FIG. 2.3.   Matrix $\mathbf{F}_u\mathbf{F}_u'/N$

factor model which requires all factors to be at right angles to one another, that is, to be uncorrelated. The matrix $\mathbf{A}$ consists of only the common factor portion of the factor loadings in matrix $\mathbf{A}_u$.

From Eq. (2.10) and (2.11), it is apparent that only the common factors enter into determining the off-diagonal elements of $\mathbf{R}$. For the diagonal elements, however, or those r_{ij} values for which $i = j$, the specific and error factors do make a contribution in Eq. (2.16) where $\mathbf{R}_u$ is reproduced as the product $\mathbf{A}_u\mathbf{A}_u'$. To show this, square both sides of Eq. (2.1) to get

$$z_{ik}^2 = a_{i1}^2 F_{1k}^2 + a_{i2}^2 F_{2k}^2 + \ldots + a_{is}^2 S_{ik}^2 + a_{ie}^2 E_{ik}^2$$
$$+ 2a_{i1}F_{1k}a_{i2}F_{2k} + \ldots + 2a_{is}S_{ik}a_{ie}E_{ik} \qquad (2.17)$$

Summing both sides of Eq. (2.17) and dividing by N gives

$$\frac{1}{N} \cdot \sum_{k=1}^{k=N} z_{ik}^2 = \frac{a_{i1}^2}{N} \cdot \sum_{k=1}^{k=N} F_{1k}^2$$

$$+ \frac{a_{i2}^2}{N} \cdot \sum_{k=1}^{k=N} F_{2k}^2 + \ldots + \frac{a_{im}^2}{N} \cdot \sum_{k=1}^{k=N} F_{mk}^2$$

$$+ \frac{a_{is}^2}{N} \cdot \sum_{k=1}^{k=N} S_{ik}^2 + \frac{a_{ie}^2}{N} \cdot \sum_{k=1}^{k=N} E_{ik}^2$$

$$+ \frac{2a_{i1}a_{i2}}{N} \cdot \sum_{k=1}^{k=N} F_{1k}F_{2k} + \ldots + \frac{2a_{is}a_{ie}}{N} \cdot \sum_{k=1}^{k=N} S_{ik}E_{ik} \qquad (2.18)$$

Every term in Eq. (2.18) that involves a sum of a single variable squared includes a variance of a standard score, like Eq. (2.7), in either a data variable or a factor, which reduces to 1.0. Every term in Eq. (2.18) that involves a sum of a product of two variables contains a correlation coefficient, like Eq. (2.6), but the correlation coefficient in each case is zero since it is a correlation between uncorrelated factors. Equation (2.18) simplifies, therefore, to

$$1 = a_{i1}^2 + a_{i2}^2 + \ldots + a_{im}^2 + a_{is}^2 + a_{ie}^2 \tag{2.19}$$

Equation (2.19) shows that all the diagonal elements of $\mathbf{R}_u = \mathbf{A}_u \mathbf{A}_u'$ are equal to 1, which is also the variance of any standard score variable. This variance may be divided up as follows:

$$1 = h_{ii}^2 + u_{ii}^2 \tag{2.20}$$

where

$$h_{ii}^2 = a_{i1}^2 + a_{i2}^2 + \ldots + a_{im}^2 \text{ and } u_{ii}^2 = a_{is}^2 + a_{ie}^2$$

The h_{ii}^2 is called the communality of variable i. It is equal to the sum of squares of the loadings for variable i in the common factors. the u_{ii}^2 is called the uniqueness of variable i. It is equal to the sum of squares of the loadings in the specific and error factors. The communality represents the portion of the total variance of a data variable which is due to common factors. The uniqueness represents the proportion of the total variance of a data variable that can be accounted for by error and specific factors. The reliability of a data variable is given by the communality plus the proportion of variance due to its specific factor, excluding only the error variance. Thus

$$r_{ii} = h_{ii}^2 + a_{is}^2 \tag{2.21}$$

where r_{ii} is the reliability for variable i and a_{is} is the specific factor loading for variable i.

Equations (2.16) and (2.11) are two forms of a very important theorem in factor analysis which has been called by Thurstone (1947) the fundamental equation of factor analysis; they both state that the correlation matrix among the data variables can be decomposed into the product of a factor matrix times its transpose. Equation (2.16), $\mathbf{R}_u = \mathbf{A}_u \mathbf{A}_u'$, reproduces the correlation matrix with 1's in the diagonals, using a factor matrix $\mathbf{A}_u$ which contains common, specific, and error factors. Equation (2.11), $\mathbf{R} = \mathbf{A}\mathbf{A}'$, reproduces the reduced correlation matrix $\mathbf{R}$ with communalities in the diagonal cells instead of 1's. All other entries are the same in the two matrices $\mathbf{R}$ and $\mathbf{R}_u$. To account for the correlations among data variables, therefore, only the common factors are needed. To account for the total data-variable variance, specific, error, and common factors are needed in this model.

2.3.   FACTOR EXTRACTION

As ordinarily carried out, the process of factor extraction starts with a matrix of correlations between data variables with communalities in the diagonals and ends up with a matrix of factor loadings $\mathbf{A}$ such that when multiplied by its transpose $\mathbf{A}'$ the correlation matrix $\mathbf{R}$ will be reproduced, at least approximately. The specific and error factor loadings are not obtained ordinarily and the $\mathbf{R}$ matrix is not usually reproduced exactly. Factor extraction, then, represents a problem in matrix decomposition, that is, the decomposition of $\mathbf{R}$ into the product of another matrix and its transpose. Many different methods have been devised to find a matrix $\mathbf{A}$ such that $\mathbf{R} = \mathbf{AA}'$. Only a few of these methods are discussed in this book.

If 1's are put in the diagonal cells to get $\mathbf{R}_u$, it is ordinarily possible to carry out a factor analysis obtaining a matrix $\mathbf{A}$ such that $\mathbf{AA}'$ reproduces $\mathbf{R}_u$ exactly, but it usually requires an $\mathbf{A}$ matrix the same size as $\mathbf{R}_u$. That is, there are as many factors in $\mathbf{A}$ as there are data variables in $\mathbf{R}_u$. In such a case, all the factors are common factors in that the error and specific factor variance has been totally absorbed by the common factors.

Traditionally, however, one of the major goals of factor analysis has been to account for a data matrix in terms of fewer factors than data variables. According to the principle of scientific parsimony, it is desirable to account for the data in a given domain making use of as few constructs as possible. In factor analysis, this principle is translated into the goal of reproducing the $\mathbf{R}$ matrix with an $\mathbf{A}$ matrix containing as few factors as possible.

To reproduce the $\mathbf{R}$ matrix exactly with real data ordinarily requires as many factors as there are data variables. It is usually possible, however, to reproduce approximately the $\mathbf{R}$ matrix with $\mathbf{AA}'$ where $\mathbf{A}$ has a number of common factors m such that m is considerably smaller than n, the number of data variables in $\mathbf{R}$. Since it is known that sampling error exists in most data, the correlation coefficients are considered to be in error to some extent, making it useless in practice to reproduce them exactly. It is considered better to tolerate some discrepancies between the computed data correlations in the matrix $\mathbf{R}$ and the reproduced correlation matrix $\mathbf{AA}'$ in order to reduce the number of explanatory constructs, or factors, needed to account for the data, that is, the **R** matrix.

In certain cases, it would be ideal to be able to account for the **R** matrix with a single factor, as in the following fictitious example:

$$
\begin{bmatrix}
.16 & .32 & .28 & .24 \\
.32 & .64 & .56 & .48 \\
.28 & .56 & .49 & .42 \\
.24 & .48 & .42 & .36
\end{bmatrix}
=
\begin{bmatrix}
.4 \\
.8 \\
.7 \\
.6
\end{bmatrix}
\times
\begin{bmatrix} .4 & .8 & .7 & .6 \end{bmatrix}
\qquad (2.22)
$$

$$
\quad\quad\quad\quad \mathbf{R} \quad\quad\quad\quad\quad\quad \mathbf{A} \quad\quad\quad\quad \mathbf{A'}
$$

If one factor is sufficient to account for the correlations, the **R** matrix shows some interesting properties. The columns are proportional to each other and consequently all the minor determinants of order 2 vanish. That is, picking out any 2×2 matrix embedded in the larger matrix and evaluating its determinant results in a value of zero. Thus, from the **R** matrix in Eq. (2.22) one of the submatrices of order 2 is

$$
\begin{bmatrix} r_{12} & r_{14} \\ r_{32} & r_{34} \end{bmatrix}
=
\begin{bmatrix} .32 & .24 \\ .56 & .42 \end{bmatrix}
$$

A 2×2 submatrix is formed by omitting all but two rows and all but two columns of the matrix. This leaves only four elements arranged in a 2×2 matrix. The minor determinant of the foregoing submatrix may be evaluated numerically as follows: $r_{12}r_{34} - r_{32}r_{14} = (.32)(.42) - (.56)(.24) = (.1344) - (.1344) = 0$

If all the minor determinants of order 2 equal zero, the matrix is said to have rank 1; then, one factor will account for the **R** matrix. This was the criterion used by Spearman in developing his famous g-factor theory of intelligence. He was attempting to account for intelligence in terms of a single common factor plus a separate specific factor for each kind of test. Thurstone employed the generalization of this principle as follows: If all the minor determinants of size 3×3 have determinants equal to zero but those of size 2×2 are not all zero, then two factors are needed to account for the **R** matrix exactly and the matrix has rank 2. In general, if all the minor determinants of size $m + 1$ equal zero, but not all those of order m, then m factors are needed to account for the **R** matrix and the matrix has rank m. Random errors in the **R** matrix and the complexities of real-life data ordinarily combine to render even the total **R** matrix nonsingular, that is, having a determinant not equal to zero. Thus, n factors are needed to account for the typical **R** matrix exactly, giving it a rank of n. More efficient methods than evaluating determinants are available, however, for deciding how many factors are needed to account for the **R** matrix.

Methods of factor extraction, designed to produce the **A** matrix, usually seek to account for as much of the total extracted variance as possible on each successive extracted factor. That is, a factor is sought at each step for which the sum of squares of the factor loadings is as large as possible. The total variance extracted in a factor analysis is represented by the sum of the computed communalities, that is the sum of the h_{ii}^2 values from 1 to m where m is the number of common factors. All the data-variable variance is not ordinarily extracted. Each variable has a variance of 1, so the total data-variable variance that could theoretically be extracted is $n \times 1$, or n, where n is the number of data variables. If the sum of the a_{ik}^2 values for all values of i from 1 to n represents the sum of squares of loadings on factor k, the proportion of the total extracted variance due to factor k is obtained by dividing this total by the sum of the communalities. Since n is the total variance for all variables combined, that is, the sum of the diagonal elements of $\mathbf{R}_u$, then dividing the sum of the communalities by n gives the proportion of the total variance that is accounted for by common factors.

After the first factor has been determined, its contribution to reproducing the $\mathbf{R}$ matrix is removed from $\mathbf{R}$ by the operation $\mathbf{R}_1 = \mathbf{R} - \mathbf{A}_1\mathbf{A}_1'$, where $\mathbf{A}_1$ represents the first factor vector, a_{11}, a_{21}, . . ., a_{n1}, and $\mathbf{A}_1'$ is the transpose of $\mathbf{A}_1$; $\mathbf{R}_1$ is called the residual matrix. It contains the residual correlations after the contribution to those correlations by factor 1 has been removed, that is, the term on the right-hand side of Eq. (2.10) associated with factor 1. If one factor is insufficient to reproduce the correlations in $\mathbf{R}$, then $\mathbf{R}_1$ will have some values which are substantially different from zero. If this is the case, another factor will be extracted from the first residual matrix by the equation $\mathbf{R}_2 = \mathbf{R}_1 - \mathbf{A}_2\mathbf{A}_2'$. Thus, the second extracted factor is removed from the first factor residuals. In general, this process is continued, extracting the mth factor from the residuals left after taking out factor $m - 1$, until the residuals are too small to yield another factor. Since at each step, as much variance is extracted as possible, the successive factors become smaller and smaller from first to last as shown by the sum of squares of the loadings in the successive columns of $\mathbf{A}$. Some methods of factor extraction, however, do not extract factor vectors in order of size of the sum of squares of their loadings. With such methods, the columns of the $\mathbf{A}$ matrix would have to be rearranged to attain this decreasing order of size of factors from first to last. This initial $\mathbf{A}$ matrix does not represent the final factor solution, however. These factors are "rotated" from their original positions by methods that are explained later. After the factors have been rotated, they are more nearly equal in size than the initially extracted factors.

2.4. FACTOR ROTATION

Factor analysis in general and factor extraction methods in particular do not provide a unique solution to the matrix equation $\mathbf{R} = \mathbf{A}\mathbf{A}'$. One of the reasons is that the **R** matrix is only approximately reproduced in practice and experimenters may differ on how closely they feel they must approximate **R**. This will lead to their using different numbers of factors. Also, different methods of determining **A** may give slightly different results. An even more important reason for lack of unique solutions, however, is the fact that even for **A** matrices of the same number of factors, there are infinitely many different **A** matrices that will reproduce the **R** matrix equally well. Consider the following:

$$
\underbrace{\begin{bmatrix} a_{11} & a_{12} \\ a_{21} & a_{22} \\ a_{31} & a_{32} \\ a_{41} & a_{42} \end{bmatrix}}_{\mathbf{A}} \times \underbrace{\begin{bmatrix} \cos\phi & \sin\phi \\ -\sin\phi & \cos\phi \end{bmatrix}}_{\Lambda} = \underbrace{\begin{bmatrix} v_{11} & v_{12} \\ v_{21} & v_{22} \\ v_{31} & v_{32} \\ v_{41} & v_{42} \end{bmatrix}}_{\mathbf{V}}
$$

This schematic matrix operation may be expressed as a matrix equation:

$$\mathbf{A}\Lambda = \mathbf{V} \tag{2.23}$$

If $\mathbf{R} = \mathbf{A}\mathbf{A}'$, then it is also true that $\mathbf{R} = \mathbf{V}\mathbf{V}'$ since if we transpose the product $\mathbf{A}\Lambda$, Eq. (2.23) may be rewritten as

$$(\mathbf{A}\Lambda)' = \mathbf{V}' \tag{2.24}$$

Since the transpose of a product is the product of transposes in reverse order, Eq. (2.24) becomes

$$\Lambda'\mathbf{A}' = \mathbf{V}' \tag{2.25}$$

By using Eqs. (2.23) and (2.25) the product $\mathbf{V}\mathbf{V}'$ becomes

$$\mathbf{V}\mathbf{V}' = \mathbf{A}\Lambda\Lambda'\mathbf{A}' \tag{2.26}$$

But $\Lambda\Lambda'$, included in the middle of the matrix product in Eq. (2.26), gives an identity matrix, as follows:

$$
\underbrace{\begin{bmatrix} \cos\phi & \sin\phi \\ -\sin\phi & \cos\phi \end{bmatrix}}_{\Lambda} \times \underbrace{\begin{bmatrix} \cos\phi & -\sin\phi \\ \sin\phi & \cos\phi \end{bmatrix}}_{\Lambda'} = \underbrace{\begin{bmatrix} 1 & 0 \\ 0 & 1 \end{bmatrix}}_{\mathbf{I}} \tag{2.27}
$$

The reason for this is that the diagonal terms of the product matrix are equal to $\cos^2\phi + \sin^2\phi$, which equals 1 for all ϕ, and the off-diagonal elements are equal to $\sin\phi\cos\phi - \sin\phi\cos\phi$, which equals zero. As a result, Eq. (2.26) simplifies to $\mathbf{R} = \mathbf{VV'} = \mathbf{AA'}$, since multiplying by an identity matrix does not alter the matrix, that is, $\mathbf{AIA'} = \mathbf{AA'}$.

As long as the matrix Λ is of such a form that $\Lambda\Lambda' = \mathbf{I}$, then $\mathbf{A}\Lambda$ will reproduce the $\mathbf{R}$ matrix as well as $\mathbf{A}$ itself. Since the value of ϕ is not specified, this means that there are as many Λ matrices that will do this as there are values of ϕ. This particular Λ matrix was of size 2×2, or order 2, because only two factors were involved in the $\mathbf{A}$ matrix. If there had been three factors in the $\mathbf{A}$ matrix, the Λ matrix required would be of size 3×3. In general, if there are m factors in the $\mathbf{A}$ matrix, the Λ matrix will be of size $m \times m$. Any such Λ matrix must meet the following requirements: (1) the sums of squares of the rows must equal 1; (2) the sums of squares of the columns must equal 1; (3) the inner product of one row by another row must equal zero for all pairs of non-identical rows; (4) the inner product of one column by another column must equal zero for all pairs of nonidentical columns. If these conditions are met, then $\Lambda\Lambda' = \mathbf{I} = \Lambda'\Lambda$. If these conditions are not met, then $\Lambda\Lambda'$ is not equal to the identity matrix and $\mathbf{A}\Lambda$ will not substitute for $\mathbf{A}$ in reproducing the $\mathbf{R}$ matrix in the same way that $\mathbf{A}$ will.

The matrix $\mathbf{A}$ or $\mathbf{V}$ represents an interpretation of the data, the correlation matrix, in terms of a set of explanatory constructs, or factors. The values in a column of the $\mathbf{A}$ or $\mathbf{V}$ matrix of orthogonal factors are correlations of the data variables with the particular explanatory construct, or factor, represented by that column. By studying these correlations between the known data variables and the hypothetical explanatory constructs (or factors), it is possible to infer something about the nature of the explanatory constructs themselves. Factor interpretation is treated at greater length in a later chapter.

The values in a given column of $\mathbf{A}\Lambda$ will be different from those of $\mathbf{A}$ itself. This means that different constructs are involved. Matrix $\mathbf{A}$ represents one set of constructs for accounting for the data. Matrix $\mathbf{A}\Lambda$ represents a different set of constructs which account for the data equally well in the mathematical sense that both reproduce the $\mathbf{R}$ matrix equally well.

The so-called rotation process in factor analysis involves finding a Λ matrix such that $\mathbf{A}\Lambda$ will represent an optimum set of constructs for scientific purposes. Because what is optimum for one investigator may not be optimum for another, this particular phase of the factor analytic process provides a fertile source of differences among investigators in the way they view the data. But, just as the artist, the engineer, the geologist, and the farmer may all describe a given piece of real estate accurately in very different ways, so can various transformations of **A** provide equally accurate but different descriptions of a body of data. An attempt is made later in this book to provide some guidelines for choosing among alternate possible interpretations, all of which are equally good mathematically for reproducing **R**.

It is sometimes proposed that the **A** matrix should be used as it is, without performing any transformations; that is, use **A** instead of **A**Λ. This approach will yield factor constructs that are highly complex because each extracted factor accounts ordinarily for approximately as much variance as possible. The only way to make a factor account for this much variance is to make the factor overlap as much as possible with as many of the data variables as possible. Since such a factor correlates substantially with many variables that are essentially uncorrelated with each other, it becomes a complex composite of uncorrelated things. After this factor is removed, the second factor will become a complex composite of as much as possible of what is left in the matrix of residuals. The position is taken in this book that factor constructs are more useful if they are relatively univocal in character, that is, if they cannot be broken down into several essentially uncorrelated components. To derive univocal factor constructs from a factor analysis, if it is possible at all in a given situation, almost always requires that the original extracted **A** matrix be rotated or transformed to a **V** matrix by the transformation $\mathbf{V} = \mathbf{A}\Lambda$ where

$$\mathbf{R} = \mathbf{AA'} = \mathbf{VV'} \tag{2.28}$$

It is understood, of course, that in practice, Eq. (2.28) is only approximate in the sense that the **R** matrix is only approximately reproduced by **AA'** and **VV'**.

2.5. GEOMETRIC REPRESENTATION OF THE FACTOR MODEL

Although the factor model can be developed without reference to geometric concepts, as done by Horst (1965) in his book on factor analysis, most students find it helpful to employ an additional medium of representation in trying to understand the basis of this complex statistical technique.

In the geometric representation of the factor model, a data variable may be represented as a vector in a space of as many dimensions as there are common factors (see Fig. 2.4). In this case, the length of the vector is h, the square root of h^2, the communality. It is also possible to represent the data variables in spaces of higher order, adding also a dimension for each specific and error factor. If all of these factors are included, h^2 rises to 1.0

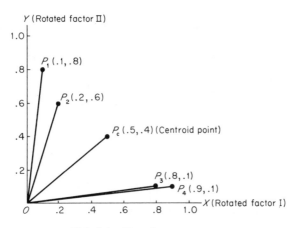

FIG. 2.4.   Four data vectors.

for each data variable and so does the vector length. In the most extreme
case, it is possible to represent each data variable by a vector in N
dimensions, requiring one coordinate axis for each person or other data-
yielding object.

As an illustration, Fig. 2.4 represents four data variables as vectors in a
two-dimensional space. A vector is a line extending from the origin to some
point in space, in this example a space of two dimensions, that is, a plane.
The coordinates of the end points (or termini) of the vectors are given.
There are two coordinates for each point because the vectors are represented in two dimensions. The vectors are represented in the common factor
space because the vectors are of length h rather than of length 1.0. If more
than two common factors were needed to account for the data, the vectors
would have to be represented in more than two dimensions and more than
two coordinates per vector would be needed.

By the Pythagorean theorem, the length of each vector in Fig. 2.4 is given
by the square root of the sum of squares of its coordinates:

$$h_1 = \sqrt{(.1)^2 + (.8)^2} = \sqrt{.01 + .64} = \sqrt{.65} = .806$$

$$h_2 = \sqrt{(.2)^2 + (.6)^2} = \sqrt{.04 + .36} = \sqrt{.40} = .632$$

$$h_3 = \sqrt{(.8)^2 + (.1)^2} = \sqrt{.64 + .01} = \sqrt{.65} = .806$$

$$h_4 = \sqrt{(.9)^2 + (.1)^2} = \sqrt{.81 + .01} = \sqrt{.82} = .906$$

(2.29)

For more than two dimensions, for example, m dimensions, vector length is
given by

$$h = \sqrt{a_1^2 + a_2^2 + a_3^2 + \ldots + a_m^2} \tag{2.30}$$

where the a_i values are the coordinates of the vector with respect to the m reference axes or dimensions. For more than three dimensions, of course, it is impossible to visualize the results. ✓

The scalar product of two vectors may be defined as follows:

$$[a_{11} \; a_{12} \; a_{13} \; \ldots \; a_{1m}] \times \begin{bmatrix} a_{21} \\ a_{22} \\ a_{23} \\ \ldots \\ a_{2m} \end{bmatrix} = [c_{12}] \tag{2.31}$$

where $c_{12} = a_{11}a_{21} + a_{12}a_{22} + \ldots + a_{1m}a_{2m}$ is a constant, i.e., a number. The values $a_{11}, a_{12}, a_{13}, \ldots, a_{1m}$ represent the coordinates of the first vector, and the values $a_{21}, a_{22}, a_{23}, \ldots, a_{2m}$ are the coordinates for the second vector. Thus, the scalar products of all possible pairs of the four test vectors in Fig. 2.4 are given as follows:

Pair	Row × Column	Scalar product
1,2	$[.1 \; .8] \times \begin{bmatrix} .2 \\ .6 \end{bmatrix}$	$= (.1 \times .2) + (.8 \times .6) = (.02 + .48) = .50$
1,3	$[.1 \; .8] \times \begin{bmatrix} .8 \\ .1 \end{bmatrix}$	$= (.1 \times .8) + (.8 \times .1) = (.08 + .08) = .16$
1,4	$[.1 \; .8] \times \begin{bmatrix} .9 \\ .1 \end{bmatrix}$	$= (.1 \times .9) + (.8 \times .1) = (.08 + .09) = .17$
2,3	$[.2 \; .6] \times \begin{bmatrix} .8 \\ .1 \end{bmatrix}$	$= (.2 \times .8) + (.6 \times .1) = (.16 + .06) = .22$
2,4	$[.2 \; .6] \times \begin{bmatrix} .9 \\ .1 \end{bmatrix}$	$= (.2 \times .9) + (.6 \times .1) = (.18 + .06) = .24$
3,4	$[.8 \; .1] \times \begin{bmatrix} .9 \\ .1 \end{bmatrix}$	$= (.8 \times .9) + (.1 \times .1) + (.72 + .01) = .73$

$$\tag{2.32}$$

Let λ_{ik} represent the cosine of the angle between vector i and coordinate axis k. The value λ_{ik} is called the direction cosine of vector i with respect to coordinate (factor) axis k. If a_{ik} is the coordinate of data vector i with respect to factor axis k, and h_i is the length of vector i, then

$$\lambda_{i1} = \frac{a_{i1}}{h_i}, \ \lambda_{i2} = \frac{a_{i2}}{h_i}, \ \ldots, \ \lambda_{im} = \frac{a_{im}}{h_i}$$

or

$$a_{i1} = h_i\lambda_{i1}, \ a_{i2} = h_i\lambda_{i2}, \ \ldots, \ a_{im} = h_i\lambda_{im}$$

and similarly for vector j

$$a_{j1} = h_j\lambda_{j1}, \ a_{j2} = h_j\lambda_{j2}, \ \ldots, \ a_{jm} = h_j\lambda_{jm}$$

Substituting these values in Eq. (2.31) gives the following representation of the scalar product of two vectors:

$$[h_i\lambda_{i1} \ h_i\lambda_{i2} \ \ldots \ h_i\lambda_{im}] \times \begin{bmatrix} h_j\lambda_{j1} \\ h_j\lambda_{j2} \\ \ldots \\ h_j\lambda_{jm} \end{bmatrix} = [c_{ij}] \qquad (2.31)$$

or

$$h_i h_j \lambda_{i1}\lambda_{j1} + h_i h_j \lambda_{i2}\lambda_{j2} + \ldots + h_i h_j \lambda_{im}\lambda_{jm} = c_{ij}$$

and

$$h_i h_j [\lambda_{i1}\lambda_{j1} + \lambda_{i2}\lambda_{j2} + \ldots + \lambda_{im}\lambda_{jm}] = c_{ij} \qquad (2.33)$$

A theorem from analytic geometry that will not be proved here states that the inner product of the direction cosines for two vectors equals the cosine of the angle between the vectors. Thus Eq. (2.33) becomes

$$h_i h_j \cos\phi_{ij} = c_{ij} \qquad (2.34)$$

The scalar product between vectors i and j is also equal to the correlation between them. The proof proceeds from Eq. (2.10): Dividing both sides of this equation by h_i and h_j gives

$$\frac{r_{ij}}{h_i h_j} = \frac{a_{i1}}{h_i} \cdot \frac{a_{j1}}{h_j} + \frac{a_{i2}}{h_i} \cdot \frac{a_{j2}}{h_j} + \ldots \frac{a_{im}}{h_i} \cdot \frac{a_{jm}}{h_j}$$

$$= \lambda_{i1}\lambda_{j1} + \lambda_{i2}\lambda_{j2} + \ldots + \lambda_{im}\lambda_{jm} = \cos\phi_{ij}$$

or

$$r_{ij} = h_i h_j \cos\phi_{ij} \qquad (2.35)$$

It should be pointed out that r_{ij} in Eq. (2.35) is the reproduced correlation based on the contributions of m common factors and hence is only approximately equal to the actual data correlation. The h_i, h_j, and ϕ_{ij} are the lengths of these vectors and the angle between them, respectively, in the common factor space.

Application of the law of cosines will show that the scalar products computed for all pairs of vectors in the series of equations in (2.32) are the same as the results of multiplying the lengths of the two vectors by the cosine of the angle between them as on the right-hand side of Eq. (2.35). For two of the vectors, P_1 and P_2, for example, the law of cosines states that

$$h_1 h_2 \cos\phi = 1/2 \, (h_1^2 + h_2^2 - d^2) \tag{2.36}$$

where d is the distance between the vector end points and is given by

$$d = \sqrt{(X_1 - X_2)^2 + (Y_1 - Y_2)^2} \tag{2.37}$$

where (X_1, Y_1) and (X_2, Y_2) are the coordinates for P_1 and P_2, respectively, in Fig. 2.1. For the first two vectors

$$d = \sqrt{(.1 - .2)^2 + (.8 - .6)^2} = \sqrt{.01 + .04} = \sqrt{.05}$$

Then, $h_1 h_2 \cos\phi_{12} = 1/2(.65 + .40 - .05) = .50$. This value is the same as that obtained for the scalar product of vectors 1 and 2 obtained in Eq. (2.32). Applying these same equations to the calculations for other vector pairs gives the same numbers as those obtained in Eq. (2.32) for the other scalar products.

The relationship between the correlation coefficient and the scalar product can be seen more clearly when the data variables are represented by vectors in a space of as many dimensions as persons, that is, in N dimensions. The lengths of such vectors are 1.0, so the coordinates for two vectors must be scaled by dividing the z scores by the square root of N. The sum of squares of such scores then equals 1.0, so the length of the vector scaled in this way is appropriately equal to 1.0. The scalar product of two such vectors is

$$\begin{bmatrix} \dfrac{z_{i1}}{\sqrt{N}} & \dfrac{z_{i2}}{\sqrt{N}} & \dfrac{z_{i3}}{\sqrt{N}} & \cdots & \dfrac{z_{iN}}{\sqrt{N}} \end{bmatrix} \times \begin{bmatrix} \dfrac{z_{j1}}{\sqrt{N}} \\[2mm] \dfrac{z_{j2}}{\sqrt{N}} \\[2mm] \dfrac{z_{j3}}{\sqrt{N}} \\[2mm] \vdots \\[2mm] \dfrac{z_{jN}}{\sqrt{N}} \end{bmatrix} = \dfrac{\sum_{k=1}^{N} z_{ik} z_{jk}}{N} = r_{ij} \tag{2.38}$$

The right-hand side of Eq. (2.38) represents an expression like Eq. (2.6) and hence is a correlation coefficient. In this case, the vector lengths are 1.0, so $r_{ij} = h_i h_j \cos\phi_{ij}$, and the correlation equals the cosine of the angle between two unit-length data vectors. In this case, the scalar product is between actual data vectors, so the correlation obtained equals the data correlation. With error-free data, or if m, the number of common factors, becomes as large as n, the scalar product in the common factor space will equal the real data correlation exactly.

Using the squared lengths of the vectors and scalar products for all non-identical pairs of vectors in Fig. 2.4, the correlation matrix with communalities as shown in Table 2.1, is obtained for the four data variables.

In Table 2.1, $\mathbf{R}$ is the correlation matrix; $\mathbf{A}$ is a factor matrix, or a matrix of extracted factors derived from $\mathbf{R}$; and $\mathbf{A}'$ is the transpose of $\mathbf{A}$. The values in parentheses along the main diagonal of $\mathbf{R}$ are the communalities h_{ii}^2 obtained by squaring the vector lengths h_i in Eq. (2.29). The off-diagonal elements of $\mathbf{R}$ are the correlations r_{ij} among the fictitious data variables, derived as scalar products of the vectors in Fig. 2.4.

Since the correlation matrix in Table 2.1 was derived from the coordinates of four vectors represented in a plane, which is a space of two dimensions, the correlation matrix is error free, and should yield exactly two factors. These two factors will give the coordinates for each variable in two dimensions.

Use of the centroid method of factor extraction, which is described in a later chapter, does indeed yield two factors which reproduce this correlation matrix perfectly, within the limits of rounding error. This reproduction of $\mathbf{R}$ is accomplished by the matrix operation $\mathbf{R} = \mathbf{AA}'$, as in Eq. (2.11). If more than two factors were necessary to reproduce $\mathbf{R}$, the four vectors could not be drawn in a plane. A space of three or more dimensions would be needed. If fewer than two factors were needed, that is, only one, the vectors would all fall on the same line. This is the case for the matrix in Eq.

TABLE 2.1

A Centroid Factor Analysis

	1	2	3	4		I	II			1	2	3	4
1	(.65)	.50	.16	.17	1	.578	−.562						
2	.50	(.40)	.22	.24	2	.531	−.344	I		.578	.531	.687	.765
3	.16	.22	(.65)	.73	= 3	.687	.422	× II		−.562	−.344	.422	.484
4	.17	.24	.73	(.82)	4	.765	.484					$\mathbf{A}'$	
		$\mathbf{R}$					$\mathbf{A}$						

(2.35) in which one pair of vectors gives $r_{12} = h_1 h_2 \cos\phi_{12}$, or $.32 = \sqrt{.16} \times \sqrt{.64} \times \cos\phi_{12}$ or $\cos\phi_{12} = 1.0$, and ϕ_{12} equals $0°$.

If the X and Y coordinates for the four vectors in Fig. 2.4 are averaged, the average X coordinate would be .5 and the average Y coordinate would be .4. These two coordinates locate the centroid point, P_c (.5,.4). Centroid factor analysis derives the factor loadings by obtaining the perpendicular projections of the data vectors onto a line extending from the origin through the centroid point P_c as shown in Fig. 2.4. The perpendicular projection of vector 1 on the centroid vector is shown as line OA in Figure 2.5. Then, the $\cos\phi_{1c}$ equals OA/OP_1 or a_1/h_1 where a_1 is the factor loading, or projection of vector 1 on the centroid vector. Using these equalities, the expression for the factor loading a_1 becomes

$$a_1 = h_1 \cos\phi_{1c} \qquad (2.39)$$

Cosine ϕ_{1c} here is the cosine of the angle between vector 1 and the centroid vector.

The scalar product between vector 1 and the centroid vector is given by

$$[.1 \quad .8] \times \begin{bmatrix} .5 \\ .4 \end{bmatrix} = (.1 \times .5) + (.8 \times .4) = h_1 h_c \cos\phi_{1c} \qquad (2.40)$$

It should be noted that the centroid factor vector has unit length, but the centroid vector, from the origin to the centroid point, with which it is coincident, does not.

Using Eq. (2.39), Eq. (2.40) becomes

$$.37 = h_c(h_1 \cos\phi_{1c}) = h_c a_1 \qquad (2.41)$$

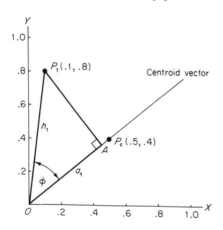

FIG. 2.5. Projection of a data vector on the centroid vector.

Solving for a_1 gives $a_1 = .37/h_c$. Since by the Pythagorean theorem h_c is given by $\sqrt{(.5)^2 + (.4)^2} = \sqrt{.41} = .6403$, this gives $a_1 = .37/.6403 = .578$. Thus, dividing the scalar product of each vector with the centroid vector by the length of the centroid vector from the origin to the centroid point gives the projection of the data vectors on the centroid vector. Performing this operation for the other three vectors in Fig. 2.1 gives $a_2 = 0.531$, $a_3 = .687$, and $a_4 = .765$.

These projections of the four data vectors in Fig. 2.1 on the centroid vector, derived from the coordinates of the vectors, are identical with the first factor loadings in matrix **A**, Table 2.1, derived by factor analysis of the correlation matrix **R**, also shown in Table 2.1.

The contribution of factor I to the **R** matrix is removed by the equation $\mathbf{R_1} = \mathbf{R} - \mathbf{A_1 A_1}'$ (see matrix equations (a) and (b) in Fig. 2.6). $\mathbf{R_1}$, the matrix of residuals after the extraction of factor I, is reproduced exactly by the product of the second factor times its transpose (see matrix equation (c) in Fig. 2.6). In matrix terms, $\mathbf{R_1} - \mathbf{A_2 A_2}' = 0$. Since the $\mathbf{R_1}$ matrix is reproduced exactly by the second factor multiplied by its transpose, no more than two factors are necessary to account for the original **R** matrix.

The sum of the original communality values is $.65 + .40 + 0.65 + .82 = 2.52$. The sum of squares of the first factor loadings, 1.6737, plus the sum of squares of the second factor loadings, .8463, also equals 2.52, showing that all of the common factor variance was extracted. The first factor was approximately twice as large as the second factor, since 1.6737 is roughly twice as much as .8463.

The factor analysis was carried out through operations with the correlation matrix only, without using directly any information about the coordinates of the vectors with respect to the X and Y axes in Fig. 2.4. The correlation matrix shows the squared lengths and scalar products of the vectors but does not refer the vectors to any coordinate system. Factor analysis can be viewed as a technique for placing coordinate axes within the same framework created by orienting the data-variable vectors in space with the appropriate angles between them.

Although each data-variable vector has N coordinates, one for each subject, there are only n vectors; so n dimensions would be enough to accomodate these vectors, even if they were all orthogonal to one another. By appropriate location of the coordinate axes, it is possible to squeeze the dimensionality of the space down still further, from n to m, without distorting the geometric representation of the data too much. The factor analytic process determines just where the m factor vectors are to be placed with respect to the data-variable vectors and derives the coordinates that the data-variable vectors will have with respect to coordinate axes drawn collinearly with the factor vectors. The factor axes, all of unit length, provide a reference frame with respect to which the data-variable vectors

(a)

$$
\begin{bmatrix} (.65) & .50 & .16 & .17 \\ .50 & (.40) & .22 & .24 \\ .16 & .22 & (.65) & .73 \\ .17 & .24 & .73 & (.82) \end{bmatrix} - \begin{bmatrix} .578 \\ .531 \\ .687 \\ .765 \end{bmatrix} \times \boxed{\begin{matrix} .578 & .531 & .687 & .765 \end{matrix}} =
$$

$\quad\quad\quad\quad$ R $\quad\quad\quad\quad\quad$ A_1 $\quad\quad\quad\quad$ A_1'

(b)

$$
\begin{bmatrix} (.65) & .50 & .16 & .17 \\ .50 & (.40) & .22 & .24 \\ .16 & .22 & (.65) & .73 \\ .17 & .24 & .73 & (.82) \end{bmatrix} - \begin{bmatrix} .334 & .307 & .397 & .442 \\ .307 & .282 & .365 & .402 \\ .397 & .365 & .472 & .526 \\ .442 & .406 & .526 & .585 \end{bmatrix} =
$$

$\quad\quad\quad\quad$ R $\quad\quad\quad\quad\quad\quad\quad\quad$ $A_1 A_1'$

$$
\begin{bmatrix} (.316) & .193 & -.237 & -.272 \\ .193 & (.118) & -.145 & -.166 \\ -.237 & -.145 & (.179) & .204 \\ -.272 & -.166 & .204 & (.234) \end{bmatrix}
$$

$\quad\quad\quad\quad\quad\quad$ R_1

(c)

$$
\begin{bmatrix} (.316) & .193 & -.237 & -.272 \\ .193 & (.118) & -.145 & -.166 \\ -.237 & -.145 & (.179) & .204 \\ -.272 & -.166 & .204 & (.234) \end{bmatrix} = \begin{bmatrix} -.562 \\ -.344 \\ .422 \\ .484 \end{bmatrix}
$$

$\quad\quad\quad\quad\quad\quad$ R_1 $\quad\quad\quad\quad\quad\quad$ A_2

$$
\times \boxed{\begin{matrix} -.562 & -.344 & .422 & .482 \end{matrix}}
$$

$\quad\quad\quad\quad\quad\quad\quad\quad\quad\quad$ A_2'

FIG. 2.6.   Calculating the matrix of first factor residuals R_1

can be located by giving coordinates or factor loadings. In Fig. 2.4, as an exercise, the coordinates with respect to the X and Y axes were used to derive a correlation matrix. Factor analysis is essentially the reverse of this process; that is, the given correlation matrix is used to find the coordinates of the vectors with respect to some system of coordinate axes.

The number of factor vectors needed is equal to the dimensionality of the space, that is, the number of dimensions in the space, into which the data-variable vectors are fitted. In the simple four-variable example given here, all the vectors lie in a plane; so two coordinate axes are adequate for a complete specification of the data-variable vectors.

The centroid method places the first reference axis through the centroid point at the center of the swarm of points that are the termini of the data-variable vectors (see Fig. 2.4). The second reference axis, or second centroid vector, is placed at right angles to the first centroid factor vector. In most methods of factor extraction, each succeeding factor extracted is placed at right angles to the preceding factors. The centroid loadings represent coordinates of the data-variable vectors with respect to the orthogonal centroid axes. It is possible to transform these coordinates with respect to the centroid loadings into coordinates with respect to any other set of reference axes, such as those in Fig. 2.4, that is, the X and Y coordinate axes. This operation would represent the rotation of the centroid factors to new factor positions with greater value for descriptive, theoretical, or other scientific purposes.

The angle between the centroid axis and the Y axis in Fig. 2.4 may be obtained as follows: The Y-axis vector terminus has coordinates (0,1). The scalar product with the centroid is given by

$$h_y h_c \cos\phi_{yc} = \begin{bmatrix} 0 & 1 \end{bmatrix} \times \begin{bmatrix} .5 \\ .4 \end{bmatrix} = (0 \times .5) + (1 \times .4) = .4$$

$$\cos\phi = .4/h_y h_c = .4/(1.0 \times .6403) = .625$$

Hence, $\phi = 51°19'$ and the sine of ϕ is .781. The angle of the centroid axis with the X axis in Fig. 2.4 is $90° - 51°19'$, or $38°41'$.

To obtain a configuration of points corresponding to those in Fig. 2.4 using the coordinates of the data points from the matrix of factor loadings **A** in Table 2.1, it is necessary to reverse the direction of factor II in matrix **A**, Table 2.1. Any factor may be reversed in direction in this manner at any stage in the factor analytic process without affecting the property that **AA'** reproduces the matrix **R**.

Reversing the direction of a factor by changing all the signs of the loadings on the factor, then, is perfectly acceptable. It merely inverts the meaning of the factor. For example, a factor named Lack of Intelligence would be converted to a factor properly named Intelligence merely by reversing the signs of all the loadings.

If the signs on the loadings for factor II in Table 2.1 are reversed in this manner, the coordinates for the four data vectors with respect to the centroid axes become P_1 (.578,.562), P_2(.531,.344), P_3(.687, $-$.422), and P_4(.765, $-$.484). Plotting these data points with respect to centroid factor axes I and II yields Fig. 2.7. Only the end points of the data vectors are plotted here. This is a more usual practice than drawing in the full vector from the origin to each data-vector end point.

Rotation of factor I away from factor II by an angle of 38°41′ will bring it into coincidence with the old X axis (see Fig. 2.7). At the same time, rotation of factor II an equivalent amount toward factor I will bring factor II into coincidence with the old Y axis. The matrix operations in Table 2.2 show how this rotation is carried out, transforming the coordinates with respect to centroid axes (after reversing axis II) into the coordinates with respect to the original X and Y coordinate axes, respectively.

In Table 2.2, $\mathbf{A}$ is the centroid matrix with factor II reversed; Λ is the transformation matrix with cos 38°41′ in cells λ_{11} and λ_{22}, $-\sin$ 38°41′ in cell λ_{21}, and sin 38°41′ in cell λ_{12}; $\mathbf{V}$ is the matrix of coordinates of the data-variable vectors with respect to the original X and Y axes. The coordinates with respect to the original X and Y axes, matrix $\mathbf{V}$, can also be transformed back to the centroid loadings. From Table 2.2 it is apparent that $\mathbf{V} = \mathbf{A}\Lambda$. Let the matrix Λ^{-1} be called the inverse of Λ, a matrix that has the following property:

$$\Lambda^{-1}\Lambda = \Lambda\Lambda^{-1} = \mathbf{I}$$

where $\mathbf{I}$ is the identity matrix as before. Then, if the matrix equation $\mathbf{V} = \mathbf{A}\Lambda$ is multiplied on both sides by Λ^{-1}, the following matrix result is obtained:

$$\mathbf{V}\Lambda^{-1} = \mathbf{A}\Lambda\Lambda^{-1} = \mathbf{A}\mathbf{I} = \mathbf{A} \tag{2.42}$$

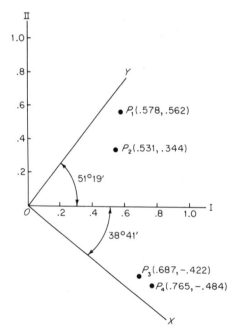

FIG. 2.7. Rotation from centroids to original coordinates axes.

TABLE 2.2

Rotation of the Centroid Axes

Unrotated factor matrix		Transformation matrix		Rotated factor matrix	
I	II			I(X)	II(Y)

$$
\begin{array}{c} 1 \\ 2 \\ 3 \\ 4 \end{array}
\begin{bmatrix} .578 & .562 \\ .531 & .344 \\ .687 & -.422 \\ .765 & -.484 \end{bmatrix}
\times
\begin{bmatrix} .781 & .625 \\ -.625 & .781 \end{bmatrix}
=
\begin{array}{c} 1 \\ 2 \\ 3 \\ 4 \end{array}
\begin{bmatrix} .1 & .8 \\ .2 & .6 \\ .8 & .1 \\ .9 & .1 \end{bmatrix}
$$

$$
\qquad\quad \mathbf{A} \qquad\qquad\qquad \Lambda \qquad\qquad\qquad \mathbf{V}
$$

Thus, if the matrix $\mathbf{V}$ is multiplied on the right by the inverse of the matrix which transforms the original centroid factors to $\mathbf{V}$, that is, by the operation $\mathbf{V}\Lambda^{-1}$, the $\mathbf{V}$ matrix will be transformed back to the centroid factors. In the case of an orthogonal matrix like Λ, the inverse Λ^{-1} is very easily obtained because it is merely the transpose of Λ. For nonorthogonal matrices, the inverse of a matrix is not so easily obtained and is not equal to the transpose.

Equation (2.42) for this example gives the following result:

$$
\begin{array}{c} 1 \\ 2 \\ 3 \\ 4 \end{array}
\begin{bmatrix} .1 & .8 \\ .2 & .6 \\ .8 & .1 \\ .9 & .1 \end{bmatrix}
\times
\begin{bmatrix} .781 & -.625 \\ .625 & .781 \end{bmatrix}
=
\begin{array}{c} 1 \\ 2 \\ 3 \\ 4 \end{array}
\begin{bmatrix} .578 & .562 \\ .531 & .344 \\ .687 & -.422 \\ .765 & -.484 \end{bmatrix}
$$

$$
\qquad\quad \mathbf{V} \qquad\qquad\qquad \Lambda^{-1} \qquad\qquad\qquad \mathbf{A}
$$

In this example, the centroid factors are complex composites of all the variables represented by the data vectors. A complex composite factor is one that has substantial loadings for variables that are slightly or not at all correlated with each other. By rotating matrix $\mathbf{A}$ to matrix $\mathbf{V}$, the factor matrix is rotated to a form in which factor I of the $\mathbf{V}$ matrix is like variables 3 and 4 but not much like variables 1 and 2. The second factor of $\mathbf{V}$ is like variables 1 and 2 but not much like variables 3 and 4. The factor constructs represented by the $\mathbf{V}$ matrix are less complex than those represented by the $\mathbf{A}$ matrix, because in the $\mathbf{A}$ matrix all variables have substantial loadings on both factors. For purposes of scientific description and explanation, the factors in the $\mathbf{V}$ matrix are more useful because they are simpler, easier to understand, and better differentiated from each other because they are defined by different variables.

3

Factor Extraction by the Centroid Method

The centroid method of factor extraction (Thurstone, 1947; Fruchter, 1954) was the best known and most widely used method of factor extraction before electronic high-speed computers became readily available. Most factor analytic studies published before 1960 used this method. As high-speed computing equipment has become more generally accessible, the centroid method has been supplanted gradually by more precise methods that would have been too laborious for application with a desk calculator. The most commonly used method today is the principal factor method, with communalities of less than 1.0, or the principal component method if the communalities are set to equal 1.0. The computational algorithms are the same for both of these methods.

The centroid method is still important to study for several reasons. First, a great many studies have been published using this method. Second, it is a method of considerable historical interest. Third, it is a method that can still be applied to very large matrices that might require too much computing time with more laborious methods. Fourth, it is a very useful method for teaching purposes because it is feasible to do a problem of sufficient size with this method using a hand-held calculator to illustrate the factor analytic process. The centroid method also has the advantage of being easily conceptualized in terms of the geometric model of factor analysis. For these various reasons, the centroid method is presented here in some detail despite the fact that it is no longer widely used in practice.

3.1.   EQUATIONS FOR THE CENTROID METHOD

In Fig. 2.4 the centroid point was located by averaging all the data-vector X coordinates to get the X coordinate of the centroid point and all the data-vector Y coordinates to get the Y coordinate of the centroid point. If there had been more than two dimensions involved, the third, fourth, and other coordinates would have been averaged to get the remaining coordinates of the centroid point.

Imagine a new set of coordinate axes at right angles to one another placed in such a way that one of the axes goes through the centroid point, as in Fig. 2.7. Suppose that the coordinates of the data vectors with respect to these new coordinate axes are known (actually they are the centroid loadings given in Table 2.2). With these new coordinates, it would be possible to recompute the coordinates of the centroid point with respect to the new coordinate axes. Because one of the axes, say the first one, goes right through the centroid point, however, the coordinates of the centroid point with respect to the new axes will be

$$\frac{1}{n} \cdot \sum_{i=1}^{i=n} a_{i1}, 0, 0, \ldots, 0 \tag{3.1}$$

That is, since the centroid point falls on the first coordinate axis, its coordinates with respect to all the other axes will be zero. In Fig. 2.7, there are only two factors, hence only two coordinates. Therefore, the coordinates of the centroid point can be found by averaging the loadings with respect to the new axes, the first of which goes through the centroid point. These loadings are given in Table 2.2. Thus, averaging the coordinates in the first column gives $1/4(.578 + .531 + .687 + .765) = .64$ as the first coordinate of the centroid point. The second coordinate of the centroid point is the average of the second column of the **A** matrix in Table 2.2; that is, $1/4(.562 + .344 - .422 - .484) = 0$, which is in accordance with Eq. (3.1).

To use Eq. (3.1) for deriving an expression for the centroid loadings, Eq. (2.10) serves as a starting point:

$$r_{ij} = a_{i1}a_{j1} + a_{i2}a_{j2} + \ldots + a_{im}a_{jm} \tag{3.2}$$

Summing both sides of Eq. (3.2) over i gives

$$\sum_{i=1}^{i=n} r_{ij} = a_{j1} \sum_{i=1}^{i=n} a_{i1} + a_{j2} \sum_{i=1}^{i=n} a_{i2} + \ldots + a_{jm} \sum_{i=1}^{i=n} a_{im} \tag{3.3}$$

Summing both sides of Eq. (3.3) over j gives

$$\sum_{j=1}^{j=n} \sum_{i=1}^{i=n} r_{ij} = \sum_{j=1}^{j=n} a_{j1} \sum_{i=1}^{i=n} a_{i1} + \sum_{j=1}^{j=n} a_{j2} \sum_{i=1}^{i=n} a_{i2} + \ldots$$

$$+ \sum_{j=1}^{j=n} a_{jm} \sum_{i=1}^{i=n} a_{im} \qquad (3.4)$$

But

$$\sum_{j=1}^{j=n} a_{jk} = \sum_{i=1}^{i=n} a_{ik} \qquad (3.5)$$

since both terms in Eq. (3.5) are merely the sum of the entries in the kth column of the **A** matrix of factor loadings. Substituting (3.5) in (3.4), therefore, gives

$$\sum_{j=1}^{j=n} \sum_{i=1}^{i=n} r_{ij} = \left[\sum_{i=1}^{i=n} a_{i1}\right]^2 + \left[\sum_{i=1}^{i=n} a_{i2}\right]^2 + \ldots + \left[\sum_{i=1}^{i=n} a_{im}\right]^2 \qquad (3.6)$$

By Eq. (3.1), however, all the sums on the right-hand side of Eq. (3.6) are zero except the first. Equation (3.6) reduces, therefore, to

$$\sum_{j=1}^{j=n} \sum_{i=1}^{i=n} r_{ij} = \left[\sum_{i=1}^{i=n} a_{i1}\right]^2 \qquad (3.7)$$

Also by Eq. (3.1) the sums of loadings for the second and subsequent factors are zero, since the second and subsequent coordinates of the centroid point derived from these sums are zero, making Eq. (3.3) reduce to

$$\sum_{i=1}^{i=n} r_{ij} = a_{j1} \sum_{i=1}^{i=n} a_{i1} \qquad (3.8)$$

Taking the square root of both sides of Eq. (3.7) and substituting in Eq. (3.8) gives

$$\sum_{i=1}^{i=n} r_{ij} = a_{j1} \sqrt{\sum_{j=1}^{j=n} \sum_{i=1}^{i=n} r_{ij}} \qquad (3.9)$$

Solving for a_{j1} gives

$$a_{j1} = \frac{\displaystyle\sum_{i=1}^{i=n} r_{ij}}{\sqrt{\displaystyle\sum_{j=1}^{j=n}\sum_{i=1}^{i=n} r_{ij}}} \tag{3.10}$$

Equation (3.10) gives the formula for a centroid loading for variable j on factor 1 (or I, using roman numerals). To get the centroid factor loading for data variable 1, for example, Eq. (3.10) calls for the following steps:

1. Add up the entries in the first column of the correlation matrix, including the diagonal cell.
2. Divide this number by the square root (or multiply by the reciprocal of the square root) of the sum of all the entries in the entire correlation matrix, including the diagonal cells.

For the second data variable, compute the sum of the entries in the second column of the correlation matrix and divide by the same square root term as for the first data variable. Continue this for all columns of the **R** matrix. Thus, the computation steps involve computing the sums of the columns of the **R** matrix, adding these column sums to get the sum of all entries, taking the square root, and dividing this square root into each column sum.

3.2.   A FOUR-VARIABLE, TWO-FACTOR EXAMPLE

Applying these steps to the four-variable correlation matrix in Table 2.1 gives the results of Table 3.1. The contribution of factor 1 must be removed from the correlation matrix by the operation $\mathbf{R} - \mathbf{A}_1\mathbf{A}_1'$, as shown in Chapter 2. The results of this operation give the matrix $\mathbf{R}_1$, the matrix of first factor residuals shown in Table 3.2. Note that in Table 3.2 the columns in each case add up to zero, within the limits of rounding error. As a check, the rows should be added also, to make sure that the row totals equal the column totals as required for a symmetric matrix.

It was established in Eq. (3.1) that the sum of the loadings on the second and subsequent centroid factors is zero, which provides the basis for a check on the computations of the first factor residuals used above. Because the sums of the columns are zero, however, it is clearly impossible to apply the steps used for computing the first centroid factor to the matrix of residuals given in Table 3.2. It is necessary first to carry out a process of reflecting the residuals to get rid of as many negative signs as possible in the matrix of first factor residuals.

TABLE 3.1

Correlation Matrix

	1	2	3	4	
1	(.65)	.50	.16	.17	
2	.50	(.40)	.22	.24	
3	.16	.22	(.65)	.73	
4	.17	.24	.73	(.82)	$T = \sum\sum r = 6.56$
t	1.48	1.36	1.76	1.96	$\sqrt{T} = 2.56125$
a_t	.578	.531	.687	.765	$1/\sqrt{T} = .3904$

TABLE 3.2

First Factor Residuals

	1	2	3	4
1	(.316)	.193	−.237	−.272
2	.193	(.118)	−.145	−.166
3	−.237	−.145	(.179)	.204
4	−.272	−.166	.204	(.234)
Sum	.000	.000	.001	.000
$\sum_0$	−.316	−.118	−.178	−.234

The basis for this procedure is as follows: First, it is known that after they are computed, the second factor centroid loadings will sum to zero. This means that approximately half of the loadings will have negative signs. On the other hand, to extract a centroid factor, all the column sums of the residual correlation matrix should be positive and as large as possible. If this is the case, the loadings will be positive too, since they are the ratios of the positive column sums to the square root of the overall sum. To make the column sums positive and as large as possible, it is necessary to reflect, or change the direction, of those residual data-variable vectors that will ultimately have negative second factor loadings. This reflection is carried out by changing all the signs the variable has with every other variable in the matrix of residuals. As many variables are reflected as necessary to get the largest possible positive column sums in the matrix of reflected residuals. When all these sign changes have been effected, positive factor loadings can be extracted by the centroid method to obtain the second factor loadings. After extraction, however, with all positive signs, negative signs will be placed on the loadings for those variables that were reflected.

Any data variable that has been reflected, therefore, must have a negative sign attached to its second factor loading so that the second factor loadings with signs attached will add up algebraically to zero. Thus, any variable that will have the sign of its factor loading reversed on this factor from what it was on the previous factor will require reflection of this factor to make the sum of its column entries positive without including the communality value. Failure to carry out the reflection process far enough to get the maximum positive sums of the columns of reflected residuals will result in smaller column sums and hence in a smaller amount of variance being extracted on the factor than would be possible with complete reflection.

In picking a data variable to reflect, start with the variable that has the largest negative total without the communality added in. The communality is not considered here because it may even change a total from negative to positive, thus stopping the reflection process too soon. In the example shown in Table 3.2, this would be variable 1, which has a negative total of $-.316$ without the h^2 added in. Reflecting variable 1, that is, changing the signs of the residuals for variable 1 with all the other variables, requires a reversal of all the signs in row 1 and column 1. This leaves the diagonal cell unchanged. The first factor residuals after reflecting variable 1 are shown in Table 3.3. In this table, only variable 2 now has a negative sum, exclusive of the communalities, so it is the next variable to be reflected. After reflecting variable 2, the values in Table 3.3 are changed to those in Table 3.4. The asterisk (*), appended to columns 1 and 2 and rows 1 and 2, indicates that the variable has been reflected and a negative sign must be attached to the second factor loadings for these variables.

After reflecting variable 2, as shown in Table 3.4, no more negative signs

TABLE 3.3

First Factor Residuals after Reflecting Variable 1

	*1	2	3	4
* 1	(.316)	−.193	.237	.272
2	−.193	(.118)	−.145	−.166
3	.237	−.145	(.179)	.204
4	.272	−.166	.204	(.234)
Sums without communalities	.316	−.504	.296	.310

TABLE 3.4

Reflected First Factor Residuals and Second Factor Calculations

	*1	*2	3	4	
* 1	(.316)	.193	.237	.272	
* 2	.193	(.118)	.145	.166	
3	.237	.145	(.179)	.204	
4	.272	.166	.204	(.234)	$T = 3.281$
t	1.018	.622	.764	.877	$\sqrt{T} = 1.81135$
a_t	.562	.343	.422	.484	$1/\sqrt{T} = .55207$

remain in the matrix of reflected residuals. In practice, some negative signs will usually remain after reflection has been carried as far as possible. In some cases, it may even be necessary to reflect back again a variable that was previously reflected. This just cancels the effect of the previous reflection of that variable, leaving it as a variable with a positive second factor loading rather than a negative one.

The computed second factor loadings in Table 3.4, obtained by the same steps applied in Table 3.1 for the first factor loadings, are all positive. Negative signs must be attached to the first two loadings, however, that is, for variables 1 and 2, since these two variables were reflected. These second factor loadings reproduce the matrix of second factor residuals exactly, as shown in the last chapter. In matrix form, the equation is $\mathbf{R}_1 - \mathbf{A}_2\mathbf{A}_2' = \mathbf{0}$. In that example, the matrix of residuals before reflection was reproduced by the product $\mathbf{A}_2\mathbf{A}_2'$ with signs attached to the second factor loadings for variables 1 and 2. In actual practice, the column of positive factor loadings $\mathbf{A}_2$ is multiplied by its transpose $\mathbf{A}_2'$ to give an $n \times n$ matrix that is subtracted from the matrix of first factor residuals after they have been reflected. Subtraction takes place by subtracting corresponding matrix elements.

Thus, in summary, the residuals are reflected to make them positive. A factor with positive signs is extracted. This positively signed factor is removed from the residuals after they have been reflected. After this, the negative signs are attached to the loadings for the variables that were reflected. The new residual matrix has sums of columns that equal zero and hence it must be reflected to start the cycle anew.

Once a variable has been reflected, all of its factor loadings will have minus signs attached to them for that and all later factors unless it is reflected again. If it is reflected again, it goes back to positive from that point on, remaining that way until it is reflected once more. It should be noted that changing all the signs on a factor will not affect the reproduction of the $\mathbf{R}$ matrix by the equation $\mathbf{R} = \mathbf{A}\mathbf{A}'$. Any variable or any factor may be reflected if appropriate changes are made in the signs of the correlations and factor loadings. If any variable has a negative column sum without the communality added in, it is necessary to carry out reflections of the data variables in the original correlation matrix before even the first factor is computed. It is also desirable in many cases to reflect a factor after it has been extracted or rotated so that the positive end of the factor vector will correspond with the positive side of a bipolar concept, for example, Adjustment versus Maladjustment, represented by the factor.

The process of reflecting a variable at any point amounts to changing the signs of all correlations of that variable with all other variables. This causes the reversal of all signs on the factor loadings for this variable from that point on. The correlations for which the signs are changed may be from the original correlation matrix or from any of the subsequent residual matrices. After extraction, the signs on the factor loadings must be adjusted to be consistent with these reflections. Once a matrix of original or residual correlations with positive column totals has been obtained, extraction of a centroid factor proceeds according to the same steps enumerated above for the extraction of the first centroid factor.

3.3. A 12-VARIABLE, FOUR-FACTOR EXAMPLE

Understanding of the factor analytic extraction process by the centroid method is facilitated by considering a somewhat larger problem based on real data. Table 11.1 (See Chapter 11) gives the matrix of intercorrelations for the 40 variables that define the eight factors on the Comrey Personality Scales, a personality inventory developed by factor analytic methods (Comrey, 1970a,b; 1980). This 44 × 44 table of correlations shown in Table 11.1 provides a source of sample problems for class exercises. By selecting four of the eight factors and three variables with high factor loadings that define each factor, a 12-variable sample problem may be generated that can serve as an exercise for the student. If desired, each student may take a different sample of factors and/or variables so that no two students in the class are working on the same exercise. It is important, however, to have at least four factors and preferably at least three variables defining each factor. In this way, the exercise will be an appropriate learning experience for the student, providing an opportunity to develop the skills needed for both factor extraction and rotation.

In choosing the variables to represent a given factor, reference to Table 11.4 (See Chapter 11) will be helpful. This table gives the final eight-factor orthogonal rotated solution for the 44-variable matrix shown in Table 11.1. To be chosen as a variable to represent a factor in a sample problem, the variable should have a factor loading over .50 on that factor in Table 11.4. Names and descriptions of the variables are given in the text of Chapter 11. From the standpoint of the student, there is no substitute for actually carrying out a sample factor analysis. Failure to do so almost inevitably will result in a poorer grasp of the subject. A sample problem of 12 variables and four factors should give sufficient scope to the problem for an initial attempt. Fewer factors will not permit adequate practice in rotation. If the size of the student problem must be reduced, such as for a one-quarter course instead of a full semester course, it is better to use only two marker variables for some of the factors rather than to reduce the number of factors.

A complete factor analytic solution is given in Chapter 11 for this 44-variable, eight-factor problem that will serve as a model solution against which solutions to sample problems may be compared. Only the rotated solutions can be compared, however, because the extracted factor loadings depend too heavily on the particular combination of variables included in the analysis. After rotation, sample problems should produce a pattern recognizably similar to the model solution to the extent that a solution for a subset of the variables can be expected to resemble the solution for the full set. The factor loadings for a sample problem, however, are expected to agree in size only approximately with the loadings for the solution based on the entire matrix, as shown in Table 11.4.

The 12-variable sample problem chosen to be used as an example in this book is given in Table 3.5. Using the numbers in the second column of Table 3.5, Table 11.1 may be entered to find the correlations among these 12 selected variables. This correlation matrix is shown in Table 3.6. The correlation coefficients are entered both above and below the main diagonal in Table 3.6 to facilitate calculation of the first centroid factor. The estimated communalities in parentheses along the main diagonal are added to the correlation matrix in the process of extracting the first centroid factor.

3.3.1.   STEPS IN COMPUTING THE FIRST CENTROID FACTOR

1. Add up algebraically (using signs) each column of the correlation matrix (Table 3.6) omitting the diagonal cell or h^2 value from the total. Record these totals in row Σ_0 at the bottom of the correlation matrix.

TABLE 3.5

12-Variable Sample Problem

Variable number	Number in Table 11.1	Variable name	Factor
1	11	Law Enforcement	C
2	12	Acceptance of Social Order	C
3	13	Intolerance of Nonconformity	C
4	21	Lack of Inferiority Feelings	S
5	22	Lack of Depression	S
6	23	Lack of Agitation	S
7	26	Lack of Reserve	E
8	27	Lack of Seclusiveness	E
9	28	No Loss for Words	E
10	36	Sympathy	P
11	37	Helpfulness	P
12	39	Generosity	P

TABLE 3.6

12-Variable Correlation Matrix and First Factor Computations

	1	2	3	4	5	6	7	8	9	10	11	12	$\sum_0$
1	(.64)	.61	.64	.07	.14	.07	.04	.08	.06	-.02	-.02	-.17	1.50
2	.61	(.61)	.50	.02	.13	.08	-.05	.02	-.02	-.07	-.08	-.15	.99
3	.64	.50	(.64)	.02	.04	-.03	-.01	.08	.01	-.01	-.02	-.04	1.18
4	.07	.02	.02	(.51)	.51	.46	.28	.29	.47	.10	.14	.05	2.41
5	.14	.13	.04	.51	(.51)	.51	.29	.31	.41	.18	.24	.09	2.85
6	.07	.08	-.03	.46	.51	(.51)	.13	.19	.31	.05	.18	.05	2.00
7	.04	-.05	-.01	.28	.29	.13	(.66)	.46	.66	.16	.16	.12	2.24
8	.08	.02	.08	.29	.31	.19	.46	(.55)	.55	.31	.39	.26	2.94
9	.06	-.02	.01	.47	.41	.31	.66	.55	(.66)	.20	.28	.17	3.10
10	-.02	-.07	-.01	.10	.18	.05	.16	.31	.20	(.60)	.60	.46	1.96
11	-.02	-.08	-.02	.14	.24	.18	.16	.39	.28	.60	(.61)	.61	2.48
12	-.17	-.15	-.04	.05	.09	.05	.12	.26	.17	.46	.61	(.61)	1.45
$\sum_0$	1.50	.99	1.18	2.41	2.85	2.00	2.24	2.94	3.10	1.96	2.48	1.45	25.10
t	2.14	1.60	1.82	2.92	3.36	2.51	2.90	3.49	3.76	2.56	3.09	2.06	
a_t	.377	.282	.321	.514	.592	.442	.511	.615	.662	.451	.544	.363	

$$T = 32.21$$
$$\sqrt{T} = 5.67538$$
$$1/\sqrt{T} = .17620$$

2. Add the rows across, computing each row total of **R**, again omitting the diagonal cells. Check the row totals against the column totals to make sure they are identical.

3. If any of these column-row totals is negative, the reflection process must be applied, as explained under the steps for computing the second centroid factor, before proceeding. If all the column totals are positive, proceed to step 4.

4. Place estimated communality values in the diagonal cells. Most commonly, the absolute values (h^2 values must be positive) of the highest correlations in the columns are used as the estimates. Sometimes other values are used.

5. Add the estimated communalities to the column totals and place these sums in row t.

6. As a check, subtract the communalities from the totals in row t to see if the column totals without communalities are recovered.

7. Add the column totals with communalities, that is, the elements of row t, to obtain T, the sum of all entries in the table.

8. Compute the square root of T to at least five decimal places.

9. Compute the reciprocal of the square root of T to at least five places.

10. Multiply the column totals with communalities, that is, the entries in row t, by $1/(T)^{1/2}$, the reciprocal of the square root of T, and enter the products in row a_i. These are the centroid loadings before any signs have been attached.

11. If any variable has been reflected prior to these computations, these centroid loadings must have the appropriate signs attached before they are entered in the first column of matrix **A**, the table of factor loadings (see Table 3.13).

12. Sum the factor loadings in row a_i and check to see that it equals $(T)^{1/2}$ within the limits of rounding error, as called for by Eq. (3.7).

The calculations for the 12-variable sample problem called for in steps 1–12 are shown in Table 3.6. Since all the columns, exclusive of h^2 values, were positive, no reflection of the original **R** matrix was necessary.

3.3.2.   COMPUTING THE FIRST FACTOR RESIDUALS

The matrix of first factor residuals R_1 is computed by the matrix equation

$$R_1 = R - A_1 A_1' \tag{3.11}$$

where **R** is the original matrix of correlations, reflected if necessary; A_1 is the first factor, a column matrix, with all positive signs attached; and A_1' is the transpose of $\mathbf{A}_1$. For a given element of $\mathbf{R}_1$, r_{1ij}, the computation is as follows:

$$r_{1ij} = r_{ij} - a_{i1}a_{j1} \tag{3.12}$$

where r_{ij} is an element of the original correlation matrix and a_{i1} and a_{j1} are the positive first factor loadings for variables i and j.

Some analysts prefer to compute an $n \times n$ matrix of the positive elements $a_{i1}a_{j1}$ and then subtract this matrix, element by element, from the original correlation matrix, reflected if that should be required. To do this, lay out a square work sheet with the n positive first factor loadings down the side and also across the top of the page. Fill in the $n \times n$ blank cells in the matrix by multiplying the loading at the side by the loading at the top. Each element of this $n \times n$ matrix, including the diagonals, is subtracted from the corresponding element of the original correlation matrix to obtain the first factor residuals. For the 12-variable sample problem, these first factor residuals are shown in Table 3.7.

3.3.3. COMPUTING THE SECOND CENTROID FACTOR

Steps 1 and 2 of the first centroid factor extraction procedure are repeated; that is, the rows and columns of the matrix of residuals are added up, omitting the diagonal elements, and the row sums are checked against the column sums. These column sums are entered in row Σ_0 and in turn are added up to give an overall sum of all elements in the table except the communality values (see Table 3.7). These column sums in row Σ_0 should be equal to the residual communality values but opposite in sign so that if the diagonal cells were added in, the column totals would be zero within the limits of rounding error. These totals should be negative in most cases, although occasionally, especially with later factors, a residual communality will go negative, requiring a positive column sum to balance it. The balancing of the column sums with the residual communality values must be satisfied before proceeding. If they do not balance, an error has been made and it must be corrected.

3.3.4. REFLECTION OF VARIABLES

Sometimes on the first factor, and always on the second and subsequent factors, the sums of some of the columns, not counting the diagonals, are negative. This requires the reflection of variables with negative column sums (without communalities added in) so that all the column sums will be positive. The steps involved in this reflection process are as follows:

1. Locate the variable that has the largest negative total without the communality added in as the first variable to be reflected. Place an asterisk (*) over this column and to the left of this row to indicate that it is a variable that is being reflected.

2. Label the row immediately below the Σ_0 row with the number of the variable to be reflected. In Table 3.7, the first variable to be reflected is variable number 3, so the first row below the Σ_0 row is labeled 3.

3. Bring down the column sum from the Σ_0 row for this variable, changing its sign from negative to positive and place it in the next row, underlining the number. Since reflecting a variable changes all the signs in the column, the sum with signs changed is just the same as before the sign changes except that the sign on the total goes from minus to plus. In Table 3.7, the positive total of .537 is recorded for variable 3 in row 3 and underlined to indicate that the total is for a reflected variable.

4. The column totals for the other variables must now be adjusted to allow for the fact that variable 3 is being reflected. The column total for variable 3 is already taken care of, but these same residuals also appear in row 3, and hence adjustments are necessary to the other column totals when these values are reflected. Before reflection, these values were added into the total with one sign. After reflection, they are added in with the opposite sign. To adjust the total correctly, therefore, the entry must be doubled, its sign reversed, and the result added to the previous column total. Thus, before reflection of variable 3, the entry in row 3 of column 4, Table 3.7, is $-.145$. When this entry is doubled, its sign changed, and the result (.290) added to the column 4 entry in row Σ_0, $-.246$, the new column total, 0.044, is obtained and entered under column 4 in row 3. The other entries in this row, except that for the variable being reflected, are obtained in a similar way.

5. As a check, the new column totals are added up by adding across row 3 at the bottom of Table 3.7. This value should equal the old sum of column totals plus four times the positive column sum for the variable being reflected, that is, $4 \times .537$, since both the row and column values must first be taken out of the old total and then added into the new total with different signs. Thus $-2.116 = -4.264 + 4(.537)$.

6. If any column totals are still negative after the first reflection, and they usually are, pick out the variable with the largest remaining negative total, put an asterisk (*) on its column and row, and proceed to reflect this variable in the same way the first one was reflected. Its total is brought down with a plus sign and underlined as the new total for that column. Proceed as before, doubling row values, changing their signs, and adding to the previous column totals. In Table 3.7 for example, the next variable to be reflected is variable 1. The entry in column 2, row 1, is .504. Doubling and changing signs gives -1.008 which is added to the previous column total,

TABLE 3.7 First Factor Residuals and Second Factor Computations

	*1	*2	*3	4	5	6	7	8	9	10	11	12	Σ_o
*1	.519 (.498)	.504	.519	-.124	-.083	-.097	-.153	-.152	-.190	-.190	-.225	-.307	-.498
*2	.504	.504 (.530)	.410	-.125	-.037	-.045	-.194	-.153	-.207	-.197	-.233	-.252	-.529
*3	.519	.410	.519 (.537)	-.145	-.150	-.172	-.174	-.117	-.202	-.155	-.195	-.156	-.537
4	-.124	-.125	-.145	.232 (.246)	.205	.232	.017	-.026	.129	-.132	-.140	-.137	-.246
5	-.083	-.037	-.150	.205	.248 (.160)	.248	-.013	-.054	.018	-.087	-.082	-.125	-.160
6	-.097	-.045	-.172	.232	.248	.248 (.315)	-.096	-.082	.017	-.149	-.061	-.111	-.316
7	-.153	-.194	-.174	.017	-.013	-.096	.321 (.399)	.146	.321	-.070	-.118	-.065	-.399
8	-.152	-.153	-.117	-.026	-.054	-.082	.146	.153 (.172)	.143	.033	.055	.037	-.170
9	-.190	-.207	-.202	.129	.018	.017	.321	.143	.321 (.222)	-.099	-.081	-.070	-.221
10	-.190	-.197	-.155	-.132	-.087	-.149	-.070	.033	-.099	.354 (.397)	.354	.296	-.396
11	-.225	-.233	-.195	-.140	-.082	-.061	-.118	.055	-.081	.354	.412 (.314)	.412	-.314
12	-.307	-.252	-.156	-.137	-.125	-.111	-.065	.037	-.070	.296	.412	.412 (.478)	-.478
Σ_o	-.498	-.529	-.537	-.246	-.160	-.316	-.399	-.170	-.221	-.396	-.314	-.478	-4.264
3	-1.536	-1.349	.537	.044	.140	.028	-.051	.064	.183	-.086	.076	-.166	-2.116
1	1.536	-2.357	1.575	.292	.306	.222	.255	.368	.563	.294	.526	.448	4.028
2	2.544	2.357	2.395	.542	.380	.312	.643	.674	.977	.688	.992	.952	13.456
t	3.063	2.861	2.914	.774	.628	.560	.964	.827	1.298	1.042	1.404	1.364	
a_i	.728	.680	.692	.184	.149	.133	.229	.196	.309	.248	.334	.324	

$$T = 17.699$$
$$\sqrt{T} = 4.20740$$
$$1/\sqrt{T} = .23768$$

65

-1.349, to give a new column total of -2.357, which is placed in row 1 (below the main table), column 2.

Coming to column 3, however, brings us to a variable that has been previously reflected. Since this variable has been previously reflected, its effective sign is therefore opposite to that which shows in the table of residuals. Another reflection has the effect of bringing the sign back to what it is in the table as shown. It is unnecessary, therefore, to change the sign after doubling before adding to the old column total to get the new column total. Therefore, the entry in column 3, row 1, is doubled and added to the previous column total *without changing its sign*. Its new total is also underlined, indicating that it is a variable previously reflected, requiring the addition of the doubled row entry without sign change. Once a variable is reflected, its column totals are underlined in each successive row during the reflection process.

7. Add up the entries of row 1. This total, 4.028, should equal the previous row total, -2.116, plus four times the positive sum of the first column, that is 4×1.536.

8. This process of reflecting variables is continued until no negative column total remains. Occasionally it may be necessary to re-reflect a variable that has already been reflected earlier. The asterisk (*) must be removed from the column and row but in carrying out the re-reflection, the row entries for previously unreflected variables are doubled and added without changing signs since the variable has been reflected previously. For the previously reflected variable entries, the signs are changed after doubling and before adding. Table 3.7 shows the completed reflection process for the first factor residuals for the 12-variable sample problem.

3.3.5.   COMPUTING THE SECOND FACTOR LOADINGS

It would be possible to use the residual communalities (in parentheses) in Table 3.7 as the communality estimates for the second factor extraction. This procedure is used where good communality estimates were available at the beginning of the analysis or where a solution with these particular communality estimates is desired. In this sample problem, and in common practice, new estimated communalities are introduced for each factor extracted.

In reestimating the communalities, then, locate the largest residual in each column (other than the diagonal cell), make it positive in sign, and place it above the residual communality value, as shown in Table 3.7. Thus, in Table 3.7, column 1, .519 is the new communality estimate and .498 is the residual communality value that will not be used further.

In this example, the reestimated communalities in Table 3.7 are added to he positive column totals without communalities in row 2 (just above row to give the column totals with communalities in row t. The second factor adings are then computed in the same way as for the first factor and the ⸤sults entered in row a_i, Table 3.7. These a_i values from Table 3.7 are also entered in the **A** matrix, Table 3.13. Since variables 1, 2, and 3 were reflected in making the columns have positive totals, the signs of the factor loadings for variables 1, 2, and 3 are made negative on factor II in Table 3.13.

3.3.6. COMPUTING THE SECOND FACTOR RESIDUALS

When the second factor residuals are computed by the formula $R_2 = R_1 - A_2A_2'$, R_1 is a matrix of reflected first factor residuals and A_2 is a single column with all positive signs. To get R_1, variables 1, 2, and 3 in Table 3.7 must be reflected. This gives Table 3.8, the R_1 matrix required, with reflected residuals. In carrying out the reflections for a given variable, both row and column signs for that variable must be changed unless the residual is with another variable that is also reflected, in which case the sign is not changed. Thus, in reflecting variable 1, entries r_{16} and r_{61}, residual elements from Table 3.7 that equal $-.097$, are changed from minus to plus. Entries r_{13} and r_{31}, both equal to .519, are left unchanged as to sign, however, since variable 3 is also reflected. If both variables 1 and 3 are reflected, this means two sign changes that cancel each other; so the residual retains the same sign. The results of the reflection process can be described in another way: If r_{ij}' represents an unreflected residual and r_{ij}'' represents the reflected residual, then $r_{ij}'' = r_{ij}' (-1)^{ni} (-1)^{nj}$ where n_i and n_j are the numbers of times variables i and j, respectively, have been reflected during this particular reflection process preparatory to extracting a factor.

After the matrix of reflected residuals is formed, Table 3.8, the matrix of products A_2A_2' is obtained by multiplying the absolute values of the second factor loadings times each other. This matrix of products, representing the contribution of factor II to the correlations, is subtracted term by term from the R_1 matrix of reflected residuals, Table 3.8, to get the second factor residuals which are shown in Table 3.9.

3.3.7. COMPUTING THE THIRD FACTOR LOADINGS

The third factor loadings are obtained by essentially the same steps used for computing the second factor loadings except that a different set of variables must be reflected. For the third factor, variables 12, 11, 10, 2, 1, and 8 are reflected in that order before the column totals without communalities

TABLE 3.8

First Factor Residuals after Reflection with Reestimated Communalities

	1	2	3	4	5	6	7	8	9	10	11	12
1	(.519)	.504	.519	.124	.083	.097	.153	.152	.190	.190	.225	.307
2	.504	(.504)	.410	.125	.037	.045	.194	.153	.207	.197	.233	.252
3	.519	.410	(.519)	.145	.150	.172	.174	.117	.202	.155	.195	.156
4	.124	.125	.145	(.232)	.205	.232	.017	-.026	.129	-.132	-.140	-.137
5	.083	.037	.150	.205	(.248)	.248	-.013	-.054	.018	-.087	-.082	-.125
6	.097	.045	.172	.232	.248	(.248)	-.096	-.082	.017	-.149	-.061	-.111
7	.153	.194	.174	.017	-.013	-.096	(.321)	.146	.321	-.070	-.118	-.065
8	.152	.153	.117	-.026	-.054	-.082	.146	(.153)	.143	.033	.055	.037
9	.190	.207	.202	.129	.018	.017	.321	.143	(.321)	-.099	-.081	-.070
10	.190	.197	.155	-.132	-.087	-.149	-.070	.033	-.099	(.354)	.354	.296
11	.225	.233	.195	-.140	-.082	-.061	-.118	.055	-.081	.354	(.412)	.412
12	.307	.252	.156	-.137	-.125	-.111	-.065	.037	-.070	.296	.412	(.412)

become all positive. These computations are shown in Table 3.9. The asterisks, for reflected variables 1, 2, and 3, are *not* carried over from Table 3.7 to Table 3.9. Each new reflection process for computing another factor starts with no asterisks on the table.

When the third factor loadings are entered in matrix **A** (Table 3.13), however, attaching the proper signs is more complicated than it was for the second factor. The sign of each variable that was reflected during the third factor computations must be reversed, but this is not just a matter of putting negative signs on the loadings for those variables in factor III.

Rather, it is a matter of changing the sign from what it was on the immediately preceding factor II. If a variable has not been reflected in computing any previous factor, the signs of all previous factor loadings will be positive; so a reflection on the current factor will merely cause its sign to go negative. This is the case in this example for variables 8, 10, 11, and 12.

Variables 1 and 2, however, were previously reflected on factor II and therefore had negative signs there. When they are reflected on factor III in computing factor III, their signs are changed back to positive because they are re-reflected. Variable 3 has a negative loading on factor III not because it was reflected in computing factor III, but because it was reflected in computing factor II, making it negative, and it was not reflected back again in computing factor III. A variable maintains its sign, whatever it is, until a reflection changes it. When changed, it remains in that state until another reflection occurs to change it back again.

3.3.8.   COMPUTING THE FOURTH FACTOR LOADINGS

After the third factor is extracted, it is necessary to carry out the reflections of the residuals before removing the contribution of the third factor by the formula $R_3 = R_2 - A_3A_3'$. The reflected R_2 matrix is not shown, but it is obtained by the same method that was used to obtain the reflected R_1 matrix in Table 3.8. In this case, however, the residuals for variables 1, 2, 8, 10, 11, and 12 had to be reflected. The third factor residuals (matrix R_3), derived from the reflected second factor residuals, are shown in Table 3.10, along with the computations for the fourth factor loadings. For the fourth factor, variables 1, 7, 9, 10, 11, and 12 must be reflected to make all the column totals positive. In entering the fourth factor loadings in matrix **A** (Table 3.13), the signs for these newly reflected variables must be made opposite to what they were for factor III. The remaining fourth factor loadings will have the same signs that were present for these variables on the third factor, since they were not reflected in obtaining the fourth factor loadings.

TABLE 3.9 Second Factor Residuals and Third Factor Computations

	*1	*2	3	4	5	6	7	*8	9	*10	*11	*12	Σ_o
*1	.071 (−.011)	.009	.015	−.010	−.026	.000	−.014	.009	−.035	.010	−.018	.071	.011
*2	.009	.065 (.041)	−.061	.000	−.065	−.046	.038	.020	−.003	.029	.006	.032	−.041
3	.015	−.061	.080 (.040)	.017	.046	.080	.015	−.019	−.011	−.017	−.037	−.068	−.040
4	−.010	.000	.017	.208 (.198)	.178	.208	−.025	−.063	.072	−.178	−.202	−.197	−.200
5	−.026	−.065	.046	.178	.228 (.226)	.228	−.047	−.083	−.028	−.124	−.132	−.173	−.226
6	.000	−.046	.080	.208	.228	.228 (.230)	−.126	−.108	−.024	−.182	−.105	−.154	−.229
7	−.014	.038	.015	−.025	−.047	−.126	.251 (.269)	.101	.251	−.127	−.195	−.140	−.269
*8	.009	.020	−.019	−.063	−.083	−.108	.101	.108 (.115)	.082	−.016	−.010	−.027	−.114
9	−.035	−.003	−.011	.072	−.028	−.024	.251	.082	.251 (.226)	−.175	−.184	−.171	−.226
*10	.010	.029	−.017	−.178	−.124	−.182	−.127	−.016	−.175	.272 (.293)	.272	.216	−.292
*11	−.018	.006	−.037	−.202	−.132	−.105	−.195	−.010	−.184	.272	.304 (.301)	.304	−.301
*12	.071	.032	−.068	−.197	−.173	−.154	−.140	−.027	−.171	.216	.304	.304 (.307)	−.307
Σ_o	.011	−.041	−.040	−.200	−.226	−.229	−.269	−.114	−.226	−.292	−.301	−.307	−2.234
12	−.131	−.105	.096	.194	.120	.079	.011	−.060	.116	−.724	−.909	.307	−1.006
11	−.095	−.117	.170	.598	.384	.289	.401	−.040	.484	−1.268	.909	.915	2.630
10	−.115	−.175	.204	.954	.632	.653	.655	−.008	.834	1.268	1.453	1.347	7.702
2	−.133	.175	.326	.954	.762	.745	.579	−.048	.840	1.326	1.465	1.411	8.402
1	.133	.193	.296	.974	.814	.745	.607	−.066	.910	1.346	1.429	1.553	8.934
8	.151	.233	.334	1.100	.980	.961	.405	.066	.746	1.314	1.409	1.499	9.198
t	.222	.298	.414	1.308	1.208	1.189	.656	.174	.997	1.586	1.713	1.803	
a_t	.065	.087	.122	.384	.356	.350	.193	.051	.293	.466	.504	.530	

$$T = 11.568$$
$$\sqrt{T} = 3.40008$$
$$1/\sqrt{T} = .29411$$

The fourth factor residuals, computed by the formula $\mathbf{R}_4 = \mathbf{R}_3 - \mathbf{A}_4\mathbf{A}_4'$, are shown in Table 3.11. Again, $\mathbf{R}_3$ is a matrix of reflected residuals and $\mathbf{A}_4$ has all positive signs; $\mathbf{R}_4$, of course, is a matrix of unreflected residuals. If a fifth factor were computed and the matrix equation $\mathbf{R}_5 = \mathbf{R}_4 - \mathbf{A}_5\mathbf{A}_5'$ applied to get fifth factor residuals, it is important to recognize that although $\mathbf{R}_4$ appears in both equations, in the first case it is unreflected and in the second case it is reflected, although the same symbol is used in both places.

No more than four factors were expected to appear in this analysis and indeed no fourth factor residual correlation exceeds 0.057 in absolute value. Factor extraction was terminated after four factors, therefore, because the matrix of fourth factor residuals contained only small residual correlations.

3.3.9. REPRODUCING THE CORRELATION MATRIX

If the computations have been carried out correctly, the following equation should hold:

$$\mathbf{R} = \mathbf{AA'} + \mathbf{R}_4 \qquad (3.13)$$

That is, if the factor matrix, consisting of four factors, is multiplied by its transpose and added to the matrix of fourth factor residuals, the original correlation matrix should be reproduced within the limits of rounding error. The matrix $\mathbf{AA'}$ is shown in Table 3.12. Before $\mathbf{R}_4$ can be added to $\mathbf{AA'}$, however, the individual residuals must be returned to their original unreflected state. Otherwise, some residual elements would have to be added to the inner product of the factor loadings in $\mathbf{AA'}$, to reproduce the original correlation, and others would have to be subtracted. To adjust the signs on the residuals, it is necessary to know how many times each matrix element has been reflected in sign.

Table 3.13 gives the number of reflections for each variable over all the factor extraction operations, that is, the number of times the factor loading sign of each variable has been reversed. For any given residual r_{ij} add up the number of sign changes for the two variables i and j. If this number is odd, the r_{ij} sign is out of phase and must be reversed from what it is in the fourth factor residual matrix, Table 3.11. If the sum of the two numbers of sign changes is an even number, however, the r_{ij} sign is correct as shown in Table 3.11. After these sign changes are made, Eq. (3.13) holds as expected, although not for the diagonal cells if communalities have been reestimated during the factor extraction process.

TABLE 3.10 Third Factor Residuals and Fourth Factor Computations

	*1	2	3	4	5	6	*7	8	*9	*10	*11	*12	Σ_o
*1	.051 (.066)	.003	-.023	-.015	.002	-.023	.002	.006	.016	-.020	-.051	.036	-.067
2	.003	.055 (.057)	.051	-.033	.034	.015	-.055	.015	-.023	-.012	-.038	-.015	-.058
3	-.023	.051	.051 (.065)	-.029	.003	.037	-.008	.013	-.047	-.040	-.025	.004	-.064
4	-.015	-.033	-.029	.099 (.060)	.041	.073	-.099	.043	-.040	-.002	.008	-.007	-.060
5	.002	.034	.003	.041	.132 (.102)	.104	-.115	.065	-.132	-.042	-.047	-.015	-.102
6	-.023	.015	.037	.073	.104	.194 (.106)	-.194	.090	-.127	.019	-.071	-.032	-.109
*7	.002	-.055	-.008	-.099	-.115	-.194	.194 (.214)	-.111	.194	.037	.098	.038	-.213
8	.006	.015	.013	.043	.065	.090	-.111	.111 (.106)	-.097	-.040	-.036	-.054	-.106
*9	.016	-.023	-.047	-.040	-.132	-.127	.194	-.097	.194 (.165)	.039	.036	.015	-.166
*10	-.020	-.012	-.040	-.002	-.042	.019	.037	-.040	.039	.042 (.054)	.037	-.031	-.055
*11	-.051	-.038	-.025	.008	-.047	-.071	.098	-.036	.036	.037	.098 (.050)	.037	-.052
*12	.036	-.015	.004	-.007	-.015	-.032	.038	-.054	.015	-.031	.037	.054 (.023)	-.024
Σ_o	-.067	-.058	-.064	-.060	-.102	-.109	-.213	-.106	-.166	-.055	-.052	-.024	-1.076
7	-.071	.052	-.048	.138	.128	.279	.213	.116	-.554	-.129	-.248	-.100	-.224
9	-.103	.098	.046	.218	.392	.533	.601	.310	.554	-.207	-.320	-.130	1.992
11	-.001	.174	.096	.202	.486	.675	.797	.382	.626	-.281	.320	-.204	3.272
10	.039	.198	.176	.206	.570	.637	.871	.462	.704	.281	.394	-.142	4.396
12	-.033	.228	.168	.220	.600	.701	.947	.570	.734	.219	.468	.142	4.964
1	.033	.222	.214	.250	.596	.747	.951	.558	.766	.179	.366	.214	5.096
t	.084	.277	.265	.349	.728	.941	1.145	.669	.960	.221	.464	.268	
a_i	.033	.109	.104	.138	.289	.373	.454	.265	.381	.087	.184	.106	

$T = 6.371$
$\sqrt{T} = 2.52252$
$1/\sqrt{T} = .39643$

TABLE 3.11

Fourth Factor Residuals

	1	2	3	4	5	6	7	8	9	10	11	12
1	(.049)	-.007	.020	.010	-.012	.010	-.013	-.014	.003	-.023	-.057	.033
2	-.007	(.043)	.039	-.048	.002	-.025	.006	-.014	-.019	.002	.018	.003
3	.020	.039	(.040)	-.044	-.027	-.002	-.039	-.015	.007	.031	.005	-.015
4	.010	-.048	-.044	(.080)	.001	.022	.036	.006	-.012	-.010	-.033	-.008
5	-.012	.002	-.027	.001	(.049)	-.004	-.016	-.011	.022	.017	-.006	-.016
6	.010	-.025	-.002	.022	-.004	(.055)	.025	-.009	-.015	-.052	.002	-.008
7	-.013	.006	-.039	.036	-.016	.025	(-.011)	-.010	.021	-.002	.014	-.011
8	-.014	-.014	-.015	.006	-.011	-.009	-.010	(.040)	-.004	.017	-.013	.026
9	.003	-.019	.007	-.012	.022	-.015	.021	-.004	(.049)	.006	-.034	-.025
10	-.023	.002	.031	-.010	.017	-.052	-.002	.017	.006	(.034)	.021	-.040
11	-.057	.018	.005	-.033	-.006	.002	.014	-.013	-.034	.021	(.064)	.018
12	.033	.003	-.015	-.008	-.016	-.008	-.011	.026	-.025	-.040	.018	(.043)

TABLE 3.12

Reproduced Correlation Matrix (AA')

	1	2	3	4	5	6	7	8	9	10	11	12
1	(.677)	.603	.620	.080	.128	.080	.053	.094	.057	-.043	-.077	-.137
2	.603	(.561)	.539	.068	.128	.105	-.044	.006	-.039	-.072	-.098	-.153
3	.620	.539	(.608)	-.024	.013	-.032	.029	.095	.003	.021	-.015	-.055
4	.080	.068	-.024	(.466)	.509	.438	.316	.296	.458	.110	.173	.058
5	.128	.128	.013	.509	(.583)	.514	.274	.299	.432	.163	.246	.106
6	.080	.105	-.032	.438	.514	(.474)	.155	.181	.295	.102	.178	.058
7	.053	-.044	.029	.316	.274	.155	(.557)	.470	.639	.158	.174	.109
8	.094	.006	.095	.296	.299	.181	.470	(.490)	.554	.327	.377	.286
9	.057	-.039	.003	.458	.432	.295	.639	.554	(.765)	.206	.246	.145
10	-.043	-.072	.021	.110	.163	.102	.158	.327	.206	(.490)	.579	.500
11	-.077	-.098	-.015	.173	.246	.178	.174	.377	.246	.579	(.695)	.592
12	-.137	-.153	-.055	.058	.106	.058	.109	.286	.145	.500	.592	(.529)

TABLE 3.13

Factor Matrix (A)[a]

	I	II	III	IV	h^2	Number of reflections
1	.377	−.728	.065	−.033	.677	3
2	.282	−.680	.087	.109	.561	2
3	.321	−.692	−.122	−.104	.608	1
4	.514	.184	.384	.138	.466	0
5	.592	.149	.356	.289	.583	0
6	.442	.133	.350	.373	.474	0
7	.511	.229	.193	−.454	.557	1
8	.615	.196	−.051	−.265	.490	1
9	.662	.309	.293	−.381	.765	1
10	.451	.248	−.466	.087	.490	2
11	.544	.334	−.504	.184	.695	2
12	.363	.324	−.530	.106	.529	2
SSQ	2.845	2.010	1.300	.739	[6.895]	

[a] The SSQ values for columns I, II, III, and IV are the sums of squares of the column elements. The value in brackets, 6.895, is the sum of the communalities. The proportion of the extracted variance accounted for by any factor is its SSQ total divided by the sum of the communalities.

3.4. ITERATING THE COMMUNALITIES

In a large matrix, say 50 variables, errors in estimating communalities usually do not affect the solution heavily because such discrepancies are typically small compared with the column sums after reflection. With smaller matrices, however, these errors can be of greater significance. For this reason, it is sometimes necessary to calculate the communalities derived from the first solution by summing the squares of the extracted factor loadings, and to use these values as estimates of the communalities for a second solution. The communalities derived from the second solution are used as estimates for a third solution, and so on, until the communalities which emerge from a given solution are close to those that were input as estimates. Usually 10 to 15 interations will be sufficient for all practical purposes although many more may be required to achieve convergence. Occasionally, convergence cannot be achieved even with a large number of iterations. Even five iterations, however, will often bring the communalities close enough to converged values for most practical purposes.

Where the communalities are being iterated by repeating the entire factor extraction process, after the first solution, the residual communalities are carried throughout the solution without reestimating communalities at each factor extraction step as was done in this sample problem. Thus, the residual communality from the first factor is used as the estimate of the communality for the second factor. The residual for the second factor is used as the estimate for the third factor, and so on. The same number of factors is extracted in each solution. For this reason, it is important to determine how many factors are needed before refactoring to stabilize communalities. Table 3.14 gives a solution after six iterations of the communalities in the sample problem used here as an illustration of centroid factor extraction. The differences in factor loadings between the first solution and the sixth iterated solution are not large, even for a small problem like this one. With matrices of 20 or more variables, iteration of the solution until stabilized communalities are obtained may not be worth the extra computation time involved, particularly if the computations are being carried out on a hand-held calculator! In actual practice, most empirical problems with real data do not require a high degree of precision in the estimated communality values to obtain useful results.

Unfortunately, there is no way of obtaining the "correct" communalities. Even converged communality values are not necessarily correct. There is no solution to the "communality problem." Methods of dealing with the communality problem are discussed further in the next chapter where a method of factor extraction is presented that does not require the use of communality estimates to obtain the factor loadings.

One of the computer programs described in Chapter 14 can be used to perform a centroid factor analysis, provided the FORTRAN program has

TABLE 3.14

Factor Matrix with Iterated Communalities[a]

	I	II	III	IV	h^2
1	.398	−.771	.037	−.012	.753
2	.265	−.651	.062	.075	.503
3	.309	−.673	−.100	−.063	.563
4	.504	.181	.368	.113	.434
5	.610	.135	.343	.304	.600
6	.443	.148	.374	.394	.514
7	.500	.242	.204	−.493	.593
8	.602	.194	−.042	−.244	.462
9	.686	.294	.276	−.382	.779
10	.428	.246	−.452	.068	.452
11	.567	.320	−.538	.162	.740
12	.350	.334	−.534	.078	.526
SSQ	2.855	2.000	1.307	0.756	[6.918]

[a] The SSQ values for columns I, II, III, and IV are the sums of squares of the column elements. The value in brackets, 6.918, is the sum of the communalities. The proportion of the extracted variance accounted for by any factor is its SSQ total divided by the sum of the communalities.

been compiled and prepared for running at your own computer center. A diskette that is available with this book contains the FORTRAN listings of the various programs described in Chapter 14. After completing the calculations for their own sample problems using a hand-held calculator, students can check their work using the centroid computer program. For some classes, students may be permitted to bypass the hand calculation and just run the analysis on the computer. In such cases, the student would learn more by at least checking here and there with hand calculations enough to be sure that how the method works is thoroughly understood. The centroid computer program uses slightly different computing procedures from those described in this chapter but with the same final outcome. Residuals are computed, for example, without making the sign changes and using all positive factor loadings. This requires keeping track of negative signs, a task that the computer can handle without error but the human being cannot. Other procedures for obtaining factor solutions similar to the centroid solution are also available but they are no longer in common use (Thurstone, 1947; Horst, 1965).

4

Methods of Factor Extraction

The centroid method of factor extraction was developed by Thurstone as a practical method for use with the desk calculator. It is an approximation to the principal factor method that, though more demanding of computation time, does extract the maximum amount of variance with each succeeding factor. The centroid method only approximates this ideal. With electronic computers, the additional computation time required for doing a principal factor solution, instead of a centroid solution, does not represent an unreasonable expenditure of resources for most factor analytic problems. Consequently, the principal factor method in recent years has replaced the centroid method as the most widely used method of factor extraction. With the principal factor method, however, it is still necessary to estimate the communalities. Because there is no clear solution to this problem, a certain indeterminacy is introduced by using estimated communalities because the solution can be affected substantially by the values chosen. It is possible, however, to obtain a solution without using any communality estimates by using the minimum residual method of factor extraction (Comrey, 1962a; Comrey & Ahumada, 1964, 1965). This method is described later in this chapter.

4.1. THE PRINCIPAL FACTOR METHOD

A theorem from matrix algebra that will not be proved here states that a symmetric matrix can be "diagonalized" by the method shown in the following diagram:

78

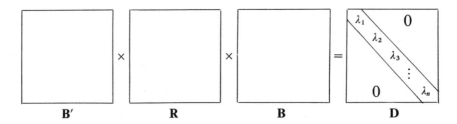

where **R** is the symmetric matrix to be diagonalized, **B** is an orthogonal matrix, **B'** is the transpose of **B**, and **D** is a diagonal matrix with zeroes every place except along the main diagonal. The reader will recall from Chapter 2 that an orthogonal matrix is one in which the sum of squares for each row and each column equal 1.0 and the inner products of any two nonidentical rows or columns equal zero. The schematic matrix operation just shown may be represented by the matrix equation

$$\mathbf{B'RB} = \mathbf{D} \tag{4.1}$$

Since **B** is orthogonal with sums of squares of rows and columns equal to 1.0 and inner products of nonidentical rows or columns equal to zero, **BB'** = **B'B** = **I**, the identity matrix. Thus, if **B** is orthogonal, **B'** is the inverse of **B** and vice versa. This fact will be used to operate on Eq. (4.1) as follows:

$$\mathbf{BB'RB} = \mathbf{BD} \tag{4.2}$$

BB' equals the identity matrix on the left in Eq. (4.2); so it drops out. Then, multiplying both sides of Eq. (4.2) on the right side by **B'** gives

$$\mathbf{RBB'} = \mathbf{BDB'} \tag{4.3}$$

But **BB'** is also an identity matrix; so Eq. (4.3) becomes

$$\mathbf{R} = \mathbf{BDB'} \tag{4.4}$$

Now, let $\mathbf{D}^{1/2}$ be a diagonal matrix that has elements in the diagonals that are the square roots of the corresponding elements in the diagonals of the diagonal matrix **D**. Then, since $\mathbf{D}^{1/2}\mathbf{D}^{1/2} = \mathbf{D}$, Eq. (4.4) may be written as

$$\mathbf{R} = \mathbf{BD}^{1/2}\mathbf{D}^{1/2}\mathbf{B'} = \mathbf{AA'} \tag{4.5}$$

That is, the matrix $\mathbf{BD}^{1/2}$ is a factor matrix **A** and the matrix $\mathbf{D}^{1/2}\mathbf{B'}$ is its transpose **A'**.

A series of steps that could produce a principal factor solution, then, may be set out as follows:

1. Form the $n \times n$ correlation matrix $\mathbf{R}$ with appropriate values selected for the diagonal cells as communality estimates.

2. Find an $n \times n$ orthogonal matrix $\mathbf{B}$ such that when $\mathbf{R}$ is premultiplied by $\mathbf{B}'$ and postmultiplied by $\mathbf{B}$, the result is an $n \times n$ diagonal matrix $\mathbf{D}$ with diagonal elements $\lambda_1, \lambda_2, \lambda_3, \ldots, \lambda_n$.

3. Multiply each element of column 1 of $\mathbf{B}$ by $\sqrt{\lambda_1}$. Multiply each element of column 2 of $\mathbf{B}$ by $\sqrt{\lambda_2}$, and so on, for the other columns until each element of the last column of $\mathbf{B}$ is multiplied by $\sqrt{\lambda_n}$. These operations in step 3 are equivalent to multiplying the matrix $\mathbf{B}$ on the right by a diagonal matrix with diagonal elements that contain the square roots of the following values: $\lambda_1, \lambda_2, \lambda_3, \ldots, \lambda_n$. Multiplying a matrix on the left by a diagonal matrix has the effect of multiplying each row by a different constant.

4. The matrix obtained in step 3 is a factor matrix $\mathbf{A}$ such that $\mathbf{R} = \mathbf{AA}'$. The sum of squares of column 1 of $\mathbf{A}$ equals λ_1, the sum of squares of column 2 of $\mathbf{A}$ equals λ_2, and so on, until the sum of squares of column n of $\mathbf{A}$ equals λ_n.

The proportion of variance extracted by factor i is λ_i divided by the sum of all the λ values from 1 to n. The sum of the λ_i values represents the total variance extracted since by a theorem in matrix algebra the sum of the λ_i values will equal the sum of the diagonal values of the $\mathbf{R}$ matrix. For each variable, the diagonal values of $\mathbf{R}$ give the proportions of variance h_i^2 that are input to the analysis, so their sum represents the total extractable variance in the matrix. If all the variance in the matrix were extracted, then the sum of the λ_i values would equal the sum of the communalities. If the communalities are set equal to 1.0 and if n factors are extracted, then the sum of λ_i values would equal n. The total variance of a set of standard scores equals 1.0, so 1.0 equals the amount of variance entered for each variable when the communalities are all equal to 1.0. The total amount of variance that can be extracted, therefore, is $n \times 1.0$ or n. This is only possible, however, using 1.0 for every communality and extracting as many factors as there are variables. This is seldom done in practice since we usually do not wish to obtain a solution that requires as many factors as there are variables.

4.1.1. THE JACOBI METHOD

There are various methods of obtaining the $\mathbf{B}$ matrix such that $\mathbf{B}'\mathbf{RB} = \mathbf{D}$. Obtaining $\mathbf{B}$ is the major part of the work since once $\mathbf{B}$ is obtained, it is a simple matter to compute $\mathbf{BD}^{1/2}$.

One method of obtaining matrix $\mathbf{B}$ is that developed in the last century by the mathematician Jacobi. The procedure begins by finding a matrix $\mathbf{B}_1$ such that (see Fig. 4.1)

$$
\begin{bmatrix}
1 & 0 & 0 & 0 & 0 \\
0 & b_{22} & 0 & b_{42} & 0 \\
0 & 0 & 1 & 0 & 0 \\
0 & b_{24} & 0 & b_{44} & 0 \\
0 & 0 & 0 & 0 & 1
\end{bmatrix}
\begin{bmatrix}
h_1^2 & r_{12} & r_{13} & r_{14} & r_{15} \\
r_{21} & h_2^2 & r_{23} & r_{24} & r_{25} \\
r_{31} & r_3^2 & h_3^2 & r_{34} & r_{35} \\
r_{41} & r_{42} & r_{43} & h_4^2 & r_{45} \\
r_{51} & r_{52} & r_{53} & r_{54} & h_5^2
\end{bmatrix}
$$

$$
\mathbf{B_1'} \qquad\qquad\qquad \mathbf{R}
$$

$$
\times
\begin{bmatrix}
1 & 0 & 0 & 0 & 0 \\
0 & b_{22} & 0 & b_{24} & 0 \\
0 & 0 & 1 & 0 & 0 \\
0 & b_{42} & 0 & b_{44} & 0 \\
0 & 0 & 0 & 0 & 1
\end{bmatrix}
=
\begin{bmatrix}
d_{11} & d_{12} & d_{13} & d_{14} & d_{15} \\
d_{21} & d_{22} & d_{23} & d_{24} & d_{25} \\
d_{31} & d_{32} & d_{33} & d_{34} & d_{35} \\
d_{41} & d_{42} & d_{43} & d_{44} & d_{45} \\
d_{51} & d_{52} & d_{53} & d_{54} & d_{55}
\end{bmatrix}
$$

$$
\mathbf{B_1} \qquad\qquad\qquad \mathbf{D_1}
$$

FIG. 4.1. One Jacobi transformation. In this schematic representation, the annihilation of one pair of elements of the 5 × 5 correlation matrix is indicated, namely, r_{24} and r_{42}. The elements of $\mathbf{B}_1$ are found as follows: b_{22} and b_{44} equal $\cos \phi_{24}$, $b_{42} = -\sin \phi_{24}$, and $b_{24} = \sin \phi_{24}$, where ϕ_{24} is found using Eq. (4.7) with $i = 2$ and $j = 4$.

$$
\mathbf{B_1'RB_1} = \mathbf{D_1} \tag{4.6}
$$

where $\mathbf{B}_1$ is an orthogonal matrix that has nonzero elements in the cells b_{ii}, b_{ij}, b_{ji}, and b_{jj}, and also in the other diagonal cells. Except for b_{ii} and b_{jj}, however, the diagonal cells have the value 1.0 placed in them. The matrix $\mathbf{D}_1$ will have a zero in cells d_{ij} and d_{ji}. Thus, this matrix operation "annihilates" one off-diagonal value in the original $\mathbf{R}$ matrix, moving it closer to the ultimate diagonal form shown in Eq. (4.1). The r_{ij} chosen for "annihilation" is the largest off-diagonal element of the matrix.

The elements of matrix $\mathbf{B}_1$ are b_{ii} and b_{jj} equal to $\cos \phi_{ij}$; $b_{ji} = \sin \phi_{ij}$; and $b_{ij} = -\sin \phi_{ij}$ where

$$
\tan 2\phi = \frac{-2r_{ij}}{h_i^2 - h_j^2} \tag{4.7}
$$

The effect of these matrix operations for a 2 × 2 correlation matrix may be shown in the following equations, which also demonstrate how Eq. (4.7) may be developed:

$$\begin{bmatrix} \cos \phi & -\sin \phi \\ \sin \phi & \cos \phi \end{bmatrix} \times \begin{bmatrix} h_1^2 & r_{12} \\ r_{21} & h_2^2 \end{bmatrix} \times \begin{bmatrix} \cos \phi & \sin \phi \\ -\sin \phi & \cos \phi \end{bmatrix} = \begin{bmatrix} \lambda_1 & 0 \\ 0 & \lambda_2 \end{bmatrix}$$

$\quad\quad$ **B'** $\quad\quad\quad\quad$ **R** $\quad\quad\quad\quad\quad$ **B** $\quad\quad\quad\quad$ **D**

$$\begin{bmatrix} (\cos \phi \cdot h_1^2 - \sin \phi \cdot r_{21}) & (\cos \phi \cdot r_{12} - \sin \phi \cdot h_2^2) \\ (\sin \phi \cdot h_1^2 + \cos \phi \cdot r_{21}) & (\sin \phi \cdot r_{12} + \cos \phi \cdot h_2^2) \end{bmatrix}$$

$\quad\quad\quad\quad\quad\quad\quad\quad$ **B'R**

$$\times \begin{bmatrix} \cos \phi & \sin \phi \\ -\sin \phi & \cos \phi \end{bmatrix} = \begin{bmatrix} \lambda_1 & 0 \\ 0 & \lambda_2 \end{bmatrix}$$

$\quad\quad\quad\quad$ **B** $\quad\quad\quad\quad\quad$ **D**

Computing the elements d_{21} and d_{12} of the product **B'RB** gives

$$d_{21} = (\sin\phi \cdot h_1^2 + \cos\phi \cdot r_{21})\cos\phi - (\sin\phi \cdot r_{12} + \cos\phi \cdot h_2^2)\sin\phi = 0$$

$$d_{12} = (\cos\phi \cdot h_1^2 - \sin\phi \cdot r_{21})\sin\phi + (\cos\phi \cdot r_{12} - \sin\phi \cdot h_2^2)\cos\phi = 0$$

$$d_{21} = \cos\phi\sin\phi \cdot h_1^2 + \cos^2\phi \cdot r_{21} - \sin^2\phi \cdot r_{12} - \sin\phi\cos\phi \cdot h_2^2 = 0$$

$$d_{12} = \sin\phi\cos\phi \cdot h_1^2 - \sin^2\phi \cdot r_{21} + \cos^2\phi \cdot r_{12} - \sin\phi\cos\phi \cdot h_2^2 = 0$$

Adding these last two equations together gives

$$2\sin\phi\cos\phi \cdot h_1^2 + 2(\cos^2\phi - \sin^2\phi)r_{12} - 2\sin\phi\cos\phi \cdot h_2^2 = 0$$

$$\sin2\phi \cdot h_1^2 + 2\cos2\phi \cdot r_{12} - \sin2\phi \cdot h_2^2 = 0$$

$$\sin2\phi(h_1^2 - h_2^2) + 2r_{12}\cos2\phi = 0$$

$$\text{Tan}2\phi = \frac{\sin2\phi}{\cos2\phi} = \frac{-2r_{12}}{h_1^2 - h_2} \tag{4.7}$$

After the matrix $\mathbf{B_1'RB_1} = \mathbf{D_1}$ is computed with a zero in element d_{ij} and d_{ji}, the largest remaining matrix element off the diagonal in $\mathbf{D_1}$ is annihilated as follows:

$$\mathbf{B_2'D_1B_2} = \mathbf{B_2'(B_1'RB_1)B_2} = \mathbf{D_2} \tag{4.8}$$

Suppose the largest off-diagonal element in $\mathbf{D_1}$ were d_{13}. Then the result of the operation in Eq. (4.8) would be to place a zero in cells d_{13} and d_{31} of matrix $\mathbf{D_2}$. The only off-diagonal elements of $\mathbf{B_2}$ that would be nonzero in this case would be b_{13} and b_{31}. The elements of $\mathbf{B_2}$ of principal interest would be as follows: b_{11} and b_{33} equal to $\cos\phi_{13}$, with other diagonal elements equal to 1.0; $b_{31} = -\sin\phi_{13}$; and $b_{13} = \sin\phi_{13}$ where

$$\tan 2\phi_{13} = \frac{-2r_{13}}{h_1{}^2 - h_3{}^2} \tag{4.9}$$

It must be emphasized, however, that the elements r_{13}, $h_1{}^2$, and $h_3{}^2$ in Eq. (4.9) are taken from the matrix $\mathbf{D}_1$ rather than from the original $\mathbf{R}$ matrix.

This entire process is repeated over and over again, always with the largest remaining off-diagonal value selected, regardless of sign, for annihilation. Each element that is annihilated requires the addition of another $\mathbf{B}_i$ matrix. Unfortunately, a matrix element of $\mathbf{D}_i$ does not stay annihilated. It will return to a nonzero value as other matrix elements are annihilated. Each time a matrix element is annihilated, however, the overall sum of squares of the off-diagonal elements is reduced. Thus, by iterating over and over again, the off-diagonal elements can be made as close to zero as the accuracy of calculation permits. At the end, the result looks like the following:

$$\mathbf{B}_k{}' \cdots \mathbf{B}_3{}'\mathbf{B}_2{}'\mathbf{B}_1{}'\mathbf{R}\mathbf{B}_1\mathbf{B}_2\mathbf{B}_3 \cdots \mathbf{B}_k = \mathbf{D} \tag{4.10}$$

where k ordinarily is a number considerably larger than n. That is, many iterations are required to complete the diagonalization of $\mathbf{R}$. After the annihilation of each off-diagonal element, a check is made to see if the largest remaining off-diagonal element in $\mathbf{D}_i$ is greater than some selected value, ϵ, close to zero. If so, another iteration is run, and another check is made. Eventually, the largest off-diagonal element of the matrix $\mathbf{D}_i$ will be less than ϵ. At this point, iteration is terminated, and the $\mathbf{D}_i$ is the $\mathbf{D}$ of Eq. (4.1) achieved by diagonalizing $\mathbf{R}$. Then, the $\mathbf{B}'$ matrix of Eq. (4.1) is given by

$$\mathbf{B}' = \mathbf{B}_k{}' \cdots \mathbf{B}_3{}'\mathbf{B}_2{}'\mathbf{B}_1{}' \tag{4.11}$$

and $\mathbf{B}$ is the transpose of $\mathbf{B}'$. Each of these intermediate $\mathbf{B}_i{}'$ matrices individually is an orthogonal matrix since $\cos^2\phi + \sin^2\phi = 1$ and the sums of squares of all rows and columns equal this expression. The inner products of nonidentical rows and columns of each $\mathbf{B}_i{}'$ equal zero. A theorem of matrix algebra that will not be proved here states that the product of orthogonal matrices is an orthogonal matrix, so $\mathbf{B}'$ in (4.11) is also an orthogonal matrix, satisfying the requirements of Eq. (4.1).

The $\mathbf{B}_i{}'$ matrix required to annihilate any particular matrix element r_{ij} can be formed as follows:

1. Put 1 in all diagonal cells of $\mathbf{B}_i{}'$ except for elements b_{ii} and b_{jj}.

2. Find $\tan 2\phi_{ij} = -r_{ij}/(h_i^2 - h_j^2)$, as in Eq. (4.9), where r_{ij}, h_i, and h_j are taken from the $\mathbf{R}$ matrix for the first transformation and from the $\mathbf{D}$ matrix in its present state of transition toward diagonal form for all subsequent transformations. From $\tan 2\phi_{ij}$ determine the angle 2ϕ and then the angle ϕ itself.

3. Determine the following elements of $\mathbf{B}_i'$: $b_{ii} = b_{jj} = \cos\phi_{ij}$; $b_{ji} = -\sin\phi_{ij}$; and $b_{ij} = \sin\phi_{ij}$. Other off-diagonal elements of $\mathbf{B}_i'$ equal zero.

If the tangent of 2ϕ is negative, then 2ϕ is a negative angle. Find 2ϕ, ignoring the sign on the tangent; find ϕ and then put a negative sign on the sine of ϕ. This will have the effect of making b_{ij} negative and b_{ji} positive. If the tangent of 2ϕ is positive, however, 2ϕ and ϕ will be positive angles and the sine of ϕ will be positive. This leaves b_{ij} positive and b_{ji} negative. In a computer program application, it is more convenient to compute $\cos\phi$ and $\sin\phi$ algebraically from $\tan 2\phi$ by trigonometric identities rather than by using tables.

A Jacobi principal factor solution to the four-variable problem treated in previous chapters by other methods is shown in Table 4.1. The $\mathbf{B}_i'$ and $\mathbf{D}_i$ matrices for each off-diagonal element annihilation are shown in order. The largest off-diagonal element of the original correlation matrix (see Table 2.1) was $r_{34} = r_{43} = .73$. The first $\mathbf{B}_i'$ matrix, then, annihilates r_{34}; this is apparent in the first $\mathbf{D}_i$ matrix which has cells d_{34} and $d_{43} = 0$. The largest element of $\mathbf{D}_1$ is .50, in elements d_{12} and d_{21}; so $\mathbf{B}_2'$ annihilates this element, leaving zero in cells d_{12} and d_{21} of $\mathbf{D}_2$. The off-diagonal elements of $\mathbf{D}_i$ are gradually reduced and after eight iterations, the largest off-diagonal element is .0002 in absolute value. The accumulated $\mathbf{B}'$ matrix, computed by Eq. (4.11), and the factor matrix are also shown in Table 4.1, after the last $\mathbf{B}_i'$ and the final $\mathbf{D}$ matrix. The final $\mathbf{D}$ matrix has the eigenvalues in its diagonals, λ_1, λ_2, λ_3, and λ_4. Ignoring the rounding error, only two nonzero eigenvalues were obtained, 1.7010 in d_{44} and .8190 in d_{11}. Because there are only two nonzero eigenvalues, there are only two factors, as expected. This is evident in the factor matrix that has only two nonzero columns. It will be noted that the factors do not emerge in the order of size in this method. The factor matrix obtained may be rearranged, if desired, to put the largest factor in the first column, the next largest in the second column, and so on.

The centroid solution to this problem (see Tables 3.1 and 3.4) gives factor loadings that appear to be very different from those for the final factor matrix in Table 4.1. Judging from this information alone, it might appear that the principal factor and centroid solutions are not comparable. A rotation of the fourth principal factor away from the first principal factor by an angle of approximately $27°$, however, recovers the initial configuration in Fig. 2.4, just as a rotation of the centroid axes recovered the same configuration (see Table 2.2). Thus, although the centroid and principal

TABLE 4.1

Principal Factor Solution to the Four-Variable Problem

	$\mathbf{B}_i'$				$\mathbf{D}_i$				
	1	2	3	4		1	2	3	4
1	1	0	0	0		.6500	.5000	.0065	.2334
2	0	1	0	0		.5000	.4000	.0047	.3255
3	0	0	.7469	−.6650		.0065	.0047	.0001	.0000
4	0	0	.6650	.7469		.2334	.3255	.0000	1.4699
1	.7882	.6154	0	0		1.0404	0	.0080	.3843
2	−.6154	.7882	0	0		0	.0096	−.0002	.1130
3	0	0	1	0		.0080	−.0002	.0001	0
4	0	0	0	1		.3843	.1130	0	1.4699
1	.8625	0	0	−.5060		.8149	−.0572	.0069	0
2	0	1	0	0		−.0572	.0096	−.0002	.0974
3	0	0	1	0		.0069	−.0002	.0001	.0040
4	.5060	0	0	.8625		0	.0974	.0040	1.6954
1	1	0	0	0		.8149	−.0571	.0069	−.0033
2	0	.9983	0	−.0575		−.0571	.0040	−.0005	0
3	0	0	1	0		.0069	−.0005	.0001	.0040
4	0	.0575	0	.9983		−.0033	0	.0040	1.7010
1	.9976	−.0699	0	0		.8189	0	.0069	−.0033
2	.0699	.9976	0	0		0	0	0	−.0002
3	0	0	1	0		.0069	0	.0001	.0040
4	0	0	0	1		−.0033	−.0002	.0040	1.7010
1	1	0	.0084	0		.8190	0	0	−.0032
2	0	1	0	0		0	0	0	−.0002
3	−.0084	0	1	0		0	0	0	.0040
4	0	0	0	1		−.0032	−.0002	.0040	1.7010
1	1	0	0	0		.8190	0	0	−.0032
2	0	1	0	0		0	0	0	−.0002
3	0	0	1	−.0023		0	0	0	.0002
4	0	0	.0023	1		−.0032	−.0002	.0002	1.7010
1	1	0	0	.0036		.8190	0	0	0
2	0	1	0	0		0	0	0	−.0002
3	0	0	1	0		0	0	0	.0002
4	−.0036	0	0	1		0	−.0002	.0002	1.7010
1	.7240	.4771	−.3250	−.3777	1	.655	0	0	.470
2	−.5883	.8042	−.0564	−.0634	2	.432	0	0	.462
3	−.0069	−.0048	.7484	−.6632	3	−.294	0	0	.751
4	.3601	.3545	.5755	.6430	4	−.342	0	0	.839
	$(\mathbf{B}_8'\cdots\mathbf{B}_3'\mathbf{B}_2'\mathbf{B}_1')$					A (Factor matrix)			

factor solutions look different, they are actually nearly equivalent in the sense that they both produce essentially the same rotated configuration if they start with the same communality estimates. The transformation of the principal factor solution to the original configuration is shown as follows:

$$
\begin{bmatrix}
.470 & .655 \\
.462 & .432 \\
.751 & -.294 \\
.839 & -.342
\end{bmatrix}
\times
\begin{bmatrix}
\cos 27° & \sin 27° \\
-\sin 27° & \cos 27°
\end{bmatrix}
\doteq
\begin{bmatrix}
.1 & .8 \\
.2 & .6 \\
.8 & .1 \\
.9 & .1
\end{bmatrix}
$$
$$
\quad\ \ \mathbf{A} \qquad\qquad\qquad \Lambda \qquad\qquad\qquad \mathbf{V}
$$

Application of the principal factor method, Jacobi-type solution, to the 12-variable sample problem, treated by the centroid method in the previous chapter (see Table 3.6), gives the results shown in Table 4.2. The four factors that were associated with positive eigenvalues are shown in the first four columns. The sums of squares of the factor loadings, the derived communalities, are shown in the column headed by h^2. The values in the column headed by R^2 are the initial communality estimates inserted in the diagonal cells of the $\mathbf{R}$ matrix. The principal factor solution obtained, therefore, was determined to some extent by these estimated communalities.

In the four-variable fictional data example, the exact communalities were known and utilized in the solutions to obtain precise results, namely, exactly two factors with essentially zero residuals, except for rounding errors. The 12-variable sample problem is based on real data, however; so the communalities are not known.

The R^2 values used here as estimates of those communalities are the squared multiple correlations (SMCs) that represent the square of the multiple correlation (Guilford, 1965, Chap. 16) of each variable with all the other variables. These SMCs have been shown under certain conditions to represent lower bound estimates of the unknown communalities (see Harman, 1967, for a more extended discussion of this topic).

Guttman (1956) showed that the value of the SMC is a function of the number of variables under study and that at times it would be equal to the true communality. In order to obtain the squared multiple correlations (SMCs), it is necessary to compute the inverse of the correlation matrix. In some studies, the correlation matrix may be singular or nearly singular. The inverse in such cases cannot be obtained. Thus, it may not be possible to compute the SMCs.

To get these SMCs, where they can be obtained, find $\mathbf{R}^{-1}$, the inverse of $\mathbf{R}$ with 1.0 inserted in each diagonal cell. Take the reciprocals of the diagonal elements of $\mathbf{R}^{-1}$ and subtract each such reciprocal from 1.0. The resulting values are the SMCs entered in Table 4.2 under column R^2. These R^2 values were computed using program 03M of the BMD series of

TABLE 4.2

Principal Factor Solution to 12-Variable Problem for Four Factors with Positive Eigenvalues[a]

	I	II	III	IV	R^2	h^2
1	.092	.768	.236	−.035	.547	.653
2	.012	.671	.185	.054	.413	.489
3	.043	.645	.317	−.081	.448	.524
4	.545	.139	−.325	.208	.387	.464
5	.589	.187	−.213	.288	.415	.509
6	.446	.133	−.263	.383	.342	.435
7	.575	.016	−.211	−.413	.467	.544
8	.642	.015	.047	−.213	.397	.457
9	.742	.052	−.249	−.270	.588	.688
10	.467	−.229	.427	.050	.390	.455
11	.590	−.263	.473	.133	.552	.660
12	.414	−.353	.433	.058	.423	.488
SSQ[b]	2.884	1.777	1.113	0.595	(5.369)	(6.369)

[a] The SMCs R^2 and communalities were computed by the BMD 03M program. This solution used these R^2 values as communality estimates for a Jacobi method solution. The BMD solution varied from this no more than .002 at any point.
[b] The sum of squares.

computer programs (Dixon, 1970a), which also computes a principal factor solution. This program has been supplanted by Program 4M in the newer BMDP series of programs (Dixon, 1983). The factor solution in Table 4.2 was obtained using a FORTRAN computer program written by the first author, with SMCs inserted as communality estimates. Most statistical computing software systems available today, for example, BMDP, SAS, SPSS, SYSTAT, offer programs for computing a principal factor solution although not necessarily by means of the Jacobi method.

In comparing the principal factor solution in Table 4.2 with the centroid solution in Table 3.13, certain similarities can be seen between the two, although the signs of factor II and III are reversed in the two solutions. There would still remain discrepancies of some magnitude between the two solutions, however. Part of this is due to the fact that the SMCs represented communality estimates that were lower generally than the high column values used in the centroid solution. This difference is reflected in the greater sum of the h^2 values after extraction for the centroid method (6.895) than for the principal factor method (6.369). Despite the greater total for the centroid method, however, the amount of variance extracted on the largest principal factor was actually greater than that for the first centroid, 2.884 compared with 2.845. This is due to the fact that the principal factor method extracts the maximum amount of variance at a given step that is possible to extract with the communalities used. The centroid method only approximates this goal. Discrepancies between two solutions due to differences in communality estimates will persist through the rotation process since rotation does not affect the communalities. Differences between solutions by different factor extraction methods using the same communalities tend to disappear, however, in the ultimate rotated solution. This phenomenon has already been illustrated by the centroid and principal factor solutions to the four-variable sample problem. Although the unrotated factors were different for the two solutions, the two rotated solutions were essentially identical.

In the principal factor solution to the 12-variable problem using SMCs as h^2 estimates, only four of the eigenvalues obtained were positive, for example, 2.884, 1.777, 1.113, and .595, as shown in the last row of Table 4.2. The remaining eight eigenvalues were all negative: $-.226$, $-.194$, $-.189$, $-.136$, $-.112$, $-.066$, $-.051$, and $-.016$. Since the sum of squares of the factor loadings for a factor is supposed to equal its eigenvalue, because the factor loadings equal the normalized eigenvector multiplied by the square root of the eigenvalue as called for by Eq. (4.5), a negative eigenvalue poses something of a dilemma. A sum of squares of real numbers cannot be negative. There can be no legitimate factors, therefore, associated with negative eigenvalues. With SMCs as communality estimates, then, only four factors can be extracted from the 12-variable sample matrix. The general problem of determining how many factors to extract from a correlation matrix is considered in greater detail later in this chapter.

4.2.   THE MINIMUM RESIDUAL METHOD

Both the centroid and the principal factor methods require communality estimates that in turn influence the nature of the results. Because there is no known way of determining the "correct" communalities, if indeed they do exist, factor analysis results are subject to some distortion by the use of inaccurate communality estimates. The first author has developed a method of factor extraction, called the "minimum residual" method, that utilizes only the off-diagonal elements of the correlation matrix and hence requires no communality estimates (Comrey, 1962a).

Let **A** represent a column of the factor matrix with elements a^1, a^2, . . ., a^n. Let F(**R,A**) be a function of the correlation matrix **R** and the column of factor loadings **A** such that

$$F(\mathbf{R,A}) = \sum_{i=1}^{i=n} \sum_{j=1}^{j=n} (r_{ij} - a_i a_j)^2, j \neq i \tag{4.12}$$

$F(\mathbf{R},\mathbf{A})$ is the sum of squares of the off-diagonal residuals after the factor $\mathbf{A}$ has been removed from the $\mathbf{R}$ matrix. The basis of the minimum residual method, as the name suggests, is to determine the factor loadings a_1, a_2, ..., a_n of the factor $\mathbf{A}$ such that $F(\mathbf{R},\mathbf{A})$ will be as small as possible. That is, a factor is sought which, after it is removed, will leave the sum of squares of the residuals as small as possible, ignoring the diagonal elements in the sum. This is indicated by the $j \neq i$ notation in Eq. (4.12). This procedure minimizes the sum of squares of the residuals at each factor extraction step, not after m factors. Harman and Jones (1966) more recently have developed a procedure, called the "minres" method, which minimizes the residuals after a specified number of factors, m, rather than at each factor extraction.

Solving for a formula to obtain the elements a_i of $\mathbf{A}$ requires some calculus, so the reader unfamiliar with this mathematical tool may wish to skip the following derivation and go directly to the end result, Eq. (4.18) below. Solution of this problem requires partial differentiation of the function $F(\mathbf{R},\mathbf{A})$ with respect to each unknown a_i, setting these n equations equal to zero, and solving them simultaneously for the n unknown a_i values. Thus

$$F(\mathbf{R},\mathbf{A}) = \sum_{i=1}^{i=n} \sum_{j=1}^{j=n} (r_{ij}^2 + a_i^2 a_j^2 - 2r_{ij}a_i a_j), \ j \neq i \tag{4.13}$$

$$F(\mathbf{R},\mathbf{A}) = \sum_{i=1}^{i=n} \sum_{j=1}^{j=n} r_{ij}^2 + \sum_{i=1}^{i=n} \sum_{j=1}^{j=n} a_i^2 a_j^2$$

$$- 2\sum_{i=1}^{i=n} \sum_{j=1}^{j=n} r_{ij}a_i a_j, \ j \neq i \tag{4.14}$$

Differentiating partially with respect to a_i and setting the result equal to zero gives

$$\frac{\delta F}{\delta a_1} = 0 + 2a_1 a_2^2 + 2a_1 a_3^2 + \ldots + 2a_1 a_n^2$$

$$- 2r_{12}a_2 - 2r_{13}a_3 - \ldots - 2r_{1n}a_n = 0$$

$$\frac{\delta F}{\delta a_1} = a_1 \sum_{j=2}^{j=n} a_j^2 - \sum_{j=2}^{j=n} r_{1j}a_j = 0 \tag{4.15}$$

Solving for a_1 gives

$$a_1 = \frac{\sum\limits_{j=1}^{j=n} r_{1j}a_j}{\sum\limits_{j=1}^{j=n} a_j^2} , \quad j \neq 1 \tag{4.16}$$

Differentiating $F(\mathbf{R},\mathbf{A})$ in Eq. (4.14) partially with respect to a_2 and setting the result equal to zero gives an expression analogous to Eq. (4.15) which can be simplified similarly to

$$a_2 = \frac{\sum\limits_{j=1}^{j=n} r_{2j}a_j}{\sum\limits_{j=1}^{j=n} a_j^2} , \quad j \neq 2 \tag{4.17}$$

The same procedure may be followed for each element of a_i resulting in a general expression

$$a_i = \frac{\sum\limits_{j=1}^{j=n} r_{ij}a_j}{\sum\limits_{j=1}^{j=n} a_j^2} , \quad j \neq i \tag{4.18}$$

Substituting in turn each value from 1 to n for i in Eq. (4.18) results in n equations in n unknowns, which would give the unknown factor loadings $a_1, a_2, \ldots, a_n$ if the equations could be solved. These equations are not linear equations, however; so the solution is not easy to obtain algebraically.

It is possible, however, to solve these equations by means of an iterative procedure. For example, if all the correct factor loadings were known except the first, these values could be substituted in Eq. (4.16) to find the correct a_1. In general, if all the correct a values are known except a_i, they may be substituted in Eq. (4.18) to find a_i.

In practice, initial estimates of the a values are made. These estimates are substituted in Eq. (4.18) to solve for each a_i value. Since the first estimates are usually incorrect, the a values derived by putting them in Eq. (4.18) are still not likely to be correct. These new values, however, can be substituted in turn in Eq. (4.18) to get still another estimate of the a_i values. These two sets of derived values may be averaged term by term to derive new estimated a values before starting the cycle anew. Such a procedure is helpful in finding the correct a_i values only if the values obtained from each iterative cycle are closer to the correct values than those with which the iterative cycle was begun, that is, if the iterative process converges. When the values put into the iterative cycle are the same as those that come out of it, then the iterative process has converged on the correct values.

The iterative process may be schematized for a four-variable example as follows:

$$
\frac{1}{\sum\limits_{j=1}^{j=4} a_j^2} \cdot
\begin{bmatrix}
0 & r_{12} & r_{13} & r_{14} \\
r_{21} & 0 & r_{23} & r_{24} \\
r_{31} & r_{32} & 0 & r_{34} \\
r_{41} & r_{42} & r_{43} & 0
\end{bmatrix}
\times
\begin{bmatrix}
a_{10} \\
a_{20} \\
a_{30} \\
a_{40}
\end{bmatrix}
=
\begin{bmatrix}
a_{11} \\
a_{21} \\
a_{31} \\
a_{41}
\end{bmatrix}
, \quad j \neq i \quad (4.19)
$$

$$
\qquad\qquad \mathbf{R} \qquad\qquad \mathbf{A_o} \qquad \mathbf{A_I}
$$

$$
\frac{1}{\sum\limits_{j=1}^{j=4} a_j^2} \cdot \mathbf{R} \cdot \mathbf{A_1} = \mathbf{A_2}, \quad j \neq i \qquad (4.20)
$$

$$
(\mathbf{A_1} + \mathbf{A_2})/2 = \mathbf{A_3} \qquad (4.21)
$$

Reinsert the $\mathbf{A_3}$ from Eq. (4.21) into Eq. (4.19) as $\mathbf{A_o}$ to calculate a new $\mathbf{A_1}$. The new $\mathbf{A_1}$ is inserted into Eq. (4.20) to get a new $\mathbf{A_2}$, and so on, until $\mathbf{A_1}$ and $\mathbf{A_2}$ are as close to one another as desired. Three-decimal-place accuracy is ordinarily quite sufficient for empirical work.

Particular note must be taken of the fact that j may not equal i in Eq. (4.18)–(4.20). This means that in getting a_1 in Eq. (4.18), the first element of the sum is omitted in both numerator and denominator. In getting a_2, the second element of these sums is omitted. In general, in computing the value a_i, the ith elements of the sums in both numerator and denominator are omitted. The appropriate numerator elements are effectively eliminated from the sums by placing zeros in the diagonal cells in the matrix multiplication in Eq. (4.19). This does *not* mean, however, that zeros are being used as communalities. This device merely eliminates the unwanted terms in the numerator summations. The denominator sums for a_i, however, must be computed separately by

$$
\left[\sum_{j=1}^{j=n} a_j^2 \right] - a_i^2 \qquad (4.22)
$$

Thus, instead of adding each time, omitting the term where $i = j$, it is more efficient to add once over all values of a_j and then to subtract out the unwanted term as in formula (4.22).

After a factor is obtained through convergence of the iterative process, it is removed from the matrix of correlations by the usual method; that is, $\mathbf{R}_1 = \mathbf{R} - \mathbf{A}_1\mathbf{A}_1'$, where $\mathbf{A}_1$ in this case is the factor vector computed previously and referred to in Eqs. (4.12)–(4.14) as $\mathbf{A}$.

If enough factors are extracted, the point will be reached where convergence on a factor vector does not occur with this method of iteration. To understand this phenomenon, it is helpful to see the relationship between the minimum residual and the principal factor methods. Equations (4.1) and (4.2) lead to the schematic matrix result:

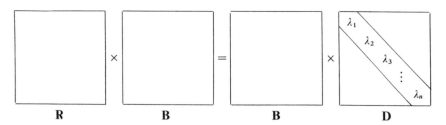

$\mathbf{R}$	$\mathbf{B}$	$\mathbf{B}$	$\mathbf{D}$

or, in matrix equation form:

$$\mathbf{RB} = \mathbf{BD} \tag{4.23}$$

The effect of the multiplication of $\mathbf{B}$ on the right by $\mathbf{D}$ is to multiply each column of $\mathbf{B}$ by a λ value. Every element of column 1 is multiplied by λ_1, every element of column 2 is multiplied by λ_2, and so on. If the first column of $\mathbf{B}$ is isolated from the rest, thus considering only the first eigenvector, we have

$$\mathbf{R} \times \mathbf{B}_1 = \lambda_1 \mathbf{B}_1 \tag{4.24}$$

That is, multiplying $\mathbf{R}$ by the column matrix $\mathbf{B}_1$, the first eigenvector, equals that same eigenvector multiplied by a constant, λ_1. It has already been indicated that λ_1 equals the sum of squares of the first factor loadings and that the vector $\mathbf{B}_1$ can be converted from a normalized vector to the first factor vector $\mathbf{A}_1$ by multiplying each element of $\mathbf{B}_1$ by $\sqrt{\lambda_1}$. Then, since $\sqrt{\lambda_1}\,\mathbf{B}_1 = \mathbf{A}_1$, multiplying both sides of Eq. (4.24) by $\sqrt{\lambda_1}$ would give

$$\mathbf{RA}_1 = \lambda_1 \mathbf{A}_1 \tag{4.25}$$

Dividing both sides of Eq. (4.25) by λ_1 gives

$$\mathbf{RA}_1/\lambda_1 = \mathbf{A}_1 \tag{4.26}$$

For a particular element a_i in the product column matrix $\mathbf{A}_1$ on the right of Eq. (4.26), the formula for that equation in algebraic terms would be

$$a_i = \frac{\sum_{j=1}^{j=n} r_{ij} a_j}{\lambda_i} = \frac{\sum_{j=1}^{j=n} r_{ij} a_j}{\sum_{j=1}^{j=n} a_j^2} \tag{4.27}$$

Equation (4.27) is just like Eq. (4.18), the expression for the minimum residual solution, except that the restriction $j \neq i$ is removed. Thus, if the diagonal elements are used in the minimum residual method of factor extraction, instead of being omitted, the minimum residual method becomes equivalent to a principal factor method and yields a principal factor solution. The principal factor solution, then, is also a minimum residual solution for the particular communality estimates employed. Thus, if a principal factor solution is desired, the minimum residual method including the diagonal cells, that is, removing the restriction $i \neq j$ in the equations, may be used provided estimated communalities are inserted in the diagonal cells and operated upon instead of omitting the diagonal cells. The ordinary minimum residual solution without communalities may or may not reduce the sum of squares of the off-diagonal residuals as well as the principal factor solution. This will depend on the communalities used for the principal factor solution.

Professor Sukeyori Shiba of the University of Tokyo, who translated the first edition of this book for publication into Japanese, proved (personal communication) that the minimum residual method results are equivalent to a principal factor solution using squares of the converged factor loadings as diagonal cells. Thus, if we apply the minimum residual method, find the converged a_i values, square them and use these values as communalities, recomputation with the principal factor method, using the diagonals, will give the same solution as the minimum residual method. A proof follows (proof by Dr. Janis Hardwick):

Let a_1 be a factor loading by the principal factor method with a_i^2 values in the diagonals where the a_i values are those derived from a minimum residual solution. Then by Eq. (4.27)

$$a_i = \frac{\sum\limits_{j=1}^{j=n} a_j r_{ij}}{\sum\limits_{j=1}^{j=n} a_j^2} = \frac{\sum\limits_{j=2}^{j=n} a_j r_{ij} + a_1^3}{\sum\limits_{j=1}^{j=n} a_j^2} \tag{1}$$

Let

$$a_1^* = \frac{\sum\limits_{j=2}^{j=n} r_{ij} a_j}{\sum\limits_{j=2}^{j=n} a_j^2}$$

Cross multiplying, we get

$$a_1^* \left[\sum\limits_{j=2}^{j=n} a_j^2 \right] = \sum\limits_{j=2}^{j=n} r_{ij} a_j \tag{2}$$

Substituting (2) in (1) above and cross multiplying gives

$$a_1 \left[\sum\limits_{j=2}^{j=n} a_j^2 + a_1^2 \right] = a_1^* \left[\sum\limits_{j=2}^{j=n} a_j^2 \right] + a_1^3$$

$$a_1 \sum\limits_{j=2}^{j=n} a_j^2 + a_1^3 = a_1^* \sum\limits_{j=2}^{j=n} a_j^2 + a_1^3$$

and therefore

$$a_1 = a_1^*$$

Since the minimum residual solution gives results equivalent to assuming that the communality values are equal only to the contributions of one factor to the total communality, in effect the minimum possible values are being used as communalities. Thus, the minimum residual method will extract less variance from the matrix than would be extracted if higher communality estimates had been employed. This will tend to make the factor loadings derived by the minimum residual method somewhat smaller on the average than would normally be the case with principal factor extraction using estimated communalities in the diagonals.

Equation (4.25) expresses the rather remarkable theorem that multiplying the correlation matrix times a factor from a principal factor solution equals the result of multiplying every term of that factor by a constant, namely, the eigenvalue associated with that factor. In the minimum residual solution, while iterating to achieve convergence by a formula like (4.26), the **A** on the left-hand side and the **A** on the right-hand side are somewhat different. As the process converges, these two **A** vectors become more and more alike. If the factor involved is associated with a negative eigenvector, however, λ will be negative and

$$\frac{\mathbf{RA}_1}{\sum\limits_{i=1}^{i=n} a_i^2} = -\mathbf{A}_1$$

That is, the successive iterated vectors will tend to be equal, term by term, in absolute value but opposite in sign. When Eq. (4.21) is applied to obtain the $\mathbf{A}_0$ for the next iteration, the approximately equal but oppositely signed elements of $\mathbf{A}_1$ and $\mathbf{A}_2$ will tend to add up to zero. This phenomenon results in a failure to achieve convergence. This does not occur, however, until all the major factors have been removed. When this failure to converge occurs, it is roughly equivalent to the situation where there are no more positive eigenvalues and hence there cannot be any more legitimate factors to extract.

An improved method of averaging the successive iterated vectors suggested by Ahumada (Comrey & Ahumada, 1964, 1965) avoids the situation where convergence fails to occur. This improved method, called the "length adjustment" method, finds a vector that has a length equal to the geometric mean of the lengths of the two vectors to be averaged. Under this system of averaging, the signs of the loadings do not affect the averaging since the vector lengths are given by the square roots of the sum of squares of the loadings. The signs of the loadings are lost in the squaring process.

To illustrate this method, consider the vector **A** with elements $a_1, a_2, \ldots,$ a_n to be a correct factor vector with length L, that is, one satisfying Eq. (4.18). Derive two other vectors $\mathbf{A}_1$ and $\mathbf{A}_2$ as follows:

$$\mathbf{A}_1 = \frac{1}{K} a_1, \frac{1}{K} a_2, \ldots, \frac{1}{K} a_n$$

$$\mathbf{A}_2 = Ka_1, Ka_2, \ldots, Ka_n \tag{4.28}$$

The lengths of vectors $\mathbf{A}_1$ and $\mathbf{A}_2$ in (4.28) are given by

$$L_1 = \sqrt{(a_1/K)^2 + (a_2/K)^2 + \ldots + (a_n/K)^2} = L/K$$

$$L_2 = \sqrt{(Ka_1)^2 + (Ka_2)^2 + \ldots + (Ka_n)^2} = KL \tag{4.29}$$

The geometric mean of the lengths of L_1 and L_2 is given by

$$\sqrt{L_1 L_2} = \sqrt{(L/K) \cdot KL} = L \tag{4.30}$$

Thus, if two vectors differ only by a constant from the correct vector, the geometric mean of their lengths will produce the length of the correct vector. This fact can be used to derive a method of averaging successive iterated vectors with the minimum residual factor extraction procedure. If $a_1, a_2, \ldots, a_n$ are the elements of $\mathbf{A}_1$ and $a_1', a_2', \ldots, a_n'$ are the elements of $\mathbf{A}_2$ where $\mathbf{A}_1$ and $\mathbf{A}_2$ are successively derived vectors in the minimum residual iterative process, the correct averaged vector may be obtained by multiplying the elements of the second vector $\mathbf{A}_2$ by the fourth root of the ratio of the squared length of the vector $\mathbf{A}_1$ to the squared length of the vector $\mathbf{A}_2$ as follows:

$$a_{i_o} = a_i' \sqrt[4]{\frac{L_1^2}{L_2^2}} \tag{4.31}$$

If L_0, the length of the vector $\mathbf{A}_0$ derived by Eq. (4.31), is computed, it will be the geometric mean of the lengths of vectors $\mathbf{A}_1$ and $\mathbf{A}_2$. This can be shown as follows:

$$L_0^2 = a_1'^2 \sqrt{\frac{L_1^2}{L_2^2}} + a_2'^2 \sqrt{\frac{L_1^2}{L_2^2}} + \ldots a_n'^2 \sqrt{\frac{L_1^2}{L_2^2}}$$

$$L_0^2 = (a_1'^2 + a_2'^2 + \ldots + a_n'^2) \sqrt{\frac{L_1^2}{L_2^2}}$$

$$L_0^2 = L_2^2 (L_1/L_2) = L_2 \cdot L_1$$

$$L_0 = \sqrt{L_1 L_2}$$

Using this method of averaging successive vectors avoids the failure to converge at some point in the factor extraction process that characterized the averaging of vectors by taking the arithmetic mean of the two. Instead of reaching the point where convergence fails, the length-adjustment method of iteration will eventually reach convergence where the two successive vectors, $\mathbf{A}_1$ and $\mathbf{A}_2$, in the iterative cycle are equal in absolute value, term for term, but opposite in sign for each element. For the principal factor solution, which requires communalities, this corresponds to the case where the factor being extracted is associated with a negative eigenvalue. This terminology is perhaps inappropriate for the minimum residual solution without communalities, because the diagonal cells of the matrix are not involved, but an analogous situation occurs; that is, a factor is reached ultimately where the iterative process converges on vectors of opposite sign. The process of extraction is terminated at this point, with the factor that converges on vectors of opposite sign being dropped.

If the arithmetic average method of averaging vectors were applied after the length-adjustment method converged on vectors of opposite sign, additional factors might be extracted before reaching a point where this method would fail to converge. These extra factors are analogous to factors with positive eigenvalues that are smaller in absolute value than the largest negative eigenvalue. Such factors are considered to be too minor to be retained.

The steps in computing a minimum residual solution with the length adjustment method of averaging successive vectors are given below. This set of steps will yield either a minimum residual solution without using communality estimates, or it will permit the calculation of a principal factor solution using the diagonal cells with communality estimates inserted.

1. Place zeroes in the diagonal cells of the correlation matrix for the minimum residual solution without communality estimates. For a principal factor solution by the minimum residual method of factor extraction, place communality estimates in the diagonal cells of the R matrix.

2. Estimate the factor loadings for the factor to be extracted. This is vector A_0. The largest column value in each column with sign attached will serve adequately. If more accurate estimates are available, the iterative process will be shortened.

3. Inner multiply each row of the correlation matrix with vector A_o. This is like multiplying R (the left-hand matrix) by A_0 (the right-hand matrix), that is, RA_0.

4. Divide the inner products from step 3 by $\left[\sum_{j=1}^{j=n} a_j^2 \right] - a_i^2$, as in formula (4.22), when communalities are *not* being used and the minimum residual solution is desired. Divide these inner products by $\sum_{j=1}^{j=n} a_j^2$ for the principal factor solution where communalities are being used. The result of step 4 is to obtain the vector A_1, the first iterated vector.

5. Repeat steps 3 and 4, substituting A_1 for A_0 to obtain a second iterated vector A_2.

6. Vectors A_1 and A_2 are averaged by the length-adjustment method to obtain a new A_0. This is done by multiplying each element of A_2 by the fourth root of the ratio of the squared length of A_1 to the squared length of A_2, as in Eq. (4.31).

7. The vectors A_1 and A_2 are compared term by term to see if they are sufficiently identical to permit termination of the iterative process. In practice, every such difference might be reduced to less than ϵ in absolute

value where ϵ equals some suitably small number, for example, $\epsilon = 0.0005$ for third place accuracy in the results.

8. If all differences are less than ϵ, terminate iteration and take $\mathbf{A}_2$ as the factor vector. If some differences are still larger than ϵ, use the new $\mathbf{A}_0$ to recycle through steps 3–7. Continue until convergence is reached.

9. Compute the residuals by the usual process. Compute the matrix $\mathbf{A}_i\mathbf{A}_i'$, where $\mathbf{A}_i$ is the second iterated vector $\mathbf{A}_2$, and subtract this matrix product from the matrix of correlation coefficients.

10. Repeat steps 2–9 for the second and subsequent factors to extract as many factors as desired, or until the iterative process converges on vectors of opposite sign. That is, each element of $\mathbf{A}_1$ will be equal in absolute value to the corresponding element of $\mathbf{A}_2$ but will be opposite in sign.

The results of applying the procedure just outlined to the four-variable sample problem are shown in Table 4.3. A minimum residual solution without communalities was obtained. The communalities derived as a result of the minimum residual solution by summing the squares of the factor loadings for each variable were .538, .469, .655, and .710. These values are considerably different from the "true" communalities of .65, .40, 0.65, and .82 which reduce the rank of the matrix to exactly 2 when a solution with communalities is obtained. The minimum residual method operating on the off-diagonal elements only, therefore, will not ordinarily yield derived communalities that can be considered to be the "correct" communalities, that is, those that reduce the rank of the correlation matrix to a minimum. In fact, the values will generally be underestimates.

In using the minimum residual method without communality estimates, factor loadings and computed communalities in excess of 1.0 may be encountered, particularly with small matrices where the number of unknown diagonal elements represents a substantial proportion of the total number of elements in the matrix. Communalities in excess of 1.0 are not allowed, of course, so such a solution is incorrect. In such cases it is necessary to refactor using the diagonal cells with communality estimates in place until no communalities or factor loadings in excess of 1.0 are encountered.

Rotating the minimum residual factor loadings and retaining only one-place accuracy gives 0.1, 0.2, 0.8, and 0.9 for factor I and 0.7, 0.7, 0.1, and 0.1 for factor II. These values are within 0.1 in absolute value of the original coordinates in every case despite the fact that the minimum residual factor loadings were derived using only six data values out of a total of ten needed to fix these coordinates. The communality values represent the remaining four data values that were not used in obtaining the solution. It would be reasonable to expect greater accuracy as the proportion of known to unknown data values rises, for example, with larger matrices.

The minimum residual solution, without communalities, for the 12-variable sample problem is shown in Table 4.4. Five factors were extracted before the iterative process converged on vectors of opposite sign, although the fifth factor was very small, accounting for only 4% of the total extracted variance. The principal factor solution gave only four positive eigenvalues suggesting a maximum of four factors, but this was using SMCs as communality estimates. The sum of these SMCs gave a total of 5.369, which is appreciably less than the sum of the communalities derived from the minimum residual solution, for example, 6.783. The communalities derived from the minimum residual solution suggest that the SMCs here were underestimates of the correct communalities. In any event, the smaller SMCs permitted the extraction of fewer factors, four instead of five.

The differences between the principal factor solution and the minimum residual solution are attributable primarily to the communalities selected for the principal factor solution. The smaller the matrix, the more pronounced this effect can be, other things being equal, because the number of diagonal values is a larger proportion of the total number of entries in the **R** matrix with smaller matrices.

Lee (1979) has investigated several methods of performing the iterations for the minimum residual method other than the averaging and length adjustment-method in an attempt to increase computational speed. The method that proved to be most efficient and sometimes faster than the length-adjustment method waited until the vector iteration sequence converged before making length adjustment. The length-adjustment procedure adjusts after each pair of iterated vectors has been obtained, thereby in some cases increasing the amount of computation somewhat. Zegers and Ten Berge (1983) have also proposed modifying the Comrey-Ahumada method of obtaining the minimum residual solution by substituting back into the solution each iterated value as it is obtained, rather than waiting until all values have been obtained. Levin (1988), however, has recently proved that convergence may not necessarily occur under these alternate methods of iteration and shows that the original Comrey-Ahumada length adjustment method will always converge. It seems, therefore, that to be sure of obtaining convergence, the original Comrey-Ahumada method of iteration with the minimum residual method is to be preferred. Even if it results in some cases in somewhat greater computation time, this is a small price to pay to guarantee that convergence will occur.

4.3.   THE COMMUNALITIES

If 1's are placed in the diagonal cells of **R**, all the eigenvalues will be positive, unless **R** has a determinant equal to zero, which would almost

TABLE 4.3

Minimum Residual Solution to the Four-Variable Problem

Initial R matrix

	1	2	3	4
1	.00	.50	.16	.17
2	.50	.00	.22	.24
3	.16	.22	.00	.73
4	.17	.24	.73	.00

Factor I

	Cycle 1			Cycle 2			Cycle 3		
	A_0	A_1	A_2	A_0	A_1	A_2	A_0	A_1	A_2
1	.500	.373	.381	.360	.342	.325	.326	.320	.315
2	.500	.445	.449	.425	.407	.388	.389	.383	.377
3	.730	.700	.801	.758	.784	.784	.787	.795	.794
4	.730	.714	.823	.779	.809	.811	.814	.825	.825

	Cycle 4			Cycle 5			Factor
	A_0	A_1	A_2	A_0	A_1	A_2	
1	.315	.313	.312	.312	.311	.311	.311
2	.377	.375	.374	.374	.373	.373	.373
3	.795	.797	.796	.797	.797	.797	.797
4	.826	.829	.829	.830	.831	.831	.831

Residual matrix I

	1	2	3	4
1	.000	.384	-.088	-.088
2	.384	.000	-.077	-.070
3	-.088	-.077	.000	.068
4	-.088	-.070	.068	.000

Factor II

	Cycle 1			Cycle 2			Cycle 3			Cycle 4	Factor
	A_0	A_1	A_2	A_0	A_1	A_2	A_0	A_1	A_2	A_2	
1	.384	1.000	.390	.627	.631	.635	.641	.644	.646	.646	.646
2	.384	.984	.379	.609	.605	.601	.595	.593	.591	.591	.591
3	-.088	-.229	-.089	-.142	-.142	-.142	-.142	-.142	-.142	-.142	-.142
4	-.088	-.222	-.085	-.137	-.137	-.137	-.137	-.137	-.137	-.137	-.137

TABLE 4.3 continued

Factor II (continued)

	A₀	A₁	A₂	A₀	A₁	A₂	A₀	A₁	A₂	A₀	A₁	A₂
1	.646	.648	.650	.650	.652	.653	.653	.655	.656	.656	.657	.658
2	.591	.589	.587	.587	.586	.584	.584	.583	.581	.581	.581	.579
3	−.142	−.142	−.142	−.142	−.142	−.142	−.142	−.142	−.142	−.142	−.142	−.142
4	−.137	−.137	−.137	−.137	−.137	−.137	−.137	−.137	−.137	−.137	−.137	−.137
	Cycle 5			Cycle 6			Cycle 7			Cycle 8		

	A₀	A₁	A₂	A₀	A₁	A₂	A₀	A₁	A₂	A₀	A₁	A₂
1	.658	.660	.660	.660	.661	.662	.662	.663	.663	.663	.664	.664
2	.579	.579	.578	.578	.577	.577	.577	.576	.575	.575	.575	.575
3	−.142	−.142	−.142	−.142	−.142	−.142	−.142	−.142	−.142	−.142	−.142	−.142
4	−.137	−.137	−.137	−.137	−.137	−.137	−.137	−.137	−.137	−.137	−.137	−.137
	Cycle 9			Cycle 10			Cycle 11			Cycle 12		

Residual matrix II

	1	2	3	4
1	.000	.002	.006	.003
2	.002	.000	.004	.009
3	.006	.004	.000	.048
4	.003	.009	.048	.000

Factor matrix

	I	II	h_2
1	.311	.664	.538
2	.373	.575	.469
3	.797	−.142	.655
4	.831	−.137	.710

TABLE 4.4

Minimum Residual Solution to the 12-Variable Problem

	I	II	III	IV	V	h^2
1	.080	.846	.160	−.046	.011	.749
2	.011	.707	.101	.048	−.058	.515
3	.037	.652	.221	−.100	−.045	.488
4	.544	.099	−.287	.261	.122	.471
5	.589	.157	−.180	.366	.092	.546
6	.435	.098	−.212	.482	.105	.487
7	.563	−.006	−.161	−.339	.310	.553
8	.661	.013	.076	−.205	.070	.489
9	.758	.023	−.210	−.230	.372	.811
10	.431	−.174	.506	.045	.019	.475
11	.537	−.197	.591	.152	.082	.706
12	.370	−.281	.522	.052	.043	.493
SSQ	2.779	1.833	1.198	.686	.288	(6.783)

never occur with real data matrices. Analyses with 1's in the diagonals are called "principal components" analyses to distinguish them from principal factor analyses where communalities are inserted in the diagonals. With 1's in the diagonals, all the eigenvalues will ordinarily be positive and then the matrix is said to be "positive definite." With some zero eigenvalues, fewer than n factors are needed to reproduce the R matrix exactly. The factors with sums of squares equal to eigenvalues of zero are obviously factors with all zero entries; hence they may be dropped. If there are m nonzero eigenvalues, then the B′ matrix in the equation B′RB = D, which diagonalizes the R matrix, will have only m nonzero rows and n columns. The matrix B, the transpose of B′, will have n rows and m nonzero columns as will the factor matrix A derived from B.

In the case where communality values less than 1 are put in the diagonal cells of R, it often occurs that the R matrix is no longer positive definite or even positive semidefinite (all eigenvalues positive or zero). When this happens, negative eigenvalues occur in the D matrix. Since the sum of squares of the loadings on a factor is supposed to equal its eigenvalue, mathematicians tend to prefer the use of diagonal values, for example 1's, which will avoid this troublesome possibility. If 1's are placed in the diagonals, however, the total variance for each variable is input to the analysis. This includes common, specific, and error variance. In the limiting case where n factors are extracted, all the variance for each variable is extracted so that both the entered and the derived communalities will equal 1.0 for every variable. This would occur even if the variable had a zero correlation with every other variable in the matrix. In this case, the specific and error variance would represent all the variance for that variable since there could be no common variance.

In most factor analytic applications, the interest is focused on studying the relationships between variables, that is, what they share in common. The variance in such analyses should be properly allocated to common and unique factor sources. Inserting values in the diagonal cells that exceed the correct communalities results in extraction of extra specific and error variance that is then treated as common variance. The more the diagonal cells are inflated, the more pronounced is this distortion. The result of such distortion is to obtain factors that are not just common factors, but factors that mix up common and unique variance in an inextricable way that obscures the view of what the variables have in common with each other. Thus, while it is true that use of 1's in the diagonals avoids a troublesome mathematical problem, the treatment has unfortunate side effects which interfere with the proper interpretation of the data. Knowledgeable factor analysts with an empirical orientation, therefore, have tended to prefer working with communalities, rather than 1's, in the diagonals, coping with the negative eigenvalue problem by dropping any factors that do not have positive associated eigenvalues.

Some factor analysts use 1's in the diagonal cells and then retain only those factors with eigenvalues greater than 1.0. This procedure is based on the fact that since a single variable contributes 1.0 to the total extractable variance by being added to the matrix, any factor must have a total variance in excess of that added by a single variable. This seems reasonable enough, but in using this procedure there is no guarantee, or even a good reason to suppose, that only common factor variance is being extracted by this approach. The communalities that emerge from such an analysis, however, could be reinserted in the matrix to institute an iterative process that would terminate when the entered communalities prove to be essentially identical to the extracted communalities. Ten to 15 iterations will usually be sufficient to achieve convergence. In some cases, a very large number of iterations may be required and in others convergence may not occur. In iterating the communalities, however, the number of factors extracted must be held constant. If the number of factors extracted is allowed to increase, the derived communalities will tend to increase and the number of factors extractable will rise until finally the process will stabilize with communalities of 1.0 and n factors. Iterating the communalities requires doing the entire factor analysis over again and again, however, so the cost is much greater than for a single uniterated solution.

Another procedure for an iterated factor analytic solution is to use SMCs as the initial communalities instead of 1's. The derived communalities from this initial solution are recycled, as before, and the iterative process continues until communalities stabilize or until the desired number of iterations has been carried out. Guertin and Bailey (1970) present an informative treatment of the distortions that can occur with the use of SMCs as communality estimates. Although they generally find the SMCs to be good estimates with a large N and a small n, which is the case with the present 12-variable sample problem, the SMCs are sometimes much too small. They recommend iterating the communalities with a fixed number of factors until the values derived from the solution are essentially identical with the communalities input to the solution (see also Tucker, Koopman, & Linn, 1969).

Still another starting point for an iterative cycle of factor analytic solutions is the set of communalities derived from the minimum residual solution. These values, derived without using the diagonal cells, are fed back into a minimum residual solution using the diagonal cells, which makes it a principal factor solution. With these derived communalities as the estimates for a second factor analysis, a new solution is obtained. The communalities derived from this solution are recycled, and so on, as before. After the first analysis, the remaining analyses are all principal factor solutions because they all use the diagonal cells filled with communality values derived from the previous solution. Table 4.5 gives the solution after 15 such cycles for the 12-variable problem. The communalities tend to rise as the process stabilizes because higher communalities in the right places will permit a greater reduction of the sum of squares of the off-diagonal elements.

Once the number of factors has been determined, iterating the solution until the communalities stabilize, starting with either SMC's or communalities derived from a minimum residual solution, gives a solution that has been shown to recover the correct communalities for a reproduced correlation matrix where these values are known (Lee & Comrey, 1979). Starting with 1's in the diagonals will not necessarily iterate to the same end point as starting with other estimates and can give values that are known to be inappropriately high, particularly for variables that have low correlations with the other variables. Such variables should have low true communalities but they may not if 1's are used as communality estimates. Even if the solution is iterated after inserting 1's as the initial estimates, communalities will not necessarily drop sufficiently during the iterative process (Lee & Comrey, 1978). This is particularly true for those variables with low SMCs. For these reasons, inserting 1's in the diagonals is not recommended, whether or not the solution is iterated.

Iteration of the communalities runs the risk of capitalizing on chance errors, elevating the communalities unduly in order to drive down the sum of squares of the off-diagonal residuals. For example, the sum of the

TABLE 4.5

Minimum Residual Solution to the 12-Variable Problem with Iterated Communalities[a]

	I	II	III	IV	h^2_{15}	$h_1{}^2$
1	.099	.835	.266	.044	.780	.749
2	.013	.678	.186	−.055	.498	.512
3	.045	.653	.316	.090	.536	.486
4	.549	.137	−.329	−.217	.475	.456
5	.603	.190	−.223	−.317	.550	.538
6	.464	.138	−.282	−.454	.520	.476
7	.585	.016	−.230	.448	.596	.457
8	.638	.013	.042	.214	.455	.485
9	.772	.053	−.279	.317	.777	.673
10	.466	−.227	.429	−.034	.454	.474
11	.628	−.289	.552	−.153	.806	.699
12	.414	−.352	.435	−.043	.486	.491
					(6.933)	(6.496)

[a] This solution is that obtained after 15 analyses using h^2 values from each analysis as h^2 estimates for the next trial. The $h_1{}^2$ values above are the values derived from the first minimum residual solution based only on off-diagonal correlation matrix entries.

derived communalities after 15 iterations with four factors in the 12-variable sample problem (see Table 4.5) is 6.933. This is only slightly larger than the corresponding sum for the five-factor minimum residual solution, 6.783. On the other hand, the communality for variable 11 is driven up to .806 in the iterated communality solution compared with .706 for the five-factor minimum residual solution. The value of .806 could be correct, but it appears to the authors to be unrealistically high.

With the uniterated minimum residual solution, the derived communalities are entirely a function of the known correlation coefficients and the factor loadings are independent of any errors in estimating communalities. As proved mathematically earlier in this chapter and as shown empirically by Lee and Comrey (1978), however, the minimum residual solution produces communalities that tend to be understimates. Once the number of factors is fixed, therefore, it is probably best to iterate the communalities at least for a few iterations, starting from some reasonable values, but not one's.[1] The investigator should be alert for evidence that some communalities may have been driven up to unrealistically high values in order to

---

[1] Recently, Widaman and Herringer (1985) found that running enough iterations to obtain convergence of the communality values to 0.001 or less removed the effect of different starting values in the kinds of matrices they studied. It may be prudent, therefore, to run more iterations of the communalities than were previously believed necessary.

maximize the amount of variance extracted. If this occurs, a new solution can be obtained using the best available estimates of the correct communalities without further iteration.

4.4. DETERMINING HOW MANY FACTORS TO EXTRACT

It is easy to establish an upper bound on the number of factors to be extracted. With communalities specified, the maximum number of factors equals the number of factors with positive eigenvalues. Using the minimum residual method without communalities, it is the number of factors extracted before the iterative process converges on vectors of opposite sign. The authors prefer the latter solution where the two disagree, because the number of factors with positive eigenvalues in the principal factor solution will vary with the particular communalities inserted. Since these are unknown, the solution is not exactly determined. With the centroid method, neither of these guidelines is available. By reestimating communalities, it is possible to continue extracting centroid factors almost indefinitely.

In actual practice with real data, the number of factors that merit retention for purposes of scientific description and explanation will be less than the upper bound, often considerably so. With such data, there are typically several factors of lesser importance trailing off into insignificance. Trying to decide precisely where to draw the line, considering the remaining factors to be too small to be retained, is somewhat like trying to decide how short someone must be to be called short. There is no precise solution to this problem in any practical sense, although a kind of precise solution may be imposed on the situation through appeal to mathematical criteria. For example, it may be determined that there is not another "significant" factor in the statistical sense to a certain level of confidence. Decisions of this kind ultimately are based on the sample size employed, which, after all, has nothing to do with the nature of the variables being studied. The sample size is determined by a decision of the investigator, not by the factor structure of a group of variables. The precision of such solutions to the problem of how many factors to extract, therefore, is more apparent than real.

Several signs are useful in trying to decide whether or not to stop extracting factors before the maximum number possible has been reached. For example, if the sums of squares of the loadings on the extracted factors are no longer dropping but are remaining at a low and rather uniform level, factor extraction may be reasonably terminated. Cattell's (1966) Scree test is based on this principle. A point is sought where there is a break in the eigenvalues. The eigenvalues can be plotted and a straight line can be drawn through the later, smaller values. The earlier, larger values will not fall on this straight line, giving an indication of how many major factors there are.

This procedure is helpful in getting a rough idea of the number of factors but cannot be depended upon to give a precise answer. Indeed, no method can because there is no definitive solution to the number of factors problem just as there is no definitive solution to the communality problem.

The underlying rationale for the Scree test is based on the fact that within a set of variables, a limited number of factors are measured more precisely than the others. As a result, the predominant factors account for most of the variance and have large eigenvalues. Because the step-wise extraction procedures available for exploratory factor analysis extract factors in order of size, the more dominant factors (with large eigenvalues or characteristic roots) are extracted first followed by the smaller, more trivial factors. By graphing the eigenvalues, Cattell found that the smaller factors form a straight line sloping downward. The dominant factors will fall above the line. Some of the smaller factors extracted immediately after the dominant factors may also be above or near the line. Cattell proposes that the number of factors is at the point where the last small factor is above the line. Figure (4.2) demonstrates a four factor solution. Some of the problems with the Scree test include the presence of several breaks in the sizes of the eigenvalues and the possibility of several sets of smaller factors. With these complications, it is often difficult to determine just where the cut-off should be. Gorsuch and Nelson (1981) have developed a procedure, called the "Objective Scree Test," which has outperformed the more subjective approach given by Cattell. Gorsuch and Nelson compute the slope for every adjacent triplet of eigenvalues. The number of factors is taken to be at that

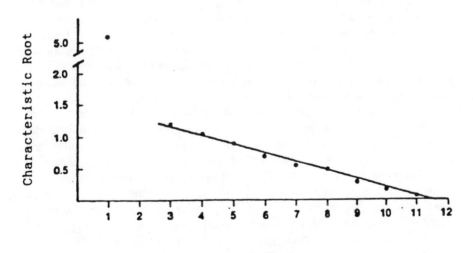

Factors

FIG. 4.2.   Determining the Number of Factors by the Scree Test point where there is a major difference in the slopes. Cattell (1978) and Gorsuch (1983) do not recommend the indiscriminate use of the Scree test. Gorsuch recommends that the potential user should practice with the Scree test using the examples provided in Cattell and Vogelman (1977) prior to using it on their own data.

The maximum remaining residual correlation gives another clue in determining when no more factoring is required. If all remaining residuals are less than .10, for example, it would be unnecessary to continue in most cases since any factor extracted would have very small loadings. Also, if the factors being extracted have no loadings as large as .30 or higher in absolute value, there is ordinarily little reason to extract more factors.

Many computer packages use a default option of extracting all principal factors with eigenvalues of 1.0 or more (the Kaiser-Guttman rule). In no case should this rule be used unless 1's have been inserted as communalities. Even where 1's have been used as communalities, this rule may not give the correct number of factors (Gorsuch & Nelson, 1981; Velicer, 1974, 1977) although it is usually not too far off. Another option sometimes offered on such programs is to extract all factors with eigenvalues greater than zero. This option will generally give a much larger number of factors than needed, particularly if 1's are used as communalities. It is more appropriate if SMCs are used as communality estimates. Even then, the number of factors extracted will be an upper bound value, similar to what can be obtained with the minimum residual method when convergence on vectors of opposite sign occurs.

The main thing to consider in deciding when to stop factoring is that it is better to err on the side of extracting too many factors rather than too few. There are two main reasons for this rule. First, if there are ten strong factors, for example, in the matrix and only eight are extracted, most of the variance for all ten factors has already been taken out with the first eight factors. Since the amount of variance extracted gets progressively smaller from the largest to the smallest factor extracted, variance is extracted on a single large factor that ultimately may be distributed to several different factors by the subsequent rotation process. In the rotation process, however, this variance for ten factors must be distributed on only eight factors. Not only are two factors lost, but the character of the remaining factors is distorted by the intrusion of variance from the two factors that are not retained in the final solution. Secondly, if too many factors have been extracted, proper management of the rotation process following factor extraction will permit discarding of the extra factors as residual factors of minimal importance without distorting the character of the major factors. In most cases, some rotation of extracted factors will be necessary before the correct number of major factors can be established.

The recommended procedure, then, is to extract enough factors to be relatively certain that no more factors of any importance remain. If in doubt, continue until the maximum number has been extracted, that is, with the minimum residual method until convergence on vectors of opposite sign has taken place using the length-adjustment procedure. In the rotation process following factor extraction, eliminate the excess factors. Just how this can be done is explained later. It should be emphasized, however, at this point, that appropriate steps *must* be taken to eliminate these extra factors. If too many factors are rotated without thought, for example, with a canned computer program, distortions to the solution may occur that are just as serious as those that result from extracting and rotating too few factors.

4.5. OTHER METHODS OF FACTOR EXTRACTION

There are many other methods of factor extraction besides those discussed here. Thurstone (1947) described the group centroid and multiple group methods as labor-saving alternatives to the centroid method.

A model of factor analysis that existed at the time the centroid method was developed but that did not receive much attention until later was the statistical inference model of factor analysis. Lawley (1940) reduced the extraction of factor parameters to a problem in maximum-likelihood estimation (See also Lawley & Maxwell, 1963). Lawley's "new" development eliminated the indeterminacies and subjective decisions required by the centroid and principal factor methods. Unlike other factor methods available at the time, Lawley's Maximum Likelihood method provided a goodness-of-fit test. Hence, statistically, a factor analyst could determine whether the obtained solution was a good fit to the observed data points. Additionally, the maximum-likelihood estimates contained a powerful invariance property. Changes in the scales of the response variates only appear as scale changes of the loadings. When using a correlation matrix or a covariance matrix, the loadings extracted only differ by a scale factor. Lawley's algorithm for maximum likelihood factor analysis, (see Harman, 1967), was beset with problems different from those found with the principal factor method. Convergence seemed to be one of the major problems and excessive computation time was another. Other attempts to deal with these problems, such as that by Morrison (1967), ran into problems with larger numbers of variables and factors. Joreskog (1967) employed newer algorithms (Newton-Raphson and Fletcher-Powell) to solve the maximum-likelihood estimation problems. With faster and more accurate computers and algorithms, Joreskog not only found a better maximum likelihood solution for factor analysis problems but also developed the methods for analyzing more complex relationships in the form of covariance structure models (described in more detail in Chapter 13).

Horst (1965) presents an exhaustive treatment of factor extraction methods and their variations. Harman (1967) also presents an extended treatment of factor extraction methods as do other more recent books cited in Chapter 1. Lee (1979) describes a number of factor extraction methods that attained some degree of popularity due to their ready availability on well-known statistical computer package programs.

Following the development of Comrey's (1962a) minimum residual method, Harman and Jones (1966) published their "minres" method. Whereas the minimum residual method minimizes the off-diagonal residuals after each factor, in a stepwise procedure, the minres method minimizes the residuals using a specified number of factors. Unfortunately, the number of factors must be known in advance. The minres method reduces the sums of squares of the off diagonal residuals, however, to a lower level than is the case for the stepwise minimum residual method. Lee and Comrey (1978) demonstrated empirically that if the minimum residual solution is iterated until the communalities stabilize, the solution obtained is virtually identical to the minres solution and requires less computation. These findings are consistent with the Joreskog and Sorbom (1981) position that iterating a principal factor solution gives the same results as the Harman-Jones minres solution.

The minimum residual algorithm and computer program described later in this book, therefore, provide a versatile tool for obtaining several kinds of solutions: minimum residual solution with or without communality estimates and with or without iteration to stabilize the communalities, minres, principal factor solutions with any specified communalities, and principal component solutions. The factor extraction methods presented in this book, therefore, are probably adequate for most ordinary empirical research purposes. In any event, the particular method of factor extraction used will usually have less effect on the final outcome than such considerations as the communalities chosen, whether or not communalities are used, how many factors are extracted, and how the rotations are carried out.

5

Orthogonal Hand Rotations

5.1. INTRODUCTION

It has already been pointed out in previous chapters that the extracted factor matrix does not usually provide a suitable final solution to a factor analysis problem. Most extraction methods are designed to extract something approximating the maximum amount of variance at each step. The factors, therefore, get progressively smaller until finally they are too small for retention. At each step, variance from many different common factor sources is being extracted because the factor vector is placed in such a way that as many of the variables as possible have substantial projections on it. It is not atypical for entirely uncorrelated data vectors to have substantial projections on the same extracted factor vector. Such extracted factor vectors are, then, complex composites of partially overlapping and even unrelated data variables rather than narrowly defined factors represented by homogeneous collections of closely related data variables.

Suppose, for example, that several verbal abilities tests and several measures of physical size were included in the same matrix. A reasonable final factor solution might give two equally prominent factors, Verbal Ability and Size. The first extracted factor, however, would be a combination of Verbal Ability and Size, with all measures having positive loadings of substantial proportions. The second factor might have positive loadings for the size variables and negative loadings for the verbal ability variables, but the second factor loadings in general would be smaller in absolute size than those for the first factor. Only by rotating the extracted factors would it be possible to obtain the expected factors of Verbal Ability and Size.

111

Failure to understand how the first factor can pull variance from uncorrelated variables has led some investigators to infer mistakenly that a general factor exists in the data just because all the variables have positive loadings on the first factor. Consider the example in Fig. 5.1. Let variables 1, 2, and 3 represent three substantially intercorrelated verbal tests: 1. Vocabulary, 2. Verbal Fluency, and 3. Verbal Analogies. Variables 4, 5, and 6 represent size variables: 4. Height, 5. Weight, and 6. Chest Volume. The two groups of variables represent essential uncorrelated clusters, yet the first extracted factor, a vector about equidistant between these two clusters, will have substantial positive projections for all these variables. These projections are indicated by the dotted lines from the data vector termini perpendicular to the factor vector I. The second factor will be bipolar, with positive loadings for variables 4, 5, and 6 and negative loadings for variables 1, 2, and 3. A rotation of the two extracted factors about 45° counterclockwise will bring the factors in line with the two independent clusters of homogeneous variables.

It is inappropriate to think of the unrotated factor I position as representing a scientifically meaningful, interpretable factor. Such a factor consists of unrelated components that do not go together. The rotated factor positions, identified with the Verbal Ability and Size factors, are much easier to interpret and use than the unrotated factors, which would represent, respectively, a Size plus Verbal Ability factor and a bipolar Size plus Lack of Verbal Ability factor.

In the event that all variables have substantial loadings on the first

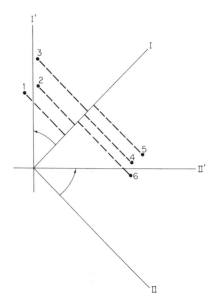

FIG. 5.1. Projection of data vectors on first extracted factor. 1: Vocabulary; 2: verbal Fluency; 3: Verbal Analogies; 4: Height; 5: Weight; 6: Chest Volume.

extracted factor and *in addition* all variables correlate positively to a substantial degree with each other, the case for a general factor would be much stronger, although still not conclusive. It could still be possible that all the variables included were themselves complex composites, making it impossible in the analysis to isolate the separate factor components. It can be stated, therefore, that having all variables in the matrix load substantially on the first extracted factor is a necessary but not sufficient condition to demonstrate the presence of a general factor.

The initial extracted factor matrix, then, usually must be rotated before the final factor solution is achieved. In Chapter 2 it was shown that a factor matrix may be transformed to a rotated factor matrix by the matrix operation $V = A\Lambda$, where V is the rotated matrix, A is the unrotated matrix, and Λ is an orthogonal transformation matrix in which rows and columns have sums of squares equal to 1.0 and inner products of nonidentical rows or columns equal to zero. As shown in Chapter 2, such a transformation does not affect the capacity of the factor matrix to reproduce the original correlation matrix because

$$VV' = (A\Lambda)(A\Lambda)' = A\Lambda\Lambda'A' = AIA' = AA' = R$$

In other words, the transformed or rotated matrix V when multiplied by its transpose V' will reproduce the R matrix just as well as A multiplied by its transpose A' does.

In order to carry out the rotation of the A matrix, it is necessary to find the appropriate Λ matrix to transform A to V by the matrix operation $V = A\Lambda$. This chapter is concerned with methods of determining this Λ matrix through inspection of plots of factors two at a time. This traditional method of determining what rotations to perform has lost popularity in recent years because of the ready availability of computer program packages that offer the user a variety of analytic rotational options. In such cases, the user does not have to carry out the rotations "by hand." Because of the availability of these easier and more convenient computerized procedures, a widely held view is that it is no longer important to teach the "old-fashioned" rotation procedures based on inspection of graphical plots of factors two at a time.

The authors take strong exception to this point of view. Computer methods of rotating factor axes by means of analytic criteria (as discussed in a later chapter) cannot replace intelligent judgment by the investigator as to what kind of rotational solution is appropriate. A computer program will carry out rotations according to some specified criterion that may be appropriate for certain situations, but it cannot be appropriate for all or even most situations. The investigator must be prepared to ascertain what criteria are suitable for guiding the rotations in the particular situation at hand and then carry out the rotations in such a way that the data are properly treated. The only way to prepare the investigator to meet all possible situation is to teach him or her how to position the rotated vectors in any mathematically possible configuration. The investigator can then use any rotational criterion desired and place the axes accordingly. The hand rotation methods described in this book offer the investigator this freedom of choice. If these procedures are not mastered, the student is left only with the alternative of choosing among available computer programs to carry out the rotation of factor axes, and none of these programs may be suitable for the particular situation at hand.

To illustrate how orthogonal rotations are carried out to place the rotated factor axes in any orthogonal position desired, a rotation of the minimum residual solution to the 12-variable sample problem (see Table 5.1) is shown in the next section. These rotations are carried out using "positive manifold" and "simple structure," rotational criteria that have been traditional guides in carrying out the rotation process in factor analysis. Many of the computer rotation procedures are designed to achieve an approximation to this solution except that the computer does it without the benefit of any human judgment. Traditional application of these criteria has involved a series of judgments by the investigator as the rotation process unfolds.

Although simple structure and positive manifold are the guiding principles used here in carrying out the rotations for the 12-variable sample problem, it should be stressed that these methods of executing rotations are not limited to use with these particular rotational criteria. Simple structure and positive manifold are poor criteria to use in many situations. The same

TABLE 5.1

Unrotated Minimum Residual Solution to the 12-Variable Problem[a]

Variable	Factors					Variable name	Factor
	I	II	III	IV	V		
1	.080	.846	.160	−.046	.011	Law Enforcement	C
2	.011	.707	.101	.048	−.058	Acceptance of Social Order	C
3	.037	.652	.221	−.100	−.045	Intolerance of Nonconformity	C
4	.544	.099	−.287	.261	.122	Lack of Inferiority Feelings	S
5	.589	.157	−.180	.366	.092	Lack of Depression	S
6	.435	.098	−.212	.482	.105	Lack of Agitation	S
7	.563	−.006	−.161	−.339	.310	Lack of Reserve	E
8	.661	.013	.076	−.205	.070	Lack of Seclusiveness	E
9	.758	.023	−.210	−.230	.372	No Loss for Words	E
10	.431	−.174	.506	.045	.019	Sympathy	P
11	.537	−.197	.591	.152	.082	Helpfulness	P
12	.370	−.281	.522	.052	.043	Generosity	P

[a] Factor names are C: Social Conformity versus Rebelliousness; S: Emotional Stability versus Neuroticism; P: Empathy versus Egocentrism; E: Extraversion versus Introversion.

methods of executing the rotations, however, may be used no matter what criterion is being used to guide the rotations. The only restriction is that the methods shown in this chapter limit the investigator to an orthogonal solution with uncorrelated factors. Oblique solutions that involve correlated factors will be considered in the next chapter.

5.1.1. POSITIVE MANIFOLD

Even if all correlations in the original matrix are nonnegative, i.e., zero or positive, except for a few chance correlations slightly below zero, the extracted factors past the first factor frequently exhibit many substantial negative as well as positive loadings. This is an arbitrary result, based on the requirement in the centroid method, for example, that the sum of the factor loadings be zero for the second and subsequent factors (if the communalities have not been reestimated at each step). Because all the original correlations are nonnegative, however, the final rotated factors should be positioned in such a way that there are no substantial negative loadings for any of the variables on any of the factors. In looking at a plot of two factors in Cartesian coordinates, therefore, the investigator looks for a rotation that will reduce or eliminate negative loadings as much as possible on the rotated factors. Trying to rotate to obtain nonnegative loadings is known as rotating to "positive manifold." The rotation of factors I and II about 45° counterclockwise in Fig. 5.1 to positions I' and II' is a good illustration of this principle. Before the rotation, variables 1, 2, and 3 had substantial negative loadings on Factor II. After the rotation, however, there are no negative loadings of any consequence on either factor I' or II'.

The idea behind positive manifold, then, is that if all the data variables in a matrix have intercorrelations that are either zero or positive, it is unreasonable to anticipate an underlying factor with substantial negative loadings for any of the data variables. Most factor analytic methods, however, will produce *extracted* factors after the first factor with substantial negative loadings for some variables, even if all the intercorrelations were nonnegative. The rotated factors that represent the meaningful constructs ordinarily should not exhibit these large negative loadings. Even with nonnegative correlations among the data variables, however, it would be theoretically possible to obtain one or more underlying rotated factor constructs with substantial negative loadings, because the extracted factors exhibit such loadings; on the other hand, such constructs would be contrary to reasonable expectation, probably complex in character, and difficult to interpret. In the absence of strong evidence suggesting the presence of such bipolar factors (that is, with both large positive and large negative loadings), therefore, extracted factors should be rotated to eliminate substantial negative loadings. Of course, if a contemplated rotation would make all or most of the factor loadings negative, this would not necessarily represent a violation of the positive manifold concept. The direction of the factor can be reversed following the rotation, thereby changing all the signs. Positive loadings become negative and vice versa. As long as none of the negative loadings after reversal is large, reversal of the factor direction would bring the factor into agreement with positive manifold rotational principles.

Computer programs often produce rotated factors in which the major loadings have negative signs. Many inexperienced factor analysts are unaware that they are permitted arbitrarily to reverse the signs of the factor loadings for all variables on such a factor, thereby reversing the direction of the factor. Suitable interpretation and representation of a factor construct often requires such a reversal of signs.

5.1.2. SIMPLE STRUCTURE

Thurstone (1947) developed the criterion of "simple structure" to guide the investigator in carrying out rotations of factor axes to positions of greater "psychological meaningfulness." A generation of factor analysts followed his lead and even today, most exploratory factor analyses are carried out using this method or some analytic procedure that was developed to approximate it without the necessity of carrying out hand rotations that require judgment on the part of the investigator.

Thurstone reasoned that if we sample widely and more or less randomly from all the possible data variables that describe a complex domain such as the domain of human characteristics, it is inevitable that a large collection of such variables will measure many factors, not just one or two. He also supposed that any one variable will be related to only a few of these many factors. Furthermore, he reasoned that no one factor will be substantially related to more than a small proportion of the variables. If these conditions are met, Thurstone deduced that the rotated factor matrix representing these factors should take on a characteristic form.

1. Most of the loadings on any one factor should be small, that is, more or less randomly distributed about zero, with only a few of the loadings being of substantial size. This means that any column of the factor matrix should have mostly small values, as close to zero as possible.

2. A given row of the factor matrix, containing the loadings for a given variable on all the factors, should have nonzero entries in only a few columns. The fewer the columns in which the variable has loadings, the closer to the expected form is the solution.

3. Any two factor columns should exhibit a different pattern of high and low loadings. Otherwise, there would be no apparent difference between the two factors represented by these two columns.

The situation represented by Fig. 5.1 does not conform to the ideal circumstances for applying simple structure because there are only two factors with three variables for each. Only half the variables on a given factor, therefore, can have low loadings. Within these limitations, it is clear that the rotation shown in Fig. 5.1 brings the rotated factors as close to a simple structure position as possible. Whereas the unrotated factors had no low loadings, the rotated factors both have 50% of the loadings at essentially zero level. Also, each variable has a major loading only in one of the two rotated factors. The pattern of loadings is markedly different in the two rotated factors because those variables with high loadings on one have low loadings on the other.

The rotation in Fig. 5.1, then, is a good one from the standpoint of meeting both positive manifold and simple structure criteria. In practice, rotations are sought that will in fact do just this. A rotation that works against one of these criteria while improving the other would be less desirable and in fact might be actually undesirable. Positive manifold is less useful as a guide to rotations with factor matrices derived from correlation matrices with large negative correlations present. There is no large negative correlation in the 12-variable sample problem correlation matrix, however, so positive manifold is very useful with this problem.

Sometimes the negative correlations in a matrix can be reduced or eliminated by the reflection of data variables. For example, suppose one variable is represented by the number of mistakes in a certain task. All the other variables represent the number of correct answers on similar kinds of tasks. The variable based on the number of mistakes will very likely have negative correlations with the other variables. This variable can be reflected by changing all the signs for all the correlations between this variable and the other variables. This will eliminate these negative signs from the matrix, making it easier to use positive manifold to guide the rotations. However, the name of the reflected variable would have to be changed as, for example, from "Mistakes" to "Lack of Mistakes."

5.2. ORTHOGONAL ROTATION OF THE 12-VARIABLE PROBLEM

The first step in the rotation process is to plot every pair of factors that are to be a part of the solution. In this case, only the first four factors from the minimum residual solution to the 12-variable problem, given in Table 4.4 and repeated in Table 5.1, will be rotated. The fifth factor could be included in all the rotation cycles, but it is a very small factor; so it will be omitted from consideration until after the main factors have been rotated. In plotting the factors, that is, I with II, I with III, and so on, until finally III with IV is plotted, the loadings for a variable in the two factors establish the location of a point on the plot in a Cartesian coordinate system. For example, if a variable had loadings of 0.60 and -0.40 in factors I and II, respectively, there would be a single point at the location $(+.60, -.40)$ on a two-dimensional plot of factor I with factor II. There would be a point on this plot for each variable. Each factor axis would extend from -1.0 to $+1.0$ to accomodate the largest possible loadings, positive or negative. These plots for the minimum residual factors are shown in Fig. 5.2.

From the first set of plots, two rotations were selected to be performed. Factor I is rotated 22°47′ away from factor IV, that is, counterclockwise in

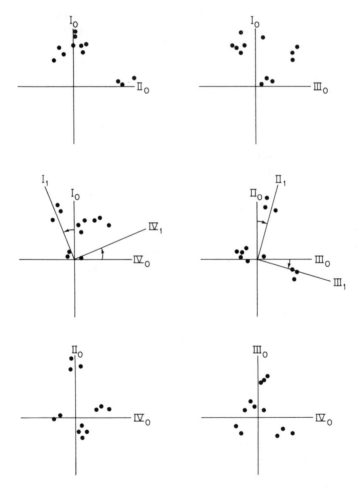

FIG. 5.2.   First set pf plots in orthogonal rotation of the 12-variable problem.

this plot, and to keep the rotations orthogonal, factor IV is rotated the same angle (22°47′) toward factor I. This keeps the angle between the new factor I and the new factor IV at 90°. Any angle approximately equal to 22°47′ would have served equally well as the angle used, for example, any angle between 21° and 23°. In this example, the angle needed to achieve a desired result was calculated, yielding a more precise angle than would be employed in actual practice. The unrotated minimum residual factors are labeled with a zero subscript, that is, I_0 and IV_0. The positions after one rotation are labeled with a subscript of 1, that is I_1, and after i rotations with a subscript i, for example, III_i.

This rotation of factor I with factor IV was selected because it eliminates the negative loadings on factor IV while bringing the formerly negatively loaded variables into the "hyperplane" of factor IV; that is, those variables have loadings close to zero on factor IV. The line perpendicular to the vector labeled IV is at once the hyperplane for factor IV and also the factor vector for factor I. Any points close to the factor axis I will have perpendicular projections onto the factor axis IV near the origin and hence will have near-zero loadings on factor I.

In the orthogonal case, the line perpendicular to the factor axis at the origin is referred to as a hyperplane. The termini of a collection of vectors in four-dimensional space have been projected onto a two-dimensional surface, that is, a plane, when we plot two factors at a time. For a three-dimensional space, we see the plane perpendicular to one of the factors as a line only because we are looking along the edge of the plane. If, for example, a square piece of plywood is held up before the eyes, it can be positioned in such a way that it will show only one edge, hence it appears as a line. If the board were clear plastic and points were imbedded in the plastic, these points would all appear along the edge, but the distances between them in the direction of the line of sight would not be apparent. Only distances along the axis perpendicular to this line would be apparent. For a three-dimensional space, the hyperplane perpendicular to a factor axis is really a plane and as such has only two dimensions. If vectors project out into space of higher dimensions, such as the four-dimensional space with this sample problem, then the space perpendicular to a factor is no longer a plane of two dimensions. It is a "plane" of many dimensions and hence is referred to as a "hyperplane." In a two-dimensional plot, however, only the "edge" of this plane or hyperplane is seen. Any data vector that has no loading on a given factor will be wholly contained in the hyperplane somewhere. The point that represents the terminus of this vector, therefore, will show up in the plot of this factor with some other factor as a point along the line perpendicular to this factor (or close to it), and hence it is said to be in the hyperplane of this factor even though it appears only as a point close to a line. When the hyperplane has several dimensions, of course, it is impossible to visualize it, just as it is impossible to visualize a space of more than three dimensions.

In determining the loadings of the data vector on the new factors I_1 and IV_1 in Fig. 5.2, perpendicular projections from the data points are dropped to the two axes I_1 and IV_1. The distances from the origin to the points where these perpendicular projections intersect with the factor axes give the factor loadings on the orthogonal factors. The loadings on the old axes I_0 and IV_0 are used to locate the points on the plot. They are the coordinates of the points with respect to axes I_0 and IV_0.

The rotation of factor I with factor IV also takes some of the variance away from factor I and puts it on factor IV. The first factor usually has maximum variance on it, representing a composite factor substantially related to as many data variables as possible. This means that the rotational process must remove variance from factor I (that is, reduce the sum of squares of loadings on factor I) and spread it around to other factors if the rotated factors are to be more nearly equal in the amount of variance they account for than were the original unrotated factors. Other early extracted factors may also have to give up some of their total variance to later factors in the rotational process.

To summarize, in Fig. 5.2 the rotation of factor I away from factor IV, and of IV toward I, improves positive manifold, moves closer to simple structure, and reduces some of the excess variance on factor I. The other rotation worth carrying out from the plots in Fig. 5.2 is that for factors II and III. Factor II is rotated toward factor III, that is, clockwise, by an angle of 15°39′ and factor III is rotated away from factor II by the same angle. This rotation improves both positive manifold and simple structure for both factors, making it an excellent choice for execution.

This series of plots (in Fig. 5.2) also offers another excellent rotational possibility. Factor I could have been rotated away from factor III about 22°, that is, counterclockwise, and factor III toward factor I by the same amount to maintain orthogonality. This rotation would be about as good as the rotation of I with IV actually performed. In a given series of rotations, however, each factor may be rotated only once without making new plots for that factor with the other factors. Factor I cannot be rotated both with IV and with III at the same time except through the use of techniques more complicated than those to be demonstrated in this text. After I has been rotated with IV, however, the new factor I, that is, I_1, can be rotated with the original, as yet unrotated, factor III, that is, III_0, if in fact factor III has not yet been rotated. In this example, factor III is rotated with factor II in the first series of rotations; so when the rotation of I with III is considered again, it will be I_1 plotted with III_1, as shown in Fig. 5.3.

Instead of rotating factor I counterclockwise away from factor III by an angle of about 22°, as considered in the preceding paragraph, we could achieve the same effect by rotating factor I clockwise toward factor III by an angle of (90–22)°. This would interchange factors I and III relative to those obtained with the 22° counterclockwise rotation. It would also reverse the direction of factor III. Since III would be rotated away from I in this clockwise rotation, the major loadings of the variables on the new factor III would be negative, whereas they were positive for the counterclockwise rotation. This clockwise rotation would not be considered a violation of the positive manifold principle, however, because the orientation of factor III can be reversed arbitrarily by changing all the signs of the factor loadings on the new III. Then, the major loadings would be positive as expected with the positive manifold principle. The signs of the third column entries in the transformation matrix would also have to be reversed to maintain consistency with the reversed signs in the third column of the rotated factor matrix. Thus, at any point in the rotation process, should $V = A\Lambda$ and the signs of any column of V be predominately negative, they may be changed, reversing the signs of all column entries, if the signs in the corresponding column of Λ are also reversed. This may be done arbitrarily and at will. It merely reverses the direction of the factor. If the factor were Introversion-Extraversion before this reflection, after the reflection it would become Extraverion-Introversion. Many rotation problems will require this type of arbitrary reflection of factors at one or more points in the rotation process to eliminate a predominance of unwanted negative signs in the factor loadings for a given factor.

The remaining plots in Fig. 5.2 are less attractive as rotational possibilities than the three already given, although factor III could be rotated a small amount with factor IV in a clockwise direction with resulting improvements in both positive manifold and simple structure. This rotation was not chosen, however, because for these factor axes, good rotations of greater magnitude (with bigger angles) were available with other factors than with each other. The rotation of III with IV will actually be chosen as the best rotation in a later series of plots (see Fig. 5.3). Higher numbered factors are rarely to be rotated with each other before they have been rotated with lower numbered factors to build up their total variance. Initially, these factors have rather low sums of squares of their factor loadings before rotation and therefore little is to be gained by rotating them with each other before they have been rotated with larger factors.

The plots of I with II and II with IV in Fig. 5.2 offer little opportunity for improving positive manifold and simple structure simultaneously. To find three good rotations in a series of plots, however, is all that the most optimistic investigator could hope for. Even one good rotation possibility is enough to keep the process moving forward.

5.2.1.   ALGEBRAIC EXECUTION OF THE FIRST ROTATION

Computations for the first rotation are shown in Table 5.2. It is possible to do the rotations entirely graphically (Zimmerman, 1946), and in precomputer days this was the usual method. Today, however, the plots are used most commonly only as a means of deciding which factors to rotate, in what direction, and by how large an angle. The actual execution of the rotation is carried out algebraically rather than graphically; it is more accurate, provides a better mathematical record of what was done, and with the availability of computing equipment, is actually less work. A computer program developed by the first author that plots the factors and carries out the rotations asked for by the investigator is described in a later chapter. Thus, "hand rotations" today can be done by computer. The investigator only has to decide what rotations the computer is to perform.

Each orthogonal rotation is carried out by multiplying the present matrix of factor loadings on the right (postmultiplying) by an orthogonal transformation matrix Λ_1. For the first rotation, the matrix equation is:

$$\mathbf{V}_1 = \mathbf{A}\Lambda_1 \tag{5.1}$$

where $\mathbf{A}$ is the unrotated matrix of extracted factor loadings, $\mathbf{V}_1$ is the matrix of rotated loadings after the first rotation, and Λ_1 is the orthogonal matrix that carries the matrix $\mathbf{A}$ into matrix $\mathbf{V}_1$.

Matrix Λ_i is determined by the rotation to be performed, which in turn is based on the plots of the factors, two at a time (see Fig. 5.2). If factor j is to be rotated with factor k, the elements of Λ_i are determined as follows: (1) $\lambda_{jj} = \lambda_{kk} = \cos\phi$ where ϕ is the number of degrees in the angle of rotation to be performed; (2) $\lambda_{jk} = \sin\phi$ when the lower numbered factor is rotated away from the higher numbered factor and $-\sin\phi$ when the lower numbered factor is rotated toward the higher numbered factor; (3) $\lambda_{kj} = -\sin\phi$ when $\lambda_{jk} = \sin\phi$, and $\lambda_{kj} = +\sin\phi$ when $\lambda_{jk} = -\sin\phi$; (4) other diagonal entries of Λ_i are equal to 1.0; (5) all other entries of Λ_i are zero.

In the first rotation, factor I is rotated away from factor IV by an angle of 22°47'. The cosine of this angle is 0.922, which appears as λ_{11} and λ_{44} of Λ_1, Table 5.2. The sine of 22°47' is 0.387 and since factor I is rotated *away* from factor IV, $\lambda_{14} = +.387$. Since $\lambda_{14} = +.387$, λ_{41} will equal $-.387$, also shown in Table 5.2. The other two diagonal cells of Λ_1 equal 1 and all other entries of Λ_1 are zero.

It should be noted in Table 5.2 that multiplying $\mathbf{A}$ by Λ_1 has the effect of subtracting a proportion of the fourth factor loadings from the first factor loadings multiplied by 0.922. Thus, when factor I is rotated *away* from factor IV, the minus sign in the fourth row, first column of Λ_1 causes the

TABLE 5.2

First Orthogonal Rotation of the 12-Variable Problem

A

	I	II	III	IV
1	.080	.846	.160	−.046
2	.011	.707	.101	.048
3	.037	.652	.221	−.100
4	.544	.099	−.287	.261
5	.589	.157	−.180	.366
6	.435	.098	−.212	.482
7	.563	−.006	−.161	−.339
8	.661	.013	.076	−.205
9	.758	.023	−.210	−.230
10	.431	−.174	.506	.045
11	.537	−.197	.591	.152
12	.370	−.281	.522	.052

$\times$

Λ_1

I	II	III	IV
.922	0	0	.387
0	1	0	0
0	0	1	0
−.387	0	0	.922

$=$

V_1

I	II	III	IV
.092	.846	.160	−.011
−.008	.707	.101	.049
.073	.652	.221	−.078
.400	.099	−.287	.451
.401	.157	−.180	.566
.214	.098	−.212	.613
.650	−.006	−.161	−.095
.689	.013	.076	.067
.788	.023	−.210	.081
.380	−.174	.506	.208
.436	−.197	.591	.348
.321	−.281	.522	.191

new factor I to be less like the old factor IV. The new factor IV, however, is being made more like the old factor I because it is being rotated toward factor I. This is reflected in the matrix multiplication by the plus sign in the first row, fourth column of Λ_1 in Table 5.2. This causes a portion of the first factor loadings to be added to the fourth factor loadings multiplied by 0.922. The placement of the minus sign in the transformation matrix, therefore, is determined by whether the lower numbered factor is to be made more like the higher numbered factor (rotated toward it), which requires a plus sign in the λ_{ji} cell of Λ, or whether it is to be made less like the higher numbered factor (rotated away from it), which requires a minus sign in the λ_{ji} cell of Λ.

Multiplying **A** by Λ_1 changes only columns I and IV, which is to be expected since only factors I and IV were being rotated. Factors II and III of V_1 are seen in Table 5.2 to be identical with factors II and III of matrix **A**. The values in columns I and IV of matrix V_1 could be obtained by taking the perpendicular projections of the test vectors on the rotated factor axes I_1 and IV_1 in Fig. 5.2. The reader may verify this to be assured that the indicated matrix operations actually carry out the desired rotation of the factor axes.

The second rotation is performed by the matrix equation

$$V_2 = V_1\Lambda_2 \tag{5.2}$$

where V_2 is the matrix of rotated factor loadings after two rotations, V_1 is the matrix of rotated factor loadings after one rotation, and Λ_2 is the orthogonal transformation matrix for the second rotation. For the 12-variable sample problem, the second rotation consisted of rotating factor II toward factor III by an angle of 15°39′. Factor III was rotated away from factor II by the same angle at the same time. The computations for this rotation are shown in Table 5.3. The cosine of ϕ, therefore, appears in λ_{22} and λ_{33} of Λ_2. Ones appear in the other two diagonal cells, λ_{11} and λ_{44} of Λ_2. Because factor II is rotated *toward* factor III, $\lambda_{23} = -\sin\phi$ and $\lambda_{32} = +\sin\phi$.

The matrix V_2 will be altered by the next rotation as follows:

$$V_3 = V_2\Lambda_3 \tag{5.3}$$

Then

$$V_4 = V_3\Lambda_4 \tag{5.4}$$

and, in general,

$$V_{i+1} = V_i\Lambda_{i+1} \tag{5.5}$$

The effect of all the rotations performed by the many orthogonal matrices, one pair of factors at a time, can be achieved through one transformation matrix Λ, which is found as follows:

$$\Lambda = \Lambda_1\Lambda_2\bullet\bullet\bullet\Lambda_q \tag{5.6}$$

where Λ_1 is the first orthogonal transformation matrix that performs the first rotation, Λ_2 is the second orthogonal transformation matrix that performs the second rotation, and so on, with Λ_q being the last transformation matrix that effects the last orthogonal rotation. Then

$$V = A\Lambda \tag{5.7}$$

where V is the final orthogonal rotated matrix of factor loadings, A is the unrotated matrix of extracted factor loadings, and Λ is the orthogonal transformation matrix that does all the rotations at once. The matrix Λ is orthogonal itself because it is a product of orthogonal matrices (see Eq. (5.6)). The product of V by its transpose gives

$$\begin{aligned} VV' &= (A\Lambda)(A\Lambda)' = A(\Lambda\Lambda')A' \\ &= AIA' = AA' \end{aligned} \tag{5.8}$$

Equation (5.8) shows that the rotated matrix VV' reproduces the R matrix just as well as AA' does; hence the matrix V is mathematically equivalent to the matrix A in this sense.

The matrix V_2 contains factors that have each been rotated once. New plots of these factors must be made to find more rotations to perform in the quest for better positive manifold and simple structure. Because two of the possible rotations have just been carried out, that is, I with IV and II with

TABLE 5.3

Second Orthogonal Rotation of the 12-Variable Problem

	I	II	III	IV
1	.092	.846	.160	−.011
2	−.008	.707	.101	.049
3	.073	.652	.221	−.078
4	.400	.099	−.287	.451
5	.401	.157	−.180	.566
6	.214	.098	−.212	.613
7	.650	−.006	−.161	−.095
8	.689	.013	.076	.067
9	.788	.023	−.210	.081
10	.380	−.174	.506	.208
11	.436	−.197	.591	.348
12	.321	−.281	.522	.191

V_1

$\times$

	I	II	III	IV
I	1	0	0	0
II	0	.963	−.270	0
III	0	.270	.963	0
IV	0	0	0	1

Λ_2

$=$

	I	II	III	IV
	.092	.858	−.074	−.011
	−.008	.708	−.093	.049
	.073	.687	.037	−.078
	.400	.018	−.303	.451
	.401	.103	−.216	.566
	.214	.037	−.231	.613
	.650	−.049	−.153	−.095
	.689	.033	.070	.067
	.788	−.034	−.208	.081
	.380	−.031	.534	.208
	.436	−.030	.622	.348
	.321	−.130	.578	.191

V_2

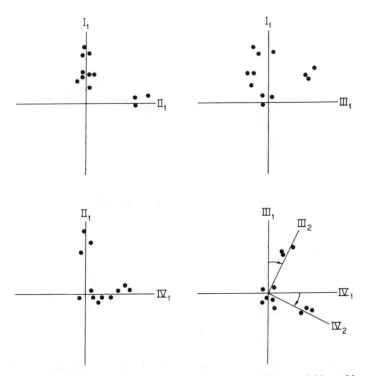

FIG. 5.3.   Second set of plots in orthogonal rotation of the 12-variable problem.

III, it is unnecessary to make these two plots in the next series of plots since these pairs will not be chosen for the next rotation. It is necessary, therefore, to make only four plots, I with II, I with III, II with IV, and III with IV. These plots are shown in Fig. 5.3. The loadings that provide the coordinates of the points for the plots in Fig. 5.3 are obtained from matrix V_2 in Table 5.3.

Inspection of the second series of plots in Fig. 5.3 indicates that the best rotation is factor III toward factor IV by an angle of 21°36'. This rotation clearly improves both simple structure and positive manifold simultaneously. Again, in actual practice, it is not necessary to determine the angle of rotation with this degree of precision. Factor I could be rotated away from factor III and factor III toward factor I, but this would involve factor III for which a more clear-cut rotation is available with factor IV. The matrix operations for this third rotation are shown in Table 5.4. The plots of factor I with II and II with IV in Fig. 5.3 offer no significant opportunities for improving either simple structure or positive manifold.

After the rotation of factor III with factor IV, new plots must be made for these two factors with factors I and II. The plot for factors I and II in Fig. 5.3 is still current and offers no rotational opportunities. The new plots are shown in Fig. 5.4. The loadings for these plots were taken from matrix V_3 in Table 5.4. Pairs II, III and II, IV in Fig. 5.4 offer no rotational opportunities. The plot of I with III is better than the plot for I with IV from the standpoint of simultaneously improving both simple structure and positive manifold. In addition, I has not been rotated previously with III, whereas I and IV have already been rotated once. For these reasons, factor I is rotated away from factor III, by an angle of 19°17', to make the fourth rotation.

Although the rotation of factor I away from factor III improves positive manifold by eliminating the small negative loadings on factor III, the improvement in simple structure is less marked. A position for factor I in between I_2 and I_1 would give a better hyperplane for factor III, but at the expense of making the three-point cluster to the right of the plot further

TABLE 5.4

Third Orthogonal Rotation of the 12-Variable Problem

	I	II	III	IV		I	II	III	IV			I	II	III	IV
1	.092	.858	−.074	−.011								.092	.858	−.073	.017
2	−.008	.708	−.093	.049								−.008	.708	−.069	.080
3	.073	.687	.037	−.078								.073	.687	.006	−.086
4	.400	.018	−.303	.451		I	II	III	IV			.400	.018	−.116	.531
5	.401	.103	−.216	.566		1	0	0	0			.401	.103	.008	.605
6	.214	.037	−.231	.613	×	0	1	0	0	=		.214	.037	.011	.655
7	.650	−.049	−.153	−.095		0	0	.930	−.368			.650	−.049	−.177	−.032
8	.689	.033	.070	.067		0	0	.368	.930			.689	.033	.089	.036
9	.788	−.034	−.208	.081				Λ_3				.788	−.034	−.164	.152
10	.380	−.031	.534	.208								.380	−.031	.573	−.003
11	.436	−.030	.622	.348								.436	−.030	.707	.094
12	.321	−.130	.578	.191								.321	−.130	.608	−.035
			V_2											V_3	

FIG. 5.4.   Third set of plots in orthogonal rotation of the 12-variable problem.

from the hyperplane of factor I. On the other hand, if factor III were placed right through the three-point cluster just above the present location of III_3 in Fig. 5.4, the hyperplane for factor I would be improved, but because this would force I_2 even further counterclockwise than it is now, the hyperplane for III would be made worse.

The rotation actually chosen for I with III in Fig. 5.4 is a compromise solution, which tries to get both hyperplanes as close as possible to the lines of maximum point density. In rotating to simple structure, the object is to get as many points in the hyperplanes as possible rather than to put the factors through clusters of points. The factor locations are determined by the hyperplane positioning rather than vice versa. The failure to get the hyperplanes right through the lines of maximum point density with factors I and III, as shown in Fig. 5.4, is due to the fact that some correlation between factors I and III is indicated by the pattern of points. When factors are correlated, an orthogonal rotated solution can only approach simple structure; it cannot reach it.

Thus, the present orthogonal solution will be taken as the best approximation to simple structure that can be achieved without going to an oblique solution. It is only by allowing the factor axes to depart from orthogonality, however, that the requirements for simple structure can ordinarily be completely satisfied. The methods of carrying out oblique rotations where the factors are allowed to depart from orthogonal positions are described and illustrated in the next chapter. There, further oblique rotations are performed on this 12-variable sample problem to bring it to a final oblique simple structure position.

Computations for the fourth rotation, factor I with III, are shown in Table 5.5. After this rotation, it is necessary to replot the remaining factors with the new factors I and III. Using the factor loadings in matrix V_4 of Table 5.5 leads to the plots for the new I and III with the other factors shown in Fig. 5.5. Inspection of these plots reveals that no improvements in simple structure and positive manifold can be attained with plots I with II, II with III, and III with IV. The plot of I with IV, however, affords a good rotation. Factor I is rotated away from factor IV by an angle of 14°2′, thereby improving the balancing of the two hyperplanes. Prior to the rotation, the hyperplane for factor IV was well located, but the hyperplane for I was too far from the three points above it. By the indicated rotation, the hyperplane for IV is made worse to gain some improvement in the positioning of the hyperplane for I. Had the first rotation of I with IV been better chosen, this rerotation of I with IV would not have been necessary. In practice, however, such rerotations are frequently necessary before the final positions for the factors are located. The computations for this final orthogonal rotation are shown in Table 5.6.

In Fig. 5.5 the plot of factor I with IV shows that simple structure is not well achieved with this final orthogonal positioning of these two factors. Factors I and III also are not close to simple structure when plotted with each other, as shown in Fig. 5.4. This fifth orthogonal rotation of factor I with factor IV, however, takes the solution about as close to simple

TABLE 5.5

Fourth Orthogonal Rotation of the 12-Variable Problem

	I	II	III	IV		I	II	III	IV		I	II	III	IV
1	.092	.858	−.073	.017							.111	.858	−.039	.017
2	−.008	.708	−.069	.080							.015	.708	−.068	.080
3	.073	.687	.006	−.086			I	II	III	IV	.067	.687	.029	−.086
4	.400	.018	−.116	.531			.944	0	.330	0	.416	.018	.023	.531
5	.401	.103	.008	.605	×		0	1	0	0	= .377	.103	.139	.605
6	.214	.037	.011	.655			−.330	0	.944	0	.199	.037	.081	.655
7	.650	−.049	−.177	−.032			0	0	0	1	.672	−.049	.047	−.032
8	.689	.033	.089	.036				$Λ_4$			.621	.033	.312	.036
9	.788	−.034	−.164	.152							.798	−.034	.105	.152
10	.380	−.031	.573	−.003							.169	−.031	.667	−.003
11	.436	−.030	.707	.094							.179	−.030	.811	.094
12	.321	−.130	.608	−.035							.102	−.130	.680	−.035
			V_3										V_4	

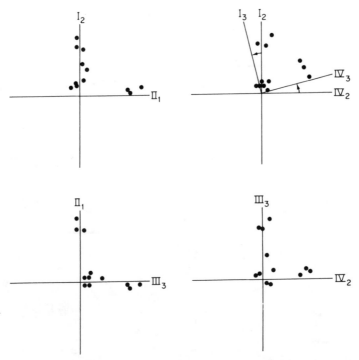

FIG. 5.5.   Fourth set of plots in orthogonal rotation of the 12-variable problem.

structure as it can get within the framework of orthogonal rotations. In the next chapter, oblique rotations between I and IV and also between I and III will improve the extent to which simple structure is achieved in the solution.

The same final solution as that in matrix V_5, in Table 5.6, may be obtained a different way. First, multiply all the orthogonal rotation matrices together as follows:

$$\Lambda = \Lambda_1\Lambda_2\Lambda_3\Lambda_4\Lambda_5 \tag{5.9}$$

Once this Λ matrix, which is the product of all the one-rotation Λ_i matrices, is obtained, the final rotated matrix V is obtained as follows:

$$V = A\Lambda \tag{5.10}$$

The computations for this operation are shown in Table 5.7. The final V matrix in Table 5.7 is seen to be identical with the matrix V_5, in Table 5.6, which was the end result of the long series of rotations, modifying the matrix of rotated loadings by one rotation at a time. Equation (5.10)

TABLE 5.6. Fifth Orthogonal Rotation of the 12-Variable Problem

$$
V_4 \times \Lambda_5 = V_5
$$

	I	II	III	IV
1	.111	.858	−.039	.017
2	.015	.708	−.068	.080
3	.067	.687	.029	−.086
4	.416	.018	.023	.531
5	.377	.103	.139	.605
6	.199	.037	.081	.655
7	.672	−.049	.047	−.032
8	.621	.033	.312	.036
9	.798	−.034	.105	.152
10	.169	−.031	.667	−.003
11	.179	−.030	.811	.094
12	.102	−.130	.680	−.035

V_4

	I	II	III	IV
	.970	0	0	.242
	0	1	0	0
	0	0	1	0
	−.242	0	0	.970

Λ_5

	I	II	III	IV
1	.103	.858	−.039	.043
2	−.005	.708	−.068	.080
3	.086	.687	.029	−.067
4	.275	.018	.023	.616
5	.219	.103	.139	.678
6	.034	.037	.081	.683
7	.660	−.049	.047	.133
8	.593	.033	.312	.186
9	.737	−.034	.105	.341
10	.165	−.031	.667	.038
11	.150	−.030	.811	.135
12	.107	−.130	.680	−.010

V_5

TABLE 5.7. Orthogonal Rotational Solution to the 12-Variable Problem

$$
A \times \Lambda = V
$$

	I	II	III	IV
1	.080	.846	.160	−.046
2	.011	.707	.101	.048
3	.037	.652	.221	−.100
4	.544	.099	−.287	.261
5	.589	.157	−.180	.366
6	.435	.098	−.212	.482
7	.563	−.006	−.161	−.339
8	.661	.013	.076	−.205
9	.758	.023	−.210	−.230
10	.431	−.174	.506	.045
11	.537	−.197	.591	.152
12	.370	−.281	.522	.052

A

	I	II	III	IV
	.711	.000	.439	.549
	.057	.963	−.237	.116
	−.201	.270	.845	−.416
	−.671	.000	.192	.716

Λ

	I	II	III	IV
1	.103	.858	−.039	.043
2	−.005	.708	−.068	.080
3	.086	.687	.029	−.067
4	.275	.018	.023	.616
5	.219	.103	.139	.678
6	.034	.037	.081	.683
7	.660	−.049	.047	.133
8	.593	.033	.312	.186
9	.737	−.034	.105	.341
10	.165	−.031	.667	.038
11	.150	−.030	.811	.135
12	.107	−.130	.680	−.010

V

permits the execution of the rotations all at once and provides a matrix Λ, which gives a final summarization of all the rotations that were performed.

In Fig. 5.6, the plots of the four rotated orthogonal factors are shown with the small fifth minimum residual factor, shown in Table 5.1. There is no way to build this factor up to an important separate factor except by splitting the variance for variables 7, 8, and 9 between factor I and this new factor, V. Factor V may be treated as a minor factor based on some surplus overlapping variance between variables 7 and 9 not shared as much with variable 8; or by rotating factor I slightly toward factor V and V slightly away from factor I, most of the variance on V can be shifted to factor I. This would reduce factor V to a residual factor with very little variance. A small rotation of IV toward V and V away from IV would complete the residualization of factor V by transferring further variance from factor V to factor IV. Residualing the small fifth factor through rotations with the other factors, however, would have the effect of making those other factors somewhat more complex in character, so the best strategy is probably to leave the fifth factor as it is. This would leave four major interpretable factors and a small fifth factor of minor importance. A four-factor solution, therefore, seems well justified for this 12-variable problem.

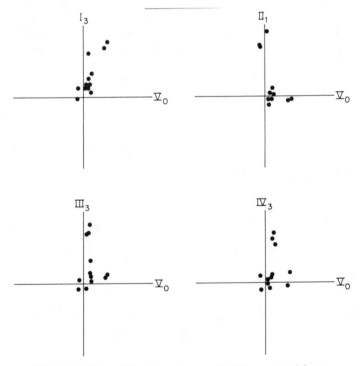

FIG. 5.6.   Plots of final four factors with fifth unrotated factor.

In Table 5.1, the variable names and hypothetical factor identifications were given for each variable. The unrotated matrix in Table 5.1 shows some tendency for variables to cluster into factors according to the hypothesized factor structure, but the rotated factor matrix **V** in Table 5.7 shows this tendency to a much more marked degree. In the rotated solution in matrix **V** of Table 5.7, factor I corresponds to Extraversion versus Introversion (E), factor II is Social Conformity versus Rebelliousness (C), factor III is Empathy versus Egocentrism (P), and factor IV is Emotional Stability versus Neuroticism (S).

Matrix **V** represents a rotational solution based on "blind" rotations to the best orthogonal simple structure that can be achieved, using positive manifold as a supplementary aid to guide the rotations. The rotations are described as "blind" because the plots showed only points without identifying variable numbers. That is, the rotational decisions were made on the basis of the configuration of points in the plots and not on the basis of the experimenter's knowledge of the variables or hypotheses regarding their factor structure. Following Thurstone's lead, Cattell (1952) has been a prominent advocate of this particular method of carrying out rotations, using it in developing his well-known Sixteen Personality Factor Questionnaire (16 PF), and teaching it to his many students. Unfortunately, this method does not always work well, as for example when the assumptions underlying simple structure are violated, so it is important to develop a familiarity with other rotational criteria that may be more appropriate in certain special situations.

6

Oblique Hand Rotations

In the previous chapter, blind hand rotation to orthogonal simple structure was illustrated for the 12-variable sample problem through the inspection of orthogonal factor plots, two factors at a time. In this chapter, the process is extended to the case of nonorthogonal factors. Plots are examined, two at a time, to determine if any oblique rotations are called for, that is, if the factor axes should depart from orthogonal positions.

6.1. OBLIQUE FACTOR AXES

The extent to which simple structure could be achieved with orthogonal hand rotations was limited by the restriction that the factors had to be kept at right angles to each other. It was necessary, for example, in the rotation of factor I with factor III, Fig. 5.4, to position the factors so that the clusters of points lay near the hyperplanes, but not actually on the lines representing the hyperplanes. This type of situation is illustrated in Fig. 6.1. If the factor axes are kept orthogonal to one another, points 1, 2, and 3 cannot be brought into the hyperplane of factor II at the same time points 4, 5, and 6 are brought into the hyperplane of factor I. One cluster or the other may be brought into the hyperplane of one of the factors, but only at the cost of putting the other cluster farther from the hyperplane nearest to it. If the factors are allowed to go to oblique (that is nonorthogonal) positions, however, both clusters can be brought into the hyperplanes nearest to them. The proper oblique positions of these factors are shown in Fig. 6.2 with the angle ϕ between them. Now the data vectors with termini

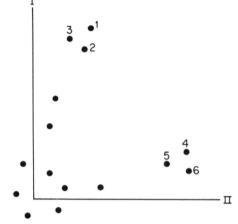

FIG. 6.1. Plot of factors requiring oblique rotation.

in points 4, 5, and 6 have near-zero loadings on factor I′, and the points 1, 2, and 3 have near-zero loadings on factor II′. For the table of oblique factor loadings, variables 1, 2, and 3 will have essentially zero values on factor II, whereas in the table of orthogonal factor loadings, the loadings were not large but were definitely nonzero. The same situation applies for variables 4, 5, and 6 with respect to factor I.

Thus, by rotating factors to oblique positions, it is possible to place the factor axes so that simple structure is more closely approximated if the clusters of points are not orthogonal to one another. For this reason, those who place great faith in the value of blind rotation to simple structure prefer to rotate obliquely, thereby enabling them to obtain a closer adherence to simple structure criteria.

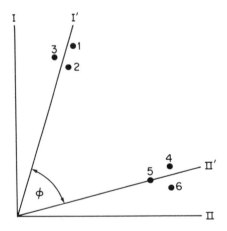

FIG. 6.2. Oblique factor positions.

6.1.1.   COORDINATES AND PROJECTIONS

In Fig. 6.2, the loadings of the points 4, 5, and 6 are essentially zero on factor axis I′ because the loadings are the distances from the origin to the points where lines from points 4, 5, and 6 *parallel* to factor axis II′ intersect with factor axis I′. The loadings are *not* determined by the distances from the origin to the points where lines from points 4, 5, and 6 *perpendicular* to factor axis I′ intersect with factor axis I′. These perpendicular projections of the vectors 4, 5, and 6 on factor axis I′ are referred to as "projections" rather than as "factor loadings" and are equal to the correlations of these data vectors with the factor vector I′. The factor loadings, on the other hand, are the coordinates of vectors 4, 5, and 6 with respect to factor axis I′, values that are not equal to the correlations between the data vectors and the factor axis.

These various relationships are illustrated by a single data vector P_1 in Fig. 6.3, a pair of orthogonal factor axes F_1 and F_2, and a pair of oblique factor axes $F_1′$ and $F_2′$. The coordinates of the data vector P_1 with respect to the orthogonal factor axes F_1 and F_2, respectively, are 0.7 and 0.5, indicated in parentheses after P_1. The coordinates of the factor vectors with respect to vectors F_1 and F_2 as coordinate axes are also given in parentheses following F_1 and F_2 as well as $F_1′$ and $F_2′$.

When it is stated that the coordinates of the data vector P_1 are (.7,.5) with respect to the factor vectors F_1 and F_2, the following is meant:

$$P_1 = .7F_1 + .5F_2 = .7\begin{bmatrix} 1 \\ 0 \end{bmatrix} + .5\begin{bmatrix} 0 \\ 1 \end{bmatrix} = \begin{bmatrix} .7 \\ 0 \end{bmatrix} + \begin{bmatrix} 0 \\ .5 \end{bmatrix} = \begin{bmatrix} .7 \\ .5 \end{bmatrix}$$

$$(6.1)$$

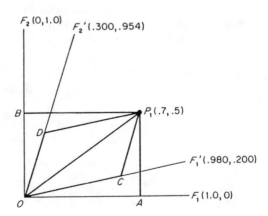

FIG. 6.3.   Oblique corrdinates.

Thus, .7 is multiplied by the coordinates of the vector F_1 and added to .5 multiplied by the coordinates of the vector F_2 to get vector P_1. Thus, P_1 is expressed as a linear combination of the two factor vectors F_1 and F_2, that is, $P_1 = .7F_1 + .5F_2$. The factor vectors F_1 and F_2 are said to provide a "basis" for the two-dimensional space in that any vector in the plane can be expressed as a linear combination of these two vectors. Even F_1 and F_2 can be expressed as a linear combination of the same basis vectors, that is, themselves:

$$F_1 = 1 \begin{bmatrix} 1 \\ 0 \end{bmatrix} + 0 \begin{bmatrix} 0 \\ 1 \end{bmatrix} = \begin{bmatrix} 1 \\ 0 \end{bmatrix}$$

$$F_2 = 0 \begin{bmatrix} 1 \\ 0 \end{bmatrix} + 1 \begin{bmatrix} 0 \\ 1 \end{bmatrix} = \begin{bmatrix} 0 \\ 1 \end{bmatrix} \tag{6.2}$$

or, $F_1 = 1F_1 + 0F_2$ and $F_2 = 0F_1 + 1F_2$. The coordinates, therefore, for F_1 and F_2 are (1,0) and (0,1), respectively, with respect to basis vectors F_1 and F_2, as shown in Fig. 6.3. Because every vector in the plane can be expressed as a linear combination of the two factor vectors F_1 and F_2, the vectors F_1 and F_2 are said to "span" the space of two dimensions represented by this plane.

The coordinates of the vector P_1 with respect to the two orthogonal basis vectors F_1 and F_2 are equal to the perpendicular projections of the vector P_1 on the two factor vectors. Thus, vector coordinates and perpendicular projections of the vectors on the coordinate axes are the same as long as the coordinate axes are at right angles to one another.

It is not necessary, however, to give the coordinates of the data vector P_1 with respect to orthogonal factors such as F_1 and F_2. It is also possible to give the coordinates of vector P_1 with respect to vectors F_1' and F_2', which are not orthogonal. The angle between F_1' and F_2' is not equal to 90°; so these vectors are said to represent "oblique" factor axes.

Both F_1' and F_2' may be expressed as linear combinations of the orthogonal basis vectors F_1 and F_2 as follows:

$$F_1' = .980 \begin{bmatrix} 1 \\ 0 \end{bmatrix} + .200 \begin{bmatrix} 0 \\ 1 \end{bmatrix} = .980F_1 + .200F_2$$

$$F_2' = .300 \begin{bmatrix} 1 \\ 0 \end{bmatrix} + .954 \begin{bmatrix} 0 \\ 1 \end{bmatrix} = .300F_1 + .954F_2 \tag{6.3}$$

The vector P_1 may be expressed as a linear combination of the oblique factor vectors F_1' and F_2' by the equation $P_1 = .592F_1' + .400F_2'$ as follows:

$$P_1 = .592 \begin{bmatrix} .980 \\ .200 \end{bmatrix} + .400 \begin{bmatrix} .300 \\ .954 \end{bmatrix} = \begin{bmatrix} .120 + .580 \\ .118 + .382 \end{bmatrix} = \begin{bmatrix} .7 \\ .5 \end{bmatrix}$$

$$(6.4)$$

Thus, Eq. (6.4) shows that the coordinates of vector P_1 with respect to the basis vectors F_1 and F_2 can be expressed in terms of the coordinates of P_1 with respect to the factor vectors F_1' and F_2' *and* the coordinates of F_1' and F_2' with respect to the basis vectors F_1 and F_2. The values 0.592 and 0.400 are the coordinates (.592,.400) of the vector P_1 with respect to the two oblique factor axes F_1' and F_2'. These two values were computed readily by letting X and Y be the unknown coordinates. Then

$$X \begin{bmatrix} .980 \\ .200 \end{bmatrix} + Y \begin{bmatrix} .300 \\ .954 \end{bmatrix} = \begin{bmatrix} .7 \\ .5 \end{bmatrix}$$

$$(6.5)$$

This gives two equations in two unknowns:

$$.980X + .300Y = .7$$
$$.200X + .954Y = .5 \qquad (6.6)$$

Solving these two linear equations simultaneously gives $X = 0.592$ and $Y = 0.400$, the coordinates of P_1 with respect to F_1' and F_2'. The coordinates of any other vector in the plane can also be determined with respect to factor axes F_1' and F_2' if their coordinates with respect to F_1 and F_2 are known. Thus, any vector in this space of two dimensions can be expressed as a linear combination of the vectors F_1' and F_2'; so these two oblique factor vectors also constitute an adequate set of basis vectors. They, too, span this two-dimensional space.

The coordinates of a data vector with respect to two oblique factor vectors cannot be obtained, however, by dropping perpendiculars to the factor axes and measuring the distance from the origin to these points of intersection. In Fig. 6.3, the line OC has a length equal to .592, the coordinate of vector P_1 with respect to the basis vector F_1'. The line OD has a length of .4 which is equal to the coordinate of P_1 with respect to the basis vector F_2'. The lines OD and P_1C are parallel as are the lines DP_1 and OC. This can be shown by demonstrating that the line CP_1 equals the line OD. This can be proved by showing that the angle COP_1 calculated from the assumption that $CP_1 = OD$ equals the angle COP_1 calculated from the scalar product (see Eq. (2.34)) of vectors P_1 and F_1'. Calculating the scalar product of vectors P_1 and F_1' gives

$$[\,.7 \quad .5\,] \times \begin{bmatrix} .980 \\ \\ .200 \end{bmatrix} = l_1 l_2 \cos\phi$$

where

$l_1 = \sqrt{(.7)^2 + (.5)^2} = \sqrt{.74}$ is the length of vector P_1,

$l_2 = \sqrt{(.980)^2 + (.200)^2} = 1.00$ is the length of vector F_1', and $\cos\phi$
is the cosine of the angle COP_1 in Fig. 6.3.

Substituting these values in Eq. (6.7) and dividing both sides by $l_1 l_2$ gives

$$\cos\phi = \frac{(.7)\,(.980) + (.5)\,(.200)}{2OC \cdot OP_1} = \frac{.686 + .100}{2(.592)\,\sqrt{.74}} = \frac{.786}{\sqrt{.74}}$$

The cosine of ϕ can also be obtained using the law of cosines:

$$\cos\phi = \frac{OC^2 + OP_1^2 - CP_1^2}{2OC \cdot OP_1} = \frac{(.592)^2 + .74 - (.400)^2}{2(.592) \cdot \sqrt{.74}} = \frac{.786}{\sqrt{.74}}$$

$$(6.8)$$

Since the angle COP_1 has the same cosine computed by both Eqs. (6.7) and (6.8), the asserted proposition is established. This means that to obtain the coordinates of a vector P_1 with respect to two factor axes F_1' and F_2', oblique to one another, draw lines through the terminus of P_1 parallel to F_1' and F_2', respectively. The distances from the origin to the points where these parallels intersect the coordinate factor axes F_2' and F_1', respectively, are the coordinates of the vector P_1 with respect to these oblique factor axes.

Dropping a perpendicular line from the point P_1 in Fig. 6.3 to the vector F_1' does *not*, then, give the coordinate of vector P_1 with respect to factor F_1'. Instead, it gives the correlation of the data vector P_1 with the factor vector F_1'. From Eq. (2.35) the following relationship holds:

$$r_{12} = h_1 h_2 \cos\phi \qquad\qquad (6.9)$$

where r_{12} is the correlation between vectors 1 and 2, h_1 and h_2 are the lengths of vectors 1 and 2, and $\cos\phi$ is the cosine of the angle between the vectors. In Fig. 6.3, the cosine of the angle between vector P_1 and factor F_1' is given by X/OP_1, where X is the distance from the origin to the point where a perpendicular projection from P_1 to the vector F_1' would intersect the vector F_1'. Therefore, $X = OP_1 \cos\phi$, where $\cos\phi$ is the cosine of angle COP_1. The length of vector F_1' is $\sqrt{(.980)^2 + (.200)^2} = 1.0$. Substituting these values in Eq. (6.9) gives the result that $X = r_{12}$, where vector 1 is factor vector F_1', vector 2 is data vector P_1, and r_{12} is the correlation between the two; X is, as before, the perpendicular projection of data vector P_1 on factor vector F_1'.

6.1.2. COORDINATES AND FACTOR LOADINGS

The coordinates of a data vector with respect to oblique factor axes are referred to as the "factor loadings" for the data variable with respect to those factors. The term "factor saturations" is used by some authors. The matrix of these factor loadings for all the data variables with respect to the factors has come to be called the "factor pattern" matrix (Harman, 1967).

The matrix of correlations of the data vectors with the oblique factor axes, the perpendicular projections of the data vectors onto the oblique factor axes, correspondingly, has come to be called the "factor structure" matrix. The structure matrix contains the correlations of each data variable with each of the oblique factors. A complete oblique factor solution requires the determination of both the pattern matrix and the structure matrix.

In the orthogonal factor model, the factor axes are all at right angles to one another. In this case, the coordinates of the data vectors with respect to the factor axes and the perpendicular projections of the data vectors onto these factor vectors coincide. Thus, with orthogonal factors, the pattern matrix and the structure matrix are identical. This permits the interpretation of the factor loadings of a data variable with respect to orthogonal factors as though they were correlation coefficients. With oblique factors, the factor loadings cannot be interpreted in this manner. Only elements of a structure matrix may be interpreted as correlations with the oblique factors.

6.2.   REFERENCE VECTOR STRUCTURE

The ultimate objective in oblique rotations is to obtain the data-variable loadings on the oblique factors, that is, the pattern matrix **P**, after the factors have been rotated to a simple structure position. When oblique rotations are being carried out through inspection of plots of factors two at a time, however, it is more convenient to work initially with the "reference vector structure." Once the reference vector structure is found, the final solution matrices may be obtained: the pattern matrix **P**, the structure matrix **S**, and the matrix of correlations among the factors, **Φ**.

The reference vector structure consists of perpendicular projections, or correlations, of the data-variable vectors onto what Thurstone (1947) and Cattell (1952) called "reference vectors." They were called "simple axes" by Fruchter (1954). The reference vector is illustrated in Fig. 6.4. This figure shows an oblique position for factor vectors I and II in which simple structure criteria are well met. In this plot, vector I is the trace of the hyperplane for factor II and vector II is the trace of the hyperplane for factor I.

If Fig. 6.4 were presented as a plot of orthogonal factors I and II', leaving out of the picture the axes I' and II, then vector I would be the trace of the hyperplane, or just "the hyperplane," for factor II', and II' would be the hyperplane for factor I. In this case factor II' would be well positioned because its hyperplane lies along the path of maximum point density. Factor I, on the other hand, would be poorly positioned because its hyperplane, vector II', does not lie along the line of maximum point density. Vector II would be a more appropriate hyperplane for factor I.

The reference vector associated with a given factor is the line from the origin perpendicular to the hyperplane for that factor. In the orthogonal case, with factors I and II' in Fig. 6.4, the reference vector I and the factor vector I coincide, as do reference vector II' and factor vector II'. This is because the factors are at right angles to one another and hence the hyperplanes are at right angles to each other in the orthogonal factor solution. With the oblique factor positions I and II in Fig. 6.4, however, vector I' is the reference vector for factor I since it is perpendicular to the hyperplane for factor I, vector II. Vector II' is the reference vector for factor II since it is perpendicular to the hyperplane for factor II, vector I.

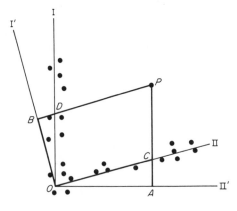

FIG. 6.4. Reference vectors: I' and II' are reference vectors; I and II are factor axes.

If only an orthogonal rotation were to be done for the plot in Fig. 6.4, factor I would be rotated a bit away from factor II', about half-way between the present I and I', and factor II' would be moved toward I' an equivalent amount to maintain orthogonality. This would balance off the two hyperplanes, making the hyperplane for I a bit better and hyperplane for II' a bit worse.

By an oblique rotation in Fig. 6.4, however, it is possible to leave the hyperplane for II' undisturbed, moving only the hyperplane for factor I. This is accomplished by rotating the reference vector for I to position I', pulling the hyperplane at right angles to the referece vector to position II where it lies along the path of maximum point density. Vector II' is now the reference vector for factor II, perpendicular to the hyperplane for factor II, which is vector I.

The perpendicular projections of the data vectors on these reference vectors I' and II' are found by dropping perpendiculars from the data points to these axes and measuring the distances from the origin to the points of intersection. In Fig. 6.4, for example, OB is the projection of data vector OP on reference vector I' and OA is the projection of data vector OP on reference vector II'. These projections are also the correlations of the data vectors with the reference vectors.

If the orthogonal factor positions I and II' were being rotated in Fig. 6.4 to new orthogonal positions I' and II, respectively, the rotation would be carried out as follows:

$$
\begin{array}{cc}
\text{I} \quad \text{II}' \\
\begin{bmatrix} a_{11} & a_{12} \\ a_{21} & a_{22} \\ \cdots & \cdots \\ a_{n1} & a_{n2} \end{bmatrix}
\end{array}
\times
\begin{bmatrix} \cos\phi & \sin\phi \\ -\sin\phi & \cos\phi \end{bmatrix}
=
\begin{array}{cc}
\text{I}' \quad \text{II} \\
\begin{bmatrix} a'_{11} & a'_{12} \\ a'_{21} & a'_{22} \\ \cdots & \cdots \\ a'_{n1} & a'_{n2} \end{bmatrix}
\end{array}
$$

$$\mathbf{V}_i \qquad\qquad \Lambda_{i+1} \qquad\qquad \mathbf{V}_{i+1} \qquad\qquad (6.10)$$

In this case, the column of values I' in matrix $\mathbf{V}_{i+1}$ would be perpendicular projections of the data vectors on orthogonal factor vector I', and the values in column II of matrix $\mathbf{V}_{i+1}$ would be the perpendicular projections of the data vectors on orthogonal factor vector II.

In doing an oblique rotation of reference vector I to position I' in Fig. 6.4, however, the reference vector for factor II is not moved. The projections of the data vectors on reference vector II' would remain unchanged. Only the projections on reference vector I would change. The projections of the data vectors on reference vector I' are the same as those found in column I' of the matrix $\mathbf{V}_{i+1}$ in Eq. (6.10). Rotating one reference vector, then, is like doing half an orthogonal rotation, using only half of the Λ_i transformation matrix. Multiplying matrix $\mathbf{V}_i$ in Eq. (6.10) by the left column of matrix

Λ_{i+1} produces the new column I' in matrix V_{i+1}. If the right-hand column of Λ_{i+1} were 0 in λ_{12} and 1 in λ_{22}, then column II of V_{i+1} would be the same as column II' of matrix V_i.

Carrying out an oblique rotation of one reference vector, then, involves changing one column of the transformation matrix. To illustrate this operation, suppose that orthogonal rotations for a given problem had been carried as far as possible and had given the results $V_0 = A\Lambda_0$, where V_0 is the final orthogonal rotated matrix, A is the matrix of unrotated loadings, and Λ_0 is the cumulated transformation matrix that carries out all the orthogonal rotations at once. Then, consider the rotation of reference vector I to position I' in Fig. 6.4 to be the first oblique rotation to be performed. Assume that there are four factors. The rotation can be performed by obtaining a new L matrix with an altered column 1 to reflect the oblique rotation of reference vector I. This matrix operation is shown in matrix equation (6.11).

$$
\begin{bmatrix}
\lambda_{11}' & \lambda_{12}' & \lambda_{13}' & \lambda_{14}' \\
\lambda_{21}' & \lambda_{22}' & \lambda_{23}' & \lambda_{24}' \\
\lambda_{31}' & \lambda_{32}' & \lambda_{33}' & \lambda_{34}' \\
\lambda_{41}' & \lambda_{42}' & \lambda_{43}' & \lambda_{44}'
\end{bmatrix}
=
\begin{bmatrix}
\lambda_{11} & \lambda_{12} & \lambda_{13} & \lambda_{14} \\
\lambda_{21} & \lambda_{22} & \lambda_{23} & \lambda_{24} \\
\lambda_{31} & \lambda_{32} & \lambda_{33} & \lambda_{34} \\
\lambda_{41} & \lambda_{42} & \lambda_{43} & \lambda_{44}
\end{bmatrix}
$$

$$\Lambda_1 \qquad\qquad\qquad \Lambda_0$$

$$
\times
\begin{bmatrix}
\cos\phi & 0 & 0 & 0 \\
-\sin\phi & 1 & 0 & 0 \\
0 & 0 & 1 & 0 \\
0 & 0 & 0 & 1
\end{bmatrix}
$$

$$\Theta \qquad\qquad (6.11)$$

The angle ϕ in matrix I is the angle of rotation of I away from II'. The sine of v has a negative sign because I is being rotated away from II'. If it were being rotated toward II', the sine of ϕ would be positive. The multiplication of Λ_0 by Θ changes only column 1, leaving Λ_1 and Λ_0 identical except for the elements of the first columns. The elements of column 1 of Λ_1 are given by

$$\lambda_{11}' = \lambda_{11}\cos\phi - \lambda_{12}\sin\phi$$

$$\lambda_{21}' = \lambda_{21}\cos\phi - \lambda_{22}\sin\phi$$

$$\lambda_{31}' = \lambda_{31}\cos\phi - \lambda_{32}\sin\phi \qquad (6.12)$$

$$\lambda_{41}' = \lambda_{41}\cos\phi - \lambda_{42}\sin\phi$$

Squaring both sides of Eq. (6.12) and adding them up gives

$$\lambda_{11}'^2 + \lambda_{21}'^2 + \lambda_{31}'^2 + \lambda_{41}'^2 =$$

$$\lambda_{11}^2 cos^2\phi + \lambda_{12}^2 sin^2\phi - 2\lambda_{11}\lambda_{12}sin\phi cos\phi +$$

$$\lambda_{21}^2 cos^2\phi + \lambda_{22}^2 sin^2\phi - 2\lambda_{21}\lambda_{22}sin\phi cos\phi +$$

$$\lambda_{31}^2 cos^2\phi + \lambda_{32}^2 sin^2\phi - 2\lambda_{31}\lambda_{32}sin\phi cos\phi +$$

$$\lambda_{41}^2 cos^2\phi + \lambda_{42}^2 sin^2\phi - 2\lambda_{41}\lambda_{42}sin\phi cos\phi$$

which simplifies to

$$\lambda_{11}'^2 + \lambda_{21}'^2 + \lambda_{31}'^2 + \lambda_{41}'^2 =$$

$$(\lambda_{11}^2 + \lambda_{21}^2 + \lambda_{31}^2 + \lambda_{41}^2)cos^2\phi +$$

$$(\lambda_{12}^2 + \lambda_{22}^2 + \lambda_{32}^2 + \lambda_{42}^2)sin^2\phi -$$

$$2(\lambda_{11}\lambda_{12} + \lambda_{21}\lambda_{22} + \lambda_{31}\lambda_{32} + \lambda_{41}\lambda_{42})sin\phi cos\phi$$

Because the sum of squares of the columns of Λ_0 equals 1.0 and the inner products of the columns of Λ_0 equal zero, the preceding equation reduces to

$$\lambda_{11}'^2 + \lambda_{21}'^2 + \lambda_{31}'^2 + \lambda_{41}'^2 = cos2\phi + sin^2\phi - 2(0)sin\phi cos\phi = 1$$

The first column of values in the Λ_1 matrix, therefore, has a sum of squares equal to 1.0; that is, the column is "normalized." The λ_{i1} values in this column are the direction cosines of the rotated reference vector with respect to the unrotated factor axes in matrix **A**. Any such set of direction cosines must have a sum of squares equal to 1.0.

That the columns of the transformation matrix Λ give the direction cosines of the rotated orthogonal factors with the original unrotated factors can be shown as follows. First, it has been shown in the last chapter that multiplying **A** by Λ gives the correlations of the data vectors with the rotated orthogonal factors. For data variable 1 and rotated factor I, this would be

$$r_{1I} = a_{11}\lambda_{11} + a_{12}\lambda_{21} + \cdots + a_{1m}\lambda_{m1} \tag{6.13}$$

But by Eq. (2.35),

$$r_{ij} = h_i h_j cos\phi_{ij}$$

and since factor vector I has length 1.0,

$$r_{1I} = h_1 cos\phi_{1I} \tag{6.14}$$

The a_{1i} values in Eq. (6.13) are projections of the data vector 1 on the unrotated factor vectors. If the angle of the data vector 1 with unrotated factor vector I is ϕ, then $\cos\phi = a_{11}/h_1$ where h_1 is the length of data vector 1 and $a_{11} = h_1\cos\phi$. Letting δ_{1i} be the cosine of the angle of the data vector 1 with unrotated factor i, Eq. (6.13) can be rewritten as:

$$r_{1I} = h_1\delta_{11}\lambda_{11} + h_1\delta_{12}\lambda_{21} + h_1\delta_{13}\lambda_{31} + \cdots + h_1\delta_{1m}\lambda_{m1} \tag{6.15}$$

$$r_{1I} = h_1(\delta_{11}\lambda_{11} + \delta_{12}\lambda_{21} + \delta_{13}\lambda_{31} + \cdots + \delta_{1m}\lambda_{m1}) \tag{6.16}$$

Using Eqs. (6.14) and (6.16) and canceling h_1 on both sides gives

$$\cos\phi_{1I} = (\delta_{11}\lambda_{11} + \delta_{12}\lambda_{21} + \delta_{13}\lambda_{31} + \cdots + \delta_{1m}\lambda_{m1}) \tag{6.17}$$

The cosine of the angle between data vector 1 and rotated factor vector I is the inner product of the δ_{1i} values and the column of λ_{i1} values from Λ. The δ_{1i} values are the direction cosines of the data-variable vector with the original unrotated factors. It was stated in Chapter 2 that the cosine of the angle between two vectors is the inner product of the direction cosines. Because the δ_{1i} values are the direction cosines of the data-variable vector with the original unrotated factors, the λ_{i1} values in Eq. (6.17) equal the direction cosines of the rotated factor vector I with respect to the same unrotated factor vectors.

With orthogonal factors, then, the Λ matrix that transforms unrotated factor loadings to rotated factor loadings has columns that represent direction cosines of the rotated factors with respect to the original unrotated factors. In oblique rotations of the matrix of reference vectors, columns of the matrix of projections on the axes are altered one at a time instead of two at a time, as in orthogonal rotations. This is accomplished through modification of the Λ matrix one column at a time. As the ith column of Λ is altered, the ith column of the rotated matrix is changed in the equation $\mathbf{V}_i = \mathbf{A}\Lambda_i$ where Λ_i includes all the rotations up to this one, orthogonal plus oblique. The matrix Λ_i is altered to Λ_{i+1} and $\mathbf{V}_i$ is altered to $\mathbf{V}_{i+1}$ to incorporate the current rotation.

6.2.1.   OBLIQUE ROTATION OF A REFERENCE VECTOR

A convenient way of changing one column of the Λ matrix to rotate one reference vector is a procedure described by Cattell (1952) that is equivalent to the multiplication of Λ by a matrix that is an identity matrix except for the column being changed. This process has already been illustrated in Eq.

(6.11). To illustrate the equivalent process recommended by Cattell, we begin with the following equation:

$$\mathbf{I'} = \mathbf{I} \Lambda \pm \tan\phi \cdot \mathbf{II} \tag{6.18}$$

where $\mathbf{I}$ represents the first column of Λ before the rotation and $\mathbf{II}$ is the second column of Λ before the rotation. In this case, vector $\mathbf{I}$ is being rotated with respect to vector $\mathbf{II}$ by an angle ϕ. If $\mathbf{I}$ is rotated *toward* $\mathbf{II}$, the plus sign is used in Eq. (6.18). If $\mathbf{I}$ is being rotated *away from* $\mathbf{II}$, the minus sign will be used in Eq. (6.18). The term $\mathbf{I'}$ represents the new column $\mathbf{I}$ of Λ *before* the column of values has been normalized. That is, the sum of squares of the values in $\mathbf{I'}$ will not usually equal 1.0. Every column of Λ must have a sum of squares equal to 1.0, because these values are the direction cosines of the rotated factor with the original factors. These values are made to have a sum of squares equal to 1.0 by "normalizing" them. To normalize the $\mathbf{I'}$ values, take the sum of squares of the values in column $\mathbf{I'}$, take the square root of this total, and divide each element of $\mathbf{I'}$ by this square root. The sum of squares of the resulting values will equal 1.0. These normalized values will replace the previous column 1 of the Λ matrix.

In Eq. (6.18), the roman numeral of whatever reference vector is being rotated is placed where the $\mathbf{I}$ is now placed. The roman numeral of the reference vector it is being rotated with goes where the $\mathbf{II}$ is now placed. The unnormalized new column of Λ goes where $\mathbf{I'}$ now is placed. The normalized values will then replace the proper column of the Λ matrix. If reference vector $\mathbf{II}$ is being rotated, for example, then column 2 of the Λ is changed. In multiplying the original unrotated factor matrix by this new Λ matrix, only the column of the rotated matrix that corresponds to the altered column of the Λ matrix will be altered.

That the procedure indicated in Eq. (6.18) is equivalent to the procedure describe in Eq. (6.11) may be shown as follows. The procedure in Eq. (6.18) is equivalent to altering the Λ matrix by the following matrix multiplication:

$$
\begin{bmatrix}
\lambda_{11} & \lambda_{12} & \lambda_{13} & \lambda_{14} \\
\lambda_{21} & \lambda_{22} & \lambda_{23} & \lambda_{24} \\
\lambda_{31} & \lambda_{32} & \lambda_{33} & \lambda_{34} \\
\lambda_{41} & \lambda_{42} & \lambda_{43} & \lambda_{44}
\end{bmatrix}
\times
\begin{bmatrix}
1 & 0 & 0 & 0 \\
\pm\tan\phi & 1 & 0 & 0 \\
0 & 0 & 1 & 0 \\
0 & 0 & 0 & 0
\end{bmatrix}
$$

$$\Lambda \qquad\qquad\qquad\qquad \Theta' \tag{6.19}$$

If the matrix Θ' on the right of Eq. (6.19) is normalized, only the values in the first column need to be changed since the other three columns already are normalized. Taking the sum of squares of the entries in the first column of $\mathbf{I'}$, taking the square root of this total, and dividing the elements of the first column of Θ' by this square root gives the values $1/\sqrt{1 + \tan^2\phi}$ and $\pm\tan\phi/\sqrt{1 + \tan^2\phi}$ in the first two rows with zeros in the last two rows as before. These two values reduce trigonometrically, however, to the cosine and $\pm$ sine of ϕ, respectively, and hence the normalized Θ' matrix is equivalent to the Θ matrix in Eq. (6.11). The more convenient procedure using Eq. (6.18) will be used, therefore, in making oblique rotations of the reference vectors.

6.3. OBLIQUE ROTATION OF THE 12-VARIABLE PROBLEM

To illustrate these procedures, the 12-variable problem treated in the last chapter will be rotated to oblique simple structure. The point of departure for the oblique rotations is the final orthogonal solution shown in Table 5.7. It is best to rotate orthogonally as far as possible toward simple structure before attempting any oblique rotations. If oblique rotations are made early in the rotation process, a greater degree of obliquity may be introduced than is actually necessary to achieve simple structure. In the interest of keeping factor constructs as independent of one another as possible, angles between factors are kept as close to 90° as possible while bringing the factors to simple structure positions. As factors become more oblique to each other, they overlap each other more and more in what they represent, introducing redundancy into the system of constructs.

Results from orthogonal rotations of the factors in the 12-variable problem suggested that factor I might require oblique rotation with both factors III and IV. Plots of the final orthogonal factors I with III and IV are shown in Fig. 6.5. These plots are based on the factor loadings in Table 5.7. The plot of factor I with factor III is shown twice in Fig. 6.5 to allow presentation of one oblique rotation on each graph for the sake of clarity. Both oblique rotations could be shown on the same graph, but the profusion of lines would be confusing.

In the first plot of factor I with factor III in Fig. 6.5, reference vector I is moved to position I_4 from the original final orthogonal position at I_3. By rotating I away from III in this fashion, the three points to the right side of the graph are brought into the hyperplane of I_4. This is the whole purpose of this rotation. The reference vector I_4 is actually further from the points with high projections on this reference vector than was I_3, so the rotation has *not* been to bring reference vector I closer to a cluster of points high on I. Since this is the first oblique rotation, for the first time reference vector I and factor I will no longer coincide. Until a reference vector is rotated obliquely with some other reference vector, it will coincide with its associated factor vector.

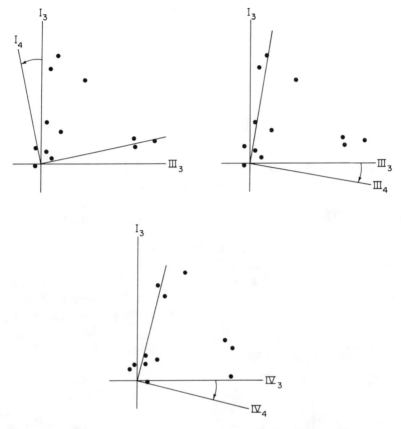

FIG. 6.5.   First series of oblique rotations for the 12-variable problem.

The calculations for altering Λ, the final orthogonal transformation matrix, to include this first oblique rotation are as follows:

$$\mathbf{I}' = \mathbf{I} - \tan\phi \cdot \mathbf{III} \tag{6.20}$$

$$\lambda'_{11} = .711 - .2(.439) = .711 - .088 = .623$$

$$\lambda'_{21} = .057 - .2(-.237) = .057 + .047 = .104$$

$$\lambda'_{31} = -.201 - .2(.845) = -.201 - .169 = -.370$$

$$\lambda'_{41} = -.671 - .2(.192) = -.671 - .038 = -.709 \tag{6.21}$$

Summing the squares of the λ'_{i1} values in Eqs. (6.21) gives $0.3881 + 0.0108 + 0.1369 + 0.5027 = 1.0385$. The square root of 1.0385 is 1.019.

Multiplying each λ'_{i1} value in Eqs. (6.21) by $1/1.019$ gives the normalized λ_{i1} values in column 1 of the Λ_1 matrix in Table 6.1. The calculations for the oblique rotation in Fig. 6.5 are shown in Table 6.1.

In Eqs. (6.21) the first column of values, $\mathbf{I'}$, the λ'_{i1} values, are the unnormalized first column transformation matrix values. The values in the $\mathbf{I}$ column are taken from the first column of the Λ matrix in Table 5.7, the final orthogonal transformation matrix, and the values in parentheses are the values from column 3 of the same Λ matrix in Table 5.7. The value 0.2 is the tangent of the angle of rotation of I and III in Fig. 6.5. The 0.2 value for the tangent has a minus sign before it because I is rotated away from rather than toward III. If I were rotated toward III by this same angle, the tangent would have a plus sign placed in front of it.

The second plot in Fig. 6.5 shows the rotation of reference vector III away from reference vector I by an angle whose tangent is 0.17. This rotation moves the reference vector away from the cluster of points with high loadings, which again demonstrates that simple structure rotations are made to improve hyperplanes rather than to move reference vectors toward clusters. The hyperplane perpendicular to reference vector position III_4 is better located than it was in the original position perpendicular to III_3 (see Fig. 6.5). The calculations for getting the new column III of the Λ matrix to make this rotation are as follows:

$$\mathbf{III'} = \mathbf{III} - .17(\mathbf{I})$$

$$\lambda'_{13} = .439 - .17(.711) = .318$$

$$\lambda'_{23} = -.237 - .17(.057) = -.247$$

$$\lambda'_{33} = -.845 - .17(-.201) = .879 \qquad (6.22)$$

$$\lambda'_{43} = .192 - .17(-.671) = .306$$

TABLE 6.1

Calculations for the First Series of Oblique Rotations

	I	II	III	IV		I	II	III	IV		I	II	III	IV
1	.080	.846	.160	−.046							.109	.858	−.056	.016
2	.011	.707	.101	.048							.009	.708	−.066	.079
3	.037	.652	.221	−.100							.079	.687	.014	−.086
4	.544	.099	−.287	.261		I	II	III	IV		.265	.018	−.023	.531
5	.589	.157	−.180	.366		.611	.000	.314	.360		.187	.103	.101	.605
6	.435	.098	−.212	.482	×	.102	.963	−.243	.099	=	.017	.037	.074	.655
7	.563	−.006	−.161	−.339		−.363	.270	.867	−.355		.638	−.049	−.064	−.031
8	.661	.013	.076	−.205		−.696	.000	.302	.857		.520	.033	.208	.037
9	.758	.023	−.210	−.230			Λ_1				.702	−.035	−.019	.153
10	.431	−.174	.506	.045							.031	−.031	.630	−.003
11	.537	−.197	.591	.152							−.012	−.030	.775	.095
12	.370	−.281	.522	.052							−.028	−.130	.653	−.035
			A										V_1	

The sum of squares of the unnormalized λ'_{i3} values in Eqs. (6.22) is 1.0284 and the square root is 1.014. Multiplying the λ'_{i3} values in Eqs. (6.22) by 1/1.014 gives the λ_{i3} values in Table 6.1, which shows the calculations for the oblique rotation of factor III. These normalized values are shown in the third column of the Λ_1 matrix in Table 6.1.

Computations for the new column **IV** of the Λ_1 matrix to rotate reference vector IV away from reference vector I are made in the same way, that is, **IV′** = **IV** - .25(**I**) to give the unnormalized column of values λ'_{i4}. These λ'_{i4} values are then normalized, giving the fourth column of Λ_1 as shown in Table 6.1.

Multiplication of the original unrotated matrix by the new transformation matrix Λ_1 gives the new matrix of projections on the oblique reference vectors, as shown in Table 6.1. Reference vectors I, III, and IV were rotated obliquely, while II was left unchanged. Thus, columns I, III, and IV of matrix V_1 in Table 6.1 are different from the corresponding columns of the final orthogonal solution, matrix V of Table 5.7, while column II remains identical in the two matrices.

After the oblique reference vector projections in matrix V_1 have been calculated by the equation $V_1 = A_1'\Lambda_1$, as shown in Table 6.1, the matrix of correlations among the reference vectors C must be calculated as follows:

$$C = \Lambda_1'\Lambda_1 \tag{6.23}$$

In Eq. (6.23), the transpose of the transformation matrix is multiplied by the transformation matrix itself to get the matrix of correlations among the reference vectors. Each row of Λ_1' in Eq. (6.23) is a row of direction cosines for a reference vector, as is each column of Λ_1. Hence a row of Λ_1' inner multiplied with a column of Λ_1 gives the inner product of direction cosines for two vectors, which is a correlation between the two vectors. It is important to avoid the mistake of multiplying Λ_1 times Λ_1' because this reversed order of multiplying the matrices does not give a matrix of correlations among the reference vectors.

The C matrix for the 12-variable problem after the first series of oblique rotations of the reference vectors is shown in Table 6.2. When the reference vectors in matrix V_1 of Table 6.1 are plotted with each other, the correlation between the two reference vectors is indicated on the plot to keep the investigator advised of the actual degree of obliquity present. This is kept in mind in planning further rotations, primarily to avoid allowing the axes to become too highly correlated with each other. If the axes are allowed to become too highly oblique with each other, two hyperplanes will collapse into one and a factor will be lost.

After the first series of oblique rotations, a new series of plots is made in order to look for additional oblique rotations. Even though the reference

TABLE 6.2

Correlations between Reference Vectors After the First Series of Oblique Rotations

	I	II	III	IV
I	1.000	.001	−.358	−.237
II	.001	1.000	.000	−.001
III	−.358	.000	1.000	.040
IV	−.237	−.001	.040	1.000
		$\Lambda_1'\Lambda_1$		

vectors are not at right angles to each other, they are plotted as if they were because it is difficult to make plots with axes at angles to each other different from 90°. In practice, the angles of rotation chosen are little affected by plotting these oblique axes at right angles to each other.

Inspection of the available plots of the oblique reference vectors in matrix V_1 of Table 6.1 with each other produces one additional oblique rotation that will make a noticeable improvement in the oblique simple structure. This last oblique rotation is shown in Fig. 6.6. Reference vector I is moved away from reference vector IV by an angle whose tangent is 0.2. Calculations for modifying column 1 of the transformation matrix Λ_1 to make this rotation are shown below:

$$\mathbf{I'} = \mathbf{I} - .2(\mathbf{IV})$$

$$\lambda'_{11} = .611 - .2(.360) = .611 - .072 = .539$$

$$\lambda'_{21} = .102 - .2(.099) = .102 - .020 = .082$$

$$\lambda'_{31} = -.363 - .2(-.355) = -.363 + .071 = -.292 \tag{6.24}$$

$$\lambda'_{41} = -.696 - .2(.857) = -.696 - .171 = -.867$$

Normalizing these λ'_{i1} values gives the λ_{i1} values found in the first column of the final Λ matrix shown in Table 6.3. Only column 1 of Λ_1 is changed to obtain the final Λ; so only column 1 of V, the final matrix of rotated oblique reference vector projections, is different from the corresponding column of matrix V_1, Table 6.1.

In Table 6.3, the matrix A contains the original unrotated factor loadings. Matrix Λ is the transformation matrix that contains the effects of all orthogonal and oblique rotations performed. The columns of Λ are the direction cosines of the reference vectors with respect to the original unrotated factor axes. The V matrix in Table 6.3 contains the perpendicular projections of the data vectors on the oblique reference vectors. These

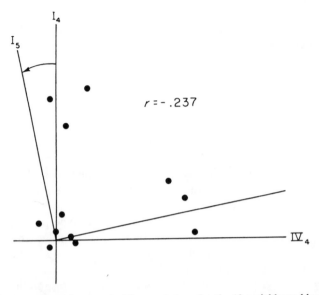

FIG. 6.6.   Second series of oblique rotations for the 12-variable problem.

values may be interpreted as correlations of the data-variable vectors with the oblique reference vectors.

Table 6.4 contains the matrix of correlations **C** among the final oblique reference vectors. The matrix is symmetric, since $r_{12} = r_{21}$, and has values of 1.0 in the diagonals, since the correlation of a reference vector with itself is 1.0. The correlations of reference vector I with reference vectors III and IV are negative, indicating an angle of greater than 90° between them. It should be noted that where the reference vectors are correlated negatively,

TABLE 6.3

Final Oblique Reference Vector Structure for the 12-Variable Problem

	I	II	III	IV			I	II	III	IV			I	II	III	IV
1	.080	.846	−.160	−.046									.099	.858	−.056	.016
2	.011	.707	.101	.048									−.007	.708	−.066	.079
3	.037	.652	.221	−.100									.090	.687	.015	−.086
4	.544	.099	−.287	.261				I	II	III	IV		.149	.018	−.023	.531
5	.589	.157	−.180	.366				.506	.000	.314	.360		.061	.103	.101	.605
6	.435	.098	−.212	.482	×			.077	.963	−.243	.099	=	−.107	.037	.075	.655
7	.563	−.006	−.161	−.339				−.274	.270	.867	−.355		.605	−.049	−.064	−.031
8	.661	.013	.076	−.205				−.814	.000	.302	.857		.482	.033	.208	.037
9	.758	.023	−.210	−.230						Λ			.630	−.035	−.019	.153
10	.431	−.174	.506	.045									.029	−.031	.630	−.003
11	.537	−.197	.591	.152									−.029	−.030	.775	.094
12	.370	−.281	.522	.052									−.020	−.130	.653	−.035
		A												**V**		

TABLE 6.4

Final Matrix of Correlations among Reference Vectors for the 12-Variable Problem

	I	II	III	IV
I	1.000	.000	−.343	−.411
II	.000	1.000	.000	−.001
III	−.343	.000	1.000	.040
IV	−.411	−.001	.040	1.000

$$C = \Lambda'\Lambda$$

the correlations between the factor axes associated with those reference vectors will be positive. If the reference vectors are correlated positively, the associated factor axes will, in general, be correlated negatively.

The factor axes coincide with the intersections of hyperplanes. If any two such lines of intersection have an angle between them of less than 90°, then the angle between the corresponding reference vectors must be greater than 90°, yielding a negative correlation. If the lines of intersecting hyperplanes are at an angle greater than 90°, however, the corresponding reference vectors must have an angle between them of less than 90°.

The plots of the final reference vectors are shown in Fig. 6.7. Although some slight further improvements could be made, for example, moving II toward III by a small angle of rotation, the plots shown in Fig. 6.7 exhibit a reasonable approximation to simple structure that is clearly better than for the orthogonal factors in Fig. 5.4. No excessively large correlations between reference vectors were needed to reach this structure. The correlations between reference vectors should be kept as low as possible consistent with reaching simple structure positions. Values less than 0.5 should be preferred and rarely should a value larger than 0.6 be permitted.

When a correlation between reference vectors is negative, rotating one vector away from the other will merely increase the size of the negative correlation. A rotation of one vector toward the other under these circumstances will reduce the size of the negative correlation. With a positive correlation between vectors, rotating one reference vector toward the other makes the correlation higher and rotating one vector away from the other reduces the size of the correlation. When reference vectors have substantial correlations between them, rotations that reduce the absolute size of the correlation, while at the same time improving simple structure, are particularly welcome.

All the oblique rotations executed for the 12-variable problem involved moving one reference vector away from the other. This was an accidental phenomenon caused by the fact that the factors represented by these 12 variables are either correlated positively or not at all. This means that the reference vectors will be correlated negatively where the factors are

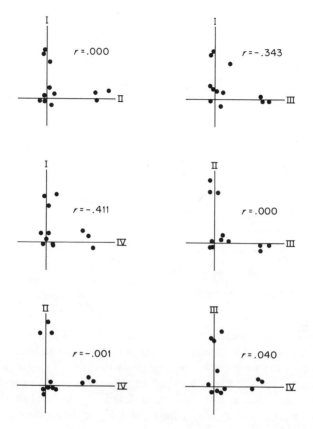

FIG. 6.7.   Plots of final reference vectors.

correlated positively. If the small rotation of reference vector II toward reference vector III were carried out, the new column II of the Λ matrix would be obtained by using the equation $\mathbf{II'} = \mathbf{II} + \mathbf{0.05(III)}$ and normalizing the λ'_{2i} values from $\mathbf{II'}$. Notice that the tangent of ϕ, 0.05, multiplied by λ_{i3} is *added* rather than subtracted because the rotation of $\mathbf{II}$ is toward rather than away from $\mathbf{III}$.

The reference vector projections in matrix $\mathbf{V}$ of Table 6.3 are not the factor loadings required for a complete factor analytic solution, although they are proportional to the factor loadings and hence are perfectly correlated with them. This can be seen in Fig. 6.8 where F_1 and F_2 are factor vectors that are the hyperplanes for the reference vectors RV_1 and RV_2, respectively. The horizontal lines from the data points are perpendiculars that intersect RV_1 at distances from the origin which equal the reference vector projections. The factor loadings on factor F_1 are the distances from the origin to the points where these horizontal lines intersect the axis F_1.

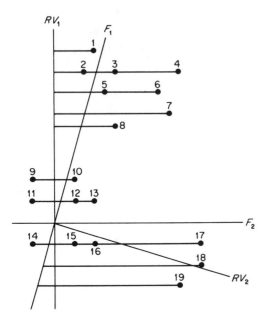

FIG. 6.8.   Correlations between factor loadings and refernce vector projections.

Point 1 has the highest value in both. Points 2, 3, and 4 are tied for the next highest reference vector projections on RV_1 and factor loadings on F_1. Points 5 and 6 are tied for the next position in the rank order, and so on, down to point 19 which has the largest negative reference vector projection on RV_1 and factor loading on F_1. The rank order is identical for the points, whether reference vector projections on RV_1 are considered, or factor loadings on F_1.

Because of the identical rank order in size of reference vector projections and factor loadings, investigators have often presented the matrices **R, A,** Λ, **V,** and **C** as the solution to an oblique factor analysis, failing to compute the factor pattern, factor structure, and matrix of correlations among the factors. This was particularly apt to be the case prior to the widespread availability of computers because the extra calculations needed to obtain these additional matrices represent a significant burden if the work is done on a desk or hand-held calculator. With computers readily available, however, there is little reason to omit these additional matrices from the final factor solution.

6.4.   OBTAINING THE ADDITIONAL MATRICES Φ, S, AND P

Consider the schematic matrix operation in Fig. 6.9, an adaptation of a similar figure presented by Thurstone (1947, p. 349). Ignoring, for the

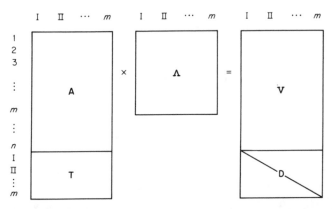

FIG. 6.9. Projections on oblique reference vectors: Rows of **A** are projections of data vectors on orthogonal unrotated factors; rows of **T** are direction cosines of oblique factor vectors with the unrotated factors and also projections of the oblique factor vectors on the unrotated factors; columns of Λ are direction cosines of oblique reference vectors with the unrotated factors; rows of **V** are projections of data vectors on the oblique reference vectors; rows of **D** are projections of oblique factor vectors on the oblique reference vectors. (Adapted from *Multiple factor analysis*, by L. L. Thurstone, Chicago, 1947, by permission of The University of Chicago Press).

moment, the bottom part **T** of the matrix on the left and the bottom part **D** of the matrix on the right, this operation is just the $A\Lambda = V$ of Table 6.3 that produced the final reference vector structure **V** by multiplying the matrix of unrotated loadings **A** by the oblique transformation matrix Λ. The columns of Λ are the direction cosines of the reference vectors with respect to the unrotated factors in matrix **A**. The sums of squares of each column of Λ equal 1.0.

The rows of **A** are projections of the data vectors on the unrotated factor vectors, that is, correlations with the unrotated factors. Since $r_{ij} = h_i h_j \cos\phi_{ij}$ where r_{ij} is the correlation between vectors i and j, h_i and h_j are the lengths of vectors i, and j, and $\cos\phi_{ij}$ is the cosine of the angle between vectors i and j, the values in a row of **A** equal $h_i \cos\phi_{ij}$ where h_i is the length of the data vector i, and j is the factor vector with length equal to 1.0. The sums of squares of the rows of **A** are the communalities h_i^2, the squared lengths of the data vectors.

Let the rows of **T** represent the projections of the oblique rotated factor vectors on the original unrotated factor vectors, that is, the correlations between the oblique rotated factor vectors and the orthogonal unrotated factor vectors. These rows in **T** of Fig. 6.9 may be considered to represent additional data vectors added to the matrix of unrotated loadings **A**. The rows of **T** have sums of squares equal to 1.0 rather than communalities less than 1.0, however, because the rotated factor vectors have unit length, as do both the unrotated factor vectors and the reference vectors.

Since the rotated factor vectors that are represented by the rows of **T** in Fig. 6.9 have unit length and the unrotated factor vectors have unit length, the correlations between these two sets of factors are given by

$$r_{ij} = h_i h_j \cos\phi_{ij} = (1.0)(1.0)\cos\phi_{ij} = \cos\phi_{ij}$$

The values in each row of matrix **T**, therefore, are also the direction cosines of the oblique rotated factor vectors with respect to the orthogonal unrotated factor vectors. Row i of matrix **T** and column j of matrix Λ, therefore, represent direction cosines of factor vector i and reference vector j, respectively. Where $i=j$, they are the factor vector and reference vector that correspond to each other in the oblique solution.

Multiplying **A** by Λ gives a matrix in which the columns consist of the projections of the data vectors on the reference vectors. Since the rows of matrix **T** in Fig. 6.9 consist of projections of rotated factor vectors on the unrotated factor vectors in **A**, multiplying **T** by Λ will produce a matrix **D** for which the columns consist of projections of the rotated factor vectors on the same reference vectors.

The matrix **D** will be a diagonal matrix, however, because a factor vector has zero projections on every reference vector except the one with which it is associated. Thus, oblique factor vector I projects only on reference vector I, factor II projects only on reference vector II, and so on. This leaves nonzero entries only in the diagonal cells of **D**. These relationships can be seen more clearly by reference to Fig. 6.10 in which one reference vector has been rotated obliquely, from OG toward OA to position OH, by an angle whose tangent is 0.2. The hyperplane perpendicular to reference vector OH, which is really only a plane when three factors are represented, is the plane $OCJI$. This plane is shown in dotted lines except for the line OC where plane $OCJI$ intersects plane $OCBA$.

The factors are the intersections of the hyperplanes. Before the oblique rotation of the reference vector, the three hyperplanes in Fig. 6.10 were $OCBA$, $OADG$, and $OCFG$. The intersections of these hyperplanes, that is, the factors, were the lines OA, OC, and OG. In the orthogonal system, the reference vectors perpendicular to the hyperplanes were coincident with the factors, that is, OA, OC, and OG.

After the rotation of the reference vector OG toward reference vector OA, however, arriving at position OH, the hyperplane perpendicular to OH has been tipped below plane $OCBA$, rotating around axis OC. The line OI is in the plane $OADG$ still because OH is in the plane of $OADG$. The rotation was performed in the plot of factor OG with factor OA; OA is the trace of the hyperplane for OG in the plane $OADG$ and OI is the trace of the hyperplane for reference vector OH in plane $OADG$.

After the rotation of OG to OH, then, the intersections of the hyper-

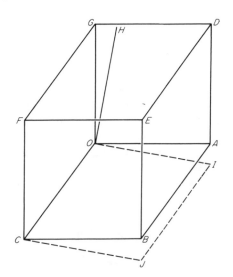

FIG. 6.10. Oblique hyperplanes
and reference vectors.

planes, and hence the factors, are the lines *OI*, *OC*, and *OG*. The reference
vectors corresponding to these factors are *OA*, *OC*, and *OH*. The reference
vector *OC* still coincides with factor *OC* because the oblique rotation took
place only in the plane perpendicular to *OC*. The hyperplanes perpendicular
to the reference vectors, then, are *OCFG*, *OADG*, and *OCJI*.

Now, it is apparent that a factor projects only on its own reference
vector. It is orthogonal to all other reference vectors. Factor *OI* projects on
reference vector *OA*, but it is orthogonal to reference vectors *OC* and *OH*.
Factor *OG* projects on reference vector *OH* but is orthogonal to reference
vectors *OA* and *OC*. Finally, reference vector *OC* projects on factor *OC*
(actually coincides with it) but is at right angles to reference vectors *OH* and
OA.

Note that the angle between reference vectors *OH* and *OA* is less than
90°, giving a positive correlation between these reference vectors, but that
the angle between their associated factors, *OI* and *OG*, is greater than 90°,
leading to a negative correlation between the factors. The diagonal cells of
the **D** matrix in Fig. 6.9, then, contain the projections of the factors on their
associated reference vectors, and the off-diagonal cells are zero because
they represent projections of these factor vectors on reference vectors other
than their own.

6.4.1. CORRELATIONS BETWEEN THE FACTORS

The matrix of correlations between the oblique factors Φ can be represented
as follows:

$$\Phi = \mathbf{TT'} \tag{6.25}$$

where $\mathbf{T}$, as before, is a matrix whose rows are direction cosines of the oblique rotated unit-length factor vectors with respect to the original orthogonal unrotated factor vectors, as shown in Fig. 6.9. The matrix $\mathbf{TT'}$ gives the inner products of the direction cosines for all possible pairs of oblique rotated factor vectors. Because these rotated factor vectors are of unit length, these inner products equal the correlations between the rotated factor vectors. The matrix Φ is symmetric, since $r_{ij} = r_{ji}$, and has 1.0 in the diagonals since the correlation of each factor with itself is 1.0. Since the matrix $\mathbf{T}$ is not known from the results of the reference vector rotations, however, Eq. (6.25) must be developed further to provide a workable equation for obtaining Φ.

From Fig. 6.9 and the accompanying discussion, the following holds:

$$\mathbf{T\Lambda} = \mathbf{D} \tag{6.26}$$

Multiplying both sides of Eq. (6.26) by Λ^{-1}, the inverse of Λ, gives

$$\mathbf{T\Lambda\Lambda^{-1}} = \mathbf{D\Lambda^{-1}} \tag{6.27}$$

Equation (6.27) simplifies to

$$\mathbf{T} = \mathbf{D\Lambda^{-1}} \tag{6.28}$$

Substituting Eq. (6.28) in Eq. (6.25) gives

$$\Phi = \mathbf{D\Lambda^{-1}(D\Lambda^{-1})'} \tag{6.29}$$

Since the transpose of a product of matrices equals the product of the transposes in reverse order, Eq. (6.29) simplifies to

$$\Phi = \mathbf{D\Lambda^{-1}(\Lambda^{-1})'D'} \tag{6.30}$$

The transpose of a diagonal matrix is identical to the matrix itself; hence $\mathbf{D'} = \mathbf{D}$. Also, the inverse of a transpose equals the transpose of an inverse; so Eq. (6.30) may be rewritten as

$$\Phi = \mathbf{D(\Lambda'\Lambda)^{-1}D} \tag{6.31}$$

Since $\Lambda'\Lambda$ is the matrix $\mathbf{C}$, the matrix of correlations between reference vectors already referred to, Eq. (6.31) reduces to

$$\Phi = \mathbf{DC^{-1}D} \tag{6.32}$$

Equation (6.32) would permit the calculation of the matrix of correlations among factors V if C^{-1} and D were available. A method of calculating the inverse of C is described in the next section. The unknown matrix D can be determined if C^{-1} is known.

The matrix Φ must have the value 1.0 in all diagonal cells. For oblique solutions, the diagonal values of C^{-1} will generally be different from 1.0 even though the diagonal values of the C matrix itself are equal to 1.0. Selecting the unknown diagonal values of D in such a way that the product matrix $DC^{-1}D$ gives diagonal values of 1.0 provides a unique solution for the diagonal values of D, that is, d_{ii}.

The values of the diagonal cells in D which will make $DC^{-1}D$ have unities in the diagonal cells are

$$d_{ii} = \frac{1}{\sqrt{c_{ii}^{-1}}} \tag{6.33}$$

where c_{ii}^{-1} is the diagonal element of the matrix C^{-1} that corresponds to the diagonal element of D, d_{ii}. Multiplying C^{-1} on the left by D has the effect of multiplying row i of C^{-1} by d_{ii}. Multiplying C^{-1} on the right (that is, postmultiplying) by D has the effect of multiplying the elements of column i by d_{ii}. Using Eq. (6.33) to obtain the d_{ii} values, an element in the diagonal of $\Phi = DC^{-1}D$ will be

$$\phi_{ii} = \frac{1}{\sqrt{c_{ii}^{-1}}} \times \frac{1}{\sqrt{c_{ii}^{-1}}} (c_{ii}^{-1}) = 1.0 \tag{6.34}$$

6.4.2. COMPUTING THE INVERSE OF C

There are many satisfactory methods of computing an inverse. Most computer centers have standard programs available for this purpose. If at all possible, the inverse of the C matrix should be obtained by computer, using one of these available standard programs. If these facilities are not available so that the inverse must be calculated with less powerful computing equipment, the following method described by Fruchter (1954) will serve. Several decimal places should be carried in the computations even though only four are reported in the following example.

Begin by placing the C matrix to be inverted on the left and the identity matrix on the right as shown in (6.35). The general procedure is to use row operations to convert the C matrix on the left into an identity matrix. The same operations carried out on the rows of the C matrix are also carried out on the right-hand matrix. As the C matrix is carried by these row operations into the identity matrix, the identity matrix on the right is carried into the inverse matrix $\mathbf{C}^{-1}$.

$$
\begin{bmatrix}
1.0000 & .0000 & -.3430 & -.4111 \\
.0000 & 1.0000 & .0000 & -.0010 \\
-.3430 & .0000 & 1.0000 & .0400 \\
-.4111 & -.0010 & .0400 & 1.0000
\end{bmatrix}
\quad
\begin{bmatrix}
1.0000 & .0000 & .0000 & .0000 \\
.0000 & 1.0000 & .0000 & .0000 \\
.0000 & .0000 & 1.0000 & 0.0000 \\
.0000 & .0000 & .0000 & 1.0000
\end{bmatrix}
$$

$$\mathbf{C} \qquad\qquad\qquad\qquad \mathbf{I}$$

$$(6.35)$$

The $\mathbf{C}$ matrix to be inverted in the following example is the matrix of correlations among reference vectors for the 12-variable problem shown in Table 6.4 and in Eq. (6.35) above.

If the entry c_{11} in matrix $\mathbf{C}$ above were not 1.0000, it would be necessary first to get a value of 1.0000 in that position by dividing every entry in row 1 of both matrices by the value in c_{11}. Since c_{11} is already 1.0000, however, it is possible to proceed to the next step. The remaining values in column 1 of the matrix on the left, that is, c_{21}, c_{31}, and c_{41}, must be made equal to zero by multiplying row 1 by a constant such that when the product is added to the row in question, a zero appears in the first column position for that row. The entry c_{21} is already zero; so there is no need to eliminate this value. The element c_{31} is $-.3430$, however; so it must be made equal to zero. Multiplying the row 1 values by 0.3430 and adding the results to row 3 will give a zero in row 3, column 1 of the matrix on the left. Correspondingly, multiplying row 1 by 0.4111 and adding to row 4 will eliminate the $-.4111$ in row 4, column 1 of the matrix on the left, making it zero. These same operations are also carried out on the matrix at right. The results of these operations are shown below:

$$
\begin{bmatrix}
1.0000 & .0000 & -.3430 & -.4110 \\
.0000 & 1.0000 & .0000 & -.0010 \\
.0000 & .0000 & .8824 & -.1010 \\
.0000 & -.0010 & -.1010 & .8311
\end{bmatrix}
\quad
\begin{bmatrix}
1.0000 & .0000 & .0000 & .0000 \\
.0000 & 1.0000 & .0000 & .0000 \\
.3430 & .0000 & 1.0000 & .0000 \\
.4110 & .0000 & .0000 & 1.0000
\end{bmatrix}
$$

$$(6.36)$$

Zeros will now be induced in the second column elements of the matrix on the left, except for the diagonal element. The process calls for making the entry $c_{22} = 1.0000$ by dividing all row 2 entries of both matrices by c_{22} and then adding multiples of the second row to the other rows to eliminate the non-diagonal second column values of the matrix on the left. The element c_{22} is already equal to 1.0000; so that step is unnecessary. The entries c_{12} and c_{32} are already zero; so only the entry c_{42}, $-.0010$, needs to be eliminated. Multiply row 2 by 0.0010 and add to row 4 obtaining

$$
\begin{bmatrix}
1.0000 & .0000 & -.3430 & -.4110 \\
.0000 & 1.0000 & .0000 & -.0010 \\
.0000 & .0000 & .8824 & -.1010 \\
.0000 & .0000 & -.1010 & .8311
\end{bmatrix}
\begin{bmatrix}
1.0000 & .0000 & .0000 & .0000 \\
.0000 & 1.0000 & .0000 & .0000 \\
.3430 & .0000 & 1.0000 & .0000 \\
.4110 & .0010 & .0000 & 1.0000
\end{bmatrix}
$$

$$(6.37)$$

To eliminate the nondiagonal elements of the third column of the matrix on the left, divide the third row by the element in the third column and third row, that is, 0.8824, to get a value of 1.0000 in the cell c_{33}. This is the third row in the matrix (6.38). Multiplication of this third row by 0.3430 and adding the result to row 1 of (6.37) gives the new row 1 of (6.38) with a zero in the third column position. In (6.37) the second row value is zero in the third column of the matrix on the left so nothing needs to be done about the second row. The second row of (6.37) is carried down unchanged to the second row of (6.38). Multiplying row 3 of (6.38) by 0.1010 and adding to row 4 of (6.37) will give the new row 4 of (6.38) with a zero in the third column position. Again, these operations are performed on both matrices. The results are

$$
\begin{bmatrix}
1.0000 & .0000 & .0000 & -.4503 \\
.0000 & 1.0000 & .0000 & -.0010 \\
.0000 & .0000 & 1.0000 & -.1145 \\
.0000 & .0000 & .0000 & .8195
\end{bmatrix}
\begin{bmatrix}
1.1333 & .0000 & .3887 & .0000 \\
.0000 & 1.0000 & .0000 & .0000 \\
.3887 & .0000 & 1.1333 & .0000 \\
.4503 & .0010 & .1145 & 1.0000
\end{bmatrix}
$$

$$(6.38)$$

Only the last column of the matrix on the left now needs further treatment. Divide row 4 of both matrices by 0.8195 to get 1.0000 in the cell c_{44} and place the result in row 4 of (6.39) below. Then, multiply row 4 in (6.39) by 0.4503 and add to row 1 in (6.38) to get the new row 1 in (6.39). This places a zero in the cell c_{14}. Multiplying row 4 of (6.39) by 0.0010 and adding to row 2 in (6.38) gives the new row 2 in (6.39). This places a zero in the cell c_{24}. Finally, multiplying row 4 in (6.39) by 0.1145 and adding to row 3 in (6.38) gives the new row 3 in (6.39). This places a zero in the cell c_{34}:

$$
\begin{bmatrix}
1.0000 & .0000 & .0000 & .0000 \\
.0000 & 1.0000 & .0000 & .0000 \\
.0000 & .0000 & 1.0000 & .0000 \\
.0000 & .0000 & .0000 & 1.0000
\end{bmatrix}
\begin{bmatrix}
1.3807 & .0005 & .4516 & .5495 \\
.0005 & 1.0000 & .0001 & .0012 \\
.4516 & .0001 & 1.1493 & .1397 \\
.5495 & .0012 & .1397 & 1.2203
\end{bmatrix}
$$
$$\quad\quad\quad\quad I \quad\quad\quad\quad\quad\quad\quad\quad\quad\quad\quad\quad\quad C^{-1}$$

$$(6.39)$$

Now, the matrix on the left in (6.39) is the identity matrix, and the matrix on the right is the inverse of C, that is, C^{-1}. By multiplying C by C^{-1}, and vice versa, it can be verified that the identity matrix is obtained as required by the definition of the inverse; for example, $\mathbf{CC}^{-1} = \mathbf{C}^{-1}\mathbf{C} = \mathbf{I}$.

6.4.3. FORMULAS FOR THE STRUCTURE AND PATTERN MATRICES

The oblique rotation of reference vectors ends up with the formula

$$\mathbf{A}\Lambda = \mathbf{V} \tag{6.40}$$

where $\mathbf{A}$ is the matrix of unrotated factor loadings, Λ is the matrix with columns of direction cosines of the reference vectors with respect to the unrotated factor vectors, and $\mathbf{V}$ is the matrix of correlations of the data variables with the reference vectors. By analogy,

$$\mathbf{A}\mathbf{T}' = \mathbf{S} \tag{6.41}$$

where the columns of $\mathbf{T}'$ are direction cosines of the oblique factor vectors with respect to the unrotated factor vectors and $\mathbf{S}$ is the matrix of correlations of the data variables with the oblique factor vectors, that is, the factor structure. The rows of matrix $\mathbf{T}$ gave the projections of the unit-length oblique factor vectors on the unrotated factor vectors. These are also direction cosines. The transpose $\mathbf{T}'$ merely puts these direction cosines in columns rather than rows. Equation (6.41) is not used in practice to obtain $\mathbf{S}$ because $\mathbf{T}$ is ordinarily not known. This equation will be used, however, in the derivation of a formula for the factor pattern $\mathbf{P}$. The formula that is actually used to obtain $\mathbf{S}$ in practice requires knowing $\mathbf{P}$, the pattern.

Equation (2.2) gave the matrix of standard scores as a product of the matrix of factor loadings multiplied by the orthogonal, unrotated factor scores:

$$\mathbf{Z} = \mathbf{A}_u\mathbf{F}_u \tag{6.42}$$

Each row of $\mathbf{Z}$ is a data-variable vector and each row of matrix $\mathbf{F}_u$ is a factor score vector. Each row of $\mathbf{A}_u$ is a set of weights for the factor scores for a given data variable. The data-variable vectors, then, are being expressed as linear combinations of the orthogonal unrotated factor score vectors. These factor vectors constitute a basis for the space.

It was explained earlier in this chapter that any set of vectors that can be expressed as a linear combination of one set of basis vectors can also be expressed as a linear combination of a different set of basis vectors spanning the same space. The basis vectors do not even have to be orthogonal. A new set of basis vectors requires new weights, or coordinates, however. Using a new set of basis vectors, Eq. (6.42) may be written as

$$\mathbf{Z} = \mathbf{P}_u\mathbf{W}_u \tag{6.43}$$

where $\mathbf{Z}$ is the matrix of data-variable scores, $\mathbf{W}_u$ is the matrix of basis vectors, and $\mathbf{P}_u$ is the matrix of weights, or coordinates, of the data variables with respect to the factor vectors in $\mathbf{W}_u$ that constitute the new basis for the space. Let the first m rows of $\mathbf{W}_u$ be the oblique rotated factor scores with the next $2n$ rows the same specific and error factor scores that appear in matrix $\mathbf{F}_u$ in Eq. (6.42). The first m columns of $\mathbf{P}_u$ in Eq. (6.43) are the coordinates of the data-variable vectors with respect to the common factors, and the next $2n$ columns are the coordinates of the data-variable vectors with respect to the specific and error factors. The portions of $\mathbf{P}_u$ and $\mathbf{W}_u$ that are concerned only with common factors will be designated as matrices $\mathbf{P}$ and $\mathbf{W}$, respectively.

The relationship in Eq. (6.43) will be used now in developing another equation for the factor structure $\mathbf{S}$. Since the factor structure is the matrix of correlations between the n data variables and the m oblique factors, it may be represented in schematic matrix form as follows:

$$\tag{6.44}$$

where $\mathbf{S}$ is the common factor structure, $\mathbf{Z}$ is the matrix of data-variable scores reproducible from all factors, and $\mathbf{W}'$ is the transpose of the matrix of oblique common factor scores. An element of the matrix on the left, s_{ik}, is given by

$$s_{ik} = \frac{\sum\limits_{j=1}^{j=n} z_{ik}w'_{jk}}{N}$$

Since this is an average cross product of standard scores, it represents a correlation coefficient for data variable i with oblique factor k.

If the specific and error factor correlations were added on as additional columns of **S** and the specific and error factor scores as additional columns of **W'**, Eq. (6.44) would become

$$S_u = \frac{1}{\sqrt{N}} Z \frac{1}{\sqrt{N}} W_u'$$
(6.45)

By Eq. (6.43), $Z = P_u W_u$. Substituting this value for **Z** in Eq. (6.45) gives

$$S_u = P_u \left[\frac{W_u W_u'}{N} \right]$$
(6.46)

The expression in brackets in Eq. (6.46) is the matrix of correlations among all the factors, common, specific, and error. Except for the self-correlations and the intercorrelations among the oblique common factors, these values are all zero because the specific and error factors are uncorrelated with any other factors. Using only the part of Eq. (6.46) relevant to the oblique common factors gives the equation

$$S = P\Phi$$
(6.47)

where **S** is the factor structure for the oblique common factors, **P** is the factor pattern for the oblique common factors, and Φ is the matrix of correlations among the oblique common factors. Equation (6.47) is the formula actually used in practice to compute the factor structure **S**. The pattern matrix **P** must be obtained first. A formula for finding **P** is developed next.

By Eq. (6.41), $S = AT'$; by Eq. (6.47), $S = P\Phi$. Equating these two expressions for **S** gives

$$P\Phi = AT'$$
(6.48)

Substituting $T = D\Lambda^{-1}$ from Eq. (6.28) in Eq. (6.48) gives

$$P\Phi = A(D\Lambda^{-1})'$$
(6.49)

But, since $A\Lambda = V$ (see Fig. 6.9), and therefore $A = V\Lambda^{-1}$, Eq. (6.49) becomes

$$P\Phi = V\Lambda^{-1}(D\Lambda^{-1})'$$
(6.50)

Equation (6.50) simplifies to

$$P\Phi = V(\Lambda'\Lambda)^{-1}D \tag{6.51}$$

By Eq. (6.31), however, $\Phi = D(\Lambda'\Lambda)^{-1}D$; hence, Eq. (6.51) can be expressed as

$$PD(\Lambda'\Lambda)^{-1}D = V(\Lambda'\Lambda)^{-1}D \tag{6.52}$$

Multiplying both sides of Eq. (6.52) by D^{-1} and substituting $C = \Lambda'\Lambda$ gives

$$PDC^{-1}DD^{-1} = VC^{-1}DD^{-1} \tag{6.53}$$

Dropping DD^{-1} from both sides and multiplying both sides by C gives

$$PDC^{-1}C = VC^{-1}C \tag{6.54}$$

Dropping $C^{-1}C$ from both sides of (6.54) and multiplying both sides by D^{-1} and simplifying produces the final equation for
P, the pattern matrix:

$$P = VD^{-1} \tag{6.55}$$

The effect of multiplying the reference vector structure matrix V by D^{-1} is merely to multiply column i of matrix V by element d_{ii}^{-1} of D^{-1}. This is consistent with the previously demonstrated fact that the factor loadings in P are perfectly correlated with and proportional to the corresponding reference vector projections in V. The matrix D^{-1} is also a diagonal matrix with elements equal to the reciprocals of the corresponding elements of matrix D.

A complete oblique solution, then, requires the following matrices: (1) R, the correlation matrix; (2) A, the matrix of unrotated factor loadings; (3) V, the reference vector structure; (4) Λ, the transformation matrix that carries A into V; (5) C, the matrix of correlations among the oblique reference vectors; (6) P, the pattern matrix of factor loadings of the data variables on the oblique common factors; (7) S, the structure matrix of correlations between the data variables and the oblique common factors; and (8) Φ, the matrix of correlations among the oblique common factors.

Some investigators would expect to carry out a second-order factor analysis of the matrix of correlations among the factors, Φ, usually with 1.0 values in the diagonal cells as communalities. This analysis is carried out to find the factors among the oblique factors at the next level of generality.

Such factors are referred to as "second-order" factors. Eysenck in particular has been an advocate of this approach, even doing third- and higher order factor analyses until the higher order factors are uncorrelated (Eysenck & Eysenck, 1969).

The $\mathbf{P}$, $\mathbf{S}$, and Φ matrices for the 12-variable sample problem are given in Table 6.5. Simple structure holds only for the pattern matrix $\mathbf{P}$. The structure matrix $\mathbf{S}$ shows the extent to which data variables correlate with the oblique factors, whereas the pattern matrix does not. Both pattern and structure matrices are needed to present a clear picture of the interrelationships among the data variables and the oblique common factors.

As solutions become highly oblique, the values in the reference vector structure often become rather small. The factor loadings in the factor pattern, however, will be large in these cases, even exceeding 1.0. The oblique factor loadings are not to be interpreted as correlations, however; so these values over 1.0 are entirely appropriate as weights in the specification equation. Wherever possible, however, it is preferable not to allow the correlations among factors to become so high that pattern matrix values in excess of 1.0 occur.

6.4.4.   REPRODUCING $\mathbf{R}$ FROM THE OBLIQUE FACTOR LOADINGS

Equation (2.2) stated that $\mathbf{Z} = \mathbf{A}_u\mathbf{F}_u$ where $\mathbf{Z}$ is the matrix of data-variable scores, $\mathbf{A}_u$ is the matrix of unrotated factor loadings, common plus specific and error factors, and $\mathbf{F}_u$ is the matrix of factor scores for the orthogonal unrotated factors. The correlation matrix can also be represented by the following equation:

$$\mathbf{R} = \frac{1}{\mathbf{N}}(\mathbf{Z}\mathbf{Z}') \tag{6.56}$$

where $\mathbf{Z}$ is the matrix of data-variable scores. Each row of $\mathbf{Z}$ inner multiplied with a column of $\mathbf{Z}'$, the transpose of $\mathbf{Z}$, gives a sum of cross products of standard scores which when divided by N gives the correlation coefficient for the pair of data variables involved. Substituting $\mathbf{Z} = \mathbf{A}_u\mathbf{F}_u$ in Eq. (6.56) gives

$$\mathbf{R} = \frac{1}{\mathbf{N}}(\mathbf{A}_u\mathbf{F}_u)(\mathbf{A}_u\mathbf{F}_u)' \tag{6.57}$$

Equation (6.57) simplifies to

TABLE 6.5

Pattern, Structure, and Φ Matrices for the 12-Variable Problem

	I	II	III	IV	I	II	III	IV
1	.117	.858	−.060	.018	.103	.858	−.016	.061
2	−.008	.708	−.071	.088	.004	.708	−.064	.076
3	.105	.687	.016	−.095	.071	.687	.042	−.049
4	.175	.018	−.025	.587	.414	.018	.107	.658
5	.072	.103	.109	.668	.394	.103	.213	.712
6	−.125	.037	.080	.723	.209	.037	.120	.679
7	.710	−.049	−.068	−.035	.671	−.049	.182	.258
8	.566	.033	.223	.040	.663	.033	.431	.306
9	.740	−.035	−.020	.169	.804	−.034	.265	.479
10	.035	−.031	.675	−.003	.275	−.031	.687	.091
11	−.034	−.030	.830	.104	.308	−.030	.830	.188
12	−.023	−.130	.700	−.039	.211	−.130	.687	.033
	Pattern matrix (P)				Structure matrix (S)			

	I	II	III	IV
I	1.000	.000	.359	.423
II	.000	1.000	.000	.000
III	.359	.000	1.000	.118
IV	.423	.000	.118	1.000

Correlations among factors
Φ matrix

$$R = A_u \left[\frac{F_u F_u'}{N} \right] A_u' \qquad (6.58)$$

The expression in brackets in Eq. (6.58) is the matrix of correlations among all the factors, common, specific, and error. Because specific and error factors do not contribute to the correlations between data variables, if communalities are used in the diagonals of R and only the common factor portions of the matrices in Eq. (6.58) are used, Eq. (6.58) simplifies to

$$R' = A\Phi A' \qquad (6.59)$$

where R' is the reproduced correlation matrix (residuals are not accounted for), A is the matrix of unrotated factor loadings and Φ is the matrix of correlations among these factors. With the unrotated, orthogonal extracted factors, no correlations exist among the factors, so the matrix Φ would be the identity matrix, leading to the equation $R' = AA'$, which corresponds to Eq. (2.11). With oblique factors, however, the correlations among the factors are not equal to zero; so Eq. (6.59) becomes

$$\mathbf{R}' = \mathbf{P}\Phi\mathbf{P}' \qquad\qquad (6.60)$$

where $\mathbf{P}$ is the pattern matrix of oblique factor loadings and Φ is the matrix of correlations among the oblique factors. To obtain the reproduced correlation matrix, $\mathbf{R}'$, from oblique factor loadings, therefore, it is necessary to use the matrix of correlations among the oblique factors as well as the pattern matrix.

6.4.5. OBLIQUE VERSUS ORTHOGONAL SOLUTIONS

The complexities of using oblique solutions and the added burden of computation involved have led many investigators to settle for the much simpler orthogonal solutions. Some investigators, for example, Cattell (1952), have insisted on using oblique solutions because they feel that factors in nature are not apt to be orthogonal and that the use of orthogonal solutions is therefore unjustified. Other investigators, such as Guilford (1959), have generally preferred to stick with orthogonal factor solutions on the grounds that they wish to develop constructs that are as independent of each other as possible. The too-easy acceptance of oblique solutions may inhibit the search for truly independent constructs.

The authors can sympathize with both these points of view. There seems to be little real doubt about the fact that the most satisfactory constructs in a given empirical domain will usually exhibit at least some degree of obliquity. Height and weight, for example, are excellent constructs for anthropometric studies, but they are obviously correlated, and to a rather substantial degree. On the other hand, just because constructs are apt to be oblique in nature does not mean necessarily that oblique factor solutions must always be employed. Often, an orthogonal solution may give for all practical purposes a perfectly adequate impression of the nature of the constructs in a domain and a reasonably adequate impression of the degree of obliquity that is involved from inspection of the orthogonal plots without actually executing oblique rotations. Furthermore, the data variables that define the oblique simple structure factors most clearly are almost invariably the same ones that have the highest loadings on the corresponding orthogonal factors.

Using the best orthogonal approximation to a simple structure solution has the advantage of avoiding the extra computation involved in an oblique solution and perhaps more importantly, it simplifies the task of reporting results. The only feasible way of publishing all the matrices for a complete oblique solution is through the use of auxiliary publication channels because scientific journals do not have sufficient space available for such voluminous results. Unless it is important to obtain a precise oblique solution for the particular study involved, therefore, it is often more practical to settle for the best orthogonal approximation to the simple structure solution. This is particularly true with crude, exploratory investigations. The latter stages of a programmatic series of factor analytic investigations will usually be soon enough to expend the additional effort to obtain and report the more refined oblique solutions. If, however, the particular investigation reveals factors of great obliquity, such that an orthogonal solution would seriously distort the true picture, an oblique solution would be preferred even in an exploratory study.

6.5.   HAND ROTATED SOLUTIONS VERSUS ANALYTIC SOLUTIONS

The vast majority of factor analyses conducted today make use of programs available in standard computer packages. In most cases, the rotations are performed as part of the solution using an analytic method where the computer generates the results according to some mathematical principle. Often the principle used represents some mathematical approximation to a simple structure solution. These kinds of factor analytic solutions are convenient because the consumer is not required to make any decisions or exercise any judgment to obtain the results. This suits most consumers quite well because many of them would have no idea how to carry out hand rotations in any event.

The problem with this approach to the application of factor analysis is that simple structure and mathematical approximations to it represent appropriate treatments of the data only under rather restricted conditions that frequently, or even usually, are not present.

Each empirical data situation requires a kind of rotational solution that fits its particular parameters. Any given rotational criterion, including simple structure, works only for a subset of possible data situations. No rotational criterion is universally appropriate.

This is why hand rotation cannot be relegated to the status of outmoded technology, as many would like to suppose. The reason that the investigator needs to become familiar with hand rotation methods is that they often offer the only way to locate the best model for the data at hand. Hand rotation methods are not constrained by the requirements of any particular rotational criterion, mathematical or otherwise. The investigator is free to place the reference vectors in any chosen positions whatever, except that with orthogonal hand rotations the axes must be kept at 90°. This makes oblique hand-rotated solutions the most versatile way of seeking an adequate representation of the data.

Later in this book, other criteria of rotation than simple structure are considered. These methods represent, however, only a small subset of possible criteria. Oblique hand rotations are method free in the sense that any criterion whatever can be used to guide them. Of course, the solution chosen by an investigator using oblique hand rotations may be far off target. Any chosen solution must be supported with evidence that points to its usefulness. It is the only kind of rotational procedure, however, that can find *any* solution that is needed, provided the investigator can apply the needed good judgment to position the factors properly. Those who would become proficient in applying factor analytic methods, therefore, must make the effort to master the techniques described in chapters 5 and 6. A computer program is described in a later chapter that can relieve the investigator of the computational burden of carrying out such orthogonal and oblique hand rotations.

7

Simple Structure and Other Rotational Criteria

7.1. INTRODUCTION

In the preceding two chapters, rotation of factor axes according to simple structure criteria has been described, with positive manifold used as a supplementary aid in achieving this goal. Thurstone (1947, pp. 140ff.) attempted to prove the value of simple structure by presenting a solution to his famous "box" problem. He collected a sample of 20 boxes and took various mathematical functions of the three basic dimensions to obtain a total of 20 variables. with x, y, and z being the basic dimensions, Thurstone used as variables x^2, logx, $x^2 + y^2$, $x^2 + z^2$, $2x + 2y$, $x^2 + y^2 + z^2$, and e^x, with similar functions for y and z. From the intercorrelations of these variables he obtained three centroid factors, none of which matched the basic dimension variables of length, width, or height, the presumed underlying factors in the system. Rotation to simple structure, however, produced factors that were readily identifiable with the three basic box dimensions of length, width, and height.

Cattell and Dickman (1962) published a similar kind of study, called the "ball" problem, designed to present a more obviously oblique set of factor constructs. In fact, two of the rotated factors ultimately derived from the solution to this problem correlated 0.76 with each other. Thirty-two properties were measured for 80 balls varying in size, weight, and elasticity. The 32 ball measures were intercorrelated over the 80 "cases" and factor analyzed. Oblique simple structure rotations produced four oblique factors corresponding to the physical influences expected in this situation. The orthogonally rotated factors, however, did not match the physical influences nearly as well.

Examples like the Thurstone "box" problem and the Cattell and Dickman "ball" problem are supposed to establish the proposition that simple structure, and oblique simple structure in particular, leads to satisfactory solutions. Cattell (1952, 1966) in particular has tended to reject as unsuitable rotational solutions that do not satisfy oblique simple structure criteria. Yates (1987) discusses this topic at length.

All that these examples demonstrate, however, is that there *exist* instances in which oblique simple structure *does* work. Pointing out two such instances, or indeed any number of examples in which a method works, is not sufficient to establish the proposition that the method *always* works or even that it will work in the next situation where it is applied.

It is the authors' view that although simple structure can often be a very valuable guide in the rotation process, as can positive manifold, it has definite limitations. In fact, the uncritical use of oblique simple structure as a criterion can lead to grossly distorted solutions. This conclusion was reached by the first author as a result of his experimentation with a computer program that he developed (described in a later chapter) that searches systematically for good hyperplane positions. The general conclusion from these unpublished investigations was that with many variables and many factors in a factor matrix, hyperplanes can be "improved" to extremely high proportions of near-zero loadings if the factors are allowed to become sufficiently oblique to one another. Furthermore, frequently found with good hyperplanes were factor positions that made no sense whatsoever. For example, unrelated and uncorrelated variables in some cases had high loadings on the same factor. This was true for matrices that had alternate rotational solutions that were entirely satisfactory and meaningful as well as exhibiting a reasonable approximation to simple structure. Earlier experimentation (Comrey, 1959) with Thurstone's oblique analytic rotation method gave additional evidence questioning the universal dependability of oblique simple structure.

Thurstone's seldom used method started with a vector coincident with some selected data variable. This vector was adjusted to a position not too far from the original position but with an improved hyperplane by minimizing a function derived through differential weighting of loadings of different size. The rotation would attempt to bring relatively small loadings into the hyperplane but would ignore variables with large loadings. Experiments with large matrices using this procedure showed that with the data analyzed, a good hyperplane could be found starting with *any* of the data variables, invariably winding up with that variable having the highest or at least a high loading on the adjusted factor vector.

The authors' conclusion from these studies is that locating good hyperplanes is not always sufficient to establish good factor positions. In fact, it is asserted that rotating to obtain the best oblique hyperplanes is neither necessary nor sufficient in general for obtaining the best factor solution, although it may have that effect in many cases.

One reason that the anomaly of a good hyperplane with a bad factor position is not encountered more often is that systematic searches for good oblique hyperplanes are not generally conducted starting immediately with the unrotated factors. Typically, orthogonal rotations are carried along until the hyperplanes have been fairly well established before going to oblique positions to improve them. Under such conditions, the degree of obliquity permitted is fairly well controlled and wildly oblique but uninterpretable factor positions with good hyperplanes are less likely to be reached.

Some problems with oblique simple structure may still remain, however, even following the procedure of carrying the solution as far as possible orthogonally before going to oblique factor positions. The difficulty is that with many variables and many factors available for rotation, it is possible to continue reducing the size of the reference vector projections by allowing the vectors to go more and more oblique relative to each other.

At a given point, for example, rotating reference vector I away from reference vector III an additional 25° will bring two more variables into the hyperplane. But, should they be brought into the hyperplane? Is the resulting factor position representative of a factor construct that is superior to the factor construct represented by the position before this rotation? It is the authors' view that the answer may sometimes be "yes;" but at other times it will be "no." The mere fact that an additional point has been brought into the hyperplane is, per se, no guarantee that the factor is better positioned than before.

The number of zero or near-zero loadings that a factor will have in the "best" scientific solution cannot be stated independently of knowledge about the variables that are included in the analysis. It is possible to select a group of variables that would be best represented by one general factor with substantial loadings for all the data variables plus several additional smaller factors that would have a high proportion of near-zero loadings. A simple structure solution would be inappropriate here, although one might approximate such a solution by rotating the big general factor obliquely with the other factors. In less spectacular fashion, the best oblique position for a given factor might be one that would leave variable 3, for instance, with a moderate loading, although by oblique rotation it would be possible to bring variable 3 into the hyperplane. In many instances it may be necessary to make a solution move away from simple structure rather than toward it to achieve the optimum positioning of factors.

How is it possible to know how oblique to let the factors go? Because this question is difficult to answer, investigators have often settled for a belief in the proposition that "simple structure" would guide them correctly. The authors have limited faith in simple structure as a guide in making such decisions. This faith is strained more and more as the criterion of simple structure calls for more and more obliquity in the solution. Where factor axes are to be placed in very oblique positions, the authors believe that not only should simple structure indicate the need for such positioning but that supporting evidence outside the geometric configuration of the data points themselves should be available to justify this type of solution. The fact that a better simple structure can be achieved by going to a more highly oblique position does not constitute a necessary and sufficient reason for doing so. If, however, apart from the configuration of data points, there are other good reasons that strongly suggest the need for a highly oblique solution, then there is some basis for accepting the guidance of simple structure as being essentially valid in this instance.

Cattell and those who share his views are so convinced of the value of simple structure as a guide to rotations that they prefer to do their rotations "blindly," that is, without knowledge of the variables represented by the data points, to be certain that simple structure and that alone will influence their decisions in the rotation process.

The authors cannot place that much faith in manipulations on a configuration of points as a royal road to truth. Few factor analyses indeed conform to the ideal situation Thurstone had in mind when he formulated the principles of simple structure. He felt that simple structure would be a good guide where a large random selection of variables was taken from the entire universe. In such a case, many factors would be represented among the variables, no factor would be related to very many variables, and no one variable would be related to very many factors. To the extent that this situation is achieved, simple structure undoubtedly provides an excellent aid in the rotation process, but even here the best possible solution may diverge from the best simple structure solution because of random effects resulting in atypical variable selection. The best position for a given factor may call for certain variables to have loadings in the region of 0.2 to 0.3; a simple structure solution could be found where these variables would be brought down into the hyperplane by making the factors more oblique.

In the real-life situation, collections of variables chosen for a factor analysis rarely if ever represent a random selection of variables from the total universe. The investigator typically has something in mind in selecting the variables or may be limited by the data that are available to work with. All this adds up to making it probable that the conditions optimum for applying oblique simple structure may not be met in the study. To obtain the best solution for the data, therefore, it may be necessary to depart from the goal of obtaining the best oblique simple structure.

A given rotational solution provides the basis for only one of many possible interpretations of the data. It was shown earlier that there are infinitely many possible rotational transformations for most real-life correlation matrices. The best oblique simple structure solution often provides the basis for an interpretation that the investigator will find useful for the purposes at hand. It has not been proved, and cannot be proved, however, that the best oblique simple structure will always constitute the most meaningful solution for scientific purposes. The authors feel, therefore, that it is a mistake to depend upon blind rotations to oblique simple structure as though this procedure takes precedence over all others.

The correctness of a factor matrix as an interpretation of the data cannot be validated by reference to anything within the analysis itself, including the conformity of the solution to oblique simple structure. To attempt to do so would be circular. The validity of an interpretation of the data must be assessed with reference to evidence that is gathered independently, that is, outside the analysis itself. This evidence may come from many sources, for example, knowledge about the characteristics of the variables that are being analyzed, previous factor analytic investigations, experiments conducted using these variables, experiments conducted using factor scores derived from this investigation, additional factor analytic studies in which variables have been added, dropped, or modified according to certain hypotheses, theoretical considerations, and so on.

Since the correctness of a factor analytic interpretation of the data can only be established by appeal to information independent of the analysis itself, it would seem to be reasonable to use all available knowledge in selecting the best possible factor interpretation to begin with. It would be absurd to select a factor solution that contradicts available knowledge when an alternate solution is available that is consistent with that information. The investigator is urged, therefore, to use, in addition to oblique simple structure, any available well-established knowledge that is available to provide a guide in arriving at a final rotational solution.

Rotation "with knowledge," therefore, is recommended by the authors in preference to "blind" rotation. Where outside knowledge and simple structure criteria point to the same path, the investigator is fortunate. When several lines of evidence point to the same conclusions, confidence in that conclusion is increased. Where outside evidence and oblique simple structure call for traveling along divergent paths, the investigator is faced with a dilemma that must be resolved. A resolution in favor of the oblique simple structure may be the correct one, but there can be no assurance that this will always be the case. The investigator must carefully assess the situation and make the most intelligent decision that circumstances permit. Knowledge about the correctness of the decision, whatever it is, may be forthcoming only after a great deal of additional research.

One example of using knowledge of the situation to guide in the rotations is that of taking advantage of what is known about the data variables in determining the degree of obliquity that will be permitted. If variables 1, 2, and 3 are good marker variables for factor I and variables 4, 5, and 6 are good marker variables for factor II, for example, the correlations of variables 1, 2, and 3 with variables 4, 5, and 6 offer some useful clues. If the correlations are all about 0.3 to 0.4 and the best oblique simple structure seems to suggest a correlation between factors I and II in the range of 0.3 to 0.4, everything holds together well and both lines of evidence point to the same conclusion. If, on the other hand, variables 1, 2, and 3 all correlate zero with variables 4, 5, and 6, to permit factor axes I and II to correlate substantially would be more open to question even if it were to improve simple structure. Other lines of supportive evidence would be needed to justify departing from orthogonality.

Adherents of the blind-rotation approach warn that the use of knowledge about the variables will make it possible for the investigator to allow preconceived notions to bias observation. This is true, of course, and the investigator must strive to avoid selective perception favoring pet hypotheses. Closing one's eyes, however, does not increase the probability that the world will be seen as it really is rather than as one might like it to be. If there were some guarantee that blind rotations to oblique simple structure would enable us to see the world as it is, this would be an excellent means of controlling this type of bias. Unfortunately, no such guarantee exists.

7.2. ALTERNATIVE CRITERIA FOR ROTATION

Although hand rotation to oblique simple structure, or to the best orthogonal approximation to it, has been the most traditionally favored method of rotation, alternate approaches have enjoyed some popularity. In fact, at the present time, few published factor analyses are actually done using hand rotations. Most are done by the use of computer programs that do not require the investigator to make rotational decisions. Most of these computer programs, however, are designed to provide approximations to simple structure without the benefit of any decision-making on the part of the investigator. As such, their validity still rests upon the same foundation used by hand rotation to simple structure. Other computer programs are based upon different principles and of course hand rotation can proceed without depending upon simple structure criteria. Some of the alternative methods of rotation are considered in the remainder of this chapter.

7.2.1. ROTATION TO PLACE FACTORS THROUGH CLUSTERS

It will be recalled that simple structure rotations are carried out to improve the hyperplanes for a factor, not to bring the factor closer to a cluster of vectors with large projections or loadings on the factor. Advocates of simple structure insist that clusters merely represent "surface traits," to use Cattell's terminology, rather than "real" factors, or "source traits." To rotate toward clusters, therefore, is an error as a general policy although it might work out in a given instance. Suppose, for example, that several psychological tests were constructed that consisted of items drawing upon two distinct mental abilities factors, A and B. Some of the tests lean more on ability A and other more on B. These tests would correlate substantially with each other because they all depend on both factors A and B. They would form a well-defined cluster. To rotate toward this cluster, however, would be to put a factor about half-way between factor position A and factor position B, while no factor would represent either A or B alone. For this reason, simple structure advocates reject the cluster as a guide to factor positioning and rely on the hyperplane instead.

Professor Robert Tryon has been one of the most prominent supporters of the cluster approach, developing with the collaboration of his students theory and procedures for carrying out cluster analyses (Tryon & Bailey, 1970). Sophisticated computer programs have been developed to implement these methods. Tryon certainly did not accept the idea that the only way to locate useful constructs through analysis of correlations among variables is by the application of simple structure rotations to an unrotated factor matrix. The authors agree with Tryon and his collaborators that rotating toward clusters in certain analyses can produce excellent solutions with good scientific utility. It is also undoubtedly true, however, that rotation toward clusters in some instances may position factors in such a way that the constructs represented by those factor positions are not univocal. This was the case in the hypothetical example previously described where the factor through the cluster of tests represented a composite of factors A and B and where neither univocal factor A nor B was represented separately by any test variable in the analysis.

The investigator thoroughly familiar with the characteristics of these particular tests would know that they are factorially complex, that is, involving more than one factor, and would not choose or accept a rotational solution that would place a factor through the cluster of such related test variables.

It should be noted in passing that the application of simple structure is no guarantee that a factor will not be placed through a cluster of complex data variables. Suppose, for instance, that in the matrix there are no variables that measure either factor A or B alone, and the only variables measuring either are the complex variables that measure both. Suppose further that the other 80% of the variables in this matrix clearly are uncorrelated with these tests and define other unrelated factors. Under these circumstances, a simple structure solution will produce a factor with substantial loadings for these complex variables A and B on a single factor. Thus, a composite A + B factor will be produced rather than two separate univocal factors, A and B. In this case, blind rotation to simple structure might give the same result as rotating toward clusters; both methods would then imply that these complex tests measure a single univocal factor when in fact they do not. Only by using knowledge of the variables involved can the investigator avoid making the mistake of accepting this type of solution. Of course, the knowledgeable investigator would design the study properly to avoid this kind of situation, given sufficient information and freedom in planning the study to do so. Proper design of factor analytic investigations is discussed in a later chapter.

In summary, the position taken here is that under certain circumstances, clusters can be used as guides in rotations. Factors should only be rotated toward clusters, however, when confirmed knowledge about the variables in the clusters suggests strongly that they are univocal in character. By the same token, knowledge about the variables in a cluster may clearly suggest a positioning of a given factor in some other relationship to one or more clusters. That is, it might be concluded that two factors should be positioned so that a given cluster lies in the plane of two factors and half-way between them rather than collinear with either. Clusters, then, can be helpful to the investigator in making rotations, but knowing how to use them requires information and intelligent judgment.

7.2.2. ROTATION TO ACHIEVE CONSISTENCY WITH PAST RESULTS

Significant scientific progress using factor analytic results is most likely to come from a series of programmatic investigations rather than from a single isolated study. Investigators involved in programmatic research naturally seek findings that will generalize across studies. They wish to be able to replicate findings in order to gain confidence in their conclusions. In studying human abilities, Guilford (1967, 1985; Guilford & Hoepfner, 1971) and his collaborators have generally been more concerned in their rotations to relate present results to past findings than to satisfy simple structure criteria. They have also adhered to orthogonal solutions for the most part.

Cattell has also extended criteria for rotation from simple structure in one single study to results from several related studies in his "parallel proportional profiles" concept (Cattell, 1944a; Cattell & Cattell, 1955). Consider two different factor analytic studies involving the same or nearly the same variables, some of which were designed to give a factor of general intelligence. One of the studies is carried out with college students, and the other uses a random sample from the general population. Because the college students would show a restriction of range in intelligence, due to the elimination of people with low IQs from the sample, the correlations among the intelligence measures would be lower in this group than they would be in the sample from the general population. This would result in lower factor loadings for these variables on the Intelligence factor in the college sample. Cattell would position the Intelligence factor in the two samples in such a way that the loadings for the variables defining the factor would be proportional to each other, although they would be higher in the general population sample than they would be in the college sample. To attain a solution of this kind, it would probably be necessary to depart from the best simple structure position in each of the two samples considered alone.

The method of "orthogonal additions" is perhaps best classified under the heading of rotating to achieve consistency with past results. An investigator may start out with a group of variables that define one well-established factor. Then, a second factor is placed at right angles to the first, using existing variables and attempting to develop new ones until the second factor is well defined. A third is developed next, orthogonal to the first two, and so on. At each new step, results are built upon and made to exhibit consistency with previous findings.

Past factor analytic investigations of course do not constitute the only kind of past results that may be used to guide present rotations. Information from other kinds of investigations, knowledge about the data variables, and generally known facts in a given field are all examples of past results that have been used to guide rotations. The position has already been taken that any well-established information that the investigator has available and that has implications for factor positioning can and should be used as circumstances permit in settling upon a rotational interpretation of the data. This is not to say that it is justifiable to position a factor in a particular manner solely because it was so positioned in one or more previous studies. After all, it may have been improperly positioned in the first place. It would seem desirable, however, to strive for rotational solutions that reveal the extent to which continuity of results does exist over a series of investigations. This may occasionally require a rerotation of all the studies in a series to make allowances for recently discovered information that is relevent to all these factor solutions. Again, it must be emphasized that any rotational solution is merely an hypothesis about nature that can only be verified by appeal to evidence that goes beyond the results of any single factor analysis, per se. If the investigator is to *prove* that a rotational interpretation is correct in some absolute sense, it will be necessary to go beyond describing the mathematical procedures used to obtain the solution. This is not often done in published descriptions of factor analytic investigations.

7.2.3. ROTATION TO AGREE WITH HYPOTHESES

This approach in some of its applications is very similar to the last one in that by rotating present results to be consistent with known facts, including findings from previous investigations, there is an attempt to achieve congruence between present results and a complex hypothesis about their nature. In other instances, the hypothesis about present results may be generated strictly by theory rather than by past results. In such cases, factor analytic results are used as a test of the adequacy of the theory, much as a set of data points is related to a theoretically generated curve. In the latter case, a statistical test may be used to determine the adequacy of the fit between the data points and the theoretical curve. In the case of the factor analysis, the rotational solution may be manipulated to achieve the maximum possible agreement with theoretical expectations consistent with the reality of the data matrix of correlations. In such instances, the number of factors rotated is usually an important part of the test of congruence between theoretical expectations and outcome.

Rotations of this kind have been criticized by some individuals, apparently on the basis of the mistaken belief that any desired degree of congruence with theoretical expectations can be achieved through the occult art of rotation by unscrupulous but clever scientific charlatans. These same critics, in their own work, may well take advantage of generous error margins in asserting that their experimentally observed data points were not statistically inconsistent with their theoretical expectations. Or they may take failure to reject the null hypothesis as supportive of their own scientific presumptions. The truth is that the unrotated factor matrix admits only a certain class of transformations. Any investigator with much experience in carrying out factor analytic rotations is painfully aware of how intractable a configuration of data points can be when a preconceived result is sought.

Rotation to agree with hypothesis may take the form of establishing a "target" matrix. An attempt is made then to rotate the unrotated matrix into a form that agrees as closely as possible with this target matrix. Such methods give rise to what are sometimes called "Procrustes" solutions where the data are made to "fit" as closely as possible to a preconceived configuration.

Solutions of the kind described in this section come under the heading of "confirmatory factor analysis" as opposed to "exploratory factor analysis." In the latter, the investigator is presumably navigating in uncharted waters, trying to explore the region and map it. After preliminary maps are developed, either from previous empirical research or from theory-driven ideas, a "confirmatory" factor analysis can be undertaken to see how well the data confirm the preconceived notions held at the start of the study. This kind of confirmatory factor analytic investigation can be undertaken using the procedures already described in this book except that the number of factors will be fixed by hypothesis and hand rotations will be used to bring the final configuration as close as possible to what was expected.

In recent years, confirmatory factor analytic methods have been the fastest growing area of factor analysis, becoming quite complex mathematically and extensive in scope. The most pressing reason for revising this book has been the need to provide students of factor analysis with at least an introduction to these newer developments. A later chapter is devoted entirely to these methods.

7.3. ANALYTIC METHODS OF ROTATION

The basic distinction between so-called "analytic" and "nonanalytic" methods of rotation is that analytic methods can be reduced to clearly specified rules that require no judgment on the part of the investigator. Nonanalytic methods, such as hand rotation to oblique simple structure, require that the investigator exercise judgment to determine what is to be done at various stages in the rotation process.

Analytic methods of rotation have an enormous inherent appeal for many reasons. First, because they require no investigator judgment, they can be applied with equal facility by novice and expert alike, giving the same results no matter who does it. Second, because the experimenter exercises no judgment, the process is more objective, giving the experimenter no opportunity to influence the results as a function of preconceived notions. Third, because such methods are reducible to a set of well-defined rules, they can be programmed for computer application. Finally, the authors of these methods ordinarily provide computer programs for the use of the scientific community, so the user is even spared the task of having to develop a computer program to carry out the calculations.

Most computer centers today have available a variety of standard computer programs to carry out factor extractions and analytic rotations by a variety of methods. Many investigators, therefore, are able to prepare data for such "package" computer treatment and to obtain factor analytic results for interpretation with little understanding of what goes on in between, or of the extent to which the program may be appropriate as a form of treatment for their data. Such applications of factor analysis often tend to be afterthoughts of the kind, "Well, what do we do with the data now that we have collected it?" Data collected with no advance plans for data analysis are apt to be poor data. Factor analysis, unfortunately, has no magical power to extract good results from poor data, especially when the investigator is making a choice of the form of factor analytic treatment with no knowledge of the relevance of that particular method for the data at hand.

Factor analysis as a tool is not responsible for the poor quality of such research investigations any more than the hammer is at fault for the imperfections in the work of an amateur carpenter. Those who would effectively exploit the potential of factor analysis as a research tool must acquire an understanding of the method and how it is to be properly applied. Proper planning of the factor analytic investigation before data collection starts is just as important in factor analytic work as it is in experimental work that is to be followed by data treatment using analysis of variance. In the remainder of the chapter, attention is given to the properties of some of the more useful analytic methods of rotation. It should be made very clear, however, that no existing analytic method of rotation can be correct or appropriate for all data situations. For any set of rotation rules, it is possible to devise a data situation that makes this set of rules inappropriate. Analytic methods of rotation do eliminate judgment of the investigator in carrying out the rotations after the method of analytic rotation has been selected. They do not eliminate, however, the necessity of judgment on the part of the investigator in determining whether the selected method of analytic rotation is appropriate for the data. The elimination of experimenter judgment with analytic methods of rotation, therefore, is more apparent than real.

There can be no doubt that the use of analytic criteria of rotation reduces discrepancies between the solutions obtained by different investigators because starting with the same matrix and using the same analytic method all solutions would be identical. This would not be the case with hand rotations. Unanimity among investigators is of limited scientific value, however, if in agreement all are wrong. This is a distinct possibility when a randomly chosen analytic criterion of rotation is applied to a randomly chosen unrotated matrix of factor loadings. The authors have yet to find an experienced factor analyst who is uniformly satisfied with any analytic method of rotation when it is applied to a wide variety of situations. Marks, Michael, and Kaiser (1960), for example, found little agreement between Varimax analytic rotation factors and factors rotated visually by the Zimmerman method. The reader is cautioned, therefore, to avoid the uncritical acceptance of computer-produced factor analytic results. They may be appropriate and they may not be. Experimenter judgment may be necessary to decide.

The fact that analytic rotation methods can be programmed for computer application provides a tremendous labor-saving advantage over traditional hand rotation using 2 × 2 plots. What is not well understood, however, is the fact that the drudgery of plotting and calculation for the traditional hand-rotation procedures can be programmed for computer, too, so that the investigator is left only with the necessity of inspecting the plots and making decisions about what factors to rotate and where (Cattell & Foster, 1963). Once this decision is made, the computer can be used to carry out the numerical operations and to produce the new plots. A program prepared by the first author that will carry out these operations is described in a later chapter. With computer assistance, then, traditional hand-rotation procedures are only slightly less convenient than analytic methods in terms of the time investment involved. Certainly the difference in labor would not be sufficient to be of any practical significance as far as the amount of effort devoted to the total research project. Of far greater importance is the choice of those procedures that will lead to the best possible solution.

7.3.1. COMPUTERIZED SIMPLE STRUCTURE SOLUTIONS

Although rotation to oblique simple structure is not classified as an analytic method, it is possible to formulate a set of rules to apply by computer for the purpose of searching for solutions that appear to meet the demands of oblique simple structure. Because such applications involve an explicit set of rules, we classify them as analytic methods.

Cattell and Muerle (1960) developed the "Maxplane" program for factor rotation to oblique simple structure. This program counts the number of points that fall "in the hyperplane" for each factor within the range, for example, of $+.10$ and $-.10$. The hyperplane could be made wider or narrower in a particular problem. Factors are rotated systematically by computer to increase the number of points falling in the hyperplanes. Cattell (1966) states that Maxplane gives higher hyperplane counts than analytic rotation programs based on satisfying some mathematical criterion. Eber (1966) has produced a more recent version of the Maxplane rotation program that starts off by spinning the factor axes to positions at 45° to the unrotated factor positions and normalizing all data vectors to unit communalities. Then, the search for hyperplane improvement begins. A weight function is used, however, to adjust the hyperplanes rather than an all-or-none decision that merely labels the variable "in" or "out" of the hyperplane. Guertin and Bailey (1970, pp. 135ff) have had some success with the Maxplane method, although they report in general that oblique analytic solutions tend to put too many points in the hyperplanes and to give angles between factors that are more oblique than necessary. The authors' experience is in agreement with that reported by Guertin and Bailey.

The first author has also developed a program for obtaining oblique simple structure solutions by computer that is made available with this book and described in a later chapter. This program operates on a principle similar to that used with the original Maxplane program. The number of points in the hyperplane for each reference vector is counted at the beginning. Then, trial rotations a specified number of degrees toward and away from each other reference vector are tried to see if the number of points in the hyperplane increases. If so, the new reference vector position is adopted if the correlation between reference vectors would not be increased beyond a specified maximum. After each reference vector has been tried out in comparison with every other reference vector, the size of the trial angle of rotation is reduced by a proportion specified in advance by the investigator, and the process is repeated. At each step, the size of the correlation between reference vectors is checked. No rotation is permitted that would result in a correlation between reference vectors that exceeds a value specified by the investigator at the beginning of the rotation process. The investigator can begin with a large search angle or limit the angle to a relatively small value. The number of times every vector is rotated with every other vector is also specified in advance. The various options available to the investigator in applying this program permit a tremendous variety of rotational possibilities in the search for a suitable solution.

Experience with this program, which is described in a later chapter in more detail, indicates that it can "clean up" a solution that is already nearing simple structure. A maximum correlation between reference vectors that is near the largest value currently found among the oblique reference vectors is selected, with the assumption that oblique hand rotations have already been completed or nearly completed. A search angle that is not too large to begin with is preferred, for example, about 15°. These constraints prevent the search for a "better" simple structure from getting out of hand. Allowing large initial search angles and greater obliquity between reference vectors tends to result in an increased number of points in the hyperplanes but at the expense of higher correlations among reference vectors. In applying this type of program, the best strategy appears to be to come as close as possible to simple structure positions that are acceptable to the investigator using hand-rotation methods. Then, apply the computer search procedure with restrictions on the size of search angle and the maximum permissible correlation between reference vectors to prevent any radical departure from the solution already achieved at the beginning of the computer run. Even with such restrictions, the computer search will usually result in significant hyperplane improvements.

It is often convenient to start this process with the best orthogonal approximation to simple structure rather than with an oblique hand-rotation solution. Under these circumstances, it is best to begin with modest search angles and permissible correlations among reference vectors. These may be increased on a rerun later if this is strongly indicated. The greatest difficulty with oblique solutions is that of determining how oblique the reference vectors may be permitted to go. The greater the freedom allowed in this respect, the more points there will be in the hyperplanes and the greater will be the correlations between the reference vectors, as a general rule. There is virtually no assurance that the angles will stabilize at reasonable values if greater latitude is permitted.

7.3.2. "PROCRUSTES" SOLUTIONS

The Procrustes-type solutions are classified here as analytic in character because a specified set of rules is laid down governing how rotations are to be carried out to transform the unrotated factor matrix into a form maximally similar in some sense to a predetermined target matrix. The target matrix may have all the values specified or only some of them. Mosier (1939) derived equations to provide a least-squares fit to a target matrix, but these equations could not be solved algebraically. More recently, Browne (1967) has developed an iterative method for solving these equations, giving rise to an oblique Procrustes-type solution. Hurley and Cattell (1962) also developed a program for this type of solution. Green (1952) presented procedures for a Procrustes-type solution in which the final factors are orthogonal to one another. See also Schonemann and Carroll (1970) and Mulaik (1972, pp. 308–314).

Guilford has found helpful in his work with mental abilities the Procrustes-type method of Cliff (1966). This method permits either the orthogonal rotation of two matrices to maximum agreement with each other or the orthogonal rotation of one matrix to maximum agreement with a specified target matrix. The target matrix may be formulated on the basis of theoretical expectation, knowledge of past results, or inspection of a preliminary rotational solution to the problem under investigation by other rotational methods.

Guilford found Cliff's Procrustes-type solution to his liking because it enabled him to maintain maximum continuity between past results and new findings. His extensive programmatic researches and exhaustive knowledge of the variables he was working with provided a wealth of constraints that could be reasonably applied in rotating the factors for a new study designed to verify or extend previous findings. He might have the knowledge, for example, that a given factor has no pure-factor tests in the battery to identify it. It may be necessary to locate a factor in a position that would never be attained by usual rotational criteria. If the hypothesis is consistent with the data in the new matrix, a properly formulated "target" matrix and a Procrustes-type solution will produce the expected factor results. For investigators with less reliable knowledge about the probably appropriate form of solution, however, this approach should be applied with extreme caution.

It should be emphasized that rotation to a target matrix does not have to proceed analytically by means of a computer program using a particular mathematical algorithm. The investigator may use hand rotations to place reference vectors in such a way as to conform as much as possible to those aspects of the target matrix that are specified. The target matrix can be specified with respect to only a few or all possible values. The more constraints there are, of course, the more difficult it is to bring the rotated matrix into conformity with the target matrix. Hand rotation methods do provide the maximum flexibility in positioning reference vectors to attain a solution similar to that represented by the target matrix in its most salient features by giving ground on less important aspects of the total configuration.

7.3.3.   ORTHOGONAL ANALYTIC ROTATION METHODS

Dissatisfaction with the subjectivity and vagueness about simple structure criteria led to an effort to provide more precise mathematical statements of the criteria that a rotational solution should satisfy. Several methods were published in the 1950s that proved to be rather similar to each other (Carroll, 1953; Ferguson, 1954; Neuhaus & Wrigley, 1954; Saunders, 1960) according to Harman (1967, p. 298). Harman refers to these similar methods collectively as the "Quartimax" method. The essential idea underlying this approach is to rotate in such a way that ideally each variable would have a major loading in one and only one factor. That is, each variable would appear to be a pure-factor measure. In practice, of course, it is not possible ordinarily to obtain such an idealized solution. It is only approached as closely as possible in the Quartimax solution.

Experience with the Quartimax approach has shown that it tends to give a general factor, that is, a factor with which all or most of the variables are substantially correlated. This undesirable property of the Quartimax class of solutions coupled with the appearance of the Kaiser Varimax method, which does not have this fault, has led to a loss in popularity of the Quartimax methods. There do exist special situations, however, in which the Quartimax method can give a solution that is more appropriate than the Varimax method, for example, when a general factor is present in the data.

The Kaiser Varimax method (Kaiser, 1958) has become perhaps the most popular rotational procedure in use today. It is a method that gives excellent results in certain situations. It is efficient and readily available at most computer centers, for example, as part of the BMD and revised BMDP packages of programs (Dixon, 1970a; 1970b; 1983). The Varimax method does not give the large general factor that the Quartimax method does, but Cattell (1966) states that is still does not pull enough variance away from the largest extracted factor. Lee and Comrey (1979) have also reported some problems with Varimax solutions. The Varimax method is of such great importance that it is considered in a separate section later in this chapter (Section 7.4). At this point, however, it can be compared briefly with the Quartimax method.

In a sense, the Quartimax method attempts to maximize the variance of squared factor loadings by rows, because if all the variance for a given variable is concentrated on one factor, leaving the other loadings essentially equal to zero, this result will be achieved. The Varimax method, by contrast, maximizes the variance of the squared factor loadings by columns. Thus, on any given factor, a pattern is desired such that there are some high loadings and lots of low loadings with few intermediate-sized loadings. This type of solution offers easy interpretability because variables with high loadings are similar to the factor in character, whereas variables with low loadings are not. A variable with an intermediate loading is neither fish nor fowl. It is of little use in telling what the factor is or is not like. Varimax rotations, then, tend to push high loadings higher and low loadings lower, to the extent that this is possible within the constraints maintained by an orthogonal reference frame. Factor positions are determined, therefore, by the locations of clusters as well as by the location of hyperplanes. A Varimax factor will tend to be drawn toward a neighboring cluster because this elevates the variance of the squared factor loadings for the factor (for further discussion of the Varimax method see Section 7.4).

7.3.4. OBLIQUE ANALYTIC METHODS OF ROTATION

Computerized simple structure search methods and Procrustes-type approaches that give oblique solutions have already been mentioned. Well before the development of these methods, however, Thurstone (1947) presented his Single-Plane method, which is a semianalytic procedure for obtaining oblique solutions. The investigator starts with a given variable thought to be a likely defining variable for a particular factor. A trial vector is placed through this variable and projections of the data-variable vectors on this trial vector are obtained. These values are plotted against all the unrotated factor vectors and an adjustment is made in the position of the trial vector simultaneously with respect to all unrotated factor axes to improve simple structure. Projections of the data-variable vectors on the new trial vector are computed and new plots are made. A new adjustment in the trial vector position is made if further adjustments are indicated. The process is continued until no further adjustments are needed. This positions the first reference vector. A second trial reference vector is placed through a variable that has a near-zero correlation with the first trial vector but still has a substantial communality. All the oblique vectors are positioned separately in this way, one after the other. Fruchter (1954) has a clear exposition of this process.

Thurstone (1954) developed a more sophisticated version of the Single-Plane method that uses a weighting function permitting calculation of the corrections to the trial vector position simultaneously with respect to all factors without plotting and without making judgments. It is more analytic in character, therefore, than the Single-Plane method. As previously mentioned, however, the first author's experience with this method suggests that it can give misleading results if not used with considerable judgment and skill (Comrey, 1959).

More recently, several strictly analytic methods of carrying out oblique rotations have been suggested. Of these, the best known at the present time appear to be the Biquartimin criterion of Carroll (1957), the Promax method of Hendrickson and White (1964), and a procedure developed by Jennrich and Sampson (1966) to get factor loadings on the oblique factors directly without first obtaining projections on the reference vectors. Computer programs in the BMD and BMDP series (Dixon, 1970a; 1970b; 1983) are available for the Carroll and for the Jennrich and Sampson methods. A good discussion of several of these oblique analytic rotation methods is found in Harman (1967). Gorsuch (1970,1983) also discusses several of these methods and indicates that the Promax method, which is becoming increasingly popular, gives results comparable to those obtained with other analytic methods but with less computer time.

The Promax method is designed to give an oblique solution that represents a modification of an orthogonal solution toward an even better oblique simple structure. It starts with an orthogonal solution that has gone as far as possible toward simple structure, or some approximation to it. The Varimax solution is a commonly used starting point.

The existing orthogonal solution loadings are raised to the second, fourth, or even higher powers. This drops the loadings in size but drops smaller loadings more precipitously, driving more points into the hyperplanes. Then, the original orthogonal solution is rotated by oblique Procrustes methods to come as close as possible to the powered matrix. Higher powers result in higher correlations among oblique Promax factors. A solution is chosen with that powered matrix that gives the best structure with the lowest correlations between factors. The better the original orthogonal solution, the better the Promax oblique factor solution is apt to be.

Guertin and Bailey (1970, p. 135) have found, however, that oblique analytic solutions tend to put too many points in the hyperplanes. There is little evidence available at the present time to suggest that any existing oblique analytic solution can perform as well with nonorthogonal situations as Varimax does with cases known to require orthogonal solutions. The lack of success in developing totally satisfactory analytic oblique methods of rotation probably can be attributed, at least in part, to the fact that it is difficult to decide how much obliquity to tolerate. Simple structure fails to provide an entirely satisfactory guide because it is possible to continue to improve hyperplanes by allowing the axes to go more oblique. The point at which the investigator calls a halt to this process is to some extent arbitrary. Because of the present uncertainty about the value of these completely analytic rotation methods in actual practice, none of them is described in detail. More experience with these methods or perhaps new methods will be required before satisfactory oblique analytic rotation becomes a practical reality, if in fact it ever does.

7.4. THE KAISER VARIMAX METHOD

Because of its great popularity and general usefulness, the Varimax method of Kaiser (1958, 1959) is described here in some detail. It has already been stated that the Varimax method is based on the idea that the most interpretable factor has many high and low loadings but few of intermediate size. Such a factor would have a large variance of the squared loadings because the values are maximally spread out. Using the square of the formula for the standard deviation, the variance of the squared factor loadings on factor j may be symbolized as follow:

$$\sigma_j^2 = \frac{1}{n} \sum_{i=1}^{i=n} (a_{ij}^2)^2 - \frac{1}{n^2} \left[\sum_{i=1}^{i=n} a_{ij}^2 \right]^2 \tag{7.1}$$

The variance should be large for all factors; so an orthogonal solution is sought where V is a maximum, V being defined as follows:

$$V = \sum_{j=1}^{j=m} \sigma_j^2 \tag{7.2}$$

In practice, V is not maximized in one operation. Rather, factors are rotated with each other systematically, two at a time in all possible pairs, each time maximizing $\sigma_i^2 + \sigma_j^2$. After each factor has been rotated with each of the other factors, completing a cycle, V is computed, and another cycle is begun. These cycles are repeated until V fails to get any larger. The fundamental problem, then, is to find an orthogonal transformation matrix Λ that will rotate two factors such that $\sigma_i^2 + \sigma_j^2$ for the rotated factors will be as large as possible. Consider the following:

$$
\begin{bmatrix} x_1 & y_2 \\ x_2 & y_2 \\ x_3 & y_3 \\ \cdots & \cdots \\ x_n & y_n \end{bmatrix} \times \begin{bmatrix} \cos\phi & -\sin\phi \\ \sin\phi & \cos\phi \end{bmatrix} = \begin{bmatrix} X_1 & Y_1 \\ X_2 & Y_2 \\ X_3 & Y_3 \\ \cdots & \cdots \\ X_n & Y_n \end{bmatrix}
$$

$$\mathbf{V}_1 \qquad\qquad \Lambda \qquad\qquad \mathbf{V}_2 \qquad\qquad (7.3)$$

where $\mathbf{V}_1$ is a matrix of factor loadings to be rotated to maximize $\sigma_i^2 + \sigma_j^2$, $\mathbf{V}_2$ is the matrix of factor loadings for which $\sigma_i^2 + \sigma_j^2$ is a maximum and Λ is the orthogonal transformation matrix that will accomplish this desired rotation. The values in $\mathbf{V}_1$ are known. The values in $\mathbf{V}_2$ are not. The values in $\mathbf{V}_2$, however, are functions of the angle ϕ and the values in $\mathbf{V}_1$ as follows:

$$X_i = x_i\cos\phi + y_i\sin\phi$$

$$Y_i = -x_i\sin\phi + y_i\cos\phi \qquad\qquad (7.4)$$

The sum of the variances to be maximized is given by

$$\sigma_k^2 + \sigma_l^2 = \frac{1}{n}\Sigma(X^2)^2 - \frac{1}{n^2}(\Sigma X^2)^2 + \frac{1}{n}\Sigma(Y^2)^2 - \frac{1}{n^2}(\Sigma Y^2)^2 \quad (7.5)$$

The development from this point requires some knowledge of calculus. Readers who are not familiar with this mathematical tool may wish to skip to Eq. (7.8).

By substituting Eqs. (7.4) in Eq. (7.5), the unknown values of X and Y can be removed from Eq. (7.5), leaving ϕ as the only unknown. The resulting expression can be differentiated with respect to ϕ, set equal to zero, and a solution for ϕ determined that maximizes the expression in (7.5). It is easier, however, to differentiate (7.5) with respect to ϕ before making the substitutions of Eqs. (7.4) into (7.5). Doing it this way requires a knowledge of values for $dX/d\phi$ and $dY/d\phi$. Dropping the subscripts from Eqs. (7.4) and differentiating with respect to ϕ gives

$$dX/d\phi = x(-\sin\phi) + y(\cos\phi) = Y$$

$$dY/d\phi = -x(\cos\phi) + y(-\sin\phi) = -X \qquad\qquad (7.6)$$

Differentiating (7.5) with respect to ϕ, substituting Eqs. (7.6) in the resulting equation, setting it equal to zero, and multiplying both sides by n^2 gives

$$n\Sigma XY(X^2 - Y^2) - \Sigma XY(\Sigma X^2 - \Sigma Y^2) = 0 \qquad\qquad (7.7)$$

Substitution of Eq. (7.4) into Eq. (7.7) gives an expression involving only the unknown ϕ and the known values of x and y, the loadings before rotation. Using a table of trigonometric identities and double angle formuli, the resulting expression can be simplified eventually and solved for ϕ to give

$$\tan4\phi = \frac{2[n\Sigma(x^2-y^2)(2xy)-\Sigma(x^2-y^2)\Sigma(2xy)]}{n(\Sigma[(x^2-y^2)^2-(2xy)^2]) - ([\Sigma(x^2-y^2)]^2-[\Sigma(2xy)]^2)} \quad (7.8)$$

Any value of ϕ that maximizes Eq. (7.7) must satisfy Eq. (7.8). To ensure that the value of ϕ gives a maximum rather than a minimum or point of inflection, however, requires that the second derivative of Eq. (7.7) with respect to ϕ shall be negative when evaluated at ϕ. The angles of rotation that will accomplish this result may be determined as follows:

$$\tan4\phi = \frac{\sin4\phi}{\cos4\phi} = \frac{num}{denom} \quad (7.9)$$

The angle 4ϕ will be in the first quadrant if both numerator and denominator of Eq. (7.8) are positive, and the angle of rotation will be ϕ itself. If both numerator and denominator are negative, the tangent will still be positive, but the required angle of rotation is $-(180° - 4\phi)/4 = -(45° - \phi)$ because the sine and cosine are both negative in the third quadrant. If the numerator is negative and the denominator is positive, the angle 4ϕ will be in the fourth quadrant and the angle of rotation will be $-\phi$. Finally, if the numerator of Eq. (7.8) is positive and the denominator is negative, 4ϕ will be in the second quadrant and the angle of rotation will be $(180° - 4\phi)/4 = (45° - \phi)$.

Then, to determine the desired rotation transformation matrix in Eq. (7.3), compute the numerator (num) in Eq. (7.8) and the denominator (denom), keeping their signs. Ignoring these signs for the moment, find a positive angle 4ϕ in the first quadrant such that the tangent of 4ϕ equals the absolute value of num/denom. Find the angle ϕ as one-fourth of the angle with this tangent. This angle must be 22 1/2° or less. The transformation matrix Λ that maximizes the function in Eq. (7.5) will then be one of the following, depending on the combination of signs in the numerator (num) and denominator (denom) of Eq. (7.8):

$$\begin{bmatrix} \cos\phi & -\sin\phi \\ \sin\phi & \cos\phi \end{bmatrix} \qquad \begin{bmatrix} \cos\phi & \sin\phi \\ -\sin\phi & \cos\phi \end{bmatrix}$$

$$\Lambda \text{ (num+,denom+)} \qquad \Lambda \text{ (num-,denom+)}$$

$$\begin{bmatrix} \cos(45° - \phi) & -\sin(45° - \phi) \\ \sin(45° - \phi) & \cos(45° - \phi) \end{bmatrix} \qquad \begin{bmatrix} \cos(45° - \phi) & \sin(45° - \phi) \\ -\sin(45° - \phi) & \cos(45° - \phi) \end{bmatrix}$$

$$\Lambda \ (\text{num} +, \text{denom} -) \qquad\qquad \Lambda \ (\text{num} -, \text{denom} -)$$

$$(7.10)$$

As an illustration, the Λ matrix is determined that gives a Varimax rotation of the two centroid factors in matrix **A** of Table 2.2, with the results hopefully approximating those in matrix **V** of Table 2.2. These calculations are shown in Table 7.1. The tangent of 4ϕ is $+.4737$, with both numerator and denominator negative. The angle 4ϕ is $25°21'$; so the angle ϕ is $6°20'$. Because the denominator is negative, the angle of rotation is $45°$ $- \phi$, or $38°41'$. This angle is rounded to $39°$ to obtain the Λ matrix. Multiplying the unrotated centroid matrix **A** by the matrix Λ does give the expected **V** matrix as shown in Table 7.1. In this example, therefore, the Varimax method recovered the original data-variable configuration very well.

With the Varimax method, it is important to rotate the proper number of factors. Rotation of too few factors with the Varimax criterion, as with any method of rotation, crowds the variance for $n+k$ factors into a space of only n dimensions, thereby losing some factors and distorting the others. Rotating too many factors, however, can also bring about distortions with the Varimax criterion. The Varimax method will tend to build up the variance on extra small factors to increase the overall variance function V, thereby splitting up major factors and "robbing" larger factors of their variance for certain data variables. The best indication that this has happened is the appearance of a Varimax factor with only one large loading and all the rest of the loadings at much lower levels. The solution should be rerotated, dropping out any factor that is artificially overinflated in this way. Some of these distortional effects with Varimax rotations have been shown in factor analyses of item data by Lee and Comrey (1979) and by Comrey, Noller, and Law (1988).

A more subtle type of distortion occurs where several variables define a major factor, but two or three of these variables are more highly correlated among themselves than with the other variables defining the factor. This often results in a small unrotated factor with modest loadings for these more highly interrelated variables in addition to the main factor with all the variables for this factor represented. If this small extra factor is rotated into the Varimax solution, the variance for the small additional factor will be inflated, pulling variance off the larger factor so that these variables appear to be considerably less related to the larger factor than they could be. The smaller factor, meanwhile, is inflated to a larger overall share of the variance than is appropriate.

Lee and Comrey (1979) showed that when ones are placed in the

TABLE 7.1

Varimax Rotation of Two Centroid Factors from the Four-Variable Problem

x	y	$x^2 - y^2$	$2xy$	$(x^2 - y^2)^2$	$(2xy)^2$	$(x^2 - y^2)(2xy)$	$(x^2 - y^2)^2 - (2xy)^2$
.578	.562	.0182	.6497	.0003	.4221	.0118	−.4218
.531	.344	.1636	.3653	.0268	.1334	.0598	−.1066
.687	−.422	.2939	−.5798	.0864	.3362	−.1704	−.2498
.765	−.484	.3510	−.7405	.1232	.5483	−.2599	−.4251
	Sum	.8267	−.3053	.2367	1.4400	−.3587	−1.2033

$$\text{Tan}\,4\varphi = \frac{2[4(-.3587) - (.8267)(-.3053)]}{4\{(-1.2033)\} - \{(.8267)^2 - (-.3053)^2\}}$$

$$= \frac{-2.8696 + .5048}{-.48132 - (.6834 - .0932)}$$

$$= \frac{-2.4580}{-4.8132 - .5902}$$

$$= \frac{-2.4580}{-5.4034}$$

$$= .47374$$

The absolute value of tan 4φ is .47374 giving an angle of 25°21′ for 4φ. The angle φ is 6°20′. With a negative denominator, the angle of rotation will be $(45° - \varphi)$ or 38°41′ which is rounded off to 39°. The cosine and sine of 39°, respectively, are .7771 and .6293. With both numerator and denominator negative, the transformation matrix chosen from (7.10) is as follows:

$$\begin{bmatrix} .578 & .562 \\ .531 & .344 \\ .687 & -.422 \\ .765 & -.484 \end{bmatrix} \times \begin{bmatrix} .7771 & .6293 \\ -.6293 & .7771 \end{bmatrix} = \begin{bmatrix} .10 & .80 \\ .20 & .60 \\ .80 & .10 \\ .90 & .11 \end{bmatrix}$$

$$\mathbf{A} \qquad\qquad \mathbf{\Lambda} \qquad\qquad \mathbf{V}$$

diagonals of a matrix of correlations between Eysenck Personality Inventory items, all factors with eigenvalues of 1.0 or more are extracted, and when all 17 of these factors are rotated by Varimax, small factors are built up in an inappropriate way while the major expected factors of Neuroticism and Extraversion almost disappear. This same phenomenon was verified in a new sample by Comrey, Noller, and Law (1988).

It is very important in using Varimax, therefore, to avoid including extra factors in the rotations. It is often necessary to inspect several solutions, varying the number of factors rotated, before the most satisfactory solution is settled upon. The most satisfactory Varimax solutions will be those in which neither too few nor too many factors are rotated. Trial and error is often the only way to establish the correct number of factors.

It also may be necessary to rotate the Varimax solution further orthogonally or obliquely, or both, before an entirely satisfactory result has been achieved. Where such hand rotations are undertaken, starting from the Varimax solution represents a great time-saver compared with starting the hand rotations from the original unrotated matrix. The Varimax solution is most apt to prove satisfactory when the factor analytic investigation has been carefully designed so that the probable solution will be likely to approximate the demands of the Varimax criterion.

Kaiser recommends the use of the "normal" Varimax in preference to the "raw" Varimax method just described, contending that "normal" Varimax solutions are more invariant from one sample to another. With the normal Varimax, all data-variable vectors are scaled to unit length by dividing each variable's loadings by the square root of its communality. Then, the raw Varimax procedure can be applied in carrying out the rotations. At the conclusion, the loadings for each variable are rescaled back down to proper size by multiplying each loading for a given variable by the square root of the communality for that variable. After this operation, the sum of squares of the loadings for the variable will again equal the communality instead of 1.0.

The "normal" Varimax method gives equal weight to all variables in determining the rotations. This seems reasonable in a well-designed study where all variables have substantial communalities. Where some of the communalities are quite low, however, the investigator is encouraged by the authors to consider the possibility that the "raw" Varimax solution may be superior to the "normal" Varimax solution. To inflate a very low communality to 1.0 and then treat that variable as if it were of equal importance to those with originally high communalities seems questionable as a general practice.

7.5. THE TANDEM CRITERIA METHOD

The first author has developed an orthogonal analytic rotation method that avoids some of the problems occasionally encountered with the Varimax method. It is called the "Tandem Criteria" method (Comrey, 1967). Although this method is not nearly as popular as the Varimax method, the authors have found it to be very useful in practice. It is also not described in most other texts on factor analysis, so it is treated in some detail in this section.

The Tandem Criteria method grew out of a conviction that available information about the correlations among the data variables could be utilized profitably in factor rotations. Experimentation with this idea led to the development of two analytic rotational criteria that are ordinarily, but not always, used in tandem, hence the name. The first of these, Criterion I, is based on the following principle:

Principle I. If two variables are correlated, they should appear on the same factor.

A mathematical interpretation of this principle is developed in the following section to provide the basis for Criterion I rotations.

7.5.1. ROTATION BY CRITERION I OF THE TANDEM CRITERIA

Principle I may be approximated mathematically by the following:

$$F = \sum_{k=1}^{k=m} \sum_{i=1}^{i=n} \sum_{j=1}^{j=n} r'_{ij}{}^2 a_{ik}{}^2 a_{jk}{}^2 \tag{7.11}$$

where

$$r'_{ij} = \sum_{k=1}^{k=m} a_{ik} a_{jk},$$ the reproduced correlation between variable i and

variable j,

a_{ik} is the factor loading of variable i on factor k,

a_{jk} is the factor loading of variable j on factor k.

The function F in Eq. (7.11) is to be maximized. This will occur when the variables that are correlated with each other are put on the same factor. As with the Varimax method, maximizing the function in Eq. (7.11) is accomplished by rotating the factors two at a time, maximizing the function in each rotation separately. After each factor is rotated with each of the other factors, and a cycle is thus completed, the function value is computed. Additional cycles are completed until the value of the function fails to increase. For two factors, the value of the function may be expressed as follows:

$$f = \sum_{j=1}^{i=n} \sum_{j=n}^{j=n} r'_{ij}{}^2 (X_i^2 X_j^2 + Y_i^2 Y_j^2) \tag{7.12}$$

where X and Y are the rotated factor loadings as defined in Eqs. (7.3) and (7.4) for the Varimax method.

The remainder of the development requires calculus. The reader may skip to Eq. (7.20) to pass around this part of the proof. The function in Eq. (7.12) is differentiated with respect to ϕ and set equal to zero, with Eqs.

(7.6) used to give the values for $dX/d\phi$ and $dY/d\phi$. The development is similar to that for the Varimax method:

$$\frac{df}{d\phi} = \sum_{i=1}^{i=n}\sum_{j=1}^{j=n} r'^2_{ij} \times$$

$$[X_i^2(2X_jY_j) + X_j^2(2X_iY_i) + Y_i^2(2Y_j)(-X_j) + Y_j^2(2Y_i)(-X_i)]$$

$$\frac{df}{d\phi} = \sum_{i=1}^{i=n}\sum_{j=1}^{j=n} r'^2_{ij}[2X_jY_j(X_i^2 - Y_i^2) + 2X_iY_i(X_j^2 - Y_j^2)] \qquad (7.13)$$

Breaking (7.13) into parts and substituting Eq. (7.4) for X and Y, we have

$$2X_iY_i = -2(-x_i^2\sin\phi\cos\phi + x_iy_i\cos^2\phi - x_iy_i\sin^2\phi + y_i^2\sin\phi\cos\phi) \qquad (7.14)$$

$$2X_iY_i = -(x_i^2 - y_i^2)\sin2\phi + 2x_iy_i\cos2\phi \qquad (7.15)$$

By analogy to Eq. (7.15),

$$2X_jY_j = -(x_j^2 - y_j^2)\sin2\phi + 2x_jy_j\cos2\phi \qquad (7.16)$$

Continuing with other parts of (7.13), we get

$$X_i^2 - Y_i^2 = x_i^2\cos^2\phi + y_i^2\sin^2\phi + 2x_iy_i\cos\phi\sin\phi$$
$$- (x_i^2\sin^2\phi + y_i^2\cos^2\phi - 2x_iy_i\sin\phi\cos\phi)$$
$$= (x_i^2 - y_i^2)\cos^2\phi - (x_i^2y_i^2)\sin^2\phi + 4x_iy_i\sin\phi\cos\phi$$
$$X_i^2 - Y_i^2 = (x_i^2 - y_i^2)\cos2\phi + 2x_iy_i\sin2\phi \qquad (7.17)$$

and by analogy with (7.17):

$$X_j^2 - Y_j^2 = (x_j^2 - y_j^2)\cos2\phi + 2x_jy_j\sin2\phi \qquad (7.18)$$

Substituting (7.15)–(7.18) in Eq. (7.13) and simplifying gives

$$\frac{df}{d\phi} = -\sum_{i=1}^{i=n}\sum_{j=1}^{j=n} r'^2_{ij}[(x_i^2 - y_i^2)(x_j^2 - y_j^2) - 4x_iy_ix_jy_j]\sin4\phi$$
$$+ \sum_{i=1}^{i=n}\sum_{j=1}^{j=n} r'^2_{ij}[2x_iy_i(x_j^2 - y_j^2) + 2x_jy_j(x_i^2 - y_i^2)]\cos4\phi$$

$$(7.19)$$

Setting Eq. (7.19) equal to zero and solving for tan 4ϕ, which equals $\sin 4\phi / \cos 4\phi$, gives

$$\text{Tan } 4\phi = \frac{2 \sum\limits_{i=1}^{i=n} \sum\limits_{j=1}^{j=n} r'_{ij}{}^2 [x_i y_i (x_j^2 - y_j^2) + x_j y_j (x_i^2 - y_i^2)]}{\sum\limits_{i=1}^{i=n} \sum\limits_{j=1}^{j=n} r'_{ij}{}^2 [(x_i^2 - y_i^2)(x_j^2 - y_j^2) - 4x_i y_i x_j y_j]} \tag{7.20}$$

Any angle of rotation ϕ that maximizes the function in Eq. (7.12) must satisfy Eq. (7.20). To ensure, however, that a maximum is reached, rather than a minimum or a point of inflection, the second derivative evaluated at ϕ must be negative. When Eq. (7.20) is expressed as tan 4ϕ = num/denom, Eq. (7.19) may be expressed as

$$\frac{df}{d\phi} = -(\text{denom})\sin 4\phi + (\text{num})\cos 4\phi \tag{7.21}$$

Differentiating (7.21) with respect to ϕ gives

$$\frac{d^2 f}{d\phi^2} = -(\text{denom})(4\cos 4\phi) + (\text{num})(-4\sin 4\phi)$$

$$= -4[(\text{denom})\cos 4\phi + (\text{num})\sin 4\phi] \tag{7.22}$$

The quadrant in which 4ϕ is placed must be such that the expression in (7.22), the second derivative, remains negative. These relationships are shown in Table 7.2.

The angle of rotation that will maximize the function in Eq. (7.12) can be found, therefore, from the following:

		num	
		−	+
denom	+	$-\phi$	ϕ
	−	$-(45° - \phi)$	$(45° - \phi)$

The angle ϕ itself is found from Eq. (7.20), by ignoring the signs on numerator and denominator, taking 4ϕ in the first quadrant, and dividing the angle 4ϕ by 4 to get ϕ. With this value of ϕ, the transformation matrix that will perform the Criterion I rotation should be chosen from (7.10) by the same rules used to select the transformation matrix Λ for the Varimax

TABLE 7.2

Sign combinations	Second derivative	Sign	4φ
num +, denom +	$-4[(+)(+)+(+)(+)]$	–	0–90°
num +, denom –	$-4[(-)(-)+(+)(+)]$	–	90–180°
num –, denom –	$-4[(-)(-)+(-)(-)]$	–	180–270°
num –, denom +	$-4[(+)(+)+(-)(-)]$	–	270–360°

rotation. An angle in the second quadrant, for example, 150° equals (180° − 30°). Dividing 180° by four gives 45° which accounts for the (45° − ϕ) angle of rotation in (7.23) when the angle 4ϕ is divided by four to get ϕ.

As an illustration, the four-variable centroid matrix in Table 2.2 is rotated by Criterion I with the computations shown in Table 7.3. Computations are based on only the off-diagonal elements because in general the communality values are not known and should not affect the rotations. The rotated values in matrix V in Table 7.3 are reasonably close to those in Table 2.2, although not so close as the Varimax values.

Criterion I rotations are not expected to and generally do not give a close approximation to simple structure. Criterion I rotations spread the variance out to make the rotated factors less unequal in size than the unrotated factors, as do other methods of rotation. To remain on the same factor, variables must be correlated with each other. This forces a spreading of the variance from larger unrotated factors to smaller unrotated factors because the large unrotated factors typically have substantial loadings for variables that in many cases are relatively orthogonal to each other. The Criterion I demand that correlated variables should be placed on the same factor puts an effective damper, however, on the process of shifting variance from larger to smaller factors. The effect of this is that all the available unrotated factors that could possibly be worth retaining can be included in the Criterion I rotations without fear of dispersing the variance too much, thereby distorting the solution. It will be recalled that this is a problem with the Varimax method. Thus, all the factors that can be extracted by means of the minimum residual algorithm before encountering vectors of opposite sign can be rotated, if desired, by Criterion I without being concerned that too many factors are being rotated. The matter of discarding unneeded small factors can be dealt with after the Criterion I rotations have been completed.When all the unrotated factors of any size are rotated by Criterion I, there are often some Criterion I rotated factors that are too small to be retained, for example, those with no loadings at all as high as 0.3 or more. Unless the sample is very large, such factors can be dropped. Some of the other Criterion I factors may be marginal, that is, with several loadings in the range of 0.3 to 0.45, possibly even a single value over 0.50.

TABLE 7.3

Criterion I Rotation of Two Centroid Factors (4 Variable Problem)

x	y	$(x^2 - y^2)$	xy		1	2	3	4
.578	.562	.0182	.3248	1	(.65)	.50	.16	.17
.531	.344	.1636	.1827	2	.50	(.40)	.22	.24
.687	−.422	.2938	−.2899	3	.16	.22	(.65)	.73
.765	−.484	.3510	−.3702	4	.17	.24	.73	(.82)

Matrix of r values

Numerator (num) values:

$i = 1, j = 2$	$(.50)^2[(.3248)(.1636) + (.1827)(.0182)] = \quad .0141$
$i = 1, j = 3$	$(.16)^2[(.3248)(.2939) + (-.2899)(.0182)] = \quad .0023$
$i = 1, j = 4$	$(.17)^2[(.3248)(.3510) + (-.3702)(.0182)] = \quad .0031$
$i = 2, j = 3$	$(.22)^2[(.1827)(.2939) + (-.2899)(.1636)] = \quad .0003$
$i = 2, j = 4$	$(.24)^2[(.1827)(.3510) + (-.3702)(.1636)] = \quad .0002$
$i = 3, j = 4$	$(.73)^2[(-.2899)(.3510) + (-.3702)(.2939)] = -.1122$

Sum of Numerator values = −.0922

Denominator (denom) values:

$i = 1, j = 2$	$(.50)^2[(.0182)(.1636) - 4(.0593)] = -.0586$
$i = 1, j = 3$	$(.16)^2[(.0182)(.2939) - 4(-.0942)] = \quad .0098$
$i = 1, j = 4$	$(.17)^2[(.0182)(.3510) - 4(-.1202)] = \quad .0141$
$i = 2, j = 3$	$(.22)^2[(.1636)(.2939) - 4(-.0530)] = \quad .0126$
$i = 2, j = 4$	$(.24)^2[(.1636)(.3510) - 4(-.0676)] = \quad .0189$
$i = 3, j = 4$	$(.73)^2[(.2939)(.3510) - 4(.1073)] = -.1738$

Sum of Denominator values = −.1770

$$\text{Tan}4\phi = \frac{2 \times \text{num}}{\text{denom}} = \frac{2 \times (-.0922)}{-.1770} = \frac{-.1844}{-.1770} = 1.04$$

The angle $4\phi = 46° \, 7'$ so $\phi = 11° \, 32'$. Because the denominator is negative, the angle of rotation will be $(45° - \phi)$ or $33° \, 28'$. Because the numerator is negative, the angle of rotation will be negative. The results of the rotation, therefore, are as follows:

$$\begin{bmatrix} .578 & .562 \\ .531 & .344 \\ .687 & -.422 \\ .765 & -.484 \end{bmatrix} \times \begin{bmatrix} .8342 & .5515 \\ -.5515 & .8342 \end{bmatrix} = \begin{bmatrix} .172 & .788 \\ .253 & .580 \\ .806 & .027 \\ .905 & .018 \end{bmatrix}$$
$$\quad\quad\; \text{A} \quad\quad\quad\quad\quad\quad\; \Lambda \quad\quad\quad\quad\quad\quad\; \text{V}$$

By inspection of the Criterion I factors, it is ordinarily possible to narrow down the choice of the correct number of factors to a small range of possibilities. This is a very major advantage of using the Criterion I method. By squeezing the variance down to as few factors as possible, given that variables that are correlated must appear on the same factors, those later factors that are unable to capture any substantial amount of variance from the earlier large unrotated factors can be detected and discarded. Some of the Criterion I factors may be expected to have two or more variables with loadings above 0.50; these are major factors that definitely will be retained.

Factors with no loadings of 0.3 or more usually will be discarded. A few factors are apt to be questionable. Through the use of Criterion II rotations (described in Section 7.5.2) of various numbers of Criterion I factors, a determination can be made as to which marginal factors can also be retained, thus establishing the correct number of factors.

In most cases, therefore, Criterion I rotations are not carried out to obtain the final rotated solution but rather to aid in the task of determining how many factors should be retained in the rotated solution. There are exceptions to this rule, however, one being where a general factor is expected or where an hypothesis of a general factor is being tested. Criterion I rotations will reveal the presence of a general factor, if it exists, because variables that are all correlated with each other will be retained as much as possible on the same factor rather than scattered around to different factors as with some other methods based on simple structure concepts. Where a general factor is expected, therefore, Criterion I rotations may well be utilized as the final solution. Other situations are described later in which the judicious use of Criterion I rotations provide the best solution (Lee & Comrey, 1979).

7.5.2. ROTATION BY CRITERION II OF THE TANDEM CRITERIA

In most situations, Criterion I rotations will not provide the final solution to a factor analytic problem. Once it has been established how many Criterion I factors are to be retained, these factors are usually rotated further by means of Criterion II, a method based on the following principle:

Principle II. If two variables are not correlated, they should not appear on the same factor.

A mathematical approximation to the idea involved in Principle II is the following:

$$F = \sum_{k=1}^{k=m} \sum_{i=1}^{i=n} \sum_{j=1}^{j=n} (1 - r'^2_{ij})a_{ik}^2 a_{jk}^2 \qquad (7.24)$$

where all terms are defined as in Eq. (7.11). By minimizing the function in (7.24), Principle II is approximately satisfied.

The mathematical development for Criterion II parallels that for Criterion I in Eqs. (7.11)–(7.20), except that wherever r'^2_{ij} appears for Criterion I, $(1 - r'^2_{ij})$ must be substituted to obtain the corresponding results for Criterion II. Thus, by analogy with Eq. (7.20), the angle ϕ that gives the desired Criterion II rotation is derived from

$$\tan 4\phi \;=\; \frac{2\displaystyle\sum_{i=1}^{i=n}\sum_{j=1}^{j=n}(1-r'^{2}_{ij})[x_{i}y_{i}(x_{j}^{2}-y_{j}^{2}) \;+\; x_{j}y_{j}(x_{i}^{2}-y_{i}^{2})]}{\displaystyle\sum_{i=1}^{i=n}\sum_{j=1}^{j=n}(1-r'^{2}_{ij})[(x_{i}^{2}-y_{i}^{2})(x_{j}^{2}-y_{j}^{2}) \;-\; 4x_{i}y_{i}x_{j}y_{j}]}$$

$$(7.25)$$

To ensure that a minimum has been reached for the function, however, the second derivative evaluated at ϕ must be positive. By reasoning analogous to that used to find the appropriate angle of rotation for Criterion I, the desired angle of rotation for Criterion II is given by the following:

num

		−	+
denom	+	$(45° - \phi)$	$-(45° - \phi)$
	−	ϕ	$-\phi$

The angle ϕ itself is found from Eq. (7.25), ignoring the signs on numerator and denominator, taking 4ϕ in the first quadrant, and dividing the angle 4ϕ by 4 to get ϕ. The transformation matrix that will perform the Criterion II rotation is then chosen from the following possibilities:

$$\begin{bmatrix} \cos\phi & -\sin\phi \\ \sin\phi & \cos\phi \end{bmatrix} \qquad \begin{bmatrix} \cos\phi & \sin\phi \\ -\sin\phi & \cos\phi \end{bmatrix}$$

Λ (num −, denom −) Λ (num +, denom −)

$$\begin{bmatrix} \cos(45° - \phi) & -\sin(45° - \phi) \\ \sin(45° - \phi) & \cos(45° - \phi) \end{bmatrix} \qquad \begin{bmatrix} \cos(45° - \phi) & \sin(45° - \phi) \\ -\sin(45° - \phi) & \cos(45° - \phi) \end{bmatrix}$$

Λ (num −, denom +) Λ (num +, denom +)

Varimax rotations could be applied in many cases and the results obtained would be similar to those for Criterion II rotations of Criterion I factors, provided that all superfluous minor factors have been eliminated and the same number of factors is rotated for both methods. If this control is not exercised, Criterion II will disperse the variance much more than will Varimax, even splitting large factors into two more or less equal halves. For this reason, Criterion II *cannot* be applied unless the correct number of factors has been determined within a relatively small margin of error. This is normally accomplished by the prior application of Criterion I, as already explained, so that only retained Criterion I factors are rotated by Criterion

II. Rotation of differing numbers of Criterion I factors by Criterion II in the region of uncertainty helps to establish what is the correct number of factors. An example of a complete solution using Criterion II rotations following Criterion I rotations is given in a later chapter.

The preceding solutions for the Tandem Criteria are the "raw" Criterion I and Criterion II solutions. As with Varimax, "normal" Criterion I and Criterion II solutions may be obtained by scaling all factor loadings to give communalities of 1.0 before starting the computations.[1] After the rotations are completed, the loadings are scaled back down to give the original communalities. The authors feel that the use of "normal" solutions with Tandem Criteria, as with Varimax, is of questionable superiority if there are many data variables with low communalities. Inflating low communalities up to 1.0 and treating such variables with the same importance as variables with large communalities in the rotation process would seem to be inappropriate in most cases, however desirable it might be when all the communalities are substantial. A computer program for carrying out Tandem Criteria rotations with various options is described in a later chapter.

As with all other rotational criteria, special examples can be conceived where the Tandem Criteria will not provide a suitable solution, quite apart from their limitation to orthogonal solutions. If it were possible to find two distinct clusters of variables that correlate highly within clusters but not at all across clusters, and all of which have substantial loadings on the same factor, Tandem Criteria would have difficulty finding this solution. Such a situation would require that both clusters have substantial loadings of opposite sign on some other factor besides the one on which both clusters have substantial positive loadings. Although such a situation is conceivable, it is not apt to be encountered very often, and certainly it would be rare to have this kind of phenomenon involved in more than a fraction of the variables in a matrix of substantial size. The user of the Tandem Criteria must be alert to the possibility, however, that the data may present special characteristics that render this method unsuitable, a caveat that applies equally well to all analytic rotational procedures.

7.6.   ONE STRATEGY FOR FACTOR ANALYTIC WORK

In the typical factor analysis performed by the average investigator, there may not be available a great deal of information about the underlying factor structure beyond the expectation that several dimensions will be

---

[1] The first author is indebted to Henry Kaiser for suggesting the use of the "normal" procedures with Tandem Criteria and also for suggesting the use of r', the reproduced correlation, instead of r, the raw-data correlation, in the equations.

needed. Under these circumstances, the authors have found the following procedures to be serviceable:

1. Extract factors by the minimum residual method until convergence on vectors of opposite sign occurs, not using communality estimates.

2. Inspect these factors and drop any obviously residual factors, for example, those with no loadings of 0.2 or more.

3. Rotate the remaining minimum residual factors by Criterion I of the Tandem Criteria, throwing away all clearly residual rotated factors, for example, those with no loading as high as 0.3 or more. Arrange the retained Criterion I factors in order of their magnitude, that is, the sum of squares of their loadings.

4. Rotate these retained Criterion I factors by Criterion II. If any minor factor of these retained Criterion I factors fails to increase in magnitude, for example, in the proportion of variance accounted for as determined by the sum of squares of its loadings, and/or fails to retain its basic character in the Criterion II rotations, it is dropped and the remaining Criterion I factors will be rerotated. Criterion II will split a major factor and dump part of its variance onto a minor factor if that factor is not "strong enough" to resist such a "takeover." When a minor factor disappears like this, it must be dropped and the remaining factors rerotated by Criterion II. The minor factor can be retained as such but it is not allowed to be rotated in with the major factors to determine the solution for the major factors. A minor Criterion I factor retains its basic character in the Criterion II rotations provided that the same variables that had high loadings on the Criterion I factor continue to have the highest loadings on the Criterion II factor.

5. This process of testing minor factors and dropping any that fail to survive continues until all the Criterion I factors rotated by Criterion II retain their basic character and at least as much variance as they had before the rotations by Criterion II. Minor Criterion I factors are not usually included in the Criterion II rotations unless they have at least two or three loadings in the region from 0.3 to 0.5, and possibly one of 0.5 or more. Some of these minor factors ordinarily will have to be dropped as a result of this winnowing process. No Criterion I factor with two or more loadings of 0.5 or more is ever dropped. Such factors are always considered to be major factors.

6. Once the correct number of factors has been determined, the entire solution can be rerun, holding constant the number of factors. The minimum residual program is used but the solution is iterated about ten times, sometimes more, to stabilize the communalities.[2] The second and

---

[2] For a different point of view, see Velicer and Jackson's (1990) discussion of the relative advantages of component analysis versus common factor analysis. Critical comments on these views by other leading factor analysts are given in the same journal issue.

subsequent iterated solutions are principal factor solutions derived by means of the minimum residual algorithm using the diagonal cells. The communalities will be larger than those for the minimum residual solution without iteration, because the derived communalities with the minimum residual solution are generally underestimates. The process of obtaining Criterion I and Criterion II rotations should be repeated to see if any additional factors can be dropped. Usually none can be. This iterated solution should not be used if it appears that the communalities have been driven up to an unrealistically high level, a possible outcome since this procedure may take advantage of chance errors to maximize the amount of variance extracted, thereby increasing the overall size of the communalities.

7. Once the final solution has been determined after rotating the iterated unrotated factors by means of Criterion I and II, if iteration appears to have been appropriate, the Criterion II factors can be rotated further by any other method desired, for example, to obtain an oblique simple structure solution. The hand rotation program described in a later chapter can be used for this purpose.

8

Planning the Standard Design
Factor Analysis

One of the most common errors committed by inexperienced research workers is to collect a mass of data before deciding how the data are to be analyzed. Despite the fact that proper planning is just as important in factor analytic research as it is in other areas, factor analysis is often called upon to rescue unplanned research endeavors from disaster. For every person who asks how to plan a project so that factor analysis can be used effectively, there seem to be ten who wait until after the data are already collected to ask for help in doing "something" with what they have. Needless to say, when factor analysis is used as an afterthought on data from a poorly planned investigation, the results are not apt to be gratifying nor representative of what factor analysis can do when used properly. Investigators who wish to get the most from this powerful analytic tool would do well to give careful attention to the principles of proper design of factor analytic research. Principles of design and other considerations involved in a well-planned factor analytic investigation are the subject of this chapter.

8.1. SOME PRINCIPLES OF DESIGN

Ideally, investigators should be free to define the area they wish to work with, obtain data from an appropriate sample of individuals they select, and then carry out the analysis. When investigators have this kind of latitude, they are in the best position to design a good study. If they have no choice of data or subjects, their freedom may be so greatly reduced that a well-designed study might be impossible to achieve. It will be assumed here that the investigators are free to proceed in the most appropriate fashion. To the extent that they are not, they can only do their best to approximate the conditions for a properly planned study as closely as possible.

The first step in planning a factor analysis is to define the domain to be studied and then to develop a hypothesized factor structure for this domain (Comrey, 1978; Guilford, 1950). That is, the investigators should use all the knowledge and deductive power at their disposal to formulate a factor model. This model will state explicitly the nature of the expected factors together with alternative hypotheses concerning their possible characteristics. Next, data variables that are expected to be related to the hypothesized factors in a particular way should be identified. For example, if a particular factor is expected to emerge from the analysis, for example, Extraversion-Introversion, what are the data variables that should have high factor loadings on that factor and what variables should have low or negligible factor loadings on that factor?

It is important to go through this type of analysis to ensure that any expected factor will be overdetermined if it does appear in the solution. That is, there will be several data variables with high loadings on the factor as well as a much larger number of data variables that will be essentially unrelated to the factor. If a factor is not overdetermined, it may appear only weakly and with a small number of defining data variables. This situation makes the factor difficult to position and hard to identify. Of course, investigators may be wrong in their hypotheses about the factors and what variables will represent them. To the extent that they are in error, the factor solution will not verify their hypotheses. If they fail to think this through ahead of time, however, it is unlikely that they will make adequate provisions to see that all important factors are properly represented. The tendency with unplanned investigations is to have one or a few factors unnecessarily overdetermined while the others are insufficiently represented in the analysis. Finding appropriate data variables to serve these functions in a factor analysis is not always easy. Research workers frequently find that they must design or create new variables with the desired characteristics to serve as marker variables for the factors they hypothesize will emerge. This is because the best marker variables are relatively pure-factor measures while the bulk of the data variables ordinarily available to the investigator are factorially complex, measuring several factors rather than just one.

The need to overdetermine factors means that each factor should have five or more data variables as good markers to represent it if at all possible. Three good, relatively factor-pure markers would constitute an absolute minimum number of variables to define a factor in the analysis. The more variables there are to define a factor, the more clearly it will be established in the analysis, and the easier it will be to locate it in the rotations. The total number of data variables included in a factor analysis, then, should be at least five or six times as great as the number of factors expected to emerge.

Factor positions are determined by the variables that are *not* related to the factor as well as by those that *are*. In fact, with simple structure, the variables not related to the factor, *rather than* those that are, determine the factor position. Simple structure can be most helpful, therefore, as a guide to rotations when there are many variables in the analysis that are essentially unrelated to the factor in question. This can be achieved best by including six or more hypothesized factors that are relatively independent of one another. Under these conditions, the great majority of the data variables will be in the hyperplane for any one factor, thereby providing a clear hyperplane to assist in locating the factor if it does emerge as predicted. A study designed in this way stands a good chance of yielding an excellent simple structure solution if the investigators' analysis of the situation has been reasonably good. At least, if the domain is at all close to their perception of it, simple structure will probably be a fairly good rotational model for the analysis.

In ascertaining whether a given hypothesized factor is likely to be overdetermined in the analysis, only relatively pure-factor data variables can be counted on. A pure-factor data variable has a major loading in only one factor. It is to be contrasted with a complex data variable that has major loadings in more than one factor. There is nothing wrong with having some complex data variables in the analysis; indeed, one of the purposes of the analysis may be to gain a better understanding of the factorial composition of one or more such variables. These complex data variables are not very useful, however, in determining the proper positioning of factors. They are apt to have moderate loadings on several factors; hence they do not contribute to defining hyperplanes nor are they helpful in identifying the nature of the factors on which they have their major loadings. The Varimax method, for example, tries to avoid precisely this type of loading because it is not readily interpreted. Where such complex data variables are included in an analysis, then, they should not be counted on to define factors. The several "marker" variables for each factor should be as factor pure as possible. This is a very difficult requirement to satisfy, of course, if the investigators are constrained to choose the data variables from a set that does not include any pure-factor measures! Unfortunately, this is all too often the case where factor analysis is applied as an afterthought.

If the hypothesized factor is not represented by several relatively factor-pure measures, and several complex data variables involving this factor appear in the matrix, there is serious risk of improper positioning of the factor. For example, if several complex variables are included that share more than one common factor, a factor may be positioned in such a way that these complex data variables appear to be pure-factor measures. The factor itself, in such cases, becomes a complex factor rather than a unitary, that is, univocal, factor, and the appropriate factor position will be missed altogether because there were not enough pure-factor measures of that factor in the matrix. The investigators may be quite unaware that the factor they have located is in fact not univocal but complex in nature.

A good example of this phenomenon would be an analysis in which the eight abnormal scale scores of the original Minnesota Multiphasic Personality Inventory (MMPI) are included in the same matrix along with some total scores in other psychological tests. The MMPI scale scores are highly complex factorially (Comrey & Levonian, 1958; Comrey, 1959) and also overlap each other considerably in factorial content. Factor analyses of the MMPI total scale scores have shown that scales Hs, D, and Hy can be expected to define one factor. It might look as if these scales were pure-factor measures of this obtained factor. In reality, however, the factor defined by these variables would not be univocal but complex, based on the combination of several factors these complex measures all share. If some data variables that measure both factors A and B are included in the matrix, there must be other data variables that measure A but not B and B but not A if separate factors A and B are to be isolated in the analysis. The number of variables that measure both A and B should be considerably smaller than the number of variables that measure these factors alone to avoid the possibility that a factor will be placed through the cluster of complex variables that measure both A and B together. If not, ordinary rotational criteria, such as simple structure, cannot be expected to locate the proper factor positions for factors A and B.

Thus, where investigators do not have the option of including several data variables that should be relatively pure-factor measures of a hypothesized factor, it may be necessary for them to rotate the factors in a rather unorthodox fashion to make allowances for the peculiarities of their sample of variables. If they know, or strongly suspect, for instance, that there is only one data variable that is likely to be a pure-factor measure of a given hypothesized factor, they may be forced to line up a factor right through that data vector regardless of what other criteria of rotation might suggest. A proper design of the factor study, of course, would obviate the need for such ad hoc manipulations.

As a scientific tool, factor analysis has its greatest application in the process of determining what the important variables are in a given scientific domain. Determining what those important variables are is a necessary preliminary step before it is possible to begin the next phase of scientific work, which is devoted to determining the nature of the functional relationships between the important variables in the field of study. The social sciences are still very much in the phase of trying to determine what variables are important and how to measure them. Although factor analysis can be a helpful aid in this endeavor, it is apt to be most useful when applied to a series of interrelated investigations rather than just a one-shot study. The process of refining factor constructs takes place slowly. Each investigation provides some clues and hypotheses that must be checked out in a subsequent study. The conceptual boundaries of a factor construct are only dimly perceived at first in many cases. Variables that relate to it initially are modified in an attempt to increase their factor purity. An effort is made to develop other variables that also will relate to the construct. Variables that fail to do so are dropped in subsequent investigations. By means of such hypothetico-deductive methods applied through a series of empirical studies, the factor construct becomes more and more clearly understood. As this is going on, the methods of assessing the factor construct are being improved. After the factor construct has been well described and good measures of it have been established, experiments of a nonfactor-analytic kind may be undertaken to pin down still more tightly what the construct represents. These studies will also seek to determine how it is related to practical criteria of interest as well as to other variables of scientific interest in the domain of investigation (Comrey, 1988). Those who would use factor analytic methods to increase scientific understanding, therefore, are urged to plan programmatic sequences of investigations, and to make changes and test hypotheses from one study to the next, rather than settling for a single analysis.

8.1.1. THE FACTOR HIERARCHY

Constructs represented by individual factors in the results of a factor analysis can range from the highly specific and narrow to the very broad and complex, depending upon the nature of the data variables being analyzed (Comrey, 1988). Factors that are very low in the hierarchy of factors are those that are based on relatively simple phenomena of limited general interest. Perhaps the most common way in which such low-level factors are produced is through the inclusion in the same analysis of very similar variables. For example, if diastolic and systolic blood pressure are included in a factor analysis of several physiological response measures, it is likely that a doublet factor will emerge from the analysis in which only these two variables have high loadings. The factor obtained in this case does not shed much light on basic underlying physiological mechanisms; it merely advises us that diastolic and systolic blood pressure overlap tremendously in what they measure, enough perhaps to be considered almost alternate forms of the same variable.

Other common examples occur where questionnaire items are being factor analyzed. If two or more of the questionnaire items bear a marked similarity to each other, much more so than with the other items, it is almost inevitable that a factor will emerge defined principally if not exclusively by these similar items. Again, the factor in question does not herald the emergence of some dramatic new construct of great taxonomic interest. It merely means that the choice of items for analysis resulted in the production of a relatively uninteresting, unimportant, low-level factor. Use of the Varimax criterion in factor rotation tends to make these low-level factors stand out in bold relief because it will tend to push the loadings for these variables as high as possible to maximize the variance of the squared factor loadings.

An example of this kind of phenomenon can be seen in Fig. 8.1. Suppose that variables 1–6 all represent items that measure to some degree a factor construct of sufficient generality to place it above the lowest level in the factor hierarchy. Suppose in addition that items 5 and 6 are rather similar items. The following personality-type questionnaire items, used with a graded frequency scale of response, might represent the situation:

1. I am tense and nervous.
2. I lack confidence.
3. I am unable to cope with life's problems.
4. My moods fluctuate easily.
5. I feel blue.
6. I suffer from depression.

Variables 5 and 6 correlate with each other very highly because they are really only alternate ways of asking the same question. Questions 1–4 are

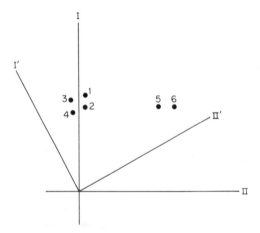

FIG. 8.1. Factors of different levels.

related to each other, and also to items 5 and 6, since they all are related to the personality factor Emotional Stability versus Neuroticism, but no two of these items are asking the same question in a different way except items 5 and 6. These last two items correlate at a higher level because they not only share the common variance due to the Emotional Stability versus Neuroticism factor they both measure, but in addition they share a substantial amount of specific variance associated with this kind of question.

In Fig. 8.1, with the factors positioned as I and II, all items are represented by vectors that project on factor I about equally and with substantial loadings. Variables 5 and 6 have substantial loadings on factor II, but the other variables do not. In this position, factor I represents the Neuroticism versus Emotional Stability factor, which is related about equally to all the variables. Factor II represents the leftover common variance in variables 5 and 6, which cannot be accounted for by the Neuroticism versus Emotional Stability factor. It is, therefore, a minor, low-level factor of limited importance in the hierarchy of factors. Factor I, on the other hand, is at a different level, higher in the hierarchy, and of much greater general scientific interest.

By poor design of this factor analytic experiment, through the use of two overly similar variables in items 5 and 6, factors of markedly different levels in the hierarchy of factors have been introduced into the same analysis. The effect of this design error can be handled by appropriate rotation of the factor axes to sort out the factors properly into one major and one minor factor, like I and II in Fig. 8.1. Unfortunately, however, typical rotational methods are not apt to give a solution like factors I and II but rather are more likely to place the factors as in positions I' and II'. These positions for the factors treat both factors more or less as equals, one with major loadings for variables 1–4 and smaller loadings for variables 5 and 6. The other factor will have major loadings for variables 5 and 6 with small loadings for variables 1–4. An oblique solution would eliminate the small loadings on both factors, leaving 1, 2, 3, and 4 on one factor and 5 and 6 on the other factor with a substantial positive correlation between the two factors. In either the orthogonal or the oblique solution of this kind, the major Emotional Stability versus Neuroticism factor would not be properly represented in the solution because of the disturbing effect of the extra-large correlation between variables 5 and 6. Neither of these solutions would correctly show all items about equally related to the same major factor as they should.

The problem created by the overlapping specific variance of variables 5 and 6 shown in Fig. 8.1 could have been avoided if one of these two variables had been eliminated from the analysis or if both had been combined to form a single variable. This could be accomplished by merely adding the two scores for variables 5 and 6 together to yield a single score for each person on these two items.

The presence of low-level factors in the hierarchy of factors through the introduction of variables with overlapping specific variance is often not anticipated by the investigator, particularly in exploratory studies. Scrutiny of the emerging factors in an analysis will often reveal that one or more factors are based either totally or partially on this kind of phenomenon. Under such circumstances, it is often wise to run the analysis again after eliminating or combining the offending variables to remove factors that are too low in the hierarchy of factors.

Another way of forcing the factors to a higher level in the hierarchy of factors is through underextraction, that is, not taking out as many factors as the data seem to call for. Because the extracted factors are ordered in a steeply graded series with respect to size, by dropping off the later factors, smaller low-level factor precursors that will produce factors in the rotations like factor II in Fig. 8.1 tend to be eliminated, leaving only the larger factors like factor I. Eysenck (1960) has used this technique in his analyses of personality variables by extracting only a few factors from his matrices of correlations between personality variables. Or, he may extract many factors, rotate them obliquely, and perform a higher-order factor analysis, forcing the variance into a space of fewer factors by this device. The difficulty with these methods of avoiding the production of low-level factors is that it requires a precise determination of the number of factors that must be extracted to be sure that only the major factors, and no low-level factors, will emerge from the analysis. Such information is normally not available to the investigators. If they are mistaken, the factor solution may be seriously distorted. In most cases, therefore, it is better to extract all the permissible factors and then gradually eliminate those of minor importance, reanalyzing, if necessary, after elimination of some variables from the analysis that cause the production of unwanted minor factors.

It should not be inferred from the foregoing discussion that a factor construct should be as high as possible in the hierarchy of factors. As a rule, factor constructs are apt to be most useful for scientific purposes if they are at an intermediate level in the hierarchy, although high-level factors can be useful for some purposes. In the domain of human abilities, General Intelligence represents a very broad factor construct, high up in the hierarchy of factors. It is based on the substantial intercorrelations that exist between such intermediate-level factor constructs as Verbal Ability, Numerical Ability, Memory, Reasoning Ability, Perceptual Speed, and so on (Guilford, 1968; Guilford & Hoepfner, 1971). Classification of people on the basis of intermediate-level factor traits permits better utilization of manpower than assessment on a single overall intelligence measure. In the latter case, all jobs requiring intelligence would be competing for the same people whereas with measures of intermediate-level ability traits, more high-level people would be available for assignment because the same individuals are not high on every trait. Correlating these intermediate-level constructs with other variables of scientific interest also provides better understanding in the field of inquiry than it is possible to achieve with the exclusive use of the fewer, broad, high-level factor constructs. Factor traits at the lowest level in the hierarchy of factors, however, are too numerous and too narrow in what they measure to be used effectively for general classification purposes and for general scientific description.

Traits like General Intelligence are legitimate factor constructs of broad character located high up in the hierarchy of factors. All broadly based factors that emerge from factor analyses do not necessarily fall in this "legitimate" category, however. It is possible to create meaningless factors high in the hierarchy of factors through faulty design of the factor analytic investigation. This occurs commonly where investigators include several highly complex data variables that overlap each other in several factors without having those factors represented in the same analyses by several relatively factor-pure measures for each factor. This phenomenon has already been illustrated earlier in this chapter using MMPI scale scores as variables. To be most useful for scientific purposes, a higher order broad factor construct should be based on the actual overlap of substantially correlated factors at a lower level in the hierarchy of factors. It should not represent merely a linear combination of essentially unrelated lower level constructs. It is unfortunately true that many of the constructs popular in the social sciences today fall in this latter category because they have been developed by armchair theorizing rather than through careful refinement by a series of factor analytic investigations. Philosophically inclined scientists who are content to believe that they are dealing with a unitary construct without checking it out with data are more often than not apt to be mistaken in their beliefs.

8.2.   DATA VARIABLES

As explained earlier in this chapter, the particular variables selected for a study have a very critical bearing on the kinds of results obtained. It is not only the general composition of the variables in some abstract sense that is important, however. The measurement characteristics of the data variables and also the subjects from which the data are obtained can have a great influence on the results obtained (Comrey, 1978, 1988).

8.2.1.   SCALES OF MEASUREMENT

The ideal situation is to have data variables that are continuous and normally distributed with normal bivariate surfaces (that is, bell-shaped joint frequency distributions) for every pair of variables. The regressions for all pairs of variables should be linear. When these ideal circumstances occur, the usual Pearson product-moment correlation coefficient gives a reliable index of the degree of correlation between data variables, and the linear factor model represents a good approximation to the data. There appears to be some confusion, however, regarding the use of the product-moment correlation coefficient on scores from scales for which interval-scale properties have not been demonstrated. If there is a normal bivariate distribution in the population for the two variables involved, the sampling distribution for the correlation coefficient does not depend on the charac-teristics of the measurement scales for the two variables. If the distributions for the data variables are reasonably normal in form, the investigators need have no concern about applying a "parametric" factor analytic model without demonstrating that their scores are measured on an equal-unit scale. Many people mistakenly believe that because means and standard deviations are computed in making various statistical tests, an equal-unit measurement scale is required. The mathematical derivations involved in statistical tests, however, typically are only concerned with the nature of the distributions involved rather than the kinds of measurement scales that led to those distributions (Burke, 1953; Comrey, Bott, & Lee, 1989).

There are many other aspects of measurement scales used for data variables that do represent a source of concern, however. For example, the correlations, and hence the factor analytic results derived from them, are affected by a reduction of the continuous measurement scale to one with fewer than a dozen categories. In the extreme, the variable is dichotomous, for example, "yes-no," "pass-fail," "married-single," and so on. Wherever possible, data variables with a reduced number of categories should be avoided. Correlations in these cases are less reliable and subject to distortions, sometimes to a very significant degree. The potential severity of these distortions increases as the number of measurement categories in the data variable decreases and as the distribution of category membership becomes more skewed. It is not always possible to avoid using such variables because in many cases there is no way of getting more categories; for example, if sex membership is being related to other variables. In many cases, however, by planning ahead, the investigator can arrange to use variables measured on scales with 12 or more steps rather than just two or three.

Data variables included in the same matrix should not be dependent on each other in some artificial way. For example, consider an ability test that gives a verbal score, a quantitative score, and a total score. The total score is just the sum of the other two and hence is linearly dependent on them. Inclusion of all three scores in a factor analysis results in the production of a spurious factor based on the forced overlap between the total score and the other two scores. The total score should be omitted from such an analysis. Another example is the inclusion of "right" and "wrong" scores. The number right is either wholly or partially dependent on the number wrong, depending on how the wrong score is calculated. If the wrong score equals the total number of items minus the number right, there is a total linear dependence of the two scores. If the wrong score is the number of items attempted and missed, the dependence may be only partial but still unacceptable. Only one or the other of these two scores should be included in the analysis to prevent the appearance of a spurious factor.

So-called "ipsative" scores (Cattell, 1944b) also introduce this kind of unwanted dependence between scores. Suppose the respondent taking an interest inventory is given a choice between two activities: A — solving an arithmetic reasoning problem, and B — designing a flower garden. If response A is chosen, a point is given on interest scale X. If response B is chosen, a point is given on interest scale Y. The score on each interest scale is the total number of times the respondent chooses the appropriate alternative for that scale from among all the relevant items. In such cases, subjects are limited as to the amount of interest they may express. They have to choose where to place their expressed interest. They cannot be "interested" in everything because they may not say, "I am interested in both these things." They also cannot say, "I am not interested in either." All subjects are treated as though they had the same amount of interest to distribute. Quite apart from being incorrect, this premise leads to interest scores that have an artificial dependence between them that makes them unsuitable for factor analytic work. If subjects' responses give them a high score in one interest area, they must compensate for this by having lower interest scores in some other interest area. The use of such scores in factor analytic work introduces spurious common factor variance. Where there is no alternative but to use such scores, a careful evaluation of the results is necessary to ascertain the extent to which the findings have been determined by the nature of the ipsative scores involved.

Spurious overlap between data variables can also be introduced through the commonly encountered practice of scoring items of a test on more than one variable. On the MMPI, for example, admission of a particular symptom may give the respondent a point on both the Depression scale and the Hysteria scale. There are so many items on the MMPI that are scored on more than one scale that substantial correlations between total scores are guaranteed. Use of these total scores in the same factor analysis, therefore, forces the introduction of overlapping specific factor variance into the common factor space, distorting the results accordingly (Comrey, 1978).

Some data variables may have a sufficient number of scoring categories and may not be artificially dependent on other scores, but they may have badly skewed distributions. Some Rorschach ink-blot test scores, for example, may have the bulk of the response-total scores close to zero with a scattering of the remaining scores over a wide range of values different from zero. With such distributions it is prudent to make scatter plots to be sure that the regressions are linear. Where the regressions are not linear, especially, it is advisable to transform the scores to eliminate such irregularities in the data. Sometimes, converting the scores to normalized standard scale scores, for example, with mean equal to 50 and standard deviation equal to 10, will be sufficient to eliminate the nonlinearity. In other cases, it may be necessary to combine categories, even reducing the variable to a dichotomy. When this is done, the variable should be dichotomized as near the median as possible to make both categories have about the same percentage of cases. If there is a genuine curvilinear relationship involved, however, it may be necessary to handle the analysis for the variable in question in an entirely different way. Some work has been done on nonlinear factor analytic models (McDonald, 1967), but as yet they have not been made operational to any great extent.

Some type of scale transformation is particularly essential in cases where a few scores in the sample depart radically from the others. An example would be to have a few high-IQ subjects thrown in with a sample of low-IQ subjects. The high-IQ subjects would be much higher than the bulk of the subjects on all ability-test variables. This would result in very high correlations for the paired ability variables. Conversion of all scores to normalized standard scores would greatly reduce this distortion because only the rank positions of the subjects are preserved by this transformation. These subjects would be high on all the tests, contributing to the elevation of the correlations, but they would not have nearly as great an effect as they would have with the untransformed scores.

8.2.2. SAMPLING

The particular sample of data objects, or subjects, upon which the investigators decide to take their measurements of the data variables has a great bearing on the final results of the factor analysis. The most obvious consideration in this respect is the size of the sample upon which the correlations are computed. As the number of observations increases, the reliability of the obtained correlations goes up, although with diminishing returns. Samples of size 50 give very inadequate reliability of correlation coefficients, whereas samples of size 1000 are more than adequate for most factor analytic purposes. The adequacy of sample size might be evaluated very roughly on the following scale: 50 — very poor; 100 — poor; 200 — fair; 300 — good; 500 — very good; and 1000 or more — excellent.

Guertin and Bailey (1970) have shown that with smaller samples the random errors of the less reliable correlation coefficients increase the absolute size of the correlations in the matrix. This results in greater communalities and a larger amount of common-factor variance, although the increase is due to spurious common-factor variance. This additional variance thrown into the analysis tends to produce distortions the seriousness of which is a function of the absolute amount of spurious variance added. The conclusion is that the investigator should use samples that are large wherever possible, preferably 500 or more. The authors have even found continued improvement in the stability of factor solutions up to 2000 cases. In most situations, however, there is probably little to be gained by going over 1000 cases.

If some other kind of correlation coefficient other than the Pearson product-moment correlation coefficient is used, larger samples are needed to achieve the same level of stability of the correlation coefficients. The tetrachoric correlation coefficient, for example, may require twice as many cases to yield comparable stability. In those cases where the investigators have no alternative but to carry out a factor analysis with samples that are too small, they must be especially conservative in their interpretation of the results.

The composition of the sample also can have a dramatic effect on the correlations obtained and consequently on the ultimate factor analytic results. The range of scores in the sample on the data variables compared to the range of scores on these variables for the entire universe constitutes an important source of modifications in factor analytic results as a function of sampling procedures. To illustrate the importance of range of data-variable scores on factor analytic results, suppose that psychological tests of Verbal Ability, Numerical Ability, Arithmetic Reasoning, Memory, and Perceptual Speed were administered to a large, random sample from the general population together with many other variables unrelated to intelligence. A factor analysis of the intercorrelations of these variables would be likely to produce a very prominent factor of General Intelligence with substantial loadings for the above-named tests.

Next, take a new sample of the same size that is made up entirely of individuals who have an IQ of exactly 100. These individuals would be chosen at random from the entire population of individuals who have IQs equal to 100. In this case, the range on intelligence for the second sample has been reduced to zero. A factor analysis of the intercorrelations of the tests in the second sample would fail to produce a General Intelligence factor because no significant variations due to differences in intelligence among the subjects are left in the test scores. The correlations among these ability tests in such a sample would be likely to distribute approximately in a random fashion about zero.

If the restriction in range on intelligence were only partial instead of complete, such as would be the case if all the subjects were graduates of prestigious American colleges and universities, the intelligence factor would still appear in the factor analytic results, but it would account for less variance than it would in a random sample from the general population. In general, the greater the degree of restriction of range for a given factor in the sample studied, the smaller will be the loadings of marker variables on that factor in the resulting analysis. If the loadings become too small, of course, the factor is not likely to be identified at all.

If a given factor is to appear in a factor analysis, then data variables that represent that factor must appear in the analysis, and the sample of data objects, or subjects, selected must vary with respect to that factor. Sometimes, variance on a given factor is reduced through restriction in range on a variable that is correlated with the factor rather than on the factor itself. This was more or less true for the previously discussed example involving graduates of prestigious colleges and universities. The same type of selection effect might be achieved by obtaining subjects who volunteered after seeing an advertisement in a particular magazine. Readers of this magazine might be, on the average, considerably higher than the general population in intelligence and, beyond this, volunteer readers might be even higher in intelligence than nonvolunteer readers.

For exploratory work, it is much more important to ensure that there is plenty of variance on the factor in the sample than it is to have a representative sample from the population at large. It is particularly important to be certain, in other words, that no restriction in range on the factor has occurred through some peculiarity of the method of sample selection. In the later stages of taxonomic research when the constructs are in the process of final refinement, representative samples from specified populations become more essential so that the sizes of factor loadings and correlations between factors can be pinpointed rather accurately.

Care must be exercized in combining subjects from different sources into the same sample for factor analytic purposes because the factor structure might be very different in the separate groups. Where this is the case, it is better to carry out the analyses in the groups separately. For example, a test that measures reasoning capacity in 6-year-old children might become a test of perceptual speed in young adults. It would be undesirable to combine 6 year olds and young adults into one sample for analysis purposes when dealing with tests that substantially vary factorially in what they measure in the two groups. Generally speaking, if two heterogeneous groups are to be combined for factor analysis, it is desirable to ascertain that the basic factor structure is essentially the same in the two groups.

Even with a specified sample of subjects, results of a factor analytic study can be influenced by the conditions under which the data are collected. The motivational circumstances surrounding the data collection, for example, are very important. The first author once had occasion to assist in the collection of data on two different ability tests that turned out to correlate with other much more highly than expected. The tests were administered to navy recruits who were informed that the test results would not go on their service record. It was later learned that they also had their liberty curtailed for involuntary participation in the testing. The subjects were also told by their superior officers that they could leave as soon as they had completed the two tests. Some of the subjects tried conscientiously to do their best on both tests. Others went through the motions of marking the answer sheets, without attempting to do well, and left as soon as they could do so without being conspicuous. The subjects that tried had the high scores on both tests while those who did not had the low scores on both tests. In effect, both tests became measures of the subjects' motivation rather than what was intended and hence correlated with each other almost as two alternate forms of the same test would correlate.

Substantial differences in factor results for the same subjects can occur if results are to be used for selection purposes as opposed to guidance purposes. An applicant for a job who takes a personality test, for example, as part of the evaluation process is often motivated to give the best possible impression and hence may answer the questions in a way calculated to have that effect. The same test administered to the same person in the context of a guidance clinic to get help in solving personal problems might be answered very differently. Tests administered to job applicants or other individuals who are concerned about the effect of the test results on their status tend to be heavily influenced by "social desirability" response sets. The respondents try to determine what kind of image is most favorable and then answer the questions in accordance with their perception. This same attitude is carried through all test performances, often introducing a considerable overlap among the variables that might not necessarily be there if the subjects had a different motivational set.

Any conditions that reduce the respondents' desire to participate intelligently, accurately, and willingly, are likely to have a deleterious effect on the data in one way or another. Thus, it is very important for the investigator to make sure that the subjects wish to participate and that they will be honest and conscientious in performing the assigned tasks. Forced participation, poor testing conditions, and inappropriate test materials are just a few of the ways in which data can be downgraded. In psychological testing, for example, even item format can significantly affect subjects' motivation. If they are asked to respond to questions for which it is difficult to decide among the available response alternatives, even motivated subjects are apt to become disgusted in due time and quit trying to do a good job. They may even shift to responding capriciously. It cannot be emphasized strongly enough that investigators must devote a great deal of care to securing the best possible data they can. No matter how skillfully the factor analytic work is done, it can never correct the deficiencies of poor data. To quote a time-worn expression that fits, "You can't make a silk purse out of a sow's ear."

The nature of the experimental treatment itself can affect the factor composition of the data variables under investigation quite apart from any motivational changes in the subjects. Fleishman and Hempel (1954) demonstrated that the factor composition of a task at an early stage in the process of skill acquisition may be considerably different from what it will be later on. If subjects practice on a given set of tasks for many trials, the factor structure at the beginning of the experiment may be considerably different from what it is at the end.

8.3. CORRELATION COEFFICIENTS

The question of what correlation coefficient to use for factor analytic work is one that comes up frequently, especially where the analysis was not planned before the data were collected. In these cases, there are typically some variables that do not have continuous, approximately normal distributions. The best approach is to design the study in such a way that the data variables will have such distributions so that the usual Pearson product-moment correlation coefficient is appropriate. Where this is not possible, it may be necessary to consider other alternatives.

8.3.1. THE PEARSON PRODUCT-MOMENT CORRELATION COEFFICIENT

The Pearson product-moment correlation coefficient may be computed by the following formula:

$$r = \frac{N\Sigma XY - \Sigma X\Sigma Y}{\sqrt{N\Sigma X^2 - (\Sigma X)^2}\sqrt{N\Sigma Y^2 - (\Sigma Y)^2}} \tag{8.1}$$

The summations in formula (8.1) are from 1 to N, the number of cases. This is the most stable of the correlation coefficients. When it is used, however, the variables should be distributed in a manner that does not depart too far from normality, and the regression for every pair of variables should be rectilinear, that is, the data points should scatter about a best-fitting straight line rather than some curved function. Ideally, the investigator would check every regression plot to see that it is linear, but in practice this precaution is not often taken. Formula (8.1) is suitable for computer or hand-held calculator applications. Short-cut methods are available where correlations must be computed without such equipment (Guilford, 1965).

8.3.2. CORRELATION COEFFICIENTS FOR DICHOTOMOUS DATA

Several different correlation coefficients have been developed to deal with the situation where one or both of the variables being correlated are dichotomous. Some of these are as follows:

1. *Phi (ϕ)*. This coefficient is used where both variables represent absolute dichotomies, such as "male versus female."
2. *Point Biserial*. This coefficient is used where one variable is an absolute dichotomy, but the other variable is continuous and approximately normal.
3. *Biserial*. This coefficient may be used where one of the variables is known to be normally distributed but has been artificially dichotomized into two categories, while the other variable is continuous and approximately normal.
4. *Tetrachoric*. This coefficient requires that both variables be normally distributed but artificially dichotomized.

If dichotomous variables are scored 1 for the higher category and 0 for the lower category, computation of the Pearson correlation coefficient with these scores will give the same results as computing the ϕ coefficient and the point biserial correlation coefficient. If an entire matrix of correlation coefficients is being obtained by computer, it is easier to use the product-moment formula to calculate all coefficients rather than to use ϕ or the point biserial formula where these methods would be appropriate. The ease of applying the same program for all coefficients would more than make up for the slightly greater computational time. The only reason for using the special formulas for these coefficients (Guilford, 1965) would be to save labor in hand computations. The authors seldom use anything but the Pearson product-moment formula (8.1) for computing the matrix of correlations for a factor analysis, regardless of the number of categories in the variables correlated.

The only reason for computing a biserial instead of a product-moment correlation coefficient would be to save labor unless for some reason the information about the full range of scores was unavailable. Investigators would do well to obtain continuous scores wherever possible, thereby avoiding the need to use biserial correlation coefficients except when it becomes very important to save labor.

The tetrachoric correlation coefficient was used in precomputer research efforts by Thurstone and others as a labor-saving device. Continuous variable regression plots were reduced to fourfold tables of frequencies that could be used to determine correlation coefficients from computing diagrams (Chesire, Saffir, & Thurstone, 1933). These tetrachoric coefficients represented shortcut approximations to the product-moment correlation coefficients. This method would be used today only if the investigator could not gain access to a computer, because such coefficients are less reliable than product-moment correlation coefficients.

One of the disturbing effects of decreasing the number of categories of measurement in variables to be correlated is a tendency to reduce the size of the maximum correlation obtainable below an absolute value of 1.0. The fewer the categories, the more pronounced this effect is likely to become. With dichotomous data, the maximum obtainable correlation may be quite small if the proportions of data objects in the categories diverge markedly for the two variables. Consider the following data for two personality test questions: (I). I am happy most of the time, and (II). I feel excitedly happy, on top of the world. A fourfold table of response proportions for these two questions might be the following:

		I		
		no	yes	
II	yes	$b = .03$	$a = .07$	$p_2 = .10$
	no	$c = .37$	$d = .53$	$q_2 = .90$
		$q_1 = .40$	$p_1 = .60$	Sum $= 1.00$

In this example, p_1 is the proportion saying "yes" to question I and p_2 is the proportion saying "yes" to question II. The proportions saying "no" are given by q_1 and q_2, respectively. The proportion saying "yes" to both questions is given by the value $a = 0.07$. Other cells give the proportions for other combinations of "yes" and "no" responses. The ϕ coefficient may be computed by the following formula:

$$\phi = \frac{ac - bd}{\sqrt{p_1 q_1 p_2 q_2}}$$

(8.2)

For the sample above, the computation of ϕ by formula (8.2) gives

$$\phi = \frac{(.07)\,(.37) - (.03)\,(.53)}{\sqrt{(.60)\,(.40)\,(.10)\,(.90)}} = \frac{.0259 - .0159}{\sqrt{(.24)\,(.09)}} = \frac{.010}{.147} = .068$$

The value .068 is very small for a correlation coefficient. Compare it, however, with the value of ϕ_{max}, the largest value of ϕ that could possibly be obtained with the same marginal totals, that is, values of p and q for the two items. This kind of hypothetical result is shown as follows:

		I		
		no	yes	
II	yes	$b = .00$	$a = .10$	$p_2 = .10$
	no	$c = .40$	$d = .50$	$q_2 = .90$
		$q_1 = .40$	$p_1 = .60$	Sum $= 1.00$

$$\phi_{max} = \frac{(.10)\,(.40) - (.00)\,(.50)}{\sqrt{(.60)\,(.40)\,(.10)\,(.90)}} = \frac{.04}{.147} = .272$$

There is no way to arrange this table to obtain a higher ϕ coefficient without changing the marginal totals; hence this table gives ϕ_{max}. The actually obtained ϕ coefficient for the data in the previous table seems more impressive when compared with a maximum possible ϕ of .272 than it does when compared with 1.0, which is the maximum that the product-moment coefficient can reach with continuous data. Some investigators have embraced the practice of dividing ϕ by ϕ_{max} as a means of correcting the ϕ coefficient for the fact that it often cannot achieve a value of 1.0 under any circumstances, given the marginal totals in the data. If this were done here, ϕ/ϕ_{max} would be .068/.272 or 0.25, which though not large is more imposing than .068, the uncorrected ϕ coefficient.

One of the reasons that ϕ/ϕ_{max} has been used for computing correlations on dichotomous variables for factor analytic work has been the widespread belief that factor solutions based on uncorrected ϕ coefficients will be dominated by "difficulty" factors. These represent factors presumed to arise because restrictions on the size of the maximum ϕ coefficient would classify variables into different categories according to the amount of restriction rather than according to content per se.

In carrying out a series of factor analyses of items on the original MMPI scales, the first author attempted to use ϕ/ϕ_{max} as the means of correlating these dichotomous personality-test items. Many of the MMPI items have rather extreme splits, with only a very small percentage of subjects in one category and with the great majority in the other. Under these conditions, the maximum ϕ is very small and the corrected ϕ/ϕ_{max} coefficients can become very large. In some factor analyses of these coefficients, communalities in excess of 1.0 were being accumulated very quickly in the factor extraction process. Such results are totally unreasonable, of course, because individual test items are unreliable at best and will seldom have a proportion of true variance that approaches 1.0. These results were disturbing because ϕ/ϕ_{max} coefficients produced impossible results and uncorrected ϕ coefficients were generally considered at the time to be inappropriate for factor analytic work because of the difficulty factor problem. The next step was to try the tetrachoric coefficient even though it requires artificially dichotomized normal distributions, an assumption clearly not met with test items. Using the $\cos\pi$ approximation (Guilford, 1965) to the tetrachoric correlation coefficient, these correlation matrices were recomputed and the factor analyses done again. The results still gave badly overinflated correlation coefficients and communalities, if anything worse than the ϕ/ϕ_{max}.

After these experiences, the first author decided to try the uncorrected ϕ coefficient even though it was contrary to accepted practice at the time to do so. There was little else to do because the other available methods failed to yield acceptable results. The factors that emerged from the analyses of ϕ coefficients did not exhibit unreasonably large item communalities, and they also were meaningful from the standpoint of content. The major factors, therefore, did not appear to represent "difficulty" factors as feared but instead seemed to be based on substantive content of the items. If difficulty factors were present, they appeared to be minor in nature rather than factors of any great significance in the analyses. These phenomena are illustrated in published analyses of the same MMPI items using ϕ, ϕ/ϕ_{max}, and the tetrachoric coefficient (Comrey & Levonian, 1958). Interestingly enough, the major factors obtained were readily matched across these analyses, although the general size level of loadings was considerably higher for the analyses based on ϕ/ϕ_{max} and the tetrachoric coefficient than for that based on the uncorrected ϕ coefficient. The smaller factors showed no correspondence across the three analyses.

The conclusion seems warranted that if dichotomous variables, for example, such as responses to test items, are to be correlated and factor analyzed, the method of choice is the ϕ coefficient. Where the proportion of individuals in the two categories departs from 0.50, item variance is diminished, and if the proportions in a given category are different in the two items being correlated, ceiling effects can be expected on the size of the coefficient obtainable. As the difference between the proportions increases between the two items, these effects become more and more pronounced. With a 99–1 split in one variable and a 50–50 split in the other, the maximum ϕ is only about 0.10, which means that only about 1% of the variance in the 50–50 variables can be predicted from knowledge about the results in the 99–1 variable. This is easily grasped intuitively by considering the amount of information available to the investigators if they know the scores on the 99–1 variable. They can only say something "different" about one person out of 100. For the other 99, they must make the same prediction because all these 99 persons have the same score on that item. If they try to predict scores on the 50–50 item, the best they can hope for is to improve very slightly on chance prediction, that is, by tossing a coin.

Dichotomous variables with extreme splits, therefore, give very little information and provide poor prediction of other variables. The ϕ coefficient gives small values for the correlations of such variables with other variables that have 50–50 splits or with continuous variables. This is appropriate because such variables provide little basis for intelligent classificatory decisions since they contain so little information. Such variables will tend to show up with small loadings in any factor analysis of common factor variance because they do not contribute much common-factor variance in most cases. As with the product-moment coefficient, however, a few extreme cases thrown into an otherwise homogeneous group can give some very high correlations with the ϕ coefficient. For example, three or four neurotics thrown in with about 96 or 97 normals could produce a number of 97–3 splits on personality items asking about psychological symptoms. If the same three or four persons are the ones admitting to the symptoms in each case, the ϕ coefficients will be very high. If only one subject out of 100 says "yes" to each of two items, and the other 99 say "no" to both items, the ϕ coefficient would be 1.0!

With dichotomous data, therefore, the ϕ coefficient may be depressed to very low values where one variable has an extreme split and the other does not. Even worse, ϕ may be elevated to an extremely high value where both variables have extreme splits, despite the fact that neither variable contains much actual information of predictive value. Naturally, if high correlations appear in the matrix to be factor analyzed, those variables will be likely to show up with high loadings on some factor. Unfortunately, these possible distortions to correlations, and hence to the factor analytic results derived from them, do not seem to be well understood by many investigators who apply factor analytic methods to dichotomous data.

The moral to this story is that investigators should try to avoid dichotomous data variables wherever possible. They should try very hard to obtain continuously measured data variables, that is, with 10 or more categories of response, if possible, and they should seek to obtain good distributions, for example, approximately normal in form. Under these circumstances, most of the aberrations in correlation coefficients and factor analytic results mentioned above can be avoided. The first author has insisted on using seven response choices for items on his personality test (Comrey, 1970) precisely to minimize such problems in factor analyses of correlations among items. Where investigators are developing verbal scales of any kind, the authors recommend the use of multiple-choice response scales rather than "yes-no," "true-false," "agree-disagree" types of scales (Comrey, 1988). Where dichotomous variables must be used, every effort should be made to dichotomize as close to the median as possible. The correlation should be computed by the ϕ coefficient, or, equivalently, by the Pearson product-moment coefficient with scores of 1 and 0 for the dichotomous variables.

8.4. COMMON ERRORS IN THE USE OF FACTOR ANALYSIS

Some of the more common errors in the use of factor analysis are enumerated in this section to provide a convenient check list that the investigator may find helpful to review when planning a factor analytic study. Most of these errors are described in Comrey (1978) and many of them were described earlier by Guilford (1952). This list represents an abbreviated summary because most of these errors have been elaborated upon previously.

1. Collecting the data before planning the factor analysis.
2. Use of data variables with bad distributions and inappropriate regression forms:
    a. badly skewed distributions, for example, with ability tests that are too easy or too hard for the subjects tested;
    b. truncated distributions;
    c. bimodal distributions;
    d. distributions with a few extreme cases;
    e. extreme splits in dichotomized variables;
    f. nonlinear regressions.
3. Use of data variables that are not experimentally independent of one another:
    a. scoring the same item response on more than one variable;
    b. in a forced-choice item, scoring one response alternative on one variable and the other on a second variable;
    c. having one data variable as a linear combination of others, for example, verbal, quantitative, and total score.
4. Failure to overdetermine the factors. The number of variables should be several times as large as the number of factors. There should be at least five good marker variables for each factor anticipated.

5. Use of too many complex data variables. The best variables for defining factors are relatively factor pure. Only a few multiple-factor data variables should be used. If complex variables measuring both factors A and B are included, there must be some variables that measure A and not B and others that measure B and not A.

6. Including highly similar variables in the analysis that produce factors at a very low level in the hierarchy of factors when constructs of greater generality are being sought. Including two similar items in an analysis of personality-test items or two variables that are alternate forms of the same test represent examples of this kind of error.

7. Failure to provide good marker variables for a factor that may be present in other factor-complex data variables that are included. Without the markers, the factor will be hard to locate, although variance for that factor will be present in the analysis and must appear on some factor.

8. Poor sampling procedures:

    a. taking a sample of cases that is too small to obtain stable correlations;

    b. combining two distinct groups with different factor structure into the same sample for factor analytic purposes;

    c. loss of a factor through biased sampling that restricts the range of variability on that factor.

9. Not including enough factors in the analysis. To have good hyperplanes for using simple structure as a guide in rotations, it is necessary to have a large number of points in the hyperplanes. Without six or more factors in the analysis that are relatively independent of one another, it is difficult to have good hyperplanes.

10. Use of inappropriate correlation coefficients such as ϕ/ϕ_{max} or use of a coefficient such as the tetrachoric in a situation that violates the assumptions underlying its use.

11. Use of inappropriate communality estimates, for example, 1.0 in the diagonals when the objectives of the investigation are concerned only with common-factor variance.

12. Extracting too few factors, forcing a factor solution for m factors into a space of fewer dimensions with consequent distortion of the factor solution.

13. Poor rotation procedures:

    a. failure to rotate at all;

    b. using an orthogonal solution when an oblique solution is necessary to give a good picture of the results;

    c. permitting an unwarranted degree of obliquity between factors in the pursuit of simple structure;

    d. use of rotational criteria that have not been determined to be appropriate for the kind of data involved;

    e. rotation of extra small factors by an analytic rotation method, such as Varimax, that spreads the variance out to minor factors to an inappropriate degree;

    f. failure to plan the study so that there will be a suitable rotational criterion that can be employed.

    14. Interpreting the first extracted factor as a general factor.

    15. Leaping to conclusions about the nature of a factor on the basis of insufficient evidence, for example, low loadings and lack of outside confirmatory information. The interpretations of factors must be verified on the basis of evidence outside the factor analysis itself. Follow-up factor analyses and construct validation studies are an important part of this verification process.

9

Alternate Designs in Factor Analysis

Up to this point, attention has been devoted exclusively to the traditional, most widely used factor analytic design, called "R-technique" by Cattell (1952) to distinguish it from other factor analytic designs such as P- and Q-techniques. The purpose of this chapter is to explore briefly some of these alternatives to the traditional R-technique factor analytic design.

9.1. Q-TECHNIQUE

The most commonly considered alternative to the R-technique factor analysis is Q-technique, which is sometimes referred to as "inverse" factor analysis. An important difference between Q- and R-techniques is illustrated in Fig. 9.1 which shows a typical data matrix. There are N data objects or subjects, as rows of the data matrix $\mathbf{Z}$ in Fig. 9.1. Each column of $\mathbf{Z}$ consists of standard scores for one data object or person for all the n data variables. In the R-technique factor analysis, a correlation is computed by taking a pair of rows of matrix $\mathbf{Z}$ and determining the average cross-product term:

$$r_{ij} = \frac{1}{N} \sum_{k=1}^{k=N} z_{ik} z_{jk} \tag{9.1}$$

For R-technique factor analysis, N, the number of cases, is normally much larger than n, the number of data variables. The number of cases N must be large to obtain stable correlation coefficients.

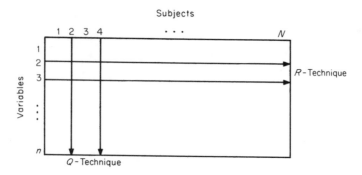

FIG. 9.1.   Data matrix for *Q*- and *R*-techniques.

In *Q*-technique factor analysis, the starting correlation matrix is computed in a different way. Instead of correlating two data variables over the sample of data objects (or subjects), two data objects (or subjects) are correlated over the sample of data variables. In Fig. 9.1 this is shown by two parallel vertical lines indicating that in order to give a correlation coefficient, two columns of the data matrix are related rather than two rows as in R-technique. For the Q-technique factor analysis, then, the correlation is computed as follows:

$$r_{ij} = \frac{1}{n} \sum_{k=1}^{k=n} z_{ki} z_{kj} \tag{9.2}$$

The limits on the summation in Eq. (9.2) are from 1 to n, the number of data variables, whereas in Eq. (9.1) the limits are from 1 to N, the number of data objects. In Eq. (9.1) the column subscript varies from 1 to N, whereas in Eq. (9.2) it is the row subscript that varies, and from 1 to n rather than 1 to N. When the data objects are people, the matrix of correlations that is factor analyzed in Q-technique contains correlations between persons rather than between variables as in R-technique.

Both formulas (9.1) and (9.2) are average cross products of standard scores. If the raw scores are correlated instead of standard scores, the raw-score correlation formula itself has the effect of reducing the scores to standard scores before the correlation is computed. In R-technique analysis, then, differences in means and standard deviations between the two variables correlated have no effect on the correlation coefficient since both variables are automatically scaled to zero means and unit variances. When two individuals are correlated over the data-variable scores in Q-technique analysis, shown by two columns of the data matrix in Fig. 9.1, there is also a rescaling of the means and standard deviations of the two individuals to 0 and 1, respectively. Differences in mean scores and variabilities of the individuals do not affect the correlation between two persons. If the scores are in the same rank order with about equal spacing between the scores for both individuals, the correlation between them will be very high even if one person's scores are considerably higher on the average and more spread out than the other person's scores.

An important difference between *Q*- and *R*-technique factor analysis is evident right at this point. With *R*-technique, the elements in a given row of the data matrix (see Fig. 9.1) are all obtained on the same measurement scale, for example, with the same test or other data-gathering instrument. With *Q*-technique, however, this is not the case. The elements in a column of the data matrix (see Fig. 9.1) are obtained ordinarily from different measurement scales since each row of the data matrix is obtained with a different measuring device.

Consider the hypothetical miniature data matrix shown in Table 9.1. Measurements of five physical size variables are shown for five fictitious subjects. Height is measured in inches, weight in pounds, shoe size on an arbitrary scale, and waist and neck size in inches. If the first two individuals (columns 1 and 2 of Table 9.1) are correlated, the value obtained is about 0.99. The correlations for each pair considered will be close to this figure.

Table 9.2 shows the scores for these same individuals after they have been standardized by rows. That is, each height measurement, for example, is converted to a standard score by the formula $z = (X - M)/\sigma$. In the case of person 1, this would be $(72 - 70.2)/2.32 = 0.78$ for the height variable. The weight scores would be standardized by the formula $(X - 168.0)/30.59$. Each row of Table 9.1 is converted to standard scores by subtracting the mean of the row from each raw score and then dividing by the standard deviation to obtain the corresponding score in Table 9.2.

If the first two columns of scores in Table 9.2, for the first two subjects, are correlated, the value obtained is 0.59, considerably below the 0.99 value obtained by correlating the unscaled raw scores. The correlations for other pairs of subjects will also be much reduced when computed with the scaled scores instead of the raw scores.

The use of raw scores for correlating persons in *Q*-technique factor analysis spuriously inflates the correlations, capitalizing on the fact that the scales of measurement differ from row to row in the data matrix. An example was chosen here that exaggerates this phenomenon, resulting in extremely high correlations between subjects. Even under ordinary conditions, however, there is often an intolerable inflation of the correlations between subjects unless the data matrix is standardized by rows before computing the correlations between persons. Of course, the data may be scaled to some mean and standard deviation other than 0 and 1, respectively, if desired. It is only essential that they be scaled to the same mean and standard deviation. For example, *T*-scores, with a mean of 50 and a standard deviation of 10, represent a popular choice.

TABLE 9.1

Unstandardized Miniature Data Matrix

Variables	Subjects					M	σ
	1	2	3	4	5		
1. Height	72	74	70	69	66	70.2	2.32
2. Weight	220	180	150	160	130	168.0	30.59
3. Shoe Size	12	14	10	9	7	10.4	2.42
4. Waist Size	36	34	33	34	28	33.0	2.68
5. Neck Size	17	15	15	15	14	15.2	.98

TABLE 9.2

Standardized Miniature Data Matrix

Variables	Subjects					M	σ
	1	2	3	4	5		
1. Height	.78	1.64	−.09	−.52	−1.81	0	1
2. Weight	1.70	.39	−.59	−.26	−1.24	0	1
3. Shoe Size	.66	1.49	−.17	−.58	−1.40	0	1
4. Waist Size	1.12	.37	.00	.37	−1.87	0	1
5. Neck Size	1.84	−.20	−.20	−.20	−1.22	0	1

One frequently encountered situation in Q-technique studies where it is easy to overlook the need for standardizing the data matrix by rows is the case where the data variables are test-item scores. In such cases, the possible scores may be only 0 and 1, or values over a very small range, for example, 1 to 5. The differences between means and standard deviations of the various rows of the data matrix are not so great under these circumstances; so the investigator may not recognize that the correlations between persons have been spuriously elevated. This is because the correlations are more moderate in size than for the example in Tables 9.1 and 9.2. Even in the case where means and standard deviations of the rows do not fluctuate greatly, however, it is necessary to scale the rows of the data matrix to equal means and standard deviations before computing the correlation matrix for Q-technique factor analysis.

The fact that computing a correlation coefficient between the scores for two individuals over a collection of data variables automatically scales the two sets of scores to the same mean and standard deviation for the two individuals has important implications for the kinds of factors derived in Q-technique analysis. Two individuals will be highly correlated if they have the same pattern of highs and lows in their scores, regardless of the absolute level of their scores. Thus, two individuals will be highly correlated and will tend to fall on the same Q-technique factor if their profiles look alike even if one profile is much higher than the other. If the investigator is looking for types of individuals who have not only similarly shaped profiles but also profiles that are at the same level, Q-technique factors cannot be counted upon to yield the desired results. Profiles of individuals who have high loadings on the same factor must be compared visually to see how much they differ in absolute level. In this way, individuals may be grouped who not only have similar profiles but actually have similar scores on the data variables sampled.

In R-technique the data variables are correlated with each other, and the factors show the relationships of the data variables with each other. In Q-technique factor analysis the subjects, or data objects, are correlated with each other, and the factors show the relationships of the subjects or data objects to each other. To put it in a somewhat oversimplified way, R-technique factors represent clusters of similar variables, whereas Q-technique factors represent clusters of similar persons or data objects.

Stability of the correlation coefficient depends on taking a large representative sample of cases from the population. In R-technique, this ordinarily means collecting data for a large number of people on a limited number of variables. With Q-technique, on the other hand, this ordinarily means taking a very large number of observations for a limited number of people or other data objects. In both cases the representativeness of the sample is important as well as the number of paired observations over which the correlation is computed. In R-technique, even if a large sample is obtained but the sampling method is biased, that is, certain kinds of individuals are systematically excluded from the sample, the sample correlations may depart substantially from the true population values. In the case of Q-technique, the correlation between two individuals is also subject to distortion because of a biased sampling of data variables over which to compute the correlation.

Correlating the item responses on a personality test for two people, for example, even if item scores are standardized, may give a very different result than if the correlation is computed over a collection of standardized ability-test scores. Theoretically, if we wish to know *the* correlation between two individuals, the correlation should be computed over a representative sample of all possible data variables.

It is manifestly impossible, however, and perhaps not desirable, to correlate people over all possible data variables or even a representative sample from that universe. Therefore in practice, Q-technique analyses must be based on a limited and usually nonrepresentative subset of the universe of all possible data variables. The clusters of similar individuals that emerge as factors in such analyses must be considered as "types" only with respect to the variables sampled. The more limited is the sampling of data variables, the more limited is the sense in which the individuals may be classified as belonging to the same type.

The practice of building up the number of observations for Q-technique analysis by using items of a single test as variables clearly does little to make the sample of observations broadly representative. On the contrary, it is picking out a very minute corner of the universe to study. This may be worthwhile where the characteristics of a particular test are being studied, but it is not a desirable procedure where the intent is to locate types of individuals in a more general sense, for example, psychopathological types, normal personality types, and intellectual ability types. When general objectives of this kind are involved in Q-technique analysis, it is essential to obtain a broader sampling of data variables on which each subject is measured, thereby coming closer to the ideal of a representative sampling of data variables from a broad and well-defined population of variables.

9.1.1.   THE ROTATION PROBLEM IN Q-TECHNIQUE ANALYSIS

One of the greatest difficulties with Q-technique analysis is the tendency for traditional rotational criteria to be inappropriate for such studies. Typically, a sample of readily available subjects is used, hopefully with an adequate battery of observations for each subject in order to give good correlations between subjects. There is usually no particular reason to suppose that such a random collection of subjects would cluster so as to give a good simple structure, for example, in rotations of Q-technique factors. To obtain a good simple structure solution, it would be necessary to have several clusters of subjects such that those within a cluster correlate substantially with each other but have low or zero correlations with subjects from other clusters.

If subjects and variables are selected for Q-technique analysis without concern for the problems of rotating the factor results, it is likely that subjects will not form very distinct clusters. The correlations between subjects are apt to be rather low after the data matrix has been properly standardized by rows so that all variables have the same mean and standard deviation. The factor structure in such cases is likely to be rather undifferentiated, giving the investigator only an arbitrary choice among several more or less equally uncompelling alternatives.

Q-technique analysis, therefore, is not apt to provide a very fruitful rescue vehicle for saving unplanned investigations from disaster. Its proper use requires as much, if not more, planning than the standard R-technique analysis. Investigators should make sure that they take the following steps:

1. Define the domain of variables over which the individuals are to be correlated.
2. Select a set of variables on which the individuals are to be measured such that the domain defined in step 1 is adequately represented. The set of variables must contain enough elements to provide stable correlations between individuals. Several hundred elements would be desirable.
3. Select several individuals to represent each pure "type" that is hypothesized to exist. At least a half-dozen, and more if possible, should be included for each type.

If the hypothesis that a given type exists is correct, and if the individuals selected to represent it are examples of this type, with respect to the set of variables over which the correlations between individuals are computed, a Q-technique factor should emerge for which these individuals all have substantial loadings. These individuals selected to represent a given type should correlate more with each other than they do with individuals selected to represent other types.

Individuals who do not represent pure types have the same status in Q-technique factor analysis that complex data variables have in R-technique factor analysis. They can be included, but they do not provide much help in determining where the factors should be located. Such individuals will have loadings of moderate size on several Q-technique factors rather than high loadings on only one factor and negligible loadings on all other factors. The pure-type individual, on the other hand, does for Q-technique factor analysis what the pure-factor data variable does for R-technique factor analysis. Such pure-type individuals, when included with others that belong to the same type, define the factors in a sharp way, permitting the common rotational criteria to locate relatively clear-cut and compelling factor positions.

It is clear that merely taking a sampling of "available" subjects for Q-technique factor analysis is not likely to provide several pure-type individuals to represent each type factor while introducing only a relatively small number of individuals who are not pure types. Since pure types are the exception rather than the rule, a random sampling of individuals is most likely to contain a preponderance of individuals who are not pure types. It would be surprising, therefore, if such sampling methods were to yield enough pure-type individuals to provide a good definition for more than a small proportion of the Q-technique factors. It is quite possible that none of the factors would be adequately represented. In any event, the large number of impure types, corresponding to complex data variables in R-technique analysis, would greatly complicate the task of achieving a good rotational solution.

These considerations emphasize the fact that subjects must be carefully selected to give meaningful Q-technique factor analytic results, just as data variables must be carefully selected to yield good R-technique factor analytic results. As with R-technique analysis, the investigator's hypotheses about the factors and individuals defining them in Q-technique analysis may prove to be incorrect, or partially so. Only through a series of carefully planned analyses, each taking advantage of what was learned in the previous one, will the investigator gradually establish what the type factors are in a given domain. This technique of analysis is very powerful and has tremendous potential for scientific explication in those areas where many data are available for relatively few data objects, such as in clinical research, but it should be emphasized that these benefits are not apt to accrue without careful planning of the research investigations in which it is to be used.

One might ask, "What good is a type after it has been located?" The location of well-defined types and knowledge of type membership can be very useful in the description, prediction, and control of human behavior. In clinical psychology, for example, "cookbooks" have been developed for use in dealing with types. A set of rules is established that permits unequivocal determination of type membership. The similarities of behavior, symptoms, etiology of pathological symptoms, typical responses to different forms of treatment, prognosis, and so on, are cataloged for each type. Once individuals are classified as belonging to a given type, a great deal is immediately known about them, how they should be treated, and what the outcome is likely to be. An example of this approach is to be found in the MMPI cookbook, for example, developed by Gilberstadt and Duker (1965) although the types described by these authors were not established on the basis of factor analytic studies.

9.2. P-TECHNIQUE

Much less commonly used than R- and Q-technique factor analyses but potentially very valuable for clinical study of the individual case is P-technique factor analysis. One of the pioneer investigations using this method was carried out by Cattell, Cattell, and Rhymer (1947). The data matrix for P-technique analysis is shown in Fig. 9.2. The correlations are computed between pairs of variables over N occasions.

In P-technique analysis, then, the subject of study is a single person, or data object. A measurement on each data variable is taken on the first occasion, for example, on day 1. On the second occasion, for example, day 2, the measurements are taken again to give the scores in column 2 of the data matrix in Fig. 9.2. The process is repeated on the third occasion, and so on, ending up with the *N*th occasion. The occasions could be repeated trials with very little time between trials or with large time intervals between trials. There is no need to standardize the scores for the matrix of correlations in *P*-technique analysis because the correlations are computed between data variables as in *R*-technique. The correlation coefficient formula automatically adjusts for the differences in mean and standard deviation between variables. Since the measurements over occasions are repeated on the same measuring instruments, there is no variation in the measurement scale from column to column that would artificially inflate the correlations. In *Q*-technique analysis, standardization of scores by rows was necessary to avoid row variations in scale. It is unnecessary in *P*-technique analysis.

The factors derived in *P*-technique, as in *R*-technique, represent clusters of substantially correlated variables. The meaning of the correlation between variables is different in the two techniques, however. If tests of Verbal Knowledge and Verbal Fluency, for example, are highly correlated and appear on the same factor in *R*-technique analysis, it means that if subjects have high scores on one of these two tests, they are also apt to have high scores on the other, and vice versa. If they have low scores in one, they are likely to have low scores in the other, and vice versa. In *P*-technique, on the other hand, a high correlation between variables means that as one variable goes up or down, the other variable moves with it over the series of occasions. For example, Heart Rate and Palmar Sweating would be two variables that tend to move up and down together over a series of occasions manipulated to expose the individual to varying amounts of stress. Heart Rate and Palmar Sweating would both be high under high-stress conditions. They would both be low in the resting state. These two variables might be selected as potential pure-factor measures of an hypothesized "Emotional

FIG. 9.2.   *P*-technique data matrix.

Arousal" factor expected in a P-technique analysis of physiological data variables.

P-technique analysis is suitable only for certain kinds of variables. There must be reliably measurable variations in scores on the variable over the series of occasions studied. This is not apt to be the case for some commonly studied variables. Ability-test scores, for example, may vary over time for a given individual, but the difference in scores for a particular test on two occasions is usually attributed to errors of measurement, practice effects, and so on, rather than primarily to real variations in the amount of ability a person has from time to time. A variable like Heart Rate, on the other hand, is ideal for P-technique analysis because it can be accurately measured and it fluctuates over wide limits as a function of events in the individual's external and internal environment, coming periodically to a steady state.

Another very important requirement for variables in P-technique analysis is that the process of taking the measurements per se should not affect the present or subsequent measurement values obtained to any appreciable degree. This is clearly not the case with those kinds of tests where subjects' performances steadily improve with each succeeding trial as they become more and more familiar with the task and expert at doing it. It is not necessarily impossible to carry out P-technique studies with such variables, but the danger of artifacts in the results is great. If the subject improves on all tasks as the trials progress, for example, this will force a fairly substantial positive correlation between all pairs of variables, tending to give one large, dominant factor which could be labeled "Practice Effect." Variables like Heart Rate do not suffer from this difficulty because the value obtained is not affected in any systematic fashion by the measurement if the individual is properly trained and appropriate measuring apparatus is employed.

P-technique analysis, therefore, has the greatest potential in clinical research involving variables that exhibit substantial real fluctuations in the individual over time. It has relatively little potential for the study of those characteristics that are stable in the individual and for which variations in scores over time can be attributed largely to practice effects and errors of measurement.

9.3. LESSER KNOWN DESIGNS

R-, Q-, and P-techniques are the best known of the basic factor analytic designs, but they by no means exhaust the possibilities, as Cattell (1952) has pointed out. With subjects, variables, and occasions representing three dimensions, it is possible to obtain three two-dimensional data matrices, each of which gives two ways of computing correlations. This gives six possible factor analytic designs. Figure 9.1 gives one of these data matrices from which R- and Q-technique designs are obtained. Figure 9.2 gives the P-technique design. It would also be possible, however, to compute the correlations in Fig. 9.2 by taking pairs of columns instead of pairs of rows. This would give correlations of pairs of occasions over the series of data-variable scores. Correlating columns from the data matrix in Fig. 9.2 yields a correlation matrix that can be factored to give what Cattell (1952) calls an "O-technique" factor analysis.

Because of the variations in means and standard deviations of the row variables in the data matrix in Fig. 9.2, the rows would have to be standardized, giving means and standard deviations that are equal from row to row, before an O-technique factor analysis can be carried out. This same step was required for a proper Q-technique analysis. The factors derived from an O-technique analysis show what occasions are clustered. Such an analysis could reveal the presence, for example, of one or more periodic states in a given individual. A particular physiological condition, characterized by a given pattern of scores on the variables, might emerge as a factor, with a period of approximately 10, 20, or even 30 days from one appearance to the next.

Correlating occasions over a sample of individuals for a given variable produces a matrix of correlations each of which is essentially a measure of test-retest reliability. This type of design is derived from a third possible data matrix, different from those shown in Figs. 9.1 and 9.2. Thus, many persons would be measured many times on the same data variable. Where the correlations are computed between occasions over a sample of individuals, the type of factor analysis obtained from the resulting correlation matrix is called "T-technique" by Cattell (1952). The factors derived would represent clusters of occasions upon which the individuals performed in a similar manner.

The same data matrix that provides the basis for T-technique can also give rise to a second design, referred to as "S-technique." In S-technique, two individuals are correlated over the series of occasions on which measurements are taken for the variable under investigation. S-technique, as Cattell points out, can be used to cluster people who respond in the same way over a series of varying social situations where all the measurements are taken with respect to a single variable, for example, the amount of overt aggression exhibited. Since O-, S-, and T-technique designs are used so little, they are not discussed further here. The interested reader is referred to Cattell (1952) for a more extended discussion of these methods.

10

Interpretation and Application of Factor Analytic Results

10.1. INTRODUCTION

The usual procedures followed in factor interpretation are very simple. Those data variables with high factor loadings are considered to be "like" the factor in some sense and those with zero or near-zero loadings are treated as being "not like" the factor, whatever it is. Those variables that are "like" the factor, that is, have high loadings on the factor, are examined to find out what they have in common that could be the basis for the factor that has emerged. High loadings in both the positive and negative direction are considered.

If a data variable were to correlate perfectly with a factor, it would ordinarily be considered identical with the factor in what it measures. Since data variables are not perfectly reliable, they cannot correlate perfectly with a factor, of course, but with a data-variable reliability of 0.81, a factor loading of 0.90 would indicate a total overlap in true variance between the data variable and the factor (see Guilford, 1965, p. 442, index of reliability). In general, a factor loading for a data variable equal to the square root of its reliability coefficient is suggestive of a completely pure-factor test or data variable. All its true variance is placed on that one factor, making it essentially identical with the factor except for its error variance.

In practice, of course, the correlations of data variables with factors generally fall well below the square roots of the data-variable reliabilities, indicating that the data variables have other true variance that is not shared with this factor. The additional true variance may be due exclusively to specific variance, but more likely it will be due to a combination of specific variance and some common variance associated with other common factors in the analysis.

Correlations of data variables with the factors, it should be remembered, are elements of the factor structure matrix rather than the factor pattern matrix (see Chapter 6) where the solutions are oblique. Only with orthogonal factor solutions are the correlations of the data variables with the factors equal to the factor loadings. With oblique solutions, the factor loadings, or pattern coefficients, might equal or exceed the square roots of the data-variable reliabilities in some cases. This would not indicate necessarily that the variable is factor pure, however, since the structure coefficient, the correlation of the data variable with the factor, would be less than 1.0.

Ordinarily, then, the correlations of the data variables with a factor they define are well below the level that would permit an easy inference of synonymity between the factor and one or more of the data variables. There must be a painstaking analysis of each highly loaded data variable into its constituent components so that the elements common to all data variables that define the factor may be identified and labeled. The process of trying to identify the nature of a factor is facilitated by several conditions:

1. The higher the factor loadings, the greater is the degree of overlapping true variance between the data variable and the factor and the more the factor is like the data variable in question. The square of the correlation of the variable with the factor is a good indication of the extent of the overlap. Dividing this figure by the reliability coefficient for the data variable gives the proportion of the data variable's true variance that it shares with the factor. It is also sometimes helpful to divide the correlation of a data variable with the factor by the square root of the reliability coefficient to get an idea about what the correlation between the two would be if the data variable were perfectly reliable.

2. The more factor pure a variable is that defines a factor, the easier it is to make inferences regarding the nature of the factor. If a complex data variable has a substantial loading on a given factor, it is difficult to determine from this information alone which of its many constituent parts is responsible. For this reason, complex data variables are not very helpful in factor interpretation just as they were not very useful in determining what rotations to perform.

3. The greater the number of variables with a substantial loading on the factor, other things being equal, the easier it is to isolate what the factor probably represents. It is still possible to obtain an erroneous impression of the factor's character despite the availability of many highly loaded variables to define it, however, if the sample of variables is biased in some sense important to the factor definition. If the data variables included fail

to represent some important aspect of the factor, for example, the picture of what the factor is like will be incomplete. The situation is somewhat analogous to the task of describing a person. Several important correct and revealing characteristics of an individual could be presented, but they might not tell the whole story. A person's employment history and background might look exceedingly impressive, but the inclusion of one addition item, for example, the information that the applicant's last two years had been spent in jail following a conviction for embezzlement, could make a significant difference to a prospective employer.

Even though a factor is prominently displayed in a given study, therefore, it cannot be assumed that all major facets of the factor have been represented by the variables defining the factor. Once a major factor has been isolated in a given domain, an important focus of further research is the search for other data variables related to the factor in a substantial way that may help to give a more complete picture of what the factor is like.

A question that frequently arises is that of how high the correlation between a data variable and a factor must be before it can be regarded as "significant" for interpretive purposes. There can be no answer to this question in any precise statistical sense since there is not available at the present time any statistical test that can establish the significance level of a rotated factor loading. The loading of a given variable on a factor can be altered easily by rotating the factor a little closer to or a little farther away from the particular data-variable vector in question. A crude index of the viability of a given data variable for interpretative purposes is the square of the correlation between the factor and the data variable. It has already been mentioned that if this value is high enough, it indicates a total overlap of the data variable's true variance with the factor. This value is also helpful at the low end to decide when the data variable is too unlike the factor to be considered in the factor intepretation.

A fairly commonly used cutoff level for orthogonal factor loadings is 0.30; that is, no variable with a factor loading below 0.30 is listed among those data variables defining the factor. A squared value $(.30)^2$ gives 0.09, which indicates that a data variable correlating with the factor less than 0.30 has less than 10 percent of its variance in common with the factor. The other 90 plus percent lies elsewhere, in common, specific and/or error variance. Some investigators have been known to list loadings less than 0.30 in interpreting factors, but in the orthogonal case where such loadings are interpreted as correlations, such values seem excessively low to us. The danger, of course, is that aspects of the variable from the 90 percent variance *not* associated with the factor will be erroneously attributed to the factor itself. This danger is particularly great where investigators have hypothesized that the data variable in question will relate to this factor, are anxious to believe that it does, and then accept a loading of between 0.2 and 0.3 as a confirmation of their hypothesis.

Whereas loadings of 0.30 and above have commonly been listed among those high enough to provide some interpretive value, such loadings certainly cannot be relied upon to provide a very good basis for factor interpretation. Table 10.1 can be used to give a rough idea of the value of variable-factor correlations (orthogonal factor loadings or structure coefficients) for factor interpretation purposes. Adjustments must be made with oblique factor solutions to consider both the factor loadings (pattern coefficients) and the correlations of the data variables with the factors (structure coefficients). If the data variable has its principal oblique factor loadings on a particular factor, then the correlation of the variable with that factor from the structure matrix may be used in Table 10.1 to judge the potential usefulness of that variable for factor interpretation.

Common sense dictates that factor interpretation based on a few variables with only "poor" or "fair" ratings in Table 10.1 must be made very cautiously and with every expectation that substantial revisions may be necessary in the future. If several data variables are available with loadings in the "very good" to "excellent" category, the investigators can afford to be somewhat more definite in what they say about the factor. Even here, however, investigators must avoid dogmatic statements because subsequent work may establish that some aspects of the factor have not been well represented, if at all, in the group of variables they have included in their investigations. Later work may force significant modifications of the factor interpretation.

Good factor interpretation requires going beyond the rudimentary steps of inspecting highly loaded variables for common content and naming the factor accordingly. The best kind of factor interpretation will also shed some light on several other areas of concern. Where does this factor lie in the hierarchy of factors? Is it a relatively specific-level factor that is too limited in scope to be of much scientific value or is it very broad and complex, perhaps too much so? How does the factor relate to previously

TABLE 10.1

Scale of Variable–Factor Correlations

Orthogonal factor loading	Percentage of variance	Rating
.71	50	Excellent
.63	40	Very good
.55	30	Good
.45	20	Fair
.32	10	Poor

developed taxonomic systems of interest in the domain under investigation? How firmly established is the factor identification? Will other studies be needed to identify more completely just what the factor represents? What potential value does the factor have for purposes of general scientific description and theory building? To what extent are variations in factor scores assignable to hereditary and environmental influences, respectively?

These questions are not easy to answer and in fact few factor analytic studies are published in which there is much of an attempt to do so. All too often, the report of a factor analysis presents a list of factors with the data variables that are highly loaded on the factors together with factor names but not a great deal else in the way of factor interpretation. The investigators should at least be aware of the need for more extensive interpretation and should attempt to provide it as their research endeavors unfold over a series of studies.

10.1.1.   ARE FACTORS "REAL?"

A persistent and recurring controversy in factor interpretation centers about the meaning that can be attached to a factor. On the one extreme there is the position expressed by Kelley (1940, p. 120): "There is no search for timeless, spaceless, populationless truth in factor analysis; rather, it represents a simple, straightforward problem of description in several dimensions of a definite group functioning in definite manners, and he who presumes to read more remote verities into the factorial outcome is certainly doomed to disappointment."

An able spokesman for the position on the other side of this controversy, Cattell (1952) feels that the psychologist or social scientist cannot be content with factors that are merely mathematical conveniences and he states that:

> in the case of factor analysis, the scientist wants each factor to correspond to some unitary influence with which he is familiar on *other* and general scientific grounds — some influence which he has reason to believe is a functional unity in nature. Consequently, he argues that there is *one* position in the rotation which corresponds to the real factors and that all other positions encountered are mathematical transformations of this real position — false claimants which we have not yet succeeded in eliminating. (p. 66)

The controversy, then, centers about the question of whether factors are to be considered as merely arbitrary descriptive variables with no more intrinsic meaning than any other set of descriptions or whether they are to be considered as "real" and meaningful structural aspects of nature, lying there waiting to be discovered by the enterprising research worker. Cattell, of course, does not take the position that the factors derived from any given factor analysis will necessarily represent examples of the real functional unities that he seeks. The location of such factors represents a desirable goal of factor analysis, in his view, whereas those who take the viewpoint expressed by Kelley deny that such a goal is attainable. Cattell obviously believes that the goal is attainable and furthermore claims that in any given study, rotation of factor axes to oblique simple structure is the most likely way to achieve success in this search.

Among active factor analysts doing empirical taxonomic research today, there appears to be more leaning toward Cattell's position than toward Kelley's in the sense that these workers like to believe that they are coming up with constructs that are not just arbitrary descriptive variables. Taxonomic investigators hope to find constructs that are better in some sense than other possible descriptors, although they may not be able to prove it nor even to specify precisely why they think their's are better.

A science consists of descriptions of the functional relationships between *the* variables in that field. To determine what the functional relationships are, it is clearly necessary first to know what *the* variables to be related are. It makes sense to believe that all possible sets of variables are not equally good for developing a particular science. Some sets may be more parsimonious than others. Some sets may be more easily integrated into unifying theoretical superstructures. Some sets of variables may have greater heuristic value than others. Variables used as the basis for development of a science, other things being equal, would seem to be superior to alternate possibilities when they are more unitary rather than complex, in closer alignment with causal forces that can be identified in the external or internal environment, easier to understand, of greater practical utility, easier to measure, and so on.

It seems clear to us that the goal of factor analysis should be to isolate constructs that *do* have greater intrinsic value for the purpose of building a science. It is going too far to say that there exists one and only one set of "correct" constructs, or "real" factors, in a given domain. On the other hand, many social science fields, for example, are burdened with a veritable avalanche of possible variables from which to choose in trying to develop a viable science. These are clearly not all equally good. An appropriate and reasonable goal of factor analysis, in our opinion, is to isolate constructs that can be shown to be superior to others in certain defined ways for the purpose of building a science.

As in most human endeavors, however, the goals of factor analysis are not always achieved in practice. The plethora of "factors" ground out by busy electronic computers is dwarfed only by the productions of armchair variable builders. If it were possible to ensure that every factor analysis would turn up at least one "good" construct, progress in the social sciences would be much faster than it is in fact. It is unfortunately true that most factor analyses do not reveal anything particularly useful in the way of scientific constructs that have not been previously isolated. Part of this is due to the fact that it is so easy to make serious mistakes in planning a factor analytic study. Another reason is that well-defined factor constructs usually emerge only out of a well-designed and integrated series of investigations. Finally, useful constructs are not necessarily revealed as such upon inspection. It is necessary to establish their claim to such status by appeal to evidence outside the factor analytic investigations themselves. This requires a great deal of painstaking work and hence it is frequently left for "other" investigators to carry out.

The task of proper interpretation of factor analytic results, therefore, is a complex one. It can be approached very simply as one of describing the putative nature of the common elements among the data variables that define the factor and giving the factor a name. On the other hand, it can be approached as a part of a long-range task of developing the best possible set of factor constructs in a given domain. In this latter case, factor interpretation must be concerned with the matters discussed above and such questions as: (a) Is this factor essentially an artifact or not? (b) What is the potential value of this factor? (c) Do the variables that define the factor reveal all its major aspects? (d) Can other data variables be found that will measure it better? (e) Will it hold up in another investigation using other variables and subjects? To answer such questions makes factor interpretation a great deal more difficult than mere factor naming. It also often involves delaying answers until additional investigations have been carried out. Factor interpretation at its best becomes an activity to be developed over a series of related studies rather than something to be based solely on a single investigation.

Mulaik (1990) has argued that one must test one's factor interpretations to see if they are consistent with the data by constructing new variables under the interpretation that supposedly reflect the influence of the same factor. The new variables can then be included with the old, new data collected and analyzed, and the interpretation tested to see if a factor appears on which the original variables have their same loadings and the new variable also loads. An interpretation, according to Mulaik, is only an hypothesis and hypotheses need to be tested with data independent of those originally inspiring the hypothesis. An interpretation is not a final judgment.

10.2. FACTOR ANALYSIS AND MULTIPLE REGRESSION ANALYSIS

Although factor analysis and multiple regression analysis have some common objectives, there is a considerable difference between them with respect to what they can be expected to accomplish. In multiple regression analysis, a data matrix is available which is used to determine the intercorrelations among predictor variables and also correlations of the predictors with one or more criterion variables, such as measures of success in training, success on the job, or success in some other kind of life adjustment. The object of the multiple regression analysis is to pick a subset of predictor variables that will best predict the criterion variable and to determine their relative weights for making that prediction.

Regression analysis has, therefore, an immediate practical goal, namely, to predict a given criterion of adjustment. The results of such studies often have considerable utility, for example, in the selection and classification of personnel. If the primary objective of a given research study is the selection of the best predictors from a specified given set of data variables, multiple regression analysis would be preferred to factor analysis as the principal method of treating the data. Factor analysis alone would not provide the most useful approach to dealing with the immediate practical problem.

Factor analysis can be a very useful supplementary method of analysis, however, in more extensive research efforts designed to improve the prediction of a given criterion of adjustment. Consider an example of a large firm that employs several hundred individuals in a particular occupational speciality. The firm finds that a substantial number of the individuals hired for this type of job fail within one year and either quit or are discharged. The firm decides to develop a testing program to select future employees in an attempt to reduce the number of failures on the job.

A simple-minded multiple regression approach to this problem could begin with the selection of a battery of available tests that might have some validity for predicting success in this occupational activity. These tests could be administered to all currently employed individuals in this kind of job. Test scores would be correlated with a numerical index of success in performing this work after dividing the sample into two randomly selected halves. Multiple regression analysis performed in each group separately would reveal those variables that contribute significantly to predicting the criterion of success on the job. Variables that prove to be significant contributors in both samples could be utilized to form a test battery for selection purposes. The total sample could be used to find optimum regression weights for these tests. This regression equation could be used to predict success for new applicants who would be hired regardless of their test scores. By follow-up evaluation of these new employess, the effectiveness of the test battery for selection purposes could be assessed.

The effectiveness of this conventional approach depends on the battery of tests selected for trial and on the quality of the criterion of success on the job. Factor analysis could be employed to improve both in a long-range research program designed to upgrade the effectiveness of personnel selection. Only by determining what the criterion of success consists of factorially is it possible to know in any precise way what kinds of data variables should be used to predict it. Factor analysis of the criterion not only helps to suggest what predictor variables should be tried, but it also can reveal possible areas of criterion improvement. This point is discussed in somewhat greater detail later in the chapter.

Available published test instruments may prove to be less than optimum as predictors for the particular criterion being predicted. Their factor composition, for example, may be complex and may contain too much variance not found in the criterion. It is also unlikely that such tests would be constructed in such a way that the proportions of variance assigned to various factors in the test would coincide with those found in the criterion itself. Factor analyses of predictor variables together with criterion variables can help to answer questions of this kind. Where it is necessary to develop new tests that are relatively pure measures of the factors identified in the criterion itself, factor analysis can be helpful in the test-development program. The use of pure-factor predictors representing the various identifiable factors in the criterion permits the choice of optimum weights for those factors in predicting the criterion. Careful research and test development of this kind, therefore, can often improve on the level of prediction for criteria of adjustment that is attainable with unanalyzed and unaltered existing predictors and criteria.

Although factor analysis can be of great practical value in this way as a means of improving prediction of important criteria, multiple regression analysis still represents the major statistical tool in this work. It is in the area of scientific understanding and taxonomic research that factor analysis plays the greater role with multiple regression retreating to a secondary position of importance. Predicting specific criteria by means of test batteries selected through multiple regression analysis represents an activity of limited general scientific interest because, among other things, the number of potential criteria to predict is very large. Even for the same general kind of occupational activity, a test battery that would be good for predicting success in one firm might not be satisfactory in another. Scientific goals call for results that have greater generality, results that are not tied to a specific criterion of practical adjustment in a specific cultural, industrial, or educational setting.

The investigator with broader scientific objectives in mind, but who nevertheless may be hopeful of achieving results with ultimate potential practical utility, is more concerned with using factor analysis to establish those variables that can provide the basis for a taxonomy describing an entire area of scientific concern. If factor analysis can be utilized to produce an adequate taxonomy for describing personality, for example, and to develop instruments to measure the data variables that make up the taxonomy, these same data variables can be utilized for predicting many different kinds of practical criteria of adjustment that contain important personality components. The multiple regression equation weights assigned to the relatively pure-factor personality measures will vary from one criterion to another, but the same pool of personality measures can be tried out for each criterion-prediction project. Many of these measures would be discarded for purposes of predicting a specific criterion, of course, since their weights would not be sufficiently different from zero. The same kind of logic applies to developing a taxonomy of cognitive abilities for the prediction of criteria that require such traits for successful performance.

The ultimate goal of taxonomic research using factor analysis is to provide a complete catalog of variables, and methods of measuring them, to cover the entire scientific domain under investigation. In psychology, for example, this would ideally involve a set of variables adequate to describe the individual completely for all practical purposes, except for errors of measurement. Such a set of variables would not only constitute the basis for a science of human behavior but would also serve practical objectives of prediction as well. Any practical criterion would be predicted by using a subset of these variables, each optimally weighted to predict this particular criterion. Taxonomic research of this kind has been conducted most intensively to date in the area of human abilities. The domain of human personality is also receiving a great deal of attention, although the progress in this field lags behind that in the mental abilities field. Work in other areas besides these two has been much less extensive. The general availability of computers, technological advances in factor analysis, and increased interest in factor analytic methods by investigators from many fields, however, offer considerable hope for an accelerated rate of progress from factor analytic applications in the future.

10.3. FACTOR SCORES

Once a factor has been isolated, investigators are eager to relate this variable to other variables of interest in a given scientific area. If a single pure-factor test of high reliability is available for a given factor, scores on this test can be used as factor scores for the factor, although they would contain error to the extent that the test is not perfectly reliable. It is more usual, however, to have several variables that are related to the factor but no one of which has anything approaching 80% of its variance concentrated in this one factor. In such cases, it is necessary to attempt to estimate factor scores utilizing the scores of those variables related to the factor in a more modest way. Some of the methods of estimating factor scores are considered briefly in the following sections.

10.3.1.   METHOD 1

One of the simplest ways of estimating factor scores is first to single out all those data variables that have factor loadings on the factor above a certain selected cutoff value, for example, 0.50. The raw scores for these data variables may be added up to provide a rough estimate of the factor score on this factor for a given individual. The same procedure is followed for each other individual. The raw score for any variable with a negative loading of $-.50$ or less would be subtracted rather than added because the data variable is negatively related to the factor. This method has the disadvantage that only an arbitrary cutoff point is used to determine which variables have high enough loadings to be used as estimators of the factor score. The higher the cutoff is set, the fewer will be the data variables used as factor score estimators. The lower the cutoff, the less related will some of the variables be to the factor and hence the more impure will be the factor scores. This method also has the disadvantage of giving disproportionate weight to those variables with greater raw-score variabilities. It is a rather crude method, therefore, but under some circumstances it may be quite adequate, such as for rough exploratory work and where the variables do not differ greatly among themselves in variability. The factor scores obtained in this fashion are not likely to be uncorrelated among the various factors even if the factor solution is an orthogonal one.

10.3.2.   METHOD 2

A somewhat more sophisticated approach than the previous one is to scale the raw scores for all variables to the same mean and standard deviation before adding scores for those variables with loadings above the cutoff. This ensures that every variable will receive the same weight as every other variable in determining the factor scores. This refinement is usually worth the effort involved unless the variables are reasonably similar in the size of their standard deviations in the raw-score form. Since standard deviations of raw scores can and do vary over a wide range, failure to standardize scores in factor score estimation can result in markedly uneven weights for the different factor score components.

10.3.3.   METHOD 3

The two methods just described do not base the weights assigned to factor score component variables on their loadings on the factor. That is, a variable with a high loading on the factor does not necessarily have a higher weight in computing the factor score than a variable with a lower loading. A further refinement in factor score estimation, therefore, is to weight the various scores after they have been scaled to the same mean and standard deviation. The weight for each score is the factor loading of that variable on the factor or perhaps an integral value approximately proportional to the factor loading. This method can be applied just to those variables with factor loadings above a specified cutoff value, or it can be applied to all the variables. Variables with small loadings, of course, would have little effect on the total factor scores.

The advantage of this method is that it allows those variables with the highest loadings on the factor to have the greatest effect in estimating the factor scores. A disadvantage is the greater computational effort required to obtain the factor scores. A more subtle disadvantage is the possibility that differences in factor loadings among those variables with loadings above the cutoff point are due more to vagaries of variable selection and rotation than to any real differences in their value for estimating the factor scores. To the extent that this is true, this method would not represent an improvement over Method 2.

10.3.4. METHOD 4

If n factors are extracted from an $n \times n$ correlation matrix, with 1's used as communalities, residuals will vanish and factor scores may be calculated as follows:

$$\mathbf{Z} = \mathbf{PF} \qquad (10.1)$$

where

$\mathbf{Z}$ is an $n \times N$ matrix of scaled scores on the data variables,

$\mathbf{P}$ is an $n \times n$ matrix of factor loadings,

$\mathbf{F}$ is an $n \times N$ matrix of scaled factor scores.

Then

$$\mathbf{P}^{-1}\mathbf{Z} = \mathbf{P}^{-1}\mathbf{PF}$$

and

$$\mathbf{F} = \mathbf{P}^{-1}\mathbf{Z} \qquad (10.2)$$

This solution for the matrix of factor scores $\mathbf{F}$ requires that $\mathbf{P}$, the matrix of factor loadings, have an inverse. This will not be true unless as many factors are extracted as there are data variables. Computing the inverse of an $n \times n$ matrix can become very time-consuming as n increases, making this a laborious method for computing factor scores. Other objections to the method, however, are even more serious. Since a primary objective of factor analysis is to account for the overlap among many data variables through the use of a much smaller number of factor constructs, the idea of extracting as many factors as there are data variables has little appeal to the empirically oriented scientist. It might well have appeal in certain kinds of problems for the theoretician.

Where unities are placed in the diagonals of the correlation matrix and a principal component solution is obtained, it is possible to derive factor scores for both rotated and unrotated factors without computing an inverse and without even extracting n factors. These procedures and other methods for obtaining factor scores have been described rather completely by Harman (1967, pp. 345–374). Some of these methods permit the calculation of factor scores that are uncorrelated with each other, a property that is important for some research purposes.

10.3.5. METHOD 5

Multiple regression methods can also be employed to estimate factor scores using the following basic equation:

$$z_{fi} = \beta_1 z_{1i} + \beta_2 z_{2i} + \beta_3 z_{3i} + \ldots + \beta_n z_{ni} \tag{10.3}$$

where

z_{fi} is a standard score in factor f for person i,

z_{1i} is a standard score in variable 1 for person i,

z_{2i} is a standard score in variable 2 for person i,

β_i is a standard regression coefficient for variable i.

The standard scores on the n variables used to predict the factor scores are known. These variables could consist of all the data variables in the factor analysis, in which case many of the β_i weights would be very low because their loadings on the factor would be low, or the variables included could be a subset of these, restricted to only those with loadings above a selected cutoff point. The development here, however, will presume that all variables are being used.

Equation (10.3) is like the standard multiple regression equation where n predictors are being used to predict a single criterion variable. To obtain the β_i weights for this equation, it is sufficient to know the correlations among the predictors and the correlations of the predictors with the criterion, that is, the validity coefficients. In the application to the problem of estimating factor scores, the factor scores become the predicted criterion scores, the variables in the factor analysis are the predictors, and the orthogonal factor loadings or the oblique structure coefficients are the validity coefficients. The unknown β_i weights are obtained through the solution of the following normal equations (Guilford, 1965, p. 409), derived using the principle of least squares:

$$\beta_1 + \beta_2 r_{12} + \beta_3 r_{13} + \ldots + \beta_n r_{1n} = r_{1f}$$

$$\beta_1 r_{21} + \beta_2 + \beta_3 r_{23} + \ldots + \beta_n r_{2n} = r_{2f}$$

$$\beta_1 r_{31} + \beta_2 r_{32} + \beta_3 + \ldots + \beta_n r_{3n} = r_{3f}$$

$$\ldots \quad \ldots \quad \ldots \quad\quad \ldots \quad \ldots$$

$$\beta_1 r_{n1} + \beta_2 r_{n2} + \beta_3 r_{n3} + \ldots + \beta_n = r_{nf} \qquad (10.4)$$

Equation (10.4) may be expressed in matrix form as follows:

$$\mathbf{R}\beta = r_f \qquad (10.5)$$

where $\mathbf{R}$ is the matrix of known correlations among variables 1 through n in Eq. (10.4); β is a column matrix containing the unknown β_i weights; and r_f is a column matrix of correlations between the variables and the factor, that is, orthogonal factor loadings or oblique structure coefficients. Provided the matrix $\mathbf{R}$ has an inverse, Eq. (10.5) and hence Eqs. (10.4) may be solved as follows:

$$\beta = \mathbf{R}^{-1} r_f \qquad (10.6)$$

Thus, the column of β_i weights to be used in Eq. (10.3) for predicting the factor scores from the data-variable scores is obtained by multiplying the inverse of the matrix of correlations among the data variables by the column matrix of correlations of the data variables with the factor.

An advantage of using all variables in the regression equation (10.3) is that the inverse $\mathbf{R}^{-1}$ may be obtained once and used in Eq. (10.6) for all factors merely by changing the r_f column, depending on which factor is being considered. If only some of the variables are used to obtain a given set of factor scores, the $\mathbf{R}^{-1}$ matrix for predicting that factor must be derived from an $\mathbf{R}$ matrix containing the intercorrelations only for those variables that are being used.

The factor scores obtained in this way are least-squares estimates, given the correlations that constitute the data. These factor scores will not be independent of one another from factor to factor, even for an orthogonal factor solution. This may be a handicap for some theoretical investigations, but it is not for most practical purposes. Obtaining these least-squares factor scores does require a considerable amount of computation. The precision obtained is a positive feature, but it must be remembered that different rotations could give substantially different factor loadings which in turn would modify the factor scores obtained. The level of precision obtained by computing factor scores in this manner may be more apparent than real. Capitalization on chance errors in multiple regression analysis is also a fact of life that must be remembered in considering whether least-squares factor scores are worth the additional cost over simpler methods.

10.3.6. OVERVIEW

Where factor scores are being derived from psychological test items, Method 1 is often the most convenient. It is desirable to compute test scores by adding item scores without weighting them because this makes test scoring easier. Where factor components have divergent variabilities that are substantial and not in accord with their relative degree of association with the factor, it may be necessary to weight the components differentially in obtaining factor scores. Scores from three separate subgroups of items might be combined to give an overall factor score using the following formula (as an example):

$$F = 4I - II + 2 \times III \qquad (10.7)$$

Rounded-off integral weights are used in Eq. (10.7) with variable II showing a negative weight, indicating that it was negatively loaded on the factor for which the factor score F is being computed. If the factor score were to be computed by adding item scores, instead of by adding total scores as in Eq. (10.7), the item scores for variable II would have to be reversed prior to being added so that the resulting reversed total of the variable II items would be positively instead of negatively related to the factor. There rarely would be any need to use weights more finely specified than rounded-off integral values for practical applications. The unstandardized factor scores obtained by Eq. (10.7) could be scaled to a mean of 50 and a standard deviation of 10, if desired, to place them on a more commonly used scale.

When test or questionnaire items are used in determining factor scores, the kind of operation indicated by Eq. (10.7) can often be avoided by appropriate selection of items to be included in the factor score. By adding an item here, deleting an item there, and so on, the component variabilities can often be adjusted close enough to equality that a simple sum of item scores will suffice to give a practically acceptable factor score. Factor scores on the first author's personality test (described in the next chapter) are obtained in this way by adding item scores where each factor is assessed by five subscales and each subscale is measured by four items. Since the subscales are not substantially different in variability and all have positive loadings on the factors, the factor scores are obtained merely by adding up the item scores over all the items representing subscales highly related to the factors. Scores for items that are negatively stated with respect to a given factor are reversed before adding them into the factor score. This is done by subtracting the item score from one point more than the maximum item score. On a seven-point item response scale, for example, if a person answers "7" to a negatively worded item, after reversal the item score becomes "8 − 7" or "1."

The factor scores obtained in this manner by adding item scores are not independent of each other from factor to factor but then neither are the factors they represent. Such procedures may be unacceptable in certain theoretical research endeavors but for most practical research objectives they are apt to be satisfactory.

10.4. REPORTING A FACTOR ANALYTIC STUDY

A proper job of reporting a factor analytic study requires that the investigators provide the readers with enough information to permit the results to be checked independently. All too often, the investigators report only the end results of their work, forcing the readers to take the findings on faith. This practice is to be discouraged. If the investigators report all of their original data, their work may be checked from the very beginning. Rarely, however, is it expected that the investigators will go this far, although it is expected that the investigators at least make available the correlation matrix that was computed from those original data and later subjected to factor analytic treatment. It would also be desirable to have the means and standard deviations of the data variables. If these statistics are made available, the readers may, if they desire, repeat all the factor analytic work and also apply other methods of analysis that they might deem more suitable.

The reader may be aware that few professional journal editors these days are willing to publish large correlation matrices with articles reporting factor analytic results because of the high cost involved and the fact that few readers will ever make use of this information. The investigators should, therefore, in most cases choose some alternate method of making the correlations matrix and other statistics available. Some authors publish in monograph form in which all the relevant tables can be included. Others, through footnotes in published articles, offer to furnish copies of the necessary tables upon written request to the authors.

Perhaps the most satisfactory method of making such tables available, however, is to take advantage of auxiliary publication services, where they exist, that permit readers to obtain the documents in question even though they are not published with the article, and without having to contact the author. Such facilities provide a more dependable and permanent record of research findings. Suppose, for example, that an author wishes to make available the correlation matrix for a factor analysis that is reported in an article submitted for publication. At an appropriate point in the article, usually in the results section, reference to a footnote such as the following would be made:

[1]The correlation matrix upon which the factor analysis in this study was based has been deposited with the National Auxiliary Publications Service. See NAPS Document No. _____ for _____ pages of supplementary material from NAPS, c/o Microfiche Publications, 248 Hempstead Turnpike, West Hempstead, N.Y. 11552. Remit in advance, in U. S. funds only, $ _____ for photocopy or $ _____ for microfiche. Outside U.S. and Canada add postage of $ _____ or $ _____ for microfiche postage.

The correlation matrix would be prepared for photocopying, even single spaced, and would be submitted along with the article manuscript to the editor, but it would be labeled for deposit with NAPS. If the article is accepted for publication, the editor or the author will send the correlation matrix to NAPS and will obtain the document number and charges. These figures will be inserted in the blank spaces indicated in the sample footnote. The footnote itself would be published in the article. The interested reader will then be able to order the correlation matrix directly from NAPS. The procedures for submitting such material change from time to time and NAPS may or may not continue to be in existence, so the reader should obtain current information on the availability of such document services and how to access them.

Although another investigator could repeat the factor analytic work from the correlation matrix, means, and variances alone, good reporting calls for submitting other matrices as well, as a convenience to other researchers who might be interested in checking the findings. For an orthogonal factor solution, for example, the following additional matrices should be submitted to NAPS or otherwise made available: unrotated factor matrix and rotated factor matrix. If available, the transformation matrix that carried the unrotated matrix into the rotated matrix should be given. In reporting the results of an oblique factor analysis, the matrices that should be made available include the correlation matrix, unrotated factor matrix, matrix of correlations of the data variables with the reference vectors, transformation matrix that transforms the unrotated factor loadings into the reference vector projections, and matrix of correlations among the reference vectors.

Unless the investigators have been forced to do the calculations without an electronic computer, they should also furnish the factor pattern, factor structure, and the matrix of correlations among the factors. Some research workers, for example, Eysenck (1960; Eysenck & Eysenck, 1969), feel that a second-order analysis of the matrix of correlations among the factors should also be provided. Where factor analytic methods are used that do not provide certain of these matrices, there would be no necessity to calculate them just for reporting purposes.

Most readers of articles, books, or monographs reporting factor analytic results may not be sufficiently interested to order the available documents needed to check the author's work for themselves. They may be interested enough, however, to attempt an evaluation of the adequacy of the procedures used in carrying out the reported factor analysis. It is incumbent upon authors, therefore, to provide readers with sufficent detail to enable them to perform such evaluations. Where possible, therefore, it is desirable for authors to provide such information as the following in reporting their study:

1. *The Sample.* How many cases of what kind were used and how they were selected.

2. *The Data Variables.* The data variables should be described in sufficient detail to enable the reader to have an understanding of what is being measured. It may be necessary to submit material on this to the auxiliary publication source, for example, variable descriptions, means, and standard deviations.

3. *The Correlations.* What method of correlation was used? Was any scaling carried out before computing the correlations? To what extent were the assumptions underlying the correlation method met by the data?

4. *Factor Extraction.* What method of factor extraction was used? What criterion was used to determine when to stop factoring?

5. *Communalities.* If communalities were used, how were they decided upon? Was there any iteration of the communalities?

6. *Rotation.* What criteria were used to carry out the rotations? What evidence is available that would suggest that these criteria were appropriate for these particular data?

When readers are provided with adequate information in the preceding areas, they are in a much better position to evaluate the results of the factor analytic study and the interpretations offered. If any question develops in their minds, the availability of the matrices through auxiliary publication sources will permit them to explore the matter to their satisfaction. If the authors do not provide these resources, their readers can only consider the results and interpretations as unsupported hypotheses. Properly documented reports generally command greater attention and respect in the scientific community. Furthermore, the life expectancy of such studies is greater because even if newer, more powerful methods of data analysis become available, they can be applied to the data at a later date, if those data are made available through such auxiliary publication services as NAPS.

Although investigators cannot usually expect to publish whole matrices with their article describing a factor analytic investigation, they can usually expect to publish a description and interpretation of each major factor. This might take the form of a major section heading entitled "Factor Results" with several subheadings, each devoted to a single major factor. The title of a subheading, for example, *Factor I. Extraversion-Introversion*, could be given followed by a description and interpretation of the factor, beginning with a table of the major loadings on the factor, such as that shown in Table 10.2. Those loadings of 0.30 or more, or some other figure such as 0.25, 0.35, and so on, would be included in the table for each factor. The reader should be told what cutoff figure is being used for including variables in the table. It is also customary to list the variables in descending order of the size of their loadings on the factor rather than in the order of the variable numbers as shown in Table 10.2. In some cases, elaboration on the meaning of the factors and their relationship to theory and previous results will be reserved for the "Discussion" section of the article.

Careful description of procedures and results is necessary for adequate scientific reporting in any area. It is especially true, however, with factor analytic studies because a factor analysis merely provides the results of one investigator's way of interpreting the data. If the reporting job is adequate, readers may evaluate how satisfactory that interpretation is for their purposes, and if they are not satisfied with the interpretation, the data are available from which they may develop their own factor interpretation. Investigators who take the trouble to do this reporting properly increase the present and potential usefulness of their work to the scientific community.

TABLE 10.2

Major Loadings on the Factor

Variable	Description	Loading
26	Lack of Reserve	.68
27	Lack of Seclusiveness	.60
28	No Loss for Words	.84
29	Lack of Shyness	.79
30	No Stage Fright	.49

10.5. APPLICATIONS OF FACTOR ANALYSIS

Thousands of articles, monographs, and books have been published in which factor analytic results have been reported. The list of areas in which it has been applied is steadily growing. The following represents a very incomplete but suggestive list of areas in which factor analytic methods have been used:

Aptitudes and Abilities	*Attitudes and Opinions*
Intellectual abilities	Political attitudes
Clerical abilities	Social attitudes
Motor skills	Judgments
Language skills	Aesthetic preferences
Social skills	Morale
Academic achievement	Ratings
Creativity	Humor

Personality Characteristics	*Physical Characteristics*
Motivation	Dimensions of physique
Temperament	Biological variables
Character	Physiological responses
Values	Perceptual phenomena
Interests	Physical symptoms

Selected Other Applications

Errors	Therapy methods
Emotions	Mental symptoms
Accidents	Group characteristics
Job performance	Structure of language
Cultural differences	Theories of color vision
Political variables	Criteria of adjustment
Economic variables	Effects of training
Geological variables	Food preferences
Item analysis	Multidimensional scaling

Although the applications of factor analysis are increasing in number and extending into more and more new areas, it is still possible to classify a substantial percentage of such applications into one or more of the categories described in the following sections.

10.5.1. TAXONOMIC RESEARCH

Perhaps the most common reason for undertaking a factor analytic study is to obtain some information concerning what are "the" factors in a comparatively unstructured area of investigation. The degree to which quantification has been achieved is sometimes used as an index of the state of development of a science. Before quantification can advance very far, however, there must be available information concerning what to quantify. Pioneer investigators in a new area frequently make use of factor analysis hoping that it will help them to navigate accurately in uncharted waters. As a result of their studies, they hope to develop better ideas of what should be measured in the domain of investigation. It is a major step in the development of any science to reach concensus on just what constructs are to provide the structural foundation for further work in the field. Most of the social sciences and many other scientific fields are still very much in the state of trying to settle on what variables are going to be most helpful for their further development. Although factor analysis does not provide a foolproof avenue to easy answers in this endeavor, it can be a valuable aid in dealing with the problems encountered at this stage of scientific development in a field.

10.5.2. ANALYZING AND IMPROVING MEASURING INSTRUMENTS

When a new construct is proposed for a given scientific field, attempts to develop methods of measuring that construct almost inevitably follow. Before it is possible to determine precisely the nature of the functional relationships in a given scientific field, it is necessary to have adequate methods of measuring the variables that are to be related. One of the most common uses of factor analysis is to analyze the characteristics of a given measuring instrument or method to assess how well it is fulfilling its mission. This sometimes takes the form of a one-shot evaluation in which the investigator is checking on the adequacy of a particular method for measuring a construct, sometimes one proposed or developed by another investigator. Through factor analysis, areas of possible improvement are located, refinements are made, and a new analysis is carried out. Such improvement attempts may involve factor analysis of individual items, subscales, or total variable scores with each other or with outside measures. The goal is to develop a highly reliable instrument that provides as pure a measure as possible of the construct in question (Comrey, 1988).

10.5.3. ANALYZING AND IMPROVING CRITERIA

A considerable amount of important applied work in psychology centers around the task of predicting criteria of adjustment, such as school achievement, job success, marital adjustment, and so on. As described earlier in this chapter, a crude frontal assault on such problems might involve the commonly used procedure of correlating available test measures and other convenient potential predictors with available criterion measures. A reasonable degree of success may be achieved by this approach if the available criterion measure is a good one and if the selected predictors account for a substantial proportion of the true variance in the criterion scores.

The use of factor analysis permits a more sophisticated approach to these important applied problems. The first objective is to determine the factor composition of the existing criterion measure or measures. This information is obtained from a series of factor analyses in which the criterion measure(s) is (are) included as variables in the analysis. In some instances, factor analyses may be carried out using only criterion measures as variables in an analysis where many possible criterion measures are available. Through such analyses, it is often possible to make substantial improvements in the criterion itself by identifying sources of unwanted variance. For example, it may be determined that ratings of "success" on the job have been heavily influenced by personal friendship between raters and ratees or by other irrelevant sources of variance.

These factor analyses of criterion measures also provide information that can facilitate decisions about what separate criterion measures should be combined into one overall variable and how many separate criterion variables should be utilized. Where one single overall criterion variable is to be derived, these factor analysis results can provide important information useful in determining what components should be included in the overall composite criterion and what their relative weights should be to provide the best possible definition of "success."

Knowledge about the factors that are represented in the criterion permits a more scientific choice of the variables that are to be tried out as potential predictors. In the absence of knowledge about the factor composition of the criterion, such decisions must be based to at least some extent upon pure guess work.

10.5.4. IDENTIFYING TYPES

The search for types, whether among people or other kinds of data objects, goes on and on because it is convenient to think in such terms. This "type" of person will do such-and-such and must be treated in this or that fashion. If people could be classified into a small number of categories or "types" for any given decision-making purpose, life would become considerably easier for decision makers, be they educators, employers, psychotherapists, or whatever. *Q*-technique analysis is specifically aimed at the objective of locating types and for this purposes represents a powerful tool that as yet has not been fully exploited. It is not the only kind of factor analysis useful for this purposes, however, because for many R-technique analyses, the experimenter's unspoken long-term goals are more concerned with locating types than with taxonomic considerations per se.

Information about types can provide aid in developing a taxonomy, and taxonomic information is useful in locating types if they exist. Unfortunately, much research aimed at locating types presumes that they exist and tends to force such distinctions on the data whether or not the data exhibit such discontinuities in fact. There is a discontinuity between male and female that permits human beings to be divided into two clear-cut types along sex lines. To divide people into "bright" and "dumb" types, however, is inappropriate because there is no discontinuity on the scale of human intelligence. Factor analysis can be a valuable aid to locating types where they exist, but it cannot create them.

10.5.5.   THEORY TESTING

Many factor analytic studies are designed to test theory-deduced hypotheses concerning the number of parameters needed to account for a given body of data. Is a two-factor theory adequate to account for certain data in color vision? Is there a single factor underlying political and social attitude variables? How many dimensions are involved in olfactory judgments? If theory X is true, variables a, b, c, and d should emerge with high loadings on the same factor; do they in fact come out this way? Factor analysis can be used to answer these and many other kinds of theory-oriented questions. Such theory-oriented applications of factor analysis are not apt to occur often in sciences where there are few variables and measurement is highly refined. In those developing sciences plagued by a plethora of imperfectly measured variables, however, factor analysis can be expected to play a more and more important role in the construction and testing of theories. It is precisely in this area that newer methods of confirmatory factor analysis have become increasingly popular in recent years. Although traditional exploratory factor analytic methods can be used effectively in a confirmatory way, these new methods are much more powerful for theory-testing purposes. An introduction to the use of such methods is presented in a later chapter.

11

Development of the Comrey Personality Scales: An Example of the Use of Factor Analysis

One of the common uses of factor analysis mentioned in the last chapter occurs in the development of psychological tests. This chapter presents an illustration of the use of factor analysis for this purpose, describing the factor analytic studies involved in the development and validation of the Comrey Personality Scales (Comrey, 1970a,1970b, 1980), an inventory of factored personality traits.

The Comrey Personality Scales, hereafter abbreviated as the CPS, were designed to measure the variables that make up a taxonomy of personality traits developed over a period of years by the first author with the aid of many of his students. The factored traits included in this taxonomy are the following: T−Trust vs Defensiveness; O−Orderliness versus Lack of Compulsion; C−Social Conformity versus Rebelliousness; A−Activity vs Lack of Energy; S− Emotional Stability versus Neuroticism; E−Extraversion versus Introversion; M−Masculinity versus Femininity; and P− Empathy versus Egocentrism. The factored personality scales for measuring these traits evolved in a series of steps as the taxonomy itself developed, with improvements in both occurring at each step. The attempt to develop this taxonomy was inspired originally by discrepancies in the personality taxonomies proposed by Guilford, Cattell, and Eysenck, three of the best known writers in the field of personal measurement. The taxonomic research undertaken by the first author had as its initial objective a resolution of the differences among these well-known writers. The intention was to independently seek out and identify the major factors of personality with the idea of comparing the resulting taxonomy of traits with those of the three authors mentioned.

As the research progressed, it became clear that the first author's own taxonomy would not closely match that of any one of these previous writers. Instead, a taxonomic system began to emerge that, while sharing much with these previous systems, was nevertheless distinct from any of them. As the form of this taxonomy took shape, methods of identifying the major factors were developed and refined, along with methods of measuring the factors, ultimately leading to the published version of the CPS.

11.1. STUDIES OF MMPI ITEMS

Since the objective of the planned research program called for the identification of the main factors needed to describe human personality, the decision was made to study the items of several well-known personality test instruments under the assumption that they would define at least some of the needed personality factors well enough to permit their identification. The MMPI was selected as the first instrument to be studied because it was the most widely used personality inventory and also because the usual scores derived from the MMPI appeared to be factorially complex and overlapping. Factor analyses of the items scored on these scales would serve the double function of (a) yielding clues to the important personality dimensions, and (b) clarifying the factor composition of these widely used scales.

It was decided, therefore, to factor analyze the items on each of the main scales of the original MMPI (Comrey, 1957a,b,c; 1958a,b,c,d,e,f; Comrey & Marggraff, 1958). Because computers were new in psychology when this work was begun, it took three years to develop a completely computerized procedure for factor analyzing the large matrices of correlations among the items on the MMPI scales. This work involved a considerable amount of experimentation with different kinds of correlation coefficients, methods of factor extraction, and methods of factor rotation. It was also necessary to devise machine-language programs to handle large matrices on an erratic early computer with a very small high-speed memory (the Bureau of Standards Western Automatic Computer, SWAC, at UCLA).

These investigations showed that the ϕ coefficient was the best available method for computing the interitem correlations, despite common belief at the time to the contrary (Comrey & Levonian, 1958). Tetrachoric and ϕ/ϕ_{max} coefficients, popular at that time, proved to be unsatisfactory. These investigations also showed that the Varimax method of Kaiser (1958), who had just developed this procedure for his Ph.D. thesis at the University of California, Berkeley, was the best method for analytic rotation available at that time. A semianalytic method developed by Thurstone (1954) was also tried out, but it failed to produce acceptable results (Comrey, 1959).

These studies demonstrated that the scales of the MMPI are indeed factorially complex with many of the same factors showing up on more than one scale. Moreover, the connections between the scale names and the apparent content of the factors found in the scale items are rather tenuous for most of the scales. Beyond this, however, these factor studies of MMPI items provided the initial identification of three of the final CPS personality taxonomy factors. The Cynicism factor in the MMPI analyses ultimately led to the Trust versus Defensiveness factor. Agitation, Sex Concern, and Neuroticism item factors from the MMPI analyses led eventually to the present Emotional Stability versus Neuroticism factor, and finally, the MMPI Shyness factor is now represented in the CPS by the Extraversion versus Introversion factor. The initial identification of these factors was poor, as were the methods of measuring them. The present-day factor measures and the factors themselves were developed through a long series of refinements over the subsequent 12 years. As newer factors were being sought and developed, work continued on the refining of factors already identified.

11.2. THE FHID APPROACH

These initial studies with MMPI items were followed by several investigations designed to locate important constructs in the personality domain through a consideration of other personality tests (Comrey & Soufi, 1960; Levonian, Comrey, Levy, & Proctor, 1961). Ideas derived from these studies and from the published works of other investigators provided the basis for the first empirical investigation by the first author aimed directly at developing a factor analytic taxonomy of personality traits (Comrey, 1961). This article also outlined a first approximation to the strategy that was to guide subsequent research efforts culminating in the publication of the CPS (Comrey, 1984).

A very important feature of this research strategy is the use of the Factored Homogeneous Item Dimension (FHID) as the basic unit of analysis in factor analytic studies designed to locate the main factors for a taxonomy of personality. A study of past factor analytic investigations, the first author's as well as those of others, revealed that many obtained factors are virtual artifacts produced by the combination of variables that are too similar in character. If a random selection of personality-test items from a specified pool is factor analyzed, for example, it is probable that some of the items will be very similar to other items in the pool, creating subsets of items that are essentially alternate ways of asking the same question. Because of the great similarity of the items in such a homogeneous subset, they will correlate considerably higher among themselves than they will with items outside the subset. Because of this, these highly related items will be very apt to define their own separate factor in the solution.

A factor produced by the unwitting or even intentional insertion of highly similar items into an analysis is not the kind of broad factor construct that is needed for a taxonomy to describe the whole of human personality. In factor analytic studies designed to locate broader and more meaningful constructs, it is necessary to take steps to avoid the production of factors that are not at an appropriate level in the hierarchy of factors.

The development and use of the FHID as the basic unit in the factor analysis has helped to accomplish this objective in the studies leading to the production of the CPS. The FHID is a total score variable calculated by summing scores over several items that are required to satisfy the following two criteria: (a) The items must be originally developed and logically conceived as measures of the variable under consideration, or chosen with this in mind; (b) the items must be found to define the same factor in a factor analysis of items. By meeting both these requirements, the items forming a FHID are shown to have both conceptual and demonstrated empirical statistical homogeneity. To control for acquiescence response bias (tendency to agree or to disagree), half the items are phrased positively with respect to the FHID name and half of the items are phrased negatively. Item scores for the negatively worded items are reversed before adding them with the positively worded item scores to obtain the total FHID score. This score reversal is accomplished by subtracting the number of the selected response from one more than the number associated with the highest numbered response. If the items are scored on a five-choice response scale, the item score for a negatively worded item would be subtracted from 6 to reverse the item score. With the CPS, which uses 7 alternative response values, the negatively worded response numbers are subtracted from 8.

The early studies carried out in this programmatic research revealed that many factors emerging from the studies were essentially nothing more than FHIDs. The experience gained from these and subsequent studies showed that it was relatively easy to develop a pool of conceptually homogeneous items that would define a single factor when included in a factor analysis of items. Not all items, of course, would emerge with loadings of sufficient magnitude to be acceptable. Items that failed to yield an adequately high loading were modified or replaced. Through a succession of analyses, a set of items could be developed that would meet the criteria for a FHID. Although it proved to be relatively easy to develop these item factors, or FHIDs, to represent numerous defined personality concepts, success was not always attained, by any means. A poorly defined concept usually leads to failure to develop a FHID. The items may split up into more than one item factor when included in a factor analysis of items or they may fail to define any factor at all. In such cases, the concept must be redefined for another attempt or dropped.

The relative ease with which such item factors were produced led the first author to reject the notion that FHID factors represent those major constructs that are needed to provide the basis for scientific development in the field of personality. In areas of measurement that do not depend on items, factors of a similarly arbitrary sort can be produced by using highly overlapping measures in the same analysis, for example, diastolic and systolic blood pressure included together in the same analysis of physiological variables. Such factors are considered to be at a very low level in the hierarchy of factors.

Factor analysis of properly selected FHIDs, however, forces the production of factors at a higher level in the factor hierarchy. The FHIDs analyzed must be selected in such a fashion as to avoid inclusion of two or more FHIDs that overlap each other too much conceptually in what they measure, that is, are alternate forms of each other. If two or more alternate-forms FHIDs are included, it is just like including two very similar items in the analysis. The effect is to drive out a factor that is very low in the hierarchy of factors. In analyses of FHIDs, this problem is avoided by making certain that each FHID included as a variable is conceptually distinct from every other FHID in the analysis. When this is done, the factors that emerge fall at a higher level in the hierarchy of factors and hence are much more likely to represent the broad constructs needed for a taxonomy to provide the basis for development of a science. Thus, factors produced by the common variance found among conceptually distinct FHIDS are presumed to represent constructs at a level of generality above the FHID level.

The advantages of factor analyzing FHIDs instead of items to locate the major constructs in a given field, such as personality, is not limited to being able to control the level in the factor hierarchy where the factors will emerge (Comrey, 1984). When items are combined to form a FHID, such as in the CPS, each FHID score is based on four items and has a range of possible scores from 4 to 28. Not only is the unreliable two-choice item replaced by a much more reliable seven-choice item, but the total FHID score itself is further enhanced in reliability through the use of several items instead of just one. Thus, the basic building blocks of the analysis are much better variables with much higher reliabilities than two-choice items. It inevitably follows that factor analytic results using FHIDs will be much more stable than those based on items, especially two-choice items.

The second level in the factor hierarchy, where factors that come from analyses of conceptually distinct FHIDs lie, might be called the "primary" level, following Thurstone's use of the term in his famous studies of the primary mental abilities. The factors at this primary level are conceived as providing the kind of constructs most likely to be useful for developing a science of personality, for example. It is extremely important to note that the number of factors that have emerged at this level is very limited in number, only eight in the CPS system. The number of factors that can be produced at the FHID level, however, is almost without limit. As long as new groups of similar items can be found, new FHID factors can be identified. The principle of scientific parsimony demands that we limit the number of main constructs that we use to form our scientific taxonomies. Primary level factors are sufficiently numerous and broad enough to cover the domain but they are limited in number. FHID factors are not.

Although these primary-level factors are considerably broader in character than FHIDs, they are not so broad as to represent "type" factors. Type factors are found at a higher level in the factor hierarchy, being based on the correlations that occur naturally among the primary-level factors. Type factors are too few, too broad, and too complex to be most useful for the purpose of building a general taxonomy for scientific purposes, although they may be very useful for certain applications. General Intelligence would be an example of a well-established type-level factor in the domain of human abilities. It is a high-level factor in the hierarchy of factors that exists because the basic primary-level human ability factors are substantially correlated in the general population.

Application of the FHID approach to the task of building a taxonomy of factored personality traits gradually led to the emergence of the following general strategy (Comrey, 1984):

1. Formulate verbal definitions of many concepts that might lead to the development of FHIDs.

2. Develop a pool of items for each of these defined concepts, half stated positively and half stated negatively with respect to the concept name.

3. Carry out factor analyses of items in which all the items for a given concept are included in the same analysis together with items designed to measure other concepts. Avoid including items in the same analysis for concepts that are expected to measure the same primary-level factor construct. If two item pools from the same primary-level factor are included in the same analysis, the factor analytic results may not produce only FHIDs but may produce the primary-level factor or some hybrid factor that represents a mixture of the two levels.

4. Revise the items and item pools and reanalyze until an acceptable FHID is available for each concept retained. Concepts that fail to produce acceptable FHIDs in the refinement process are dropped out.

5. Factor analyze the FHIDs to develop a first approximation impression of the number and nature of the primary-level factor constructs. On the

basis of these results, formulate a verbal conception of each factor construct identified at the primary-factor level.

6. Develop new FHIDs and revise or drop old ones with the objective of providing several variables with high loadings on each factor. Diversity of content is desirable among the variables chosen to define a factor so that all important aspects of the factor construct will be represented. FHIDs that prove to be factorially complex, that is, with major loadings on more than one primary-level factor, are eliminated.

7. Carry out new analyses in which the primary-level factors expected are specified along with the FHIDs that are supposed to define them. Drop, modify, or redefine factors and FHIDs that fail to replicate in successive studies with different subjects. Retain the factors, and the FHIDs defining them, that replicate successfully in a series of studies. Continue, however, to search for FHIDs that might do an even better job of defining these replicated factors.

8. Formulate hypotheses about new factor constructs that might constitute useful additions to the taxonomy of replicated factors. Try to expand the taxonomy, in other words, into as yet unrepresented but important areas of the domain. Develop FHIDs that should define such hypothesized factors, and carry out new analyses to determine if such factors do emerge and whether or not they can be replicated. Continue the attempt to expand the taxonomy until no new primary-level factors can be found.

11.3. FACTOR ANALYTIC STUDIES TO DEVELOP THE CPS TAXONOMY

The research strategy using the FHID, as described in the previous section, was applied in a series of investigations undertaken during the 1960s to develop the personality taxonomy upon which the CPS is based. The early studies (Comrey, 1961, 1962b; Comrey & Schlesinger, 1962; Comrey & Soufi, 1960, 1961) concentrated on methodology, developing FHIDs, and some preliminary identification of primary factors. Trust versus Defensiveness, Orderliness versus Lack of Compulsion, Emotional Stability versus Neuroticism, and Extraversion versus Introversion were already identified by this time, although under other names, for example, Hostility, Compulsion, Neuroticism, and Shyness, respectively.

These factors continued to emerge in subsequent studies, undergoing successive refinements and improvements in the FHIDs designed to measure them, although the Shyness factor did fail to separate from Neuroticism in the very next study (Comrey, 1964). The first strong identification of the Empathy versus Egocentrism factor occurred in 1965, under the name "Empathy." The previously identified four factors were replicated in this same study (Comrey, 1965). These early studies also showed promise for the development of a Dependence factor. Attempts to refine and replicate this factor in essentially the same form through a series of investigations were not successful, however; so it was not included in the final CPS taxonomy. Some aspects of this factor, however, suggested the possibility of a new factor that was ultimately identified and replicated as the Social Conformity versus Rebelliousness factor.

In the next study (Comrey & Jamison, 1966), the four previously identified factors were well defined. Dependence was also a major factor in this analysis. The Dependence factor split into two parts in the next study, however (Jamison & Comrey, 1968), one part retaining the name Dependence, which was ultimately dropped for failure to replicate, and the other part, named "Socialization," which exhibited a character very close to the final Social Conformity versus Rebelliousness factor. The previously established factors were also replicated in this study.

The remaining two factors in the taxonomy, Activity versus Lack of Energy and Masculinity versus Femininity, were added to the taxonomy as a result of the next investigation (Comrey, Jamison, & King, 1968) in which FHIDs from the previous studies were analyzed together with quasi-FHIDs derived from an analysis of the Guilford-Zimmerman Temperament Survey. These "quasi-FHIDs" were groups of items found in the Guilford-Zimmerman Temperament Survey that appeared to meet the criteria for FHIDs reasonably well. In this particular analysis, all the previously established CPS factors were replicated but in addition, the Guilford-Zimmerman General Activity and Masculinity factors emerged as distinct from the CPS factors. Additional studies were carried out in which these two factors were replicated using new items and FHIDs to define them, so they were added to the taxonomy as Activity versus Lack of Energy and Masculinity versus Femininity. The Guilford-Zimmerman Emotional Stability factor proved to be very similar to the Neuroticism factor (Emotional Stability versus Neuroticism) and the Guilford-Zimmerman Personal Relations factor was closely identified with the Hostility factor (Trust versus Defensiveness).

The next investigation (Comrey & Duffy, 1968) failed to establish any new factors for the taxonomy, although it provided information about replication of the factors ultimately selected for the final taxonomy. This study did establish the essential similarity between Eysenck's Neuroticism and the CPS Neuroticism, previously replicated so often. Eysenck's Extraversion-Introversion was also found to be closely identified with the CPS Shyness factor. In view of the similarities among these Guilford-Zimmerman, Eysenck, and CPS factors, the CPS Neuroticism factor was renamed as "Emotional Stability versus Neuroticism" and the CPS Shyness factor was renamed as "Extraversion versus Introversion." Other name changes in the CPS factors were initiated to provide a bipolar name for each factor with the more culturally approved pole mentioned first.

In this same investigation, an unsuccessful attempt was made to locate FHIDs from the Cattell 16PF test to analyze in the same matrix with the CPS FHIDs for the purpose of locating possible additional factors. Since the Cattell items could not be broken down into subgroups meeting the criteria for FHIDs, the Cattell total factor scores were analyzed with the CPS FHIDs. The Cattell factor scores overlapped with many of the CPS factors but did not match any of them on a one-to-one basis. Cattell's second-order Neuroticism and Extraversion-Introversion factors, however, appeared to be reasonably well matched with the correspondingly named CPS primary-level factors. Howarth and Browne (1971) also had difficulty replicating Cattell's factors at the primary-factor level.

The last study in this series before the publication of the CPS (Duffy, Jamison, & Comrey, 1969) represented an unsuccessful attempt to replicate the Guilford-Zimmerman Thoughtfulness factor as a possible addition to the CPS taxonomy. This study also failed to replicate the Masculinity factor satisfactorily, although later unpublished studies did so. The results of the final empirical replication study, described fully in the CPS manual (Comrey, 1970b), are summarized in the next section.

11.4. FACTOR ANALYSIS OF THE FHIDS IN THE CPS

After the final decision had been made about what primary-level factors had demonstrated sufficient independence and replicability to be included in the CPS personality taxonomy, a new sample of subjects was drawn to serve as the basis for deriving normative data and for obtaining a final factor solution. The final version of the CPS was administered to 746 volunteer subjects, 362 males and 384 females. About one-third of these subjects were visitors to a university Open House day at UCLA, comprising friends, acquaintances, and family of students for the most part. The remaining two-thirds of the cases consisted of university students and their friends and UCLA employees. The sample, therefore, represented predominantly the educated upper-middle class with a heavy concentration of subjects in the college-age group but some representation for all adult age groups.

11.4.1. THE VARIABLES

Forty-four variables were included in the analysis, 40 FHIDs defining the eight CPS factors, two validity scale scores, V and R, plus the variables of Age and Sex. Each of the personality factors was represented by five

FHIDs. Each FHID in turn contained four items, two positively stated with respect to the FHID name and two negatively stated. Each item was answered by using one of the following two response scales:

Scale *X*: 7. Always   6. Very Frequently   5. Frequently
4. Occasionally   3. Rarely   2. Very Rarely   1. Never
Scale *Y*: 7. Definitely   6. Very Probably   5. Probably   4. Possibly
3. Probably Not   2. Very Probably Not   1. Definitely Not

The validity scales, *V* and *R*, were designed to provide information about the genuineness of the test protocol. The *V* scale presents items to which the respondent should give a particular extreme response, either a "1" for a positively stated item or a "7" for a negatively stated item. Since there are eight items on this scale, the expected total score is 8 due to the fact that an item score of 7 becomes 1 when the score is reversed for a negatively stated item. If the respondent has a score that departs too far from 8 on the *V* scale, for example if values approach 25 or more, the test protocol becomes suspect. Random marking should produce on the average a score of 32 on the *V* scale.

The *R* scale, on the other hand, is designed as a "response bias" scale, to indicate whether the subjects are responding in a "socially desirable" way, that is, making themselves look good. Very low scores on the R scale would suggest that the subjects might be deliberately giving a socially undesirable impression of themselves for some reason. The 44 variables included in the analysis are listed below. Following each FHID name (variables 1 to 40) a letter is given in parentheses to show what factor this FHID is supposed to measure. A sample item is also given with its item number in the CPS test booklet. The *X* or *Y* after the item number indicates the preferred scale to be used by the respondent in choosing a test statement answer. If the item number is underlined, the item is negatively stated with respect to the FHID name.

1. Lack of Cynicism (T).
2. Lack of Defensiveness (T).

3. Belief in Human Worth (T).
4. Trust in Human Nature (T).

5. Lack of Paranoia (T).

6. Neatness (O).

7. Routine (O).

8. Order (O).
9. Cautiousness (O).

1*X*. The average person is honest.
19*X*. You can get what is coming to you without having to be aggressive or competitive.
37*Y*. Most people are valuable human beings.
10*X*. Other people are selfishly concerned about themselves in what they do.
28*X*. Some people will deliberately say things to hurt you.
2*Y*. I could live in a pig pen without letting it bother me.
20*Y*. Living according to a schedule is something I like to avoid.
38*X*. My room is a mess.
11*X*. I am a cautious person.

10. Meticulousness (O).

29X. I will go to great lengths to correct mistakes in my work which other people wouldn't even notice.

11. Law Enforcement (C).

3Y. This society provides too much protection for criminals.

12. Acceptance of Social Order (C).

21Y. The laws governing the people of this country are sound and need only minor changes, if any.

13. Intolerance of Nonconformity (C).

39Y. Young people should be more willing than they are to do what their elders tell them to do.

14. Respect for Law (C).

12X. If the laws of society are unjust, they should be disobeyed.

15. Need for Approval (C).

30X. I ignore what my neighbors might think of me.

16. Exercise (A).

4X. If I think about exercising, I lie down until the idea goes away.

17. Energy (A).

22X. I seem to lack the drive necessary to get things done.

18. Need to Excel (A).

40Y. Being a big success in life requires more effort than I am willing to make.

19. Liking for Work (A).
20. Stamina (A).

13X. I love to work long hours.
31X. I can work a long time without feeling tired.

21. Lack of Inferiority Feelings (S).
22. Lack of Depression (S).

6X. I feel inferior to the people I know.
24X. I feel so down-in-the-dumps that nothing can cheer me up.

23. Lack of Agitation (S).
24. Lack of Pessimism (S).
25. Mood Stability (S).

42X. My nerves seem to be on edge.
15X. I expect things to turn out for the best.
33X. My mood remains rather constant, neither going up nor down.

26. Lack of Reserve (E).
27. Lack of Seclusiveness (E).

7X. I am a very talkative person.
25X. At a party I like to meet as many people as I can.

28. No Loss for Words (E).
29. Lack of Shyness (E).

43X. It is easy for me to talk with people.
16X. I find it difficult to talk with a person I have just met.

30. No Stage Fright (E).

34Y. It would be hard for me to do anything in front of an audience.

31. No Fear of Bugs (M).

8X. Big bugs and other crawling creatures upset me.

32. No Crying (M).
33. No Romantic Love (M).

26X. A sad movie makes me feel like crying.
44X. I like movies which tell the story of two people in love.

34. Tolerance of Blood (M).

17Y. I could assist in a surgical operation without fainting if I had to.

35. Tolerance of Vulgarity (M).
36. Sympathy (P).

35X. I can tolerate vulgarity.
144X. I am rather insensitive to the difficulties that other people are having.

37. Helpfulness (P).

27Y. I enjoy helping people even if I don't know them very well.

38. Service (P).

39. Generosity (P).

40. Unselfishness (P).

41. Validity Scale (V).

42. Response Bias Scale (R).

43. Age (recorded as a two-digit number)

44. Sex (scored 1 = male, 0 = female)

45 Y. I would like to devote my life to the service of others.

18 Y. I would hate to make a loan to a poor family I didn't know very well.

36 X. I take care of myself before I think about other people's needs.

5 Y. If I were asked to lift a ten-ton weight, I could do it.

41 X. My morals are above reproach.

11.4.2. THE ANALYSIS

The 44 variables described in the previous section were intercorrelated using the Pearson product-moment correlation coefficient. This 44 × 44 matrix of correlation coefficients is shown in Table 11.1 (Tables 11.1 through 11.10 are grouped following the end of this section). The correlation matrix in Table 11.1 was factor analyzed by the minimum residual method (see Chapter 4), with 15 factors extracted to be certain that more than enough factors would be taken out. By the fifteenth factor, the loadings were of negligible importance and the residuals contained no appreciable true variance remaining to be extracted. No iteration of the minimum residual solution was carried out, hence the obtained communalities and factor loadings are underestimated to some extent. The first 12 of these minimum residual factors are shown in Table 11.2.

The 15 minimum residual factors were rotated by Criterion I of the Tandem Criteria for orthogonal analytic rotation (see Chapter 7). This procedure spreads the variance from the minimum residual solution out but only as far as the intercorrelations among the variables permit because the method seeks to place as much variance on one factor as possible given that the variables placed on the same factor must be correlated with each other. Most extraction methods can squeeze the variance down even more than Criterion I rotations do because they can place variables on the same factor that are not correlated with each other, and they typically do.

Only eight of the Criterion I factors were of appreciable importance; the remaining Criterion I factors were too small in the proportion of variance accounted for to be considered further. The largest 12 criterion I factors are shown in Table 11.3, revealing clearly the negligible character of the last four factors. Only the first 12 minimum residual factors are shown in Table 11.2 since it was clearly unnecessary to extract more than 12 and since only 12 Criterion I factors were large enough even to be reported. Because only the first eight of the Criterion I factors had enough high loadings to be considered as possible major factors, only these eight factors were rerotated by Criterion II of the Tandem Criteria in the attempt to produce a solution in which the variance is distributed more evenly among the retained factors, such as is customarily obtained in a simple structure solution.

The eight rotated Criterion II factors are shown in Table 11.4. These results represent the final orthogonal rotated loadings for the 44 variables defining the eight CPS taxonomy factors. The sharp break in the number of important Criterion I factors at exactly eight when there were eight factors expected would not normally occur. These results were achieved after a long series of studies in which the factors and the variables defining them had been carefully refined to produce a very sharp factor structure.

Although the orthogonal solution in Table 11.4 presents a sharp factor structure, plots of the factors with each other suggest the need for oblique rotations if simple structure criteria are to be satisfied. To obtain a simple structure solution, rotations of factor axes to oblique positions were carried out in two stages. The first stage consisted of "hand" rotations based on inspection of visual 2 × 2 graphs of the factor loadings plotted on a Cartesian coordinate system (see Chapter 6). These rotations were carried out using Program 8, the Hand Rotation Program, described in Chapter 14. These rotations were planned to make the obvious gross oblique adjustments of the reference vector axes suggested by simple structure criteria without introducing any changes that clearly contradicted available psychological knowledge about the probable relationships among the factors.

Once the rough oblique positions for the reference vectors had been established, fine adjustments were carried out analytically using computer Program 9, Analytic Oblique Rotation, described in Chapter 14. This program searches for alternate new positions on either side of the current reference vector positions that have a greater number of points in the hyperplanes than at present. In this particular use of the program, the permissible search angles were kept small so that only modest adjustments in the reference vector positions could be achieved. Even with small adjustments, however, the hyperplanes counts for the eight factors were increased appreciably, as follows: I. 33 to 35; II. 31 to 34; III. 25 to 29; IV. 34 to 35; V. 34 to 35; VI. 35 to 38; VII. 23 to 31; and VIII. 25 to 30.

The final oblique reference vector projections are shown in Table 11.5. The transformation matrix that carries the eight Criterion II factor loadings into the oblique reference vector projections is given in Table 11.6. Had hand rotations been used for the orthogonal rotations, the transformation matrix carrying the minimum residual factor loadings into the oblique reference vector projections would have been obtained because the final orthogonal transformation matrix could have been modified as the oblique rotations were carried out. The computer program that carries out the Tandem Criteria rotations, however, does not output the transformation matrix that would accomplish these rotations. The oblique rotation process,

Table 11.1[a]

Correlations among FHIDs[b]

	1	2	3	4	5	6	7	8	9	10	11	12	13	14	15	16	17	18	19	20	21	22
1																						
2	37																					
3	44	32																				
4	54	43	44																			
5	45	42	50	46																		
6	-01	-19	-04	-04	-10																	
7	09	-12	-01	03	00	43																
8	14	-04	03	04	07	54	48															
9	04	-08	02	-03	00	23	33	22														
10	14	-10	03	03	02	28	28	42	13													
11	16	-27	00	02	-04	32	30	21	19	19												
12	33	-08	11	15	08	22	28	15	12	07	61											
13	13	-19	02	10	-03	42	41	25	23	21	64	50										
14	30	-07	18	16	09	29	34	26	30	22	58	52	56									
15	15	-12	12	09	-02	28	34	14	26	13	34	33	40	36								
16	06	06	08	-02	13	-02	-02	00	-21	00	07	02	-03	-01	-09							
17	11	02	12	07	16	10	10	22	-12	27	11	01	08	14	00	38						
18	03	-25	01	-03	-03	27	21	24	-05	37	25	14	23	20	18	16	43					
19	20	00	13	17	12	15	24	25	-02	43	14	09	20	16	05	24	42	36				
20	13	03	09	03	18	-03	00	11	-22	23	09	05	-01	03	-11	41	63	35	45			
21	08	07	12	05	21	-02	-02	12	-12	09	07	02	02	07	-16	19	44	27	12	34		
22	23	21	32	18	34	00	04	14	-04	07	14	13	04	17	-01	20	43	22	12	34	51	
23	07	14	19	12	26	-08	-03	06	-08	-08	07	08	-03	08	-14	21	27	07	07	31	46	51
24	26	19	33	21	30	-06	-04	09	-15	03	06	04	-01	09	-06	19	38	20	15	32	48	62
25	14	10	11	07	19	00	13	15	06	01	12	16	12	14	-01	14	22	08	10	26	36	42
26	-01	-01	09	09	06	-02	02	04	-09	02	04	-05	-01	04	01	04	36	16	04	15	28	29
27	06	02	24	10	14	02	-02	07	-08	11	08	02	08	16	08	12	38	26	11	16	29	31
28	09	11	19	13	23	-02	06	13	-11	06	06	-02	01	08	-05	19	44	14	14	30	47	41
29	11	12	14	14	20	-03	09	12	-10	05	03	-02	04	10	-05	15	38	12	14	24	40	31
30	01	05	02	06	09	-02	-02	-17	03	-04	-01	-05	-04	-07		16	22	20	15	23	28	20
31	00	05	-05	-02	07	-27	-15	-15	-24	-08	-12	-08	-17	-24	-26	20	00	-03	07	20	10	-02
32	-11	-10	-14	-13	-02	-06	-04	-06	-12	-08	02	-04	-06	-11	-11	22	-03	10	-03	17	16	05
33	00	07	-07	-03	10	-09	-09	-04	-08	-02	-05	-06	-06	-10	-14	09	00	-06	06	17	10	00
34	01	-02	-01	00	05	-14	-06	-11	-20	00	-02	-04	-10	-12	-14	22	08	08	13	30	12	10
35	-19	00	-12	-17	-04	-31	-20	-15	-27	-18	-33	-27	-44	-42	-29	10	-08	-12	-18	06	00	-07
36	12	08	32	14	14	02	-03	05	09	20	-02	-07	-01	12	06	05	29	19	21	16	10	18
37	19	18	36	27	25	-09	-08	-02	-04	17	-02	-08	-02	14	-03	13	30	16	31	26	14	24
38	12	14	30	18	10	-02	-03	00	02	13	-12	-13	-04	08	04	-02	15	16	22	10	00	16
39	11	18	23	20	14	-08	-14	-06	-03	11	-17	-15	-04	04	-03	04	16	07	24	10	05	09
40	15	08	24	23	17	06	03	06	04	13	19	11	23	24	07	10	24	16	24	19	12	18
41	-04	-06	-13	-03	-03	-02	00	-01	-13	06	12	10	12	00	-04	10	-02	12	06	06	00	-06
42	27	09	17	25	23	18	21	26	20	29	28	23	35	39	15	04	26	20	33	18	17	17
43	19	04	13	12	16	07	18	16	10	06	11	12	17	18	05	-06	08	-11	14	06	06	03
44	-13	-14	-16	-18	-08	-08	-03	-09	-16	-06	-05	-06	-13	-19	-09	18	-03	11	-02	10	05	-04

[a]From Comrey, 1970b.
[b]Variables 1–40 are FHIDs; 41 = V; 42 = R; 43 = Age; 44 = Sex.

23	24	25	26	27	28	29	30	31	32	33	34	35	36	37	38	39	40	41	42	43	44
44																					
51	36																				
13	23	08																			
19	31	07	46																		
31	36	26	66	55																	
24	29	21	53	57	82																
21	15	14	36	27	46	43															
17	-01	14	-07	-09	-02	05	22														
23	-01	30	-07	-15	-01	-06	14	35													
08	-03	18	-14	-17	-04	-04	10	34	32												
14	06	11	04	-01	11	09	26	42	26	20											
05	-06	02	05	-12	01	00	08	31	28	14	26										
05	24	00	16	31	20	17	04	-14	-26	-25	-11	-22									
18	26	05	16	39	28	26	15	06	-14	-03	07	-20	60								
02	13	-05	13	25	12	08	08	-06	-13	-15	01	-15	50	57							
05	14	-01	12	26	17	16	10	-05	-18	-08	-07	-17	46	61	52						
13	19	12	10	23	16	15	12	-04	-09	-07	-04	-31	52	54	36	38					
05	-04	08	-02	-02	-03	-02	07	15	18	06	04	04	-13	-06	-06	01	00				
15	16	14	00	18	13	16	04	-10	-09	-03	-11	-43	32	37	21	34	37	13			
-03	09	17	-02	-03	14	18	00	-05	-10	14	-01	-06	-01	-02	-12	-08	05	-04	14		
07	-08	12	-04	-15	-11	-13	13	38	49	25	18	37	-20	-16	-11	-19	-09	11	-24	-15	

TABLE 11.2[a]

Minimum Residual Matrix

	1	2	3	4	5	6	7	8	9	10	11	12	h^2
1	.39	.13	−.11	.52	.07	.08	.18	−.20	.06	.03	.05	.09	.56
2	.19	−.22	−.31	.47	−.03	.16	.06	.02	−.01	.12	.06	−.12	.46
3	.45	−.02	−.30	.37	.00	.01	.00	−.11	.22	−.13	.06	.00	.51
4	.37	.03	−.26	.46	.02	.04	.21	−.10	.09	.15	.04	.01	.50
5	.41	−.14	−.13	.50	.00	.13	.07	.00	.06	.00	.05	−.04	.49
6	.14	.52	.22	−.16	−.01	.22	−.06	.05	.12	.07	.03	−.06	.46
7	.19	.48	.28	−.02	−.04	.25	.09	.13	.17	−.08	.02	−.02	.47
8	.29	.35	.23	−.06	−.02	.46	−.04	.14	.10	.07	.06	.04	.52
9	.01	.47	−.05	.04	−.07	.09	−.10	.27	.08	−.16	−.03	.04	.35
10	.31	.27	.10	−.20	.24	.32	.08	−.03	.02	.07	.04	.23	.45
11	.26	.52	.40	.04	−.01	−.35	.03	−.12	−.07	−.06	.04	.08	.65
12	.22	.45	.29	.27	−.03	−.28	.07	−.18	.00	.00	.02	.05	.52
13	.27	.63	.28	.03	.00	−.23	.10	.02	−.07	.05	.03	.02	.62
14	.40	.57	.13	.13	−.04	−.21	.02	.00	−.01	−.08	.07	.07	.58
15	.13	.52	.05	.01	−.06	−.09	.06	−.10	.23	−.08	.00	−.04	.37
16	.25	−.26	.24	−.01	.20	−.02	.02	−.15	−.04	−.05	.11	−.35	.39
17	.63	−.16	.20	−.25	.07	.17	−.08	−.20	−.14	−.08	.19	−.14	.69
18	.39	.11	.28	−.34	.21	.02	−.04	−.19	.18	.14	.08	.12	.52
19	.46	.08	.11	−.11	.39	.24	.19	−.07	−.11	−.02	.10	.04	.51
20	.48	−.28	.30	−.08	.30	.12	−.01	−.18	−.18	−.13	.20	−.07	.63
21	.49	−.30	.28	.00	−.14	.01	−.21	.08	−.08	.09	.09	.12	.52
22	.60	−.21	.14	.17	−.14	−.02	−.36	−.05	.10	−.01	.15	.09	.64
23	.40	−.31	.23	.21	−.04	−.12	−.30	.19	.00	.06	.14	−.02	.52
24	.56	−.24	.04	.16	−.11	.00	−.33	−.12	−.01	.01	.10	.11	.55
25	.35	−.14	.34	.26	−.02	−.04	−.21	.31	.02	−.06	.08	.01	.48
26	.39	−.21	.02	−.27	−.43	−.06	.16	−.04	.14	.02	.12	.00	.52
27	.55	−.11	−.10	−.27	−.28	−.13	.09	−.05	.08	.06	.09	.01	.52
28	.61	−.30	.09	−.16	−.48	.00	.25	.13	−.01	−.04	.21	−.03	.85
29	.55	−.25	.07	−.15	−.43	.02	.32	.16	−.07	−.02	.14	−.01	.73
30	.31	−.32	.17	−.14	−.08	−.08	.27	.08	.08	.08	.04	.04	.36
31	−.06	−.44	.24	.12	.30	−.10	.24	.13	.02	−.03	−.03	.06	.46
32	−.10	−.28	.48	.09	.23	−.14	−.03	.21	.20	.06	−.02	−.10	.50
33	−.07	−.22	.26	.20	.22	.05	.11	.20	−.12	−.05	−.04	.03	.29
34	.05	−.35	.26	.03	.20	−.05	.20	−.04	.05	−.13	.03	.11	.31
35	−.30	−.55	.17	−.01	−.01	.10	.07	−.03	.18	−.11	−.05	.00	.48
36	.48	.04	−.45	−.23	.17	−.06	−.12	.04	.06	−.16	.10	.02	.57
37	.58	−.12	−.43	−.12	.30	−.16	.06	.14	.02	−.08	.15	.05	.72
38	.36	−.03	−.45	−.18	.25	−.07	.00	.06	.25	−.01	.12	.06	.52
39	.38	−.08	−.49	−.16	.24	−.09	.04	.16	−.02	.14	.12	−.02	.54
40	.50	.10	−.22	−.06	.24	−.23	−.01	.13	−.03	−.06	.05	−.06	.44
41	−.01	−.02	.20	−.01	.15	−.14	.10	.03	−.06	.29	−.01	−.03	.18
42	.52	.32	−.07	.05	.20	−.02	.02	.19	−.20	.20	.05	.02	.54
43	.16	.14	.08	.21	−.10	.17	.14	.11	−.23	−.25	−.04	.09	.29
44	−.19	−.28	.39	−.02	.25	−.09	.03	.05	.31	−.02	−.06	−.09	.45

[a] From Comrey, 1970b.

TABLE 11.3[a]

Criterion I Loadings

	1	2	3	4	5	6	7	8	9	10	11	12	h^2
1	.10	.25	-.09	.67	.02	.00	.02	-.08	.01	.00	.01	.13	.56
2	.10	-.22	-.09	.60	-.06	.01	-.03	.03	-.12	.04	.03	-.13	.46
3	.20	.07	-.28	.56	-.09	-.05	-.05	.02	.22	-.06	-.02	-.01	.51
4	.10	.11	-.19	.64	-.03	-.03	.10	.02	-.05	.10	.00	.04	.50
5	.26	.00	-.11	.63	.06	.03	-.06	.01	-.02	-.05	-.02	-.06	.49
6	-.02	.52	.05	-.14	-.12	.35	-.02	-.02	.05	.09	.00	-.11	.45
7	.03	.54	.10	-.01	.01	.35	.07	.05	.08	-.09	.00	-.12	.47
8	.16	.41	.05	.03	-.07	.56	-.06	.01	-.04	-.02	.01	-.06	.52
9	-.18	.37	-.04	-.01	-.18	.14	-.09	.24	.03	-.21	.00	-.14	.35
10	.08	.34	-.20	-.04	.03	.45	.02	-.14	-.06	.00	.00	.23	.45
11	.10	.73	.08	-.09	.09	-.25	-.03	-.07	.01	.00	.01	.10	.65
12	.03	.62	.13	.17	.07	-.26	-.02	-.06	.03	.05	.01	.10	.52
13	.01	.77	-.01	-.05	.02	-.11	.05	.00	-.11	.04	.00	.01	.62
14	.10	.72	-.11	.11	-.07	-.13	-.03	.04	.01	-.07	.02	.03	.58
15	-.10	.52	-.02	.04	-.12	-.01	.11	.03	.24	.03	-.02	-.04	.37
16	.30	-.05	-.05	.02	.30	-.05	-.03	-.39	.04	.08	-.02	-.22	.39
17	.62	.12	-.20	-.05	.02	.17	-.06	-.45	.00	-.02	-.02	-.04	.69
18	.30	.32	-.18	-.21	.14	.23	-.02	-.20	.16	.25	-.01	.22	.52
19	.20	.25	-.32	.08	.20	.31	.06	-.35	-.13	-.06	.00	.10	.51
20	.48	.02	-.16	.01	.31	.11	-.12	-.49	-.04	-.09	.05	.03	.63
21	.66	.01	.02	.01	.10	.04	-.23	.04	-.10	.02	-.02	.08	.52
22	.65	.09	-.07	.22	-.02	-.01	-.36	.02	.14	.03	.01	.05	.64
23	.53	-.02	-.02	.13	.20	-.10	-.37	.13	-.05	.03	.04	-.11	.52
24	.59	.00	-.10	.24	-.07	-.04	-.34	-.05	.06	.02	-.03	.11	.55
25	.42	.14	.06	.12	.28	.01	-.32	.19	-.06	-.12	.02	-.15	.48
26	.59	-.02	-.04	-.08	-.16	-.02	.34	.08	.14	.05	.01	.01	.52
27	.57	.07	-.26	-.03	-.20	-.07	.24	.04	.08	.10	-.05	.04	.52
28	.82	.00	-.06	.04	-.08	.00	.35	.10	-.05	-.11	.06	-.09	.85
29	.72	.01	-.06	.05	-.07	.01	.40	.11	-.14	-.12	.01	-.07	.73
30	.45	-.07	-.07	-.03	.24	.01	.28	.07	-.02	.06	-.02	.05	.36
31	.06	-.26	.01	.04	.61	-.04	.06	.01	-.07	-.05	.00	.07	.46
32	.08	-.07	.17	-.12	.61	.00	-.15	.11	.07	.12	.00	-.14	.50
33	-.01	-.10	.12	.07	.44	.04	-.08	.02	-.19	-.15	-.01	-.02	.29
34	.16	-.14	.03	.02	.45	-.02	.09	-.10	.07	-.10	.02	.14	.31
35	.04	-.51	.27	-.06	.30	.06	.07	.01	.20	-.05	.00	.01	.48
36	.20	.04	-.68	.02	-.22	.02	-.05	-.05	.12	-.10	-.02	-.01	.58
37	.27	-.01	-.78	.14	.03	-.04	.03	-.01	-.01	-.07	.02	.02	.72
38	.09	-.04	-.66	.09	-.07	.08	.03	.07	.18	.06	.04	.04	.52
39	.12	-.10	-.68	.09	-.09	.01	.05	.04	-.13	.10	.04	-.03	.54
40	.19	.22	-.57	.07	.03	-.12	-.04	-.01	-.04	-.04	-.06	-.08	.44
41	.00	.08	.03	-.07	.24	-.05	.03	-.01	-.20	.26	.00	.03	.18
42	.16	.43	-.40	.15	-.02	.08	-.09	.00	-.35	.06	-.03	-.02	.54
43	.07	.20	.10	.19	-.02	.06	.04	-.01	-.18	-.40	-.05	.00	.29
44	-.03	-.14	.15	-.15	.55	.04	-.03	.02	.24	.13	-.03	-.07	.45

[a] From Comrey, 1970b.

279

TABLE 11.4[a]

Criterion II Loadings[b]

	T	O	C	A	S	E	M	P	h^2
1	.68	.09	.21	−.10	−.08	−.01	−.01	−.06	.54
2	.59	−.13	−.21	.04	−.12	.01	−.05	−.07	.43
3	.57	−.03	.06	−.04	−.19	.07	−.10	−.27	.45
4	.66	.01	.10	.00	−.04	.08	−.03	−.17	.49
5	.63	.00	−.02	−.07	−.25	.08	.04	−.09	.48
6	−.12	.57	.26	−.05	.02	−.04	−.14	.05	.43
7	.02	.59	.28	−.02	.02	.05	.00	.09	.44
8	.06	.69	.05	−.10	−.13	.05	−.08	.06	.52
9	−.02	.35	.22	.28	.00	−.13	−.15	−.08	.29
10	.00	.54	.05	−.25	.03	.01	−.03	−.17	.39
11	−.08	.16	.76	−.12	−.10	.02	.02	.06	.64
12	.17	.10	.67	−.05	−.08	−.04	.02	.12	.51
13	−.03	.31	.72	−.03	.00	.02	−.02	−.03	.61
14	.12	.26	.67	−.01	−.12	.04	−.12	−.13	.57
15	.06	.26	.44	.06	.12	.00	−.13	−.03	.31
16	.04	−.12	.00	−.51	−.13	.07	.19	.01	.33
17	.00	.15	.00	−.67	−.30	.31	−.11	−.13	.68
18	−.17	.34	.15	−.38	−.13	.14	.06	−.16	.38
19	.14	.34	.06	−.51	.02	.05	.10	−.26	.48
20	.04	.04	−.03	−.70	−.27	.12	.17	−.09	.62
21	.01	.05	−.03	−.20	.59	.32	.07	.01	.50
22	.20	.03	.05	−.19	.69	.22	−.07	−.08	.62
23	.09	−.08	.01	−.09	.66	.14	.18	−.06	.51
24	.22	−.04	−.01	−.22	.61	.18	−.13	−.10	.54
25	.09	.10	.10	−.03	.57	.08	.27	.02	.44
26	−.02	−.01	−.01	−.08	−.12	.68	−.11	−.04	.50
27	.02	.00	.08	−.13	−.17	.60	−.18	−.26	.50
28	.11	.03	−.01	−.15	−.26	.84	−.02	−.06	.82
29	.12	.04	.00	−.12	−.17	.79	−.01	−.06	.69
30	.02	−.02	−.05	−.14	−.09	.49	.28	−.07	.36
31	.04	−.18	−.16	−.12	−.01	.02	.61	.01	.45
32	−.14	−.03	−.03	−.04	−.21	−.07	.60	.14	.46
33	.05	−.02	−.09	−.06	−.08	−.10	.43	.11	.23
34	.03	−.11	−.08	−.23	−.03	.10	.43	.04	.27
35	−.07	−.21	−.44	−.02	.02	.06	.34	.28	.44
36	.06	.04	−.02	−.16	−.10	.11	−.26	.66	.55
37	.18	−.05	−.01	−.20	−.11	.19	.00	.77	.71
38	.12	.06	−.10	−.05	.00	.10	−.07	.66	.48
39	.12	−.04	−.11	−.06	.00	.13	−.10	.67	.51
40	.09	.01	.23	−.15	−.13	.08	−.02	.57	.43
41	−.07	.00	.11	−.06	.01	.00	.23	.02	.07
42	.18	.28	.31	−.12	−.16	.03	−.07	−.40	.41
43	.20	.15	.14	−.02	−.03	.06	−.03	.11	.10
44	−.16	−.04	−.11	−.08	−.03	−.08	.54	.14	.37

[a] From Comrey, 1970b.

[b] The signs of all loadings for factors A, S, and P must be reversed to be consistent with the direction of the factor names.

280

TABLE 11.5

Oblique Reference Vector Projections (V)[a]

	I	II	III	IV	V	VI	VII	VIII
1	.64	.01	.10	.09	.00	-.07	-.04	-.06
2	.54	-.06	-.27	-.04	.07	.00	-.06	-.04
3	.49	-.06	.01	-.01	.10	.01	-.09	.15
4	.62	-.03	.03	-.02	-.04	.05	-.01	.04
5	.57	.01	-.09	.03	.16	.02	.03	-.02
6	-.13	.43	.24	.07	-.02	-.05	-.10	-.05
7	.03	.46	.27	.02	-.03	.04	.06	-.10
8	.02	.62	.03	.09	.09	.01	-.03	-.08
9	-.04	.24	.26	-.26	.08	-.07	-.08	.07
10	-.03	.49	.05	.23	-.10	-.05	.01	.15
11	-.08	-.08	.72	.10	.08	-.03	.01	-.03
12	.17	-.12	.59	.05	.06	-.08	.00	-.13
13	-.03	.06	.69	.02	-.01	-.01	.01	.03
14	.08	.02	.63	-.02	.09	-.01	-.08	.10
15	.06	.09	.41	-.04	-.12	.00	-.09	.00
16	.03	-.08	-.05	.46	.01	-.06	.10	.01
17	-.09	.13	-.07	.59	.09	.09	-.15	.09
18	-.21	.29	.17	.32	.03	.03	.07	.18
19	.10	.32	.03	.46	-.15	-.09	.08	.23
20	-.01	.08	-.09	.62	.09	-.08	.07	.10
21	-.08	.06	-.03	.10	.47	.21	.07	.00
22	.07	.01	.02	.09	.57	.09	-.08	.04
23	.00	-.05	.04	-.02	.58	.06	.16	.07
24	.10	-.05	-.06	.14	.49	.05	-.15	.04
25	.03	.10	.15	-.07	.53	.04	.26	.01
26	-.05	-.02	-.02	.00	-.02	.62	-.01	.00
27	-.05	-.04	.08	.04	.02	.50	-.08	.20
28	.05	.03	-.02	.04	.07	.74	.08	.01
29	.08	.04	.00	.02	.00	.71	.10	.01
30	.02	.04	.00	.04	-.02	.45	.32	.09
31	.10	-.04	-.09	.06	-.01	.03	.55	.07
32	-.10	.06	.06	-.02	.23	-.05	.55	-.01
33	.09	.06	-.05	.03	.09	-.09	.37	-.05
34	.06	-.02	-.06	.17	-.03	.07	.38	.01
35	.00	-.02	-.41	.02	-.01	.10	.29	-.21
36	-.06	.02	.04	.08	.00	.03	-.19	.59
37	.07	-.03	.08	.08	-.02	.10	.06	.71
38	.03	.08	.00	-.03	-.06	.06	.01	.60
39	.03	.00	-.02	-.01	-.08	.08	-.02	.61
40	.00	-.06	.29	.06	.04	.00	.02	.53
41	-.04	-.01	.13	.04	-.02	.00	.21	.03
42	.09	.16	.33	.06	.09	-.04	-.02	.35
43	.20	.09	.08	.03	.00	.04	-.03	-.14
44	-.09	.07	-.03	.04	.05	-.06	.49	-.02

[a] To compute this matrix by the formula $V = A\Lambda$, where A is the matrix of Criterion II factor loadings, requires a rearrangement of the columns of A from the present order, TOCASEMP, to the order ECPTMOSA.

281

TABLE 11.6

Transformation Matrix (A)

	1	2	3	4	5	6	7	8
1	−.003	−.001	.014	−.099	−.161	.959	.153	−.031
2	.009	−.318	.945	−.008	.001	−.033	−.007	.014
3	.112	−.017	−.184	.111	.045	.029	−.102	−.973
4	.976	−.005	−.148	.010	−.083	−.030	−.026	−.174
5	.101	.131	.155	−.105	.020	.062	.964	.148
6	−.019	.939	.039	−.004	−.003	.011	.100	−.012
7	.150	.000	−.038	.106	−.960	.079	.023	−.014
8	.028	−.005	.155	−.977	.210	.258	.161	.015

TABLE 11.7

Correlations among Reference Vectors (C)

	1	2	3	4	5	6	7	8
1	1.000	−.014	−.143	.000	−.212	−.004	.067	−.265
2	−.014	1.000	−.240	−.012	−.002	.026	.223	.020
3	−.143	−.240	1.000	−.203	.075	.028	.195	.243
4	.000	−.012	−.203	1.000	−.288	−.342	−.283	−.139
5	−.212	−.002	.075	−.288	1.000	−.172	.003	−.005
6	−.004	.026	.028	−.342	−.172	1.000	.249	−.041
7	.067	.223	.195	−.283	.003	.249	1.000	.243
8	−.265	.020	.243	−.139	−.005	−.041	.243	1.000

TABLE 11.8

Factor Pattern for the CPS (P)

	I	II	III	IV	V	VI	VII	VIII
1	.71	.01	.11	.11	.00	-.08	-.04	-.06
2	.60	-.07	-.30	-.06	.08	-.01	-.07	-.04
3	.53	-.06	.01	-.01	.11	.01	-.10	.17
4	.68	-.03	.03	-.03	-.05	.06	-.02	.05
5	.63	.01	-.10	.04	.18	.02	.04	-.02
6	-.14	.47	.27	.08	-.02	-.06	-.11	-.06
7	.03	.50	.30	.03	-.03	.05	.06	-.11
8	.02	.67	.04	.11	.10	.01	-.04	-.10
9	-.04	.25	.29	-.31	.08	-.08	-.09	.08
10	-.03	.53	.06	.28	-.11	-.06	.01	.17
11	-.09	-.09	.80	.12	.09	-.04	.01	-.04
12	.18	-.13	.66	.06	.07	-.09	-.01	-.14
13	-.04	.07	.77	.02	-.01	-.01	.01	.04
14	.08	.02	.70	-.02	.10	-.01	-.09	.11
15	.07	.10	.46	-.05	-.13	.00	-.10	.00
16	.03	-.09	-.06	.55	.01	-.07	.11	.01
17	-.10	.14	-.08	.71	.11	.10	-.17	.10
18	-.23	.31	.18	.38	.04	.03	.08	.20
19	.11	.35	.04	.55	-.18	-.10	.09	.26
20	-.01	.08	-.10	.74	.10	-.09	.08	.11
21	-.09	.07	-.03	.12	.54	.25	.08	.00
22	.08	.01	.02	.11	.65	.11	-.09	.04
23	.00	-.06	.05	-.02	.66	.07	.18	.08
24	.10	-.06	-.06	.17	.56	.06	-.17	.04
25	.03	.11	.16	-.08	.60	.05	.30	.01
26	-.06	-.02	-.02	.01	-.02	.72	-.01	.00
27	-.06	-.05	.09	.05	.02	.58	-.09	.23
28	.05	.03	-.02	.04	.08	.86	.10	.01
29	.08	.04	-.01	.02	.00	.82	.11	.01
30	.02	.04	.00	.05	-.02	.52	.38	.10
31	.11	-.04	-.10	.07	-.01	.03	.64	.08
32	-.11	.07	.07	-.03	.26	-.06	.63	-.02
33	.10	.06	-.06	.04	.10	-.11	.43	-.05
34	.07	-.02	-.06	.21	-.03	.08	.44	.02
35	.00	-.02	-.46	.02	-.01	.11	.34	-.24
36	-.07	.02	.04	.10	.00	.03	-.22	.65
37	.08	-.03	.09	.09	-.02	.11	.07	.79
38	.04	.09	.00	-.04	-.07	.06	.01	.67
39	.04	-.01	-.03	-.01	-.09	.10	-.02	.68
40	.00	-.06	.32	.08	.05	.00	.02	.60
41	-.05	-.01	.15	.05	-.02	.00	.24	.03
42	.10	.18	.36	.07	.10	-.05	-.03	.39
43	.22	.10	.09	.03	.00	.04	-.03	-.16
44	-.10	.08	-.04	.05	.06	-.06	.56	-.02

TABLE 11.9

Factor Structure for the CPS (S)

	I	II	III	IV	V	VI	VII	VIII
1	.71	.11	.23	.17	.19	.07	−.14	.14
2	.57	−.09	−.24	.00	.20	.07	−.09	.20
3	.63	.01	.06	.13	.28	.17	−.22	.37
4	.69	.04	.10	.08	.15	.14	−.16	.25
5	.66	.02	−.02	.19	.36	.17	−.05	.21
6	−.07	.57	.43	.05	−.04	.00	.24	−.11
7	.07	.58	.46	.08	−.01	.06	−.12	−.15
8	.10	.69	.28	.15	.15	.11	−.20	−.05
9	.02	.36	.32	−.27	−.06	−.12	−.25	.00
10	.07	.54	.22	.24	.00	.06	−.13	.16
11	.02	.14	.77	.24	.10	.06	−.08	−.16
12	.23	.08	.66	.15	.10	.00	−.07	−.18
13	.07	.29	.78	.12	.00	.04	−.16	−.08
14	.24	.26	.72	.13	.14	.11	−.28	.07
15	.11	.27	.51	−.04	−.13	.00	−.24	−.04
16	.07	−.14	−.03	.54	.21	.13	.23	.07
17	.10	.17	.07	.76	.41	.46	−.13	.26
18	−.07	.33	.26	.45	.17	.21	−.01	.16
19	.22	.34	.17	.51	.08	.12	.00	.29
20	.11	.03	−.01	.76	.38	.23	.17	.20
21	.09	.04	.00	.42	.64	.44	.04	.10
22	.31	.06	.07	.41	.75	.40	−.14	.21
23	.18	−.08	−.01	.31	.69	.25	.14	.14
24	.31	−.01	−.01	.40	.68	.35	−.17	.24
25	.17	.08	.13	.24	.59	.17	.20	.02
26	.04	.00	.01	.27	.20	.70	−.14	.12
27	.13	.02	.10	.31	.25	.66	−.25	.33
28	.19	.04	.03	.43	.39	.89	−.09	.18
29	.19	.05	.05	.37	.29	.82	−.08	.16
30	.06	−.04	−.04	.31	.17	.47	.24	.11
31	.02	−.24	−.22	.17	.05	−.05	.63	−.01
32	−.15	−.10	−.06	.13	.19	−.12	.62	−.18
33	.02	−.07	−.10	.09	.09	−.14	.44	−.11
34	.02	−.15	−.12	.28	.09	.07	.45	−.02
35	−.17	−.25	−.49	.01	−.01	−.02	.47	−.23
36	.19	.09	.01	.17	.14	.22	−.36	.70
37	.33	−.01	−.02	.27	.19	.28	−.14	.81
38	.23	.09	−.07	.06	.04	.15	−.19	.68
39	.23	.00	−.11	.08	.05	.19	−.20	.71
40	.24	.03	.22	.23	.17	.17	−.15	.57
41	−.06	−.04	.09	.09	−.01	−.03	.22	−.06
42	.31	.30	.39	.20	.20	.13	−.24	.39
43	.20	.15	.18	.07	.07	.08	−.08	−.09
44	−.19	−.10	−.13	.10	.02	−.16	.59	−.18

TABLE 11.10

Correlations among Factors (Φ)

	1	2	3	4	5	6	7	8
1	1.00	.08	.13	.14	.26	.15	−.17	.30
2	.08	1.00	.30	.01	.01	.04	−.28	.00
3	.13	.30	1.00	.14	.01	.06	−.20	−.14
4	.14	.01	.14	1.00	.39	.39	.13	.14
5	.26	.01	.01	.39	1.00	.32	−.02	.15
6	.15	.04	.06	.39	.32	1.00	−.20	.18
7	−.17	−.28	−.20	.13	−.02	−.20	1.00	−.23
8	.30	.00	−.14	.14	.15	.18	−.23	1.00

therefore, proceeded as if the Criterion II rotated matrix were the starting point in the entire rotational process. In reproducing the rotated solution using the transformation matrix shown in Table 11.6, therefore, the Criterion II solution must be taken as the starting point rather than the minimum residual solution. The matrix of correlations among the reference vectors, the C matrix, is shown in Table 11.7.

The final oblique solution consists of the factor pattern, shown in Table 11.8, the factor structure, shown in Table 11.9, and the matrix of correlations among the factors, shown in Table 11.10. These matrices were computed using the methods described in Chapter 6 with the aid of computer Program 9, Analytic Oblique Rotation, which is described in Chapter 14.

11.4.3. RESULTS

It will be noted in Table 11.8, the factor pattern or matrix of factor loadings with respect to the oblique factors, that the major loadings for factors A, S, and P are positive. These factors were reversed in direction in the orthogonal Criterion II solution shown in Table 11.4; that is, by chance they emerged from the orthogonal rotations 180° out of phase. They may be reversed at will by changing the signs on all the loadings for the given factors. The orientation for these factors in Table 11.8, however, is consistent with the direction of the factors as named. The reversal of the direction of factors A, S, and P from the Criterion II solution to the opposite and correct direction in the pattern matrix (Table 11.8) was accomplished here by reversal of all the signs in the columns of the transformation matrix (Table 11.6) that correspond to factors A, S, and P. Because the directional orientation for all the factors in Table 11.8 is consistent with the direction of the factors as named in the CPS taxonomy, the correlations among the factors, as shown in Table 11.10, have the proper signs for interpretation of the relationships among the CPS factors. The order of the factors as they emerge in a rotated solution will be arbitrary as well, and hence Table 11.4, the table of Criterion II loadings, was rearranged to have the factors listed in the desired order.

The major correlations to be noted in Table 11.10 are the two values of 0.39 between Activity versus Lack of Energy (A) and Emotional Stability versus Neuroticism (S) and Extraversion versus Introversion (E); these two latter factors correlate 0.32 with each other. Orderliness versus Lack of Compulsion (O) correlates 0.30 with Social Conformity versus Rebelliousness (C). The computed factor scores correlate somewhat higher than 0.30 since the variables that define one of these factors also tend to contain some variance related to the other. Trust versus Defensiveness (T) correlates 0.30 with Empathy versus Egocentrism (P) and 0.26 with Emotional Stability versus Neuroticism (S). Masculinity versus Femininity (M) correlates − .23 with Empathy versus Egocentrism (P), − .20 with Extraversion versus Introversion (E), and − .20 with Social Conformity versus Rebelliousness (C).

Each of the eight rotated factors is presented in the following together with a brief description and the FHIDs with loadings of 0.30 or more in either the Criterion II orthogonal solution or the oblique factor pattern solution.

I. *Trust versus Defensiveness* (T).   Individuals who are high on this personality factor indicate that they believe more than the average person in the basic honesty, trustworthiness, and good intentions of other people. They believe that others wish them well and they have faith in human nature. Individuals who are low on T are cynical, defensive, suspicious, and have a low opinion of the value of the average man. More extensive clinical interpretations of the CPS factor scores are given in Comrey (1980). Variables with loadings of 0.30 or more on this factor are as shown in Table 11.11.

TABLE 11.11

Variables with Loadings of .3 or More on Factor T

Variable	Orthogonal	Oblique
1. Lack of Cynicism	.68	.71
2. Lack of Defensiveness	.59	.60
3. Belief in Human Worth	.57	.53
4. Trust in Human Nature	.66	.68
5. Lack of Paranoia	.63	.63

II. *Orderliness versus Lack of Compulsion* (O).   Individuals who are high on this factor tend to be very concerned with neatness and orderliness. They report being cautious, meticulous, and say they like to live in a routine way. Individuals who are low on this factor are inclined to be careless, sloppy, unsystematic in their style of life, reckless, and untidy. Variables with loadings of 0.30 or more on this factor are shown in Table 11.12.

III. *Social Conformity versus Rebelliousness* (C).   Individuals who are high on this factor depict themselves as accepting the society as it is, respecting the law, believing in law enforcement, seeking the approval of society, and resenting nonconformity in others. Individuals who are low on this factor are inclined to challenge the laws and institutions of the society, resent control, accept nonconformity in others and are nonconforming themselves. Variables with loadings of 0.30 or more on this factor are shown in Table 11.13.

IV. *Activity versus Lack of Energy* (A).   Individuals who are high on this factor report liking physical activity, hard work and exercise, having great energy and stamina, and striving to excel. Individuals who are low on A are inclined to be physically inactive, lack drive and energy, tire quickly, and have little motivation to excel. Variables with loadings of 0.30 or more on this factor are shown in Table 11.14.

The signs of the orthogonal solution loadings have been reversed here to make them consistent with the oblique solution loadings and the direction of the factor name.

V. *Emotional Stability versus Neuroticism* (S).   Individuals who are high on this factor report being happy, calm, optimistic, stable in mood, and having confidence in themselves. Individuals who are low on the factor have inferiority feelings, are agitated, depressed, pessimistic, and have frequent

TABLE 11.12

Variables with Loadings of .3 or More on Factor O

Variable	Orthogonal	Oblique
6. Neatness	.57	.47
7. Routine	.59	.50
8. Order	.69	.67
9. Cautiousness	.35	.25
10. Meticulousness	.54	.53
18. Need to Excel	.34	.31
19. Liking for Work	.34	.35

Table 11.13

Variables with Loadings of .3 or More on Factor C

Variable	Orthogonal	Oblique
2. Lack of Defensiveness	−.21	−.30
7. Routine	.28	.30
11. Law Enforcement	.76	.80
12. Acceptance of the Social Order	.67	.66
13. Intolerance of Nonconformity	.72	.77
14. Respect for Law	.67	.70
15. Need for Approval	.44	.46
35. Tolerance of Vulgarity	−.44	−.46
40. Unselfishness	.23	.32
42. Response Bias Scale (R)	.31	.36

Table 11.14

Variables with Loadings of .3 or More on Factor A

Variable	Orthogonal	Oblique
9. Cautiousness	−.28	−.31
16. Exercise	.51	.55
17. Energy	.67	.71
18. Need to Excel	.38	.38
19. Liking for Work	.51	.55
20. Stamina	.70	.74

mood swings. Variables with loadings of 0.30 or more on this factor are shown in Table 11.15.

As with the previous factor, the orthogonal solution loadings have been reversed in sign to make them consistent with the directional orientation of the factor as named.

Table 11.15

Variables with Loadings of .3 or More on Factor S

Variable	Orthogonal	Oblique
17. Energy	.30	.11
21. Lack of Inferiority Feelings	.59	.54
22. Lack of Depression	.69	.65
23. Lack of Agitation	.66	.66
24. Lack of Pessimism	.61	.56
25. Mood Stability	.57	.60

TABLE 11.16

Variables with Loadings of .3 or More on Factor E

Variable	Orthogonal	Oblique
17. Energy	.31	.10
21. Lack of Inferiority Feelings	.32	.25
26. Lack of Reserve	.68	.72
27. Lack of Seclusiveness	.60	.58
28. No Loss for Words	.84	.86
29. Lack of Shyness	.79	.82
30. No Stage Fright	.49	.52

VI. *Extraversion versus Introversion* (E).   Individuals who are high on this factor depict themselves as outgoing, easy to meet, seeking the company of others, meeting strangers easily, and speaking before groups with little fear. Individuals low on the factor are reserved, seclusive, shy, cannot easily find things to talk about with others, and suffer from stage fright. Variables with loadings of 0.30 on this factor are shown in Table 11.16.

VII. *Masculinity versus Femininity* (M).   Individuals who are high on this factor report being rather tough-minded individuals who are not bothered by crawling creatures, the sight of blood, vulgarity, who do not cry easily, and who have little interest in love stories. Individuals who are low on this factor are inclined to cry easily, are bothered by blood and crawling things such as snakes and insects, are disturbed by vulgarity, and have a high interest in romantic love. Variables with loadings of 0.30 or more on this factor are shown in Table 11.17.

TABLE 11.17

Variables with Loadings of .3 or More on Factor M

Variable	Orthogonal	Oblique
25. Mood Stability	.27	.30
30. No Stage Fright	.28	.38
31. No Fear of Bugs	.61	.64
32. No Crying	.60	.63
33. No Romantic Love	.43	.43
34. Tolerance of Blood	.43	.44
35. Tolerance of Vulgarity	.34	.34
44. Sex (Male versus Female)	.54	.56

VIII. *Empathy versus Egocentrism* (P). Individuals who are high on this factor describe themselves as sympathetic, helpful, generous, unselfish, and interested in devoting their lives to the service of other people. Individuals who are low on this factor are not particularly sympathetic or helpful to others, tend to be concerned about themselves and their own goals, and are relatively uninterested in dedicating their lives to serving other people. Variables with loadings of 0.30 or more on this factor are shown in Table 11.18.

Masculinity versus Femininity (M) has several FHIDs with rather small loadings so it is the least homogeneous of the CPS factors and the one that needs the most work to find additional FHIDs with high loadings. As with factors A and S, the orthogonal factor loadings on factor P were reversed to make them consistent with the orientation of the factor as named.

11.4.4.   DISCUSSION OF THE RESULTS

The orthogonal Criterion II solution (Table 11.4), the oblique factor pattern solution (Table 11.8), and the factor structure matrix (Table 11.9) all agree rather well in showing that in most cases the variables had major loadings on the factors they were expected to define and not elsewhere. The two variables that were most disappointing in this respect were FHIDs 9 and 35. Variable 9, Cautiousness, was expected to have a major loading on factor O, Orderliness versus Lack of Compulsion. It had loadings of 0.35 in the orthogonal solution and 0.25 in the oblique solution while exhibiting loadings of comparable magnitude in two other factors, C and A. The structure coefficient was highest for O, 0.36, but not much lower for C and A, 0.32 and $-.27$, respectively. This FHID, therefore, would be regarded as a prime candidate for revision or replacement in carrying out another study designed to improve the factor taxonomy and the test instrument.

In this study, variable 35, Tolerance for Vulgarity, appears to be too complex factorially, measuring factor C as much as it measures factor M

TABLE 11.18

Variables with Loadings of .3 or More on Factor P

Variable	Orthogonal	Oblique
36. Sympathy	.66	.65
37. Helpfulness	.77	.79
38. Service	.66	.67
39. Generosity	.67	.68
40. Unselfishness	.57	.60
42. Response Bias Scale (R)	.40	.39

since its loadings and structure coefficient are of comparable magnitude in both factors. If such results are replicated, in a revision of the test instrument, this particular FHID would also be marked for revision or replacement. Variable 18, Need to Excel, has its highest loadings and structure coefficient on the factor it is supposed to define, factor A, but the loading is only 0.38 in both solutions, although the structure coefficient on factor A is 0.45. An attempt would be made to modify this FHID to obtain a higher loading on factor A in a new study aimed at revising the test.

The loadings for variables 33 and 34 are not very high on factor M, about 0.43, in both solutions, but they have no appreciable loadings on any other factors. This tends to make factor M somewhat broader and less homogeneous in composition compared to other factors, but this is not necessarily unacceptable. It would be desirable, however, to increase these loadings in a revised version of the taxonomy and test, if at all possible.

The study reported above represents an example where the oblique solution gives very little more than the orthogonal solution in the way of useful information. In reporting the study, therefore, it would not be unreasonable to report only the orthogonal solution in detail with verbal comments on the nature of the oblique solution and its relationship to the orthogonal solution. All the oblique solution tables except perhaps the table of correlations among the factors could be omitted to save on costs where it appears to be important to do so.

11.5.   VALIDATION OF A FACTOR ANALYTIC TAXONOMY

It has already been pointed out in Chapter 10 that good factor analytic interpretation requires the investigator to go beyond a mere intuitive description of the factors from a single study based on a cursory analysis of the variables with major loadings on the factors obtained. Hypothetico-deductive factor studies are an important part of a good program aimed at validating a taxonomy by improving the accuracy and expanding the richness of factor interpretation. In successive studies, new hypotheses are formulated about variables that should and others that should not appear on the factor if it is indeed what it is presumed to be. These hypotheses are tested empirically and conceptions about the factor constructs are revised accordingly. Many such studies were carried out in developing the final CPS taxonomy as described in the CPS manual (Comrey, 1970b).

It is important, however, to go beyond these kinds of factor studies with the same general population to understand more fully the true nature of the factor constructs and how well they generalize to other settings. It is also important to know what conditions affect the stability of the factor taxonomy. Factor analytic investigations can be undertaken with other kinds of samples, for example, in different cultures, to see how well the taxonomy will be replicated with different kinds of subjects and different motivational conditions.

The validity and potential usefulness of a factor analytic taxonomy can be further enhanced by relating the system to existing knowledge and theory in a field. To the extent that the factor constructs making up the taxonomy can be related in a meaningful way to what is already known, additional support for the validity of the system is obtained. One way of doing this is to attempt to relate the factor constructs to other theoretical systems developed from an entirely different perspective. Another way is to relate the factor constructs in this taxonomy to those of a similar kind in other systems. Where two tests, for example, are supposed to measure similar constructs, a study relating them is commonly referred to as a "concurrent validation" study. For example, studies have been conducted in which CPS factor scores have been correlated with scores for similar factors in other well-known tests such as the Guilford-Zimmerman Temperament Survey, the Cattell 16PF, and the Eysenck Personality Inventory.

Another important research technique for validating a taxonomy and the interpretive meaning of its factor scores is the "construct validity" study. Such studies can take many forms but most of them share the following ingredients: (a) If the factor construct is as it is thought to be, data collected in a certain way can be expected to yield a predicted result. (b) The data are collected and the prediction is tested. (c) If the prediction is upheld, confirmatory evidence for the factor interpretation is obtained; if not, the factor construct or its interpretation may require revision. Thus, a prediction might be made that diagnosed paranoid schizophrenics should have lower than average scores on Trust versus Defensiveness (T) if it is measuring what it is presumed to measure. By administering the test to a sample of such individuals this hypothesis can be tested. Finding that paranoid schizophrenics do in fact have a significantly lower score than the "normal" individual, on the average, would be consistent with the hypothesis that the factor score is measuring what it is supposed to measure. As more and more hypotheses about the factor are confirmed in such studies, confidence in the factor interpretation is increased. Studies of this kind can substantially enhance the meaningfulness of factor score interpretation and at the same time provide important evidence for the utility of the factor constructs involved. Several studies of this kind that have been conducted with the CPS are described in the next section.

11.6.   VALIDITY OF THE FACTORS MAKING UP THE CPS TAXONOMY

An example of a simple construct validation investigation of the CPS is contained in the factor analytic study reported above through the inclusion of "sex" as a variable. It was predicted that the variable 44, Sex, should have a substantial positive loading on factor M, Masculinity versus Femininity. Both loadings and the structure coefficient were above 0.50 on M for this variable. There are easier ways of determining sex than by giving the CPS, of course, but the verification of this deduction is a point in favor of the intepretation advanced for the M factor.

That is, if the CPS Masculinity versus Femininity (M) factor is measuring something that is associated with differences in men and women, gender identity should be substantially loaded on this factor and indeed it is.

11.6.1.   REPLICATION OF THE CPS TAXONOMY

Many studies have been undertaken since the CPS was published to determine how well the CPS taxonomy would replicate in other settings and under varying motivational conditions. Noller, Law, and Comrey (1988) report a replication of the norm group study, described earlier in this chapter, using a stratified sample of 669 Australian volunteer subjects balanced for age, sex, and social class. They summarize (see Table 11.19) their results (AU) and compare them with those from the norm group (NO) and several other previously published studies using roughly comparable kinds of samples, for example, Forbes, Dexter, and Comrey (NZ) (1974), Rodrigues and Comrey (BZ) (1974), Vandenberg and Price (DE) (1978), and Zamudio, Padilla, and Comrey (MA) (1983). The letter pair in parentheses with each reference identifies the group involved in the results summarized in Table 11.19 (see Note for Table 11.19).

Table 11.19 shows that there was a remarkable degree of stability in the major factor loadings from these various studies despite vast differences in the populations from which these samples were drawn. Comparable findings were obtained in another study using a sample of 394 psychiatric outpatients (Comrey & Schiebel, 1985b). The subjects in all these studies, however, were volunteers. In a similar study of Israeli applicants for drivers' licenses (Montag & Comrey, 1982b), all the CPS factors were replicated reasonably well except Social Conformity versus Rebelliousness (C). This was attributed to the reluctance of applicants to admit to anti-establishment attitudes and values. A similar study with 226 Hare Krishna subjects (Weiss & Comrey, 1987c) also verified all the CPS factors except Social Conformity versus Rebelliousness (C). Although these were volunteer subjects, they were very homogeneous with respect to their scores on the FHIDs defining the C factor, preventing its emergence in the analysis.

11.6.2.   THE CPS TAXONOMY AND ERIKSON'S AGES OF MAN

As the CPS taxonomy took shape through a series of factor analytic investigations, the first author was struck by the fact that there appeared to

TABLE 11.19

Loadings of CPS FHIDs in Six Different Samples

Factor	FHID	Loadings for 6 Samples					
		NO	BZ	NZ	MA	DV	AU
T	1. Lack of Cynicism	68	56	63	71	78	66
T	2. Lack of Defensiveness	59	51	43	48	54	49
T	3. Belief in Human Worth	57	52	58	52	59	61
T	4. Trust In Human Nature	66	54	61	63	69	57
T	5. Lack of Paranoia	63	43	49	46	67	62
O	6. Neatness	57	57	48	58	65	60
O	7. Routine	59	59	70	42	56	59
O	8. Order	69	59	73	62	79	75
O	9. Cautiousness	35	51	45	21	35	45
O	10. Meticulousness	54	29	54	09	38	40
C	11. Law Enforcement	76	56	64	55	67	66
C	12. Acceptance of Social Order	67	66	57	39	03	48
C	13. Intolerance of Nonconformity	72	69	63	46	68	75
C	14. Respect for Law	67	51	57	65	49	66
C	15. Need for Approval	44	26	49	06	36	30
A	16. Exercise	51	61	64	35	56	56
A	17. Energy	67	35	73	66	65	66
A	18. Need to Excel	38	26	58	36	53	56
A	19. Liking for Work	51	69	50	48	66	56
A	20. Stamina	70	59	61	58	66	64
S	21. Lack of Inferiority Feelings	59	38	44	49	49	54
S	22. Lack of Depression	69	64	68	68	58	61
S	23. Lack of Agitation	66	47	64	54	69	61
S	24. Lack of Pessimism	61	60	60	52	55	60
S	25. Mood Stability	57	41	63	65	71	64
E	26. Lack of Reserve	68	71	67	71	73	71
E	27. Lack of Seclusiveness	60	57	54	70	71	73
E	28. No Loss for Words	84	77	82	77	92	88
E	29. Lack of Shyness	79	77	78	72	85	84
E	30. No Stage Fright	49	52	55	38	58	52
M	31. No Fear of Bugs	61	40	59	70	64	65
M	32. No Crying	60	57	67	53	59	62
M	33. No Interest in Love Stories	43	43	38	32	52	43
M	34. Tolerance of Blood	43	39	46	37	38	42
M	35. Tolerance of Vulgarity	34	35	50	34	28	32
P	36. Sympathy	66	53	52	53	64	54
P	37. Helpfulness	77	72	73	70	74	68
P	38. Service	66	60	64	59	57	62
P	39. Generosity	67	63	56	70	71	70
P	40. Unselfishness	57	60	55	52	63	58

Note. Decimal points have been omitted. The samples referred to in the columns of this table are: NO = normative group , BZ = Brazil college students, NZ = New Zealand college students, MA = Mexican-American students, DV = Denver residents, AU = Australian residents. Factor names are T = Trust vs Defensiveness, O = Orderliness vs Lack of Compulsion, C = Social Conformity vs Lack of Rebelliousness, A = Activity vs Lack of Energy, E = Extraversion vs Introversion, M = Masculinity vs Femininity, and P = Empathy vs Egocentrism.

be a close correspondence between the emerging factor constructs and the eight ages of man proposed by Erik Erikson (1963), a neo-Freudian psychoanalyst. Elaborating on Freud's psychosexual theory, Erikson proposed a social theory of development, describing eight stages through which an individual should progress in passing from infancy to maturity. Each of these stages has a characteristic developmental task and characteristic modes of behavior designed to achieve the goals of that period. Erikson elaborated eight ages of man, but the eighth one, Ego Integrity versus Despair, represents the end result of the accumulated effects of adjustments made in the first seven stages. The CPS taxonomic traits and their hypothesized corresponding ages of man are shown below:

	CPS Traits	Erikson Ages of Man
T	Trust vs Defensiveness	Basic Trust vs Mistrust
O	Orderliness vs Lack of Compulsion	Autonomy vs Shame and Doubt
C	Social Conformity vs Rebelliousness	Initiative vs Guilt
A	Activity vs Lack of Energy	Industry vs Inferiority
S	Emotional Stability vs Neuroticism	Identity vs Role Confusion
E	Extraversion vs Introversion	Intimacy vs Isolation
M	Masculinity vs Femininity	Intimacy vs Isolation
P	Empathy vs Egocentrism	Generativity vs Stagnation
		Ego Integrity vs Despair

Two CPS factors are paired with Intimacy versus Isolation, one related to social adjustment in a non-sexual role (E) and the other in a sex-specific role (M). Erikson's theory merges these kinds of adjustments but empirical findings establish that these are distinct types of adjustment that require separate constructs. At the time of publication, the order of the CPS factors was chosen to be identical to that for the Erikson ages of man due to the apparent correspondence of these constructs.

At this point in time, the putative correspondence between the CPS factor traits and Erikson's ages of man enjoys the status of a plausible hypothesis that needs more substantial confirmation through further empirical research. To the extent that such a correspondence can be verified, a wealth of additional interpretive possibilities for CPS factor scores becomes available through the use of psychoanalytic theory. These possible interpretations are elaborated at greater length in Comrey (1980). The foregoing represents an example of enhancing and validating factor interpretation by relating factor analytic results to outside theory and knowledge.

11.6.3.   CONCURRENT VALIDATION STUDIES

Comrey, Jamison, and King (1968) administered an early version of the CPS and the Guilford-Zimmerman Temperament Survey to the same subjects. Analyses of the Guilford-Zimmerman items were undertaken to find any FHIDs among the items that could be factor analyzed with the CPS FHIDs. Factor analysis of the matrix of intercorrelations of FHIDs from both tests led to the conclusion that Neuroticism (an earlier version of Emotional Stability versus Neuroticism) in the CPS is very close to the Emotional Stability factor in the Guilford-Zimmerman test.

In another concurrent-validation study (Comrey & Duffy, 1968), an earlier version of the CPS was administered along with the Eysenck Personality Inventory and the Cattell 16PF to the same subjects. It was established that the Eysenck items factor analyzed into two factors, as expected, Neuroticism and Extraversion versus Introversion. It was further shown that these two factors are highly related to the CPS Neuroticism and Shyness factors, now renamed Emotional Stability versus Neuroticism and Extraversion versus Introversion, respectively. These findings were confirmed in a similar study several years later with a large, representative sample of Australian subjects (Noller, Law, & Comrey, 1987). Cattell 16PF scales were also shown to be related to these factors although these major factor constructs emerge at the second-order level in the 16PF rather than at the primary level as in the CPS and EPI.

Knapp and Comrey (1973) administered the Shostrum Personal Orientation Inventory (POI) and the CPS to the same subjects predicting that self-actualization as measured by major POI scales Time Competence (Tc) and Inner Directed (I) would be significantly related to Emotional Stability versus Neuroticism (S), a prediction that was confirmed. Also predicted and confirmed was a positive relationship between the POI Nature of Man-Constructive (Nc) and the CPS Trust versus Defensiveness (T) scale, both of which measure a basic belief in the goodness of human nature. Finally, a negative relationship was predicted and confirmed between the POI Existentiality (Ex) scale and the CPS Social Conformity versus Rebelliousness (C). The Ex scale measures the ability situationally to react without rigid adherence to principles.

In an entirely different kind of study, translated versions of the Minnesota Multiphasic Personality Inventory, the Eysenck Personality Inventory, and the CPS were administered to 179 applicants for driving licenses in Israel (Montag & Comrey, 1982a). Intercorrelations were obtained for three Lie Detection scales, three Emotional Stability scales, three Extraversion-Introversion scales, and two Masculinity-Femininity scales. Using a modified multitrait-multimethod procedure, these correlations were evaluated to show good convergent and discriminant validity for most of these measures.

11.6.4.   CONSTRUCT VALIDATION STUDIES

A doctoral dissertation study by Fabian, also reported in Fabian and Comrey (1971), has provided evidence for the construct validity of the

Emotional Stability versus Neuroticism factor. As a part of the study, she administered an early version of the factor scale designed to measure factor S to 69 normal, nonneurotic general medical and surgical hospital patients, 31 neuropsychiatric outpatients, and 68 neuropsychiatric inpatients. All of the neuropsychiatric patients had been diagnosed as neurotics. The prediction was that the lowest mean Neuroticism score (or highest Emotional Stability score) would be shown by the general medical and surgical patients with the highest Neuroticism mean score occurring for the inpatient neurotics. Outpatient neurotics were expected to have an intermediate mean Neuroticism score. The mean Neuroticism scores for the normals, outpatients, and inpatients, respectively, were 85.1, 110.1, and 119.1, giving a highly significant F-ratio of 32.6 in a one-way analysis of variance test of the differences between means.

Comrey and Backer (1970) administered the CPS and a biographical inventory to 209 male and female volunteer students at UCLA. The questions on the biographical inventory were hypothesized to show a relationship in a predicted direction with one or more of the CPS. The most striking degree of confirmation occurred for the Social Conformity versus Rebelliousness (C) scale. Variables correlated significantly at the 1–percent level with Social Conformity versus Rebelliousness in this study were the following; amount of marijuana consumed, $-.54$; having some religious preference versus having none, 0.39; degree of participation in campus demonstrations, $-.39$; amount of addictive drugs used, $-.36$; extent of premarital sexual activity, $-.27$; amount of interest in joining the Peace Corps, $-.26$; number of mental problems listed, $-.26$; degree of unconventionality of dress, $-.25$; and several other variables with lower but still significant values. All the significant relationships except one had been predicted in advance on the basis of what the factor should represent. The association of substance abuse with low scores on Social Conformity versus Rebelliousness (C) has also been confirmed by Knecht, Cundick, Edwards, & Gunderson (1972). Comrey and Wong (1978) showed that Asian students scored higher than non-Asians on the CPS C scale and that it is also positively correlated with political conservatism, both outcomes as predicted.

Weiss and Comrey (1987a, 1987b) compared the personality characteristics of 132 males and 94 females of the Hare Krishna movement with those of normals and psychiatric patients using the CPS. They found that the main way in which Hare Krishnas differed from normals was that they exhibited a very high average score on the Orderliness versus Lack of Compulson (O) scale, indicating a strong tendency to compulsivity. This finding is consistent with an analysis of the daily living habits of cult members. In other respects they were more similar to normals than to psychiatric patients.

The value of the CPS for detecting emotional disturbance has been demonstrated rather conclusively in studies of psychiatric patients compared with normals (Comrey, Soufi, & Backer, 1978; Comrey & Schiebel, 1983, 1985). Results from a study with normal subjects are in substantial agreement (Comrey, 1981). What these studies were able to show is that extreme scores on most of the CPS scales, whether high or low, are indicative of serious adjustment problems. The nature of the indicated difficulty varies, of course, from scale to scale. Thus, the CPS factor scales have been shown to have considerable clinical utility in diagnosis and treatment. These empirically demonstrated relationships greatly expand the possibilities for interpreting the meaning of CPS factor scores (Comrey, 1980).

The studies described briefly above only scratch the surface of what needs to be done to fully validate a personality taxonomy system. It is never possible to complete the job (Comrey, 1988). A description of what has been done with the CPS, however, will provide the reader with some notion of what is required to translate factor analytic findings into knowledge and measuring instruments that can be applied effectively in the real world for understanding, prediction, and control of human behavior.

12

Confirmatory Factor Analysis

The methods of factor analysis described up to this point represent traditional procedures that are now commonly referred to as "exploratory factor analysis," or EFA. Newer methods with a stronger base in statistical hypothesis testing theory have been developed in recent years. These new methods are referred to as "confirmatory factor analysis," or CFA, and are generally noted by the absence of factor rotation. Confirmatory factor analysis, hereafter referred to as CFA, is actually a special case of a more general set of statistical analysis methods that are called "covariance structure analysis." This chapter provides an introduction to CFA and show how it differs from EFA. A brief introduction to covariance structure analysis is given in Chapter 13.

12.1. SOME MATHEMATICAL BACKGROUND

Both EFA and CFA use the same basic specification equation that was given in Chapter 2 as:

$$z_{ik} = a_{i1}F_{1k} + a_{i2}F_{2k} + \ldots + a_{im}F_{mk} + a_{is}S_{ik} + a_{ie}E_{ik} \qquad (2.1)$$

By assuming that all the common, specific, and error factors were uncorrelated with each others, it was possible to derive the equation for the reproduced correlation matrix, $\mathbf{R}'$:

$$\mathbf{R}' = \mathbf{AA}' \qquad (2.11)$$

299

$\mathbf{R}'$, the reproduced correlation matrix, has communalities in the diagonals in common factor analysis, since not all the variance is accounted for by the common factors. Furthermore, the values in the off-diagonal cells of $\mathbf{R}'$ are only approximately equal to $\mathbf{R}$, the observed correlation matrix. Of course, it is hoped that the discrepancies between $\mathbf{R}'$ and $\mathbf{R}$, that is, the final residuals, will be small.

In the chapter on oblique rotations, it was shown that the common factors need not be uncorrelated, leading to a revised equation for the reproduced correlation matrix in terms of the factor pattern matrix and the matrix of correlations among factors:

$$\mathbf{R}' = \mathbf{P}\Phi\mathbf{P}' \tag{6.60}$$

The specific and error factors are still assumed to be uncorrelated with each other and with the common factors, hence they will not affect the off-diagonal values of $\mathbf{R}'$. They do affect the diagonal cells, however, since the total variance is apportioned to h^2, a_s^2, and a_e^2. The sum of the specific and error variance components make up the uniqueness of the variable. The communality and the uniqueness add up to 1.0 for each variable, the total variance of a variable in standard score form. Thus if the uniqueness is to be included, equation (6.60) must be rewritten as follows:

$$\mathbf{R}_e = \mathbf{P}\Phi\mathbf{P}' + \mathbf{U} \tag{12.1}$$

Where $\mathbf{U}$ is a diagonal matrix that contains the uniquenesses for the variables. The off-diagonal elements of $\mathbf{U}$ are zero because the specific and error factors are all uncorrelated. $\mathbf{R}_e$ appears in equation (12.1) instead of $\mathbf{R}'$ because it contains 1.0 in all the diagonals instead of h^2 values. $\mathbf{R}_e$ will be compared with $\mathbf{R}$, the observed correlation matrix with 1.0 values in the diagonals, to see how well the model accounts for the observed data.

Exploratory factor analysis methods have not had very good procedures for comparing $\mathbf{R}_e$ and $\mathbf{R}$ to determine how well they agree. Confirmatory factor analysis methods, on the other hand, permit an actual statistical test by means of chi-square to determine how good the fit is, provided that certain assumptions about the data can be met. This is an important advantage that CFA has over EFA.

In EFA, there are many acceptable methods, some of which have been covered in previous chapters, of obtaining the pattern matrix, $\mathbf{P}$, and the matrix of correlations among the factors, Φ. CFA approaches the problem of obtaining estimates for the elements of the $\mathbf{P}$ and Φ matrices in a different way from EFA. CFA can also permit the off-diagonal elements of the $\mathbf{U}$ matrix to depart from zero, an option considered to be of major importance by Mulaik (1975). In EFA, values are estimated for all the elements of **P** and **Φ**. The elements of **U** follow as a consequence of estimating the other parameters because these elements equal $1 - h_{ii}^2$.

In CFA, the parameters of the model include all the elements of **P**, **Φ**, and **U**, including the off-diagonal elements of **U**, which are all zero in EFA. In CFA, linear regression equations based on Equation (2.1) are set up containing a subset of the parameters of the model as parameters to be estimated by solving these linear regression equations. Because there are so many unknowns, regression equations cannot be set up and solved for all of the possible parameters. Some of the parameters are fixed, therefore, to reduce the number of parameters to be estimated to a manageable number. One of the most important ways that the number of parameters to be estimated is reduced in CFA is to fix a great many of the values at zero. For example, in a good simple structure solution, most of the values in the column of the **P** matrix fall in the hyperplane, that is, roughly plus or minus 0.10. In CFA, values expected to fall in the hyperplane would be fixed at zero. Even when it is possible to obtain a unique solution for the system of linear regression equations, that is, the model is "identified," the parameters obtained in the solution will not permit an exact reproduction of the data matrix, **R**. Rather, the $\mathbf{R}_e$ matrix reproduced by means of equation (12.1) will only approximate **R**. If the data fulfill certain requirements, however, a chi-square based test can be employed to determine if $\mathbf{R}_e$ is significantly different from **R**. CFA has drawn considerable interest in the behavioral sciences because it allows the researcher to partially define the target factor loading matrix and then uses the data to estimate the undefined portions of the factor loading matrix, within the confines of obtaining the best fit possible.

12.2. APPLYING CFA TO THE 12-VARIABLE SAMPLE PROBLEM

An oblique, rotated simple structure solution for the 12-variable sample problem was given in Chapter 6. The oblique EFA solution had a clear-cut simple structure with four factors. Four factors are used, therefore, in the CFA solution. Note that one must specify in advance exactly how many factors are to be used in the CFA solution. In EFA, the correct number of factors is often determined only after a good deal of exploratory work. At the present time, the two most popular structural equations computer programs that can do CFA are the LISREL program by Joreskog and Sorbom (1981, 1984, 1988) and the EQS program by Bentler (1985, 1989). Setups for running the 12-variable sample problem on these two programs are shown below. These are only two of many possible setups that could run the same problem using these programs. Readers will need to consult the LISREL and EQS manuals to see how to set up their own problems.

LISREL and EQS will seek a solution that can be represented schematically by the following Φ and $\mathbf{P}$ matrices:

$$
\Phi = \begin{array}{c}
 \\ F1 \\ F2 \\ F3 \\ F4
\end{array}
\begin{bmatrix}
F1 & F2 & F3 & F4 \\
1.00 & & & \\
* & 1.00 & & \\
* & * & 1.00 & \\
* & * & * & 1.00
\end{bmatrix}
$$

Φ is the matrix of correlations between factors. The asterisks indicate the parameters to be estimated by the data. The diagonal elements of this matrix are fixed at the value 1.00.

Notice that only the lower half of the matrix is estimated. The upper half does not need to be estimated because those elements are equal to those below the diagonal.

$$
\mathbf{P} = \begin{array}{c}
 \\ X_1 \\ X_2 \\ X_3 \\ X_4 \\ X_5 \\ X_6 \\ X_7 \\ X_8 \\ X_9 \\ X_{10} \\ X_{11} \\ X_{12}
\end{array}
\begin{bmatrix}
F1 & F2 & F3 & F4 \\
* & 0 & 0 & 0 \\
* & 0 & 0 & 0 \\
* & 0 & 0 & 0 \\
0 & * & 0 & 0 \\
0 & * & 0 & 0 \\
0 & * & 0 & 0 \\
0 & 0 & * & 0 \\
0 & 0 & * & 0 \\
0 & 0 & * & 0 \\
0 & 0 & 0 & * \\
0 & 0 & 0 & * \\
0 & 0 & 0 & *
\end{bmatrix}
$$

In the $\mathbf{P}$ matrix, the asterisks indicate loadings estimated by the data. The other elements of this matrix are all fixed at the value of zero (0).

LISREL Setup for 12-Variable Problem

```
TWELVE VARIABLE FACTOR ANALYSIS BOOK SAMPLE PROBLEM
DA NI=12 NO=727 MA=KM
LA
*
'LAW-ENF' 'ACC-SOC' 'INTOL-NC' 'NO-INF-F' 'NO-DEPR' 'NO-AGIT'
'NO-RESV' 'NO-SECL' 'WORDY' 'SYMPATHY' 'HELPFUL' 'GENEROUS'
MO NX=12 NK=4 PH=ST
KM SY
(20F4.2)
 100
  61   100
  64    50   100
  07    02    02   100
  14    13    04    51   100
  07    08  - 03    46    51   100
  04  - 05  - 01    28    29    13   100
  08    02    08    29    31    19    46   100
  06  - 02    01    47    41    31    66    55   100
- 02  - 07  - 01    10    18    05    16    31    20   100
- 02  - 08  - 02    14    24    18    16    39    28    60   100
- 17  - 15  - 04    05    09    05    12    26    17    46    61   100
LK
'CONFORM' 'STABLE' 'EXTRAVRT' 'EMPATHY'
FR LX(1,1) LX(2,1) LX(3,1) LX(4,2) LX(5,2) LX(6,2)C
   LX(7,3) LX(8,3) LX(9,3) LX(10,4) LX(11,4) LX(12,4)
OU SE TV RS VA MI FS
```

The first line gives the title. The DA or DATA line indicates the number of variables input (NI = 12), the number of cases (NO = 727), and MA = KM tells the program that a correlation matrix will be input as data. The next line starting with "LA" for labels and the three following lines specify eight-digit, or less, names for the input variables. The MO (MODEL) line states that the solution matrix will have 12 rows (NX = 12), four factors (NK = 4), and PH = ST indicates that phi is a symmetric correlation matrix with ones in the diagonals. The KM SY row indicates that a symmetric data matrix is to be input with ones in the diagonals and the format specified on the next row indicates that each correlation will occupy a four-column field with two digits to the right of the decimal point. The decimal points are supplied by the program itself. The correlation matrix follows.

The LK row and the one following specify the labels for the factors. The row beginning with "FR" tells which elements of the solution factor matrix will be free, that is, subject to estimation by the program. Variables 1–3 are supposed to define factor I, variables 4–6 are supposed to define factor II, and factors III and IV, respectively are supposed to be defined by variables 7–9 and 10–12. The other entries in the model matrix are fixed at zero. The last row, beginning with "OU" for output, tells the program which items to produce for the printed output. The reader should consult the LISREL manual for more details.

EQS Setup for 12-Variable Problem

```
/TITLE
EQS ANALYSIS OF FACTOR ANALYSIS BOOK SAMPLE PROBLEM
/SPECS
CAS = 727; VAR = 12; ME = ML; MA = COR; AN = COR;
/LABELS
V1 = LAW ENF; V2 = ACC SOC; V3 = INTOLNC; V4 = NO INF F;
V5 = NO DEPR; V6 = NO AGIT; V7 = NO RESERV; V8 = NO SECL;
V9 = WORDY; V10 = SYMPATHY; V11 = HELPFUL; V12 = GENEROUS;
F1 = CONFORM; F2 = STABLE; F3 = EXTRAVRT; F4 = EMPATHY;
/EQU
V1  = .7*F1 + E1;
V2  = .7*F1 + E2;
V3  = .7*F1 + E3;
V4  = .7*F2 + E4;
V5  = .7*F2 + E5;
V6  = .7*F2 + E6;
V7  = .7*F3 + E7;
V8  = .7*F3 + E8;
V9  = .7*F3 + E9;
V10 = .7*F4 + E10;
V11 = .7*F4 + E11;
V12 = .7*F4 + E12;
/VAR
F1 TO F4 = 1.0;
E1 TO E12 = .5*;
/COV
F2,F1 = .1*; F3,F1 = .1*; F3,F2 = .6*;
F4,F1 = -.2*; F4,F2 = .3*; F4,F3 = .4*;
/PRINT
CORRELATION = YES;
EFFECT = YES;
/MAT
 1.00
  .61   1.00
  .64    .50   1.00
  .07    .02    .02   1.00
  .14    .13    .04    .51   1.00
  .07    .08  -.03    .46    .51   1.00
  .04  -.05  -.01    .28    .29    .13   1.00
  .08    .02    .08    .29    .31    .19    .46   1.00
  .06  -.02    .01    .47    .41    .31    .66    .55   1.00
 -.02  -.07  -.01    .10    .18    .05    .16    .31    .20   1.00
 -.02  -.08  -.02    .14    .24    .18    .16    .39    .28    .60   1.00
 -.17  -.15  -.04    .05    .09    .05    .12    .26    .17    .46    .61   1.00
/END
```

The first two lines of the EQS setup give the title and the next two lines give the specifications, that is, the number of cases is 727, the number of variables is 12, the method of estimation (ME) is the maximum likelihood method (ML), the input matrix is a correlation matrix (MA = COR), and the matrix to be analyzed is a correlation matrix (AN = COR).

The next several lines give the labels for the variables. The twelve regression equations that follow the /EQU line show which variables are to be related to which factors. The numbers preceding the asterisks are beginning estimates of the factor loadings. Without the asterisks, the parameters would be fixed at the assigned values. That is, variables with numbers preceding the asterisks are free parameters and are estimated using the observed data. Variables with numbers only are fixed parameters. Variance estimates must be given for each factor and for each error term. These follow the /VAR line. Estimates of the correlations between the factors are given following the /COV line. Printed output controls and the data matrix follow.

12.2.1. OUTPUT FROM LISREL AND EQS

Both EQS and LISREL programs gave identical estimates of the factor loadings and chi-square values ($X^2 = 228.4$ with 48 df) for the 12-variable sample problem. Although this chi-square is highly significant, indicating a lack of fit, these chi-square values are inflated because the sample is large. Both programs, therefore, give other indications of the degree of fit that are less subject to influence by the size of the sample. The LISREL program gave three such indices, the goodness of fit index (.950) the adjusted goodness of fit index (.918), and the root mean square residual (.053). The EQS program gave three different kinds of indices for the same purpose, the Bentler-Bonett normed fit index (.927), the Bentler-Bonett nonnormed fit index (.919), and the comparative fit index (.941). All these indices run from 0 to 1 (with rare exceptions), with values of 0.9 or more indicating a reasonably good fit. Thus, a fit can be reasonably good but still yield a highly significant chi-square, especially with larger sample sizes, as was the case here. The estimated factor loadings obtained from both programs are shown in Table 12.1.

Note in Table 12.1 that there are many loadings that are forced to be exactly zero in this solution. The sizes of the non-zero loadings, the uniquenesses ($1 - h^2$ values), and the elements of the Φ matrix must be adjusted to make this possible. Because variables typically have non-zero loadings on factors other than the one where they have their principal loadings in EFA, CFA introduces some distortion into the final results in these cases in order to keep the unestimated parameters equal to zero.

In another 12-variable problem using artificial data with no errors, the distortions become more apparent. Table 12.2 gives the true factor load-

TABLE 12.1

LISREL and EQS Estimated Factor Loadings for 12-Variable Problem

Variable Number	Social Conformity	Emotional Stability	Extraversion Introversion	Empathy vs. Egocentrism
1. Law Enforcment	.888	.000	.000	.000
2. Accept Society	.690	.000	.000	.000
3. Intolerance of Non-Conformity	.719	.000	.000	.000
4. No Inferiority	.000	.708	.000	.000
5. No Depression	.000	.755	.000	.000
6. No Agitation	.000	.639	.000	.000
7. No Reserve	.000	.000	.711	.000
8. No Seclusiveness	.000	.000	.621	.000
9. Wordiness	.000	.000	.915	.000
10. Sympathy	.000	.000	.000	.669
11. Helpfulness	.000	.000	.000	.900
12. Generosity	.000	.000	.000	.678

ings. By multiplying this four-factor matrix of loadings by its transpose, a 12 variable correlation matrix was obtained. This correlation matrix was used in a CFA with LISREL where parameters allowed to be free were only those known to have a true loading of 0.40 or higher. All others were set to zero (0). The values in parentheses in Table 12.2 are the non-zero parameter estimates obtained from the LISREL CFA solution. Correlations among the factors for the LISREL solution are shown in Table 12.3 together with information on goodness-of-fit measures.

It is apparent, therefore, from inspecting Table 12.2, that forcing some loadings to be zero when in reality they are not affects the final CFA solution. Also, the chi-square goodness-of-fit test was statistically significant, indicating a lack-of-fit. However, as more parameters were set free for estimation by CFA in the factor loading matrix, the chi-square decreased in size until it became statistically insignificant. Without knowledge about which variables should have minor non-zero loadings, the researcher can easily become involved in an extended odyssey trying to find the best fitting model. Furthermore, as more and more parameters are set free to be estimated, finding a unique solution for the model parameters becomes increasingly unlikely.

12.2.2. RESPECIFYING THE MODEL TO IMPROVE FIT

The oblique simple structure solution to the 12-variable sample problem obtained by EFA and shown in Chapter 6 had several loadings out of the

TABLE 12.2

True Factor Loadings and a CFA Solution for Fictitious Data

Variable Number	Factor 1	Factor 2	Factor 3	Factor 4
1	90(91)	00	05	00
2	70(71)	00	21	00
3	80(79)	00	00	00
4	00	62(62)	00	10
5	00	70(74)	00	20
6	00	53(50)	00	00
7	00	00	80(80)	00
8	00	00	65(65)	20
9	00	00	71(71)	00
10	30	00	00	45(58)
11	20	10	00	48(53)
12	10	00	00	51(43)

Note. Decimal points have been omitted. Values not in parentheses are the artificial data **P** matrix values. Values in parentheses are the non-zero model parameters obtained by LISREL in analyzing the correlation matrix generated by the artificial data.

TABLE 12.3

Correlations Among Factors

	Factor 1	Factor 2	Factor 3	Factor 4
Factor 1	1.000			
Factor 2	.000	1.000		
Factor 3	.076	.013	1.000	
Factor 4	.410	.242	.058	1.000

Note. The chi-square measure of goodness of fit for the whole model was 80.58 with 48 degrees of freedom (p < .002). The goodness of fit index was .982; the adjusted goodness of fit index was .970; the root mean square residual was .037.

hyperplane for variables on factors other than their main factor. Variable 8, for example, had a loading of 0.22 on what is shown in Table 12.1 as the fourth factor. Several other pattern coefficients ranged from 0.10 to 0.20 on factors where they were not necessarily expected to have loadings out of the hyperplane. It seems reasonable to suppose that making some adjustments in the original model specification should permit a revised solution that would yield a smaller chi-square, that is, a better fit of the model to the actual data.

Both LISREL and EQS provide information about which elements of the solution could be freed up and what the potential effect might be on reducing the chi-square value. Thus, the researcher can make changes in the model, permitting more parameters to be freely estimated instead of being held to zero, and then checking to see if the chi-square and fit indices are improved. Tinkering with the model in this way, especially without a theoretical justification for making the adjustments, encourages a capitalization upon chance variations to bring about the appearance of a better fit of the model to the data. Verification of the adjusted model with new data, if successful, would remove the cloud of suspicion surrounding the legitimacy of such ad hoc adjustments.

It should also be noted that making such adjustments to the model involves other difficulties. As the size of the problem increases, the number of possible adjustments rises sharply as do the labor and computation costs connected with making them. Yet another difficulty is that making adjustments increases the number of parameters that must be estimated, which will lead sooner or later to an "unidentified" model, that is, one for which there is no unique solution for the unknown parameters. Another problem that can be encountered is that reasonable estimates must be made for the parameters to start the estimation process or the solution may not converge. It is often difficult to decide what the starting values should be, especially when a variance-covariance matrix is being analyzed. Trial and error may be the only way out, but this can result in substantial computation costs with large matrices.

12.2.3. MODEL IDENTIFICATION

As indicated in the last section, if there is no unique set of values that produce the matrices making up the CFA solution, the model is considered to be "not identified." To obtain a unique solution for the parameter estimates in the model, there must be enough constraints in the system to lead to a unique solution. For starters, the number of known data values must exceed the number of parameters to be estimated. The greater the excess, the better. This is only a necessary but not sufficient condition, however, to ensure unique parameter estimates.

Joreskog and Sorbom (1981) indicate that the factor model will be identified if the following conditions are met: (1) The matrix of correlations between the factors is a symmetric, positive definite matrix (all eigenvalues > 0) with unities in the main diagonal of the matrix; (2) The unique variance matrix is a diagonal matrix; (3) The factor matrix has at least (m − 1) fixed zero elements in each column, where m is the number of common factors; and (4) the submatrix of the factor matrix consisting of rows that have fixed zero elements has rank of (m − 1). See also Long (1983) for more details. In any event, if the model is not identified, both LISREL and EQS will indicate this fact to the user so that adjustments can be made until the indeterminancy has been removed.

12.3. ANALYSIS OF COVARIANCE MATRICES

The examples given above have involved the analysis of correlation matrices by means of the maximum likelihood method. If the underlying distributions of the variables are multivariate normal and if the samples are large, such analyses are appropriate and provide dependable chi-square values. Where these conditions are not met, as they frequently are not, more reliable results are to be obtained by analyzing the variance-covariance matrix rather than the correlation matrix (Bentler, 1989; Cudeck, 1989). In fact, devotees of structural equation modeling typically prefer to work with the variance-covariance matrix rather than the correlation matrix. In this particular case where the 12-variable CPS sample problem constituted the data, however, analysis of the covariance matrix by EQS gave standardized pattern coefficients identical to those obtained by analyzing the correlation matrix.

In the EQS program, it is possible to input the correlation matrix and have the program obtain the variance-covariance matrix for further analysis if the standard deviations of the data variables are provided as part of the program input. Because analysis of variance-covariance matrices is often preferred in CFA and structural equation modeling, researchers who publish EFA results should be careful to include the means and standard deviations of their data variables as well as the correlation matrix, or else make the raw data themselves available. If they do so, other researchers can apply CFA methods to the data. Some structural equation models also make use of the mean data as well as the standard deviations.

Typical notation with CFA and structural equation modeling where the variance-covariance matrix is analyzed is somewhat different from that which has been used thus far in this book with EFA. For example, Equation (12.1) for EFA and correlation matrices would be written as follows for CFA with variance-covariance matrices:

$$\Sigma = \Lambda \Phi \Lambda' + \Psi \tag{12.2}$$

where

Σ = the variance-covariance matrix

Λ = the matrix of factor loadings

Φ = the matrix of correlations among factors

Ψ = the diagonal matrix of unique variances

It should be noted that in CFA, the requirement that Ψ be diagonal is relaxed to permit the unique factors to be correlated with one another. There are certain empirical situations in which it is clear that the unique factors are correlated with each other, contrary to the assumptions of the EFA model.

12.4. ESTIMATING THE UNKNOWN CFA PARAMETERS

The most commonly used methods for estimating the CFA parameters are unweighted least squares (ULS), generalized (weighted) least squares (GLS), and maximum likelihood (ML). Each of these methods assumes multivariate normal distributions for all measured variables. The GLS and ML methods also assume that the correlation or covariance matrices are positive definite (all eigenvalues > 0). In addition to these methods, Bentler's EQS program provides estimation methods based on elliptical error distributions and also "distribution free" procedures. We confine ourself here to a discussion of the LS, GLS, and ML methods.

In each of these methods, initial starting values are needed for the elements of each matrix in the model: P, Φ, and U when the correlation matrix is being analyzed, or Λ, Φ, and Ψ when the variance-covariance matrix is being analyzed. Some of the starting values are fixed at zero, or some other constant, and remain fixed, while the "free" parameters begin with initial estimates and change as the iterative process proceeds. The starting values are input to equation (12.1) to obtain an R_e matrix (if analyzing a correlation matrix) or to Equation (12.2) to obtain a Σ matrix (if analyzing a variance-covariance matrix). The reproduced matrices are compared with the observed data matrices to see how closely these initial estimates serve to reproduce the observed data values. If the fit is not very close, as it never is with the initial starting values, then the starting values must be modified before trying again.

The comparison of the model generated (fitted) matrix with the observed data matrix is done through the use of a "fitting function" which is to be minimized by making suitable modifications in the current estimates. As the estimates are improved, the value of the fitting function decreases. The iterative process terminates successfully if convergence to a minimum value of the fitting function occurs with a unique set of parameter estimates.

Each of the three methods, ULS, GLS, and ML, uses a different fitting function that must be minimized. These fitting functions are as follows:

Unweighted Least Squares ULS.

$$F(\mathbf{R},\mathbf{R}_e) = (1/2) \text{ tr } [(\mathbf{R} - \mathbf{R}_e)^2] \tag{12.3}$$

$$F(\mathbf{S}^*,\Sigma) = (1/2) \text{ tr } [(\mathbf{S}^* - \Sigma)^2] \tag{12.4}$$

Generalized (Weighted) Least Squares (GLS).

$$F(\mathbf{R},\mathbf{R}_e) = (1/2) \text{ tr } [(\mathbf{R} - \mathbf{R}_e)\mathbf{R}^{-1}]^2 \tag{12.5}$$

$$F(\mathbf{S}^*,\Sigma) = (1/2) \text{ tr } [(\mathbf{S}^* - \Sigma)\mathbf{S}^{*-1}]^2 \tag{12.6}$$

Maximum Likelihood (ML).

$$F(R,R_e) = tr(RR_e^{-1}) + \ln |R_e| - \ln |R| - q \qquad (12.7)$$

$$F(S^*,\Sigma) = tr(S^*\Sigma^{-1}) + \ln |\Sigma| - \ln |S^*| - q \qquad (12.8)$$

In equations (12.3) through (12.8), the terms are defined as follows:

R is a sample correlation matrix

R_e is a reproduced (fitted) correlation matrix

S* is the sample variance-covariance matrix

Σ is the reproduced (fitted) variance-covariance matrix

q is the number of free parameters to be estimated

$\ln |R|$ means to take the natural logarithm of the determinant of the matrix **R**

$tr (RR_e^{-1})$ means to take the trace of the matrix product RR_e^{-1} where the trace is the sum of the main diagonal elements of the matrix

In each case, the fitting function is at a minimum when the set of parameter estimates is found that minimizes the difference between **R** and R_e or between **S*** and Σ.

Joreskog (1977) indicates that GLS and ML give scale-free solutions, which means that the minimum found for the fitting function is independent of the scale of the variables. Thus, the minimum value found for the fitting function using the correlation matrix or the variance-covariance matrix will be the same. For the ULS method, this is not the case. Changing the variables to different means and standard deviations will result in a different minimum for the fitting function. Unweighted least squares (ULS) should be restricted to the use of the correlation matrix for data whereas the other two methods can be used to analyze either the sample correlation matrix or the sample variance-covariance matrix. An additional problem with the unweighted least squares estimation method (ULS) for CFA is that the chi-square test takes more computation than just finding the minimum of the fitting function. Bentler's EQS (1989) makes this test and also provides standard error estimates. This feature was not available on earlier versions of the program. On the positive side, Long (1983) states that for large samples, the estimates from ULS are unbiased and Joreskog (1977) reports that the method will work with matrices that are not positive definite, that is, those with some negative eigenvalues.

12.4.1. ADJUSTING THE PARAMETER ESTIMATES

Joreskog (1969, 1977) recommends adjusting the parameter estimates to minimize the fitting functions through the use of a two-step iterative procedure. Since each fitting function is a function of P, Φ, and U or Λ, Φ, and Ψ, the first step involves specifying the contents of the U matrix or the Ψ matrix and then finding the p largest eigenvalues and their associated eigenvectors for the matrix $R - U^2$ or the matrix $S^* - \Psi^2$ in ULS and the matrix $UR^{-1}U$ or the matrix $\Psi S^{*-1}\Psi$ for GLS and ML, where p is the number of hypothesized factors, S^* is the sample covariance matrix and R is the sample correlation matrix. This first step provides a conditional minimum for the fitting function. These eigenvectors are then used in the second step to define a new matrix function which in turn is also minimized. This second step involves using the Newton-Raphson, the Davidon-Fletcher-Powell, or the Fisher scoring optimization algorithms. In all of these methods, the matrix starting values are used to generate an R_e or a Σ matrix. After the generation of this initial fitted matrix, the optimization algorithm is applied to the fitting function. This process generates reestimates of the free parameters in the system. With these new estimates, the fitted matrices are generated again and the fitting function recomputed. This iterative process terminates when the fitting function is at a minimum, that is, when R_e is close to R or Σ is close to S^*.

A detailed mathematical explication of these optimization procedures is beyond the scope of this introductory text. The reader is referred to other sources for a fuller discussion of these methods (Beightler, Phillips, & Wilde, 1979; Bentler, 1989; Fletcher & Powell, 1963; Kennedy & Gentle, 1980; McMillan, 1975; Mulaik, 1972). Lee and Jennrich (1979, 1984) have also explored the possibility of using other optimization algorithms.

12.5. GOODNESS OF FIT

Lawley and Maxwell (1971) proposed two likelihood ratio tests (L^2) for comparing R and R_e (or S^* and Σ). One is for the generalized least squares (GLS) fitting function and the other is for the maximum likelihood (ML) fitting function. Both tests are goodness-of-fit tests similar to the chi-square test. Lawley and Maxwell's generalized least squares test involves computing:

$$L^2_{gls} = (N-1)/2 \, \text{tr} \, [(R - R_e)R^{-1}]^2 \tag{12.9}$$

$$L^2_{gls} = (N-1)/2 \text{ tr } [(S^* - \Sigma)S^{*-1}]^2 \qquad (12.10)$$

For the maximum likelihood criterion fitting function, the test involves computing:

$$L^2_{ml} = (N-1) [\text{tr } (RR_e^{-1}) + \text{Ln } |R_e| - \text{Ln } |R| - q] \qquad (12.11)$$

$$L^2_{ml} = (N-1) [\text{tr } (S^*\Sigma^{-1}) + \text{Ln } |\Sigma| - \text{Ln } |S^*| - q] \qquad (12.12)$$

where N is sample size or number of observations and q is the number of variables under study in the sample. Other terms are defined as in previous equations. These equations are also reported in Brown (1986).

Both L^2_{gls} and L^2_{ml} are evaluated as chi-square statistics with the number of degrees of freedom equal to $[q(q+1)/2] - t$, where t is equal to the number of independent parameters estimated.

Bentler and Bonett (1980) state that if the L^2 statistic is large when compared with the degrees of freedom, then the model specified does not fit the observed data. An insignificant L^2, on the other hand, indicates that the observed data are consistent with the model.

Joreskog and Sorbom (1981) and Bentler and Bonett (1980) have indicated that the chi-square test is not necessarily the best statistic to use in most real-life situations. The chi-square test has some restrictions, such as the requirement that the observed variables be normally distributed, the sample sizes be large enough to satisfy the assumptions underlying the chi-square test, and the sample covariance matrix be used instead of the sample correlation matrix. For ordinary CFA maximum likelihood solutions, however, the X^2 will be the same for both correlation and covariance matrices (Cudek, 1989). It is difficult to claim in most cases that all of the assumptions mentioned above have been met. As a result of these limitations, other tests have been developed.

Joreskog and Sorbom (1984) developed two other measures of goodness-of-fit, the "goodness-of-fit" index (GFI) and the "adjusted goodness-of-fit" index (AGFI). These two statistics have the following form:

$$\text{GFI} = 1 - \text{tr } (R_e^{-1}R - I)^2/\text{tr } (R_e^{-1}R)^2 \qquad (12.13)$$

$$\text{GFI} = 1 - \text{tr } (\Sigma^{-1}S^* - I)^2/ \text{tr } (\Sigma^{-1}S^*)^2 \qquad (12.14)$$

$$\text{AGFI} = 1 - (q(q+1)/2 \ df)(1 - \text{GFI}) \qquad (12.15)$$

where df is the number of degrees of freedom, which in this situation is $[q(q+1)/2] - t$ where q is the number of variables in the problem and t is the number of parameters to be estimated. Other terms are defined as in previous equations in this chapter. Thus, the AGFI is really the GFI adjusted for the number of variables and the degrees of freedom.

These indices vary from 0 to 1, as previously indicated, are independent ple size, and are relatively unaffected by departures from normality in the measured variables. Unfortunately, no statistical distribution has been established for the GFI statistic and as a result, no complete standard has been developed to evaluate the values of GFI. However, through the work of Bentler and Bonnet (1980), the recommendation is that values below 0.9 indicate the need to change the model to obtain a better fit to the observed data.

Also produced by the LISREL program is a goodness-of-fit measure called the "Root Mean Square Residual" or RMR. RMR is defined as

$$RMR = [2\Sigma\Sigma \ (S^*_{ij} - \Sigma_{ij})^2/[k(k+1)]]^{1/2} \tag{12.16}$$

$$RMR = [2\Sigma\Sigma \ (R_{ij} - Re_{ij})^2/[k(k+1)]]^{1/2} \tag{12.17}$$

where k is the total number of variables, S^*_{ij} is the observed covariance for variables i and j, R_{ij} is the observed correlation between variables i and j, Σ_{ij} is the reproduced covariance between variable i and j, and Re_{ij} is the reproduced correlation for variables i and j.

Whereas the goodness-of-fit measures such as GFI indicate a "good" fit if the statistic is high, the RMR statistic indicates a "good" fit if its value is small. This is similar to the chi-square test, where a insignificant statistic is an indication of a good fit. RMR is useful in two ways. It can be used to compare the fit of two different specifications on the same data as well as comparing the same specification using different data.

Another popular fit criterion is the "normed fit index" (NFI), developed by Bentler and Bonett (1980). This statistic is calculated by the EQS program whereas the GFI and AGFI are given by the LISREL program. The NFI is similar to the modified Tucker-Lewis coefficient (Bernstein, 1988). The modified Tucker-Lewis coefficient is given by:

$$I = \frac{F(L) - F(O)}{F(L) - F(U)} \tag{12.18}$$

where $F(L)$ is the lower limit of fit imposed by the model with no structure. This is analogous to finding a solution to the fitting function with a P or Σ matrix filled with zeros, a correlation matrix that is an identity matrix, or a correlation matrix with all off-diagonal values equal (Loehlin, 1987). That is, $F(L)$ is derived from the fitting function of either the maximum likelihood or generalized least squares method where every value is identical. $F(O)$ is the computed value of the fitting function using either maximum likelihood or generalized least squares with the researcher's hypothesized values in the P, Φ, and U (or Λ, Φ, and Ψ) matrices, with some parameters freed and others restricted. $F(U)$ is the upper limit imposed by an unconstrained solution with all relevant parameters set free.

$F(U)$ is difficult to obtain because CFA does not allow the user to leave all parameters free to be estimated by the data. In order to make the modified Tucker-Lewis method usable, the researcher can only specify the maximum number of free parameters allowed by the model. The coefficient essentially describes the relative distance of the observed model from the mathematically defined upper and lower bounds of the model. A coefficient close to zero would indicate a good fit with the "null" model or the model with no structure.

The Bentler-Bonett NFI coefficient avoids some of the problems with the modified Tucker-Lewis coefficient:

$$NFI = 1 - F(O)/F(L) \qquad (12.19)$$

using the same definitions of symbols as in Equation (12.18). Models that yield NFI values of 0.9 or more will yield little improvement in fit through changes in the model specification. NFI values less than 0.9 indicate room for improvement in the specification of the model (Bentler & Bonett, 1980).

The EQS program also provides two other fit indices. These are the Bentler-Bonett nonnormed fit index (NNFI) and the comparative fit index (CFI) (Bentler, 1988, 1989). The NNFI takes into account the degrees of freedom of the model and can exceed the normed NFI in magnitude, even being outside the 0–1 range. It is essentially the same as the original Tucker-Lewis (1973) coefficient, extended to cover a wider range of models and fit functions. The CFI has the advantage, also obtained with the NNFI, of reflecting the degree of fit relatively well at all sample sizes, and avoids the underestimation of fit sometimes found in true models with the NFI. For a more extended discussion of this topic, consult Bentler (1988, 1989).

Mulaik, et al., (1989) contend that current goodness-of-fit indices can be misleading because they do not take into account the fact that higher values can be achieved by freeing up parameters to get a better fit. They propose a "parsimony ratio" adjustment to goodness-of-fit indices to correct for the loss of degrees of freedom in freeing up more parameters to obtain a better fit. They also point out that these indices are insensitive to misspecifications of causal relations among the latent variables under certain conditions and offer a method for testing the fit just for this part of the model.

In summary, the reader should again be forewarned that despite the indications of a "good fit," these goodness-of-fit statistics should not be used as the sole criteria by which to judge the quality of the CFA model specified. The goodness-of-fit refers only to the comparison between two correlation or two covariance matrices and does not support any conclusion about the significance of the actual relationship between the variables in the model specified. Dillon and Goldstein (1984) have pointed out that there is a negative relationship between the strength of relationship among the variables and the goodness-of-fit statistics. That is, the weaker the observed relationships between variables, the better the chances of obtaining a desirable goodness-of-fit statistic. In trying to reproduce the correlations or covariances as closely as possible, very low observed correlations or covariances will give rise to even lower residuals. Because the goodness-of-fit statistics evaluate the magnitude of the residuals, the chances of a good fit as indicated by the goodness-of-fit statistic are increased.

12.6.   A TWO-SAMPLE EXAMPLE

An important capability of CFA that is more difficult to realize in EFA is the possibility of testing an hypothesized factor structure in two separate samples simultaneously. Noller, Law, and Comrey (1988) replicated the factor analysis of 40 CPS FHIDs described in Chapter 11 using a representative sample of 669 Australian volunteers. The 12-variable sample problem used throughout this book represents a subset of the original data and so from the Australian data a comparable 12-variable sample problem can be extracted. The question to be answered is whether the hypothesized factor structure for these 12 variables fits the data for both samples simultaneously. A setup to test this hypothesis using EQS is as follows:

```
/TITLE
EQS ANALYSIS OF FACTOR ANALYSIS BOOK SAMPLE PROBLEM – GROUP 1
/SPECS
CAS = 727; VAR = 12; MA = COR; GROUPS = 2;
/LABELS
V1 = LAW ENF; V2 = ACC SOC; V3 = INTOLNC; V4 = NO INF F;
V5 = NO DEPR; V6 = NO AGIT; V7 = NO RESERV; V8 = NO SECL;
V9 = WORDY; V10 = SYMPATHY; V11 = HELPFUL; V12 = GENEROUS;
F1 = CONFORM; F2 = STABLE; F3 = EXTRAVRT; F4 = EMPATHY;
/EQU
V1 = 3*F1 + E1;
V2 = 3*F1 + E2;
V3 = 3*F1 + E3;
V4 = 3*F2 + E4;
V5 = 3*F2 + E5;
V6 = 3*F2 + E6;
V7 = 3*F3 + E7;
V8 = 3*F3 + E8;
V9 = 3*F3 + E9;
V10 = 3*F4 + E10;
V11 = 3*F4 + E11;
V12 = 3*F4 + E12;
/VAR
F1 TO F4 = 1.0;
E1 TO E12 = 10*;
```

/COV
F2,F1 = .1*; F3,F1 = .1*; F3,F2 = .6*;
F4,F1 = .1*; F4,F2 = .1*; F4,F3 = .4*;
/PRINT
CORRELATION = YES;
EFFECT = YES; /MAT
1.00
.61   1.00
.64   .50   1.00
.07   .02   .02   1.00
.14   .13   .04   .51   1.00
.07   .08 − .03   .46   .51   1.00
.04 − .05 − .01   .28   .29   .13   1.00
.08   .02   .08   .29   .31   .19   .46   1.00
.06 − .02   .01   .47   .41   .31   .66   .55   1.00
− .02 − .07 − .01   .10   .18   .05   .16   .31   .20   1.00
− .02 − .08 − .02   .14   .24   .18   .16   .39   .28   .60   1.00
− .17 − .15 − .04   .05   .09   .05   .12   .26   .17   .46   .61   1.00
/STANDARD DEVIATIONS
4.63   4.74   4.82   4.28   3.86   4.23   4.10   4.30   4.42   3.54   3.57   4.39
/END
/TITLE
EQS ANALYSIS OF FACTOR ANALYSIS BOOK SAMPLE PROBLEM – GROUP 2
/SPECS
 CAS = 669; VAR = 12; MA = COR;
/LABELS
 V1 = LAW ENF; V2 = ACC SOC; V3 = INTOLNC; V4 = NO INF F;
 V5 = NO DEPR; V6 = NO AGIT; V7 = NO RESERV; V8 = NO SECL;
 V9 = WORDY; V10 = SYMPATHY; V11 = HELPFUL; V12 = GENEROUS;
 F1 = CONFORM; F2 = STABLE; F3 = EXTRAVRT; F4 = EMPATHY;
/EQU
 V1 = 3*F1 + E1;
 V2 = 3*F1 + E2;
 V3 = 3*F1 + E3;
 V4 = 3*F2 + E4;
 V5 = 3*F2 + E5;
 V6 = 3*F2 + E6;
 V7 = 3*F3 + E7;
 V8 = 3*F3 + E8;
 V9 = 3*F3 + E9;
 V10 = 3*F4 + E10;
 V11 = 3*F4 + E11;
 V12 = 3*F4 + E12;
/VAR
 F1 TO F4 = 1.0;
 E1 TO E12 = 10*;
/COV
F2,F1 = .1*; F3,F1 = .1*; F3,F2 = .6*;
F4,F1 = .1*; F4,F2 = .1*; F4,F3 = .4*;

```
/PRINT
CORRELATION = YES;
EFFECT = YES;
/MAT
1.00
 .30   1.00
 .60    .31   1.00
 .06    .00    .03   1.00
 .05    .13   -.03    .43   1.00
 .05    .12   -.06    .40    .49   1.00
-.12   -.04   -.13    .20    .16    .09   1.00
-.04   -.03   -.04    .33    .22    .24    .57   1.00
-.05   -.01   -.06    .40    .30    .25    .66    .67   1.00
 .02    .03    .14    .04    .12    .05    .11    .16    .14   1.00
 .08    .06    .11    .14    .19    .10    .05    .27    .16    .52   1.00
 .04   -.08    .12   -.02    .08    .03    .07    .17    .12    .40    .49   1.00
/STANDARD DEVIATIONS
4.38   4.45   5.32   4.18   3.75   4.31   4.18   4.59   4.28   3.43   3.57   4.14
/CONSTRAINTS
(1,V1,F1)  = (2,V1,F1);
(1,V2,F1)  = (2,V2,F1);
(1,V3,F1)  = (2,V3,F1);
(1,V4,F2)  = (2,V4,F2);
(1,V5,F2)  = (2,V5,F2);
(1,V6,F2)  = (2,V6,F2);
(1,V7,F3)  = (2,V7,F3);
(1,V8,F3)  = (2,V8,F3);
(1,V9,F3)  = (2,V9,F3);
(1,V10,F4) = (2,V10,F4);
(1,V11,F4) = (2,V11,F4);
(1,V12,F4) = (2,V12,F4);
(1,F2,F1)  = (2,F2,F1);
(1,F3,F1)  = (2,F3,F1);
(1,F3,F2)  = (2,F3,F2);
(1,F4,F1)  = (2,F4,F1);
(1,F4,F2)  = (2,F4,F2);
(1,F4,F3)  = (2,F4,F3);
/LM TEST
/END
```

The setup for Group 1 is essentially the same as previously described for the EQS analysis of the 12-variable sample problem, except that this time standard deviations for the variables are entered. This will cause EQS to calculate and analyze the variance-covariance matrix instead of the correlation matrix, which was analyzed in the previous example. Also, in the specifications statement, the program is informed that the number of

groups to be analyzed is two, causing it to look for mo
/END card for the first data set.

The EQS control cards for the second data set, derived
Australian data, follow immediately. They are essentially the same a
the first 12-variable data set except for a couple of additions. The first of
these is the specification of constraints following the /CONSTRAINTS
control card. Twelve constraints are specified that force the group 1 and
group 2 factor loading estimates to be equal. Six additional constraints
force the correlations between factors to be equal in the two groups. It
should be noted that it is also possible to constrain correlations between
factors and other estimated parameters to be equal to each other within a
single analysis.

The /LM TEST row entry requests that the program calculate the effect
on the overall chi-square value of relaxing certain constraints. The LM
(Lagrange Multiplier) test can provide information about how much a
previously fixed parameter would change if it were left free to vary and how
much freeing the parameter would reduce the size of the overall chi-square
index of model fit. Use of univariate and multivariate LM tests, therefore,
can help the investigator make changes that will improve the model fit. Of
course, such successful model adjustments are shown to work only with the
data set at hand and they may not work out in a new sample. For this
reason, the adjusted model must be tested in a new sample before
concluding that the adjustments were warranted.

The overall chi-square value for this problem was 546.5 with 114 degrees
of freedom, which is highly significant. The samples are large, however, so
a look at the fit indices is called for. The Bentler-Bonett normed fit index
was 0.900, the Bentler-Bonett nonnormed fit index was 0.906, and the
comparative fit index was 0.919. These values give a more favorable
indication of fit in the two samples than the chi-square value. The LM
TEST information indicated that forcing the second variable loadings on
Factor I to be identical created the greatest increment in chi-square. Noller,
Law, and Comrey (1988) also found this variable to have a lower loading
(.48) on the Social Conformity versus Rebelliousness factor in the Australian data than had been the case in the U. S. normative sample (.67). The
solution matrix of standardized pattern coefficients for this two-sample
analysis by EQS is given in Table 12.4. Values in parentheses are the EQS
solution values for the 12-variable problem run as a single sample (see Table
12.1). Decimal points are omitted in Table 12.4. It will be noted that the
largest discrepancy is for variable 2, factor I.

The correlations between the factors in the two-sample solution, with
comparable values for the 12-variable single sample in parentheses, were as
follows: I vs. II, .107 (.134); I vs. III, −.011 (.051); I vs. IV, .008 (−.074);

or 12-Variable Problem

	Emotional Stability	Extraversion Introversion	Empathy vs. Egocentrism
	000	000	000
	000	000	000
	000	000	000
	676(708)	000	000
5. N.	723(755)	000	000
6. No A	630(639)	000	000
7. No Reserv.	000	713(711)	000
8. No Seclusiven.	000	699(621)	000
9. Wordiness	000	922(915)	000
10. Sympathy	000	000	655(669)
11. Helpfulness	000	000	833(900)
12. Generosity	000	000	643(678)

Note. Decimal points have been omitted. Values in parentheses are comparable loadings for the 12-variable problem run as a single sample, as shown in Table 12.1.

II vs. III, .549 (.601); II vs. IV, .248 (.270); and III vs. IV, .305 (.353). These values clearly did not differ in any major way in the two solutions.

12.7.   A SECOND-ORDER FACTOR ANALYSIS

In EFA, the usual way of carrying out a second-order factor analysis is to obtain an oblique solution in which the factors are correlated, yielding a Φ matrix that has non-zero values in the off-diagonal cells. This Φ matrix is then factor analyzed by the usual EFA methods. In CFA, it is possible to combine the first- and second-order analyses using a single model. In the CFA analysis of the 12-variable problem, the first factor correlated very little with the other factors while the other three factors showed substantial intercorrelations. Only factors two, three, and four, therefore, will be related to the second-order factor. An EQS setup to perform such an analysis is shown below:

```
/TITLE
EQS ANALYSIS OF FACTOR ANALYSIS BOOK SAMPLE PROBLEM
/SPECS
CAS = 727; VAR = 12; ME = ML; MA = COR; AN = COR;
/LABELS
V1 = LAW ENF; V2 = ACC SOC; V3 = INTOLNC; V4 = NO INF F;
V5 = NO DEPR; V6 = NO AGIT; V7 = NO RESERV; V8 = NO SECL;
V9 = WORDY; V10 = SYMPATHY; V11 = HELPFUL; V12 = GENEROUS;
F1 = CONFORM; F2 = STABLE; F3 = EXTRAVRT; F4 = EMPATHY;
/EQU
```

```
V1  = .7*F1 + E1;
V2  = .7*F1 + E2;
V3  = .7*F1 + E3;
V4  = 1F2 + E4;
V5  = .7*F2 + E5;
V6  = .7*F2 + E6;
V7  = 1F3 + E7;
V8  = .7*F3 + E8;
V9  = .7*F3 + E9;
V10 = 1F4 + E10;
V11 = .7*F4 + E11;
V12 = .7*F4 + E12;
F2  = .7*F5 + D2;
F3  = .7*F5 + D3;
F4  = .7*F5 + D4;
/VAR
F1 = 1.0; F5 = 1.0;
E1 TO E12 = .5*;
D2 TO D4 = .6*;
/PRINT
CORRELATION = YES;
EFFECT = YES;
/MAT
```

1.00											
.61	1.00										
.64	.50	1.00									
.07	.02	.02	1.00								
.14	.13	.04	.51	1.00							
.07	.08	−.03	.46	.51	1.00						
.04	−.05	−.01	.28	.29	.13	1.00					
.08	.02	.08	.29	.31	.19	.46	1.00				
.06	−.02	.01	.47	.41	.31	.66	.55	1.00			
−.02	−.07	−.01	.10	.18	.05	.16	.31	.20	1.00		
−.02	−.08	−.02	.14	.24	.18	.16	.39	.28	.60	1.00	
−.17	−.15	−.04	.05	.09	.05	.12	.26	.17	.46	.61	1.00

```
/END
```

Most of the lines in this setup are the same as in the previously explained EQS setup for the first-order CFA illustrated earlier in this chapter. Several important changes, however, should be noted. Whereas before there were 12 equations, one for each of the 12 variables in the analysis, in this set up there are 15, that is, three additional equations, one for each of the factors, 2, 3, and 4. The first factor has no equation because it is not hypothesized to be related to the second-order factor, factor 5, in this model. This is because the previous analysis showed factor 1 to be essentially uncorrelated with the other three factors.

The equations relating factors 2, 3, and 4 to factor 5 have error terms D2, D3, and D4, respectively, whereas the error terms for the measured variables are labeled E1 to E12. The EQS program labels measured and unmeasured variables and their error terms differently. Thus, measured variables are designated by "V" and unmeasured variables, that is, factors, are designated by "F".

The EQS program makes a further distinction between dependent and independent variables. Any variable appearing on the left side of one of the equations is designated as a dependent variable, regardless of whether it is a V or an F variable. In this situation, therefore, V1 to V12 and F2 to F4 are all dependent variables. F1 and F5, however, do not appear on the leftside of any equation so they are treated as independent variables. All the error terms, E1 to E12, and D2 to D4, are also considered to be independent variables. Estimates or fixed values for the variances of all independent variables must be specified, but not for the dependent variables. Hence, in the /VAR section of the setup, F1 and F5 are fixed at 1.0 and estimates are given for the E and D error variances. In addition, any unmeasured dependent variable, here F2, F3, and F4, must have its scale fixed in order to obtain a solution. This is done in this example by fixing a weight at 1.0 for one of the variables defining each of these factors, F2, F3, and F4. In the set up, notice that the weight next to these factors is 1 (with no *) for measured (V) variables 4, 7, and 10.

The EQS solution to the second-order model yielded **P** matrix values that were all within .01 of the values obtained for the first-order CFA solution (see Table 12.1). The first-order solution allowed these factors to be correlated whereas the second-order solution does not, only permitting factors 2, 3, and 4 to be related to the second-order factor, i.e., factor 5. The weights attached to factor 5 for factors 2, 3, and 4, were 0.680, 0.886, and 0.397, respectively.

The various fit indices for this second-order solution are given as follows with corresponding values for the first-order solution in parentheses: chi-square, 242 (230); normed fit index, 0.922 (.927); nonnormed fit index, 0.919 (.919); comparative fit index 0.937(.941). The level of fit in the second-order analysis is slightly lower than in the first-order analysis because one second-order factor does not quite account for all the variance in the matrix of correlations among the factors in the first-order analysis.

12.8.   OTHER CFA APPROACHES

Structural equation approaches to confirmatory factor analysis as implemented through LISREL and EQS are powerful new factor analytic procedures that often may represent the method of choice in a given situation. They are not the only approaches, however, that could be employed, and in many cases other methods may be preferred.

In the earlier chapters in this book, it was emphasized that exploratory factor analytic methods are most powerful when employed in a hypothesis-testing manner. That is, an hypothesis is developed about the factors to be found in a given domain and what variables measure them. Several variables are chosen for each hypothesized factor that should provide relatively pure-factor measures of that factor. Data are collected for a large sample and factor analyzed to see how well the obtained factors and the variables loaded on them correspond to the originally hypothesized factor structure. On the basis of the first analysis, revisions are made in the hypothesis and in the variables designed to measure each factor, and the study is repeated. This process is continued programmatically until the factor structure that emerges corresponds reasonably well to the factor structure hypothesized in advance.

This approach represents a type of confirmatory factor analysis in which the number of factors that emerges from the analysis is not restricted to a preconceived number. If the "correct" number happens to be what was hypothesized, fine, but it is not pre-specified, as in EQS or LISREL. Furthermore, the loadings are allowed to fall where they may rather than being forced to conform as much as possible to a pre-specified pattern. In particular, large numbers of parameters are not forced to zero. The proportion of variance attributed to unique factors for each variable emerges as an end result of the analysis rather than being a parameter to be estimated, per se. Thus, in EFA, one can evaluate how well the obtained solution fits a preconceived factor pattern but without using powerful optimization techniques to force a fit that may hold up poorly with new data. In many cases, it may be best to proceed with EFA through a series of programmatic studies, as described earlier, and when the factor structure seems well confirmed, apply CFA methods, such as EQS and LISREL, to make a more precise statistical test of the degree of fit. Parenthetically, it could be stated that if the number of variables is large, this may be the only feasible way to proceed. CFA methods become increasingly difficult to use as the number of variables and the number of factors increase.

Precursors to the CFA approach have been the Procrustean solutions in EFA, already referred to somewhat in earlier chapters (Cattell, 1944a; Cliff, 1966; Mosier, 1939; Schonemann & Carroll, 1970). This approach can take various forms. One can rotate a given unrotated matrix as closely as possible to a target matrix, either orthogonal or oblique. The target matrix could be an hypothesized matrix based on theory or upon expectations developed from previous research. Least squares methods are typically employed to find the transformation matrix that will accomplished the desired rotations. These methods probably will become less popular now that LISREL or EQS can perform the same kind of task in most cases and also provide a statistical test of goodness of fit along with indications on how to improve the model.

The use of LISREL and EQS for the purpose of CFA appears to be the trend for the future. CFA may become the preferred method of factor analysis as the structure in various behavioral science research areas become stronger and contain better hypothetical concepts supported by real data. However, as pointed out out by Cattell (1978):

> "One may well fear, after seeing certain liberties taken with Procrustes, that it (CFA) may suffer similar abuse, e.g., by testing the targeting of one experimental result to another before the first has been well enough substantiated by two independent experiments independently rotated to simple structure" (p. 401).

Gorsuch (1983) has pointed out that CFA has its roots in the Maxwell-Lawley Maximum Likelihood factor analysis method. In its present form, CFA is attributed by many to Joreskog and his associates (Joreskog, 1967, 1969, 1970; Joreskog & Goldberger, 1972) although Bock and Bargmann (1966) had suggested something similar at an earlier date.

The Bock and Bargman (1966) procedure requires the researcher to specify all of the parameters in the factor loading matrix, the matrix of correlations among the factors, and the unique variance matrix. Using these a priori specified matrices, an estimated correlation or covariance matrix is created. This matrix is then compared to the sample correlation or covariance matrix via a goodness-of-fit statistic such as the Bartlett test (see Morrison, 1967). This procedure is generally difficult to carry out unless the researcher knows what initial matrix values would be appropriate. Bernstein (1988) refers to this as the "weak constraint solution."

Joreskog (1969) recognized that only some, but not all, of the parameters could be estimated. Joreskog's development allows the researcher to specify some of the parameters and allow the others to be estimated from the data. These modifications made Joreskog's method an important improvement over previous procedures. As with EFA, however, proper use of such methods as LISREL and EQS requires the researcher to have a thorough knowledge of the area being studied and what represents a good hypothesis concerning the underlying factor structure. It is not a method that can be successfully applied to a large body of data with many variables where the investigator has no idea about what the underlying factor structure might be.

CFA should not be confused, however, with the power vector method of factor analysis developed by Overall and Porterfield (1963). The power vector method seeks a simple structure solution without the use of rotation but it is really exploratory (an EFA method) in that relationships between the components of the factor model are not specified in advance.

In developing the CFA model, the researcher must choose the parameters to be fixed and those that are to be estimated. Constraints can be imposed upon certain parameters, such as by specifying a range of values within which they must fall. Bock and Bargmann suggested fixing the loadings of the factor pattern matrix and then allowing the variances and covariances to be estimated from the data with the constraints posed by the fixed loadings of the pattern matrix. These estimated variances and covariances are then compared to the actual sample variances and covariances. LISREL and EQS, however, permit the testing of more general models than the one proposed by Bock and Bargmann.

In CFA, the researcher can specify in advance which factors are correlated and which are uncorrelated. This can also be done with exploratory factor analysis in oblique or Procrustean solutions. Bernstein (1988) is a strong supporter of the "oblique multiple groups (OMG) test of weak structure." Bernstein feels that the use of LISREL for many confirmatory factor analysis problems is a drastic "overkill" and that many problems can be and should be solved using OMG. OMG, however, is classified as an EFA method in that all observed variables are potentially affected by all common factors whereas in CFA the observed variables are affected by only some of the factors. Bernstein (1988) gives some examples showing the benefits OMG has over LISREL.

Whatever method researchers may find to be the most appropriate for their data, it is clear that factor analysis has undergone a major revolution in recent years. Powerful new methods are now available that dramatically expand research workers' capacity to examine the implications of their data. It must be emphasized, however, that these newer methods should be viewed as complementing rather than supplanting older EFA methods that may continue to be the most effective procedures for dealing with many data analysis situations. For the foreseeable future, therefore, students of factor analysis will need to become familiar with both EFA and CFA methods.

13

Structural Equation Models

The previous chapter provided an introduction to confirmatory factor analysis or CFA. Confirmatory factor analysis is only one of a number of multivariate statistical methods that fall under the broad category of structural equation models, which includes methods variously referred to as multiple regression, path analysis, causal modeling, latent structure analysis, and covariance structure analysis. As was the case with CFA, the computation required to estimate the parameters for these models is extensive. The work of setting up the models and carrying out the computations to estimate the model parameters for many of these methods, however, has been greatly simplified by the availability of the LISREL (Joreskog & Sorbom, 1988) and EQS (Bentler, 1989) computer programs. Although many authors have contributed to the development of various kinds of structural equation models and methods for estimating their parameters, the LISREL and EQS programs have become the currently most popular means of implementing this methodology. In this chapter, the reader is introduced to some of the theory and procedures for utilizing these programs. This chapter is designed to provide a general idea of what these programs can do rather than to serve as a self-contained operations manual. The reader interested in applying these methods should consult the LISREL and EQS program manuals for essential additional details as well as more advanced treatises on the topic (e.g., Hayduk, 1987).

In developing a structural equation model, it is helpful to construct a path diagram that provides a visual representation of the hypothesized linear relationships among the different variables involved in the model. This diagram serves as a roadmap that can help to guide the researcher through the steps required to use LISREL or EQS to set up the necessary linear equations, solve for the model parameters, and test to see how well the model fits the data. LISREL and EQS use somewhat different procedures and labeling conventions in constructing path diagrams, although an EQS path diagram can usually be converted readily into a LISREL path diagram. EQS path diagrams are more completely specified and easier to understand, so EQS diagramming procedures and labeling conventions are followed in this chapter. A comparison between earlier versions of EQS and LISREL may be found in Brown (1986). After mastering the EQS system, the reader will be able to learn the LISREL system without a great deal of additional effort. The rules for preparing EQS path diagrams are developed a bit at a time as we progress from simpler to more complicated models.

13.1. REGRESSION MODELS

The simplest type of linear structural model is the familiar regression model in which there is only one regression equation. One measured variable is predicted as a linear combination of several other measured variables, as, for example, in Eq. (13.1a) or Eq. (13.1b):

$$x_1' = B_2x_2 + B_3x_3 + B_4x_4 \tag{13.1a}$$

$$x_1 = B_2x_2 + B_3x_3 + B_4x_4 + e \tag{13.1b}$$

The scores in Eq. (13.1a) are in deviation-score form, that is, as deviations about their means. This removes the need for an intercept term in the linear equation while preserving differences in scale between the variables. If all predictor variables were normalized, that is, converted to zero means and unit standard deviations, then the B values in Eq. (13.1a) would become standardized beta weights. For most structural equation models, however, variables are not standardized, so that the data input includes the unscaled variances and covariances of all the measured variables. A correlation can be converted to a covariance term as follows: $s_{ij} = r_{ij}s_is_j$. In EQS, the correlation matrix can be input and the program will convert it to a variance-covariance matrix using the s_i values that are also input as part of the data. Means are not entered except for some of the more complicated models involving growth curves or multiple data samples.

The single equation regression model shown in Eq. (13.1b) can be represented by the path diagram in Fig. 13.1. Measured data variables are represented in boxes or rectangles and contain within them identifying numbers, for example, V1, V2, V3, and V4, or more, as required. Variable V1 in Fig. 13.1 corresponds to x_1 in Eq. (13.1b) and is the dependent variable that is being predicted as a linear combination of the independent

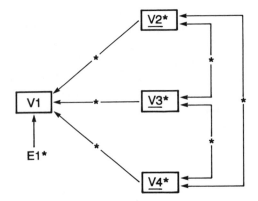

FIG. 13.1.   Regression Model.

variables V2, V3, and V4, represented in Eq. (13.1b) by x_2, x_3, and x_4, respectively. There is a one-way arrow from each of the independent variables V2, V3, and V4 pointing toward variable V1. Every variable that has a one-way arrow pointing to it generates one linear regression equation in the model. There is only one such variable here, V1, and hence only one equation.

There is an asterisk or star (*) imbedded in each of the arrows from V2, V3, and V4 to V1 indicating that there are free parameters to be estimated in connection with these paths, one for each star. There is also a one-way arrow pointing from E1 toward V1, indicating that the regression equation contains an error variable, E1, which is also an independent variable in the model. The error term is implicit in Eq. (13.1a) because x_1', the predicted x value, is on the left side of the equation, rather than the actual value of x. Eq. (13.1b) gives the error explicitly. The actual x value is on the left side of the equation and an error term, e, is introduced on the right side. The error term, e, makes up the difference between x' and x. Thus, the regression equation in the EQS system program setup for the regression model in Fig. 13.1 could be written as follows:

$$V1 = 2*V2 + 2*V3 + 2*V4 + E1; \qquad (13.2)$$

The 2* coefficients represent initial rough guesses about the values of the three regression coefficient parameters to be estimated by the program. The star (*) notifies the program that the preceding value is an estimate and not a fixed value. The star also identifies a free parameter in the model. Counting the number of stars in the EQS program setup enables the researcher to determine the total number of free parameters being estimated for the model. E1 is presumed to be uncorrelated with V2, V3, and V4, hence no two-way arrows appear between these variables in the path diagram.

Additional free parameters in the model include all the covariances among the independent measured variables, V2, V3, and V4. Free covariance parameters are indicated by two-way arrows with a star in the middle. The arrow lines may be straight or curved, depending upon diagramming needs for clarity. This adds three more free parameters. Estimates of these covariance parameters would be indicated in the /COVARIANCES section of the EQS program setup, for example, by: V2,V3 = 3*; V2,V4 = 2*; V3,V4 = −4*; or something similar.

Additional free model parameters include the variances of the independent measured variables, which are V2, V3, and V4. The fact that these variances are free parameters is indicated in the model by underlining V2, V3, and V4 in their boxes and placing stars (*) beside their symbols. Alternatively, instead of underlining the variable symbols, the boxes could be shaded to a darker color, as is done in the EQS manual when the variance is a model parameter for that variable. It is easy to lose sight of the fact that the variances of these independent variables are parameters in the model. The underlining (or shading in the EQS manual) makes it easier to remember that the EQS program setup must contain either estimates or fixed values for these variance parameters. That these variables have variances as free parameters in the model would be indicated in the /VARIANCES section of the EQS setup by something like the following: V2 = 6*; V3 = 8*; V4 = 5*; which adds three more free parameters (indicated by the *'s).

One more variance must be estimated in the model because the general rule is that all independent variables have variances as parameters in the model, which includes all the *error* variables as well as the independent *measured* variables. Dependent variables, however, do not have variances as parameters in the model. Thus, in the section for specifying variances, because E1 is an independent variable, one more term must be added to the EQS /VARIANCES setup, namely, E1 = 3*; with the number preceding the star (*) being an initial estimate. A star (*) is also placed beside E1 in the path diagram in Fig. 13.1 to show that its variance is a free parameter in the model. This now gives a total of 10 stars in the EQS setup, and in the path diagram, indicating that there are 10 free parameters to be estimated.

There is one additional parameter in the model that is fixed at 1.0, namely, the regression coefficient for E1. All independent unmeasured variables in the model must have their scale fixed in one of two ways: (a) set a regression coefficient at a fixed value, usually 1.0, which was done here for E1, or (b) fix its variance at some known value, usually 1.0. In most cases, the E values have their regression coefficients fixed at 1.0 and consequently in the path diagram no star (*) appears within the arrow pointing to the dependent variable with which that error variable is associated.

It is not possible to fix both the regression weight *and* the variance for an E variable because the product of these two numbers must be free to accomodate the amount of error in predicting the dependent variable correctly. Thus, one or the other is fixed but not both.

There are 10 free parameters to be estimated for the regression model in Fig. 13.1 from a total of 10 data points. The data points consist of the variances and covariances of the measured variables, V1, V2, V3, and V4, or $(n(n+1))/2$ where n is the number of variables. That is, there are 6 covariances and 4 variances. The number of degrees of freedom for estimating the model is given by the number of data points minus the number of free parameters in the system, which in this case is 10 − 10 or zero.

When there are no degrees of freedom, the model is said to be "saturated," that is, values can be obtained for the free parameters that will reproduce the input data exactly. Thus, there is no question about the model fitting the data and no chi-square test or other statistical test is needed to see how good the fit is because the fit is perfect. For this reason, regression models are not considered to be of much interest to structural equation modelers. In general, they wish to develop a model that has considerably more data points than free parameters to be estimated. In such cases, it is a challenge to find a model and a set of parameters that will reproduce the data reasonably well, that is, give a good fit. Only when the number of degrees of freedom for estimating the model is greater than zero can a good model fit convey any scientific information of theoretical significance.

In summary, the equations, variances, and covariances part of the EQS setup for the model in Fig. 13.1 might be as follows:

/EQUATIONS

V1 = 2*V2 + 2*V3 + 2*V4 + E1;

/VARIANCES

V2 = 6*; V3 = 8*; V4 = 5*; E1 = 3*;

/COVARIANCES

V2,V3 = 3*; V2,V4 = 2*; V3,V4 = −4*;

Other parts of the EQS setup would be similar to those shown in Chapter 12. Parameter estimates, of course, could be different. Variations in size and sign of parameter estimates should reflect the researcher's best guess as to what the final values will be. The EQS manual should be consulted for further details.

13.2.   MEASURED VARIABLE MODELS

The regression model described in the preceding section contained only one regression equation and had zero degrees of freedom. Most models of any scientific interest will contain more than one regression equation, that is, will have more than one dependent variable, and will have more data points than free parameters. Models that contain only measured variables are often referred to as "measured variable models." More complicated models also contain latent variables, such as the factor variables in the models described in Chapter 12.

Fig. 13.2 contains a path diagram for a measured variable model describing a set of hypothesized linear relationships among several demographic variables measured on a fictitious data sample of 25 year old males ($N = 600$) born and raised in American inner-city environments. The following scores are presumed to be available for each subject:

1. Number of years of schooling completed
2. I. Q. (scaled by dividing by 10)
3. Level of past drug use (rated on a scale of 1 to 7)
4. Level of past gang involvement (on a scale of 1 to 5)
5. Last adjusted gross income reported to IRS (scaled by dividing by 3000)

For the model in Fig. 13.2, IQ (V2) and gang involvement (V4) are not to be explained; they are independent variables that are correlated (a two-way arrow connects them). Schooling (V1) is expected to be positively affected by IQ (V2). Drug use (V3) is expected to be positively affected by gang involvement (V4). Finally, it is hypothesized that reported income (V5) is positively affected by schooling (V1) and negatively affected by drug use (V3). Measured *independent* variables in Fig. 13.2 (i.e., those without

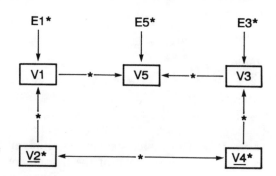

FIG. 13.2. Measured Variable Model.

arrows pointing to them) requiring variances and covariances as free parameters in the model are V2 and V4, which account for three free parameters, two variances, and one covariance. In Fig. 13.2, V2 and V4 are underlined and have stars (*) affixed to indicate that as independent variables they have variances as free parameters to be estimated. Given that V2 and V4 are measured variables, their actual sample variances and covariances are known from the data. The best estimates of these parameters, therefore, will turn out to be the sample data values, but this does not alter the fact that these are parameters to be estimated in the model.

Unmeasured independent variables requiring variances as free model parameters to be estimated in Fig. 13.2 are the error variables associated with the dependent variables, namely, E1, E3, and E5. As previously indicated, the stars (*) beside E1, E3, and E5, respectively, indicate that the variances of these error variables are free parameters and estimates for them must be contained in the variances section of the EQS program setup.

The measured dependent variables requiring regression equations, but no variances, are variables V1, V3, and V5. Each of these dependent variables has one or more unidirectional arrows pointing toward it in Fig. 13.2. Each one-way arrow requires a regression coefficient parameter in the model. The two-way arrow between V2 and V4, however, represents a covariance parameter and the star (*) indicates that it is a free parameter in the model to be estimated. This gives a total of ten free parameters to be estimated plus three regression parameters fixed at 1.0 for the error factor paths from E1 to V1, E3 to V3, and E5 to V5. These fixed parameters are set at 1.0 to fix the scale for these unmeasured independent variables. Because they are fixed, they are not included in the count of free parameters that must be estimated. The number of data points is given by $(5(5+1))/2 = 15$ so the number of degrees of freedom in the model is $15 - 10 = 5$. The part of the EQS setup that gives the initial estimates of the regression equation, variance, and covariance parameters is as follows:

/EQUATIONS

V1 = 2*V2 + E1;
V3 = 2*V4 + E3;
V5 = 2*V1 − 2*V3 + E5;

/VARIANCES

V2 = 3*; V4 = 2*; E1 = 4*; E3 = 2*; E5 = 5*;

/COVARIANCES

V2,V4 = −2*;

Notice that there are ten stars in this setup, and in the path diagram shown in Fig. 13.2, one for each of the free parameters to be estimated. If the initial estimates are poor, the program may have difficulty converging to an optimal set of values. Improving the initial estimates will often solve this problem.

Proceeding from the initial estimates and model characteristics as outlined in the EQS setup given above, EQS will operate on the input data, that is, the matrix of variances and covariances of the measured variables, to generate optimum parameter values. These optimum parameter values, in turn, are used by the program to generate a reproduced variance-covariance matrix that is then compared to the original data matrix to see how well the two agree. A chi-square test is generally used for this purpose, although both LISREL and EQS manuals provide other indications of the quality of fit of the model to the data. Some of these other indicators of fit were described briefly in Chapter 12. Where the model does not appear to reproduce the original data well, both EQS and LISREL provide clues to suggest possible changes in the model that could be tried out in an attempt to improve the degree of fit. Needless to say, there is danger in this model-modification process of capitalizing on chance, so results should be interpreted with caution, especially in small samples.

13.3. FACTOR ANALYTIC MODELS

Chapter 12 described two structural equation models that are generally referred to as factor analytic models, a first-order confirmatory factor analysis model (CFA), and a second-order factor analysis model. In both cases, the models were applied to the 12-variable problem data used throughout the book to illustrate various factor analytic methods. Both these models were discussed in some detail in Chapter 12 so their treatment here is confined to a brief analysis of their path diagrams and how these models fit into the broader context of structural equation modeling.

The path diagram for the 12-variable CFA problem described in Chapter 12 is shown in Fig. 13.3. Variables V1 to V12 are the measured personality variables. This model goes beyond the measured-variable model described in Section 13.2 by introducing unmeasured latent variables, or factors, namely, the variables F1, F2, F3, and F4. Notice that the latent variables are given different letter series designations, F's instead of V's, and they are enclosed in circles (or sometimes in ellipses) rather than in the rectangles or squares that enclose the measured variables. These F variables are classified as latent, unobservable variables. To save space, in this illustrative example, there are only three defining variables for each latent variable. In actual practice, however, at least four to five indicators should be used for each latent variable.

The variances of the hypothetical factor (F) variables in Fig. 13.3 are fixed at 1.0 in the EQS setup, as shown in Chapter 12, thereby determining

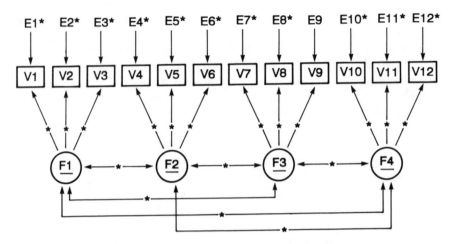

FIG. 13.3.   Path Diagram for 12-variable Problem.

their scale. The symbols for these F variables have been underlined, however, to show that the variances of these unmeasured independent variables are parameters of the model. Because the variances of these latent variables have been fixed at 1.0, however, they are not *free* parameters and hence no stars (*) have been affixed to their symbols in the path diagram. In the EQS system manual, these F-variable circles would be shaded (also with no stars) instead of underlining the symbols as was done here. Underlining is easier to produce in ordinary document preparation than shading. The convention used to indicate that the variable has a variance as a parameter, whether shading, underlining, or some other method, is arbitrary.the paths from the latent variables, or factors, to the measured variables (V's) they are presumed to affect, provide 12 free parameters to be estimated. These free parameters are regression coefficients in the equations relating the 12 measured (V) variables to the 4 factor (F) variables. In factor analysis literature, these F to V paths are known as factor loadings or factor pattern coefficients, as was noted in Chapter 12. Since the measured variables have not been standardized here, however, these regression coefficients are not the typical standardized coefficients ordinarily found in factor analysis. Each V variable has a one-way arrow pointing toward it, hence each V variable requires a separate regression equation in the EQS setup.

Each regression equation also has an error variable term with a unit weight and each such unmeasured error variable requires a free parameter for its variance, indicated in Fig. 13.3 by the stars (*) placed beside each E variable symbol. The error variables all have one-way arrows pointing toward the variables with which they are associated. Thus, for the factor model in Fig. 13.3, there are 12 regression coefficient free parameters and

12 error variable variance free parameters. The remaining free parameters of the model are the 6 covariances represented in Fig. 13.3 by two-way arrows connecting the circled latent-factor variables. Because the variances of these latent variables have been set equal to one, the resultant estimated covariances can be interpreted as correlations. Fig. 13.3 has 30 stars (*), indicating a total of 30 free parameters to be estimated. The number of data points in the model is (12)(13)/2, or 78, so the number of degrees of freedom for testing the model fit to the data is 78–30 = 48.

As with other models, if the initial estimates of the free parameters input to the EQS setup are poor, the program may take longer to obtain a solution, or it may not be able to find a solution at all. In this case, it is necessary to rerun the program with improved estimates of the parameters.

In Fig. 13.3 there are no two-way paths between error (E) variables, indicating that these covariances are set at zero. It is possible, however, to introduce paths with two-way arrows between error variables, introducing covariance parameters between error terms that are believed not to be independent. This is an important model-fitting capability in CFA that is not available in EFA where all the error variable covariances are presumed to be zero.

It should be noted, too, that each measured (V) variable in Fig. 13.3 has a path from only one factor. There is nothing, however, to prevent making a given V variable dependent on more than one F variable, thereby making it factorially complex. In some situations, such complexity may be necessary if the model is to fit the data. On the other hand, the addition of each new free parameter reduces the number of degrees of freedom available for testing the model. Care should be taken not to introduce more free parameters than necessary because it is desirable to retain as many degrees of freedom as possible. EQS offers the capability of fixing some parameters at the same value, where this seems appropriate, thereby saving degrees of freedom. In some cases, such restrictions upon parameter values may be required to even permit a test of the model.

13.4. UNRESTRICTED LATENT-VARIABLE MODELS

Although the first-order factor model described in the previous section involved both measured and latent variables, such models do not have one-way arrows going from one latent variable to another. When this restriction is removed, the range and complexity of structural equation models that can be tested expands enormously.

Fig. 13.4 shows a path diagram for the second-order factor analysis described in Chapter 12. This diagram differs from that in Fig. 13.3, which describes the first-order factor analysis model, in several ways, although

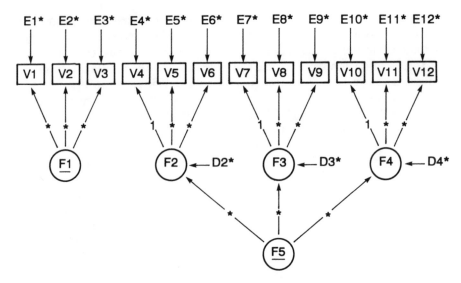

FIG. 13.4.   Path Diagram for Second Order Factor Analysis.

both models are fit to the same data. There is an additional latent variable in Fig. 13.4, F5, which is the second-order factor. Factors F2, F3, and F4 now have one-way arrows pointing toward them indicating that they are dependent variables. They are functions of the second-order factor, F5, where F1 is not shown to be affected by F5 and hence has no one-way arrow pointing toward it from F5. In this more general model, therefore, direct paths are permitted between latent variables.

Since F2, F3, and F4 are now dependent variables, they do not have variances as parameters of the model and, since they are unmeasured variables, each of them must have a path with a regression coefficient fixed (usually at 1.0) to determine their scale. The other way of fixing scale is not available since dependent variables do not have variances as parameters in structural equation models. Thus, V4, V7, and V10 now show fixed regression coefficients of 1, instead of stars indicating free parameters, in their paths from Factors F2, F3, and F4, respectively. The choice of which path to fix at 1.0 for each factor is arbitrary, so V5, V8, and V11 might have been chosen instead of V4, V7, and V10. Fixing of just one path is sufficient to determine the scale for any unmeasured variable, and fixing more than one would be unnecessarily restrictive.

The independent factor variables F1 and F5 (no one-way arrows pointing toward them), however, can have their variances set at 1.0 which fixes their scale, thereby leaving all the regression coefficients for the paths emanating from them free to vary. That is, none of these paths has to be fixed at 1.0 because the scales for F1 and F5 have already been fixed by setting their variances at 1.0. The symbols for F1 and F5 are underlined, indicating that these unmeasured variables have variances as model parameters. There are no stars (*) beside F1 and F5, however, because their variances have been fixed at 1.0 and therefore are not *free* parameters to be estimated.

Note that the covariances between factors in Fig. 13.3 are missing in Fig. 13.4 because dependent variables do not have covariances. F1 and F5 are not dependent variables, so they could have a covariance but the absence of a path between F1 and F5 indicates that these variables are independent of each other in the model.

Since F2, F3, and F4 are now dependent variables in Fig. 13.4, and hence cannot be presumed to be predicted perfectly from F5, the second-order factor, they must have error variables, called "Disturbances." There error variables are labeled D2, D3, and D4, respectively. As with the E variables, the scale of the D variables is fixed by setting their regression coefficents to 1.0 and their variances become model parameters to be estimated. Both E and D variables function similarly and have one-way paths to their associated measured and latent variables, respectively, but they are given different letter designations to distinguish what kinds of error variables they represent.

There are 27 stars (*) in Fig. 13.4, 12 for E variable variance estimates, 3 for D variable variance estimates, and 12 for regression coefficient estimates. With $12(13)/2 = 78$ data points in the variance-covariance matrix input, this leaves 78–27 or 51 degrees of freedom for testing the model.

13.5.   STRUCTURAL EQUATION MODELS AS "CAUSAL" MODELS

The measured-variable model in Fig. 13.2 might be interpreted as a "causal" model in that the one-way paths could be considered to indicate actual causal effects, as opposed to mere correlational phenomena. Thus, if the model fit the data adequately as specified, the regression coefficient indicated by the star between V2 and V1 could be taken as indicative of the extent to which years of schooling completed in this group was determined by IQ. Correspondingly, the V4 to V3 regression coefficient in the model could be interpreted as indicating the extent to which involvement with gangs leads to drug use. Finally, the regression coefficients from V1 and V3 to V5 could be taken as indicative of the extent to which reported income is determined by years of schooling and past drug use, respectively. The relative effect of schooling and past drug use could be evaluated by comparing the sizes of the two regression coefficients for these variables in predicting income values. EQS provides estimates of the standard errors of regression coefficients. Thus, the "statistical significance" of a regression coefficient can be tested.

Structural equation models are often referred to as "causal" models precisely because the researchers are interested in making causal inferences of this kind. The very essence of scientific inquiry, after all, is to find out what causes what and to what extent. The original development of path analysis for purposes of making causal inferences is generally credited to the geneticist Sewell Wright (1921, 1923). Wright distinguished between direct and indirect effects using correlations and regressions and found a way to use tracing rules in path diagrams to perform the types of matrix manipulations that current structural modeling programs perform algebraically. In Fig. 13.4, for example, all one-way arrows represent direct effects. Variable F5's influence on the measured variables, however, is indirect. That is, F5 affects V4 only via F2. EQS computes such indirect effects and also tests their significance. Wright's work was also popularized in sociology by such writers as Duncan (1966) and Blalock (1971, 1972). These methods became popular in psychology and education during the 1970s and 1980s. An historical overview is provided by Bentler (1986).

Attempts to make causal inferences as a result of structural-equation analysis has been greeted with a good deal of skepticism by some segments of the scientific community. After all, generations of psychologists have been warned often and well that correlation does not necessarily indicate causation. Textbooks are replete with examples of instances where naive misinterpretations of research results have been made precisely because of this kind of logical error (see Comrey, Bott, & Lee, 1989). Hence, when the input for structural equation modeling consists of variances and covariances (or correlations), the skeptics want to know how *causal* inferences can be made from such data.

The answer, of course, is that causal inferences cannot be made with any certainty. The best that can be said is that the data are consistent with the proposed causal inferences, provided the model fits adequately. Thus an adequate model fit would be consistent with a causal hypothesis, while a model that does not fit the data is certainly evidence against the causal hypothesis. Cliff (1983, 1987) cautions about the dangers of making causal inferences from correlational data. Freedman (1987) indicates that the validity of causal inferences from structural equation analysis depends upon numerous assumptions that are difficult to check and that may be false in any particular application. While it is generally true that in scientific research one may never be able to check *all* assumptions in any given study, nevertheless it would be desirable to check specific modeling assumptions. While some of these (e.g., multivariate normality of variables) can be evaluated using diagnostics such as those provided in EQS, others (e.g., linearity) are not yet easy to evaluate. Mulaik (1987) provides a good discussion of assumptions that are needed in using modeling for purposes of causal inference. Perhaps the most important point to remember is the fact that if a given model fits the data this does not preclude the possibility that some other very different model could also fit the data just as well or better.

Blalock (1972) mentions that path analysis appears to be useful in those situations where practically all of the variation in a given dependent variable can be associated with other variables *explicitly* included in the model. This kind of situation would require a very high multiple correlation between the dependent and independent variables, which is hard to achieve in practice. Blalock also indicates that these methods are most helpful when applied to data for which the underlying theory is well developed. It is apparent, however, that a path diagram could hardly be drawn when hypotheses about influences among the variables cannot be formulated. Dillon and Goldstein (1985) also point out that statistical methodology alone cannot prove cause and effect.

Despite these concerns, however, structural modeling does provide a mechanism for testing whether a particular causal hypothesis is consistent with the data. Ordinary correlational methods and simple regression analysis do not provide this kind of capability. Many researchers who have refrained from implying causality have still found structural modeling techniques to be very useful in defining research problems and building theory. Although "causal" modeling cannot furnish uncontestable experimental evidence that A causes B to such and such a degree, this should not obscure the fact that it does provide a set of investigative techniques that can be very helpful in the attempt to learn something about fundamental underlying causal effects. It is incumbent upon the investigator, however, to exercise considerable caution in making causal interpretations based upon results of statistical analyses of structural equation models.

13.5.1. AN UNRESTRICTED "CAUSAL" MODEL

A more complex unrestricted latent-variable model with causal implications is shown in Fig. 13.5. This model presents an expanded version of the hypothetical model described in Section 13.2, introducing latent variables as well as additional measured variables. The measured variables represented in Fig. 13.5 are as follows:

V1. Number of years of schooling completed
V2. I.Q. (scaled by dividing by 10)
V3. Number of A's earned in High School
V4. Stanine score on a Wide-Range Achievement Test
V5. Level of past drug use (rated on a scale of 1 to 7)
V6. Level of past gang involvement (on a scale of 1 to 5)

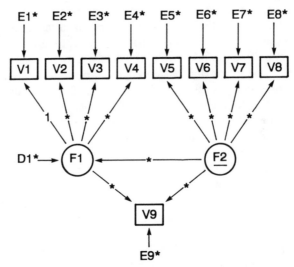

FIG. 13.5.   Path Diagram for Unrestricted Model.

V7. Past level of church attendance (on a scale of 1 to 5)

V8. Social Conformity vs Rebelliousness (C) score on the Comrey Personality Scales (scaled by dividing by 10)

V9. Last adjusted gross income reported to IRS (scaled by dividing total by 3000)

The measured V variables, enclosed in squares, are all observable and dependent variables indicated by one-way arrows pointing toward them. Each V variable also has an E variable with a one-way arrow pointing toward it and each E variable has a star (*) affixed indicating that its variance is a free parameter to be estimated.

There are two latent, unmeasured variables, F1 and F2, that are enclosed in circles. F1 represents Educational Level and F2 represents Conformity. As in factor analysis, the directional interpretation of the factor depends on the sign of the factor loadings and how the variables are scored. Some factor loadings may be negative. Because F1 is positively associated with V1 (loading 1.0), higher scores on F1 indicate higher scores on V1 and hence F1 can be interpreted as reflecting degree of education. However, if V5 and V6 have larger numbers representing less conformity, and if their factor loadings were positive, F2 would be more appropriately labeled as "Nonconformity." F2 is underlined, indicating that its variance is a parameter in the model. There is no star (*) beside F2, however, so its variance is not a free parameter. The scale of this variable is fixed by fixing its variance at 1.0 in the /VARIANCE section of the EQS setup.

Latent variable F1 is not underlined, that is, its variance is not a parameter in the model, because it is a dependent variable, as shown by the one-way arrow pointing toward it from F2. Dependent variables do not have variances as parameters. Since F1 is a dependent latent variable, it must have an error variable associated with it, shown as D1 in the path diagram. The regression coefficient for D1 is fixed at 1.0, as usual, and the variance is free to be estimated, as shown by the star (*) next to D1.

There are three stars (*) in the paths from F1 to variables V2, V3, and V4 while the path toward V1 has its coefficient fixed at 1.0. This is because the scale of F1 cannot be fixed by fixing its variance, because dependent variables do not have variances as parameters, so the scale must be fixed by fixing one of the paths from F1 to a dependent variable. It could have been toward V2, V3, or V4 as well, but of course only one of these paths need be fixed to determine the scale of the unmeasured latent variable F1.

Note that all the paths from F2 to V variables have stars (*), indicating that none is fixed at 1.0, as was done with F1. This is because F2 is not a dependent variable and its scale could be fixed by fixing its variance at 1.0, thereby leaving its regression parameters free to vary. The model in Fig. 13.5 is more general than a CFA model in that it has a one-way path from one latent variable to another. This was not permitted in the factor analytic model, which would require a two-way arrow between F1 and F2 (i.e., a covariance term). The model in Fig. 13.5 permits a possible interpretation that factor 1 is directly affected in a causal sense by factor 2 whereas in the factor analytic model, these factors could only be considered as being correlated with each other rather than causally related.

Variable V9, income, is the main variable of interest. It is a dependent variable that has paths from F1, Educational Level, and F2, Conformity, as well as a path from its associated error variable, E9. These regression coefficients can provide an indication of the relative importance of Level of Education and Conformity to Reported Income. Educational Level is itself hypothesized to be influenced by Conformity, so the model should reveal if there is any additional impact of Conformity on Income over and above its effect on Level of Education. The extent of its effect on Level of Education would be shown by the regression coefficient for the path from F2 to F1.

If the effect of Conformity on Reported Income were zero (no path from F2 to V9), then the effect of Conformity on Reported Income would be entirely mediated by Level of Education. The possibility of evaluating such mediational models is one of the main advantages of structural modeling over other methods of analysis. Another key feature is that errors of measurement have been removed from the predictor variables, here F1 and F2, so that the reliability of the V variables is not a factor in the regression. This can be seen diagrammatically in that added error variance in a V variable would be reflected by an increased variance in the associated E variable.

A possible setup of the /EQUATIONS, and /VARIANCES sections for the EQS program for the model in Fig. 13.5 would be as follows:

/EQUATIONS

```
V1 = 1F1 + E1;
V2 = 2*F1 + E2;
V3 = 2*F1 + E3;
V4 = 2*F1 + E4;
V5 = 2*F2 + E5;
V6 = 2*F2 + E6;
V7 = 2*F2 + E7;
V8 = 2*F2 + E8;
V9 = 2*F1 + 2*F2 + E9;
F1 = 2*F2 + D1;
```

/VARIANCES

```
E1 TO E9 = 3*; D1 = 4*; F2 = 1.0;
```

There is no /COVARIANCES section because Fig. 13.5 does not contain any covariances as parameters to be estimated. This is evident because of the absence of two-way arrows in Fig. 13.5.

At the risk of being too repetitive, the reader is reminded that the validity of possible causal inferences made on the basis of structural analysis of the model shown in Fig. 13.5 is conditional upon having all relevant variables represented in the model, the correctness of the assumptions upon which the statistical theory is based, as well as upon the extent to which the model conforms to the data.

13.6.   ADVANCED MODELS

The kinds of structural equation models described in previous sections of this chapter cover the most common applications of LISREL and EQS, but they do not by any means exhaust the possibilities. There are "nonstandard" models, for example, that permit one-way paths from error (E) variables to variables other than their own associated measured (V) variables. Other nonstandard latent variable models include paths from one V variable to another, a practice that is not normally permitted in the current LISREL system. Other advanced models utilize data from multiple samples with or without information about means. These various kinds of advanced models are considered briefly in the next section.

13.6.1.   UNUSUAL ERROR VARIABLE PATHS

Normally, each measured variable (V) has an associated error variable (E), which has a one-way arrow pointing toward it from E to V. Usually, this regression coefficient is set at 1.0 to fix the scale of the error variable and the variance of the E variable is allowed to vary, thereby allowing it to become a free parameter of the model to be estimated. Factor analytic CFA models do permit these E variables to have covariances, that is, to have two-way arrows connecting them, which is a capability CFA enjoys that EFA does not. These covariances are set at zero in EFA. Correlated errors, that is, covariances between E variables, are commonly postulated, for example, when two variables are included in the analysis each of which represent the same variables measured at two different points in time.

Present standard LISREL models do not permit paths to emanate from E variables to V variables with different numbers or to any F variables. EQS, however, permits the analysis of models to include such nonstandard paths for E variables. This is sometimes useful because there can be possible specific causal effects associated with these error variables that are not captured by a model without such paths. Of course, this feature makes clear that "error" variables are not just random noise or pure error, but also represent specific reliable variance like specific (as opposed to common) factors in EFA (see Chapter 2). In fact, these error variables in latent variable models are often referred to as "unique" variables rather than as "error" variables.

In Fig. 13.5, for example, measured variable V5 has an error variable (E5) with a unit-weight path to V5, as is customary. Variable V5 is predicted by factor F2, identified in this model as Conformity. Variable V9, Reported Income, in turn, is affected directly by Conformity (F2). A somewhat different, nonstandard, model might include an additional direct path (one-way arrow) from E5 to V9. As it is now in Fig. 13.5, this path is absent and hence its regression coefficient is presumed to be zero.

A non-zero, negative estimated direct path coefficient from E5 to V9 would suggest that the part of Drug Use not explained by the general Conformity construct has a specific negative impact on Reported Income over and above the impact of nonconformity, per se. For example, drug-using dealers might not want to report their income to the IRS. The standard design, without the E5 to V9 link, would show the effect of Drug Use on Reported Income only to the extent that it is part of the latent variable, Conformity (F2). Where clear-cut rationales can be formulated for postulating specific causal effects, such as that outlined above, the use of direct paths from error variables to other variables can result in models that mirror reality more accurately than standard models. Fortunately, EQS has the flexibility to permit the testing of such nonstandard models. It should be noted that direct paths from error variables to *latent* variables (F's), indicating specific effects on latent constructs, can also be postulated and tested, if appropriate to one's substantive theory.

13.6.2. UNUSUAL PATHS FOR MEASURED VARIABLES

In standard latent-variable models, direct one-way paths ordinarily occur from latent F variables toward measured V variables. Thus, measured variables are explained as functions of the latent variable constructs. Direct paths are not permitted in these standard models from one V variable to another.

There are instances, however, in which a logical analysis of the possible causal effects in a dynamic system calls for a direct one-way path from one measured variable to another, in addition to the usual direct paths from the F variables to the V variables.

In Fig. 13.5, for example, suppose that a direct, one-way path were added between V5, Drug Use, and V9, Reported Income. In the previous section, a path from E5 to V9 was discussed and described as a possible specific causal effect. If the postulated path from V5 to V9 generates a substantial, or definitely non-zero regression coefficient, it would suggest that the part of Drug Use predicted by the general latent variable Conformity (F2) has an additional, albeit indirect, effect on V9, Reported Income, over and above that due to the general Conformity construct of which it is a part. Thus the total effect of F2 on V9 is the direct effect of F2 on V9 plus the indirect effect mediated by V5.

There is a subtle but distinct difference in the causal effect implications of the E5 to V9 and V5 to V9 paths. The former says there is an impact of Drug Use on Reported Income over and above any effect concerned with general Conformity. For example, the heavy user might have incurred some brain damage that would have a deleterious effect on performance, and hence on income, which has nothing to do with Conformity, per se.

A significant path from V5 to V9, on the other hand, although a specific effect of Drug Use on Reported Income, would nevertheless be an effect of the part of that variable that is associated with Conformity (F2) and predicted from it. Thus, Drug Use helps to define Conformity and Conformity affects Reported Income but the part of Drug Use predicted by Conformity plays a bigger role in affecting Reported Income than can be accounted for merely by its level of overlap with the general trait of Conformity.

The unusual paths from E and V variables discussed earlier with reference to Fig. 13.5 have been directed at the measured variable, V9, Reported

Income. Such paths can also be directed at latent (F) variables as well. Covariances can also be introduced between independent V and F variables in EQS. Another non-standard practice. In such cases, two-way arrows would connect the variables, rather than one-way arrows, suggesting mutual covariation but with no directional or possible causal effects implied.

A very careful analysis is usually necessary to determine if such non-standard paths are called for, and if so, from which E or V variables to which other V or F variables. It is also necessary to determine if these paths should utilize one-way arrows (putative causal effects) or merely two-way arrows (non-causal effects). With presently available software, it is easier to set up and test such nonstandard models with EQS than with LISREL.

13.6.3.   MULTIPLE SAMPLE MODELS

In Chapter 12, an example was presented in which the same CFA factor analytic model was tested in two samples simultaneously using EQS. This procedure was represented as a powerful way of determining if an earlier set of factor analytic results could be confirmed at a later date, sampling from the same population, or if the same factor analytic model would fit samples of data from two different populations.

Although sample correlation matrices were input as data for the multiple sample problem in Chapter 12, such analyses operate on covariance matrices. EQS uses the standard deviations of the variables, also input as data, to convert correlations to covariances prior to estimating the parameters. Upon completion of the analyses, standardized versions of the parameters are computed which can be interpreted as factor loadings and correlations between factors in the same way as in exploratory factor analysis (EFA).

In the two-sample factor analysis model tested in Chapter 12, all the factor loadings and factor covariances were constrained to be equal. No error variance terms, however, were constrained to be equal across samples. Such constraints on error variances could have been added at the cost of making it more difficult to obtain a model fit. If a good fit were obtained without such constraints, however, reanalyses could be carried out to see how many of the error variances could be constrained to be equal without getting a significant chi-square, an outcome that would imply rejection of the model.

In the two-sample factor analytic model tested in Chapter 12, the data were obtained from two rather different populations, one in the U.S.A., with a large proportion of university students, and the other from Australia, with a more balanced distribution of subjects across different socioeconomic and educational levels. Given two such diverse sources of data, it would be remarkable if the same model fit both samples. Even if the correlation matrices were very similar in the two samples, differences in standard deviations of the variables between the American and Australian samples would probably cause a lack of model fit. Multiple-sample tests make more sense in the case where the samples could reasonably be assumed to come from the same or from similar populations. Where the populations from which the samples were drawn are clearly different, it is usually more appropriate to fit different models to the various samples individually rather than to attempt to make the same model work for all samples.

Multiple sample model tests are not confined, of course, to two samples, nor to factor analytic models, as was the case of the example in Chapter 12. Any of the various kinds of models described earlier in this chapter can be adapted for testing in two or more samples simultaneously if it appears appropriate to do so.

Cross-sample parameter constraints can be imposed in a variety of ways that go well beyond what was done in the Chapter 12 factor analysis two-sample model. For example, some of the factor loadings could have been constrained to be equal while others could have remained free to vary in the two groups. Similarly, some or all of the factor covariances could have been allowed to vary from one group to the other. Of course, where parameters are permitted to vary in the various samples, the models are not identical across samples, merely the same in certain respects.

If all parameters were constrained to be equal, which is the most restrictive case, all reproduced covariance matrices generated for the various samples would be identical and they would be generated from identical models, that is, all regression coefficients, all factor variances and covariances, and all error variances and covariances would be constrained to be equal.

The probability that a fit could be obtained for such a restrictive model over several good-sized samples would be very low in practice. There are almost always differences between samples of sufficient magnitude to generate a significant chi-square in such cases. Some of these differences, however, may not be that important, so relaxing certain constraints on some parameters (particularly error variances) will often make it possible to obtain a reasonable fit. In such cases, the models that fit the various samples are not shown to be identical but may, nevertheless, appear to be essentially equivalent for all practical purposes.

13.6.4. MEAN AND COVARIANCE STRUCTURES

All the models considered so far have operated on data that excluded information about means of the variables. That is, calculations based on deviation scores about the means for the various variables are unaffected by differences that exist between means of the variables. All variables are treated as though they had zero means, which is the case with deviation scores. In such models, only the variances and covariances are reproduced as a function of the model parameters, not the means. There are structural equation models, however, that make use of information about the means of the variables. In such models, data input include means of the measured variables as well as their variances and covariances. When the various parameters of these models have been estimated, they are used to generate means as well as variances and covariances. These generated values are then compared with the sample values to see how well the model fits. Such models, called "mean and covariance structures," are considered briefly in this section.

It only makes sense to apply mean and covariance structures to those situations where there is some compelling reason to consider data about means as significant in the situation. For most research analyses, the scaling of the variables is of minor significance, and the variables can be transformed to different means without affecting the analysis. This is actually done with most models where deviation scores, with means equal to zero, are employed.

There are other situations, however, where the information about means is significant and represents something worth explaining in the model. An example of such a case is illustrated by the path diagram in Fig. 13.6, which uses the following measured variables:

1. Picture Absurdities scores for subjects at age 7
2. Comprehension scores for subjects at age 7
3. Digit Span scores for subjects at age 7
4. Vocabulary scores for subjects at age 7
5. Picture Absurdities scores for subjects at age 9
6. Comprehension scores for subjects at age 9
7. Digit Span scores for subjects at age 9
8. Vocabulary scores for subjects at age 9

All tests are subtests of a general intelligence test. The four subtests, however, were administered twice to the same subjects, two years apart. Other possible aspects of this model, such as correlated errors, are ignored here for the sake of simplicity in exposition. One latent variable or factor (F1) is hypothesized to "explain" the commonality among the various intelligence subtests on the first occasion. This factor would be General Intelligence. A second latent factor (F2) is presumed to "explain" the commonality among the various intelligence subtests on the second occasion. Intelligence factor F1 directly affects intelligence factor F2, as shown

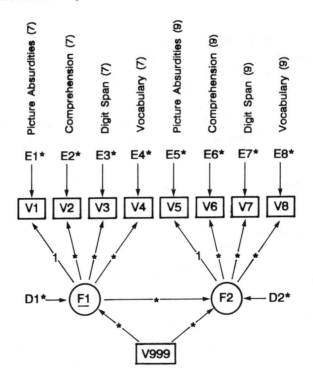

FIG. 13.6.   Mean and Covariance Structure.

by the one-way arrow from F1 to F2 in Fig. 13.6. This represents the stability of intelligence across the two-year time span.

In the normal factor analytic model, means of the variables would not be input and the path diagram would show no direct paths pointing to F1 or to F2. Also, the variances for F1 and F2 would be fixed at 1.0 and the paths to V1 and V5 would contain stars (*), indicating free parameters to be estimated. In this diagram, F1 and F2 are dependent variables, showing direct paths from the "variable" V999 with imbedded stars (*) indicating free parameters to be estimated. Because F1 and F2 are now designated as dependent variables (with direct paths pointing toward them), they must have disturbance variables, D1 and D2, which also have variances as free parameters to be estimated in the model. Because F1 and F2 are now dependent variables, they do not have variances in the model, so their scales must be fixed in some other way besides setting their variances equal to 1.0. This is done in Fig. 13.6 by fixing the path coefficients to V1 and V5 at 1.0.

A new type of independent, measured variable appears in Fig. 13.6, and in all mean and covariance structure path diagrams, which is designated as V999. It is a "constant" variable, one consisting entirely of unit values, that functions in the regression equations like a variable even if all values are the same. Because all the values are the same, the variance of this "variable" is zero. Its symbol designation is underlined (or the box shaded) nevertheless since all independent variables have variances as parameters. In this case, however, the variance of V999 is a parameter fixed at zero. In practice, EQS does not require values for this variable to be read in. They are provided internally by the program. In this sense, V999 is an unmeasured variable.

The regression equation for the now dependent variable F1 will be F1 = 20*V999 + D1, where the 20 is an estimated value that will be replaced ultimately by the optimally estimated parameter. F2 is affected both by V999 and F1, because Intelligence at time one is expected to affect Intelligence at time two. The other stars (*) in Fig. 13.6 indicate the usual kinds of free parameters to be estimated. The other regression equations, for V1 to V8, are composed as usual.

The equations and variances section of the EQS setup for the path diagram in Fig. 13.6 might be as follows:

/EQUATIONS

V1 = F1 + E1;
V2 = 2*F1 + E2;
V3 = 2*F1 + E3;
. . .

V8 = 2*F1 + E8;
F1 = 20*V999 + D1;
F2 = .9*F1 + 10*V999 + D2;

/VARIANCES

D1 = 10*;
D2 = 8*;
E1 TO E8 = 6*;

In this model, the estimated mean for each variable from V1 to V4 would be generated by multiplying the regression coefficient with respect to F1 for that variable by the regression coefficient for V999 from the regression equation for F1. The mean is an indirect effect of V999 on the measured variable, as can be seen by path tracing. Similarly, the estimated means for variables V5 to V8 would be generated by multiplying the regression coefficient with respect to F2 by the regression coefficient for V999 from the regression equation for F2. The estimated mean for F1 is just the value of the path from V999, while the mean for F2 is the product of the paths V999 to F1 and F1 to F2 plus the value of the V999 to F2 path.

The input data stream will contain either raw data from which both means and standard deviations of the measured variables can be computed, or if a covariance or correlation matrix is input, the means and standard deviations will be directly input. EQS uses the information about the sample means of the V variables, in addition to the sample variances and covariances, to estimate the parameters of the model represented by Fig. 13.6. In turn, using these parameter estimates, EQS can generate estimated means as well as variances and covariances that are implied by the model. The sample and generated values are tested for similarity using a chi-square test, or other indication of goodness of fit. A poor fit may occur because the sample means are poorly estimated, because the sample variances and covariances are poorly estimated, or both.

The use of a mean and covariance structure is appropriate for this kind of situation because mean intelligence and the means of the indicator variables are expected to increase from time one to time two, due to maturation of intellectual functioning. Whether a two latent-factor model can account for the variances and covariances of these variables on both occasions, *and* for the changes in their mean values, is the question to be answered by testing a model such as that represented in Fig. 13.6.

13.7.   DIFFERENCES BETWEEN EQS AND LISREL NOTATION

The EQS notation has been used in this chapter despite the fact that LISREL has been around longer and historically has been more widely used. The EQS system can be absorbed more easily, specifies the diagrams more fully, and avoids Greek letters that seem to terrify many social science students. The LISREL manual presents the complete model in all its complexity and then shows how various application models represent submodels of the more general LISREL model. The EQS manual and system, on the other hand, permit a more gradual approach to this complex topic, simplifying the learning task for the uninitiated.

Whereas EQS uses measured (V) variables, latent (F) variables, and two kinds of error variables, that is, E's (errors) for the V variables, and D's (disturbances) for the F variables, LISREL is more complicated. The V variables of EQS are divided into x and y variables in LISREL. The x variables are those measured variables that can be expressed as linear combinations of the *independent* latent variables. The y variables, on the other hand, are those measured variables that can be expressed as linear combinations of the *dependent* latent variables, that is, those that themselves can be expressed as linear combinations of other latent variables.

The latent (F) variables of EQS are thus divided into two different types in LISREL, the ξ (xi) variables and the η (eta) variables. The ξ (xi) variables in LISREL are the *independent* latent variables, that is, those *not* expressed as linear combinations of other variables. The η (eta) variables are those latent variables that are *dependent* , that is, they are expressed in the structural equation model as linear combinations of other latent variables. In Fig. 13.4, F1 and F5 are the ξ (xi) variables and F2, F3, and F4 are the η (eta) variables.

In addition to these four kinds of variables, the general LISREL model has three kinds of error variables. These are ϵ (epsilon) variables, which are errors for the y variables, δ (delta) variables, which are errors for the x variables, and ζ (zeta) variables which are "disturbances" for the dependent latent variables, that is, the η (eta) variables. The latent *independent* variables (ξ's) do not have associated error variables. The ϵ and δ error variables of LISREL are treated as E's in the EQS system while the LISREL ζ (zeta) error variables are called D's in the EQS system.

Hayduk (1987) and others have represented the general structural equation model for LISREL with three basic equations:

$$\eta = \mathbf{B}\eta + \Gamma\xi + \zeta \tag{13.3a}$$

$$\mathbf{y} = \Lambda_y\eta + \epsilon \tag{13.3b}$$

$$\mathbf{x} = \Lambda_x\xi + \delta \tag{13.3c}$$

These three equations involve eight parameter matrices in the complete LISREL model:

1. Ψ (Psi): covariance matrix for the ζ (zeta) error variables (associated with the η variables)
2. Theta-epsilon: covariance matrix of the ϵ (epsilon) error variables (associated with the y variables), i.e., θ_ϵ
3. Theta-delta: covariance matrix of the δ (delta) error variables (associated with the x variables), i.e., θ_δ
4. Φ (Phi): covariance matrix of the ξ (xi) variables, the independent latent variables
5. Λ_y (Lambda-y): the matrix of regression weights for expressing the y variables as a function of the *dependent* latent variables (η's) in the measurement model equation for the y variables: $y = \Lambda_y\eta + \epsilon$
6. Λ_x (Lambda-x): the matrix of regression weights for expressing the x variables as a function of the *independent* latent variables (ξ's) in the measurement model equation for the x variables: $x = \Lambda_x\xi + \delta$
7. B (Beta) and 8. Γ (Gamma), the matrices of regression weights for predicting the *dependent* latent variables (η's) as a linear combination of the η's themselves *and* the *independent* latent variables (ξ's), respectively, as in the structural equation model: $\eta = \mathbf{B}\eta + \Gamma\xi + \zeta$

Fig. 13.7 shows a representation of Eqs. (13.3a), (13.3b), and (13.3c) in schematic matrix form. As an example, these equations are given here for the LISREL path diagram in Fig. 13.8. Each path in Fig. 13.8 is labeled with the appropriate structural coefficient. Equations 13.3a, 13.3b, and 13.3c for the LISREL model in Fig. 13.8 could be written in schematic matrix form as follows:

$$\begin{bmatrix} \eta_1 \\ \eta_2 \end{bmatrix} = \begin{bmatrix} 0 & \beta_1 \\ 0 & 0 \end{bmatrix} \begin{bmatrix} \eta_1 \\ \eta_2 \end{bmatrix} + \begin{bmatrix} \gamma_1 & 0 \\ 0 & \gamma_2 \end{bmatrix} \begin{bmatrix} \xi_1 \\ \xi_2 \end{bmatrix} + \begin{bmatrix} \zeta_1 \\ \zeta_2 \end{bmatrix} \quad \text{(13.4a)}$$

$$\begin{bmatrix} x_1 \\ x_2 \\ x_3 \\ x_4 \end{bmatrix} = \begin{bmatrix} \lambda_1 & 0 \\ \lambda_2 & 0 \\ 0 & \lambda_3 \\ 0 & \lambda_4 \end{bmatrix} \begin{bmatrix} \xi_1 \\ \xi_2 \end{bmatrix} + \begin{bmatrix} \delta_1 \\ \delta_2 \\ \delta_3 \\ \delta_4 \end{bmatrix} \quad \text{(13.4b)}$$

$$\begin{bmatrix} y_1 \\ y_2 \\ y_3 \\ y_4 \end{bmatrix} = \begin{bmatrix} \lambda_5 & 0 \\ \lambda_6 & 0 \\ 0 & \lambda_7 \\ 0 & \lambda_8 \end{bmatrix} \begin{bmatrix} \eta_1 \\ \eta_2 \end{bmatrix} + \begin{bmatrix} \epsilon_1 \\ \epsilon_2 \\ \epsilon_3 \\ \epsilon_4 \end{bmatrix} \quad \text{(13.4c)}$$

The other parameter matrices to be estimated are shown below.

Ψ, the covariance matrix for the ζ (zeta) error variables associated with the η latent variables is given by:

$$\begin{bmatrix} \psi_{11} & \\ 0 & \psi_{22} \end{bmatrix}$$

In this model, ζ_1 and ζ_2 are not connected by a two-way arrow, hence ψ_{21} is zero.

Φ, the covariance matrix for the independent latent variables is given by:

$$\begin{bmatrix} \phi_{11} & \\ \phi_{21} & \phi_{22} \end{bmatrix}$$

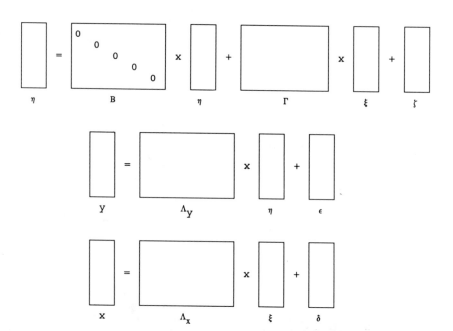

FIG. 13.7. Matrix Representation for 3 Basic Structural Equations.

Note. Matrices B, Γ, Λ_y and Λ_x are matrices of structural coefficients. Columns ϵ, δ, and ζ are vectors of errors for the x variables, y variables, and the η variables, respectively. The column η is a vector of endogenous (dependent) latent variables. Column y is a vector of observed endogenous variables, that is, those associated with the endogenous (dependent) latent variables (η). Column x is a vector of observed exogenous variables, that is, those associated with the exogeneous (independent) latent variables (ξ).

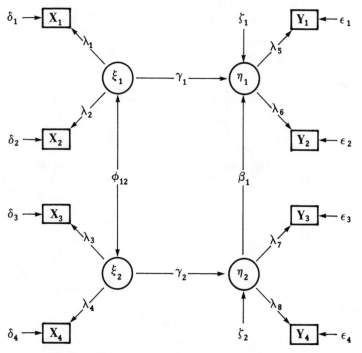

FIG. 13.8. LISREL Path Model.

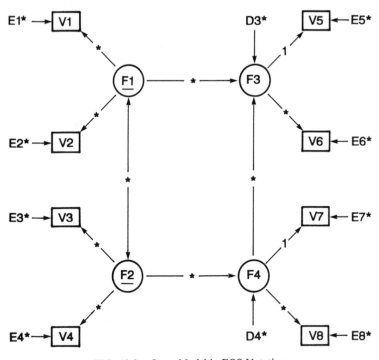

FIG. 13.9.   Same Model in EQS Notation.

The covariance matrix of the ϵ error variables, Θ_ϵ that is associated with the y variables is given by:

$$\begin{bmatrix} \theta_{\epsilon_{11}} & 0 & 0 & 0 \\ 0 & \theta_{\epsilon_{22}} & 0 & 0 \\ 0 & 0 & \theta_{\epsilon_{33}} & 0 \\ 0 & 0 & 0 & \theta_{\epsilon_{44}} \end{bmatrix}$$

The covariance matrix of the δ error variables, Θ_δ that is associated with the x variables is given by:

$$\begin{bmatrix} \theta_{\delta_{11}} & 0 & 0 & 0 \\ 0 & \theta_{\delta_{22}} & 0 & 0 \\ 0 & 0 & \theta_{\delta_{33}} & 0 \\ 0 & 0 & 0 & \theta_{\delta_{44}} \end{bmatrix}$$

As usual, some paths or variances must be fixed for identification purposes. Such values would be known nonzero elements of these matrices. The EQS path diagram that corresponds to the LISREL path diagram in Fig. 13.8 is given in Fig. 13.9.

In the complete, or general, LISREL model, the unknown elements of all eight matrices represent the parameters that are estimated to generate a reproduced covariance matrix, Σ, which is compared with the sample covariance matrix, S^*, to see how well the model fits the data. Thus, the general LISREL model involves two kinds of measured variables, two kinds of latent variables, and three kinds of error variables, generating eight parameter matrices. Different kinds of submodels are generated by dropping some of these parameter elements.

Factor analytic model. For a LISREL model like the EQS model described in section 13.3, drop the y variables and the η variables. This leaves Eq. (13.3c) with three parameter matrices instead of eight as in the general LISREL model, namely, Λ_x, Φ, and Θ_δ.

Second-order factor analytic model. For a LISREL model like the EQS model described in Section 13.4, drop the x variables in Eq. (13.3c) and make the parameter matrix B contain all zeroes. This leaves only five parameter matrices, namely, Λ_y, Γ, Φ, Ψ, and Θ_ϵ.

Measured variable model. For LISREL models like the EQS model described in Section 13.2, there are no latent variables, so the η's and the ξ's are eliminated. In this case, the x variables are treated as ξ variables and the y variables are treated as η variables and the model equation reduces to: $y = B_y + \Gamma_x + \zeta$. Only three parameter matrices are involved, B, Γ, and Ψ.

As with EQS, LISREL can also analyze multisample data and can incorporate means into the structural equation model. The reader is referred to the LISREL manual for further details.

14

Computer Programs

The computations involved in factor analysis are so extensive that it has only been since the appearance of the electronic computer that this method has begun to gain the acceptance it deserves. This chapter provides a description of the programs developed by the first author to execute various kinds of computations needed in factor analytic work. FORTRAN listings and PC versions of these programs are available on diskettes from the publisher of this book. These programs were developed by the first author to carry out the operations in factor analysis that he prefers to use. They do not represent a complete package of programs to do all kinds of factor analytic computations. They also are not professionally developed, hence they lack the polish and documentation that characterize professionally developed and marketed computer packages such as SAS, BMDP, SPSS, SYSTAT, and others. Despite these limitations, the programs listed here perform some operations that are not available elsewhere and hence may be useful to the reader. Aside from the main computer packages, other factor analytic programs can be found in Horst (1965) and in Cooley and Lohnes (1962).

In their present form, the programs described here are suitable for running on intermediate-sized and mainframe computers. They can also be adapted for use on minicomputers with adequate speed, memory, and the capability of compiling FORTRAN programs. Downsized compiled versions of the programs for IBM AT or compatible personal computers may be obtained from the publisher.

The computer programs described in this chapter were written in the FORTRAN IV language and/or later FORTRAN updates. Many of the programs require special job control language (JCL) instructions because of the use of tapes, data set output, and so on. Readers may find it necessary to consult with experts at their own computer centers to see what is required to compile and run these programs on their own systems. Program five, for example, designates tapes 1 and 2 as "scratch" tapes for intermediate output. Several programs use tape 7 for outputting intermediate results on external data sets (punch files) to serve as input for further computations. The programs use tape 5 for reading input and tape 6 for writing output. In general, most of the programs are limited to 115 variables or less with the present dimension statements. Of course, the FORTRAN programs can be modified to change these various parameters. Computer center consultants can help users to get these programs up and running.

There are frequent references to "control lines" in the program descriptions. These are the initial data entry rows, 80 columns each, on which the information is entered that will control how the program performs its functions. The number of cases and the number of variables are examples of the kinds of information that is supplied to the program in these control lines. In the program descriptions, you will be told what information to "enter" on the control lines of data. Many of the programs contain provisions for outputting data to a separate external data set, sometimes referred to as a "punch file." This possibility is very useful since it permits the results of one set of computations to be used as part of the entry data for a later set of operations. The procedures for outputting results to these external data sets will vary from computer center to computer center. An example of one procedure used at the UCLA computing facility with the IBM 3090 is supplied with the program listings. The external data set output is on tape 7.

For each program to be described, the purpose and general nature of the program are presented first, followed by a description of the data to be input, including the control lines, variable format lines, if any, and other special instruction data lines provided to the program in addition to the other data input. All of the programs have at least one control line at the beginning, often followed by several other data lines that tell the program how to process the data. These instruction data lines are part of the data that are input and are necessary for the program to process the actual data themselves properly. Depending on how the particular computer center operates, various JCL and program lines may or may not be required to precede the data themselves.

The authors have used these programs extensively and have endeavored to eliminate errors in them as much as possible. No warranty is intended, however, that all errors or "bugs" have been removed. Readers who use them, therefore, do so at their own risk. The authors are not responsible for any loss the reader may incur as a consequence of using these programs.

Users must accept the responsibility to check the results themselves to be certain that the programs have functioned correctly.

14.1.   PROGRAM 1. SCORING

This program was designed to compute raw scores by summing scores over smaller units, such as items on a test. Through the dimension lines (described below), the program is informed which items are to be included in the total score. The program will then add up those item scores and output a total score for each person on that variable. Scores may be computed for many different variables for a given person on the same run. If some of the items are negatively stated with respect to the variable name, to control for acquiescence response set, these item scores may be reversed before adding the scores into the total raw score. Items that are to be reversed are specified on the item reversal lines (described below). Composite scores based on a sum of subscores can be obtained with this program even though they are not items, however. After the scores for each person are computed on the different variables, they are printed out before the data for the next person are input for score computation. If desired, the computed scores may be output on an external data set for later input to another program, depending on which options are available at the computer center you are using.

Variable Format Lines.   The first control line is the first data line. The next *three* data lines following the first control line are the variable format lines that specify how the data are arranged on input, either from directly entered data or from an external data set. If item scores were the data, they might be arranged one column per item, 72 items on a data row, with columns 73–80 reserved for identification purposes. This program accepts only integer (I) formats, for example (72I1) in the case of entering 72 single digit item scores per person. The number of data items indicated on the variable format lines must be compatible with the number of scores input per person as indicated in columns 7–9 of the first control line. If all the format is contained on the first line within the first 72 columns, the second two variable format lines will be left blank but they must be included in the data for this program. Only columns 1 to 72 on each format line are used before going to the next format line.

Dimension Lines.   For each total score variable or dimension to be scored by adding up component or item scores, one or more dimension lines must be included as data following the three variable format lines. The same number of dimension lines must be included for each variable, even though

TABLE 14.1

First Control Line Information for the Scoring Program

Columns	Values Input to the Columns
1–3	N, the number of subjects or data objects, 999 maximum
4–6	NUDIM, the number of dimensions to be scored, 135 max
7–9	NSCORE, the number of items of data input per subject, 999 maximum
10–12	NCARDS, the number of lines needed to hold item numbers of the items of data to be scored on a given dimension or variable; this number may be 1, 2, 3, or 4 and is that number needed for the variable with the largest number of data items
13–15	NREV, the number of items to be reversed in direction, 001 minimum; if no reversal of data items is needed, use a dummy data item and reverse it.
16–18	NMISP, the maximum data item score plus the lowest score. If items start with 1, NMISP is the maximum item score plus 1. If item scores start with 0, NMISP equals the maximum item score itself. Used in reversing score for negatively-worded items.
19–21	NCOL, the number of columns allowed for the scores in the external data set output; if the computed scores will be three digits, or if three columns per score are desired, 003 must be input in these three columns; if the computed scores will be two digits and only two columns per score are desired in the external data set output, put 004 here. If you wish to output the computed scores in some other format, place a value of 001 here and add one output variable format line in integer format, for example (4X, 3I2, 2X, 4I3), and add this line following the item reversal lines and before the regular data lines. Do not insert this output format line, however, if 003 or 004 is entered in columns 19–21.
22–24	NPUN, put 001 here to obtain both printed output and data set output; put 000 for printed output only, or if the other is not possible at your computer center.

some variables may not require as many, for example, when fewer items are scored for some variables. The extra line(s), if any, are left blank. The first entry on each set of dimension lines for each variable is the number of items to be scored on that dimension. This entry is placed in columns 1–3 of the first dimension line for that variable. Following this entry, the data-item numbers of the data items to be added up for this total score are placed in three column fields, ending with column 72 on line 1. If more items are to be scored than the 23 that can be fitted on dimension line one, continue on to a second line and so on. The data-item numbers are based on the order in which the lines are input as specified on the input variable format lines. The dimension lines are assembled in the order in which the variables are to be scored and output and they follow the input variable format lines.

Item Reversal Lines. These are the next data lines following the dimension lines. The data-item numbers of the data items to be reversed before adding up data items to obtain the total scores are placed on these lines, three columns per number and 24 numbers per line, in columns 1–72. If more than 24 data items are to be reversed, their numbers are placed on a second, third, and subsequent item reversal lines, until all such number have been entered, 24 per line. The program subtracts the data-item value for such items from NMISP, the entry in columns 16–18 of the first control line, and places the result back in storage as a replacement for the original data-item value. At least one item reversal line with at least one data-item number is required by the program. If all data items are positive, add an extra dummy data item at the end of the data and reverse it to satisfy the demands of the program.

Output Variable Format Line. If 2 or 3 column external data set output is unsuitable for all variables, place a value of 001 in columns 19–21 and add a single integer variable format line here specifying the desired output format. If 003 or 004 has been placed in columns 19–21, omit this output format line.

The Data-Item Lines. The data items to be operated on are placed on lines that follow the item reversal lines, or the output variable format line if there is one. All the data items for a single individual or subject are placed on consecutive lines according to the integer format specified on the input variable format lines. These data items may be responses to test items, total scores over several items, or other kinds of numerical measures.

Tapes Used. In addition to tapes 5 and 6 for reading data and written output, respectively, this program uses tape 7 for data set output. The JCL lines and the computer system must allow the use of this tape command for the program to function properly.

Data Line Order. The lines that constitute the data are arranged in the following order: control line, three variable format lines, dimension lines, item reversal line, one output variable format line, if called for, and data-item lines.

Printed Output. The total scores for all the variables scored are printed out for the first person, then for the second person, and so on, until they have been printed out for the last person.

14.2. PROGRAM 2. REGRESSION PLOT

This program is designed to prepare a scatter plot for pairs of selected variables so that nonlinear regressions may be detected visually. A matrix of scores is input, such as that output from Program 1. Pairs of these variables may be selected for plotting. The scores for a given variable are scaled to be proportions of the total range from the lowest to the highest score. These proportions are plotted against each other. The distributional characteristics of the variables are preserved by this kind of transformation, revealing skewness as well as nonlinearity. Frequencies up to 9 are printed as numerals. Any cell in the scatter plot with a frequency higher than 9 will contain a letter from A to Z if the frequency is between 10 and 35. Any cell with a frequency of 36 or larger will contain a printout of the symbol *, an asterisk.

Control Line. The control line is the first data line. The information to be placed on this line is summarized briefly in Table 14.2.

Variable Format Lines. The five data lines following the control line must be variable format lines describing the form in which the scores for the variables to be plotted are stored on the data lines. For example, (24F3.0) on the first variable format line would state that the scores are entered three columns per score in the first 72 columns of each line. Only fixed-point (F) formats are used for this program, not integer (I) formats. The remaining four variable format lines would be left blank in this case because the variable format is entirely contained within the first 72 columns of the first variable format line.

Score Lines. The scores (raw data) for each subject are placed on one or more lines in the same format for every subject as shown on the five variable format lines. Lines for the first subject are followed by those for the second subject, and so on. These lines follow the variable format lines.

Plot Lines. If a value of 001 has been entered in columns 7–9 of the control line, indicating that only some plots are to be done, a separate plot data line must be inserted here for each plot desired. For example, a plot line with 001 in columns 1–3 and 002 in columns 4–6 will cause variable 1 to be plotted with variable 2. The plot lines follow the score data lines. They are omitted if 000 is entered in columns 7–9 of the control line.

TABLE 14.2

Control Line Information for the Regression Plot Program

Columns	Information to be Placed in Columns
1–3	N, the number of subjects or data objects, 800 max
4–6	NSCR, the number of scores per subject stored consecutively by subject, 50 maximum
7–9	JPLOT, enter 001 if only pairs of variables are to be plotted for which plot lines are read in; enter 000 here if all pairs of variables are to be plotted

End Line.   If there are any plot lines used, an *end* line with 999 entered in columns 1–3 must follow the plot lines to signal the program that no more plots are to be made. This line should be omitted if columns 7–9 of the control line contain 000.

Data Line Order.   The lines that constitute the data are arranged in the following order: control line, five variable format lines, score lines (raw data), and optional plot lines and end line if only some of the plots are called for on the control line.

Printed Output.   The scores input as data are printed out first with all the scores for the first subject, followed by all the scores for the second subject, and so on, until the scores for the last subject are printed out. Following the printout of the raw-score matrix, the scaled scores are printed out in transposed form. That is, the scaled scores for variable 1 are printed out for all subjects, then the scaled scores for variable 2, and so on. The scaled scores are proportions and are the values that are plotted. After the scaled score matrix is output, the plots themselves are printed out in the sequence 1–2, 1–3, up to 1–n, 2–3, 2,4, and so on. If only some plots are called for, the plots are printed in order of the plot lines. The first-mentioned variable is plotted on the vertical axis and the second-mentioned variable is plotted on the horizontal axis.

14.3.   PROGRAM 3. FREQUENCY DISTRIBUTION

This program will select from 1 to 15 variables from the data input and prepare a frequency distribution for each. The frequencies for each raw score are tallied and the centile, or percentile, equivalent calculated.

Control Line.   The control line is the first data line. The information to be placed on this line is summarized briefly in Table 14.3.

Variables-to-be-Distributed Line.   Although 135 one-, two-, or three-digit integer scores may be input if desired, only 15 or fewer of these variables can be processed to produce frequency distributions in one run. The variable numbers, from 1 up to 135, of the variables for which frequency distributions are desired are entered as three-digit numbers on the variables-to-be- distributed line; for example, 001, 005, and 065 entered on this line in columns 1–9 would result in preparation of frequency distributions for the first, fifth, and sixty-fifth variables.

Data Score Lines.   The raw score data are entered by subject in columns 1–72 only and in one-, two-, or three-digit integer form, unless a variable

TABLE 14.3

Control Line Information for the Frequency Distribution Program

Columns	Information to be Placed in Columns
1–4	N, the number of subjects or data objects, 0999 maximum
5–7	NVAR, the number of variables or scores input per subject, 135 maximum
8–9	NFD, the number of frequency distributions to be done, 15 maximum
10–11	Enter 01 for one column per score on input, 72 scores per line in columns 1–72; enter 02 for two columns per score on input, 36 scores per line in columns 1–72; enter 03 for three columns per score on input, 24 scores per line in columns 1–72. For some other format see information in columns 12–13
12–13	To input data using an integer variable format, input the number of variable format lines here (01 to 10) and place the(se) line(s) following the control line and before the variables-to-be-distributed line. Leave columns 12–13 blank if no variable format is used.

format is used as indicated in columns 12–13 of the control line. The lines for the first subject are followed by those for the second subject, and so on.

Data Line Order. The lines that constitute the data are arranged in the following order: control line, variable format lines, if any, variables-to-be-distributed line, and data score lines.

Printed Output. The printed output consists of the frequency distributions, output consecutively in the order of the variable numbers on the variables-to-be-distributed line. The distributions are labeled consecutively beginning with the number 1, however, rather than with their numbers as shown on the variables-to-be-distributed line. Each score is listed with the frequency and cumulative frequency associated with it, from the lowest score to the highest score. The centile, or percentile, value corresponding to the score is also printed out. A median is also computed and output.

14.4. PROGRAM 4. SCALED SCORE EQUIVALENTS

This program converts raw scores to corresponding scaled scores using a table that is input for conversion purposes. It can convert raw scores to centile scores or McCall T-scores, for example, or make any other kind of transformation called for by the table of equivalents. The table of equivalents is input to the program as data in the form of scaled score equivalents (description below). These data lines contain scaled scores that are to be the equivalents for each possible raw score. The program reads the raw score, looks up the scaled score equivalent in the table, and outputs the appropriate scaled score. The most common usage of the program would be for getting centile or T-score equivalents for the raw scores with a large sample of subjects so that profile sheets could be made out to return to to the individuals taking the tests. This conversion can be carried out in one operation for as many as 15 different raw scores per person.

Control Line.   The control data line is the first data line. The information to be entered on this line is summarized briefly in Table 14.4.

Scaled Score Equivalent Lines.   The possible scaled scores are the 101 values from 0 to 100. For a given variable, the raw scores that are to correspond to these 101 scaled scores are placed on five scale score equivalent lines in the format (24I3). That is, 24 three-digit numbers go on the first such line, the next 24 on the next line, and so on, until the final five go on the fifth line. The number entered in columns 1–3 of the first scaled score equivalent line is that raw score such that all raw scores less than or equal to it receive a scaled score of 0. The fifth number on the fifth line is a raw score such that all raw scores greater than or equal to it receive a scaled score of 100. The second number on the first scaled score equivalent line, in columns 4–6, contains the smallest raw score that is to receive a scaled score of 1. In columns 7–9, place the smallest raw score that is to receive a scaled score of 2, and so on, until the fourth position on line five, in columns 10–12, contains the raw score that is the smallest raw score to receive a score of 99.

If a *T*-score equivalent transformation is desired and no *T*-score less than 20 nor greater than 80 is desired, a number lower than any score to be encountered would be entered as the raw score in the first 20 positions on the scaled score equivalent lines. A number higher than any raw score to be encountered must be entered in the last 20 positions. In between will be the

TABLE 14.4

Control Line Information for the Scaled Score Equivalents Program

Columns	Information to be Placed in Columns
1–3	IMAX, the number of scores per person, 15 maximum
4–6	JCT, the ID number of the first subject for labeling
7–10	N, the number of subjects, a four-digit number less than or equal to 9999, for example, 0085.
11–12	If the data are to be input using an integer variable format, place the number of variable format lines here (01 to 10) and place these lines immediately after the control line. Leave columns 11–12 blank if no variable format lines are used.

raw-score equivalents that are the lowest raw scores to be given the corresponding T-scores between 20 and 80. There will be five scaled score equivalent lines for each variable to be converted to scaled scores.

Raw-Score Lines. One raw-score data line is prepared for each person, with the first score in columns 1-2, the second raw score in columns 4-6, and so on. No more than 15 variables can be processed in one run. If some other format than (15I3) is desired, use a variable format (see control line, columns 11-12).

14.5. PROGRAM 5. FACTOR ANALYSIS

This program computes means and standard deviations, and correlations, extracts factors by either the minimum residual or the principal factor method (see Chapter 4), and rotates the extracted factors by the Kaiser Varimax method (see Chapter 7). If data are input as scores, the program will compute means and standard deviations and produce a correlation matrix for factor analysis. The program will also accept a correlation matrix as the basic data, however, in which case no means and standard deviations are computed. Estimated communalities may be input to be used in the factor calculations in which case the solution is a principal factor solution. If I's are input as communalities, a principal components solution is obtained. If no communalities are input, the solution is by the minimum residual method itself, which does not employ the diagonal cells in extracting the factors. These various options are controlled by appropriate entries on the control data line.

The factor solution may be iterated, if desired, in which case the computed communalities from the first factor extraction sequence will be fed back as the estimated communalities for the second solution. If the first factor extraction is done by the minimum residual method (no communalities input), the second and subsequent iterated solutions will yield principal factor solutions because the communalities calculated from the preceding solution are inserted as estimates for the next solution. Use of these options, including the number of iterated solutions to be obtained, is controlled through entries on the control line.

If the solution is iterated, normally from five to ten iterations will stabilize the communalities sufficiently for most practical purposes. The minimum residual solution without communalities underestimates the communalities somewhat so iteration of the solution is usually to be preferred once the number of factors has been clearly determined. The number of factors extracted is held constant when the solution is iterated.

Where the minimum residual solution without communalities is being obtained, factor loadings and communalities over 1.0 may occur in some small or ill-conditioned matrices. The number of unknown diagonals is large in comparision with the total number of entries in a small matrix, sometimes yielding such anomalous factor loadings. In such cases, the solution must be recomputed with estimated communalities using the principal factor method. Iteration of the solution may or may not be indicated.

Either of two iterative procedures may be chosen for obtaining convergence on a solution within the calculations for the extraction of a single factor (this type of iteration is not to be confused with iterating the entire solution to stabilize communalities). The first of the two iterative methods for extracting a factor was developed as the original form of the minimum residual solution (Comrey, 1962a) and is referred to as the "averaging method" of iteration. The second iterative method is referred to as the "length-adjustment method." The length-adjustment method is usually preferred because it has a more definite and appropriate criterion for terminating factor extraction. When the iterative process by which the factor is computed terminates with paired vectors of opposite signs, the factor extraction process is automatically terminated. This would correspond to a principal factor with an associated negative eigenvalue. The averaging method of iteration may extract more small factors after this point, but such factors would not be regarded usually as being sufficiently large to warrant retention. The averaging method terminates by failure to reach convergence in the allowed number of iterations specified in columns 4–6 on the control data line.

The program user specifies how many factors are to be extracted in columns 7–9 on the control line. The number of factors extracted will be equal to this number or less if the iterative process terminates earlier. The authors usually specify a maximum number of factors wanted large enough to be sure that all important factors will be extracted. It is better to err on the side of taking out too many rather than too few. If the program fails to extract that many, no harm is done. Extracting too few factors can lead to serious distortions in the solution.

The number of factors to be rotated by the Kaiser Varimax method is specified in columns 20–22 of the control card. It is often desirable to call for the rotation of fewer factors than have been extracted. One may expect about 10 meaningful factors, and hence call for the rotation of 10, but call for the extraction of 13 factors so that the last three extracted factors can be inspected to determine if they are sufficiently large to warrant their being included in the rotation process. If the number of factors actually extracted is less than the number called for in columns 20–22, only the smaller number will be rotated. If no rotations are desired, specify 001 in columns 20–22 of the control data line.

The criterion of convergence is specified in columns 10–15 on the control line. Successively iterated pairs of vectors must have all corresponding entries agree to less than or equal to this figure before the iterative process is considered to be converged. When the process reaches this point, the last vector in the iterative sequence is taken as the extracted factor. The smaller the value specified here, the more iterations will be required to attain convergence. Values that are too large permit termination of the iteration before adequate convergence has taken place. Values that are too small may make it impossible to obtain convergence in the allowed number of iterations, if at all. Some value between 0.0050 and 0.0005 will suffice for most practical purposes.

It may be desirable to retain some of the computed matrices and store them on an external data set to be used as input for further computations. This option may be exercised by placing a 1 in column 24, 25, and/or 26 of the control card to output the correlation matrix, the minimum residual (extracted) matrix, or the Varimax matrix, respectively, in the format (12F6.3). The computer facility must have the capability of handling output on tape 7 for this purpose. Thus, such output will be placed in a data set where it can be retrieved later. With this format, the data output are stored 12 numbers per card, six columns per number, with three digits to the right of the decimal place. Data lines for the first column of the matrix are output first, followed by those for the second column, and so on, until the lines for the last column are output. If these matrices are not needed for further operations, columns 24, 25, and 26 of the control line should have zeros placed in them.

In the iterative process to obtain a given factor, many intermediate vectors are computed before convergence takes place. Normally only the final converged vector is output. If the intermediate vectors computed in the iterative process are desired for some reason, they can be printed out by placing a 1 in column 28 of the control line. If these are not wanted, as they usually are not, place a zero in this column.

If a correlation matrix rather than scores is input, this is indicated by placing a 1 in column 23 of the control line. If scores are to be input, a zero is entered in column 23.

If the entire factor solution is to be iterated several times, the amount of output becomes rather voluminous, requiring many printed pages, if all the results are printed for each of the intermediate solutions. Where many iterations are called for by specifying more than 01 in columns 32–33 of the control line, it is possible to limit the amount of printed output to just the final computed factor matrices for each cycle by placing a 1 in column 31 of the control line. If the entire printed output of all information for each cycle is desired, a zero is entered in column 31. All information would normally be called for if only one cycle of factor extraction is being requested, that is, if 01 is placed in columns 32 and 33.

This program is set up for using a fixed point variable format. The number of data lines (01 to 10) needed to hold the variable format, in columns 1–72 only, is specified in columns 34–35 of the control line. If 34–35 are left blank, then there must be five variable format lines whether or not that many are needed to hold the format. A format of (12F6.3), for example, all fits on part of line one. Four following blank lines would be needed in addition to the one holding the format if zeros or blanks appear in columns 34–35. If 01 is placed in columns 34–35, then only one variable format data line is allowed or needed.

Control Line. The control line is the first data line. The information to be entered on this line is summarized briefly in Table 14.5.

Variable Format Lines. The variable format lines inform the program how the data are stored, regardless of whether scores are input or whether a correlation matrix is input. Complicated formats require skipping columns, repetitions of format descriptions, and hence can spill over onto several lines for some data situations. Only the first 72 columns are used on any variable format line. A format of (18F4.3) might be used for a correlation matrix as data. Each correlation would be allowed four columns on the line to accomodate a sign and a three-digit number. The decimal point need not be entered on some computer systems. The first 18 correlations in column 1 would be entered on the first line, the next 18 on line 2, and so on, until all the correlations in column 1 have been entered. The second column would start with a new line, and so on.

A typical format for inputting scores instead of a correlation matrix would be (36F2.0). This would call for two columns for each score, 36 scores per line. An individual's scores would be entered in consecutive fields of two digits, 36 on line 1, the next 36 or part thereof on line 2, until all scores are entered. The scores for the second person start on a new line. If any of the scores runs to three digits, of course, this format would not be acceptable. Integer formats may not be used for inputting data to this program; for example, (36I2) is unacceptable.

Lines for Scores or Correlation Coefficients. The control line and variable format line(s) come at the beginning. The data proper begin after that. The data lines will be either a correlation matrix, in which case a 1 must be entered in column 23 of the control line, or these lines will contain scores on all the variables for each subject, in which case a 0 will be entered in column 23.

TABLE 14.5

Control Data Line Information for the Factor Analysis Program

Columns	Information to be Placed in Columns
1–3	N, the number of variables, 115 maximum
4–6	NITER, number of iterations to be allowed without convergence in computing one factor before terminating factor extraction for failure to converge. Use 200 as the maximum and as the usual value unless the averaging method is used; then use 025 to 050 as the maximum
7–9	MNFAC, maximum number of factors to be extracted
10–15	ERROR, criterion of convergence in iteration; a value between 0.0050 and 0.0005 is ordinarily chosen
16–19	NCASES, the number of subjects, cases, or data objects; leave blank if a correlation matrix is input as data
20–22	MFROT, the maximum number of factors to be rotated
23	ISCMC, enter 1 if a correlation matrix is to be input as data; enter 0 if scores are input and **R** is computed
24	IRMPO, enter 1 to output **R** matrix; 0 if not wanted
25	IMRPO, enter 1 to output extracted factor matrix to be used in further computations; 0 if not wanted
26	IVMPO, enter 1 to output the Varimax matrix; 0, no
27	IKSH2, enter 1 if communality estimates are to be input to the program as data; use format (18F4.3); enter 0 if no estimated communalities are input. These cards must follow all the other data cards
28	ITOP, enter 1 if all intermediate trial vectors before convergence are to be printed out; enter 0 if only converged vectors are to be output (put 0 most times)
29	ITYPE, enter 1 for length-adjustment iteration; enter 0 for averaging iteration (1 is usually entered)
30	JTP, put zero here; tape input is no longer used
31	IOS, enter 1 for limiting the amount of printed output to only the summary final matrices; enter 0 to obtain all output (0 is entered usually for only a single solution, 1 is often entered for iterated solutions)
32–33	IZAG, indicate how many times the entire solution is to be iterated; 01 gives a single, uniterated solution; to obtain converged communalities, 10 or more iterations of the entire solution may be required
34–35	Indicate the number of variable format cards (01 to 10). A zero or blank here will require five format lines

Lines for Estimated Communalities.   If estimated communalities are to be input, leading to a principal-factor-type solution, or a minimum residual solution using the diagonal cells, a 1 is entered in column 27 of the control line and the estimated communalities are put on lines that follow the lines for the other data. These communalities must be entered in the fixed point format (18F4.3), that is, 18 per line in order from first to last, allowing four columns per entry. The first column in each field is left blank unless unities are to be inserted, in which case the entered value would be 1000, or .999 if the computer system requires entry of decimal points.

Tapes Used.   This program uses tapes 1 and 2 for temporary storage scratch tapes in addition to the usual tapes 5 and 6 for reading and writing. Tape 7 is used for storage of matrices for external data set ouput. The JCL system cards used with the program must allow for the use of these tapes.

Data Line Order.   The lines that constitute the data are arranged in the following order: control line, variable format line(s), lines for scores or for the correlation matrix, and lines for the communalities if estimated values are to be input.

Printed Output.   Printed output begins with a line giving three entries from the control line, NITER, MNFAC, and ERROR. Following this, the means and standard deviations are printed out if scores are input. The correlation matrix is printed out next. Prior to the calculation of each factor, the matrix is examined for the largest residual entry and its absolute value is printed. Also, the sums of squares and the standard deviation of the residuals above the main diagonal are output before the computations for the factor are begun. Following the output of the number of the factor being computed, the largest discrepancies between entries in pairs of vectors are output, one for each iteration cycle within a single factor computation sequence. If convergence is obtained, the last value will be less than the ERROR entry on the control line and the converged factor results will be output. First, the sum of squares of the factor loadings for the factor will be output. Following this, the factor loadings will be output. The communalities are output next. These include the sums of squares of previous factor entries plus the squares of the present factor entries. After this, the cycle begins anew for another factor.

If convergence is not reached in the number of iterations allowed, the last two trial vectors will be output and factor extraction will stop. If the length-adjustment iterative process is used and convergence takes place on vectors of opposite sign, these last trial vectors will be printed out showing equal but opposite signed values. In the event that all intermediate trial vectors are called for, by placing a 1 in column 28 of the control line, these vectors will be printed out before the highest absolute residual is printed.

After the last factor has been computed and printed out, the residual matrix is printed. The extracted factor matrix is printed next, although the values have already been output one factor at a time. The last column of the extracted factor matrix contains the communalities although it is not labeled as such and appears to be just the last factor in the matrix.

If suppression of the intermediate output is called for by placing a 1 in column 31 of the control line, much less output will be obtained. After the correlation matrix, each extracted factor matrix will be output with communalities in the last column. Following this, the usual information for the Varimax rotations and the final Varimax rotated matrix will be printed out with communalities in the last column. The remainder of the printout described above will be suppressed.

The Varimax subroutine used as part of this program was written by Lynn Hayward as a term project while he was a student in the first author's class in factor analysis. Essentially the same program was used for Varimax rotations in the original BMD series of programs (Dixon, 1970a,b), since Hayward was working on those programs at the time.

14.6. PROGRAM 6. TANDEM CRITERIA

This program was designed to carry out orthogonal analytic rotations by the Tandem Criteria method (see Chapter 7). The program operates on an unrotated factor matrix such as that output during the execution of program 5, or the data lines may be prepared from other data for input to this program. The user may elect to compute any one of four kinds of solutions: (a) unnormalized Criterion I solution; (b) unnormalized Criterion II solution; (c) normalized Criterion I solution; or (d) normalized Criterion II solution. The normalized solutions correct all communalities to 1.0, do the rotations, and then rescale the results to the original communalities. This procedure has the effect of giving equal weight to every variable in the rotations. Such a procedure is justifiable and probably preferable if all or most of the variables have substantial communalities. In the case where many variables have very low communalities, however, it does not seem appropriate to inflate their communalities to 1.0 and permit them equal weight in the rotation process. Under these circumstances, the authors would prefer the unnormalized solution.

Criterion I should be applied first in carrying out the rotational solution, making certain to include too many rather than too few factors since Criterion I has the capacity to extract any useful variance from extra factors without the tendency to build them up at the expense of the major factors. Criterion I tends to put as much variance on one factor as possible, consistent with the principle that variables with high loadings on the same factor should be substantially correlated. Thus, if a general factor appears in the data, Criterion I can allow it to appear, but it will not permit a general factor to be produced by placing a factor midway between two uncorrelated clusters. If two correlated factors appear in the data, Criterion I will tend to put more variance on one of the two, leaving the remainder of the variance for a smaller second factor.

Criterion II will attempt to distribute the variance on as many factors as possible, as long as the variables with substantial loadings on each factor are sufficiently correlated with each other. For this reason, Criterion II cannot be applied where extra factors of small variance are included in the matrix to be rotated. With the inclusion of such extra small factors, Criterion II is likely to split a major factor into two parts, superimposing one part of the major factor onto one of the small extra factors. If there are only k major factors, however, and exactly k factors are rotated by Criterion II, the variance will be distributed rather evenly among the factors without building up one factor at the expense of another. Criterion II rotations, therefore, are ordinarily applied after Criterion I rotations have been completed and a determination has been made of the number of major factors that the solution contains. Then, only this number of factors is rotated by Criterion II. Thus, Criterion I is applied first and the results inspected to permit elimination of factors of negligible importance. Then, the surviving factors are rotated by Criterion II. It may be necessary to try several solutions with Criterion II to see which is the best because it may not be possible to determine exactly how many factors should be retained from an inspection of the Criterion I solution alone. The Criterion I solution will usually permit a determination of approximately how many factors should be retained.

Control Line.   The control line is the first data line. The information to be entered on this line is summarized briefly in Table 14.6.

Variable Format Lines.   When the unrotated matrix is input, the format in which the data are arranged must be specified on three variable format lines that follow the control line. If the entire format fits on the first line, in columns 1-72, the second and third lines must still be included even though they are blank. A typical format for input would be (12F6.3) because this is the format in which other programs output results to be input to this program and which this program uses for its output. If the data lines were prepared from a printed matrix, a different format might be used, although it must be an F format, not an I format.

Lines for Unrotated Factor Matrix.   The lines containing the matrix of factors to be rotated follow the three variable format lines. Each factor is contained on the same number of data lines, a new factor starting with a new line. The order of the factors can be rearranged by reordering the rows of data. This is often done when rotating by Criterion II because the Criterion I factors that are input as data for the Criterion II rotations may

TABLE 14.6

Control Data Line Information for the Tandem Criteria Program

Columns	Information to be Placed in Columns
1–3	N, the number of variables, 114 maximum
4–6	M, the number of factors to be input, 29 maximum
7–9	IC, the number of cycles of rotation desired; each factor is rotated with each other factor during each cycle; eight to ten cycles is normally sufficient, for example, 008 to 010
10–12	Enter 000 for normal card image input as data lines; 001 formerly called for tape input
13–15	KIK, enter 000 if rotation by Criterion I is desired; enter 001 for rotation by Criterion II
16–18	INC, enter 000 for a "raw" or unnormalized solution; enter 001 for a normalized solution
19–21	IPUN, enter 000 if no external data set output of of the rotated factor matrix is desired; enter 001 if output of the matrix in format (12F6.3) is desired; this output may be taken from the Criterion I solution to be used as data input for the Criterion II rotations; any unwanted factors may be removed before rotating by Criterion II or by other programs.

require rearranging to be in order of descending size with respect to the total sums of squares of the factor loadings. Sometimes a particular factor may be dropped and the Criterion II rotations done again. This requires removing the data lines or rows for that particular Criterion I factor before performing the Criterion II rotations.

Tapes Used. In addition to tapes 5 and 6 for reading data and writing printed output, this program uses tape 7 for storage of matrices for external data set output.

Data Line Order. The lines that constitute the data are arranged in the following order: control line, three variable format lines, and lines for the matrix to be rotated.

Printed Output. The first printed output is the reproduced correlation matrix, obtained by summing the inner products of the factor loadings over all the factors for each pair of variables. Following this, the unrotated factor matrix input as data is printed out, with the communalities in the last column. The sum of squares of the entries in each column are output next and the sum of the communality values. If the normalized criteria are used, the scaled correlation matrix and the scaled unrotated factor matrix are printed out. These matrices are based on adjusting the communalities to unity for purposes of the computations. The differences between unrotated and rotated communalities follow and should be zero. The Tandem Criteria function values for each complete rotational cycle, rotating each factor with each other in one cycle, are output next. These values increase and stabilize for Criterion I rotation; they decrease and stabilize for Criterion II rotations. Following these values, the rotated factor matrix is output with either Criterion I or Criterion II factors, depending on which method was called for. The sums of squares of the entries in each factor are output following the matrix. The communalities for the variables are printed in the last column of the rotated matrix, and the sum of these communality values is printed out as the last item of information output.

14.7. PROGRAM 7. VARIMAX ROTATION

This program is designed to accept an unrotated factor matrix as data and perform a normal Varimax rotation. It utilizes the same Varimax subroutine, written by Lynn Hayward, that was used in Program 5.

Control Line.   The control line is the first data line. The information to be placed on this line is summarized briefly in Table 14.7.

Variable Format Line.   The second line is the single variable format line that indicates how the unrotated factor matrix is arranged. A typical format would be (12F6.3) because the unrotated matrix lines from program 5 would be in this form. Integer format is not acceptable.

Lines for Unrotated Factor Matrix.   These lines, or data rows, are prepared in the same way as for input to Program 6, that is, by columns of the matrix. These lines follow the control line and the variable format line.

Data Line Order.   The lines that constitute the data are arranged in the following order: control line, one variable format line, and lines for the unrotated matrix.

Printed Output.   The unrotated matrix input as data is printed out first. Following this, the differences in communalities between the unrotated and

TABLE 14.7

Control Data Line Information for the Varimax Rotation Program

Columns	Information to be Placed in Columns
1–3	N, the number of variables, maximum 115
4–6	L, the number of factors

rotated matrices are output. These should be zero. Next, the variance function values for the cycles of rotation are output, as in the Program 5 output. Finally, the rotated Varimax matrix is printed out.

14.8. PROGRAM 8. HAND ROTATION

This program permits the rotation of factors or reference vectors relative to each other in any way desired, utilizing any preferred criterion of rotation. For convenience, the term "factor" will usually be substituted for the term "reference vector" in the discussion that follows. Any factor may be rotated obliquely relative to any other factor, or orthogonal rotations may be carried out. Any orthogonal unrotated matrix may be input as data to this program. A previously rotated matrix can also be input for further rotations.

The matrix input may be a matrix of extracted, unrotated factors, or it may be a previously rotated orthogonal matrix, such as a Varimax matrix or a matrix output from one of the Tandem Criteria rotation treatments. A transformation matrix may be input as data with the unrotated matrix if some rotation of the unrotated matrix has already taken place and the object is to carry out additional rotations. This transformation matrix contains the effects of all rotations that have been performed previously. Any further rotations performed will result in a modification of this transformation matrix to take into account the new rotations. If no rotations have been performed on the input matrix, even though it may itself be a matrix resulting from previous rotations, it is not necessary to input a transformation matrix. An identity matrix will be supplied by the program as the beginning transformation matrix. Subsequent rotations will modify this identity matrix.

This program permits the plotting of factors against one another. These graphs are inspected to determine what rotations are to be performed, if any. Use of the program may be solely for plotting factors without rotation, or factors may be rotated and graphing of the resulting factors with each other called for so that the next round of rotations may be planned. If plots are desired for a given factor with the other factors, its factor number is shown on a plot line, which is one of the data lines to be described below. The factor in question will be plotted with all the other higher numbered factors in order up to and including the factor number specified on the control line as the last factor to be plotted. Plots for more than one factor may be called for. To obtain all plots, use $NP = NFAC - 1$ in columns 16–18 of the control line, $LAST = NFAC$ in columns 19–21 of the control line, and list all but the last factor on the plot line.

Rotation lines are input as data lines to the program to describe any rotations to be performed. Each axis that is to be rotated requires one rotation line. If no rotations are to be performed, no rotation lines are input. An end line, another data line, is placed after the last rotation line, signaling the program that no more rotations are to be performed. The sequence of operations is as follows: (a) the unrotated matrix, that is, the matrix to be operated on, is read in together with a transformation matrix if previous rotations have been performed already on this unrotated matrix; (b) the unrotated matrix is postmultiplied by the transformation matrix input to get the rotated factors—this is an identity matrix supplied by the program if no transformation matrix is input because no previous rotations have been performed on this matrix; (c) the transformation matrix is modified to take into account any rotations called for on the rotation lines, and the original unrotated matrix is multiplied by this modified transformation matrix to give the new rotated matrix; (d) the transformation matrix is premultiplied by its transpose to give the matrix of correlations among the reference vectors (simple axes); (e) the transformation matrix will be output to an external data set, if 001 is punched in columns 10–12 of the control line, providing a stored input matrix that can be fed into the program as data along with the unrotated matrix for the next series of rotations; (f) plots of the rotated factors with each other will be made if 001 has been entered in columns 13–15 of the control line. It should be noted that the plots can be called for without actually carrying out any rotations.

Control Line.   The control line is the first data line. The information to be placed on this line is summarized briefly in Table 14.8.

Blank-Dot-Asterisk Line.   Column 1 is left blank; a dot or period is put in column 2; column 3 contains an asterisk. The dot is used to make a border for the plot and the asterisk marks a data point. Other symbols may be substituted for these if desired.

Unrotated Factor Matrix.   This matrix is input by columns (column 1 first, column 2 second, etc.). Each new column starts a new line or data row. This is the matrix with which the rotations start. It is always input for each series of rotations. It is only the transformation matrix that changes as the series of rotations progresses. The transformation matrix is an identity matrix at the start. The "unrotated" matrix could, of course, be a matrix that has been rotated before in some other rotational sequence. It is merely the matrix that is the starting point for this series of rotations.

Transformation Matrix.   This matrix is not input for the first series of rotations as a rule since the series of rotations ordinarily starts with an unrotated matrix. In this case, the program supplies the identity matrix as

TABLE 14.8

Control Data Line Information for the Hand-Rotation Program

Columns	Information to be Placed in Columns
1–3	N, the number of variables, 115 maximum
4–6	NFAC, the number of factors, 50 maximum
7–9	Enter 001 if a transformation matrix is to be input by the format (12F6.3), entered by columns, i.e., the first line(s) contain(s) column 1, the next line(s) hold(s) column 2, and so on; enter 000 if no transformation matrix is input; the program supplies an identity matrix as the initial transformation matrix
10–12	Enter 001 if the computed transformation matrix incorporating the current rotations is to be output by columns (column 1 first, column 2 second, and so on) in format (12F6.3); enter 000 for no matrix output
13–15	Enter 001 if some plots are to be made of the factors against each other; enter 000 for no plots to be made
16–18	NP, the number of factors to be plotted with the other factors, where NP may not exceed NFAC minus 1
19–21	LAST, the number of the last factor to be plotted with lower numbers; LAST must be greater than NP.

the starting transformation matrix. The first series of rotations occurs as a result of modification of this identity transformation matrix (see Chapters 5 and 6) as a function of the rotations desired. The transformation matrix may be output in each series of rotations to be used as input for the next series of rotations. The format is (12F6.3) and the matrix is output by columns.

Rotation Lines.   For each rotation to be performed, a line is prepared as shown in Table 14.9. If an orthogonal rotation is desired, this requires two rotation lines. The first rotates one factor against the other by a certain angle and the second rotates the other factor against the first by the same angle but with an opposite sign to maintain orthogonality of the rotated factors. If only one factor is rotated at a time, the solution will become oblique.

End Line.   Each rotation line results in one rotation of one factor. A factor may be rotated only once in each set of rotations as a rule. To carry out more than one such rotation risks overshooting the mark. Each factor may be rotated once in each series with reasonable safety. After the last rotation line, an end line is placed with 999 entered in columns 1–3. This signals the program that there are no more rotations to be done.

Plot Line.   The numbers of the factors for which plots with other factors are to be obtained are placed on this line in numerical order using the format (24I3). Each of these factors will be plotted against factors with

TABLE 14.9

Rotation Data Line Information for the Hand-Rotation Program

Columns	Information to be Placed in Columns
1–3	IXVAR, the number of the factor that is to be rotated
4–6	IYVAR, the number of the other factor against which the first factor is to be rotated
7–12	TAN, the tangent of the angle of rotation; for example, − 0.250 would call for the rotation of the factor listed in columns 1–3 away from the factor listed in columns 4–6 by an angle for which the tangent is 0.250; if the entry had been + 0.400, the first-named factor would have been rotated *toward* the second-named factor by an angle with a tangent of 0.400; note that the second- named factor is not rotated by this rotation line

higher numbers up to and including the factor designated as the last factor to be plotted in columns 19–21 on the control line.

Tapes Used. In addition to the usual tapes for reading and writing, this program uses tape 7 for storage of the transformation matrix output as an external data set.

Data Line Order. The lines that constitute the data are arranged in the following order: control line, blank-dot-asterisk line, lines for the unrotated factor matrix, lines for the transformation matrix, if any, rotation lines, if any, end line, and plot line if any plots are to be done.

Printed Output. The unrotated factor matrix input as the starting point for the rotation process is printed out first followed by the starting transformation matrix. If a transformation matrix has been input, it will be output. If none has been input, the identity matrix will be printed out as the starting transformation matrix. The contents of the rotation lines, if any, and the end line will be printed out next. The rotated factor matrix is output next followed by the modified transformation matrix used to obtain the rotated factor matrix. The **C** matrix, the correlations among the reference vectors, is output next. Finally, the plots of the factors with each other are printed last, if any plots have been called for.

14.9.   PROGRAM 9. ANALYTIC OBLIQUE ROTATION

This program is used to make improvements in the simple structure solution through additional analytic rotations and also to compute the pattern matrix, the structure matrix, and the matrix of correlations among factors (see Chapter 6). The program performs either of these functions separately or both of them together. Thus, if a hand oblique solution has been obtained using the previous program, the unrotated matrix and the transformation matrix may be input as data for this program. Then, the solution may be adjusted further analytically, or merely the computation of the pattern, structure, and Φ matrices called for. It is also possible to merely do the analytic rotations, output the transformation matrix, and use the previous program to plot the rotated factors for inspection before considering the rotation process terminated. This solution may even be adjusted further by hand rotations, using Program 8, and the results returned to Program 9 for calculation of the final matrices.

The analytic rotation procedure, developed by the first author, is basically a trial-and-error method for improving simple structure. For each factor, a trial rotation toward and away from each other factor in turn is made. A count of the number of points in the hyperplane, for example, $+.10$ to $-.10$, is made for the present factor position and for the two trial positions. If one of the trial positions has a higher hyperplane count than the present position, the new factor position is accepted provided it does not bring the solution to a degree of obliquity exceeding the maximum specified on the control line. The program cycles through all the possible rotations and then repeats the process as often as called for on the control line. The program starts off with a search angle that is specified on the control line. The search angle is ordinarily made to be rather modest in size because the intent is to adjust an existing solution rather than to obtain an entirely new one. The size of this angle is progressively reduced on successive repetitions of the rotational cycle so that smaller and smaller search angles are used in the late stages to make only fine adjustments. It is possible to use this program starting with an original extracted, unrotated factor matrix, using a large initial search angle. The authors' experience has been that poor results are obtained in this way. It is better to start with a Tandem Criteria solution or a Varimax solution, or some other first approximation solution, and then only make comparatively small changes in the character of the initial solution by means of this analytic rotation program. When applied with relatively small initial search angles, this method will usually increase the hyperplane count for an initial solution considerably without grossly modifying the nature of the solution input. It operates to "clean up" the solution relative to simple structure criteria.

Control Line.   The control line is the first data line. The information to be put on this line is summarized briefly in Table 14.10.

TABLE 14.10

Control Line Information for the Analytic Oblique Rotation Program

Columns	Information to be Placed in Columns
1–3	N, the number of data variables, 115 maximum
4–6	NFAC, the number of factors to be rotated, 50 maximum
7–9	NITER, the number of rotation cycles desired; during each cycle, each factor is rotated with each other factor; eight to ten cycles is normally sufficient
10–12	HYPW, the hyperplane width desired; 0.10 gives a width of 0.20, that is, from −.10 to +.10, the typical value used; a smaller value may be used with a large sample
13–15	TAN, the tangent of the initial search angle; the trial positions of the reference vectors will be toward and away from the other factor by an angle with this tangent; for adjusting a rotated solution, a value above .20 would seldom be used and a smaller one would often be preferred
16–18	PROP, the proportion of the tangent of the search angle that is to be used for the next cycle; for example, if .80 is used, and if the initial search angle tangent is .20, the tangent of the search angle for the second cycle will be .16, for the third .13, and so on
19–21	RMAX, the largest correlation in absolute value between reference vectors to be tolerated; if a trial rotation yields a higher hyperplane count but would cause a correlation between reference vectors higher than this value, for example, .55, the rotation will not be carried out
22	Enter 1 if the transformation matrix is to be output in format (12F6.3); enter 0 for no data set output
23	Enter 1 if a transformation matrix is to be input following the matrix of unrotated factors; enter 0 if no transformation matrix is to be input
24	Enter 1 if analytic rotation of reference vectors is to be omitted; enter 0 to carry out analytic rotations
25	Enter 1 to bypass the computation of the pattern matrix, structure matrix, and the Φ matrix; enter 0 if these matrices are to be computed and output
26	Enter 1 if the Φ matrix of correlations between factors is to be output to an external data set; enter 0 for no output; this output may be input to the factor analysis program (Program 5) for a second-order factor analysis

Unrotated Factor Matrix Lines.   Each unrotated factor matrix column is entered as row(s) in the format (12F6.3). These data rows ordinarily would be output as an external data set by a previous program. Each column begins a new data row.

Transformation Matrix Lines.   The columns of the transformation matrix, if any, are entered as lines or rows in the format (12F6.3). These lines ordinarily would be output by a previous computer run. Each column starts on a new line.

Tapes Used.   In addition to tapes 5 and 6 for data input and printed output, tape 7 is used for external data set output.

Data Line Order. The lines that constitute the data are arranged in the following order: control line, unrotated matrix lines, and transformation matrix lines.

Printed Output. The unrotated matrix, or previously rotated matrix, input as data is printed out first followed by the oblique reference vector projections. The transformation matrix is output next. This matrix multiplied by the unrotated matrix produces the oblique reference vector projection matrix. The next matrix output is the matrix of correlations among the reference vectors, **C**. The hyperplane counts for the factors for each cycle of rotations are output next. The oblique reference vector projections following analytic rotations, the new transformation matrix, and the new **C** matrix follow if analytic rotation has been called for. Finally, the pattern matrix, the Φ matrix, and the structure matrix are printed out in that order if called for.

14.10. PROGRAM 10. MULTIPLE REGRESSION

This program was designed to compute the multiple correlation and the β weights for predicting a given criterion variable from several predictor variables. The multiple correlations and β weights may be obtained for several criterion variables on one run, using the same predictor variables in each analysis. The data consist of a correlation matrix in which the predictor (independent) variables constitute the lower numbered variables. The criterion (dependent) variables follow in order after the predictor variables. The portion of the matrix that involves correlations among the criterion variables may be left blank, although data lines must be input for this section of the matrix, blank or not. The program extracts the matrix of correlations among the predictors from this larger matrix and inverts it. This inverse matrix is multiplied by the columns of correlations of the predictor variables with the criterion variables to obtain columns of β weights, one column for each criterion variable. The squared multiple correlation is obtained as the inner product of the β weights and the correlations of the predictor variables with the criterion variable. (See Chapter 10 for a description of this method of obtaining the multiple correlation and the β weights). Care must be taken to see that the matrix of correlations among the predictors is nonsingular, that is, that it *has* an inverse. A correlation matrix will be singular, and hence will have no inverse, when linearly dependent variables are included in the same matrix. For example, if odd-item scores, even-item scores, and total scores are included as three variables in the same matrix, linear dependence exists because the total score is the sum of the other two.

Control Line.   The control line is the first data line. The information to be placed on this line is summarized briefly in Table 14.11.

Variable Format Lines.   The next three data lines following the control line are the variable format lines, which specify how the data are arranged on the input data lines. Only columns 1–72 may be used. The data consist of a full correlation matrix including all the predictor variables first followed by the criterion variables. Entries are entered both above and below the diagonal except that the section of the matrix for correlations among the criterion variables may be left blank. The diagonals may be left blank also as unities will be supplied for these cells by the program. The lines are entered for the first column of the matrix, followed by those for the second column, and so on. A typical format might be (12F6.3), which would allow six columns for each correlation coefficient. This would give an entered value, for example, of -0.358 for a single entry. If it is desired to remove a certain predictor that is entered in the data lines, in order to do another run with fewer predictor variables, the variable format must be changed to eliminate that variable from the appropriate row of the correlation matrix. The lines, or data rows, for that column, however, must be physically removed from the data.

Data Lines for the Correlation Matrix.   The lines for the correlation matrix follow the three variable format lines and are prepared in accordance with the instructions given above. Each column of the correlation matrix is started on a new line. It is helpful to label the data lines or data rows for each column of the matrix by the number of the variable they represent. Then, if a predictor or criterion variable is to be omitted on a given run, the lines for that variable can be removed easily and the variable format lines adjusted to eliminate the appropriate row or rows of the matrix.

Data Line Order.   The lines that constitute the data are arranged in the following order: control line, variable format lines, and lines for the correlation matrix.

TABLE 14.11

Control Data Line Information for the Multiple Regression Program

Columns	Information to be Placed in Columns
1–3	N, the number of predictor variables
4–6	NC, the number of criterion variables; N + NC must be less than or equal to 50

Printed Output. The matrix of correlations among the predictors and criterion variables is printed out first just as input. Following this, the inverse of the matrix of correlations among the predictor variables is printed out. Finally, the multiple correlation and the β weights are printed out for each of the criterion variables.

14.11. PROGRAM 11. CENTROID FACTOR ANALYSIS

This program is designed to carry out a centroid factor analysis. Its main use is to provide a computer check on the hand calculations done for student exercise problems, although there are certain problems where a centroid analysis might be preferred to other solutions. This program was written by Cris Thomas while he was a student in the first author's factor analysis class.

Control Line. The control line is the first data line. Information required for the control line is summarized in Table 14.12. Where blanks are called for, do *not* put zeros.

Data Lines Input. This program is designed to accept a correlation matrix as data. Correlation matrix data lines follow other lines in the data listing, entered in format (12F6.3), or in some other format if another input format is specified.

14.12. PROGRAM 12. OUTLIER DETECTION

This program is designed to detect bad data, such as may occur as a result of faked responses, errors in data entry, or other difficulties that might cause distortions in the correlations among the variables. The method used in this program is based on comparing the given subject's cross product of standard scores for all variables with the average over all correlations in the matrix (Comrey, 1985). This method detects some of the same outliers that would be found by the better known Mahalanobis D squared method, and vice versa, but both methods find outliers not identified by the other. Rasmussen (1988) used a Monte Carlo simulation to show that removing the outliers by Mahalanobis D squared gave correlations that were somewhat closer to the population values than with the Comrey method. Any outlier identified by either method, however, should be examined to see if there is some problem with the data that would require removal of the case involved to obtain better factor analytic results. A brief description of the program is given here. For more information, consult Comrey (1985).

TABLE 14.12

Control Line Information for the Centroid Factor Analysis Program

Columns	Information to be Placed in Columns
1–3	N, Number of variables
4	Leave blank
5–7	Number of factors to be extracted
8	Leave blank
9	Enter 1 to print out residual matrix after each factor; Enter 0 to omit these matrices
10	Leave blank
11	Enter 1 here *AND* in column 15 to output factor matrix to an external data set. Leave blank otherwise
12	Leave blank
13	Enter 1 if a variable input format is given on a line inserted right after the control line. If FORMAT (12F6.3) is used, omit format line and leave 13 blank
14	Leave blank
15	Enter 1 *AND* include an output format line, for example, (12F6.3), if output of the factor matrix to an external data set is desired. This output format line follows the control line and the input format line, if one is used, but precedes the data. Leave blank if no external data set output is desired
16	Leave blank
17	Enter 1 if communalities are input in the same format as the correlation matrix following the format line(s) or immediately after the control line if there are no format lines. Leave column 17 blank if high column values are to be used as communality estimates

For each case, the program computes a D_k value, which is the average squared deviation of the individual's cross product of standard scores from the correlations based on all cases. Outliers are those cases with large D_k values since they are deviating substantially from the group response tendency while those with low D_k values are responding in a manner representative of the entire sample.

Control Line.   The control line is the first data line. The information required on the control card is summarized on Table 14.13.

Variable Format Line(s).   One or more variable format lines follow the control line, depending on what is placed in columns 1–3 of the control line. Use F format only, for example, (36F2.0/8F2.0).

Data Lines.   The *n* raw scores for each person are entered consecutively on one or more lines (data rows) according to the format specified on the variable format line(s). The format listed above would have 36 two-digit scores on line 1 followed by 8 two-digit scores on line 2. Scores for each new

TABLE 14.13

Control Data Line Information for the Outlier Detection Program

Columns	Information to be Placed in Columns
1–3	Enter number of variable format lines on which the data format is contained in columns 1–72 (001 to 010)
4–6	Enter n, the number of data variables, maximum 060
7–9	Maximum number of outliers to remove. The program will halt after removing this many outliers if it has not already halted for some other reason; e.g., 020
10–12	If it is desired to have the raw scores input printed out, put 001 in columns 10–12; If no print out of these scores is desired, put 000 in columns 10–12
13–15	Minimum McCall T-score value, T_k, for removal of an outlier (where M = 50, SD = 10). If the largest remaining T_k value is less than this value, the program will halt. A value of 076 here would correspond roughly to the .01 probability level and 070 would correspond roughly to the .05 probability level.

subject must start on a new line. The number of subjects, N, must be less than 800.

Printed Output. If 001 has been entered in columns 10–12 of the control line, the raw scores that have been input to the program will be printed out. If 000 is entered, no scores will be printed out. Following this, the same kind of printout is repeated prior to the elimination of each outlier:

1. The means and standard deviations of the raw score variables for those cases that have not been eliminated as outliers.
2. The mean and standard deviation of the raw discrepancy scores, D_k, for those cases that have not been eliminated as outliers.
3. The standardized discrepancy scores, T_k, for those cases that have not been eliminated as outliers. A zero is substituted for T_k if the case has already been eliminated as an outlier.
4. The largest T_k value for those cases not yet eliminated as outliers and the case number of this subject. This case is the next one to be removed as an outlier.
5. The raw scores for the case to be removed next as an outlier.

14.13. COMMERCIAL COMPUTER PACKAGES

There are many other statistical computer software packages available to the interested researcher. Several of them contain programs for performing exploratory factor analysis. In general, the researcher who wants to use confirmatory factor analysis or structural equation modeling, such as the topics covered in Chapters 12 and 13, will be required to use specialized software that is not part of a standard computer program package. Many of these computer program packages, and even some of the specialized software programs, are available for mainframes, mini-computers, and micro-computers.

This section examines only the most commonly used software packages available at most computer centers and service bureaus. The three most popular commercially available computer packages on the market today are BMDP (Biomedical Computer Programs-P Series), SAS (Statistical Analysis System), and SPSS (Statistical Package for the Social Sciences). In the social and behavioral science literature over the past five years, these packages have been utilized by factor analysis researchers more than any other package or stand-alone computer program. Even though the computer programs written by the first author of this book are available from the publisher of this book on computer diskette, the three most popular statistical packages must be purchased or rented from the organizations involved in their distribution. University users usually would have them available at their computer center. For those in industry, larger organizations will usually rent one or more of the programs. Smaller firms usually make use of a service bureau that would have available one or more of these packages.

This section explains to the reader how to set up exploratory factor analysis problems using three popular software packages. The reader will find that each package is equipped with slightly different options and different syntax for instructing the program to do exploratory factor analysis. None of these "canned" statistical packages can perform all analyses described in the early chapters of this book, for example, Comrey's minimum residual method of factor extraction (Comrey, 1962) or Comrey's tandem criteria method of rotation (Comrey, 1967). All three of the packages, BMDP, SAS, and SPSS, however, can do principal components analysis and principal factor extraction with various kinds of orthogonal and oblique rotations.

The major entries for each package are the same. As mentioned above, only their syntax, or how to specify the program statements, is different. The major categories for entries are:

I. Data Entry
    1. The number of variables in the problem.
    2. The name of the variables.
    3. The form of the data.
    4. Format for entering data into program.
II. Factor Analysis
    5. Factor extraction method.

6. Number of factors.
7. Initial communality estimates.
8. Method of Rotation.

To illustrate the use of the packages, the twelve variable problem that has been presented throughout the text is used. The instructions given here are far from being complete. For a complete description, the reader should consult the appropriate user's manual.

14.13.1. SETUP FOR THE BMDP COMPUTER PACKAGE

The first example is the setup for using BMDP Program BMDP4M. This is the specific program named and designated in the BMDP package to perform exploratory factor analysis. There are 12 variables for this example problem. The names of the variables are abbreviated to represent those selected. The data are in the form of correlations. The format of the input data is in fields of five columns in width. That is, each variable's data will occupy 5 columns of data entry space, and the data will be numerical. Writing a format statement using this convention requires some programming knowledge on the part of the user. Later, a simpler method of input is described. The extraction method is the principal factor method and the communalities will be iterated a maximum of 25 times. Squared multiple correlations will be used as initial communality estimates. There will be a maximum of four factors extracted and the extracted factors will be rotated using Kaiser's normal varimax method. The setup follows:

```
Problem title is 'BMDP4M Iterated Principal Factor, SMCs, Varimax'./
input type is correlation.
        shape is square.
        variables is 12.
        format is '(12F5.0)'./
variable names are le,aso,in,lif,ld,la,lr,ls,nlw,sym,hlp,gen./
plot    initial is 0.
        final is 0.
        fscore is 0./
factor method is pf.
        number is 4.
        constant is 0.
        iterate is 25.
        commun is smcs./
rotate method is vmax.
        normal./
end/
```

1.00	.61	.64	.07	.14	.07	.04	.08	.06	−.02	−.02	−.17
.61	1.00	.50	.02	.13	.08	−.05	.02	−.02	−.07	−.08	−.15
.64	.50	1.00	.02	.04	−.03	−.01	.08	.01	−.01	−.02	−.04
.07	.02	.02	1.00	.51	.46	.28	.29	.47	.10	.14	.05
.14	.13	.04	.51	1.00	.51	.29	.31	.41	.18	.24	.09
.07	.08	−.03	.46	.51	1.00	.13	.19	.31	.05	.18	.05
.04	−.05	−.01	.28	.29	.13	1.00	.46	.66	.16	.16	.12
.08	.02	.08	.29	.31	.19	.46	1.00	.55	.31	.39	.26
.06	−.02	.01	.47	.41	.31	.66	.55	1.00	.20	.28	.17
−.02	−.07	−.01	.10	.18	.05	.16	.31	.20	1.00	.60	.46
−.02	−.08	−.02	.14	.24	.18	.16	.39	.28	.60	1.00	.61
−.17	−.15	−.04	.05	.09	.05	.12	.26	.17	.46	.61	1.00

finish/

The options available for the type of data are as follows: DATA (raw data), CORR (correlation matrix), COVA (covariance matrix), LOAD (factor loadings), and FSCF (factor score coefficients).

If the user is entering the correlation matrix or covariance matrix, the SHAPE of that matrix is specified as either SQUARE or LOWER. LOWER is used to enter the lower triangular part of a square matrix. The format of the data input can be FREE or fixed. With FREE, each data value is separated by a comma or a space. In the fixed specification, the user can write a FORTRAN type format statement to describe the positions of the input data. For the 12 variable problem above, format is free./ could have been specified instead of the fixed format (12F5.0), and the results of the analysis would have remained unchanged.

There are four major methods of factor extraction available in BMDP: PC (principal components), PF (principal factor), ML (maximum likelihood) and LJ (Kaiser's Second generation Little Jiffy) (Kaiser, 1970). To change the problem above to do maximum likelihood factor extraction, the statement would be entered as factor method is ml.. The number of factors to extract is done using the statement number is 4., if the researcher wants to extract a maximum of four factors. The constant is 0. statement is also used to control the number of factors extracted. Whatever number is specified in this statement, the program will extract all factors that have corresponding eigenvalues greater than or equal to that value. With the example above, the statement says to extract all factors that have an eigenvalue of 0 or higher. In those problems where the user calls for principal components extraction, this value is set equal to 1 by the statement constant is 1..

If the user specifies principal factor, PF, as the method of extraction, BMDP will automatically iterate the communalities. By using the iterate is statement, the user can control the maximum number of iterations. If the user does not want to iterate the communalities, the user should specify iterate is 1.. The type of communalities used with principal factor could be ones (UN), squared multiple correlations (SM), or the largest correlation in that row of the correlation matrix (MAX). So as an example, if a researcher wanted to use ones in the main diagonal of the correlation matrix as communality estimates, the statement would be commun is un./.

There are eight options available for rotation. In the example above, VMAX is specified. VMAX tells the program to perform varimax rotation on the unrotated factors. The other options are NONE (no rotation), QRMAX (Quartimax), EQM (Equamax), DQ (Direct quartimin), DOBL (direct oblimin with gamma), ORTHOG (Orthogonal with gamma), and ORTHOB (Orthoblique). For example, if the user decides to use the direct quartimin method of rotation, the statement would be changed to read rotate method is DQ.. The user can also specify whether or not the Kaiser normalization procedure should be performed during rotation.

The end/ statement is used to tell BMDP4M where the program statements end and the data begin.

The output of the 12-variable example given above is:

PAGE 1 BMDP4M

BMDP4M - FACTOR ANALYSIS

Copyright 1977, 1979, 1981, 1982, 1983, 1985, 1987, 1988
          BMDP Statistical Software, Inc.

Version: 1988 (IBM PC/DOS)

PROBLEM TITLE IS
BMDP4M Iterated Principal Factor, SMCs, Varimax

```
NUMBER OF VARIABLES TO READ IN ......................        12
NUMBER OF VARIABLES ADDED BY TRANSFORMATIONS .......         0
TOTAL NUMBER OF VARIABLES............................        12
CASE WEIGHT VARIABLE.................................
CASE LABELING VARIABLES .............................
NUMBER OF CASES TO READ IN ..........................    TO END
MISSING VALUES CHECKED BEFORE OR AFTER TRANS ........   NEITHER
BLANKS ARE ..........................................   MISSING
NUMBER OF WORDS OF DYNAMIC STORAGE ..................     16298
NUMBER OF CASES DESCRIBED BY INPUT FORMAT ...........         1
```

VARIABLES TO BE USED

1 le	2 aso	3 in	4 lif	5 ld
6 la	7 lr	8 ls	9 nlw	10 sym
11 hlp	12 gen			

PAGE 2 BMDP4M BMDP4M Iterated Principal Factor, SMCs, Varimax

INPUT FORMAT IS
(12F5.0)

MAXIMUM LENGTH DATA RECORD IS 60 CHARACTERS.

I N P U T   V A R I A B L E S . . . . .

VARIABLE NO.	NAME	RECORD NO.	COLUMN BEG	COLUMN END	INPUT FORMAT
1	le	1	1	5	F5.0
2	aso	1	6	10	F5.0
3	in	1	11	15	F5.0
4	lif	1	16	20	F5.0
5	ld	1	21	25	F5.0
6	la	1	26	30	F5.0
7	lr	1	31	35	F5.0
8	ls	1	36	40	F5.0
9	nlw	1	41	45	F5.0
10	sym	1	46	50	F5.0
11	hlp	1	51	55	F5.0
12	gen	1	56	60	F5.0

NUMBER OF VARIABLES TO BE USED   12

WEIGHT VARIABLE . . . .
INITIAL COMMUNALITIES ARE SQUARED MULTIPLE
   CORRELATIONS OR COVARIANCES. . . . .
ITERATED PRINCIPAL FACTOR ANALYSIS IS PERFORMED . . .
NUMBER OF ITERATIONS FOR INITIAL FACTOR EXTRACTION.   25
MAXIMUM NUMBER OF FACTORS   4
NUMBER OF FACTORS IS LIMITED TO THE NUMBER OF
   EIGENVALUES GREATER THAN 0.000
TOLERANCE LIMIT FOR MATRIX INVERSION. 0.00010
VARIMAX ROTATION IS PERFORMED . . . .
GAMMA 1.0000
MAXIMUM NUMBER OF ITERATIONS FOR ROTATION   50
CONVERGENCE CRITERION FOR ROTATION 0.0000100
KAISERS NORMALIZATION. . . . .   YES

PAGE 3 BMDP4M BMDP4M Iterated Principal Factor, SMCs, Varimax

SQUARED MULTIPLE CORRELATIONS (SMC) OF
EACH VARIABLE WITH ALL OTHER VARIABLES

1 le	0.54724
2 aso	0.41286
3 in	0.44845
4 lif	0.38730
5 ld	0.41496
6 la	0.34153
7 lr	0.46723

8 ls	0.3967 l
9 nlw	0.58843
10 sym	0.38964
11 hlp	0.55169
12 gen	0.42268

COMMUNALITY ESTIMATES ARE SQUARED MULTIPLE CORRELATIONS (COVARIANCES).

ITERATION FOR INITIAL FACTORS

ITERATION	MAXIMUM CHANGE IN COMMUNALITY
1	0.10782
2	0.05111
3	0.02880
4	0.01848
5	0.01283
6	0.00928
7	0.00687
8	0.00514
9	0.00388
10	0.00294
11	0.00223
12	0.00170
13	0.00130
14	0.00099

PAGE 4 BMDP4M BMDP4M Iterated Principal Factor, SMCs, Varimax

COMMUNALITIES OBTAINED FROM 4 FACTORS AFTER 14 ITERATIONS.

THE COMMUNALITY OF A VARIABLE IS ITS SQUARED MULTIPLE CORRELATION WITH THE FACTORS.

1 le	0.7779
2 aso	0.4983
3 in	0.5369
4 lif	0.4754
5 ld	0.5506
6 la	0.5194
7 lr	0.5983
8 ls	0.4546
9 nlw	0.7752
10 sym	0.4547
11 hlp	0.8051
12 gen	0.4869

PAGE 5 BMDP4M BMDP4M Iterated Principal Factor, SMCs, Varimax

FACTOR	VARIANCE EXPLAINED	CUMULATIVE PROPORTION OF VARIANCE IN DATA SPACE	IN FACTOR SPACE	CARMINES THETA
1	3.0204	0.4237	0.4356	0.8764
2	1.9198	0.6931	0.7126	
3	1.2531	0.8689	0.8933	
4	0.7398	0.9727	1.0000	
5	0.0807	0.9840		
6	0.0642	0.9930		
7	0.0396	0.9986		
8	0.0102	1.0000		
9	− 0.0118			
10	− 0.0386			
11	− 0.0698			
12	− 0.0752			

TOTAL VARIANCE IS DEFINED AS THE SUM OF THE POSITIVE EIGEN VALUES OF THE CORRELATION MATRIX.

NEGATIVE VALUES FOR VARIANCE EXPLAINED INDICATE THE DEGREE TO WHICH THE COMMUNALITIES HAVE BEEN UNDERESTIMATED. LARGE NEGATIVE VALUES FOR VARIANCE EXPLAINED INDICATE THAT THE COVARIANCE OR CORRELATION MATRIX IS POORLY ESTIMATED.

PAGE 7 BMDP4M BMDP4M Iterated Principal Factor, SMCs, Varimax

UNROTATED FACTOR LOADINGS (PATTERN)

		FACTOR 1	FACTOR 2	FACTOR 3	FACTOR 4
le	1	0.098	0.834	0.266	− 0.044
aso	2	0.012	0.678	0.187	0.055
in	3	0.044	0.653	0.317	− 0.090
lif	4	0.548	0.138	− 0.329	0.217
ld	5	0.603	0.191	− 0.223	0.317
la	6	0.464	0.139	− 0.282	0.453
lr	7	0.586	0.017	− 0.230	− 0.449
ls	8	0.638	0.014	0.043	− 0.214
nlw	9	0.771	0.054	− 0.278	− 0.316
sym	10	0.466	− 0.228	0.429	0.035
hlp	11	0.628	− 0.289	0.551	0.153
gen	12	0.414	− 0.352	0.435	0.044
	VP	3.020	1.920	1.253	0.740

THE VP FOR EACH FACTOR IS THE SUM OF THE SQUARES OF THE ELEMENTS OF THE COLUMN OF THE FACTOR LOADING MATRIX CORRESPONDING TO THAT FACTOR. THE VP IS THE VARIANCE EXPLAINED BY THE FACTOR. ORTHOGONAL ROTATION, GAMMA = 1.0000

ITERATION	SIMPLICITY CRITERION
0	− 2.915814
1	− 7.005107
2	− 7.147428
3	− 7.148119
4	− 7.148120

PAGE 8 BMDP4M BMDP4M Iterated Principal Factor, SMCs, Varimax

ROTATED FACTOR LOADINGS (PATTERN)

		FACTOR 1	FACTOR 2	FACTOR 3	FACTOR 4
le	1	− 0.055	0.875	0.057	0.073
aso	2	− 0.090	0.692	− 0.052	0.096
in	3	0.013	0.730	0.032	− 0.046
lif	4	0.028	0.013	0.294	0.623
ld	5	0.132	0.102	0.229	0.686
la	6	0.052	0.016	0.058	0.716
lr	7	0.071	− 0.021	0.760	0.123
ls	8	0.338	0.078	0.545	0.193
nlw	9	0.140	− 0.003	0.798	0.345
sym	10	0.659	− 0.008	0.134	0.052
hlp	11	0.876	− 0.011	0.114	0.158
gen	12	0.681	− 0.123	0.087	0.002
	VP	1.836	1.811	1.700	1.587

THE VP FOR EACH FACTOR IS THE SUM OF THE SQUARES OF THE
ELEMENTS OF THE COLUMN OF THE FACTOR PATTERN MATRIX
CORRESPONDING TO THAT FACTOR. WHEN THE ROTATION IS
ORTHOGONAL, THE VP IS THE VARIANCE EXPLAINED BY THE FACTOR.

PAGE 9 BMDP4M BMDP4M Iterated Principal Factor, SMCs, Varimax

SORTED ROTATED FACTOR LOADINGS (PATTERN)

		FACTOR 1	FACTOR 2	FACTOR 3	FACTOR 4
hlp	11	0.876	0.000	0.000	0.000
gen	12	0.681	0.000	0.000	0.000
sym	10	0.659	0.000	0.000	0.000
le	1	0.000	0.875	0.000	0.000
in	3	0.000	0.730	0.000	0.000
aso	2	0.000	0.692	0.000	0.000

nlw	9	0.000	0.000	0.798	0.345
lr	7	0.000	0.000	0.760	0.000
ls	8	0.338	0.000	0.545	0.000
la	6	0.000	0.000	0.000	0.716
ld	5	0.000	0.000	0.000	0.686
lif	4	0.000	0.000	0.294	0.623
VP		1.836	1.811	1.700	1.587

THE ABOVE FACTOR LOADING MATRIX HAS BEEN REARRANGED SO THAT THE COLUMNS APPEAR IN DECREASING ORDER OF VARIANCE EXPLAINED BY FACTORS. THE ROWS HAVE BEEN REARRANGED SO THAT FOR EACH SUCCESSIVE FACTOR, LOADINGS GREATER THAN 0.5000 APPEAR FIRST. LOADINGS LESS THAN 0.2500 HAVE BEEN REPLACED BY ZERO.

PAGE 10 BMDP4M BMDP4M Iterated Principal Factor, SMCs, Varimax

FACTOR SCORE COVARIANCE (COMPUTED FROM FACTOR STRUCTURE AND FACTOR SCORE COEFFICIENTS)

THE DIAGONAL OF THE MATRIX BELOW CONTAINS THE SQUARED MULTIPLE CORRELATIONS OF EACH FACTOR WITH THE VARIABLES.

		FACTOR 1	FACTOR 2	FACTOR 3	FACTOR 4
FACTOR	1	0.842			
FACTOR	2	− 0.018	0.846		
FACTOR	3	0.033	0.002	0.787	
FACTOR	4	0.030	0.021	0.106	0.716

CPU TIME USED   17.360 SECONDS
PAGE 12 BMDP4M

BMDP4M – FACTOR ANALYSIS

PROGRAM INSTRUCTIONS

finish/

NO MORE CONTROL LANGUAGE.

PROGRAM TERMINATED

At the end of all programming statements, BMDP requires the user to enter the statement finish/. This tells BMDP that there are no more programming statements and exits from the program. BMDP4M perhaps gives more output than the other two popular software packages. The plot section of the BMDP program is used to graphically plot the factor analysis solution. The optional output in the example given above has been eliminated to save space.

14.13.2. SETUP FOR THE SAS COMPUTER PACKAGE

Using SAS to analyze the same sample problem would require the following SAS programming statements:

```
data a(type=corr);
__type__ = 'corr';
input __name__ $ lawe aso inc lif ld la lr ls nlw sym hlp gen;
cards;
lawe    1.00    .61    .64    .07    .14    .07    .04    .08    .06  -.02  -.02  -.17
aso      .61   1.00    .50    .02    .13    .08  -.05    .02  -.02  -.07  -.08  -.15
inc      .64    .50   1.00    .02    .04  -.03  -.01    .08    .01  -.01  -.02  -.04
lif      .07    .02    .02   1.00    .51    .46    .28    .29    .47    .10    .14    .05
ld       .14    .13    .04    .51   1.00    .51    .29    .31    .41    .18    .24    .09
la       .07    .08  -.03    .46    .51   1.00    .13    .19    .31    .05    .18    .05
lr       .04  -.05  -.01    .28    .29    .13   1.00    .46    .66    .16    .16    .12
ls       .08    .02    .08    .29    .31    .19    .46   1.00    .55    .31    .39    .26
nlw      .06  -.02    .01    .47    .41    .31    .66    .55   1.00    .20    .28    .17
sym     -.02  -.07  -.01    .10    .18    .05    .16    .31    .20   1.00    .60    .46
hlp     -.02  -.08  -.02    .14    .24    .18    .16    .39    .28    .60   1.00    .61
gen     -.17  -.15  -.04    .05    .09    .05    .12    .26    .17    .46    .61   1.00
;
proc factor  method=prinit  rotate=varimax  mineigen=0  nfact=4
             maxiter=25  norm=kaiser;
priors smc;
run;
```

The first four statements of this program are used to communicate to SAS that the data entered are correlations. The __type__ = 'corr'; and (type=corr); statements are unnecessary if the researcher is using raw data and the correlations will be computed. Like BMDP4M, SAS can handle a variety of different formats: Raw data, correlations, covariances (__type = 'cov';), factor scores (__type__ = 'score';), and factor pattern (__type__ = 'pattern';).

The statement input __name__ $ lawe aso inc lif ld la lr ls nlw sym hlp gen; is used to input the correlation data into SAS and identify each of the 12 variables used in the analysis. To input a correlation matrix, the __name__ $ is necessary to insure that the proper information is passed onto the FACTOR procedure. Unlike BMDP, using a pre-existing correlation matrix in SAS means that the user will be required to add on to the beginning of each row of thè correlation matrix the name of the variable that row represents. In the example given above, the reader will see that the correlation matrix used is the same as that used in the BMDP example. The only difference is that the variable names have been added to each row. If the values in each row are separated by blanks or commas, the user can elect to use the free format option of data entry. This is done by specifying the variable names only in the order of input in the input statement, shown above. SAS offers a number of different ways for formatting input. Users should consult the SAS User's Guide to find the most appropriate method for their own data.

The cards; statement tells SAS that the input data are following. After the last data entry, it is customary to enter a line with a ;, as shown above. This will tell SAS that all the data have been entered and that the statements that follow will be SAS programming statements.

PROC FACTOR is the actual SAS routine that will perform the factor analysis on the input data. The user can specify a number of different factor extraction methods. This is done with the method = xxx parameter. The user would substitute one of the following for the xxx: PRIN is for principal components, PRINIT is for iterated principal factor, ULS is for unweighted least squares factor analysis, ALPHA is for alpha factor analysis (Kaiser & Caffry, 1965), ML is for maximum likelihood, HARRIS is for Harris components analysis, IMAGE is image factor analysis (Kaiser, 1963), and PATTERN is used to analyze an existing factor solution input through SAS's DATA step. SAS's PROC FACTOR has more extraction methods to choose from than BMDP. If the user wanted to do alpha factor analysis, for example, the specification would be proc factor method = alpha;.

The number of factors extracted is controlled by two parameters: nfact = n and mineigen = k. The nfact = n parameter tells PROC FACTOR the maximum number of factors, n, to extract. It is identical to the number is statement in BMDP4M. The mineigen = k parameter tells PROC FACTOR to retain all the factors that have an eigenvalue greater than or equal to the value k. This parameter is identical to constant is in BMDP4M. These two statements may tell PROC FACTOR to retain different numbers of factors. PROC FACTOR will actually retain a number of factors equal to the smaller of the two numbers suggested.

The maxiter = n parameter of PROC FACTOR specifies the maximum number of times, n, the communalities are iterated. This is the same as iterate is in BMDP4M.

SAS's PROC FACTOR has eight basic options for rotating the extracted factors. The desired method is specified by using the parameter ROTATE = xxxxx. In the example given above, a varimax rotation is used: ROTATE = VARIMAX. The other options are NONE (no rotation), QUARTIMAX (quartimax rotation), EQUAMAX (equamax rotation), ORTHOMAX (general orthomax rotation with gamma), HK (Harris-Kaiser case II orthoblique rotation), PROMAX (promax rotation), and PROCRUSTES (oblique Procrustes rotation with a target pattern). The user can specify the method for normalizing the rows of the factor pattern coefficients used in rotation through the norm = xxx statement. The options are NONE or RAW (no normalization), KAISER (Kaiser's method of normalization) and WEIGHT (Cureton-Mulaik technique of weighting; Cureton & Mulaik, 1975).

Initial communality estimates are specified for the program using the priors xxx; statement. The xxx is replaced by one of the options given below. This statement is written on a separate line after the PROC FACTOR statement. The ; is very important in the syntax of SAS. It is a delimiter. It tells the program when one statement ends and when another begins. The options for priors are as follows: ONE (sets all initial communalities equal to 1.0), MAX (the maximum absolute correlation in each row of the correlation matrix is used as an initial communality estimate), SMC (the initial estimates are squared multiple correlations), ASMC (adjusted squared multiple correlations), RANDOM (initial estimates are random numbers between 0 and 1), and INPUT (initial estimates are read in from another data set). For the example above, the initial communality estimates are squared multiple correlations, that is, priors smc;.

For some computer operating systems, such as DOS which is available for the IBM Personal Computers, the run; statement is necessary to execute the program. On some mainframe computers, this statement may not be necessary to complete a successful run.

PROC FACTOR in SAS has many other options in addition to those that have been mentioned here. The reader is advised to consult the SAS User's Manual for more information about the possible variations. The output from executing the SAS program statements as they are written above is presented here.

SAS

Initial Factor Method: Iterated Principal Factor Analysis

Prior Communality Estimates: SMC

LAWE	ASO	INC	LIF	LD	LA
0.547237	0.412862	0.448450	0.387298	0.414961	0.341532

LR	LS	NLW	SYM	HLP	GEN
0.467228	0.396709	0.588426	0.389641	0.551686	0.422684

Preliminary Eigenvalues: Total = 5.36871487 Average = .447392906

	1	2	3	4	5	6
Eigenvalue	2.882370	1.776515	1.113367	0.593724	− 0.016330	− 0.050843
Difference	1.105855	0.663148	0.519643	0.610054	0.034513	0.017472
Proportion	0.5369	0.3309	0.2074	0.1106	− 0.0030	− 0.0095
Cumulative	0.5369	0.8678	1.0752	1.1858	1.1827	1.1732

	7	8	9	10	11	12
Eigenvalue	− 0.068315	− 0.113452	− 0.135734	− 0.190064	− 0.195827	− 0.226696
Difference	0.045137	0.022282	0.054330	0.005762	0.030869	
Proportion	− 0.0127	− 0.0211	− 0.0253	− 0.0354	− 0.0365	− 0.0422
Cumulative	1.1605	1.1394	1.1141	1.0787	1.0422	1.0000

4 factors will be retained by the NFACTOR criterion.

Iter	Change	Communalities				
1	0.107824	0.65346	0.48940	0.52413	0.46363	0.50910	0.43457
		0.54399	0.45742	0.68780	0.45497	0.65951	0.48798
2	0.051111	0.70113	0.50869	0.54605	0.48192	0.54071	0.47256
		0.57581	0.46654	0.73027	0.46898	0.71062	0.50344
3	0.028795	0.72619	0.51091	0.55048	0.48380	0.55112	0.49031
		0.58972	0.46415	0.75037	0.46907	0.73942	0.50430
4	0.018481	0.74137	0.50880	0.54956	0.48196	0.55414	0.49993
		0.59595	0.46070	0.76069	0.46621	0.75790	0.50148
5	0.012826	0.75155	0.50617	0.54731	0.47989	0.55456	0.50583
		0.59866	0.45821	0.76633	0.46332	0.77072	0.49824
6	0.009282	0.75877	0.50397	0.54501	0.47834	0.55412	0.50976
		0.59970	0.45668	0.76957	0.46100	0.78000	0.49542
7	0.006867	0.76407	0.50230	0.54301	0.47730	0.55344	0.51252
		0.59995	0.45580	0.77151	0.45924	0.78687	0.49316
8	0.005143	0.76801	0.50108	0.54138	0.47663	0.55277	0.51452
		0.59983	0.45530	0.77274	0.45793	0.79201	0.49141

Initial Factor Method: Iterated Principal Factor Analysis

Iter	Change	Communalities				
9	0.003879	0.77098	0.50019	0.54009	0.47620	0.55218	0.51599
		0.59956	0.45501	0.77354	0.45695	0.79589	0.49007
10	0.002939	0.77322	0.49954	0.53908	0.47591	0.55169	0.51709
		0.59926	0.45484	0.77409	0.45621	0.79883	0.48904
11	0.002234	0.77491	0.49907	0.53830	0.47572	0.55130	0.51791
		0.59896	0.45475	0.77449	0.45566	0.80107	0.48826
12	0.001702	0.77620	0.49871	0.53769	0.47559	0.55100	0.51853
		0.59869	0.45469	0.77478	0.45524	0.80277	0.48767
13	0.001299	0.77718	0.49845	0.53723	0.47550	0.55076	0.51900
		0.59846	0.45465	0.77500	0.45492	0.80407	0.48722
14	0.000992	0.77793	0.49825	0.53688	0.47544	0.55057	0.51935
		0.59827	0.45463	0.77518	0.45467	0.80506	0.48687

Convergence Criterion Satisfied

Eigenvalues of the Reduced Correlation Matrix:
Total = 6.93244358   Average = .577703632

	1	2	3	4	5	6
Eigenvalue	3.020384	1.919824	1.253078	0.739814	0.080658	0.064201
Difference	1.100560	0.666746	0.513264	0.659156	0.016457	0.024555
Proportion	0.4357	0.2769	0.1808	0.1067	0.0116	0.0093
Cumulative	0.4357	0.7126	0.8934	1.0001	1.0117	1.0210

	7	8	9	10	11	12
Eigenvalue	0.039646	0.010205	−0.011784	−0.038644	−0.069773	−0.075167
Difference	0.029441	0.021989	0.026860	0.031129	0.005393	
Proportion	0.0057	0.0015	−0.0017	−0.0056	−0.0101	−0.0108
Cumulative	1.0267	1.0282	1.0265	1.0209	1.0108	1.0000

Factor Pattern

	FACTOR 1	FACTOR 2	FACTOR 3	FACTOR 4
LAWE	0.09775	0.83411	0.26591	−0.04393
ASO	0.01229	0.67840	0.18680	0.05459
INC	0.04388	0.65304	0.31674	−0.09033
LIF	0.54845	0.13796	−0.32946	0.21693
LD	0.60302	0.19088	−0.22333	0.31722
LA	0.46373	0.13872	−0.28220	0.45325
LR	0.58591	0.01654	−0.23023	−0.44911
LS	0.63795	0.01393	0.04251	−0.21366
NLW	0.77138	0.05365	−0.27832	−0.31592
SYM	0.46645	−0.22752	0.42910	0.03472
HLP	0.62823	−0.28883	0.55100	0.15285
GEN	0.41441	−0.35235	0.43484	0.04358

Initial Factor Method: Iterated Principal Factor Analysis

Variance explained by each factor

FACTOR 1	FACTOR 2	FACTOR 3	FACTOR 4
3.020384	1.919824	1.253078	0.739814

Final Communality Estimates: Total = 6.933101

LAWE	ASO	INC	LIF	LD	LA
0.777927	0.498254	0.536877	0.475438	0.550570	0.519355

LR	LS	NLW	SYM	HLP	GEN
0.598270	0.454631	0.775175	0.454672	0.805059	0.486873

Rotation Method: Varimax

Orthogonal Transformation Matrix

	1	2	3	4
1	0.53572	0.05821	0.63286	0.55597
2	− 0.36037	0.91062	0.04893	0.19621
3	0.74995	0.40587	− 0.29121	− 0.43364
4	0.14392	− 0.05142	− 0.71575	0.68143

Rotation Method: Varimax

Rotated Factor Pattern

	FACTOR 1	FACTOR 2	FACTOR 3	FACTOR 4
LAWE	− 0.05513	0.87543	0.05668	0.07276
ASO	− 0.08995	0.69149	− 0.05250	0.09614
INC	0.01271	0.73043	0.03214	− 0.04637
LIF	0.02824	0.01268	0.29452	0.62269
LD	0.13242	0.10197	0.22895	0.68572
LA	0.05203	0.01548	0.05803	0.71627
LR	0.07063	− 0.02119	0.76010	0.12280
LS	0.33787	0.07806	0.54496	0.19339
NLW	0.13971	− 0.00296	0.79797	0.34480
SYM	0.65868	− 0.00766	0.13426	0.05228
HLP	0.87586	− 0.01067	0.11359	0.15783
GEN	0.68137	− 0.12249	0.08720	0.00240

Rotation Method: Varimax

Variance explained by each factor

FACTOR 1	FACTOR 2	FACTOR 3	FACTOR 4
1.836246	1.810599	1.699554	1.586702

Final Communality Estimates: Total = 6.933101

LAWE	ASO	INC	LIF	LD	LA
0.777927	0.498254	0.536877	0.475438	0.550570	0.519355

LR	LS	NLW	SYM	HLP	GEN
0.598270	0.454631	0.775175	0.454672	0.805059	0.486873

14.13.3. SETUP FOR THE SPSS COMPUTER PACKAGE

The following is the same identical problem analyzed using the SPSS computer package factor analysis program. Again, the basic structure of the program statements is the same, but the syntax, or how the instructions are written, varies. Note that the program written below is similar to BMDP and SAS in that the data must be defined and specified before any analysis is performed on them. Defining and inputting the data into the computer is often referred to as creating a data set. After the data set is properly created, the program for factor analysis is called to act upon it. The SPSS program setup is as follows for this sample problem:

```
data list  FREE  MATRIX/  lawe,aso,inc,lif,ld,la,lr,ls,nlw,sym,hlp,gen.
begin  data.
 1.00     .61     .64     .07     .14     .07     .04     .08     .06   -.02   -.02   -.17
  .61    1.00     .50     .02     .13     .08   -.05     .02   -.02   -.07   -.08   -.15
  .64     .50    1.00     .02     .04   -.03   -.01     .08     .01   -.01   -.02   -.04
  .07     .02     .02    1.00     .51     .46     .28     .29     .47     .10     .14     .05
  .14     .13     .04     .51    1.00     .51     .29     .31     .41     .18     .24     .09
  .07     .08   -.03     .46     .51    1.00     .13     .19     .31     .05     .18     .05
  .04   -.05   -.01     .28     .29     .13    1.00     .46     .66     .16     .16     .12
  .08     .02     .08     .29     .31     .19     .46    1.00     .55     .31     .39     .26
  .06   -.02     .01     .47     .41     .31     .66     .55    1.00     .20     .28     .17
 -.02   -.07   -.01     .10     .18     .05     .16     .31     .20    1.00     .60     .46
 -.02   -.08   -.02     .14     .24     .18     .16     .39     .28     .60    1.00     .61
 -.17   -.15   -.04     .05     .09     .05     .12     .26     .17     .46     .61    1.00
end  data.
factor variables lawe to gen/READ CORRELATION/extraction=pa2
/rotation=varimax/CRITERIA=FACTORS(4)  MINEIGEN(0.0)
ITERATE(25)  KAISER.
```

The first statement line defines the 12 variables used in the problem. The FREE MATRIX specification tells SPSS that the data are input in the form of a matrix or table and that the data are in FREE format form, that is, the data values are separated by commas or blanks. If the user omits the MATRIX parameter of this SPSS statement, SPSS will assume the data entered are raw data values. The type of data, whether correlations, covariances, factor scores or loadings, is specified in another SPSS program statement. Just as in BMDP and SAS, the user can input the data in FREE form or formatted form. Only the FREE format is used in this example. The user should consult the SPSS User's Manual on the different variations of formatted input. Unlike SAS, the specification of the variables within the data list statement must be written with commas between each variable name. The data list statement must end with a period (.).

After the input data have been described, the begin data. statement marks the end of data description and tells SPSS that the data to be read into SPSS follow. In the example program statements given above, the complete correlation matrix follows this statement. To let SPSS know when data input ends, the end data. statement is used. With the end data. statement, SPSS now knows that the program statements follow, in-structing the computer on what to do with the data.

For factor analysis, the user tells SPSS to select the factor analysis program. This is done with the factor variables statement. In this statement the user tells SPSS which variables are used and the form of the data. So variables lawe to gen/ tells SPSS to use all the variables, lawe through gen. The READ CORRELATION tells SPSS that the matrix read in the data entry part of the program is really a correlation matrix. The options here are CORRELATION (a square matrix of intercorrelations is input), TRIANGLE (the lower left triangular portion of the matrix of intercorrelations is input), and FACTOR(n) (a factor matrix is input, i.e., a matrix of factor loadings, where n is the number of factors). Note that the parameters of the factor variables statement are separated by a forward slash (/).

There are six (6) options available for factor extraction in SPSS. They are PC or PA1 for principal components, PAF or PA2 for iterated principal factor, ALPHA for alpha factor analysis, IMAGE for image analysis, ULS for unweighted least-squares factor analysis, GLS for generalized least-squares factor analysis, and ML for maximum likelihood factor analysis. With GLS, the user can perform some of the operations mentioned in Chapter 12. The method of extraction is specified in SPSS with the parameter extraction = xxx/, where the xxx is replaced by one of the options mentioned above. In the example above, it is extraction = pa2/. The user also could have used extraction = paf/ with the same results.

The number of factors extracted is controlled by the FACTORS(n) parameter or the MINEIGEN(k) parameter. The FACTORS(n) parameter tells SPSS the maximum number of factors to extract. The n is the maximum number of factors. MINEIGEN(k) tells SPSS to retain all those factors whose eigenvalues are either greater than or equal to k. Just like BMDP and SAS, SPSS will retain as the number of factors the smaller number. That is, if MINEIGEN(k) tells SPSS to keep a smaller number of factors than FACTOR(n), SPSS will use the value given by MINEIGEN(k). Likewise, if FACTOR(n) tells SPSS to keep a lower number of factors than MINEIGEN(k), then SPSS will retain that number as the number of factors.

SPSS supports five (5) different rotational methods. There is NOROTATE, for no rotation, VARIMAX for varimax rotation, EQUAMAX for equamax rotation, QUARTIMAX for quartimax rotation, and OBLIMIN for direct oblimin with gamma. The method of rotation is specified by the parameter rotation = xxxxx/, where xxxxx is replaced by one of the options mentioned above. For the twelve-variable example represented above, the statement is written as rotation = varimax/. NOKAISER or KAISER is used to specify if the loadings are to be normalized or not during rotation by the Kaiser method.

The ITERATE(n) is used to specify the maximum number of times, n, the communalities are to be iterated. This parameter is only to be used when PA2 or PAF is the method of extraction. Also specific to PA2 or PAF is the specification DIAGONAL = h_1, h_2, h_3, h_4, h_5, h_6, h_7, h_8, h_9, h_{10}, h_{11}, h_{12}/. This parameter is used to tell the SPSS principal factor analysis program what values to use as initial communality estimates. The actual values themselves must be specified. Unlike BMDP and SAS, SPSS cannot be instructed to compute and insert the squared multiple correlations (SMCs) in the diagonals as initial communality estimates. These must to be computed separately and entered manually using the diagonal parameter statement. The SPSS output for this example follows.

This FACTOR analysis requires 18696 (18.3K) BYTES of memory.

Page 1 SPSS/PC+

- - - - F A C T O R   A N A L Y S I S - - - -

Analysis Number 1 Matrix input

Extraction 1 for Analysis 1, Principal Axis Factoring (PAF)

Initial Statistics:

Variable	Communality	*	Factor	Eigenvalue	Pct of Var	Cum Pct
LAWE	.54724	*	1	3.42576	28.5	28.5
ASO	.41286	*	2	2.30828	19.2	47.8
INC	.44845	*	3	1.66523	13.9	61.7
LIF	.38730	*	4	1.15983	9.7	71.3
LD	.41496	*	5	.56604	4.7	76.0
LA	.34153	*	6	.55431	4.6	80.7
LR	.46723	*	7	.51361	4.3	84.9
LS	.39671	*	8	.45491	3.8	88.7
NLW	.58843	*	9	.43703	3.6	92.4
SYM	.38964	*	10	.35128	2.9	95.3
HLP	.55169	*	11	.29526	2.5	97.8
GEN	.42268	*	12	.26847	2.2	100.0

PAF Extracted 4 factors. 14 Iterations required.

Page 2 SPSS/PC+

- - - - F A C T O R   A N A L Y S I S - - - -

Factor Matrix:

	FACTOR 1	FACTOR 2	FACTOR 3	FACTOR 4
LAWE	.09775	.83411	.26591	− .04393
ASO	.01229	.67840	.18680	.05459
INC	.04388	.65304	.31674	− .09033
LIF	.54845	.13796	− .32946	.21693
LD	.60302	.19088	− .22333	.31722
LA	.46373	.13872	− .28220	.45325
LR	.58591	.01654	− .23023	− .44911

LS	.63795	.01393	.04251	− .21366
NLW	.77138	.05365	− .27832	− .31592
SYM	.46645	− .22752	.42910	.03472
HLP	.62823	− .28883	.55100	.15285
GEN	.41441	− .35235	.43484	.04358

Page 3   SPSS/PC+

- - - - F A C T O R   A N A L Y S I S - - - -

Final Statistics:

Variable	Communality	*	Factor	Eigenvalue	Pct of Var	Cum Pct
LAWE	.77793	*	1	3.02038	25.2	25.2
ASO	.49825	*	2	1.91982	16.0	41.2
INC	.53688	*	3	1.25308	10.4	51.6
LIF	.47544	*	4	.73981	6.2	57.8
LD	.55057	*				
LA	.51935	*				
LR	.59827	*				
LS	.45463	*				
NLW	.77518	*				
SYM	.45467	*				
HLP	.80506	*				
GEN	.48687	*				

Page 4   SPSS/PC+

- - - - F A C T O R   A N A L Y S I S - - - -

Varimax Rotation 1, Extraction 1, Analysis 1 − Kaiser Normalization.

Varimax converged in 6 iterations.

Rotated Factor Matrix:

	FACTOR 1	FACTOR 2	FACTOR 3	FACTOR 4
LAWE	− .05509	.87542	.05703	.07270
ASO	− .08991	.69153	− .05223	.09609
INC	.01275	.73042	.03244	− .04643
LIF	.02822	.01261	.29449	.62270
LD	.13242	.10192	.22897	.68573
LA	.05204	.01551	.05801	.71627
LR	.07056	− .02149	.76009	.12284
LS	.33783	.07783	.54501	.19340
NLW	.13965	− .00327	.79796	.34484
SYM	.65867	− .00775	.13431	.05228
HLP	.87585	− .01075	.11366	.15782
GEN	.68135	− .12256	.08721	.00240

Page 5   SPSS/PC+

- - - - F A C T O R   A N A L Y S I S - - - -

Factor Transformation Matrix:

	FACTOR 1	FACTOR 2	FACTOR 3	FACTOR 4
FACTOR 1	.53567	.05797	.63290	.55599
FACTOR 2	−.36033	.91064	.04926	.19615
FACTOR 3	.74999	.40591	−.29096	−.43370
FACTOR 4	.14399	−.05108	−.71579	.68140

Page 6   SPSS/PC+

This procedure was completed at 20:20:09

14.13.4. COMPARISON OF PACKAGES

The factor analysis novice can become confused by the different parameters and syntax used in the various packages. Faced with the decision as to which program to use, the researcher may have difficulty choosing. From the sample outputs already shown, it is clear that the results can be pretty much the same with the three programs. In an earlier discussion, all three packages were shown to have similar setups. Their major differences were in the syntax of the program language. This section briefly examines the similarities and differences between the packages and points out some common and unique features of each package. Table 14.14 summarizes the different data input, factor extraction method, and rotation method options available on these program packages.

The common factor model extraction procedures available in all these packages are (1) principal factor, (2) principal components, and (3) maximum likelihood. The common rotational methods are (1) Varimax, (2) Quartimax and (3) Equamax. If the researcher wants to use the same combination of these methods, it would matter little as to which package is chosen. The same combination of extraction method and rotational method would give the same results with all three packages.

Table 14.14 shows the types of data each statistical package will accept. BMDP is perhaps the easiest one to use regardless of the data type. BMDP accepts raw data as easily as a correlation matrix. In terms of matrix input, SAS is the most difficult. Each row of the matrix must be labeled. It may be difficult for a novice to take an existing correlation matrix and modify it to suit SAS's requirements. The difference in input style is shown in the examples of the previous section. SPSS is nearly as easy to use as BMDP for data input.

TABLE 14.14

Data Input, Factor Extraction and Factor Rotation Options

Operation	BMD-P	SAS	SPSS
Data Input			
	raw data	raw data	raw data
	correlations	correlations	correlations
	covariances	covariances	covariances
	factor matrix	factor matrix	factor matrix
Factor Extraction			
	Principal Factor	Principal Factor	Principal Factor
	Principal Components	Principal Components	Principal Components
	Maximum Likelihood	Maximum Likelihood	Maximum Likelihood
	Kaiser's 2nd generation		
	Little Jiffy	Image factor analysis	Image factor analysis
		Unweighted Least Squares	Unweighted Least Squares
		Alpha factor analysis	Alpha factor analysis
			Generalized Least Squares
Rotation			
	Varimax	Varimax	Varimax
	Quartimax	Quartimax	Quartimax
	Equamax	Equamax	Equamax
	Direct Quartimin	Orthomax	Direct Oblimin
	Direct Oblimin	Orthoblique	
	Orthoblique	Promax	
	Orthogonal	Procrustes	
	with gamma		

SPSS has the most extraction options but the fewest rotation options. SPSS and SAS both permit extraction of image factors, alpha factors, and unweighted least squares factors. Only SPSS offers generalized least squares as a factor extraction option (See Section 12.4).

Image Analysis.   All three program packages offer image analysis as an alternative to common factor analysis. In BMDP, image analysis is part of Kaiser's Second Generation Little Jiffy (1970). Image analysis is based upon a different model than common factor analysis (Guttman, 1953; Harris, 1962; Joreskog, 1962; Kaiser, 1963). In common factor analysis, what is "common" and what is "unique" in a given variable is only estimated since there is no known solution to the "communality problem." In image analysis, what is "common" variance is explicitly equated to what can be predicted from a linear combination of the remaining variables in the matrix. Thus, the squared multiple correlation (SMC) is equated to the proportion of common factor variance. The part of the variable that can be predicted is called the "image" and the part that cannot be predicted is called the "anti-image." When squared multiple correlations are inserted in the diagonals as communalities, however, principal factor extraction generally produces some negative eigenvalues since the matrix is not Gramian. In image analysis, this problem is solved by adjusting the off-diagonal elements of the correlation matrix before factoring by the principal factor method so that there will be no negative eigenvalues.

It is well known that SMCs are lower-bound estimates of the true communalities so there is little reason to suppose that factor loadings derived through image analysis will be superior to those derived by means of an insightful application of common factor analysis methods. This is true despite the fact that what is "common" and what is "unique" is more explicitly defined in image analysis. Although there are no negative eigenvalues in the solution, this has been accomplished at the cost of underestimating communalities and altering the observed off-diagonal values of the correlation matrix. At the present time, there appears to be little evidence to suggest that image analysis will become as widely used as common factor analysis.

Alpha Factor Analysis. Another alternative to common factor analysis is alpha factor analysis (Kaiser & Caffrey, 1965). This method takes as its point of departure the model of Cronbach's (1951) alpha, or generalizability coefficient, and Lord's (1958) multivariate extension of Cronbach's development. In developing a test scale, the homogeneity of the scale is a function of the intercorrelations among the items. The higher the average interitem correlation, the higher will be the homogeneity of the scale, and the higher will be the coefficient alpha. In alpha factor analysis, a factor is sought that has high internal consistency, which will occur if the variables defining the factor have high intercorrelations. An index of the degree of internal consistency for the factor, alpha, is calculated. That factor which yields the highest alpha is removed first, and subsequent alpha factors are removed sequentially until there are no more factors with positive alphas.

Alpha factors are supposed to be the best representatives of the factors that would be found if the entire population of variables were factored instead of just a limited subset. The extent to which this is true obviously depends upon, among other things, how representative this subset is of the population of variables. Once the alpha factors have been extracted, in most cases they must be rotated. Rotation would, of course, alter the homogeneity characteristics of the factors. Cattell (1978) questions the assumptions underlying the model and whether the method will result in the extraction of enough factors. At the present time there is little evidence to suggest that alpha factor analysis is superior to common factor analysis for most research purposes, or that it will become as widely used as common factor analysis.

Unweighted Least Squares.   Unweighted least squares factor extraction, available in SAS and SPSS, can be carried out by a number of different algorithms. Joreskog (1977) proposes one method, Harman and Jones (1966) offer another, and Lee and Comrey (1978) describe yet another. The unweighted least squares method is traditionally known as the iterated principal factor solution. As described elsewhere in this book, this method begins with a correlation matrix. The researcher may use communality estimates such as squared multiple correlations. Unities as communality estimates may also be used. The user must specify the number of factors to be extracted. After the factors are extracted, new communality estimates are computed. These values are inserted in the main diagonal of the correlation matrix and the same number of factors is extracted. When two successive iterations produce computed communalities that are sufficiently close to one another, the iterative factor extraction process stops. Browne (1968) states that principal factoring with iterations will give a factor loading matrix such that the sums of squares of the off-diagonal elements of the residual matrix will be at a minimum.

Joreskog's method involves using a nonlinear search algorithm, for example, the Fletcher-Powell, to find the appropriate values that minimize a fitting function (see Equation 12.3). Harman and Jones derives this same minimum by first extracting a set of factors. Next, the reproduced correlation matrix is computed by multiplying the factor coefficient matrix by its transpose. The differences between the reproduced and observed correlations are computed. Then using a nonlinear search routine, Gauss-Seidel, the factor loadings are adjusted until the differences are at a minimum.

Rotation Methods.   The Varimax and Quartimax methods of rotation are both described in Chapter 7. Equamax was proposed by Saunders (1962). It represents an attempt to combine the best features of Quartimax and Varimax. Harman's (1960) first edition of *Modern Factor Analysis,* also presented a method combining the Varimax and Quartimax criteria. This method of rotation, called "Orthomax," is available on SAS.

The principle underlying Quartimax involves simplification of the variable complexity within the rows of the factor matrix. As mentioned previously, this has the effect of trying to concentrate as much of the variance of a given variable on only one factor as possible. Most reseachers have found that Quartimax tends to give a general factor. In Varimax, the emphasis is on simplifying the columns of the factor matrix. This tends to give factors with some high loadings, only a few intermediate-sized loadings, and many low loadings. Both Quartimax and Varimax are attempts at approximating orthogonal simple structure.

BMDP has a option called "orthogonal rotation with gamma." This rotational method allows the researcher to vary the emphasis between variables (Quartimax) and factors (Varimax) by changing the value of gamma.

Quartimin and Biquartimin are Carroll's (1957) generalization of Quartimax to the oblique case. Quartimin was found to be undesirable because it tends to produce solutions with factors that are more highly correlated than they should be. Later, Kaiser (1958) generalized Varimax to the oblique case with his Covarimin method. Unfortunately, Covarimin appears to produce merely orthogonal solutions more often than desirable. Carroll (1957) combined his Quartimin with Kaiser's Covarimin to produce Biquartimin, which was a compromise between the two. For this method, Carroll introduced a parameter, k, to control the relative emphasis on the two methods. A value of k near 1 would give factors that are highly correlated with each other. A k value of 0 would give a factor solution with somewhat correlated factors. As the k value becomes negative, the solution becomes less and less oblique, and at -4, the solution is orthogonal. None of the three current packages offers any of these rotational methods. There are older mainframe computer versions of BMDP, however, that allow the researcher to pick one of these methods.

The current version of BMDP offers a rotation method developed by Jennrich and Sampson (1966) called Direct Quartimin, which was inspired by the earlier works of Carroll and Kaiser. The Direct Quartimin method allows one to go directly from the initially extracted, unrotated, factors to the rotated primary-factor pattern without the computation of an intermediate reference vector structure, unlike some earlier methods. Jennrich and Sampson also developed a generalized form of Direct Quartimin which they call "Direct Oblimin." Both Direct Quartimin and Direct Oblimin use the same criterion but Direct Oblimin involves a parameter, gamma, that is used to control the degree of obliqueness permitted between factors. Direct Quartimin fixes this parameter at a value of zero and gives what Jennrich and Sampson call "simple loadings," which still constitute an oblique solution.

When the Direct Quartimin option is selected, BMDP performs Direct Oblimin with gamma equal to zero. When the researcher wishes to use a different value of gamma, the option selected is Direct Oblimin. Only BMDP makes this distinction. SPSS only refers to Direct Oblimin. In SPSS, instead of gamma, the Greek letter delta is used to represent the same control parameter as gamma in BMDP. In SPSS, specifying delta equal to zero would give the Jennrich and Sampson Direct Quartimin solution. If this parameter is increased above zero, the solution becomes more oblique.

As it is reduced below zero, the solution becomes more orthogonal. The current version of SAS as this book is being written does not offer Direct Quartimin as an option.

The Promax rotational method is a development of Hendrickson and White (1964) that makes use of the Procrustes method. The Procrustes method of rotation is described in Chapter 7, Section 7.3.2. With Promax, an orthogonal solution, such as Varimax, Quartimax, or Tandem Criterion II, is obtained first. Then, the loadings are powered one or more times, thereby making each powered loading smaller. When powered, however, the relative differences among the loadings become more accentuated. That is, large loadings become smaller, but small loadings become really small. This has the effect of creating a matrix that approximates simple structure. This altered orthogonal matrix is used as the target matrix for a Procrustes rotation. Gorsuch (1983) states that this procedure is fast and easy to program and expects its popularity to increase in the future. This method is available only on SAS.

BMDP and SAS both offer the Orthoblique rotational solution developed by Harris and Kaiser (1964). This method seeks a transformation matrix that will convert the unrotated factors into an oblique solution. The process starts by finding an initial orthonormal transformation matrix that would give an orthogonal solution when multiplied by the unrotated matrix. Harris and Kaiser recommend Varimax for this purpose, but any other method would do. Next, a diagonal matrix is created with diagonal elements equal to the eigenvalues found during the factor extraction procedure. This diagonal matrix is then powered to some value p. Harris and Kaiser recommend using $p = 0.5$. A p value of 1.00 would give orthogonal results. The original orthogonal transformation matrix is multiplied by this powered diagonal matrix and its inverse to obtain a new transformation matrix that will transform the original unrotated factor matrix into an oblique pattern matrix. In the final step, this matrix is multiplied by another diagonal matrix to rescale each factor to unit length. By varying the value of p, the degree of obliquity in the solution can be controlled. A major problem with the Orthoblique solution is that of deciding what value of p to use.

Communality Options.   Table 14.15 presents the communality options for each package. In SPSS, to use the squared multiple correlations (SMCs) as communality estimates, they must be computed outside the factor analysis program and then inserted via an option statement. If a correlation matrix is input, SPSS will normally expect 1.00s to be placed in the main diagonal of the matrix. The user may change the main diagonal values, however, for example, to SMCs, through an input option. The other packages have a variety of options available for initial communality estimates.

TABLE 14.15

Initial Communality Options

Option	BMD-P	SAS	SPSS
Input the values	yes	yes	yes
Squared Multiple Correlations (SMCs)	yes	yes	no
Unities (1.0's)	yes	yes	no
High row values	yes	yes	no
Leave diagonals of R matrix unaltered	yes	no	no
Random values	no	yes	no
Adjusted SMCs	no	yes	no

Default Options. Table 14.16 presents the default values for each of the factor analysis packages. It is apparent that each program has its own unique default values. These differences have also been pointed out by Hubbard and Allen (1989) and by Gorsuch (1983). As a result, the researcher who only uses the default values will discover that each package will generate different results. Such differences have been documented in part by Hubbard and Allen (1989), who show solutions with different numbers of factors and different significant loadings. We recommend that the researcher using any of these programs specify each extraction and rotational parameter explicitly rather than relying upon the default values set by the program developers.

Other Options. The Scree test discussed in Chapter 5 is available on SAS and SPSS. Another option available only on SAS is that of determining the number of factors extracted by the proportion or percentage of common variance accounted for by the retained factors. SAS is also the

TABLE 14.16

Default Settings

BMD-P	SAS	SPSS
Input Correlations	Input Raw Data	Input Raw Data
Principal Components	Principal Components	Principal Components
Initial h^2 values remain unaltered	Initial h^2 values equal 1.0	Initial h^2 values equal 1.0
Maximum number of factors equals number of variables	Maximum number of factors equals number of variables	Maximum number of factors determined by minimum eigenvalue specified
Minimum eigenvalue is 1.0	Minimum eigenvalue is 1.0	Minimum eigenvalue is 1.0
Varimax rotation	No rotation	Varimax rotation

only package that uses a communality estimate called ASMC. Factor analysts are familiar with the use of the largest absolute correlation in the column of the correlation matrix as the initial communality estimate for that variable. Cureton and D'Agostino (1983) have found the use of this value, which they call $|r|_{max}$, to give fairly good estimates under a variety of conditions. Cureton and D'Agostino have found SMCs to underestimate the communalities at times and on other occasions to overestimate them. They propose using initial communality estimates that are proportional to the SMCs while making their sum equal to the sum of the $|r|_{max}$ values.

All three packages are capable of producing graphical plots of the final factor solution. These plots are most manageable if the solution contains only a few factors. A general exploratory run with a large number of factors will produce a large amount of output.

References

Beightler, C. S., Phillips, D. T., & Wilde, D. J. (1979). *Foundations of Optimization.* Englewood-Cliffs, NJ: Prentice Hall.

Bentler, P. M. (1986). Structural modeling and Psychometrika: An historical perspective on growth and achievements. *Psychometrika, 51,* 35-51.

Bentler, P. M. (1989). *Theory and implementation of EQS a structural equations program.* Los Angeles: BMDP Statistical Software, Inc.

Bentler, P. M. (1990). Comparative fit indexes in structural models. *Psychological Bulletin, 107,* 238-246.

Bentler, P.M., & Bonett, D. G. (1980). Significance tests and goodness of fit in the analysis of covariance structures. *Psychological Bulletin, 88,* 588-606.

Bernstein, J. H. (1988). *Applied multivariate analysis.* New York: Springer.

Blalock, H. M., Jr. (1971). *Causal models in the social sciences.* New York: Norton.

Blalock, H. M., Jr. (1972). *Causal inferences in nonexperimental research.* New York: Norton.

Bock, R.D., & Bargmann, R. E. (1966). Analysis of covariance structures. *Psychometrika, 31,* 507-534.

Brown, R. L. (1986). A comparison of LISREL and EQS programs for obtaining parameter estimates in confirmatory factor analysis studies. *Behavior Research Methods, Instruments, and Computers, 18,* 382-388.

Browne, M. W. (1967). On oblique Procrustes rotation. *Psychometrika, 32,* 125-132.

Browne, M. W. (1968). A comparison of factor analytic techniques. *Psychometrika, 33,* 267-334.

Burke, C. J. (1953). Additive scales and statistics. *Psychological Review, 60,* 73-75.

Carroll, J. B. (1953). An analytic solution for approximating simple structure in factor analysis. *Psychometrika, 18,* 23-38.

Carroll, J. B. (1957). Biquartimin criterion for rotation to oblique simple structure in factor analysis. *Science, 126,* 1114-1115.

Cattell, R. B. (1944). Parallel proportional profiles and other principles for determining the choice of factors by rotation. *Psychometrika, 9,* 267-283. (a)

Cattell, R. B. (1944). Psychological measurement: Normative, ipsative, interactive. *Psychological Review, 51,* 292-303. (b)

413

Cattell, R. B. (1952). *Factor analysis*. New York: Harper, 1952.

Cattell, R. B. (Ed.) (1966). *Handbook of multivariate experimental psychology*. Chicago: Rand McNally, 1966.

Cattell, R. B. (1978). *The scientific use of factor analysis in the behavioral and life sciences*. New York: Plenum Press.

Cattell, R. B., & Cattell, A. K. S. (1955). Factor rotation for proportional profiles: Analytic solution and an example. *British Journal of Statistical Psychology*, *8*, 83–92.

Cattell, R. B., Cattell, A. K. S., & Rhymer, R. M. (1947). P-technique demonstrated in determining psychophysiological source traits in a normal individual. *Psychometrika*, *12*, 267–288.

Cattell, R. B., & Dickman, K. A. (1962). A dynamic model of physical influences demonstrating the necessity of oblique simple structure. *Psychological Bulletin*, *59*, 389–400.

Cattell, R. B., & Foster, M. J. (1963). The rotoplot program for multiple single-plane, visually guided rotation. *Behavioral Science*, *8*, 156–165.

Cattell, R. B., & Muerle, J. L. (1960). The "maxplane" program for factor rotation to oblique simple structure. *Educational and Psychological Measurement*, *20*, 569–590.

Cattell, R. B., & Vogelman, S. (1977). A comprehensive trial of the scree and KG criteria for determining the number of factors. *Multivariate Behavioral Research*, *12*, 289–325.

Chesire, L., Saffir, M., & Thurstone, L. L. (1933). *Computing diagrams for the tetrachoric correlation coefficient*. Chicago: University of Chicago Press.

Cliff, N. (1966). Orthogonal rotation to congruence. *Psychometrika*, *31*, 33–42.

Cliff, N. (1983). Some cautions concerning the application of causal modeling methods. *Multivariate Behavioral Research*, *18*, 115–126.

Cliff, N. (1987). Comments on Professor Freedman's paper. *Journal of Educational Statistics*, *12*, 158–160.

Comrey, A. L. (1957). A factor analysis of items on the MMPI Hypochondriasis scale. *Educational and Psychological Measurement*, *17*, 568–577. (a)

Comrey, A. L. (1957). A factor analysis of items on the MMPI Depression scale. *Educational and Psychological Measurement*, *17*, 578–585. (b)

Comrey, A. L. (1957). A factor analysis of items on the MMPI Hysteria scale. *Educational and Psychological Measurement*, *17*, 586–592. (c)

Comrey, A. L. (1958). A factor analysis of items on the MMPI Psychopathic Deviate Scale. *Educational and Psychological Measurement*, *18*, 91–98. (a)

Comrey, A. L. (1958). A factor analysis of items on the MMPI Paranoia scale. *Educational and Psychological Measurement*, *18*, 99–107. (b)

Comrey, A. L. (1958). A factor analysis of items on the MMPI Psychasthenia scale. *Educational and Psychological Measurement*, *18*, 293–300. (c)

Comrey, A. L. (1958). A factor analysis of items on the MMPI Hypomania scale. *Educational and Psychological Measurement*, *18*, 313–323. (d)

Comrey, A. L. (1958). A factor analysis of items on the MMPI F scale. *Educational and Psychological Measurement*, *18*, 621–632. (e)

Comrey, A. L. (1958). A factor analysis of items on the MMPI K scale. *Educational and Psychological Measurement*, *18*, 633–639. (f)

Comrey, A. L. (1959). Comparison of two analytic rotation procedures. *Psychological Reports*, *5*, 201–209.

Comrey, A. L. (1961). Factored homogeneous item dimensions in personality research. *Educational and Psychological Measurement*, *21*, 417–431.

Comrey, A. L. (1962). The minimum residual method of factor analysis. *Psychological Reports*, *11*, 15–18. (a)

Comrey, A. L. (1962). A study of thirty-five personality dimensions. *Educational and Psychological Measurement*, *22*, 543–552. (b)

Comrey, A. L. (1964). Personality factors compulsion, dependence, hostility, and neuroticism.

Educational and Psychological Measurement, 24, 75–84.

Comrey, A. L. (1965). Scales for measuring compulsion, hostility, neuroticism, and shyness. *Psychological Reports, 16*, 697–700.

Comrey, A. L. (1967). Tandem criteria for analytic rotation in factor analysis. *Psychometrika, 32*, 143–154.

Comrey, A. L. (1970). *The Comrey Personality Scales.* San Diego: Educational and Industrial Testing Service. (a)

Comrey, A. L. (1970). *Manual for the Comrey Personality Scales.* San Diego: Educational and Industrial Testing Service. (b).

Comrey, A. L. (1973). *A first course in factor analysis.* New York: Academic Press.

Comrey, A. L. (1978). Common methodological problems in factor analytic studies. *Journal of Clinical and Consulting Psychology, 46*, 648–659.

Comrey, A. L. (1980). *Handbook of interpretations for the Comrey Personality Scales.* San Diego: Edits Publishers.

Comrey, A. L. (1981). Detecting emotional disturbance with the Comrey Personality Scales. *Psychological Reports, 48*, 703–710.

Comrey, A. L. (1984). Comparison of two methods to identify major personality factors. *Applied Psychological Measurement, 4*, 397–408.

Comrey, A. L. (1985). A method for removing outliers to improve factor analytic results. *Multivariate Behavioral Research, 20*, 273–281.

Comrey, A. L. (1988). Factor analytic methods of scale development in personality and clinical psychology. *Journal of Consulting and Clinical Psychology, 56*, 754–761.

Comrey, A. L., & Ahumada, A. (1964). An improved procedure and program for minimum residual factor analysis. *Psychological Reports, 15*, 91–96.

Comrey, A. L., & Ahumada, A. (1965). Note and Fortran IV program for minimum residual factor analysis. *Psychological Reports, 17*, 446.

Comrey, A. L., & Backer, T. E. (1970). Construct validation of the Comrey Personality Scales. *Multivariate Behavioral Research, 5*, 469–477.

Comrey, A. L., Bott, P. A., & Lee, H. B. (1989). *Elementary statistics: A problem solving approach* (2nd ed.) Dubuque, Iowa: Wm. C. Brown.

Comrey, A. L., & Duffy, K. E. (1969). Cattell and Eysenck factor scores related to Comrey personality factors. *Multivariate Behavioral Research, 3*, 379–392.

Comrey, A. L., & Jamison, K. (1966). Verification of six personality factors. *Educational and Psychological Measurement, 26*, 945–953.

Comrey, A. L., Jamison, K., & King, N. (1968). Integration of two personality factor systems. *Multivariate Behavioral Research, 3*, 147–160.

Comrey, A. L., & Levonian, E. (1958). A comparison of three point coefficients in factor analyses of MMPI items. *Educational and Psychological Measurement, 18*, 739–755.

Comrey, A. L., & Marggraff, W. (1958). A factor analysis of items on the MMPI Schizophrenia scale. *Educational and Psychological Measurement, 18*, 301–311.

Comrey, A. L., Noller, P., & Law, H. (1988). Eysenck Personality Inventory item factor structure. *Multivariate Behavioral Research, 23*, 159–170.

Comrey, A. L., & Schiebel, D. (1983). Personality test correlates of psychiatric outpatient status. *Journal of Consulting and Clinical Psychology, 51*, 757–762.

Comrey, A. L., & Schiebel, D. (1985). Personality test correlates of psychiatric case history data. *Journal of Consulting and Clinical Psychology, 53*, 470–479. (a)

Comrey, A. L., & Schiebel, D. (1985). Personality factor structure in psychiatric outpatients and normals. *Multivariate Behavioral Research, 20*, 419–426. (b)

Comrey, A. L., & Schlesinger, B. (1962). Verification and extension of a system of personality dimension. *Journal of Applied Psychology, 46*, 257–262.

Comrey, A. L., & Soufi, A. (1960). Further investigation of some factors found in MMPI items. *Educational and Psychological Measurement, 20*, 779–786.

Comrey, A. L., & Soufi, A. (1961). Attempted verification of certain personality factors. *Educational and Psychological Measurement, 21*, 113-127.

Comrey, A. L., Soufi, A., & Backer, T. E. (1978). Psychiatric screening with the Comrey Personality Scales. *Psychological Reports, 42*, 1127-1130.

Comrey, A. L., Wong, Cynthia, & Backer, T. E. (1978). Further validation of the Social Conformity scale of the Comrey Personality Scales. *Psychological Reports, 43*, 165-166.

Cooley, W. W., & Lohnes, P. R. (1962). *Multivariate procedures for the behavioral sciences*. New York: Wiley.

Cronbach, L. J. (1951). Coefficient alpha and the internal structure of tests. *Psychometrika, 16*, 297-334.

Cudek, R. (1989). Analysis of correlation matrices using covariance structure models. *Psychological Bulletin, 105*, 317-327.

Cureton, E. E., & Mulaik, S. A. (1975). The weighted varimax rotation and the promax rotation. *Psychometrika, 40*, 183-195.

Cureton, E. E., & D'Agostino, R. B. (1983). *Factor analysis: An applied approach*. Hillsdale, NJ: Lawrence Erlbaum and Associates.

Dillon, W. R., & Goldstein, M. (1984). *Multivariate analysis: Methods and applications*. New York: Wiley.

Dixon, W. J. (Ed.) (1970). *BMD biomedical computer programs*. Berkeley: Univ. of California Press. (a)

Dixon, W. J. (Ed.) (1970). *BMD biomedical computer programs. X-series supplement*. Berkeley: Univ. of California Press. (b)

Dixon, W. J. (Ed.) (1983). *BMDP statistical software*. Berkeley: Univ. of California Press.

Duffy, K. E., Jamison, K., & Comrey, A. L. (1969). Assessment of a proposed expansion of the Comrey personality factor system. *Multivariate Behavioral Research, 4*, 295-308.

Duncan, O. D. (1966). Path analysis: sociological examples. *American Journal of Sociology, 72*, 1-16.

Eber, H. W. (1966). Toward oblique simple structure: A new version of Cattell's Maxplane rotation program for the 7094. *Multivariate Behavioral Research, 1*, 112-125.

Erikson, E. H. (1963). *Childhood and society* (2nd ed.). New York: W. W. Norton and Company, Inc.

Eysenck, H. J. (1960). *The structure of human personality*. London: Methuen, 1960.

Eysenck, H. J., & Eysenck, S. B. G. (1969). *Personality structure and measurement*. San Diego: Knapp, 1969.

Fabian, J. J., & Comrey, A. L. (1971). Construct validation of factored neuroticism scales. *Multivariate Behavioral Research, 6*, 287-299.

Ferguson, G. A. (1954). The concept of parsimony in factor analysis. *Psychometrika, 19*, 281-290.

Fleishman, E. A., & Hempel, W. E. (1954). Changes in factor structure of a complex psychomotor test as a function of practice. *Psychometrika, 19*, 239-252.

Fletcher, R. & Powell, M. J. D. (1963). A rapidly convergent descent method for minimization. *Computer Journal, 6*, 163-168.

Forbes, A. R., Dexter, W. R., & Comrey, A. L. (1974). A cross- cultural comparison of certain personality factors. *Multivariate Behavioral Research, 9*, 383-393.

Freedman, D. A. (1987). As others see us. A case study of causal modeling methods. *Journal of Educational Statistics, 12*, 101-128.

Fruchter, B. (1954). *Introduction to factor analysis*. New York: Van Nostrand-Reinhold.

Gilberstadt, H., & Duker, J. (1965). *A handbook for clinical and actuarial MMPI interpretation*. Philadelphia: Saunders.

Gorsuch, R. (1970). A comparison of Biquartimin, Maxplane, Promax, and Varimax. *Educational and Psychological Measurement, 30*, 861-872.

Gorsuch, R. L. (1983). *Factor analysis* (2nd ed.). Hillsdale, NJ: Lawrence Erlbaum Associates.

Gorsuch, R. L., & Nelson, J. (1981). *CNG scree test: An objective procedure for determining the number of factors.* A paper presented at the annual meeting of the Society for Multivariate Experimental Psychology, 1981.

Green, B. F. (1952). The orthogonal approximation of an oblique structure in factor analysis. *Psychometrika, 17,* 429–440.

Guertin, W. H., & Bailey, J. P. (1970). *Introduction to modern factor analysis.* Ann Arbor: Edward.

Guilford, J. P. (1950). Creativity. *American Psychologist, 5,* 444–454.

Guilford, J. P. (1952). When not to factor analyze. *Psychological Bulletin, 49,* 26–37.

Guilford, J. P. (1959). *Personality.* New York: McGraw-Hill.

Guilford, J. P. (1965). *Fundamental statistics in psychology and education* (4th ed.). New York: McGraw-Hill.

Guilford, J. P. (1967). *The nature of human intelligence.* New York: McGraw-Hill.

Guilford, J. P. (1985). The structure-of intellect model. In B. B. Wolman (Ed.), *Handbook of intelligence.* New York: Wiley.

Guilford, J. P., & Hoepfner, R. (1971). *The analysis of intelligence.* New York: McGraw-Hill.

Guttman, L. (1953). Image theory for the structure of quantitative variates. *Psychometrika, 18,* 277–296.

Guttman, L. (1956). Best possible systematic estimates of communalities. *Psychometrika, 21,* 273–285.

Harman, H. H. (1960). *Modern factor analysis.* Chicago: University of Chicago Press.

Harman, H. H. (1967). *Modern factor analysis* (2nd ed.). Chicago: University of Chicago Press.

Harman, H. H. (1976). *Modern factor analysis* (3nd ed.). Chicago: University of Chicago Press.

Harman, H. H., & Jones, W. H. (1966). Factor analysis by minimizing residuals (Minres). *Psychometrika, 31,* 351–368.

Harris, C. W. (1962). Some Rao-Guttman relationships. *Psychometrika, 27,* 247–263.

Harris, C. W., & Kaiser, H. F. (1964). Oblique factor analytic solutions by orthogonal transformations. *Psychometrika, 29,* 347–362.

Hayduk, L. A. (1987). *Structural equation modeling with LISREL: Essentials and advances.* Baltimore, MD: Johns Hopkins University Press.

Hendrickson, A. E., & White, P. O. (1964). Promax: A quick method for rotation to oblique simple structure. *British Journal of Statistical Psychology, 17,* 65–70.

Horst, P. (1965). *Factor analysis of data matrices.* New York: Holt.

Howarth, E., & Browne, J. A. (1971). An item factor-analysis of the 16 PF. *Personality, 2,* 117–139.

Hubbard, R., & Allen, S. J. (1989). On the number and nature of common factors extracted by the eigenvalue-one rule using BMDP vs SPSS. *Psychological Reports, 65,* 155–160.

Hurley, J. R., & Cattell, R. B. (1962). The Procrustes program: Producing direct rotation to test a hypothesized factor structure. *Behavioral Science, 7,* 258–262.

Jamison, K., & Comrey, A. L. (1968). Further study of Dependence as a personality factor. *Psychological Reports, 22,* 239–242.

Jennrich, R. I., & Sampson, P. F. (1966). Rotation for simple loadings. *Psychometrika, 31,* 313–323.

Joreskog, K. G. (1967). Some contributions to maximum likelihood factor analysis. *Psychometrika, 32,* 443–482.

Joreskog, K. G. (1962). On the statistical treatment of residuals in factor analysis. *Psychometrika, 27,* 335–354.

Joreskog, K. G. (1969). A general approach to confirmatory maximum likelihood factor analysis. *Psychometrika, 34,* 183–202.

Joreskog, K. G. (1970). A general method for analysis of covariance structures. *Biometrika, 57,* 239–251.

Joreskog, K. G. (1977). Factor analysis by least-squares and maximum-likelihood methods. In K. Enslein, A. Ralston, and H. Wilf (Eds.), *Statistical methods for digital computers.* New York: Wiley, pp. 125–153.

Joreskog, K. G., & Goldberger, A. S. (1972). Factor analysis by generalized least squares. *Psychometrika, 37,* 243–260.

Joreskog, K. G., & Sorbom, D. (1981). *LISREL V: Analysis of linear structural relationships by maximum likelihood, instrumental variables and least squares methods.* Chicago: National Educational Resources.

Joreskog, K. G., & Sorbom, D. (1984). *LISREL VI: Analysis of linear structural relationships by maximum likelihood, instrumental variables and least squares methods.* Mooresville, IN: Scientific Software, Inc.

Joreskog, K. G., & Sorbom, D. (1988). *LISREL VII: Analysis of linear structural relationships by maximum likelihood, instrumental variables and least squares methods.* Mooresville, IN: Scientific Software, Inc.

Kaiser, H. F. (1958). The Varimax criterion for analytic rotation in factor analysis. *Psychometrika, 23,* 187–200.

Kaiser, H. F. (1959). Computer program for Varimax rotation in factor analysis. *Educational and Psychological Measurement, 19,* 413–420.

Kaiser, H. F. (1963). Image analysis. In C. W. Harris (Ed.) *Problems in measuring change,* pp. 156–166. Madison, WI: University of Wisconsin Press.

Kaiser, H. F. (1970). A second generation Little Jiffy. *Psychometrika, 35,* 401–415.

Kaiser, H. F., & Caffry, J. (1965). Alpha factor analysis. *Psychometrika, 30,* 1–14.

Kelley, T. L. (1940). Comment on Wilson and Worcester's "note on factor analysis." *Psychometrika, 5,* 117–120.

Kennedy, W. J., & Gentle, J. E. (1980). *Statistical computing.* New York: Marcel Dekker.

Knapp, R. R., & Comrey, A. L. (1973). Further construct validation of a measure of self actualization. *Educational and Psychological Measurement, 33,* 419–425.

Knecht, S. D., Cundick, B. P., Edwards, D., & Gunderson, E. K. E. (1972). The prediction of marijuana use from personality scales. *Educational and Psychological Measurement, 32,* 1111–1117.

Lawley, D. N. (1940). The estimation of factor loadings by the method of maximum likelihood. *Proceedings of the Royal Society of Edinburgh, 60,* 64–82.

Lawley, D. N., & Maxwell, A. E. (1963). *Factor analysis as a statistical method.* London: Butterworth.

Lawley, D. N., & Maxwell, A. E. (1971). *Factor analysis as a statistical method* (2nd Ed.) London: Butterworth.

Lee, H. B. (1979). *An empirical comparison of some factor analytical methods.* Unpublished doctoral disseration, University of California, Los Angeles.

Lee, H. B., & Comrey, A. L. (1978). An empirical comparison of two minimum residual factor extraction methods. *Multivariate Behavioral Research, 13,* 497–508.

Lee, H. B., & Comrey, A. L. (1979). Distortions in a commonly used factor analytic procedure. *Multivariate Behavioral Research, 14,* 301–321.

Lee, S. Y., & Jennrich, R. I. (1979). A study of algorithms for covariance structure analysis with specific comparisons using factor analysis. *Psychometrika, 44,* 99–113.

Lee, S. Y., & Jennrich, R. I. (1984). The analysis of structural equation models by means of derivative-free nonlinear least squares. *Psychometrika, 49,* 521–528.

Levin, J. (1988). Note on the convergence of Minres. *Multivariate Behavioral Research, 23,* 413–417.

Levonian, E., Comrey, A. L., Levy, W., & Procter, D. (1959). A statistical evaluation of the Edwards Personal Preference Schedule. *Journal of Applied Psychology, 43,* 355–359.

Loehlin, J. C. (1987). *Latent variable models: An introduction to factor, path and structural analysis.* Hillsdale, NJ: Lawrence Erlbaum Associates.

Long, J. S. (1983). *Confirmatory factor analysis: A preface to LISREL*. Beverly Hills, CA: Sage.

Lord, F. M. (1958). Some relations between Guttman's principal components of scale analysis and other psychometric theory. *Psychometrika, 23*, 517–548.

McDonald, R. P. (1967). Numerical methods for polynomial models in nonlinear factor analysis. *Psychometrika, 32*, 77–112.

McMillan, C., Jr. (1975). *Mathematical programming* (2nd. Ed.). New York: Wiley.

Marks, A., Michael, W. B., & Kaiser, H. F. (1960). Comparison of manual and analytic techniques of rotation in factor analysis of aptitude test variables. *Psychological Reports, 7*, 519–522.

Montag, I., & Comrey, A. L. (1982). Comparison of certain MMPI, Eysenck, and Comrey personality constructs. *Multivariate Behavioral Research, 17*, 93–97. (a)

Montag, I., & Comrey, A. L. (1982). Personality construct similarity in Israel and the United States. *Applied Psychological Measurement, 6*, 61–67. (b)

Morrison, D. (1967). *Multivariate statistics*. New York: McGraw- Hill.

Mosier, C. I. (1939). Determining a simple structure when loadings for certain tests are known. *Psychometrika, 4*, 149–162.

⦿Mulaik, S. A. (1972). *Foundations of factor analysis*. New York: McGraw-Hill.

Mulaik, S. A. (1987). Toward a conception of causality applicable to experimentation and causal modeling. *Child Development, 58*, 18–32.

Mulaik, S. A. (1990). Blurring distinctions between component analysis and common factor analysis. *Multivariate Behavioral Research, 25*, 53–59.

Mulaik, S. A., James, L. R., Van Alstine, J., Bennett, N., Lind, S., & Stilwell, C. D. (1989). Evaluation of goodness-of-fit indices for structural equation models. *Psychological Bulletin, 105*, 430–445.

Neuhaus, J. O., & Wrigley, C. (1954). The quartimax method: An analytic approach to orthogonal simple structure. *British Journal of Statistical Psychology, 7*, 81–91.

Noller, P., Law, H., & Comrey, A. L. (1987). Cattell, Comrey, and Eysenck personality factors compared: More evidence for the five robust factors? *Journal of Personality and Social Psychology, 53*, 775–782.

Noller, P., Law, H., & Comrey, A. L. (1988). Factor structure of the Comrey Personality Scales in an Australian sample. *Multivariate Behavioral Research, 23*, 397–411.

Overall, J. E., & Porterfield, J. L. (1963). Powered vector method of factor analysis. *Psychometrika, 28*, 415–422.

Rasmussen, J. L. (1988). Evaluating outlier identification tests: Mahalanobis D Squared and Comrey Dk. *Multivariate Behavioral Research, 23*, 189–202.

Rodrigues, A. & Comrey, A. L. (1974). Personality structure in Brazil and the United States. *Journal of Social Psychology, 92*, 19–26.

Rummel, R. J. (1970). *Applied factor analysis*. Evanston, IL: Northwestern University Press.

Saunders, D. R. (1960). A computer program to find the best-fitting orthogonal factors for a given hypothesis. *Psychometrika, 25*, 199–205.

Schonemann, P. H., & Carroll, R. M. (1970). Fitting one matrix to another under choice of a central dilation and a rigid motion. *Psychometrika, 35*, 245–255.

Thomson, G. H. (1951). *The factorial analysis of human ability* (4th Ed.). Boston: Houghton.

⦿Thurstone, L. L. (1947). *Multiple factor analysis*. Chicago: University of Chicago Press.

Thurstone, L. L. (1954). An analytic method for simple structure. *Psychometrika, 19*, 173–182.

Tryon, R. C., & Bailey, D. E. (1970). *Cluster analysis*. New York: McGraw-Hill.

Tucker, L. R., Koopman, R. F., & Linn, R. L. (1969). Evaluation of factor analytic research procedures by means of simulated correlation matrices. *Psychometrika, 34*, 421–459.

Tucker, L. R., & Lewis, C. (1973). A reliability coefficient for maximum likelihood factor analysis. *Psychometrika, 38*, 1–10.

Vandenberg, S. G., & Price, R. A. (1978). Replication of the factor structure of the Comrey Personality Scales. *Psychological Reports, 42,* 343-352.

Velicer, W. F. (1974). An empirical comparison of the stability of factor analysis, principal components analysis and image analysis. *Educational and Psychological Measurement, 34,* 563-574.

Velicer, W. F. (1977). An empirical comparison of the similarity of principal components, image, and factor analysis. *Multivariate Behavioral Research, 12,* 3-22.

Velicer, W. F., & Jackson, D. N. (1990). Component analysis versus common factor analysis: Some issues in selecting an appropriate procedure. *Multivariate Behavioral Research, 25,* 1-28.

Weiss, A. S., & Comrey, A. L. (1987). Personality characteristics of Hare Krishnas. *Journal of Personality Assessment, 51,* 399-413. (a)

Weiss, A. S., & Comrey, A. L. (1987). Personality and mental health of Hare Krishnas compared with psychiatric outpatients and 'normals'. *Personality and Individual Differences, 8,* 721-730. (b)

Weiss, A. S., & Comrey, A. L. (1987). Personality factor structure among Hare Krishnas. *Educational and Psychological Measurement, 47,* 317-328. (c)

Widaman, K. F., & Herringer, L. G. (1985). Iterative least squares estimates of communality: Initial estimate need not affect stabilized value. *Psychometrika, 50,* 469-477.

Wright, S. (1921). Correlation and causation. *Journal of Agricultural Research, 20,* 557-585.

Wright, S. (1923). Theory of path coefficients: A reply to Niles' criticism. *Genetics, 8,* 239-255.

Yates, A. (1987). *Multivariate exploratory data analysis: A perspective on exploratory factor analysis.* Albany, NY: State University of New York Press.

Zamudio, A., Padilla, A. M., & Comrey, A. L. (1983). Personality structure of Mexican-Americans using the Comrey Personality Scales. *Journal of Personality Assessment, 47,* 100-106.

Zegers, F. E. & ten Berge, J. M. F. (1983). A fast and simple computational method of minimum residual factor analysis. *Multivariate Behavioral Research, 18,* 331-340.

Zimmerman, W. S. (1946). A simple graphical method for orthogonal rotation of axes. *Psychometrika, 11,* 51-55.

Author Index

P

Padilla, A. M., 293, *420*
Phillips, D. T., 312, *413*
Porterfield, J. L., 324, *419*
Powell, M. J. D., 312, *416*
Price, R. A., 293, *420*
Procter, D., 265, *418*

QR

Rasmussen, J. L., 383, *419*
Rhymer, R. M., 236, *414*
Rodrigues, A., 293, *419*
Rummel, R. J., 4, *419*

S

Saffir, M., 222, *414*
Sampson, P. F., 188, 409, *417*
Saunders, D. R., 186, 408, *419*
Schiebel, D., 293, 298, *415*
Schlesinger, B., 269, *415*
Schonemann, P. H., 185, 323, *419*
Shiba, Sukeyori, 93
Sorbom, D., 110, 301, 308, 313, 326, *418*
Soufi, A., 265, 269, 298, *415–416*
Stilwell, C. D., 315, *419*

T

TenBerge, J. M. F., 99, *420*
Thomson, G. H., 4, *419*
Thurstone, L. L., 4, 34, 52, 77, 116, 140, 154, 171, 186–188, 222, 264, *414, 419*
Tryon, R. C., 177, *419*
Tucker, L. R., 104, 315, *419*

UV

Van Alstine, J., 315, *419*
Vandenberg, S. G., 293, *420*
Velicer, W. F., 108, 203, *420*
Vogelman, S., 108, *414*

W

Weiss, A. S., 293, 297, *420*
White, P. O., 188, 410, *417*
Widaman, K. F., 105, *420*
Wilde, D. J., 312, *413*
Wong, C., 297, *416*
Wright, S., 338, *420*
Wrigley, C., 186, *419*

YZ

Yates, A., 172, *420*
Zagers, F. B., 99, *420*
Zamudio, A., 293, *420*
Zimmerman, W. S., 122, *420*

Subject Index